Also by Ian Hamilton

POETRY
The Visit
Returning

CRITICISM
The Little Magazines
A Poetry Chronicle

The Poetry of War 1939–45 (editor)
The Modern Poet (editor)

ROBERT LOWELL

ROBERT LOWELL

A Biography

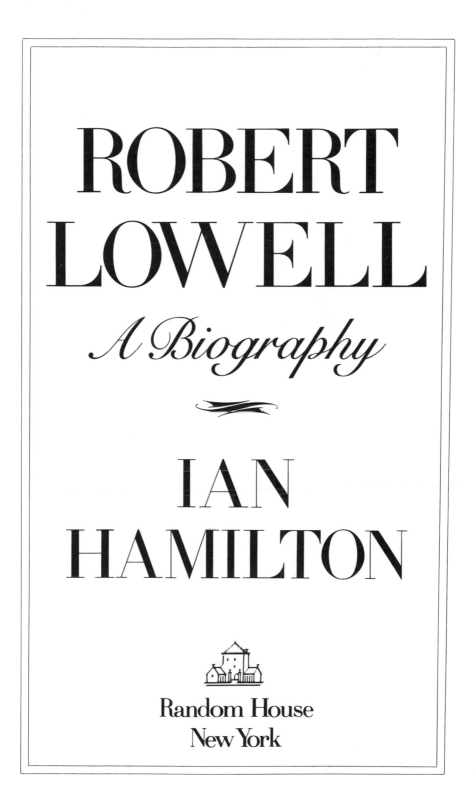

IAN HAMILTON

Random House
New York

All rights reserved under International and Pan-American Copyright Conventions.
Published in the United States by Random House, Inc., New York, and simultaneously
in Canada by Random House of Canada Limited, Toronto.

Library of Congress Cataloging in Publication Data

Hamilton, Ian, 1938-
Robert Lowell, a biography.
Includes index.
1. Lowell, Robert, 1917–1977. 2. Poets,
American—20th century—Biography. I. Title.
PS3523.089Z68   811'.52 [B]   82-40121
ISBN 0-394-50965-X   AACR2

Manufactured in the United States of America
24689753
First Edition

DESIGN BY BERNARD KLEIN

Special acknowledgment is made to the following libraries for permission to use material in their collections: The Collection of American Literature, Beinecke Rare Book and Manuscript Library, Yale University; the Henry W. and Albert A. Berg Collection, New York Public Library, Astor, Lenox and Tilden Foundations; the Kenyon College Archives, Chalmers Memorial Library; the Richard Chase Papers, Rare Book and Manuscripts Library, Columbia University; the Richard Eberhart Collection, Dartmouth College Library; Rare Books and Special Collections, Firestone Library, Princeton University; Houghton Library, Harvard University; Malcolm Cowley Papers, Newberry Library; Manuscripts Division, University of Minnesota Libraries; Manuscripts Collection, University of Washington Libraries; and the Merrill Moore Collection, Library of Congress.

Special acknowledgment is made to the following for permission to use previously unpublished material:

William Alfred; the estate of W. H. Auden, copyright © 1982 by the estate of W. H. Auden, not to be reprinted without written permission; Frank Bidart, literary executor for Robert Lowell; Lawrence E. Brinn and Louise Crane, executors for the estate of Marianne Moore; Blair Clark; Donald Davie; Kate Donahue, literary executor for John Berryman; Richard Eberhart; Alfred C. Edwards, trustee for the estate of Robert Frost; Mrs. T. S. Eliot; Robert Fitzgerald; Robert Giroux; Elizabeth Hardwick; Mary von S. Jarrell; Stanley Kunitz; Dwight Macdonald, literary executor for Delmore Schwartz; William Meredith; Anne Leslie Moore; Curtis Prout; Adrienne Rich; Russell & Volkening, Inc., agent for the estate of Jean Stafford; Helen H. Tate; Peter Taylor; John Thompson; and Liberty Winter.

Grateful acknowledgment is made to the following for permission to reprint previously published material:

American Poetry Review: Excerpt from "Caryatid: A Column" by Adrienne Rich, published in *American Poetry Review,* Sept.–Oct. 1973. Copyright © 1973 by Adrienne Rich.

Atheneum Publishers: Excerpt from *Language and Silence: Essays on Language, Literature and the Inhuman* by George Steiner. Copyright © 1967 by George Steiner. Reprinted with the permission of Atheneum Publishers.

Commentary: Excerpt from a letter by Robert Lowell reprinted from *Commentary,* April 1969, by permission of *Commentary* and Robert Lowell's literary executor.

Commonweal: Excerpt from a book review by Anne Fremantle, *Commonweal,* vol. 45. Copyright © Commonweal Publishing Co., Inc.

Doubleday & Company, Inc. and Faber & Faber, Ltd.: Excerpt from "Four for Sir John Davis," from *The Collected Poems of Theodore Roethke.* Copyright 1952 by The Atlantic Monthly Company. Reprinted by permission of Doubleday & Company, Inc. and Faber & Faber, Ltd.

Farrar, Straus & Giroux, Inc.: From *His Toy, His Dream, His Rest* by John Berryman, copyright © 1965, 1966, 1967, 1968, 1969 by John Berryman. From *The Complete Poems* by Elizabeth Bishop, copyright © 1969 by Elizabeth Bishop. From *Day by Day* by Robert Lowell, copyright © 1975, 1976, 1977 by Robert Lowell. From *Imitations* by Robert Lowell,

ACKNOWLEDGMENTS

My thanks to the following: William Alfred, A. Alvarez, Betty B. Ames, Rolando Anzilotti, Alison Armstrong, James Atlas, Steven Gould Axelrod, Elizabeth Bettman, Frank Bidart, Caroline Blackwood, Philip Booth, Keith Botsford, Christina Brazelton, Cecile Boyajian, Cleanth Brooks, Esther Brooks, Peter Brooks, Shepherd Brooks, Alan Brownjohn, Gertrude Buckman, Alistair Cameron, Brainard Cheney, Frances Neel Cheney, Blair Clark, Alexander Cockburn, Malcolm Cowley, Carley Dawson, Richard Demenocal, Liberty Dick, Harry Duncan, Richard Eberhart, Philip Edwards, Holly Eley, Valerie Eliot, Barbara Epstein, Richard J. Fein, Robert Fitzgerald, Sally Fitzgerald, George Ford, Jonathan Galassi, Robert Giroux, Grey Gowrie, Simon Gray, Matthew Hamilton, Stuart Hamilton, Xandra Hardie, Elizabeth Hardwick, Lillian Hellman, Dan Jacobson, Mary Jarrell, James Laughlin, Andrew Lytle, Robie Macauley, Giovanna Madonia, John P. Marquand, Eugene McCarthy, William Meredith, Dido Merwin, Jonathan Miller, Karl Miller, Charles Monteith, Sidney Nolan, Jacqueline Onassis, Frank Parker, Lesley Parker, Jim Peck, J. F. Powers, Patrick Quinn, Jonathan Raban, Craig Raine, Christopher Ricks, Martha Ritter, Frederick Seidel, Robert Silvers, Eileen Simpson, Natasha Spender, Stephen Spender, Donald Stanford, Hugh Staples, Richard Stern, Joan Stillman, William Styron, Peter Taylor, John Thompson, Helen Vendler, Vija Vetra, Robert Penn Warren, Peter White, Richard Wilbur, Marcella Winslow, Dudley Young, Thomas Daniel Young.

I am also indebted to the following librarians and libraries: Rodney Dennis and the staff of the Houghton Library, Harvard University; Walter W. Wright, Dartmouth College Library; Thomas B.

Greenslade, Chalmers Memorial Library, Kenyon College; Jean F. Preston, Firestone Library, Princeton University; Eve Lebo, University of Washington, Seattle; Paul T. Heffron, Manuscripts Division, Library of Congress; Alan M. Lathrop, Manuscripts Division, University of Minnesota Libraries; Diana Haskell, Special Collections, Newberry Library, Chicago; Saundra Taylor, Lilly Library, Indiana University, Bloomington; Mary Long, St. Mark's School Library, St. Mark's School, Southborough, Mass.; the Curator, Beinecke Library, Yale University; the Curator, Berg Collection, New York Public Library; the Librarian, Columbia University Library; Mary Rider, Vanderbilt University Library, Nashville, Tenn.

I am grateful to Jason Epstein of Random House for commissioning the book and for helping me to get it written, and to my agent, Gillon Aitken, for three years of friendship and encouragement. And finally, a special—yet still inadequate—note of thanks to Charis Ryder: her research assistance has been patient and resourceful, her editorial vigilance often unnervingly precise. In the actual making of this book, my chief debt is to her.

ROBERT
LOWELL

Like Henry Adams, I was born under the shadow of the Dome of the Boston State House, and under Pisces, the Fish, on the first of March, 1917. America was entering the First World War and was about to play her part in the downfall of five empires.[1]

The setting for this ominous nativity was a brownstone high on Boston's Beacon Hill, the town house of Arthur Winslow, Robert Lowell's maternal grandfather. The house was fronted by two pillars copied from the Temple of Kings at Memphis, and every afternoon Grandfather Winslow, "a stiff-necked, luxurious ramrod of a man," would station himself between these "loutish" props and survey his social gains. On the afternoon of March 1, 1917, he was probably well pleased. This new child—first son of the union between two celebrated Boston names—would surely prove another asset. Certainly, it was hard to see how such a flawless pedigree could engender positive embarrassment.

And this would have mattered quite a lot to Arthur. A Boston boy who had made his middle-sized pile as a mining engineer in Colorado, he was almost ridiculously proud of his descent from the New England Winslows who had supported George III. He wrote a history of the family that traced the Winslows back to Worcestershire. With manly lack of detail, he established that in 1620 Edward Winslow had come to America on the *Mayflower;* a year later, his brother John had followed, on the *Fortune.* John married Mary Chilton, who was "credited with having been the first woman from the *Mayflower* to have stepped ashore on Plymouth Rock." And in 1817 Arthur's grandfather had married Sarah Stark of Dunbarton in New Hampshire. Sarah was a daughter of John Stark, a renowned general in the Revolutionary War. Arthur thus had both sides of the conflict in his blood.

Secretly, though, Arthur would have preferred *all* his neighbors to have been prerevolutionary. But he also had a taste for the celebrity conferred by guidebooks, and on this reckoning Chestnut Street already rated several stars. If a neighbor was of faulty stock, the chances were that he would make up for this by being famous. All in all, it wasn't the *wrong* street for a Winslow/Lowell to be born on.

Edwin Booth, for instance, had lived just across the street, and nearby Julia Ward Howe was still in residence (by this time so old and distinguished that "one could forget she was a woman"). So too was the neo-Gothic architect Ralph Adams Cram. Arthur had his doubts about Cram, but still made sure that he kept several of his drawings on display, "thus continually enjoying the exalted ceremonial of seeing his own just derision continually defeated by his good nature."

Farther along Chestnut Street there were still richer pickings. Twenty buildings down the street, Francis Parkman had once lived, Oliver Wendell Holmes had just died, and on a clear day you didn't need a telescope to sight the late residence of Percival Lowell, the celebrated Boston astronomer who believed that there was also life on Mars.

The Winslows and the Lowells: on paper it was a spectacularly correct match. Perhaps because he was married to a whimsical Southerner from North Carolina and had spent five years at school in Stuttgart as a youth, Arthur Winslow espoused a brand of New England integrity that even hard-line Bostonians considered somewhat over-rhetorical and Prussian. Few, therefore, were surprised when, after having famously discouraged several of his daughter Charlotte's suitors (Arthur would always place himself prominently within earshot when they came to visit her), he decided to smile upon the overtures of Robert Traill Spence Lowell. The Somerset Lowles [*sic*] may not have come over on the *Mayflower,* but they had been New Englanders since 1639, and were now firmly on the list of Massachusetts' "first families." The historical appropriateness comfortably overshadowed any judgment of the young naval lieutenant's personality—which, even at this early stage, was widely thought to be oafish and compliant. In the words of R.T.S.L.'s aunt Beatrice: "Bob hasn't a mean bone, an original bone, a funny bone in his body! That's why I can't get a word he says. If he were mine, I'd lobotomize him and stuff his brain with green peppers."

Most people seem to have felt this way about Bob Lowell, but Arthur Winslow was not looking to be replaced as the dominant figure in his favorite daughter's life. Nor was Charlotte herself in need of any extra restraints upon her own natural bossiness. She had a man she worshiped; now she wanted one who would unquestioningly worship her. For both father and daughter, Bob's combination of weak character and strong lineage was indeed perfectly correct.

The union had been easily arranged. Charlotte's best friend, Kitty Bowles, had become engaged to Alfred Putnam Lowell in the winter of 1915. It was at the engagement party that Charlotte first met Alfred's cousin Bob. Afterwards she said to Kitty: "A Lowell and a naval officer. He must be a genius and a buccaneer." And Kitty replied, "Bob is the most gentle, the most cheerful, the most modest, the most Euclidian man I have ever met." And Charlotte and Kitty's friends in the Reading Club soon reported that the one sentence *everyone* used about R.T.S. was: "Can't say much about Bob. I hear he got straight A's at Columbia for his work in radio."

Well before the couple's engagement, and almost certainly before Bob knew what was being planned for him, Charlotte had done her homework on the Lowells. At the Reading Club, she mounted a charade called "The Lowells: have they tails or have they wings?" It was a slightly hysterical afternoon, and years later her son reconstructed it from the recollections of friends:

A few of Mother's skits have been remembered. There was her A. Lawrence Lowell, the genial President of Harvard, awarding Alfred his A.B. and saying lugubriously: "Go west, young man, avoid Miss Bowles." There was Percival Lowell, the brilliant but unsociable astronomer, who looked through the wrong end of my Grandfather Winslow's telescope and said, "I have discovered *Percival*, the minutest living planet." Then there was Mother all padded out with pillows and laundry bags, and with a clothes-pin in her mouth: pretending to be Amy Lowell, and exclaiming: "Hold me, John Keats, I am as light as the Lusitania." There was Judge James Lowell, himself a charader, for Mother made him talk with a Jewish accent and play the role of King Solomon giving judgment. "Oi yoi, scut de kiddo in pieces." There was Cornelius Lowell, the historian of the French Revolution, writing an article for the Atlantic Monthly entitled "Notes on the Monetary Background of Charlotte Corday." There was Guy Lowell, the architect, being consulted on a building for the Boston Fine Arts Museum. He was holding up photographs of St. Peter's, the Pitti Palace, the Taj Mahal, the Parthenon and the Eiffel Tower, and saying: "Take your pick."

And so it went on. The Reading Club politely "almost died laughing"; and on the way home, Connie Codman said, "Well I must admit Charlotte is an uproarious sport." Kitty agreed that, yes, Charlotte *was* "emphatic." But Fanny Kittredge supplied the final words: "Sometimes I worry."

The potency of the Lowell name was such that Charlotte Winslow was prepared to overlook not just Bob's less than forceful personality but also (more surprisingly) his relatively humble station in the Lowell clan. Bob was from the poor (i.e., the merely comfortably off) branch of the Lowells—priests and poets figured prominently among his immediate forebears. James Russell Lowell was a great-great-uncle and Robert Traill Spence Lowell I, James Russell's elder brother, was moderately well known for his verses and for a novel, *The New Priest in Conception Bay.* The Lowell millions, though, were elsewhere, with the bankers and the lawyers and the cotton magnates: cousins all, but hardly intimates, and in a quite separate financial league. From the late eighteenth century, the Traill/-Spence line of Lowells had been the pious poor relations, admired for their good (and even for their mediocre) works, but viewed as somehow quirkily irrelevant to the main thrust of the Lowell enterprise. Bob's feebleness, for instance, would have been seen by "real" Lowells as the to-be-expected outcome of four generations of worship and word-spinning. The view was: remove the vocation or the talent from the Traill/Spence line and you are likely to be left with a wispy, agreeable abstractedness; the Traills and the Spences had, after all, originated in the Orkneys—being a bit out of things was in their blood.

Bob Lowell's father had died before he was born, and his mother was left to languish on Staten Island. She lived on there with her mother, and had no thought of ever marrying again. Her terrible early bereavement (after only five months of marriage) had left her in a state of transfixed bewilderment, and over the years her son had grown expert in not asking unanswerable questions, not challenging the unjust fates. His marriage to Charlotte Winslow might thus, for all he knew, have been externally decreed; certainly, it would not have occurred to him to challenge its inevitability. Bob's response to any daunting situation was to smile, and on his wedding day in the spring of 1916, he is remembered as having particularly "smiled and smiled":

> He smiled and smiled in his photographs, just as he smiled and smiled in life. He would look into the faces of others as if he expected to find himself reflected in their eyes. He was a man who treated even himself with the caution and uncertainty of one who has forgotten a name, in this case his own.

Even in his wedding photographs, and in spite of the smile, Bob contrived to recede into the background, as if all too anxious to surrender the stage to Charlotte from the very start. And Charlotte showed no signs of being ruffled by his self-effacement:

> I see her strong, firmly modeled chin, her pulled-in tiny waist, her beaver muff, and her neck, which was like a swan's neck crowned with an armful of pyramided hair and an ostrich feather.

The Lowells spent their honeymoon at the Grand Canyon, a choice that baffled everyone who knew them, or knew Charlotte: "The choice was so heroic and unoriginal that it left them forever with a feeling of gaping vacuity. The Canyon's hollow hugeness was a sort of bad start for us all."

After the Canyon, it dawned on Charlotte that she had somehow become a married woman. The engagement was over. And, worse than that, she saw that far from having married into the heart of Boston's social whirl, she had committed herself to the nomadic drudgery of the low-rank "naval wife." The one thing everybody knew about Bob's work was that it kept him "on the move." Thus, immediately after the honeymoon, Charlotte found herself transferred to Jamestown, near Newport, Rhode Island, a pointless backwater where she learned that naval wives were expected to order their own groceries. Her stylishly incompetent housekeeping quite failed to irritate her agreeable new husband, and she was soon chafing for Boston, for the drawing rooms, the Reading Club, and —most of all—for "the urgent domination" of her father. Bob thought that things were going rather well.

By the fall of 1916, though, Charlotte was pregnant, and Bob's bungling response was to find himself posted to California. Charlotte went into retreat on Staten Island and there fretted through the winter. The Lowell household she found sapless and depressed, a household with no men, no arguments or explosions; and most irritating of all, Bob's mother so evidently looked to *her* to bring some long-awaited spark into the home. After a month or two of fidgety resentment "the only thing she enjoyed was taking brisk walks and grieving over the fact that she was pregnant. She took pride in looking into the great Atlantic Ocean and saying, without a trace of fear or illusion: I wish I could die."

By the time Robert (Traill Spence) Lowell IV was ready to be born, Charlotte had engineered a move back to Boston, the first of many intense returns from wherever her husband's work had ludicrously landed her. Out of Boston, she would say, she wilted: she needed the iron in the air for her will. And she needed her father. Although she had married a naval lieutenant, all her notions of military glamour were invested in Arthur—she saw him as a Prussian, tidied-up version of Napoleon.

Six years before her marriage, Charlotte had read the Duchesse d'Abrantès' *Memoirs of Napoleon,* and had fallen for the conqueror's majestic slovenliness. For a period she insisted on sleeping on an army cot, taking cold dips in the morning, bolting her food. Worst of all, she actually began calling her father "Napoleon." Small wonder that her meek husband's martial anecdotes, his uniform and his ceremonial sword came to seem neither enticing nor intimidating. When Bob tried to resist the move back to Boston, she simply took no notice, but cajoled her father into some nifty mortgage-juggling which eventually produced the house on Brimmer Street where Robert Lowell was to spend the first and—by his account—perhaps the least precarious years of his life:

When I was three or four years old I first began to think about the time before I was born. Until then Mother had been everything; at three or four she began abruptly to change into a human being. I wanted to recapture the mother I remembered and so I began to fabricate. In my memory, she was a lady preserved in silhouettes, outlines and photographs, she sat on a blue bench; she smiled at my father, a naval lieutenant in a collarless blue uniform. Blue meant the sea, the navy and manhood. Blue was the ideal defining color Mother had described to Father as his "Wagnerian theme," the absolute he was required to live up to. I was a little doll in a white sailor suit with blue anchors on the pockets, a doll who smiled impartially upon his mother and father and in his approbation thus made them husband and wife. But when I was at last three years old all that began to change. I could no longer see Mother as that rarely present, transfigured, Sunday-best version of my nurse. I saw her as my mother, as a rod, or a scolding, rusty hinge—as a human being. More and more I tried to remember Mother when she was happier, when she had been merely her father's daughter, when she was engaged but unmarried. Perhaps I had been happiest then too, because I hadn't existed and lived only as an imagined future.

The infant Robert Lowell may have come to see his mother as an adversary, a "scolding, rusty hinge," but he was utterly enthralled by her; even to make small inroads on her appalling power would be to achieve victories that seemed quite beyond his father's wit or inclination. From a tender age, Lowell became a keen student of enslavement. And from his father he learned that decency and good intentions can be abject.

One of Lowell's earliest insights into how power within the family operates came when a flu epidemic struck the household. Bob caught the bug first, and to protect his wife he improvised a resting place in the corridor outside the still "germ-free" master bedroom:

> In his quiet, smiling, feverish banishment, he meant to be an ideal husband whose demands were infinitesimal. But nevertheless, every time we moved we stumbled gracelessly upon the unselfish invalid. The strain brought about by his effort to make himself invisible was extreme; all was hushed, vexed and ajar.

After a day or two of this disruption, Bob was obliged to declare himself fully recovered; and then it was Charlotte's turn to show how it was done:

> She lay in warmth and splendour in her bedroom, supported by hot-water bottles, gardenias, doctors and trays with pink napkins on them. In her self-indulgent illness nothing was set at odds in the household; instead, everything was more smooth than ever, as if music were playing and we were all living in a floating palace.

It was for triumphs of this sort that Lowell began to see his mother as a "young Alexander, all gleam and panache." In Charlotte's copy of Plutarch, there was a picture of Alexander conferring with his aide-de-camp before the battle of Granicus. Lowell used to study this picture and compare the conqueror's strong chin with his mother's. How in the world, the child would wonder, might such a commanding, brilliant presence be undone?

One possible weak point, he noticed, had to do with Charlotte's "nerves"—*should* the imperial be quite so irritable? Lowell's earliest impressions of his mother invariably remark on her apparently unappeasable discontent. Nothing was ever quite as it should be. Charlotte was expert in haughty bon mots, glacial put-downs; she never stopped playing her "fearfully important game of keeping the world guessing what was on her mind," but it wasn't a game she seemed to get much final pleasure out of winning. But then pleasure was not one of her favorite pursuits. She never liked the presents she received; she either exchanged them or had them remodeled: "If you gave her a traveling case she would say with a sigh that she hoped never to see another train or boat as long as she lived."

At first it seemed that Boston was the key to her headachy, flamboyant petulance. During the first eight years of Lowell's life there were two enforced two-year stretches out of Boston, the first in Philadelphia, the second in Washington. Charlotte despised both places. Philadelphia society, she announced, was "limp and peripheral"; the city itself was "an over-sized and ersatz Boston." She delighted in patronizing Bob's naval colleagues and in snubbing their drab wives: she would spend whole afternoons waiting for the doorbell to ring so that her servant could announce that she was not at home. Much the same happened in Washington, although here her chief quarrel was with the steamy climate. She compared Washington to "a herd of tepid elephants sinking in seedy mud" and became obsessed with the threat to her son's health. There were regular medical alarms:

> "Dr. Talbot says that if it weren't for cod liver oil," her voice broke mockingly, "no children would survive this Washington climate. What Bobby needs are bracing winters and a daily walk around the Basin in Boston."

This was the argument Charlotte used when, after his two years in Washington, Bob was in line for his next posting. Strings were pulled, and in 1925 a transfer was arranged to a job as second in command at Boston's Naval Shipyard. Charlotte was triumphant and quite unabashed by the naval regulation that insisted on the three of them actually living in a house provided by the Yard. Her response was to purchase their own house on Boston's Revere Street. The commanding officer was furious and accused Bob of "flaunting private fortunes in the face of naval tradition." So for the next year and a half Charlotte and young Bobby lived in town while poor Bob reported nightly to his assigned quarters at the base:

> My parents' confidences and quarrels stopped each night at ten or eleven o'clock, when my father would hang up his tuxedo, put on his commander's uniform, and take a trolley back to the naval yard at Charlestown. . . . Each night he shifted back into his uniform, but his departures from Revere Street were so furtive that several months passed before I realized what was happening—we had two houses!

The "private fortune" that Bob's commanding officer objected to was a legacy left to Bob by his cousin Cassie: it was to provide him with a regular monthly income—"not grand enough to corrupt us," Charlotte would explain, "but sufficient to prevent Bob from being at the mercy of his salary." Cousin Cassie also left vanloads of rather grand furniture, which enabled Charlotte to inject a certain style into a house that was worryingly close to Boston's North End slums:

> My mother felt a horrified giddiness about the adventure of our address. She once said: "we are barely perched on the outer rim of the hub of decency." We were less than fifty yards from Louisburg Square, the cynosure of old historic Boston's plain-spoken, cold-roast elite—the hub of the Hub of the Universe. Fifty yards!

Perhaps part of Charlotte's trouble was that she was always a tantalizing fifty yards or so from the Hub. Certainly, as Robert Lowell describes it in his memoir "91 Revere Street," there was no lessening of tension as a result of the yearned-for move back to Boston. And for the eight-year-old boy Lowell, there was an even fiercer erosion of his father's dignity and general substance. The nightly exits to the Navy Yard were a painful embarrassment:

> On our first Revere Street Christmas Eve, the telephone rang in the middle of dinner; it was Admiral De Stahl demanding Father's instant return to the Navy Yard. Soon Father was back in his uniform. In taking leave of my mother and grandparents he was, as was usual with him under pressure, a little evasive and magniloquent. "A woman works from sun to sun," he said, "but a sailor's watch is never done." He compared a naval officer's hours with a doctor's, hinted at surprise maneuvers, and explained away the uncommunicative arrogance of Admiral De Stahl: "The Old Man has to be hush-hush." Later that night, I lay in bed and tried to imagine that my father was leading his engineering force on a surprise maneuver through arctic wastes. A forlorn hope! "Hush-hush, hush-hush," whispered the snowflakes as big as street lamps as they broke on Father—broke and buried.[2]

Later still on the same night, a dramatically distraught Charlotte burst into her son's bedroom, hugged him and declared, "Oh Bobby, it's such a comfort to have a man in the house." Bobby replied, "I am not a man. I am a boy."[3]

Although Commander Lowell's humbling at the hands of Admiral de Stahl was consistently difficult to bear, it nonetheless permitted some room in which father and son could conspire towards a fantasy accord. For the boy, whatever his private doubts, there were always the glamorous martial trappings—the uniforms, the dress sword, the late-night mariner's yarns. And having a naval father did win him prestige among his friends at school. There was enough, almost, on which to build a version of the father he would wish to have had—a version that his mother, perhaps in ironic desperation, helped to feed with her constant tales of the exploits of Siegfried and Napoleon, tales told with special fervor during those tranquil periods when Bob was away on sea duty in California. For Bob himself, the navy provided a screen to hide behind; the slang gave him a way of talking, the "comradeship" gave him people he could talk to, and the naval hierarchies offered simple, clear "career objectives" as well as an utterly dependable sense of "where he stood."

The next stage of Charlotte's discontent was to destroy all this. She set about nagging Bob into retiring from the navy, and when she succeeded—after two years of steady pressure—she came close to rendering her son fatherless. Bob took a job with Lever Brothers, the soap firm, and when that didn't work out, he declined from job to job, still smiling but, in his son's eyes, a ruined man, emasculated: "In his forties, Father's soul went underground."

Even in his new civilian job, Bob remained the butt of Charlotte's not quite witty enough taunts: "Don't you think Bob looks peaceful? They call him the undertaker at Lever Brothers. I think he is in love with his soap vat," or, "Bob is the only man in America who really believes it is criminal to buy Ivory Soap instead of Lux." Even in an account as studied and pitying as "91 Revere Street"—written nearly thirty years after the event—Lowell found it hard to suppress an exasperated loathing of his father's spinelessness. At the time, a child of ten, he could merely look and listen—and wonder repeatedly: "Why *doesn't* he fight back?"

Fighting back was one of the few things Robert Lowell got high marks for during his schooldays. He is remembered as dark, menacing, belligerent; always bigger, stronger, shaggier than his contemporaries—always ready to take his own unpopularity for granted.

From Brimmer kindergarten (which he attended for one "happy" year when he was five), he moved to schools in Washington and Philadelphia. At kindergarten, he had "enjoyed every minute"; he had

> learned those stories, illustrated and edifying, of Samuel and King David, also how to play soccer, and the game of the good deed, making some one smile once a day.[1]

In Washington and Philadelphia there were no such sunnily improving chores; long division replaced the game of the good deed, and the outsider from Boston elected to sulk his way through the first stages of his education. His mother would try to persuade him that the Potomac School, say, was every bit as congenial as Brimmer, but Lowell's triumph here was *never* to reply, "Washington sure isn't Boston." If he had said anything of the sort, "Mother could have explained to herself, my father and above all, me, why all my tortures came from living in Washington."

Rather than permit any such easy alliance, Lowell remained churlishly stoical, or was needling and argumentative, until the great move back to Boston in 1925 saw him reenrolled at Brimmer. Brimmer, though, was not the haven he remembered. Junior school was rather more demanding than kindergarten; smiles were no longer on the syllabus. Already aware of his unusual size and strength, Lowell seems at this point to have adopted the persona that was to serve him for most of his early adolescence: "Thick-witted, narcissistic, thuggish" was how he described it. Certainly, he was never thought to flaunt much boyish charm.

He now saw Brimmer as an awesome and perplexing place. Its eight upper grades were all-girl and therefore the "school's tone, its *ton*, was a blend of the feminine and the military." The lower, coeducational grades were incidental to the school's real spiritual thrust, and the gawky, girl-shy Lowell soon identified the regime of Brimmer with the regime of 91 Revere Street. Both worlds were, unnervingly, worlds ruled by women. "I wished I were an older girl. I wrote Santa Claus for a field hockey stick. To be a boy at Brimmer was to be small, denied and weak."

To boys of his own age, though, Lowell was neither small nor weak, and he was able to establish his own local tyranny by regularly bloodying the noses of schoolroom rivals like Bulldog Binney and Dopey Dan Parker or by spraying enemy third-graders with wet fertilizer: such deeds were sufficient to win him a reputation for being "difficult," if not "impossible," but were of little substance when it came to making an impression on the Amazons who towered over him at Brimmer. Mostly he had to take refuge in dark, vengeful fantasies:

The "contract" with Mother and Father had been that I could stay home from the Trinity Church Sunday School, if I would write my weekly English theme for Miss Bundy at the Brimmer Boys and Girls' School on Brimmer St. One shoe was untied. One stocking was wrinkling down to my ankle. I was wearing a "Byronic" as Mother called it, a soft collar which had been specially fitted to my ordinary shirt to ease my breathing because I was still thought to be suffering from asthma. I sat in my Father's favorite chair, spread out his mechanical drawing board, and began my composition. Miss Bundy had said that the script I had learned at my school in Washington D.C. was a snake-dance. I was learning to print. I wrote in ugly legible letters:

Arms-of-the-Law, a Horrid Spoof

Arms-of-the-Law was a horrid spoof most of the time, but an all-right guy on the 29th of February. He was also a Bostonian, an Irish policeman and a bear. I wish you could hear Arms talking big about his mansion with a mansard roof on Commonwealth Avenue. He realy [sic] and truly lived in a calcified tooth, which the neighbors mistook for a sugar-loaf. The room he like [sic] better than all other rooms in the whole world was a mushy brown abcess [sic] called "my cave." Arms like sleep better than liquor or living. He also like to take Sunday afternoon tours with Father on the Fenway in the Old Hudson. Arms thought belly-aching at Father's driving was more fun than a barrel of monkeys. The blood that Arms' heart beat up was the tobacco-colored juice of a squashed grasshopper in a lawn-mower.

Lowell's educational destiny had, of course, been mapped out for him at birth. His name had been entered for St. Mark's, the upper-crust Episcopalian boarding school in Southborough, Massachusetts. He was due to go there at thirteen, but was obliged to quit Brimmer at eleven. In 1928, therefore, a "respectable stop-gap" had to be found, and for several weeks Mr. Lowell was forced to spend his Sunday afternoons inspecting the posher country day schools in the Boston neighborhood. Charlotte was determined to have nothing "suburban" or "middle-class," so on his return from each tour of inspection, Bob was subjected to an exacting quiz. Invariably, he had somehow managed to botch the assignment. He rarely got to see the headmaster in person; at best he would listen to the grumbles of a very junior staff member, at worst he would find himself soliciting advice from the school janitor. At each school he visited he learned something unpleasant about all the others, and by the end of the day he was always comfortably undecided. Charlotte announced her astonishment that "a wishy-washy desire to be everything to everybody had robbed a naval man of any reliable concern for his son's welfare" and set about fixing things herself.

The chosen school was Rivers, "an open-air, i.e. unheated school where scholarship was low, health was high, manners were hearty." Lowell's own recollections of Rivers are all to do with freezing or with fighting. He played a lot of marbles and (reluctantly) some baseball. Academically, he thought he was doing pretty well if he came nineteenth in a class of twenty-seven. But his real triumphs were triumphs of brute strength. In his two years at Rivers he graduated to the status of school tough via a series of spectacular playground victories. Once, with his arm broken from an earlier dust-up, he strode into battle against an enemy gang's "flying pears" and "stood off multitudes with only my garbage can lid as a shield, a little girl a head shorter than I was, and a boy hardly tall enough to walk on two feet."

Lowell's army of course won the day; and this was how he loved to see himself: the one against the many, the victor against daunting odds. He delighted in his battle scars and would fall asleep at night fondling his newly lacerated chin:

I wanted to handle and draw strength from my scar. David Howe did it in a battle with sawed-off broomsticks. When the blood came I was friends with David, a hero to his sister and later, when the scar formed, Mother called me "old soldier."

For the eleven-year-old warrior, there could have been no sweeter praise.

Lowell's most intense friendship at Rivers was with a boy we will call W.A.—selected by Lowell, no doubt, because he was "a little less everything than I was,—less strong, less unpopular, less a C-minus student, less a child of fortune, less his mother's son." For an exciting period, the two were inseparable, comrades in delinquency and "bound *closer than life, closer than breath,* we used to say." They bullied and shoplifted together, terrorized the school bus, stole smaller boys' marbles and made themselves ever more dashingly disliked. W.A. was perhaps the first of the poet's disciples, and—as with others he recruited in later years—Lowell believed himself to be far more than just a master to his slave. At night now, when he had finished sifting the day's martial glories, Lowell would murmur to himself, "Every day, in every way, I am becoming a better and better friend to W.A." What W.A. thought remains (perhaps happily) unknown.

Although Lowell accepted the inevitability of his transfer to St. Mark's, he was unable to go there without putting up a decent fight. As the time approached, he would devise ever more ingenious debater's points to counter his mother's plea that St. Mark's was a "gift," a "sacrifice," as well as a revered family tradition (Lowell's great-grandfather, Robert Traill Spence Lowell I, had been headmaster there, and his father was a former student). For example, if Charlotte refused to buy him new fishing tackle, he would argue that she ought not to spend two thousand dollars a year on St. Mark's if it meant that he had to be denied the things he really wanted: "You ask me to thank you for giving me what I hate." "Why wear Sunday clothes seven days a week? Why want to be better than everyone else if you aren't? Why must I owe my parents two thousand dollars when my allowance is twenty-five cents a week?" And finally, when none of these strong arguments could make its mark, he would simply plead, "Mother, wouldn't it be fun to fish twelve months a year?"

These wrangles were a kind of love-play—"Mother and I loved knocking our heads together until they bled. We couldn't do without it for a day." And it was from these early jousts that Lowell had his first taste of rhetoric, of argument pursued for the sake of wit and wordplay rather than for any just or true solution. He relished his mother's "wonderfully detailed and good-humoured exaggerations" and strove hard to match her in comic outrageousness. A subject like St. Mark's was in fact far too "real-life" for them to indulge the full range of their talents—and, in any case, each of them knew that the outcome was unshakably decided. But the teasing had to be kept up. It was a vital, if complicated, bond—and for Lowell an early training that was to have ambiguous rewards.

St. Mark's itself was not the wittiest of institutions, and still made much of its high-minded origins, its similarity to the British public school, and its annual football match with Groton. In theory, it molded the young spirit to an Episcopalian design; in practice, it provided Boston with an annual supply of clean-limbed bankers, lawyers and junior executives. Founded in 1865, it was an efficient, solemnly benign academy; its buildings were modeled on the cloisters and quadrangles of an Oxford or Cambridge college, its aimed-for style was effortless, agreeable superiority.

The original devout conception of St. Mark's was still in evidence, though not overemphatically. The headmaster, for example, was permitted to be a layman, but

> He must be a man of personal religion not first because he is the headmaster of a church school but because the faith, chivalry and mystery of religion are essential to the upbuilding of an American boy's education and character. And being the headmaster of a church school his loyalty will be to the church and his heart will be in its worship. Only thus can the whole school, masters and boys, be one sympathetic family.[2]

Lowell had his doubts about the "family" atmosphere when, as a new boy at St. Mark's, he was introduced to the pettily sadistic rituals of Bloody Monday and Sanguinary Saturday. On these days of "initiation" the prefects would set the new boys silly tests or send them on complicated errands; the punishment for a less than perfect performance was to be thrashed with a paddle or a piece of kindling wood. In October 1930 (after over thirty years' rule by William Greenough Thayer) St. Mark's had acquired a new headmaster. A cautiously liberal historian from Harvard, Francis Parkman was to phase out some of the school's more barbaric customs, but for most of Lowell's stay there the British-style monitor system remained intact: big boys beating small boys, with old men watching fondly from the wings.

Lowell's own bloodthirstiness was maturing with the years. His hobby was collecting toy soldiers; his favorite reading was military history, or, more accurately, the history of solo, high-rank brilliance: he showed little interest in, say, the trench stalemate of World War One—unlike his contemporaries in Britain, his childhood had not been saturated with eyewitness horror stories or marked by the deaths in war of uncles, cousins, family friends.

Aside from history, Lowell was a below-average student. It was only in his last two years at St. Mark's (1933–35) that he began to see himself as distinctively an "intellectual." At the end of his first year, for example, he was fifth from the bottom of his class, and his letters at this time are appallingly misspelled, with each block capital carved out as if it had cost him an excruciating effort (this childlike "printing," and a good deal of the bad spelling, were to stay with him for the rest of his life—and a number of his friends vaguely thought of him as "dyslexic").

As at Rivers, Lowell joined forces with the second most unpopular boy in the class: Smelly Ben Pitman or "a boy called Everett from Colorado." He and Everett had to room together "because nobody else would room with them," and "they did nothing but fight, from the beginning of the day to the end." In football games, Lowell always contrived to be at the bottom of every scrimmage: "as if he were defying," the coach remembered, "the combined might of both teams to crush him under." At football, he was given to a bull-like domination of the mid-field, scattering opponents and teammates alike. An ex–St. Marker has recalled:

> Once years ago I returned to St. Mark's as a reuning [*sic*] alumnus. The aging master (Roland Sawyer) who had coached football in Lowell's time and had taught me trigonometry recognized me. "Still fighting the world?" he said. He appeared to remember me as a quixotic schoolboy rebel and I paraphrase what he told me. "You were always fighting the world, a little like Robert Lowell. But Lowell was stronger and a whole lot wilder than you. He was ready to take on everybody. That's why they called him Caligula."[3]

The nickname "Cal," which Lowell stuck to all his life, was part Caligula and part Caliban. Indeed, it appears that the Caliban came first, after a class reading of *The Tempest,* and that Lowell somehow had it transmuted to the (to him) more glamorous Roman tyrant. His classmates considered both models thoroughly appropriate:

> He was called Caliban. He was also called Caligula—the least popular Roman emperor with all the disgusting traits, the depravity that every-one assumed Cal had. So between the two, well, Caligula stuck and Caliban disappeared. When I began to know him well, I refused to use those names, but I couldn't find another name that he would accept. Bobby was out, his parents called him that. I called him Traill Spence and he complained that it sounded as though I was summoning a butler and so I too had to call him Cal.[4]

The "disgusting traits, the depravity" which Frank Parker speaks of here seem to have been fairly mild—unlaundered clothes, untied shoelaces and an intimidating physical awkwardness—but in the starchy atmosphere of St. Mark's it is easy to see how Lowell came to be marked out as a "wild man." He was also prone to intermittent fits of rage. These were "cautious rages," according to one friend; "They weren't really mad, challenging rages." Even so, in someone of Lowell's dark, disheveled bulk, they were vivid enough to isolate him from the spruce and orthodox achievers in his class. Not that Lowell was the only "Caliban" at St. Mark's. Thirty years later he was still afraid of Billy Butler:

> I can remember when everybody and his dog began to tease me with the jingle about Boston being the city of beans, Cabots and cod, where the Lowells spoke only to God. I was at St. Mark's Boarding School in Southborough, and away from home for the first time. My class-mates mostly came from Tuxedo Park and Westport. They found the school's tone penurious and chafing; they felt out of sorts with the New England climate. One afternoon, Billy Butler chased me under the stone hood of the chateau-sized fire-place in the junior common room. We had been reading in Roman history about the Burgundian braves who greased their long yellow hair with rancid butter. Billy's hair was like that, or like a girl's. His nose was arched like Garbo's. He was sensitive, power-ful, backward and cruel. Billy so terrified me that afternoon, that today, almost thirty years later, I have no need to close my eyes to see him. In front of my nose, he is shaking an expensive compass stolen from me-

chanical drawing class. The legs open and shut like the claw of a lobster. "Lowell R." Billy shouts, "If God talks to the Lowells in Boston, God talks Yiddish, by God!"

I asked my Father about this Yiddish business. Father was a naval officer by profession and faith. Despite his name and connections, he felt like an outsider in Boston. "I don't know about the Lowells," he said, "but of course God talks Yiddish." Father then slipped off into his typical whimsy. "God," he said, "has promised the Zionists that he will brush up on his Hebrew. He finds it hard work talking the King's English and Beacon Hill Brittish [sic] to Bishop Lawrence." Suddenly, Father dropped his eyes, as though he had been blinded by sunlight. He studied the blue eagle tatooed [sic] on his fore-arm. He said, "You Bostonians want everyone, even God and Calvin Coolidge, to be cold fish and close as clams." I was no more than twelve years old and a blithe second-former, but something in my Father's voice made me feel meant [sic] and insulted.

In Lowell's fourth year, though, he made two important allies— and this time they weren't just comrades-in-mayhem. Frank Parker was one of them, and the other, Blair Clark, recalls:

We were half intellectuals, half rebels. I never thought of Lowell, when he approached me and Parker, as an *intellect*, though God knows what I thought an intellect was, at the age of fifteen. He certainly wasn't a jock, although he was the strongest boy in the class; people left him alone —although they thought he was crazy—because he was so strong. And now and then he proved he ought to be left alone.[5]

In Blair Clark's account, there was an awesome deliberateness in Lowell's metamorphosis from lout to man of sensibility: "he created himself as an intellect, as a creative spirit. It was astonishing to see such focus."[6] Certainly, until the age of fifteen, Lowell's natural competitiveness had had no focus. It found its expression in explosive showdowns with his parents when they came to see him on weekends, in dormitory punch-ups or carnage on the sports field. The association with Parker and Clark gave him a new sort of gang to lead:

We were a mini-phalanx that he was head of—and there were only three members. But it had a definite moral function and he was unquestionably the leader—to the aggravation of both Parker and myself, as time went on. It was really the imposition of a will on us. And there was a slightly crazy element to it, even then.[7]

Late-night bull sessions on "the meaning of life"; immersion in translated Homer; unmerciful self-scrutiny—"What do you do with yourself, how do you make yourself better?": these were the terms for membership of Lowell's alternative academy. As to the regular curriculum, the whole point of his rebellion was to find St. Mark's sadly inadequate to the requirements of the really serious truth-seeker:

> On a cultural side, one art is taught, literature. In the modern languages this study is dilatory: the student never learns to speak the language; he reads, if at all, its classics without taste. Latin and Greek are better taught than at other schools but even at that with incomparably less discipline than in the last century. English is studied without enthusiasm or perception. After six uncomfortable years the student, still bordering on illiteracy, has no notion of literature's urgency and value.[8]

Lowell wrote this some five years after leaving St. Mark's, so one can imagine that, at the time, the arrogance might have been even more nakedly emphatic. It was by force of self-righteousness and exclusivity that the trio conducted their dissident maneuvers, as Blair Clark recalls:

> We were never subversive of the order at St. Mark's, however contemptuous we were of it, with its athletic values and its stockbrokers' sons, and so on. The compulsion was moral—it wasn't literary or cultural. It was an entirely priestly thing. He was the leader—and we were rather laggard acolytes in his view. We did challenge him a bit. But there was definitely a bullying aspect as time went on.[9]

Lowell, indeed, showed that he had lost none of his old taste for fisticuffs when a new master, Richard Eberhart, made his appearance at St. Mark's. Eberhart had studied at Cambridge with the Experiment group that included I. A. Richards and William Empson, he had a small but visible reputation as a poet, he had heard of Eliot and Picasso. Frank Parker showed signs of falling under Eberhart's spell, and was instantly disciplined: "Cal beat me up because I was going to see Eberhart." But Lowell eventually saw that the amiable Cousin Ghormley (as Eberhart was nicknamed) was no threat to his domination of trio ideology and there was a softening. And when, after reading Eberhart's "The Groundhog," Lowell perceived that the man might even be a genuine artist, he decided to adopt him as a kind of senior adviser to the group—a provider of booklists, and of books.

During his final year at St. Mark's, Lowell became associate editor of the school magazine, *Vindex* (Frank Parker was art editor), and published a few trifling and pretentious pieces in free verse. His most notable contribution, though, was an essay called *War: A Justification.* [10] It was an effort Caligula himself might not have been ashamed of. Lowell's aim is to counter the view that war merely "brings bloodshed, depravity and confusion." He concedes that "these are very serious objections" but goes on to demonstrate that "not only the good that [wars] bring far outweighs the evil, but also that they are essential for the preservation of life in its highest forms." In peacetime, he avers, the world is in a "pitiful condition," there is a "spirit of listlessness and decay. The people are united by no common goal. They do not have to make any great sacrifices. Success comes to them almost without effort." He cites Ulysses as "the man of hardship and war" who "radiates life, energy and enthusiasm." But war is not only the test of the individual spirit: "It unites mankind, for it shows that greatness is to be achieved, not by individualism, but by co-operation." It also gives "cowards and thieves . . . a chance to gain self-respect and honour." And as to the preferred outcome:

> The more deserving side may not always win; but war is the fairest test of which we know. The nation which succeeds must have the greater moral, physical, mental and material resources.

The year was 1935, but there is no evidence that Lowell was subscribing to any European periodicals. His toy soldiers had given way to a growing library of Napoleoniana, and he was already trying to reconcile his unruly energies with his almost monastic reverence for the disciplined, the harsh, self-abnegating Way.

Up to the time of Eberhart's arrival at St. Mark's, Lowell seems not to have thought of poetry as his calling; indeed, at that stage, Parker was regarded as the likely writer in the group. Under the shadow of Eberhart's example, the group's literary self-awareness started to take over. For the summer of 1935, a trip to Nantucket was decided on. Lowell had rented a small cottage—not for frivolous holidaying, but for a stretch of intense, Lowell-directed self-improvement. Both Parker and Clark still remember this and later retreats with a kind of horrified puzzlement. What *was* Lowell's power over them that they should have submitted to his reading programs, his rules of conduct, his imposition of roles? Parker (still quakingly) recalls:

> I wasn't physically afraid of him. I wasn't really *afraid* of him. I think my picture of our friendship is of Aesop's bronze vessel and clay vessel crossing the stream. The bronze vessel says: "Come and help me, give me company." And the clay vessel foolishly does it and is jostled and of course the clay breaks and the bronze goes on. I think I rather saw myself as the clay vessel there. I didn't want to go jostling across any stream with Cal.[11]

But jostle he did, and so did Clark, whose chief memories of Nantucket are to do with Lowell's "brutal, childish" tyranny. Lowell prescribed not just the trio's intellectual diet; he was also in charge of the daily menu: "We had dreadful health food all the time. The diet was eels—cooked by me, badly—and a dreadful cereal with raw honey. All decided by Cal." On one occasion, Lowell decided that Blair Clark should give up smoking, and when Clark resisted "he chased me around and he knocked me down, to make me give up." On another, it was decided that Experience required the trio to know what it felt like to be drunk. Lowell announced that the brew would be rum mixed with cocoa:

> I remember I made the cocoa. And we drank it as if we were mainlining heroin. I remember the chair falling over and my head hitting the floor. We got blind drunk in about twenty minutes. Next thing I remember was staggering onto the porch outside—and how I didn't choke on my own vomit, I don't know. Why *did* we go along with it?[12]

Like all "natural leaders," Lowell was probably only dimly aware of his troops' private agony, and if he did give heed to their misgivings, he would no doubt have seen them as weaknesses which it was his duty to correct—for their sakes. In letters to Eberhart from Nantucket, he makes it clear that certain essential decisions had been made:

Dear Mr. Eberhart,

Frank has probably told you all about our surroundings. They are in many ways almost ideal. The climate is cool and we are secluded; yet it is not too cool to be comfortable and we are not so secluded as to be shut off from life. The material side of living is not very difficult, although I am afraid we are not maintaining a particularly high standard.

For the first fifteen days we studied the Bible (especially the book of Job) and I expect we will return to it off and on during the summer. I shall refrain from giving any critical opinions. It suffices to say that I now believe parts of the Bible rank with Homer and Shakespeare and that for vigour and force the Hebraic poetry is unequalled. I have been reading lately Wordsworth's "Prelude" and Amy Lowell's life of Keats. I have come across many magnificent passages in the "Prelude" and have found Amy Lowell invaluable as a critic. But what has impressed me most is the picture both give of the young poet forming into a genius, their energy, their rapid growth and above all their neverending determination to succeed.

During the short time that has elapsed since school ended, I have come to realise more and more the spiritual side of being a poet. It is difficult to express what I wish to say, but what I mean is the actuallity [sic] of living the life, of breathing the same air as Shakespeare, and of coordinating all this with the actuallities of the world. My beliefs haven't changed at all only now I am beginning to *feel* what before I merely thought in a more or less impassioned or academic sense.[13]

A month later Lowell writes again to Eberhart. He has completed twenty poems, and is planning a long work called "Jonah" in Spenserian stanzas; he has read Blake, Coleridge, *Lear*, *The Tempest*, *Cymbeline* and a life of Christ. He also reports that "Frank is making good progress, although it is hard to define. I feel that he is standing on his own two feet, that he has a growing devotion for the highest forms of art, and he has the creative desire." As to the group itself, its sense of a religious as well as a cultural mission had become a good deal more explicit than it was at St. Mark's, where, although Lowell sneered at the school's pretense to godliness ("In place of Christ the God of St. Mark's is the Discobolus"), he had never been thought of as a particularly vehement believer. In August 1935 he submits to Eberhart the trio's new aesthetic:

Our aims have narrowed down to an expression of God which I feel as an infinite and ever-present power, always working objectively on man for what is good. That he always forgives, suffers when we suffer, and that he seeks only to serve, and never punishes. This is the highest, and only duty of art, for here only is truth. My only doubt is in myself not in what I am trying to do. Of course God is not a physical being with likes and dislikes, but rather a force striving to perfect man. Personifying him is not however so foolish as it sounds. For man is the highest thing we know of and what can be greater than the highest virtues in man infinitely expanded. I hope you follow me, for I realise the inability of expression.

What I have done this summer has been to begin understand [*sic*] God, and I have grown to love my art, and those who were great in it.[14]

Two months earlier, Robert T. S. Lowell, Jr., '35, had celebrated his first verse publication; called "Madonna," it shows him to be more at ease with God than with his art:

> Celestial were her robes;
> Her hands were made divine;
> But the Virgin's face was silvery bright,
> Like the holy light
> Which from God's throne
> Is said to shine,
> Giving the angels sight.
> Sleep on in thy serenity;
> Breathe on thy constant joy.
> When I look on thee,
> A vision meets my eyes,
> A maiden calmly singing,
> The Savior's message bringing.
> Her song will never cloy;
> She will not mar the quietness
> Which in eternal Paradise
> Is through the silence ringing.[15]

3

Some years after Lowell left St. Mark's, Richard Eberhart composed a verse play called *The Crystal Sepulcher;*[1] a strikingly inept work, it featured as its hero a tormented schoolboy poet, for whom Lowell was the model. The "action" of the play involves the anguished hero-figure being examined and pronounced upon by a succession of baffled but well-meaning adults: the parents, the schoolmaster, the school psychiatrist and then a second professional psychiatrist. The "facts" the play deals in must be seen as questionable, but there is a value in its general view of the adolescent Lowell: for those grown-ups who took an interest in him he was clearly thought to be more than just ordinarily odd or mixed-up. The character portrayed by Eberhart is demonic and possessed, not really human.

Eberhart's personal view is (presumably) stated in the advice offered by the schoolmaster:

> I am for you but I am also against you.
> The cost is too great, the prize you seek too high.
> The world is rough. Torn too, I give my advice:
> Keep your feet on the ground, renounce the sky.

The college psychiatrist is even less sympathetic; to him the Lowell figure is quite simply "mad," he "eats toenails," is "rude, vain, cruel, gloomy" and "talks with bitter cryptic wit": "Furthermore, I must point out that he is unclean."

Small wonder that the playwright enlists more specialized assistance. The professional psychiatrist is called in and delivers the following summary of symptoms to the boy's mother:

> I note here especially the trauma at his birth,
> That he growled when young, with stance of an animal
> Much too long, that as a little fellow he was vicious,
> Delighted in sharp instruments, was like a cannibal
> In being violently able to get his way;
> That early he developed the solitary and lonely, the surly.
> And that with the others he did not choose to play.
> He refused you as nurse, and that was early.

All this fits rather too neatly with the Caliban cartoon of Lowell as half-man, half-beast, but what does seem certain is that before Lowell left St. Mark's, his mother had had consultations with a Boston psychiatrist called Merrill Moore and that Moore had talked to Eberhart. *The Crystal Sepulcher* amalgamates all the prevailing anxieties and prejudices and suggests that by 1935 Lowell had indeed become a "case."

Merrill Moore was thought to be the right man to opine on Lowell because he was himself a poet of some reputation. He had been a fringe member of the Southern "Fugitive" group led by John Crowe Ransom and Allen Tate and was famous for writing only—but voluminously—in sonnet form. One of his books was called simply *M* because it contained one thousand sonnets, and a current story was that Moore kept a note pad on the dashboard of his car and could scrawl out fourteen-liners while waiting for the lights to change. At any rate, the sheer bulk of his output was usually sufficient to quell any very severe critical objections, and from Charlotte's point of view he offered a perhaps unique combination of medical and literary know-how. She herself had been seeing him about her own "nerves" and had left Moore in little doubt that *her* mental balance depended largely on the balance of her errant son.

The consultations with Moore were all part of Charlotte's continuing campaign to "tidy up" her no longer small Napoleon. Her efforts had intensified as they had become more self-evidently hopeless. Both Frank Parker and Blair Clark have memories of her incessant, fruitless nagging:

> She was very uncomfortable about him—he was so clumsy, so sloppy, so ill-mannered. She would say things to him like "See what nice manners Blair has." And I played that role because it was helpful to him. I

really think there was a psychological fixation on dominating Cal by that woman. And what does an only child do—with an obsessed mother and a weak father who goes along with that obsession?[2]

Inevitably, one of Charlotte's chief obsessions was that—after St. Mark's—Lowell should take his rightful place at Harvard. Cousin A. Lawrence Lowell was president of the college, and while still at St. Mark's, Lowell had spent evenings with him rather as he spent evenings with Eberhart. In both cases, the extramural guidance Lowell sought was in the interests of poetry, not of academic scholarship, but for Charlotte both mentors seemed reassuringly solid and conventional. Her hope was that Harvard orderliness would eventually tame Lowell, and in the fall of 1935 she was relieved to find her son actually enrolled and attending classes. His grades at St. Mark's had improved during his last year, and on leaving school he had been able to muster enough courtesy to write a "proper"—if slightly ambiguous—letter to his grandfather:

I have had five very pleasant years at school and I will be sorry to leave. I have at last found myself and now feel confident that I can and shall accomplish what I set out to do. College in spite of certain objections will on the whole I think prove very profitable.[3]

This was written before Lowell's summer at Nantucket. By the time he actually entered Harvard, his self-educating impulse had hardened to a state of near rebellion. And, as always, the rebellion would be all the more enticing if it could be directed at his mother. Charlotte believed in Harvard; it was to be expected that Lowell would therefore decide to treat Harvard with contempt. He enrolled in an all-English course, a clear declaration of his intention merely to *use* the university, and, after dabbling in this for a while, simply gave up going to classes.

There were higher matters to attend to. He announced to Frank Parker and Blair Clark that the trio's energies should henceforth be directed exclusively towards the arts. Parker, he declared, would be a painter; Clark would be a musician—or, failing that, a philosopher. He, Lowell, was the poet. Parker's obedience was so complete that he left Harvard during his first year in order to devote himself to his new calling:

I thought myself that I'd never amount to much, perhaps no more than a cartoonist, even. But Cal thought there was no limit to what one could do. We were reading the commentary on Dante where a man can put himself into heaven or hell, and Cal sort of believed that, and made me believe it: that I was going to paint and he was going to write. It was like that—the splendours, the terrors.[4]

Blair Clark was less easily swayed; or maybe it was just that Lowell did not press him so hard as he pressed Parker. It is possible that he had already discerned a different role for this competent lieutenant: Clark would provide a link with the world of practical affairs and serve as a buffer between Lowell and the Lowells. As it turned out, Clark spent most of Lowell's freshman year in California, recovering from illness.

In May 1936 Lowell was introduced to Anne Tuckerman Dick, a distant cousin of Frank Parker's. A slightly over-age (at twenty-four) ex-debutante, Anne was viewed with suspicion by the smart-stuffy Boston set in which her family moved. She was thought to be too vehement and "driven," not at all a safe marriage bet for any of the grander Boston sons. Sitting out at a ball one evening, Anne had been told by Charles Francis Adams III: "You know, none of *us* would marry you because we've heard you've been to a psychiatrist."[5] And she had taken this to summarize her plight. By the time she met Lowell, Anne felt herself to be drifting towards a mildly wayward spinsterhood; certainly, she was ready enough to be intrigued by the overtures of a nineteen-year-old poet:

The first time we met I said the only thing I knew how to say. "Do you like dances?" And he said, "I've never been to one." Well, I'd been to maybe a thousand. I'd never spoken to anyone who hadn't been to one. It was different.

In their first meetings, it was almost as if Lowell was weighing Anne up as a possible recruit to his exclusive tribe. Girls had not so far featured in the Lowell curriculum (not even, as with drunkenness, under the heading of "Experience"): the fear—as Lowell later described it—was that sex might enervate the group's elevated purposes. But what if Anne was "serious" as well as pretty? At his second meeting with her, Lowell showed her a poem he had written "about sitting in a rowing boat waiting for a bite," and she was somewhat scornful of it (indeed, she claimed much later to have found it "the most pathetic, wretched thing"). Afterwards, the poet regretfully reported back to Parker: "She won't do." And Anne (on hearing this from Parker) remembers wondering: "Is this some new kind of meatball?" As for Parker, he was not at all dismayed—he had originally thought of Anne as *his* girl.

It seems, however, that Anne was pretty enough to be given one more chance, and serious enough to accept it. An invitation was sent, via Parker, for her to have supper with "the boys." Lowell had by this time extended his group to include Blair Clark's brother, Bill, and a promising young Harvard poet, Harry Brown. All five of them were present for supper in a Cambridge restaurant, with Anne the only female guest: the idea was to see how Lowell's candidate would stand up to a feast of brilliant chat. This time, Anne was willing to be dazzled:

> The talk was all about the kings and queens of England. And they were talking about them as if they were so-and-so at the Porcellian Club. If I hadn't had such a terrible background, it would have just seemed regular. But to someone who'd been with such gross people, that Social Register grossity, to have this *light* conversation. There was nothing pedantic about it. It was completely spontaneous and humorful and yet learned in the right way. . . . I felt the happiest I think I've ever felt in my entire life.

The following weekend Lowell visited Anne at her grandmother's house at Appleton Farms near Ipswich, and during the course of an early evening walk in the garden he asked her—with much *gravitas* —if he could become one of her "suitors."

> And I said "Yes." And then we walked back to the house. And it was still light. It was June. We sat downstairs for a while. I thought I was in a dream, a very gentle dream. We went upstairs to the landing outside my room and there was a sofa there. And I think it was then he kissed me, maybe before—probably downstairs. I don't know if it was then or not that he told me he didn't like kissing. I guess he'd never kissed anyone before. But that was very disturbing because kissing was all I was interested in, with anybody. It was my main thing. But it's true, there was very little kissing after that.

For Lowell, though, this first kiss was of almost ceremonial significance; it meant, quite simply, that he had "become thoroughly and
firmly engaged, almost married." He gave Anne his grandfather's
watch to mark their (at this stage) secret pact. And immediately he
made a start on her reeducation. With Parker or Clark in tow,
he began to pay nightly visits to Anne's house and would there
stage readings of Milton, Donne and Shakespeare—and consume
a hearty dinner. "My father hated their guts because they didn't
even say 'Good evening, Mr. Dick.' They sat at his table and
acted as if he didn't exist." But Anne was still in her "gentle
dream":

> I kept thinking, "I'm engaged. I'm *engaged.*" It seemed very unreal. "I'm
> engaged." Hardly thinking who to, because who was he? What did I
> know except that he could talk about kings and queens?

She resolved to study, because her fiancé wanted her to study, and
if being a good fiancée meant nightly readings from *Samson Ago-
nistes,* then she was happy to put up with it. Lowell had indeed
acquired a new, and utterly devout, disciple.

For Lowell, Anne's house was more than just a night school or a
place to eat; it was also a sanctuary from his steadily deteriorating
relations with his parents. His year at Harvard had not been a
success; he was contemptuous of most of the English faculty, he had
had poems rejected by the *Harvard Advocate,* and he had been
patronized by Robert Frost. The *Advocate* rejection was particularly
wounding: Lowell was an applicant for a position on the magazine's
literary board, but when he went for an interview "he was asked to
tack down a carpet in the sanctum and, when he was finished, told
that he needn't come round anymore." Frost seems to have been
more subtle. Lowell had sought him out (Frost was the Norton
Lecturer that year) and asked for his opinion on an epic he was
writing on the subject of the Crusades. Frost read a few lines and
commented that it "goes on rather a bit," then recited Collins's
"How sleep the brave," as a model of conciseness.

Both rebuffs were to be recalled by Lowell in later years and no
doubt hurt him at the time. By the end of his first year he was in
a mood to reject Harvard rather than give it another chance to reject

him, and most of his quarrels with his parents seem to have centered on his future at the university. Lowell wanted to drop out at the end of his freshman year; Charlotte made it clear that if he did drop out he would have to survive without help from the family:

> Neither Daddy nor I wish in any way to force you into our way of life or behavior. You are now practically a man and free to do largely as you choose, only if you choose to be independent you must also be responsible and self-supporting. . . . We have thought this all over very carefully and this is a final decision. We will help you when we approve of what you do but we will not help you to do things of which we do *not* approve.[6]

Lowell already planned to spend a second summer in Nantucket, and his mother and father had arranged to go to Europe. Each side sensed that the other ought to be avoided for a time, and Lowell was now holding an important card. There could be no doubt that Charlotte would share Boston society's opinion of Anne Dick. Even so, just before Lowell set off for Nantucket, Anne wrote hopefully to Mrs. Lowell:

> Bobby has decided to go back to college—he is leaving here Monday and spending that night with the Swifts on his way to Nantucket. We are happy about this final decision as I am sure you are. . . .
>
> Bobby and I are planning to announce the engagement—Saturday. This seems best considering all things—unless for some reason you do not wish it.[7]

At the end of June 1936 Lowell left for Nantucket with Blair Clark, knowing that he had constructed the beginnings of what might turn out to be a complete break with his parents. In the meantime he was anxious to consolidate the gains of the previous summer. This summer's reading program was to include Elizabethan drama, and Clark and Parker (Parker joined them later) were given seventy-five plays to read before the end of "term." Anne Dick was instructed to read *Troilus and Cressida* and to mail him her comments, which he would then return with his tart annotations ("I loved being mocked so wittily. I adored it. The more he criticized me, the more I adored it"). Lowell's "campaign" style is well captured in this letter to Frank Parker:

Dear Frank:

I suppose I am the goat and write first. Of course I don't dare to affirm positively that you have not written. Perhaps you wrote a letter and forgot to mail, perhaps you mailed and forgot to stamp, perhaps you stamped and forgot to envelope, perhaps you dreamt your epistle ect. ect. ad infitum. With this off my chest I can begin.

I have written two fairly long poems and a mass of scrap work. Extracts are hardly worth while, you will see what I have done when you arrive here. When do you think you can join us? I am looking forward to seeing you tremendously.

Anne wrote me about the 25th and her day with you, and your bewitching. I swear Ipswich has the weirdest power: sorcery and death. I think "Cousin Annie" deserves a sound spanking. I don't know how much Anne has told you, but we are engaged. Reality and time crawl on us fast before we know it. 2 months ago marriage, working for a living ect. seemed far away at least 3 or 4 years in the future and now the curtain appears to have fallen almost overnight. I love her and know her as deeply and as much as anyone could in a few weeks, but must admit that she has not yet the same reality to me as you have and that the trial and tempering of the blade all lie in the future. The realities and problems are extremely powerful perhaps glorious, but at the same time infinitely sober. Can she or should she burn thru her neurosis? My indirect work with her this summer will partially answer the question perhaps. Will we be able to float our feather against the winds. All I should like to consider definite about the future is that you and I and Anne (Bobo? More?) will live and fight thru life together always working toward realizing our ideals. We have got to think about living conditions, making money; we must not compromise and sink into school teaching, we must break away from our relations and throw aside all convention that we cannot believe in. I want you to think on these things, to be a friend of Anne's just as you are mine, to help her and tell me what is happening and to realise that you are and always will be a definite and imperative factor. I am afraid this letter has the tone of a campaign speech, but after all that's just what we are beginning.

Could buy a cheap one volume Shakespeare for Bobo [Blair Clark]. The Oxford (Cambridge) at Grolier also Marlow *complete* you can get one of those green volumes in Cambridge for a dollar or two. Let me hear from you in a day or two.

Cal.

P.S. Try and persuade Anne to come down to Nantucket with you.[8]
[All misspellings are in the original.]

Lowell himself intended to spend the summer "wrestling with technique" and would try his hand at "satire and prose." He was also dabbling in the fashionable moderns: Aldous Huxley he was to find "so insipid and dull that I could endure but sixty pages," but Wyndham Lewis's *Snooty Baronet* won marks for "rough-hewn craftsmanship." There is no evidence that he was reading Auden at this time, but who else might have caused him to "wonder if the Old Anglo-Saxon alliterative poetry isn't coming back, loosened up a bit and strengthened by assonances and off-rhymes"?[9]

What is certain is that Lowell had been deep in Eliot and Pound during his year at Harvard (and also William Carlos Williams, under the encouragement of James Laughlin), and a comparison between the work he was sending to Richard Eberhart in the summer of 1935 and his work in 1936 shows an immense gain in directness and self-confidence. In 1935 he was blusteringly Miltonic, and most of his verse was, as he later called it, "grand, ungrammatical and had a timeless, hackneyed quality":[10]

> Turn back, look down, then turn thy face away
> Look up, away, thy eyelids to the ground
> See! God is shining forth in midst of day
> There see! He stands on yonder sloping mound
> The air is vibrant, swollen with the sound;
> His voice is sung by birds, the song of mirth,
> Of Eden lost and now forever found,
> Of love immortal, Spring, and mercy's birth
> Of Lord and Savior wandering on the earth.

All the 1935 poems are in this vein: awesome revelations of the deity ("a gleaming face is bursting through the clouds," "a mighty soul was sailing out to sea") or prostrated hymns to the potency of Art ("O Art, I am a beggar at thy shrine"). The voice is always mechanically grandiloquent; archaisms and inversions abound and the meter has a textbook regularity. By the following year all this has changed, and there is a pervading caution in Lowell's poems, as if he genuinely *has* become humble about the difficulties of his art: his modest aim now is for accuracy of observation, for natural—if not neutral —speech rhythms, and for some sparing exercise of the ironic intelligence. He had begun to grope towards the idea of himself as a "modern" poet, and in 1936 one way of being modern was to play it safe. This typical poem from the 1936 summer is possibly a reworking of the poem he showed to Anne Dick:

> I pulled up anchor well after mid-day
> Swishing the prongs back and forth in the water
> To shake off the mud:
> Washed the entrails and fish scales
> From my fingers
> And rowed thru the lily pads to shore
> My rods, a waving tuft of grass
> In the bow,
> Little perch with white-holes
> Between their back-fins
> Flapping against the sides of the bait-pail
> Cool water, loggy faded fish
> Prospect of picnic lunch ahead
> The shadow of tall trees above me.[11]

And a prose piece called "Grass Stroke," which seems to date from this year—it is headed "Robert T. S. Lowell, Lowell A.41, Harvard University, Cambridge, Mass."—has a sharp, surrealistic power; its transformations issue from feverishly intent scrutiny—if you look hard enough, and fiercely enough, it seems to say, you might injure your brain, but you will be rewarded by strange visions and elisions:

> Sometimes, when we are in disorder, every pinprick and scraping blade of grass magnifies. A pebble rolls into the Rock of Gibraltar. I got a sunstroke regarding the gardener mow the lawn. He dumped matted green grass into a canvas bag and emptied the bag into a rut pond behind a clump of shrubbery. People had emptied ashes into the pond; which otherwise might have been wild and unsullied with turtles flopping from rotten logs. I watched him dunp grass on the surface where there ought to have been frogs. I smelled the odor of dried verdure in my sleep; tons of it, wet and lifeless, floating and stifling. At morning the grass tide rose up gruesome.
>   The sea lay grass green and ever so serene. Sharks' fins ripped the ripe slick. The fish rythmically approximated each others' courses and crossed at intervals. The water was toothed with their tusks. Oil dripped from the tusks. Short cropped grass drooped over their round eyes. Whales spouted, and their flat tails flopped and towered, making me conscious of umbrageous trunks surrounding the sea; a Nether World

or antideluvian scene; shimmer of shiners, floating logs and submerged shadows.

The grass adjoining the garden house on a golf links was grisled, bleached to hay, and piled in heaps. As I handled it the grass came off in layers. The underneath was damp. Maggots crawled and crawled, searching after a putrifying rat, buried under grass. Fermentation and stagnation had set in. The grass was a sieve for their seething. They had bright colors; orange with black spots (bees fly in front of the blazing sun); grayish-white with pale gray spots on a soft sloat torso; sheeny brittle beetle shells, unbreakable with a sledge. And the maggots seethed and seethed, searching for the rats, with eyes that could not see in terrible grass smell.

I perceived a golf ball, hidden among weathered boards, near-by the hay pile. The ball was imbedded in a rut and had perhaps hibernated out the winder frozen. Rubber wrapping was visible through a dent. The cover was discolored and already undergoing the process of return. The earth devours her offspring: I am observing the earth-process, a huge globe masticating a little ball. I am addressing the earth; I have been addressing the earth some time. Earth, I am able to momentarily retard your dinner. I have not time to wait until you have finished your meal. I have leisure because I have a pain in my head; but you are tortoise-paced beyond reason, only tortoises are numbered among the rapid. I could swallow your golf ball; or, if I were profound, I could place it in a glass case with crossed brassies and a little white card inscribed "Pre-served"; or I could throw it into the rut pond behind the clump of shrubbery, where the gardener deposite mown grass. I observed the golf ball sinking through water; and the grass settles in layers in the rut pond. I have seen grass settling and descending for days, blade by blade. Gravitation is very grave in her demeanor, gravitation is the grave of grass blades. At noontide her odor increases as a rat putrifying, and at evening decreases as cobwebs crumbling. Gravitation is as the growth of a rose deified.

When I woke up and lay for months in bed, the membranes of my brain sprained, I wondered if the coincidence existed between noon, the putrifying rat, and my sunstroke.[12] [All misspellings are in the original.]

On July 4, 1936, Lowell permitted himself a brief holiday from Nantucket. It was Anne's twenty-fifth birthday and he decided to visit her at Appleton Farms. He had barely seen her since the engagement, and his letters had been more concerned with her instruction than with any sentimental small talk. Anne's memory of his visit (recorded some forty years after the event) may have to be treated cautiously, although both Parker and Clark have said that it rings true:

> The night he arrived, or the next night, he comes into my bedroom. I'm glad to say this now, because I want to. And he got into my bed. There were two twin beds in his room, with straw matting everywhere. . . . and I was a virgin, in the sense . . . well, I was a virgin, but a lot of necking. But I was engaged. I somehow felt I wanted it to be a complete rounded experience. Now this is the irony, and this is the sour part. He got into my bed, and said in a very unCal-ish, very unloving way, "You know, I've been to a whorehouse, twice." And that was awfully depressing. He didn't say anything about love, anything about me personally—he just said: "I've been to a whorehouse, twice. And I can tell you what the whores do. I can tell you and you can try and do it." That was that. I guess I did try a little bit, but that was the only time we ever . . . we went downhill from then on.[13]

Nonetheless, they persisted with their engagement, and on his return from Nantucket, Lowell took Anne to meet his parents at Marlborough Street. The effect was as he might have wished:

> There they were, at the door. Mr. Lowell had the most inane smile on his face. He was in the background. He was like some kind of flabby Halloween pumpkin, long after Halloween, long after it had any point. And it had started to smell a little. And she wore a mask, hiding nothing, hiding not the power of zero, but zero simply. They didn't know what to say. They were speechless.

This is Anne Dick's account, told with the vindictiveness that the Lowell parents managed to arouse in most of their son's women, but there seems no reason to question the outline of her recollection.

A liaison with an older, manifestly unsuitable woman seems to have been rebellion enough for Lowell at this point. He agreed to return to the university for another year, although in a letter to Eberhart about Frank Parker he made it clear that his view of Harvard was unchanged. "College, and especially the life it forces on one became a lid squashing down all [Parker's] energies and sufferings, so that he got into a neurotic condition, confusion piling up inside and nothing able to gain an outlet."[14] For the moment, though, Charlotte had the problem of Anne Dick to grapple with,

and Lowell could content himself with now and then threatening
to elope with Anne to Europe and with adopting an even more
offhand attitude to his Harvard classes.

Charlotte was not moved to oppose the Anne Dick affair openly
until it was proposed that the couple's engagement be made official.
She then wrote to Anne saying that Lowell "cannot possibly marry
with our consent until he is at least 21 and self-supporting." Why
could not Anne be patient and postpone any formal announcement
for a year or so? "Continue to consider yourself engaged if you want
to, and give him an inspiration to work for."[15]

In Charlotte's mind, it was not entirely a question of Lowell's
tender age. It was, she thought, his general instability that had led
him into the relationship in the first place, and his stubbornness that
obliged him to hold on to it. She was still attending her sessions with
Merrill Moore and had picked up enough psychoanalytic jargon to
enable her to see Anne as just another symptom of her son's disor-
derly attachment to his mother. But, like the writing of poetry,
Anne was also a source of "over-excitement" and therefore to be
warned against until she too was happily outgrown.

A marriage, though, would be disastrous, and it was perhaps
Charlotte's mounting nervousness on this score that prompted the
events of Christmas, 1936. On December 22, Lowell's father had
written to Anne's mother, again warning against the consequences
of an official engagement: "We feel we cannot co-operate in an
engagement which would not be for Bobby's good at present."[16] On
the following day, Anne's father, Evans Dick, received a call from
Mr. Lowell's lawyer cousin Alfred: could he meet with Alfred
and with Mr. Lowell at the Gourmet Club "on a matter of vital
importance." Evans Dick turned up and was lectured by both
Lowells on his daughter's immodesty; she had, it was charged,
been visiting Lowell in his rooms at Harvard, without a chaper-
one. That same evening Mr. Lowell followed up his lecture with
a note:

> In continuation of our conversation this evening, I wish to ask that you
> and Mrs. Dick do not allow Ann [*sic*] to go to Bobby's rooms at college
> without proper chaperonage. We know that she has been there once,
> and rather think that she is in the habit of doing so. Such behavior is
> contrary to all college rules, and most improper for a girl of good
> repute.[17]

On December 27 Anne's father wrote back to Mr. Lowell, denying that there had been any impropriety: "Cal and Anne both tell me this, and I believe them. . . . [I] wonder whether there is not some person trying to make a situation already bad enough—even worse."[18]

Next day, Anne gave Mr. Lowell's note to her "fiancé." Thirty years later, Lowell recollected his response as follows:

> My father's letter to your father, saying
> tersely and much too stiffly that he knew
> you'd been going to my college rooms alone—
> I can still almost crackle that slight note in my hand.
> I see your outraged father; you, his outraged daughter;
> myself brooding in fire and a dark quiet on
> the abandoned steps of the Harvard Fieldhouse,
> calming my hot nerves and enflaming my mind's
> nomad quicksilver by saying *Lycidas*—[19]

In Anne Dick's account, Lowell instructed her to drive to Marlborough Street and then wait in the car "for a minute." Fifteen minutes later he reappeared and told her that he had handed the note back to his father and then struck him to the ground. He had stormed out of the house with Mr. Lowell still half prostrate on the floor:

FROM THE STEPS OF THE HARVARD GYM

> Crossing a new
> hour's athletic credit from my debit card,
> I blanked on the steps of the gym at Harvard;
> furies muscled in on me from the blue,
> from my paranoia's Hawawiian azure—
> their mission was to reasure.
>
> In my velvety polo coat's pocket
> was my allowance's last dollar,
> Father's letter to my "fiancee's" father:
> "We have heard your daughter has made a habit
> of visiting our son
> in his rooms at Lowell House without a chaperon."

I hummed the adamantine
ore rotundo of *Lycidas* to cool love's quarrels,
and clear my honor
from Father's branding Scarlet Letter. . . .
"Yet once more, O ye laurels"—
I was nineteen!

In the Marlborough Street Parlor,
where oat meal roughened
the ceiling blue as the ocean,
I torpedoed my Father to the floor—
How could he stand
without Mother's helmsman hand?

With the white lipped masochistic
coolness of Billy the Kid or a stoic,
I streaked for my borrowed station wagon—
and girl! I could hear
Mother in slippers at the bannister:
"Bobby? Oh Bobby!" This happend.[20]
[All misspellings are in the original.]

For Charlotte, who had witnessed the beating from the top of the stairs, this was *the* crisis: her son had finally gone mad. Frank Parker, who called at Marlborough Street the next day, found Mrs. Lowell "raging like a tiger":

If you had a German shepherd, taking care of it and getting the best food and care and so on, and then it bit you, wouldn't you shoot it? Or wouldn't you have it shut out—that's what she said to me. Anger, fear, you know. Mr. Lowell was nowhere to be seen. He was nursing his jaw.[21]

Charlotte's first outraged reaction was to contact Merrill Moore in order to have Lowell committed to an institution. It is impossible to know how serious she was in this, but Moore is to be given credit for taking a placatory line. His first move was to persuade Lowell to apologize to his father. This wasn't difficult. Lowell was already remorseful and had told Frank Parker that the blow had been provoked by Mr. Lowell's description of Anne Dick as "no better than a whore." He hadn't "meant" to do it.[22] By March 24 he was able to write to Aunt Sarah Cotting:

> You probably know that I am back in the family. Daddy could not have been more reasonable, and I think everyone realizes that a great deal of the friction was needless and merely the result of misunderstanding. Nevertheless I sometimes feel rather uncertain about the future, the atmosphere is strained. My father is leaning over backwards too much, more than he can enjoy. Intercourse creaks: I have been home once. I haven't spoken with my mother, set times are made for meetings. All this is inevitable after a wide rupture. I hope above all that a mutual sympathy can be reached. Individual demands are relatively trivial.
>
>   I want to formally thank you for being so kind to both Anne and myself during this awkward "interregnum." It has meant a great deal to both of us.[23]

And on the same day he wrote to his grandmother Winslow:

> I have apologized to my father, and believe myself to be back in the family. I do not know how things will work out but chances are rosy. A small amount of experience has taught me to be less intolerant, less headstrong, a state of cooperation is above all necessary.
>
>   I have been trying out for the Harvard Advocate and have every chance of making it. . . . If I make it you will have the doubtful pleasure of seeing me in print.[24]

With the temperature thus reduced, Moore suggested that Lowell be put in touch with Ford Madox Ford, who was at Harvard on his way to visit Moore's friend Allen Tate in Tennessee. The idea was that Lowell should meet a "real writer," and if Ford agreed to help, perhaps some arrangement could be arrived at by which Lowell could be separated from his parents without abandoning either his academic prospects or his ambitions as a poet. Such an arrangement would also entail a separation from Anne Dick. The Lowells agreed, and a cocktail party was held at the Dicks' house. Frank Parker and Blair Clark were detailed to round up the local poets and to make themselves agreeable to Ford. As a social event the party was a flop. When Clark introduced himself to Ford, he was told that Ford spoke only in French; and Parker committed the supreme faux pas by dismissing the work of Gaudier-Brzeska as "admirable but trivial." But Lowell fared rather better. After the party, Ford announced that Lowell was "the most intelligent person he'd met in Boston." In later years Lowell modestly added, "I think that was more his low opinion of Boston than his high opinion of me."[25] In any event, Ford agreed to give assurances to A. Lawrence Lowell that the young malcontent had enough seriousness to warrant the kind of apprenticeship Moore had in mind. It was agreed that Lowell travel South with Moore in the spring of 1937.

En route, Lowell wrote to Anne Dick from a hotel in Pittsburgh, Pennsylvania: he told her that Merrill Moore might be willing to "take her on" as "a voluntary patient." Moore also intended to improve the quality of her social life:

> He has several "voluntary" jobs up his sleeve and is going to pass on all his literary invitations to you, i.e. going to parties, not giving them. Keep on the point of marriage! Perhaps you'll get an invitation to dinner with Robert Frost in a few days.
>
> Reading over the "Fugitive" poets on the train I decided Allen Tate is very topnotch, a painstaking tecnician [sic] and an ardent advocate of Ezra Pound. Three things I want to do. I doubt if Moore is in sympathy with any: Reach Ezra, keep up my organization, *and have you prepare for our marriage.* [26]

I was wearing the last summer's mothballish, already soiled white linens, and mocassins, knotted so that they never had to be tied or untied. What I missed along the road from Nashville to Clarksville was the eastern seaboard's thin fields, chopped by stone walls and useless wildernesses of scrub. Instead, plains of treeless farmland, and an unnatural, unseasonable heat. Gushers of it seemed to spout over the bumpy, sectioned concrete highway, and bombard the horizon. Midway, a set of orientally shapely and conical hills. It was like watching a Western and waiting for a wayside steer's skull and the bleaching ribs of a covered wagon.

My head was full of Miltonic, vaguely piratical ambitions. My only anchor was a suitcase, heavy with bad poetry. I was brought to earth by my bumper mashing the Tates' frail agrarian mailbox post. Getting out to disguise the damage, I turned my back on their peeling, pillared house. I had crashed the civilization of the South.[1]

The sneakily whimsical but condescending tone adopted here was to become familiar to Lowell's Southern friends throughout his later life. It is unlikely, though, that he was feeling specially satirical when he first arrived at Allen Tate's "Benfolly," in Clarksville, in April 1937. A fugitive from the victorious North, he was seeking refuge with the Fugitives; and Allen Tate was perhaps the most lordly and dogmatic of that heavily embattled group. Tate had helped found the *Fugitive* magazine (with John Crowe Ransom, his professor at Vanderbilt, and Robert Penn Warren, his room-mate at the same university); he had contributed to Agrarian manifestos, such as *I'll Take My Stand* and *Who Owns America;* he had written biographies of Stonewall Jackson and Jefferson Davis. If Ransom was the Southern writers' spiritual chief, Tate was their unflagging, impetuous polemicist. For Tate, to have captured a Lowell from

Boston was almost a political victory. Lowell viewed such postures as mere "themes" or "foibles";[2] for him the pilgrimage was wholly literary: it was not Tate's secessionist fervor that had drawn him down to Tennessee, it was his status as an international man of letters. Tate and Ransom, in Lowell's mind, connected America with the exhilaratingly convinced narrowness of European modernism. Ransom had studied at Cambridge, was admired by T. S. Eliot. Tate had served his time in Greenwich Village in the mid-twenties, and then in Paris and London from 1928 to 1930:

> He felt that all the culture and tradition of the East, the South and Europe stood behind Eliot, Emily Dickinson, Yeats and Rimbaud. I found myself despising the rootless appetites of middle-class meliorism.[3]

As to the Southernism, Ransom and Tate's regional self-consciousness simply had the effect of intensifying Lowell's sense of his own significance; it led him to "discover what I had never known. I too was part of a legend. I was Northern, disembodied, a Platonist, a Puritan, an abolitionist."[4]

Evidence of this legendary status was provided shortly after Lowell's arrival in Tennessee. Part of Merrill Moore's plan for Lowell had been that if his trip South was a success, he might switch from Harvard to Vanderbilt to study under Ransom. With this possibility in mind, Lowell attended some of Ransom's poetry classes at Vanderbilt during what was left of the academic year. In May, though, Ransom was offered a handsomely paid job as head of the English Department at Kenyon College, in Gambier, Ohio. Vanderbilt refused to match Kenyon's offer, and Ransom, perhaps piqued by this, was publicly toying with the idea of abandoning the South. To Tate, this was unthinkable, and he at once fired off an open letter to the local newspaper—a letter which, in the end, had the effect of making it impossible for Vanderbilt to keep its negotiations with Ransom on a discreet and friendly basis. In the short term, though, it stirred a merry row. And for Lowell the letter flatteringly implied that in the eyes of the South he was more than just "a torn cat, [who] was taken in when I needed help."[5] His presence in Tennessee was offered as a significant measure of Ransom's national renown:

> It is now common knowledge that Mr. John Crowe Ransom is about to leave Vanderbilt to join the faculty of a college in Ohio. I know

nothing of the reasons that may prompt Mr. Ransom to go, after twenty-five years at his Alma Mater, to another institution. If he goes, it will be a calamity from which Vanderbilt will not soon recover.

Mr. Ransom is, I fear, a little more famous internationally than locally. He is one of the most distinguished men of letters in the world today. Where Vanderbilt is known outside her Alumni Associations and similar groups of persons whose enlightenment of interest is not quite perfect, she is known as the institution where John Crowe Ransom profoundly influences, through his teaching and writing, the course of modern literature. I need not cite any of his more brilliant achievements, but I should like to bring to your attention two recent incidents that illustrate the far-reaching character of his reputation. The Lowell family of Boston and Harvard University has just sent one of its sons to Nashville to study poetry with Mr. Ransom—I do not say Vanderbilt, because young Mr. Lowell will follow Mr. Ransom to Ohio. In the past few months a correspondent of mine at Cambridge, England, has informed me that his fellow students repeatedly express a wish to study under John Crowe Ransom.[6]

The following week, Lowell did in fact travel to Kenyon with Ransom. Ransom had proposed that should he take the job, then Lowell should enroll at Kenyon in the fall. Lowell wrote to his mother that "the conditions would be almost ideal."[7]

During the first month after his break with Boston, Lowell returned home twice. "The atmosphere seemed less strained and more sympathetic" than before.[8] Both parents adopted a cautiously polite approach, taking pains not to seem either interfering or indifferent. Evidently, they were resigned to whatever prospects Lowell might eventually decide on. Mr. Lowell still had hopes that his son would graduate from Harvard, but for the moment he was keeping these hopes to himself. Lowell may have extended the olive branch to his family, but he could as easily snatch it back. This much is clear from the letter he wrote to Charlotte just before setting off on his trip to Kenyon:

> It is poor strategy but good ethics to call to your attention that charity begins in the home, and that the finest thing you could do would be to be kind to Anne, who I know would greatly appreciate it. Nothing could make me happier or love you more. The hardest and only things that matter in life demand relinquisment [*sic*], development or sacrifice. I am under the impression Dr. Moore would agree with me.

I have always believed that people must to remain healthy speak those things they feel most otherwise relationships become an arid frosting of useless courtesies. I enjoyed both book and maple sugar. In fact the book is one of the five or six unselected presents given me by anyone that I have really wanted. I really appreciate actions of that sort and am only unresponsive when no kindness is shown where it matters most.

To go back to my last two visits home. For the first time I really felt that your [sic] interested in my wellfare [sic] and happiness as such unconnected with whether you directed it or not. If you can only go on with what you have started everyone will be much the happier. I wish that both you and Daddy in writing would write what is in your minds. You are both prone to allowing an ambiguous state of affairs to exist. I am afraid this letter sounds like a sermon, but I have never been good at proprieties and concealments, if my feelings are right I cannot lose by expressing them.

Much love,
Bobby

P.S. See if you can't get Daddy to write a real letter of his [own] accord.[9]

Aside from being exasperated by the letter's pompous tone, the Lowells would certainly have noticed that Bobby still could not prevent himself from balancing each tentative compliment with a solemn admonition. Even so, a wobbly truce had been achieved, and the parents were not going to be the first to wreck it.

And in this, Merrill Moore continued to be the sturdy go-between, not only in his repeated praise of Tate and Ransom, but in offering to handle all the small but potentially disruptive practicalities. Moore, for instance, arranged for his friend Milton Starr to act as Lowell's Southern banker. Mr. Lowell could thus grumblingly hand over his son's allowance to Moore; Moore could then mail it to Starr, and Lowell would remain protected from any direct money transactions with his family. As Lowell later remarked, "For my Father money was the oxygen he survived on. Spending and even using money made him tired."[10]

Moore's other charitable gesture may well have been less selfless than it seemed. He invited Charlotte to take a part-time job in his office; her tasks were mainly secretarial, but after a time Moore allowed her to "take on" a few of his milder "cases." Apparently, her brisk approach to mental illness could now and then jolt self-pitying society ladies into health. Lowell snootily approved of his mother's new career, feeling it to be "more lasting than needles and lampshades"—though here again he felt he should remind her "that any occupation in order to be sustaining requires hard work and discipline."[11]

In spite of Tate's politicking, and in spite of a student petition organized by Randall Jarrell (who was just completing his final year at Vanderbilt), Ransom finally decided for Kenyon. It wasn't simply the money or Kenyon's offer of a rent-free campus house. Ransom had fought one or two losing battles against the gradual liberalization of the Vanderbilt curriculum, and he had no taste for the fairly heavy administrative load that his professorship entailed. Kenyon would give him time to write, and a teaching brief vague enough for him to do more or less what he wanted. He also knew that Jarrell, along with a few of his brighter undergraduates, would follow him to Kenyon.

As soon as Ransom had made the decision, Lowell set about organizing his summer. In July and August he would follow Ford and Tate to two writers' conferences that they had signed up for, and he would enroll at Kenyon in the fall. In the meantime he would stay in Tennessee. Ford—together with his mistress, Janice Biala, and his secretary, who was in fact Biala's sister-in-law—was now installed at the Tates' house for a two-month stay, and it seemed only sensible to Lowell that he should be as close as possible to his new mentors. He asked Tate if he could lodge at Benfolly until the writers' conferences began. Tate gave him a polite brush-off; the house was so crowded, he said, that any new visitor would have to pitch a tent on the lawn. Lowell, with "keen, idealistic, adolescent heedlessness," took this as a command: "A few days later, I returned with an olive Sears-Roebuck-Nashville umbrella tent. I stayed three months."[12]

Lowell parked his tent under a lotus tree, and with barnyard stock meandering around him—"occasionally scratching the tent side or pawing the mosquito net"[13]—could not have felt more thoroughly agrarian. There were occasions too when he was glad not to be a full member of the household. Ford was in a grumpy mood most of the time, and there was a running dispute over Tate's fierce guardianship of the water supply. It was a brutally hot summer, and when the cistern ran dry, Tate blamed Ford and his entourage for their too profligate flushing of the toilets. Ford retaliated by attempting to build a dew pond. He sank a bathtub in a nearby meadow, filled it up with twigs, and was baffled and outraged when it failed to produce a drop of liquid. There were also grumbles about the Southern cooking, which Ford loathed, and intermittent squabbles about politics; both Biala and her sister-in-law had left-wing attachments and didn't take kindly to Tate's magisterial pronouncements on behalf of the old Southern aristocracy: "The South of course should have seceded, it would have been better for the North. Communism is just a ruse to maintain the New York supremacy."[14]

Despite all this, work did get done. "It's awful here," wrote Janice Biala to a friend in New York:

In every room in the house there's a typewriter and at every typewriter there sits a genius. Each genius is wilted and says that he or she can do no more but the typewritten sheets keep on mounting.[15]

Allen Tate was writing *The Fathers*, Mrs. Tate (Caroline Gordon) was working on *The Garden of Adonis*, and Lowell was experimenting, on the Tate model, with "grimly unromantic poems—organized hard and classical." He had sent a few of these to periodicals and had them rejected, but "I'm in no hurry for recognition. I have no doubt of my ability to produce in the end."[16] The obsessed and frantic industry of Benfolly did not admit of failure or self-doubt and was a perfect match for Lowell's own rather self-consciously ferocious dedication. He wrote to his mother at the beginning of July:

I feel convinced that I have never worked so hard or reaped such favourable results before. This interim between Harvard and the writers schools has convinced me more than ever that my vocation is writing and that if I should fail at that I should certainly fail in anything else: fail to make good and fail to gain happiness.[17]

Lowell's hopes of "happiness" no longer seemed to include marriage to Anne Dick. Frank Parker had organized an expedition to the South, bringing with him Anne and "the boys," Harry Brown, Blair and Bill Clark. The trip was not a success. Lowell was unresponsive, and Anne had to content herself with the attentions of Parker and Bill Clark. Without any explicit declarations, the message from the master's tent was that the master was now living in a different world. Blair Clark recalls: "I still don't understand the theory of the trip. Part of it was to wind up the Anne Dick affair, but not in any neat and orderly way."[18] Whatever the theory, the effect certainly was that the affair became wound up. Anne was quietly acquiescent; after all, she barely knew what she had lost: "I guess Cal cared for me—loved me, as he would say—for about 10 days, the first 10 days of our engagement."[19]

In July 1937 the Tate ménage transferred itself to Olivet College in Michigan. The Tates, Ford, Janice and Lowell squeezed into the Tates' car, but at the end of the first day's drive Ford was so exhausted that he and Janice continued the journey by train. By this stage, Ford had had enough of the Tates' argumentative intensity: "consorting with the Tates is like living with intellectual desperadoes in the Sargoza [*sic*] sea."[20] He was also nervous of Lowell; Lowell had written to Richard Eberhart earlier in the summer: "I am not on speaking terms with Mr. Ford, the explanation given being that he is afraid I will write memoirs 30 or 40 years from now in which I will describe him as an over-stout, gouty old gentleman deluded by the poetry of Christina Rossetti and potentialities of the ideogram."[21] Ford's own version was: "That boy will write something terrible about me one day."[22]

At Olivet, Lowell listened admiringly to lectures by Ford, Tate and Katherine Anne Porter—"all of whom," wrote Lowell to his mother, "I think would be numbered among the score of living writers worth reading"—and he showed around his poems: "Everyone I have seen here appears to be convinced that should I keep on as I have been doing I should be a really good poet, and good poets are rare."[23]

The "rarity" of the good poet was one theme on which Ford and Tate could be depended to agree. Ford's lectures at Olivet, for example, were rambling, anecdotal, and now and then inaudible, but invariably they communicated "Ford's conviction of the sacred character of the writer's function, the unqualified dedication it required of anyone committed to it." Robie Macauley, a student at Olivet in 1937 (and another who was to follow Ransom to Kenyon), commented: "This is a very subversive idea and, if it were taught clearly enough, it would probably . . . reduce all creative writing classes . . . to a couple of students here and there."[24] Of all possible subversive notions, none could have been more congenial to Robert Lowell.

From Olivet, Lowell followed Ford to the University of Colorado at Boulder, where the conference starred John Peale Bishop, Sherwood Anderson and Ransom. The main attraction, though, was to be Ford's formal lecture on "The Literary Life"; and this proved to be a symbolic enactment, almost, of the truly serious man's separateness from the uncomprehending mass. Lowell certainly saw it in this way:

> I watched an audience of three thousand walk out on him, as he exquisitely, ludicrously, and inaudibly imitated the elaborate periphrastic style of Henry James. They could neither hear nor sympathize.[25]

Ford's biographer, Arthur Mizener, has modified this description by pointing out that the Boulder auditorium held only six hundred and fifty, that Ford refused to use a microphone even though his voice had been weakened by a recent illness, and that much of the lecture was a description of his relations with Jozef Korzeniowski, whom most people failed to identify as Joseph Conrad. As to the mass walkout, Mizener says:

> The audience behaved with sympathy and respect, but about halfway through, little clusters of them began quietly to slip away until, by the time Ford had finished, very few were left.[26]

For Lowell, however, Boulder did boast some local seriousness; among the assembled literary hopefuls he was particularly struck by Jean Stafford, a graduate student who had taken her master's degree there, and who had been delegated by the college to act as receptionist for the visitors. She herself had not yet published, but she was the daughter of a well-known writer of Western yarns (he called himself Jack Wonder but was sometimes known as Ben Delight), and she had been born and brought up in cowboy country. "As soon as I could," though, "I hotfooted it across the Rocky Mountains and across the Atlantic Ocean,"[27] so that by the time Lowell met her she had spent two years at a German university and was sparklingly eloquent on the "European scene." She knew the latest on Auden and Isherwood; she was witty and attractive. Lowell was impressed, and although nothing developed between them during his eleven days at Boulder, Jean promised to write to him at Kenyon in the fall.

Ford's fear of future biographical barbs did not prevent him from taking Lowell back to Olivet at the end of August to serve "as a sort of conscripted secretary . . . taking dictation in the mornings, and typing it out afternoons."[28] Ford was desperately trying to meet a deadline for *The March of Literature* and did not mind if a few lines of the manuscript were refashioned by his young admirer; he did briefly panic, though, when he heard a (Stafford-inspired) rumor from Boulder that Lowell was planning to be on the boat when he and Biala eventually returned to Europe. His Boulder informant, Natalie Davison, tried to calm him with some commonsense advice: "If I were in your boots, and he succeeded in his little plan, I am sure I would push him off the rail before we reached Cherbourg."[29] Lowell seems to have been unaware of the small dramas of discomfiture that tended to erupt around him; so far as he was concerned, his work for Ford was all part of the essential apprenticeship he had embarked on: "As he is a very great master of English prose the training is very valuable and I would not want to miss the opportunity."[30]

On September 12, Lowell returned to Nashville to prepare himself for enrollment at Kenyon on the fourteenth. As he saw it, the initiation stage was over; he had found his true masters and the way ahead was finally uncluttered:

> The summer has been very hard work and very much worth all the sweat that has gone into it. Much credit is due to Dr. Moore for his initial decisions which made it all possible. Many of the people I have met are above average but the Tates and Ford and Ransom are in a class by themselves.[31]

The bemused response from Boston simply underscored the victory Lowell knew he had already won:

> I am glad to hear that you met so many interesting people and think your plans for next winter with Prof. Ransome [*sic*] sound very pleasant.[32]

5

Ransom's arrival at Kenyon was viewed with some resentment by a proportion of the forty-strong and fairly close-knit faculty: rumors of his inflated salary had been "confirmed" by a story about the Vanderbilt controversy that had appeared in *Time* magazine, and also a popular junior instructor had been removed in order to make room for this Southern interloper. The Agrarians were thought of by some Kenyon Northerners as a somewhat cranky, perhaps even near-fascist Southern sect, and it was some time before Ransom's courtly and benign manner, and his immense conscientiousness, persuaded his new colleagues that he was no reactionary firebrand, nor even a grand poet come to exploit the idealism of the college's new president.

At first, though, he did feel isolated and was glad to have "his" students to support him. He arranged for Lowell and Jarrell to share a second-floor bedroom in the large campus house he had been given and was grateful for their company. They are, he wrote to Tate, "both good fellows in extremely different ways. Randall has gone physical and collegiate with a rush: tennis is the occasion. . . . Cal is sawing wood and getting out to all his college engagements in a businesslike but surly manner."[1]

Ransom's isolation at Kenyon didn't last too long; any personal opposition gradually fell away as people got to know him, and his own involvement with the college became instantly more deep and durable with the founding—in 1938—of the *Kenyon Review*. A literary magazine of international pretensions (it aimed to fill the gap left by the demise of *The Criterion*), the *Review* enabled Ransom to transform Kenyon from a sleepy Midwest backwater into an acknowledged center of high-powered literary bustle.

At first, however, his separateness from the faculty was thoroughly congenial to his disciples. For Lowell, certainly, it meant that he could legitimately keep himself to one side of the college-boy routine. He was still noticeably the wild man: "loud-humoured, dirty and frayed, I needed to be encouraged to comb my hair, tie my shoe-laces and say goodbye when leaving a house."[2] His tactics on the football field were as before: "the man of the Kenyon squad who played sideways into his own team-mates, but strong as a bull, spilling them over, [he] never won a game."[3] And the room he shared with Jarrell was soon reduced to such chaos that it was only a matter of time before "alternative accommodation" had to be sought.[4]

The "alternative accommodation" turned out in fact to be the perfect move for Lowell. Douglass House, a "carpenter-Gothic" construction in the center of the Kenyon campus, was earmarked as the ideal "isolation block" for Ransom's studious, eccentric followers. In 1938 Lowell moved in (after an interlude lodging in the house of another Kenyon professor: "There was a certain unpleasantness and Cal was asked to leave"[5]) and shared a room with Peter Taylor, a student of Ransom's whom Lowell had briefly met between classes at Vanderbilt. As Taylor has recalled, Douglass House proved to be "the ideal thing. . . . Kenyon was a very small school and a rich boys' school, and we were rather out of things. People lived in fraternities and dormitories and we didn't want to do that."[6]

The eleven residents of Douglass House—with Jarrell also living in as a chaperon or "housemother"—had a common interest in Kenyon. Each of them wanted to be a writer, and each considered himself to be a "Ransom man." John Thompson, Robie Macauley, David Macdowell—and, of course, Jarrell and Taylor—were to become Lowell's lifelong friends; others—and conveniently Douglass House provided Lowell with the essential raw material for his compulsive teasing—remained figures of fun in his automythology for years to come. Douglass House offered Lowell what he had never really had: a small, manageable community inhabited by gods, fools and equals—and set at a superior distance from the dull, conforming herd:

> We were regarded by the rest of the community as being just eggheads and longhairs. One time, there was a tradition at Kenyon that on Sunday

everyone stayed on in the great hall after lunch and sang songs—the college songs, of which Kenyon had a great many. But Cal and I got up to leave and as we went out the whole student body booed. We'd left before the singing. And that was generally how we were regarded there.[7]

And even in the bohemian set Lowell was considered to be something special: "he was usually the most slovenly and ragged looking of us all. He really went about in tatters, sometimes even with the soles hanging loose from his shoes."[8] Peter Taylor, his room-mate at Douglass House, noticed that in his closet Lowell always kept his "good" set of clothes—a suit, a hat, a pair of shoes. These had been bought from Brooks Brothers by his mother, and Lowell made sure that they were kept in mint condition.

Taylor's accounts of rooming with Lowell are a mixture of affection and recalled exhaustion (not unlike Clark's and Parker's recollections of him at Nantucket). Lowell would read aloud to Taylor late into the night, and at one point recruited him as a rather passive co-editor of an anthology of English poetry. There were occasional quarrels, usually about when to put the lights out, but only one real fight. Lowell now and then teased Taylor about his interest in Catholicism; he called it "a religion for Irish servant girls"—remembering here his mother's advice to an Irish maid who wanted to become Episcopalian: "No, you have your church and we have ours and it's better to keep it that way." And now and then Taylor would get exasperated by his friend's grand-scale untidiness. Lowell's bed was surrounded by a tumbledown but ever-mounting wall of books, dirty socks, letters from Boston, football boots and drafts of poems; when he'd read a book, he would simply toss it onto the pile and grab another. It could not be long, surely, before Taylor's own side of the room became engulfed by stray Lowelliana.[9]

There was also the business of the bears. Lowell had dreamed up a world peopled by "bear-characters"—or "berts," as he called them —and his favorite off-duty sport was to invent bear-dramas or bear-parables, which incorporated caricatures of friends and relatives. Each friend would be given a bear-name and an appropriate bear-voice. Lowell himself seems to have been the chief bear, known as Arms of the Law (the hero of his "horrid" childhood "spoof"). John Thompson remembers that Lowell

had a funny singsong whine he told these stories in and they were
endless. They became compulsive, but I didn't think they were all that
funny. He would tease people with them. They were familiars of some
kind—totems that he needed. I don't know where they came from.
Arms was like a sheriff—he was always arresting people and scolding
people. They all had names, and they were all sorts of bears. They'd do
outrageous things, get drunk and carry on, and then Arms would scold
them—or *he'd* be drunk. I can't remember.[10]

Peter Taylor—whose bear-name was "Sub"—takes a more charitable view, simply pleading that "There are things which can be
funny between friends at a particular time, and Cal's bears were that
way."[11] Lowell seems not to have been nervous that his bear-game
might be boring for his friends; being made into a bear was, after
all, a mark of his friendship and regard. It would have been a sour
companion who didn't even pretend to go along with it. For Taylor,
as his room-mate, there was consolation in reminding himself that
he "never felt Eliot's Practical Cats were very funny."[12]
But these were details. Taylor was, in his own way, as intent on
self-improvement as his more overtly fierce and dedicated room-
mate. Taylor wrote fiction; Lowell wrote poetry. There was no
rivalry, and no leader-disciple arrangement as with Clark and
Parker. The two of them were allies in a huge, world-altering adventure:

> We walked the country roads for miles in every direction, talking every
> step of the way about ourselves or about our writing, or if we exhausted
> those two dearer subjects, we talked about what we were reading at the
> time. We read W. H. Auden and Ivor Winters and Wyndham Lewis
> and Joyce and Christopher Dawson. We read *The Wings of the Dove*
> (aloud!) and *The Cosmological Eye* and *In Dreams Begin Responsibili-
> ties.*[13]

"And how sad and serious we were," wrote Taylor. "We didn't
hesitate to say what we wanted to be and what we felt we must have
in order to become that. We wanted to be writers. . . ."[14]

Robert Lowell had come to Kenyon knowing "more about Dryden
and Milton than any other student,"[15] but such accomplishment
soon seemed narrow and too recent. On Ransom's advice, he de-

cided to take classics as his major, and of all the bits of advice that Lowell was bombarded with throughout his adolescence, this may well have been the bit that mattered. Certainly, he was always to be grateful to Ransom for setting him tasks large enough to match his energy and (at least some of) his youthful arrogance:

> I often doubt if I would have survived without you. I was so abristle and untamed, nor would any discipline less inspired and kind than yours have held me.[16]

Lowell wrote this to Ransom in 1961. And at Ransom's death in 1974 Lowell again named him as the most decisive of all guiding hands:

> The kind of poet I am was largely determined by the fact that I grew up in the heyday of the New Criticism. From the beginning I was preoccupied with technique, fascinated by the past and tempted by other languages. It is hard for me (now) to imagine a poet not interested in the classics.[17]

Lowell's tributes to Mr. Ransom (as Ransom continued to be called by his students long after they had left the college) were always to a rather remote, avuncular presence. They had little of the nervous edge, the intimacy, that went into his relationship with Tate or Jarrell. If Ransom was the wise and kindly uncle, and Tate the revered but comically exasperating father figure, then Jarrell was the exciting older brother: possibly the first person of more or less his own generation that Lowell genuinely held in awe. Not all the late-night chat at Douglass House was about Henry James or Homer; a good deal of it was about Jarrell—his tennis, the girlfriend he had in town, his sometimes scathing view of Ransom, and also his conceit, his intransigence, his primness: "Randall never in his life used a four-letter word. He couldn't stand a joke about sex. He wouldn't have it."[18]

The tough guys in Douglass House found Jarrell hard to take—two of them even wrecked his newly done-up room one night—but everyone was agreed about his talents. "He was very bright—preternaturally bright. He knew everything," recalls John Thompson (who found Jarrell *very* hard to take). Lowell, though, never wholeheartedly joined in the Jarrell-baiting. He could see what the others meant and was prepared to gossip and to tease, but he never lost sight of Jarrell's worth—or usefulness. Peter Taylor remembers:

> Jarrell treated everybody pretty badly. Cal and I were the only ones who stuck by him through thick and thin. We would take his insults because —and I think Cal taught me something here—Cal was *determined to learn what he could from Randall.* From the very beginning. He wouldn't reject him the way other people did. Because Randall *was* hard to take. Have you read his early reviews? They were just acid.[19]

Lowell published half a dozen poems in the college magazine during his two and a half years at Kenyon, but the first one of these did not appear until December 1938. In his first year he continued to solicit the good opinion of Richard Eberhart, although his regard for Eberhart's homely pieties was beginning to crumble in the shadow of the New Criticism's care for detail. In November 1937 Eberhart sent Lowell a group of his own poems and was shocked to find that his ex-pupil had become confident enough to issue a few lessons of his own: "Your generalities are commonplace . . . If you want to write poems that will outlast the age you must condense."[20] Eberhart, much piqued, attempts in his reply to outpatronize the upstart. Only the immature, he says, have ambitions to "outlast the age"; wise types like himself simply aim "to get through life without pain." Lowell, he suggests, has been spoiled by Tate's good opinion and will probably "peter out by 25"—but that need not worry anyone: "You'll always be able to relapse into the soft arms of your Harvard background. Your name will probably get you down before it will set you up."[21] Lowell wrote back in icy terms:

> If you mention my relapsing into the soft arms of a Harvard background, I'll ask you about becoming a celibate in a fancy boarding school. . . . I have had little praise that would allow me to spoil and am not expecting to peter out at 25. The underlined words in your letter are undecipherable. Please reproduce them in the established alphabet.[22]

Lowell continued to send poems to Eberhart over the next three months (in January 1938 he sent "Elegy," "Epitaph," "Maternal Disorder," "Refusal," "Narcissus" and "The Flame Coloured Satin of Lust"). At best, Eberhart found them "so-so"; at worst, repugnant: "You have a hard lesson to learn," he wrote, "that poetry is supposed to please."[23] For Lowell, this kind of cozy motto was opposed to everything he was beginning to believe about what poetry is "supposed to be." It was clear to him that he had already outgrown Eberhart.

Lowell's own manifesto was not fully worked out at this stage, but near the end of 1938 a review he wrote of Ransom's *The World's Body* gives an idea of what he must have been groping towards around the time of his correspondence with Eberhart. He would certainly have thought that "Popular poetry is as worthless as popular science" and (almost certainly) that "Our best and typical poetry is characterized by its strenuous, alexandrian complexity. Alexandrians are circuitous; they are needfully so." In many ways, the review —when it appeared—would have struck Eberhart as a riposte to his "poetry should please" requirement:

> Proudly we declare that common and quotidian experience is beneath the grace of art. . . . Physical poetry is valuable because it is concrete. Two varieties are imagist and pure poetry. Imagist would present the particular in all its contingencies, and actually is, in varying degrees, artificial, filled with submerged intentions of its author. Pure poetry presents fanciful fictions in objective forms, and religiously avoids moral application and generality. Metaphysical poetry makes the miraculous explicit: epically, Christ or heroic actors; lyrically, the agony of departing lovers. Christ is not reducible to the good, or to modesty. He is an ejaculation of nature decently vested in an inseparable humanity. If the tears seem to have a cosmic importance, blotting out all else, becoming a flood which destroys the whole world, destroying at last the lovers themselves, such poetry substantiates its hypothesis. It preserves the richness of particulars and can, as in the great religions, make explicit the most supernatural reality, God.[24]

The "difficulty" that Lowell prizes is evident in the poems he was sending off to Eberhart, and in those that appeared in *Hika*, the Kenyon College magazine. Eberhart is not to be mocked for finding them unpalatable—they are awkward, overpacked and rhythmically laborious. In aiming for an exalted tone, they usually end up sounding ludicrously stiff and self-important. Classical references and a proudly Latinate vocabulary contribute to the hoped-for "density," but they always seem forced in for grandiose effect. And often the crushed syntax will make whole stretches of a poem unintelligible. At this stage there is no evidence of anything distinctive or spontaneous; Lowell's college poems are as artificial and pretentious as most other people's college poems. Here, as an example, is a poem called "Walking in a Cornfield, After Her Refusing Letter":

> The sun was forward and to him the sky,
> pale or at least sooty, wan without cloud
> harshly precluded penitrance [*sic*]; its glare
> abashed his eyes upon mollases [*sic*] shocks.
> The cold October corn defiling, passed
> pedestrian in stepping jolt his eyes,
> his eyes diffusely focussed on the ground;
> —O felly blank, O general review!
>
> Thus outwardly, this inwardly the view;
> loose paper blew about his voided eyes,
> his sinewed eyes, wildish elliptic orbs,
> compressed intensity in jellied meat,—
> a last dismissive crashed his moated eyes;
> uncombed hair and his sleavy [*sic*] coat not neat
> or clean sprawled on his sight, and shovel-fuls
> of sprawling print and longish finger-nails
> such as left humid gloats of jet-black earth
> on linnen sheats [*sic*]; the climax having reached
> of corn he looked down and a long league down
> clearly a cool brook ran on his chafed shoes
> A rillet classical since grass implied
> the cold rusticity of Maro's sedge.[25]

Eberhart, it should be said, also complained about Lowell's spelling and received the following reply: "In my defense I might add that mis-spelling seldom obscures meaning."[26]

It is not known who sent Lowell a "refusing letter," but it may well have been Jean Stafford. Lowell had kept in touch with her since their meeting in Boulder, and during 1938 he "wooed her something fierce"[27]—presumably by post. This could account for the nervous overstatement of a letter Lowell wrote to Frank Parker in that year. Parker had evidently met a girl who he thought might be "the real thing" and seems to have applied to Lowell for advice. The reply

from Lowell perfectly combines a flushed adolescent awkwardness
with the heavy didacticism of a headmasterly ascetic:

> In living maintain morality and coolness. Don't marry until you're
> passed thru puberty. Punning, I would add, until you've approached
> property.
>   We dangle (actually and vocally) sensualizations after flitting females.
> "That's just what I'm looking for, the real thing" etc. Such sensations
> should be understood as ebullitions of the blood. In reality you must
> ceaselessly search for regions of artistic florility [sic]. Art may be found
> flourishing in a group, in a single artist stuffed somewhere in your
> populous city, and always in your own imagination compounded with
> aesthetic products. But whenever you uncover the growing flowers you
> must chew and suck them, rembering [sic] that they are your staple.
> Women until you surpass puberty are sweets, not to be ignored, not to
> be lived on.[28]

Peter Taylor's story "1939" provides a further insight into Lowell's lumpish and lordly view of how to handle the troublesome
"ebullitions." In the story two Kenyon students—the first-person
narrator and his friend Jim Prewitt (Lowell)—set off to see their
girlfriends in New York. On the way, the two complacently discuss
the girls' "suitability":

> We agreed that the quality we most valued in Nancy and Carol was their
> "critical" and "objective" view of life, their unwillingness to accept the
> standards of "the world." I remember telling Jim that Nancy Gibault
> could always take a genuinely "disinterested" view of any matter—
> "disinterested in the best sense of the word." And Jim assured me that,
> whatever else I might perceive about Carol, I would sense at once the
> originality of her mind and "the absence of anything commonplace or
> banal in her intellectual make-up."[29]

On arrival in New York, things speedily go wrong for the narrator.
Nancy is flippant and offhand, she has been seeing a lot of an old
boyfriend, she laughs at the proud three days' growth of fluff on the
narrator's chin. The trouble was: "Nancy had never seen me out of
St. Louis before and since she had seen me last, she had seen Manhattan." Even so, things might improve when they meet up for dinner
with Jim and his girl. Not so: the conversation is stilted; Jim's girl

is more interested in the other diners than she is in Nancy; and worst of all, Jim's verdict—when they discuss the evening afterwards—is that "Nancy's just another society girl, old man. . . . I had expected something more than that." The narrator makes a handsome effort to strike back:

> Out of the corner of my eye I caught a glimpse of Carol at the newsstand and took in for the first time, in that quick glance, that she was wearing huaraches and a peasant skirt and blouse, and that what she now had thrown around her shoulders was not a topcoat but a long green cape. "At least," I said aloud to Jim, "Nancy's not the usual bohemian. She's not the run-of-the-mill arty type."
>
> I fully expected Jim to take a swing at me after that. But, instead, a peculiar expression came over his face and he stood for a moment staring at Carol over there by the newstand. I recognized the expression as the same one I had seen on his face sometimes in the classroom when his interpretation of a line of poetry had been questioned. He was reconsidering.[30]

In the story, Jim decides that Carol, after all, "won't do"—in spite of her beauty, wit and talent (she is a coming writer, and on the day Jim Prewitt visits her in New York she hears that her first novel has been accepted and that two sections of it are to appear in *Partisan Review*).

The real-life Carol, though, fares differently. By Christmas, 1938, Lowell's courtship of Jean Stafford had advanced to the point where he could invite her to Boston for the holidays. It was a fateful, indeed almost fatal, visit. On December 25, Lowell borrowed his parents' car and, with Jean in the passenger seat, crashed it into a wall at the end of a Cambridge cul-de-sac. Jean's nose was badly crushed. Lowell may or may not have fled the scene; according to Eberhart's verse play, he does. He may or may not have been drunk; according to Blair Clark, he'd bought a bottle of cheap wine, but he was also a notoriously bad driver. The upshot was that Jean was taken to the hospital to begin a long saga of dreadful operations on her nose: "She had months in hospital— she had, as her story "The Interior Castle" very savagely describes,[31] bits of bone picked out from near the brain. It was terrible. She had massive head injuries—everything fractured, skull, nose, jaw, everything."[32] Lowell was fined seventy-five dollars in the Cambridge District Court for "driving an automobile while under the influence of liquor and driving dangerously."[33]

Lowell returned to Kenyon in January 1939, with Jean still in the hospital and his parents hugely angry and distraught: for them the incident was further evidence of Lowell's instability (or, worse, in his father's eyes, his irresponsibility). As for Lowell, his guilt was painful enough; Boston-style recriminations simply goaded him into a deeper fury. Mr. Lowell's attitude to his son had now hardened into blank hostility; Mrs. Lowell still believed that psychiatric help was what was needed. Both were dreading the further scandal that would soon erupt: it had been agreed by Lowell and Stafford that she should sue him for insurance against her medical expenses. A trial had been scheduled for the summer of 1939. On hearing this, the Lowell parents decided that a summer trip to Europe was necessary in order to soothe their shattered nerves—and Charlotte was able to convince herself that she was "doing something" for her son by persuading Merrill Moore to arrange a consultation with Carl Jung. On May 27 she writes thanking Moore for his assistance: "Your very complete presentation of the case to Dr. Jung will be of the greatest help."[34] Unluckily, no notes have come to light revealing Dr. Jung's diagnosis —but years later Lowell wrote:

> That year Carl Jung said to mother in Zurich,
> "If your son is as you have described him,
> he is an incurable schizophrenic."[35]

Lowell struggled through an uneasy spring at Kenyon. His classics professor there was Frederick Santee, and Lowell spent a good deal of time in the Santees' "open house" across the street from Douglass House. It was a dramatic and chaotic household, and Lowell recalled it later on with some affection. Santee, he wrote,

> was a child-prodigy, who entered Harvard at thirteen, wrote the best Greek verse by an American in England, and later married another classics-child-prodigy—egregious people but fated for divorce and tragedy. They were plain and Socratic yet their divorce was marked with violence and absurdity; a sheet wetted to cause pneumonia, a carving knife left threateningly on a stairpost, a daughter held incommunicado by the Ransoms from both parents, insomnia, evidence, floods of persua-

sive, contradictory and retold debate. On the much adjourned day of the trial, the presiding judge, the master of sarcasm, was kicked and incapacitated by a mule.[36]

Stories of this sort surround the figure of Santee, and Lowell must have been attracted by the farce and the melodrama; Santee's chief usefulness in 1939, though, was that he had medical connections at Johns Hopkins and held views about how Jean's injuries should be treated. In the early summer, Blair Clark—who had been appointed to look after Jean in Boston—received instructions from Kenyon:

> I was told to bring Jean from Boston to Baltimore. Santee had recommended to Cal that she have another big operation at Johns Hopkins. Jean was of course being taken care of by all sorts of doctors in Boston —but she was simply told by Cal that she should have this operation. Sort of on the spot, without consultation with her regular doctors. I was in the middle. Santee was all for the operation—though I don't think he knew the nasal passage from the other passages. But Jean said to me, "Don't let them do this operation to me." And I said, "They can't if you don't want them to.". . . So there was a scene then, and she decided to leave Baltimore: a scene on the railroad platform, when I was taking Jean away. There was no fight about it. Cal had to give in. But Cal and Santee felt that they had lost a battle.[37]

It is clear from this and other evidence that Lowell's feelings of guilt about the accident ran fairly deep. Jean was not one to make light of her injuries—indeed, according to some who knew her she was a chronic exaggerator; nonetheless, she *had* suffered considerably and, Clark says, "There was about a 25 percent reduction in the aesthetic value of her face."[38] At times during the summer, Lowell considered leaving Kenyon to marry Jean (they had become "engaged" at Easter). Not only did he feel himself to have an obligation to her, but he also knew that his parents strongly disapproved of the association. Jean could not even boast the "society" advantages of an Anne Dick; and she came from Colorado: the source of grandfather Winslow's wealth but—or maybe "therefore"—impossibly nonsmart.

When the Lowells left for Europe, Merrill Moore was asked to serve as Lowell's acting guardian and he seems to have played a skillful double role. In June 1939, for example, shortly after a visit to Boston by Ransom, he wrote to Lowell's father:

> Please do not worry about him or his problems. I am only too happy to do this and act in loco parentis. Apparently Ransom's visit did a lot to calm them all down and keep them busy. I wrote Charlotte some notes about Ransom and what he told me, particularly about Cal's plans. I think all will go smoothly. Ransom expects Cal to come right back to Kenyon and tells me that Jean will not be welcome there of course. He said it in a polite way.[39]

In July, though, he writes to Lowell:

> I resent your father's putting me in the role of holding the purse strings. I would not want this position and had he not surreptitiously done it on the eve of his departure to Europe I would have refused. As it so happens the information about it came to me in a letter the day after he left Boston. I did not have an opportunity to suggest other arrangements.[40]

Moore goes on to describe Mr. Lowell as "relatively hopeless . . . problem child no. 1"; he feels that the "flight to Europe" is a mistake, a "running away from things," and he fears too that Lowell's father is heading for serious financial trouble: "It is possible that you and your mother can do something to prevent further dissipation of his property."

Lowell was responsive to Moore's man-to-man approach and particularly liked the suggestion that it was the parents who needed guidance and mature goodwill:

> My family are still a triffle [sic] difficult, but I think with your aid and good will everything will go on amicably. . . . the past year has been the most enlightning [sic] I have ever spent, so I am confident that given anything like an even break, I shall in the future achieve things of considerable value. By an even break I mean chiefly to be able to act without the autocratic guidance of friends and parents.
>
> My carreer [sic], I hope, will be exceptional rather than queer. That is I have become more and more aware of the need for an at least surface conformity, dressing inconspicuously and neatly, living by a stable economy, flaunting [sic] convention by penetration rather than by ec-

centricity. Poetry depends on beauty, passion and comprehension, but even here the above remarks on conduct have a preliminary appropriateness.[41]

As a postscript, Lowell asks Moore for the address of Milton Starr, the friend who had handled his finances in 1937; he wants to thank Starr for a summer invitation; but as if further to persuade Moore of his unremitting seriousness, he adds, "Also I feel that in this era of accumulating inhumanity every artist and thinker should do all he can to preserve and maintain the rights of the Jews." Moore was suitably respectful: "I appreciate your attitude toward economy and dealing with conventions. After all, it does have to be dealt with," and "I have the same feeling about the Jews as you have."[42]

Moore's main interest, though, seems to have been to impress Charlotte Lowell with his astute handling of a tricky situation: thus to Charlotte he represents Lowell as volatile and in need of sensitive manipulation. Towards the end of July he writes to her that Lowell has returned to Boston and is lodging as his guest at the Harvard Club; the letter reads like a medical report:

> Yesterday, Wednesday, July 19, Cal spent the day rather quietly. He dropped into the office once or twice. I had lunch with him and continued to make suggestions about interesting and constructive things to do. When he is in a friendly attitude he accepts suggestions readily and easily. I told him about some interesting poetry magazines in the library and he went down in the afternoon to see them.[43]

Moore also describes a lunch he has had with Lowell and Blair Clark, at which his two guests spent most of the time vigorously attacking the medical profession (possibly in relation to Jean's treatment). Moore realized, or thought he realized, that "they were being unconsciously aggressive towards me." But, he boasts, the wise physician refuses to be drawn into the trap:

> In other words I accepted their aggressions and turned it [*sic*] back to them, with sweetness and like [*sic*] and with insight on my part. I think my insight saved the situation. . . . At times I see how much Cal has developed and at others I see how far he has to go. . . . Of course I realize that Cal is coming up for trial and that latent guilt reactions are working. That is why I am treating him with so much consideration.[44]

Both Frank Parker and Blair Clark recall that there was some speculation at the time about Moore's relationship with Charlotte Lowell, and there is evidence that over the years some intimacy did develop. In 1939, though, the letters between them focus either on "Cal's problems" or on Charlotte's growingly confident sense of her own psychiatric skills. Her job with Moore involved two afternoons a week "taking case records, doing therapy and prehaps [sic] the Rorahach [sic] teat [sic]," but she was always ready to lecture her employer on basic principles:

> 1. To make the patient feel that he can be helped, but to throw the responsibility for the case as much as possible upon the patient himself. Trying to show him the great benefits he will derive from earnest and faithful work towards this end.
> 2. To find the most constructive way of escape, for each particular patient and to induce him to use this way in preference to his former destructive methods.[45]

Charlotte's son might have read this with a familiar thrill of horror, but Moore was ponderously titillated. He later praised Charlotte for being marvelously unspoiled by any medical-school training:

> I think you have a strength in your own character, a healthy balance in your own personality and a vigorous ego and a charming exterior personality that cannot be anything else but psycho-therapeutic.[46]

By 1941 the exchange of letters had become more coy and whimsical —she sends him rose petals, and he sends her seashells, "for you to give away to patients whom you think might be interested in conchology as a hobby or as vocational therapy."[47] By 1951 (after a visit to *The King and I*), Charlotte had become Moore's strong-willed "Anna"; and Moore himself was bizarrely self-promoted to "Yul Brynner alias the King."[48]

Lowell resumed at Kenyon in the fall of 1939, and one of his first tasks there was to master the art of public speaking. Kenyon made two requirements of its graduates: whatever their academic prowess, they would not be permitted a degree unless they passed tests in swimming and oratory. Swimming presented no difficulty for Lowell, but—along with the other Douglass House verbalizers—he had a dread of making speeches. Peter Taylor has amusingly described what happened:

> We were all shy of public speaking. So we signed up together for Mr. Black's public-speaking course. And we were all terrible. But Cal was the worst. You had to make speeches and so we talked about everything under the sun. I remember talking about popular dances like the Bunny Hug and the Bear Trot and that sort of thing. But Cal would get up, and behind there was a blackboard, and all the time he was speaking he'd be rubbing his bottom against the blackboard. He couldn't keep still. So he was the worst. And of course it was a delight to all of us to see each other do it.[49]

According to Taylor, Lowell was so stung by these humbling sessions that he set about turning himself into a speaker—and not just a competent speaker, but the best: "that old New England grit and drive." Sure enough, Lowell came out first in the class, won a twenty-five-dollar prize, and with it the right to give the valedictory address on graduation. The address itself was taken to be Lowell's revenge on those who had made him so exert himself: it was a densely worded attack on St. Mark's and similar schools for rich young athletes. Many of the Kenyon trustees were convinced that it was really aimed at them:

> . . . customs are not a culture, Boston is no longer Athens. I am emphasizing a glaring problem, our aristocracy . . . has special advantages but no superior way of life. Its manners are the automatic accident of wealth.
> Think of the motto of St. Mark's: *Age Quod Agis*. Unlike most mottoes, Do What You Do, is insanely accurate. *Do* in our American idiom means to do one's job and more to plug and sweat at one's job. Do What You Do, this is a fine utilitarian prescription for man and master. A scholar before a scholarly audience, I hesitate to invoke as my symbol our great, ox-eyed Statue of Liberty, Liberty brandishing her cyclopean incandescent torch; but as runners in a great race, it is our pleasant and devout ambition—not merely to Do What We Do, not run with a painted stick—but to hand on a torch. And so it is with aristocracies, they must have aspirations. For all of you know that as the Philistines and Goths proceed in their spiritless way to dismember civilization, they will come to all the golden palaces of learning, they will come at last to Milton, Groton, St. Paul's and St. Mark's [all fashionable East Coast

boarding schools] and there, the students who are neither efficient nor humane nor cultured will be doing what they are doing. And the indignant Goths and Philistines will turn these poor drones out of the hive and there will be no old limbs, for the new blood, and the world will revert to its unwearied cycles of retrogression, advance and repetition.[50]

In Boston, the Lowells were less concerned with "golden palaces of learning" than they were with the problem of What to Do About Jean Stafford. There were rumors (which reached Lowell at Kenyon) that Jean was being "got at" by his parents, or by intermediaries: that attempts were being made to persuade her to give Lowell up on the grounds that he would "go insane" if he married. Lowell was incensed:

> Kenyon has an unfortunate location. Everything said in Boston blows in my ears. I might as well be sitting in Dr. Moore's office or dining at the Chilton Club, . . . I beseech you to observe the negative virtues of keeping quiet.[51]

Letters of this sort (written to his mother) particularly irked Mr. Lowell, whose temper was shortening as his business affairs continued to decline. For a brief period at the beginning of 1940, Lowell toyed with the idea of seeking a Harvard fellowship; during his Kenyon examinations he wrote to his mother asking her to "confer *right away* with Cousin Lawrence,"[52] and in February he followed this up with a penciled note to Lawrence Lowell setting out a plan of studies:[53]

> Dear Cousin Lawrence:
>
> I appear to be embarked on the turbid waters of poetry and scholarship. And a career of poetry and knowledge is as hard to guide as Plato's horses. On the one hand I must range about discovering the fundamentals of knowledge, dipping into science, politics and other arcana, forever seeking an education that is both profound and practical; on the other, I must keep spiritually alive and brilliantly alive, for poetry is, as the moral Milton conceded in practice and precept, a sensuous, passionate, brutal thing. I put in the last adjective because I am modern and angry and puritanical.
>
> So much for my rhetoric, but something such as the above must be stated. My qualifications are a wide reading in English and an ability to read poetry extremely closely; a knowledge of the classics which should

enable me, in say three or four years, to read fluently not only Greek and Latin but all the Romance Languages. I have need of a thorough acquaintance with history, particularly with American history (I use the term *history* widely and vaguely but mean cultural history: and again I use *cultural* widely and mean the varieties of life man has been through). I have need of a knowledge of sciences and mathematics, and here I am totaly [*sic*] ignorant.

The relevance of such schedule to poetry is obvious. I cannot think it pedantry that a man desiring to speak (or sing) something important should also desire to speak with certainty. Also if he lack scope, such as an acquaintance with science and an acquaintance with other languages, he will be romantic and an anachronism.

This letter is written principally for general advice. I also wanted to ask you about "Harvard Fellowships." I remember, when I was a freshman or a sophomore at Harvard, that you mentioned such. I think their advantages are that they pay well, demand no thesis, suggest a variety of fields along with men with various proficiencies. Then, as you said last vacation Caesar was probably wrong about being "second in Rome"; success in a big place counts for more than in a small. There is some question as to whether I am qualified for a Harvard Fellowship.

This letter might pleasantly be re-written in English and with something less disgusting than a soft lead pencil; that would be much better but I am not sure of the gain.

I was distressed that you were unwell when I left, and I would say much more that I really feel; but there is something gross and mercenary about concluding a letter of rant with amenities.

Affectionately,
Robert

Lawrence Lowell was jauntily off-putting—"for you, not yet! not yet!"—but he made it clear that in some large part he was acting here on Merrill Moore's advice: "Dr. Moore thinks you had better not come back to Harvard at present, and I suspect that in this he is wise."[54] A letter to Lowell from Moore later in the same month suggests that Moore's objections had been fairly vehement:

Dear Cal,

I hesitate to write to you since it is not easy by letter to go into detail but I believe you can understand if I simply say to you that I am having a great deal of difficulty with your father at present on several scores most of which do not involve you at all but do importantly concern his personal problems and result in considerable friction and unhappiness at home. Accordingly and on account of that I should like to ask you (if you would like to be extremely helpful) *NOT* to come home unless absolutely necessary and, if it is and you do, would you not live at home or see him, if it can be tactfully done, and stay as my guest, if your stay is a short one, at the Harvard Club, and if it is a longer stay, take a room on Newbury Street. I would like to help you to do this, if you wish to. He is so deeply and so unconstructively antagonistic to your plans that contact can only lead to conflict and destructive outbursts that boomerang on the atmosphere of 170 Marlborough Street, on your mother, her work and on me, and wastes your creative energy in struggle and adjustment that is useless. The less you see of him (and he of you) the better, indefinitely. You may be sure that I want to help you in any possible way achieve the success you desire, hence this note.[55]

Quite what Lowell's objectionable "plans" were at this point it is hard to say. His father was an essentially amenable figure; for example, although he had opposed Lowell's abandonment of a Harvard education, he had—in the spring of 1937—taken pains to assure his son that "No two people think alike and you and I are very different, though each striving for a worthy end. We must each try to accept the other as he is. I want to help you in every way that I can."[56] He was gratified by Lowell's progress at Kenyon, and even took pride in his small successes as a poet. In December 1938—five days before the car crash—Mr. Lowell sent a copy of the first issue of the *Kenyon Review* to Richard Eberhart: "As you were the one to start Robert writing poetry, I thought that you might like to have a copy of the *Kenyon Review*, which is the first to print two of his poems." In the same letter—and rather touchingly, since both his son and his wife were in the habit of mocking his passionate interest in radios—he writes:

> You might also be interested to know that Dr. Moore and Robert will each read some of their poems at 7:30 p.m. on Dec. 30 over the local short wave radio station WIXAL on 6.05 megacycles.[57]

It is likely, therefore, that the "plans" were marriage plans. Lowell's first serious breach with his father had been over the Anne Dick affair; the second had centered on the Stafford car crash and its aftermath. In both cases, Mr. Lowell had been obliged to adopt the kind of censorious posture that it was not in his nature to carry off with any subtlety or style. Lowell's response to this heavy-handedness had in the past been crushing and contemptuous, even violent: and it was here that his father's tolerance was always likely to give way. A typical example of the at-one-remove dialogue between them can be seen in a letter Lowell wrote to Charlotte in July 1939 —just before his parents left for Europe:

> About Boston, I gather many people think you have behaved shabbily about Jean's accident. Such opinion is not my concern yet I cannot feel the action of my family has in all cases been ethicilly [sic] ideal. I say this not in anger but as a suggestion for a better understanding which seemed to be making such strides this winter.[58]

To this, Charlotte took the trouble to append a simple note: "This made Bob see red." In the same letter, it should be said, Lowell complains about the financial arrangements that have been made for him during their absence in Europe: "both Merrill and I," he writes, "are distressed with the secrecy with which it was done."

Poor Mr. Lowell must have been baffled by the reference to "secrecy"; had not Moore assured him that he was "only too happy" to concur in the arrangements? He might have been even more baffled, perhaps, if he had overheard Moore's conversation with A. Lawrence Lowell on the subject of the Harvard fellowship. So far as Mr. Lowell was concerned, the obstacle to the fellowship was simple: if Lowell married Jean Stafford, he would not be able to support her; why—as with Anne Dick—could he not wait until his studies were concluded? So far as is known, no stiff notes were sent to Colorado, nor did Lowell and his father come to blows, but there were clear echoes of the Anne Dick confrontation. And it should not, of course, be thought that Charlotte was indifferent to the outcome.

In April 1940 Lowell married Jean Stafford at a church in New York with the entirely happy name of St. Mark's—although *this* St. Mark's was in the Bowery; he graduated from Kenyon "summa cum laude, phi beta kappa, highest honors in classics, first man in my class, and valedictorian";[59] and he accepted a junior fellowship at Louisiana State University at Baton Rouge. He was going South again; this time to study under Cleanth Brooks and Robert Penn Warren, and with a letter of recommendation from Ransom that sent many a pang of envy through his Kenyon classmates: "Lowell is more than a student, he's more like a son to me."[60]

As to his real parents—their view of all this can, as usual, be measured by the grandeur of their son's defiance:

> You may enjoy talking about my sacrificed fellowship and forced marriage. The first is uncertain and the second untrue. Naturally I find such gossip very undignified and annoying. . . .
>
> I am not flattered by the remark that you do not know where I am heading or that my ways are not your ways. I am heading exactly where I have been heading for six years. One can hardly be ostracized for taking the intellect and aristocracy and family tradition seriously.[61]

For the first time, Lowell doesn't sign the letter "Bobby." He is now "affectionately, Cal."

6

When Lowell's train pulled into Memphis in the summer of 1940, he peered out of the carriage window at the ugly, run-down Southern freightyard and proclaimed: "All this must change. All this must go." His companions, Peter Taylor and Jean Stafford, put it down to overtiredness, though Taylor was privately "outraged"—fond as he was of Lowell, he didn't feel that the South was in need of any messiahs from New England.[1]

But with Taylor, the fondness usually prevailed and Lowell was always susceptible to his deflating banter: the standing joke between them was that—in Lowell's mock opinion—the Southerner lacked "intellectual power." Taylor was prepared to play the whimsical buffoon, provided the play remained a play; Lowell had sufficient sense of Taylor's actual strength to keep his tyrannical impulses carefully in check. It was hard for the two friends to have a lasting quarrel—between them there was a mutual, unshakable respect, a balance of both style and temperament that Lowell found almost impossible to catch with other friends. He was never in any doubt, it seems, that Taylor really liked him.

The plan was that Lowell and Stafford would stay with Taylor's family in Memphis before moving on to Baton Rouge, and in spite of the unpromising beginning these were relaxed and pleasant weeks:

My parents loved Cal and Jean, and my sister did. And we had parties. And Cal—he looked so awful, his long hair, his shoes—worse in those days than later—but he was still an attractive person and I remember a girl in Memphis saying: "That marriage won't last long. He's such an attractive man."[2]

And for the first few weeks at Baton Rouge, Lowell and Stafford found themselves "unexpectedly normal and happy." Lowell was intrigued by the exotic appearance of the place—"a mushroom fake Mexican set-up, very relieving after the Gothic-heavy North"[3]—and he enjoyed watching Stafford fix up their new three-room apartment, even though at first the "fixing up" seems to have involved puzzling over where to put the "23 chairs and 22 imitation Navajo carpets" that had been "sent down" from Boston. Stafford took a secretarial job at the *Southern Review* (based at Baton Rouge and co-edited by Cleanth Brooks and Robert Penn Warren), and Lowell began attending classes: "The climate here," he wrote his mother, "is humid, the people are affable, the architecture parvenue, and the work is tough but useful."[4] And to his grandmother (Mrs. Arthur Winslow):

Of course we have been daily enjoying your furniture and my slowness in answering is not a sign of ingratitude. Other articles from other people have also come until our apartment has grown to opulence; nothing more is needed.

I wonder where you have been this summer. I think mother mentioned Mattapoisett. Baton Rouge is the utter opposite, inland, windless, waterless, suburban. In place of Mrs. Curtiss, the Casino, the wharf, the ocean etc. are immense twentieth-century-Mexican dormitories, iron pipes blazing with crude oil, palm-beachy trees and Huey Long's two million dollar sky-scraper capitol. This world is new to me; so is a coëducational summerschool and a negro woman, named Loyola who arrives at six-thirty every other day to give us a grand house-cleaning. We have entertained with an elaborate dinner and now have a guest.

The war and our coming draft are "leveling." Nobody, conventional or unconventional, has good, unclouded prospects. I am neither a member of our military reserve, nor driving an ambulance in England; I am not looking for a vocation or marking time. If war comes and they want me, I'll gladly go; if not, I'll continue in this peaceful and sedentary occupation of university work. I suppose writing is something of a career, something that steadily grows more secure and substantial.[5]

To his old Kenyon classmate Robie Macauley, he wrote in a more sardonic vein:

About L.S.U. I have taken as my motto, "In Rome consort with the Romans and never do as they do". Here reign the critical approach, "the

aesthetic approach", "metaphysical poetry", "drama in the lyric" etc.
The students are weak and worthy: Brooks and Warren/Brooksandwar-
ren are excellent. Especially Warren; result: I am reading English theology.

This, as perhaps Randall Jarrell would say, is not as crazy as it sounds,
but it's pretty crazy and must not be amplified. My poetic terminology
using: heresy, diabolic, frivolous gnosticism etc, should worry the solemn and liberal English majors.[6]

As to poems, Lowell seems at this point to have run into a trough.
He had been writing a long, blank-verse "hell and damnation poem
against England"; he was to continue to rework and revise this piece
for several years but never seemed really to take it very seriously.
It was almost certainly clear to him that his Kenyon poems were stiff
and manufactured: Ransom, for example, after printing two poems
in the *Kenyon Review*'s first issue, had turned down all subsequent
submissions as "forbidding," "clotting," "too ambiguous." It was to
be five years before Lowell appeared again in Ransom's pages. A
poem called "The Protestant Dead in Boston"[7] reveals something
of Lowell's predicament in 1941. Knowing what we do about his
later development, we can see that Lowell already has his subject,
the subject that was to become thought of as peculiarly *his*, but is
a long way from having any confident, let alone individual poetic,
voice:

THE PROTESTANT DEAD IN BOSTON

Alas, the rosaries, how they have broken down

Crutches for the jaded gravestones, the trunks
of columns, to the visitors are soapstone or sandstone
and the cluttering plaques of obelisks are placards,
platters for the antique surnames: Adams
or Otis or Hancock or Prescott or Revere
or Franklin. Flittering leaves and bunches of lilac
liven a presbyter's horticulture with baroque
and prodigal embellishment, but the settled ground
admits no outlets, the play and pedantries,
the paradises and baits of the simonist, gothic
eschatologies that fascinate with the Walpurgis
Nacht, the additions of an animal; hallowed,
impassive, appalling, its expression is painted

with facts, the filagreed swaths
and bathos of samplers of forget-me-nots.

And forged with animation, integer
and the individual is a link in an unending chain,
the animal whose dissolution is private, publishing
no revelation of its unnatural properties.
Où sont les rangs de l'hierophante Aquin,
et leurs corps, les incarnations d'Alighieri?
And, Necropolis of Boston's skeletons and flowers,
your creed is neither magnificent nor natural,
its morals extort labored and identical
lucubrations, the fanatical caution
of the Calvinist . . . The masochistic rote
of Sisyphus relapses at the peak of achievement.

Boston cemetery is the world—here in the heyday,
the spirit hawked elections, and the decemvirate
of Morals, Ten Commandments, fostered
the perfection of a faction, regimented a mortal
yard of provincial, enterprising, prolific
Protestants. These dissenters, now the servants
of the earth were fatally chosen and beatified:
secured from temporal torrents, the ocean's
masterless surges, the contagion of human
contact, their lives were as single as their skeletons.
Ah, diet and raw material for a creation's consumption,
this was an unbaptized inattention to Epicurus,
who, basket in hand, rambled through worlds
and worlds, the basket his garner of perishable
flowers.

                                    R.T.S. Lowell

The movement is leaden and disgruntled; the onslaught, willed, gratuitous. Boston-style Calvinism may have become the enemy, but Lowell's old New England sensibility continued to crave Order— rules and tests; ideally, he required for himself the sort of regime that he imposed on others, a regime whose disciplines could be seen as different from those of Boston in their antiquity, their opulence, their intellectual distinction: rules for a better life, not rules made to protect the mediocre, rules that would engender art, not view it with suspicion. He would have seen that in a poem like "The

Protestant Dead in Boston" he was attacking Boston in a Boston voice: bleak, crabbed and vengeful. And the heavy prose rhythms were the rhythms of a sour utilitarianism, whatever the avowed meaning.

After a couple of months at Baton Rouge, Lowell began to extend his reading of "English theology" to include the work of the French theologian Etienne Gilson: in particular, his *Spirit of Medieval Philosophical Experience*—shortly afterwards described by Lowell as *the* key book during this period—and his *Philosophy of Thomas Aquinas.* From there he moved into Newman, Maritain, and E. I. Watkin: "the best English philosopher, a bit off the Thomist line."[8] He was also reading Hopkins and Pascal, and had formed a friendship with a Catholic student of philosophy called Patrick Quinn. As Peter Taylor commented, "In Louisiana, very French, Catholicism was in the air."[9]

Jean Stafford had been converted to Roman Catholicism a few years earlier but had soon lapsed—"my mission had not been accomplished, despite my fervor and my need"[10]—and she watched with a mild horror as Lowell buried himself in ever more weighty and more hallowed texts: "Except for meals and two games of chess after dinner he does nothing but read. I think he'll die soon and die blind."[11] In a short story called "An Influx of Poets" (published in 1978) Stafford has a nakedly autobiographical narrator describe the first months of her marriage to the poet Theron:

> Half a year after we were married, Theron, immersed in the rhythms of Gerard Manley Hopkins the poet, was explosively ignited by Gerard Manley Hopkins the Jesuit and, as my mother would have said, he was off on a tear. We were in Louisiana then—in steaming, verminous fetor; almost as soon as the set of Cardinal Newman's works arrived from Dauber & Pine, the spines relaxed, for the Deep South cockroaches, the size of larks, relished the seasoned glue of the bindings and banqueted by night. Like Father Strittmater [in the story, the heroine's original Catholic instructor], Theron's instructor was Pennsylvania Dutch—a coincidence that only mildly interested me but one by which my husband set great store: Our Lord (he adopted the address with ease) had planned likenesses in our experience.[12]

Lowell's instructor at Louisiana State University was in fact called Father Shexnayder, and he may or may not have chosen Baton

Rouge as his parish "because it afforded him so excellent a chance to chasten his chaste flesh," but what does seem to have been accurate is that "his austerity was right up Theron's alley, and before I knew what had happened to me I had been dragged into that alley which was blind."[13]

Patrick Quinn remembers that it was in the spring of 1941 that he received a call from Shexnayder asking him to act as sponsor for Lowell's baptism into the Roman Catholic Church:

> So I went along and there was a group of about four students, including Cal. It was the full ceremony and vows were taken. I'd never heard them before. It was a very forbidding, oppressive signing in. I'd never bothered to look up that bit of the ritual, and listening to it for the first time I felt overwhelmed at the magnitude of the promises made. I thought that was enough, but it then turned out that the neophyte had the opportunity to go to confession, which seemed to me almost untheological because, you see, baptism is a complete clearance of all your sins from birth on up. But Cal went to confession and he was in there half an hour, with Father Shexnayder. Meanwhile Jean and Peter Taylor and I were cooling our heels—it was all most embarrassing.[14]

A week later, at his own insistence, Lowell remarried Jean Stafford in a Catholic church; the previous year's marriage had been, he said, invalid. And from this point on, according to Stafford, their life together went into a decline. Her own view of Catholicism was "lighthearted . . . though she had serious moments about it," but for Lowell it had become a round-the-clock obsession: "Once Cal went for Romanism, he was all Roman."[15]

Jean started drinking heavily and also began falling victim to a series of minor illnesses—six-week flu, kidney infections, lung conditions, strange fevers that came and went for no diagnosable reason. Lowell imposed a stern domestic regimen: mass in the morning, benediction in the evening, two rosaries a day. Reading matter was vetted for its "seriousness"—"no newspapers, no novels except Dostoevsky, Proust, James and Tolstoy."[16] Food was similarly scrutinized: "Jean said that she once tried to serve him soup on a Friday, and he tasted meat stock, or thought he tasted meat stock, so he took the soup and dumped it in the sink."[17] There were frequent quarrels

about Stafford's smoking and drinking, or about her minor lapses
from full piety, and Lowell's rages were no less intimidating than
they had been at St. Mark's or Kenyon. On one occasion, in a hotel
in New Orleans, Lowell hit her in the face and broke her nose for
the second time. The incident was witnessed by Frank Parker and
Blair Clark—they were on a trip to Mexico and had met up with
Lowell and Stafford for a "night out" in New Orleans. I quote from
my interview with Parker:

> Jean and Cal had been having some sort of argument and Jean came
> down to our room, wanting to stay with us, and she did for a long time.
> We were sort of talking on the beds and so on. And then finally she went
> back to her room. And the next thing, we were taking her to the hospital
> in Baton Rouge. The nose which had been carefully repaired was bro-
> ken again. She had to start all over again repairing the nose, after the
> awful time she'd had getting it repaired in the first place. I really don't
> understand how Cal could have done that.

> *Did he do it? It wasn't just Jean saying he did?*

> No. No.

> *He admitted it?*

> Oh yes. He said he hadn't meant to. But he tried to strangle her. Jean
> was never afraid of him. I don't know why, because he was one of those
> people who didn't know his own strength. No, Cal said he really did
> hit her and he felt the nose go and everything, so there's no question of
> that. Mind you, we none of us ever thought Cal was crazy or anything.
> He was just a violent man doing his own thing.[18]

People who knew Jean Stafford advise caution when dealing with
her versions of events: she tended, they say, to get the spirit of the
thing right but to inflate or wittily distort the facts. In this case,
though, there are two "witnesses"; and it was Blair Clark who had
the job of getting Jean into a hospital in New Orleans. There is (as
there would have to be) no such direct evidence to substantiate
Stafford's most dramatic claim about the marriage: that she had no
sexual relations with Lowell from the day they were remarried in
the Catholic Church. She told this to Blair Clark and to Joan Stillman, who made notes of an interview she did with Stafford in 1952:
"She told me they had had a glorious affair before they were married, but after he became a Catholic, they never slept together."[19]
And in "An Influx of Poets" Stafford writes:

What had become of the joking lad I'd married? He'd run hellbent for election into that blind alley—that's what had become of him—and he yanked me along with him, and there we snarled like hungry, scurvy cats. If I had stubbornly withstood him from the beginning, or if I had left him when he left me for the seraphim and the saints—but I had tried to withstand and had got for myself only wrath and disdain. Leaving him had not really occurred to me, for I had married within my tribe, and we were sternly monogamous till death.[20]

In September 1941—his year at Louisiana State completed—Lowell took a job in New York with the Catholic publishers Sheed and Ward. For Lowell, Catholicism had three prongs: reason, faith and practice. Since he was a good Thomist, the first two presented him with no difficulties:

Reason permeates faith. . . . The Incarnation is only a probability, under examination it becomes more probable, after a while you believe. . . . the point is the religious coincidences are all in favor of the Incarnation. Science, medical practice, psychology etc. These are ultimately irrelevant.[21]

Thus, faith stands to reason. As to practice, Lowell concedes in this same letter that the Church's social achievements have been far from satisfactory: "Incompetence, stupidity, cruelty, conservatism, compromise and dogmatism all abound." In personal terms, though, he believes that every Catholic should "work for a corporate state, guild systems etc." His work with Sheed and Ward, although it involved only modest copy-editing, would provide the chance for a necessary extension to his Catholic reading: it qualified as practice under the heading of "self-preparation."

And in New York there were opportunities also for Stafford to do her bit, as she amusingly relates in a letter to Peter Taylor—a letter that does something to lighten the blacker presentations of their marriage. Even as Stafford was most bitterly complaining about her life with Lowell, she still would boast that he was "terribly beautiful," "brilliant," "I was fascinated by him," and so on. "I should tell you about the Catholic Worker," she writes Taylor:

Cal insisted that I do Catholic work so finally I went down to the offices of the newspaper which is run, as I suppose you know (or ought to) by a woman who . . . has written her autobiography which is called "From

Union Square to Rome." The first time I went down I was terrified just by the approach to the place. It is a block from Pell St. and two from the Bowery, just off Canal. I had to walk seven blocks through the kind of slums you do not believe exist when you see them in the movies, in an atmosphere that was nearly asphyxiating. The Worker office was full of the kind of camaraderie which frightens me to death and I was immediately put at a long table between a Negro and a Chinese to fold papers, a tiring and filthy job. The second time it was about the same except that Mott St. seemed even more depressing and that time I typed. After I had described the place to Cal, he immediately wanted to go down and live there. I vainly argued against it. Finally a priest whom he admires told him his work should be intellectual. And now we are quite happy here in a respectable neighborhood and henceforth I do not have to go to the Worker but instead I have to go to work in a friendship house in Harlem under a Baroness de something.[22]

Jean had by this time completed a large section of her first novel, *Boston Adventure,* and had had an interested response to this from Robert Giroux, a newly appointed editor at Harcourt, Brace. It did not ease the domestic atmosphere that this success of hers coincided with a period when Lowell seems to have been writing no poetry at all. After eight months in New York it was decided that they would move back to the South to share the Tates' house at Monteagle, Tennessee—an attempt, perhaps, to recapture the spirit of Lowell's first, crucial Southern summer. Jean had received an advance from Harcourt, Brace, and Lowell had his modest income from the family trust fund; they would be able to live cheaply at Monteagle, and Tate's presence would be a guarantee against idleness—at any rate, against literary idleness.

Lowell later described the winter of 1942–43 as "the winter of four books: Allen's novel; C's [Caroline Gordon's] novel; J's novel—Allen and I write poems—all of *Land of Unlikeness,* most of *Winter Sea.* "[23] By March 1943 Lowell had completed sixteen poems, and they were different from anything he'd done before. They had none of the withheld, stiffly censorious tone of his adolescent work, none of the heavy-handed literary artifice. The air of willed composition is no longer there. Instead, there is a high fever, a driven, almost deranged belligerence in both the voice and the vocabulary, as if poems had become hurled thunderbolts, instruments of grisly retribution. These Monteagle poems are unreachable, irresponsibly obscure much of the time; they flail around in a perplexing mix of local, mythological and Catholic reference. But what marks them is a blind faith in their own headlong momentum; whatever anyone else might make of them, the author believes himself to be both urgent and authoritative:

All of them are cries for us to recover our ancient freedom and dignity, to be Christians and build a Christian society. I think of Blake's hymn:

> I shall not cease from mental fight
> Nor shall my sword sleep in my hand
> Till we have built Jerusalem
> In England's green and pleasant land.[24]

This warriorlike stance is certainly evident in almost every poem, but it is never very clear how Lowell thinks the good fight should be fought—except in the most general or apocalyptic terms. And he finds it impossible to eliminate a tinge of relish from his evocations of the current European horrors:

> . . . the ship
> Of state has learned Christ how to
> sail on blood.
> Great Commonwealth, sail on and on and roll
> On blood, on my free blood . . .[25]

Most of these poems were to be rewritten at least twice over the next two years and should be evaluated in their final shape. In 1943, though, it was evident to Tate and others that Lowell, for all his bombast and confusion, was surely on to *something*, and the periodicals began publishing his work. During the summer of '43, he had poems appearing in *Sewanee Review* ("On the Eve of the Feast of the Immaculate Conception, 1942," "In Memory of Arthur Winslow," "Leviathan" and "Dea Roma"), *Partisan Review* ("Song of the Boston Nativity," "Christmas Eve in Time of War," "Salem" and "Concord") and *Kenyon Review* ("Satan's Confession"). At Allen Tate's prompting he sent the sixteen poems to the Cummington Press, a small hand-setting outfit run by Harry Duncan and Katherine Frazier in Cummington, Massachusetts. There was an enthusiastic response, and Duncan suggested that Lowell send him a few more to make up a book, and also perhaps a preface by Tate. The manuscript had been sent to Duncan on March 18; by April 2

Lowell was able to send six more poems—a rate of output entirely new for him: even before his barren stretch in Louisiana and New York he had sometimes spent a year laboring over two shortish pieces. Tate agreed to supply the preface, and the book—to be called *Land of Unlikeness*—was optimistically scheduled for publication in September 1943.

Not only do Lowell's poems of this period suggest inner turmoil, they are victimized by it. But three elements in the turmoil can be thought of as consistent: Boston, Catholicism, War. The essential drift is that if the worst of Boston could learn from the best of Rome, then wars would at least have dignity and noble purpose. This is crudely put, but the poems don't put it much more subtly: how could they, since Lowell in the spring of 1943 was irritably unsure of his own principles? Most of his childhood heroes had been military heroes, and he had shown himself to have a rare appetite for both tyranny and violence; but he could see little that was splendid in the way modern wars were fought. Could the "good fight" ever be fought with bombs? Lowell had, it is said by Frank Parker, supported the Franco side during the Spanish Civil War, and his conversion to Catholicism had engendered an even fiercer hostility to Communism. Thus, America's alliance with the Soviet Union would have seemed to him a repugnantly high price to pay for the defeat of Hitler. Much of this is conjecture: Lowell's letters of the period are strikingly free of any comment on the war, and in poems the nearest he comes to revealing the direction of his sympathies is in thoroughly ambiguous passages like this:

> Freedom and Eisenhower have won
> Significant laurels where the Hun
>   And Roman kneel
> To lick the dust from Mars' bootheel
> Like foppish bloodhounds; yet you sleep
> O'er our distemper's evil day
>   And hear no sheep
>   Or hangdog bay![26]

Many years later, Lowell was to summarize the development of his poetry up to around this stage of his biography:

When I was growing up in the twenties, moving into the thirties, it was a very peculiar period, it seems to me, particularly in America. It was a time of enormous optimism. The kind of argument that the world was getting better and better, and there would be no more wars, and so forth, that seemed very much in the air, I think more here than in Europe. Yet there was the huge jar of the first world war behind us, that hit us, of course, less hard than Europe, but yet was there, and soon you had a feeling that the violence was arising, the left and the right, in Hitler and Stalin, these two currents were going on at the same time, that maybe things were getting better, or that they were headed for disaster. And it seems to me at quite an early age that I felt it couldn't be anything but disaster, that one lived in that time, and someone writing poetry perhaps had three choices. One, which was hardly a choice, was the kind of poetry the public wanted, which was a rather watered-down imitation of 19th century poetry, that really had gone completely dead. The other was an *engagé* poetry, and the only kind that really seemed to inspire that kind of conviction was the Marxist, usually quite pro-Russian. And the third group, which I more or less belonged to, I think it derives somewhat from Yeats and from Eliot, and in this country friends of mine, Allen Tate and John Crowe Ransom. And a rather strange position was built up. There were great arguments that poetry was a form of knowledge, at least as valid as scientific knowledge, and in certain ways more so, because it didn't abstract from experience. We claimed any—the whole man would be represented in the poem. I think that was a sort of aggressive stance, that we felt at a disadvantage, and my friend and teacher John Crowe Ransom wrote a book of critical essays which might illustrate this, which he called, the book, *The World's Body*, that poetry was the world's body, it took the whole man. I don't think one would say that now exactly. And we believed in form, that that was very important, and for some reason we were very much against the Romantics. We would say that the ideal poet is Shakespeare, who is not a poet of ideology but a poet of experience, and tragedy, and the sort of villains to us were people like Shelley—that he used much too much ideology —and Whitman, the prophet, who also seemed formless. And one felt that what poetry could do was have nothing to do with causes, that if you—that might get into what you wrote but you couldn't do it at all directly; and something like Aristotle's purging by pity and terror, that of going through a catharsis, that that is what was suitable, rather than to persuade people to do anything better or to make the world better. And I think that is the position that is perhaps only intelligible in the thirties, when the danger of being swept into a cause was so great.[27]

In September 1943, though, came the event that Lowell describes in this same speech as "the most decisive thing I ever did, just as a writer"—although, at the time, "it was not intended to have anything to do with that."

America had entered the war in December 1941. Lowell in that year had registered for the draft and throughout 1942 had attempted to enlist: "so that he can go to officer's school."[28] During his time in Louisiana and with Sheed and Ward he had never known for certain if he would be called up: at one moment, there is talk of his being permanently deferred because of his eyesight; at another (November 1942), Jean Stafford resolves to give up drink because she doesn't want him "to worry about me when he goes into the army."[29]

By March 1943 Lowell was still assuming that he would be accepted for military service. He filled out "an employment questionnaire" for the army and it was probably genuine absentmindedness that led him to list himself as having "one dependent under 18, and one not living with him but deriving its whole support from him." Lowell also claimed "that he was a graduate of a trade school to which he had gone for four years, that his surname was Robert and that he could read 'forig' languages."[30] (Stafford corrected this testimony before mailing it.) And in July 1943 he wrote to his mother:

> The other day I got a notice from my draft board and expect to be examined (the 7th time) some time in the next ten days. The chances are that I will be rejected on account of vision. However there is no telling.[31]

Shortly after this, Lowell was given a date for his induction: September 8, 1943.

During July and August, Lowell took lodgings in New York and idly looked for jobs ("there are plenty of jobs but the problem is to get the right one")[32] while Jean Stafford went off to Yaddo, the writers' colony at Saratoga Springs, to complete *Boston Adventure*. For some weeks before, Jean had been suffering from a recurrence of her mysterious low fevers, and at Yaddo these seem to have suddenly got higher and more worrying. In July she writes to Peter

Taylor that she has "either a tubercular or a streptococchic infection of the kidneys" and that she has lost "13 pounds in a month."[33] A fortnight later, the symptoms were diagnosed as "nervous exhaustion," but the diagnosis didn't stop them:

> I continued to lose weight and I grew weaker and weaker. . . . I suppose I'm on the verge of some kind of nervous crack-up which the fever isn't helping any. . . . I'll be in bed somewhere within a week. This time, Peter, you'll be glad to know that I am really and truly scared to death. Write to me and think of me and pray for me.[34]

It is noticeable that Lowell receives no mention in these outcries: Stafford doesn't appear to expect his help or even his concern. In August, though, Caroline Tate approached Lowell's mother for money to arrange a thorough diagnosis. Lowell was "taken aback" by this intrusion, but it does seem to have shocked him into a more active interest in the matter. He writes to his mother agreeing to the expenditure:

> Jean has been having these fevers off and on for three years. No one has been able to cure her or tell her what the matter is. I worry about this night and day and can't resign myself to the army with her illness still unsettled.[35]

During the first week of September, Jean Stafford—her illness still "unsettled"—joined Lowell in New York. On September 7, Lowell wrote a letter to President Roosevelt:

> Dear Mr. President:
>
> I very much regret that I must refuse the opportunity you offer me in your communication of August 6, 1943, for service in the Armed Forces.
>
> I am enclosing with this letter a copy of the declaration which, in accordance with military regulations, I am presenting on September 7 to Federal District Attorney in New York, Mr. Matthias F. Correa. Of this declaration I am sending copies also to my parents, to a select number of friends and relatives, to the heads of the Washington press bureaus, and to a few responsible citizens who, no more than yourself, can be suspected of subversive activities.
>
> You will understand how painful such a decision is for an American whose family traditions, like your own, have always found their fulfill-

ment in maintaining, through responsible participation in both the civil and the military services, our country's freedom and honor.

> I have the honor, Sir, to inscribe myself, with sincerest loyalty and respect, your fellow-citizen,
>
> Robert Traill Spence Lowell, Jr.

Attached was the DECLARATION OF PERSONAL RESPONSIBILITY, which read as follows:

ORDERS FOR MY INDUCTION INTO THE ARMED FORCES ON SEPTEMBER EIGHTH 1943 have just arrived. Because we glory in the conviction that our wars are won not by irrational valor but through the exercise of moral responsibility, it is fitting for me to make the following declaration which is also a decision.

Like the majority of our people I watched the approach of this war with foreboding. Modern wars had proved subversive to the Democracies and history had shown them to be the iron gates to totalitarian slavery. On the other hand, members of my family had served in all our wars since the Declaration of Independence: I thought—our tradition of service is sensible and noble; if its occasional exploitation by Money, Politics and Imperialism is allowed to seriously discredit it, we are doomed.

When Pearl Harbor was attacked, I imagined that my country was in intense peril and come what might, unprecedented sacrifices were necessary for our national survival. In March and August of 1942 I volunteered, first for the Navy and then for the Army. And when I heard reports of what would formerly have been termed atrocities, I was not disturbed: for I judged that savagery was unavoidable in our nation's struggle for its life against diabolic adversaries.

Today these adversaries are being rolled back on all fronts and the crisis of war is past. But there are no indications of peace. In June we heard rumors of the staggering civilian casualties that had resulted from the mining of the Ruhr Dams. Three weeks ago we read of the razing of Hamburg, where 200,000 non-combatants are reported dead, after an almost apocalyptic series of all-out air-raids.

This, in a world still nominally Christian, is *news*. And now the Quebec Conference confirms our growing suspicions that the bombings of the Dams and of Hamburg were not mere isolated acts of military expediency, but marked the inauguration of a new long-term strategy, indorsed and co-ordinated by our Chief Executive.

The war has entered on an unforeseen phase: one that can by no possible extension of the meaning of the words be called defensive. By demanding unconditional surrender we reveal our complete confidence in the outcome, and declare that we are prepared to wage a war without quarter or principles, to the permanent destruction of Germany and Japan.

Americans cannot plead ignorance of the lasting consequences of a war carried through to unconditional surrender—our Southern States three quarters of a century after their terrible battering down and occupation, are still far from having recovered even their material prosperity.

It is a fundamental principle of our American Democracy, one that distinguishes it from the demagoguery and herd hypnosis of the totalitarian tyrannies, that with us each individual citizen is called upon to make voluntary and responsible decisions on issues which concern the national welfare. I therefore realize that I am under the heavy obligation of assenting to the prudence and justice of our present objectives before I have the right to accept service in our armed forces. No matter how expedient I might find it to entrust my moral responsibility to the State, I realize that it is not permissible under a form of government which derives its sanctions from the rational assent of the governed.

Our rulers have promised us unlimited bombings of Germany and Japan. Let us be honest: we intend the permanent destruction of Germany and Japan. If this program is carried out, it will demonstrate to the world our Machiavellian contempt for the laws of justice and charity between nations; it will destroy any possibility of a European or Asiatic national autonomy; it will leave China and Europe, the two natural power centers of the future, to the mercy of the USSR, a totalitarian tyranny committed to world revolution and total global domination through propaganda and violence.

In 1941 we undertook a patriotic war to preserve *our lives, our fortunes, and our sacred honor* against the lawless aggressions of a totalitarian league: in 1943 we are collaborating with the most unscrupulous and powerful of totalitarian dictators to destroy law, freedom, democracy, and above all, our continued national sovereignty.

With the greatest reluctance, with every wish that I may be proved in error, and after long deliberation on my responsibilities to myself, my country, and my ancestors who played responsible parts in its making, I have come to the conclusion that I cannot honorably participate in a war whose prosecution, as far as I can judge, constitutes a betrayal of my country.[36]

Although Lowell addressed the letter as from his parents' holiday home at Manchester-on-Sea, Massachusetts, he wrote to his mother on the same day from New York:

After your touching letter about my picture and poems, I fear you will find this a rather shocking return. Please believe that I have taken the only course that was honorable for me.

I cannot ask you to support or even in any way concern yourself with my ideas. I do ask for your love, above all for Jean whose part in this is much the hardest. Don't be too alarmed about any consequences to me, they will be within just limits.[37]

He also wrote to his grandmother:[38]

Dear Gaga:

I hardly know what to say in writing you and have hesitated to send you the enclosed statement. Finally I decided that writing you was my duty. You know more about American history than I do and can certainly judge whether our recent actions in this war are justifiable. I think only a Southerner can realize the horrors of a merciless conquest.

I love you immensely and want you to pray for us.

love,
Bobby

Lowell's letter to Roosevelt was immediately handed over to the relevant U.S. Attorney, to whom Lowell repeated his refusal. By this time the case was headline news. The front-page story in the *New York Times* was tersely headed "To Act on Draft Evader," but in more obscure journals there was considerable excitement: "Member of Famed Family Balks at Military Service" (Bowling Green *Sentinel*); "Lowell Scion Refuses to Fight" (Providence *Journal*); and in the Boston *Post*, September 10, the story ran:

SOCIALITE'S MOTHER TO UPHOLD SON

"This would be the seventh time he would take a test for war service induction," said Mrs. Lowell. "When he phoned me at midnight last night from New York City, he said he had acted in the conventional way and had notified the district attorney of his refusal to appear before the Draft Board. I believe it was a question of poetic temperament which had caused him to protest against the bombing, and especially of Rome. I really feel that if he had appeared for induction he would have again been turned down for poor eyesight."

It is worth noting that Lowell did not mention the bombing of Rome in his letter to Roosevelt—for his mother, though, this was the significant connection. Lowell himself some years later suggested that there was a further incentive: in a draft for the poem "Memories of West Street and Lepke" he writes of "my conscientious objector statement meant to blow the lid off/ the United States Roosevelt and my parents."[39]

On October 12, he wrote again to his grandmother "Gaga":

I don't [know] what to say to you except that I love you and am sorry to have caused you so much worry. That troubles me more than anything else.

I have talked at great length to my priest in New York and written the priest who baptized me in Louisiana. They are both very shrewd and experienced men. They are also very good men. They have told me to *follow my conscience and trust in God.* I have prayed for light and tried to persuade myself that I was mistaken; I cannot.

I shall be sentenced this Wednesday. I shall have to go to jail, but there is good reason to hope that in a short time I shall [be] transferred to the medical corps or to an objectors' camp.

Please forgive me for you[r] disappointment and anxiety, and pray for us.[40]

On October 13, after a month in which he was treated "with almost alarming courtesy. (No-one has questioned my sincerity),"[41] Lowell was arraigned before the Southern U.S. District Court in New York and sentenced to a year and one day in the Federal Correctional Center at Danbury, Connecticut. While waiting to be shifted there, he spent a few days in New York's tough West Street Jail. Lowell's famous poem on the subject is augmented by the recollections of a fellow inmate:

Lowell was in a cell next to Lepke, you know, Murder Incorporated, and Lepke says to him: "I'm in for killing. What are you in for?" "Oh, I'm in for refusing to kill." And Lepke burst out laughing. It was kind of ironic.[42]

7

After ten days at West Street Jail, Lowell was driven up to Connecticut, "handcuffed to two Porto Rican draft-dodgers":

> The Porto Ricans scratched their crotches
> with handcuffed hands, snatched matches
> and photos of children from their trouser-cuffs.
> Near Tarrytown, we passed a sand-red sow,
> grubbing acorns by a cinder pile,
> and line of women's trousers.
> Then some miles of artificial lakes,
> a canoe as scarlet as a maple leaf,
> finally, Danbury and "the country club"
> our model prison.
> Glassbricks blased over fields of blue denim men
> Smashing rocks with pneumatic drills.
> The cement building was as functional
> as my fishing tackle box.[1]

Danbury specialized in housing CO's and first offenders—bootleggers and black marketeers—and it prided itself on being correctional as well as punitive. The cell blocks were reassuringly named after the New England states, and the rules on visiting hours and letter writing were far more relaxed than they had been at West Street, where Jean Stafford had been allowed to see her husband only once, and then through a plate-glass wall.

At first, Lowell was viewed with suspicion by the other Danbury inmates: he had been given a comparatively light sentence (the usual term was three years), and Jim Peck, a CO jailed at around the same time, was in no doubt that the judge had been lenient simply "because he was a Lowell":

We got three years. He got a year and a day—it had to be a year and a day to be a felony. He got parole after four months. They didn't usually grant parole to objectors—he got it because he was a Lowell. I did three years minus seven months' remission.[2]

Peck and others tried to involve Lowell in a strike against the segregation of black and white prisoners, and Peck also berated him for A. Lawrence Lowell's part in the conviction of Sacco and Vanzetti (Lowell had served on the review commission that decided they had had a fair trial and should be executed), but Lowell made it clear that he had larger matters to attend to: "He was 'spaced out' —he was only interested in one thing, Catholic communities." Even so, Peck—along with most of the others—gradually warmed to this abstracted, shabby "man of God"; he may not have been *their* kind of protesting pacifist, but he was manifestly not a fraud:

> Lowell was on one of those pick-and-shovel gangs. Dig up a hole, fill it in again, you know. Usually, these privileged characters got the best jobs. I mean rich men who were in there for defrauding the government on war contracts. There were several of them. They were the only men who got out at the earliest parole eligible. Others, they'd maybe get out three months after. But these, they never failed. But Lowell was definitely not an organization person. He didn't play it uppity at all. You see, I mean, like a lot of these guys who played big shot, they get pressed pants and connection pants and all that. He just dressed sloppy like all of us, ill-fitting clothes, shoes.[3]

Ten years later, Lowell reminisced about his fellow inmates:

> I belonged to a gang that walked outside the prison gates each morning, and worked on building a barn. The work was mild: the workers were slow and absent-minded. There were long pauses, and we would sit around barrels filled with burning coke and roast wheat-seeds. All the prisoner[s] were sentenced for a cause, all liked nothing better than talking the world to rights. Among the many eccentrics one group took the prize. They were negroes who called themselves Israelites. Their ritual compelled them to shave their heads and let their beards grow. But the prison regulations forced them to shave their beards. So with unnaturally smooth and shining faces and naked heads wrapped in Turkish towels, they shivered around the coke barrels, and talked wisdom and non-sense. Their non-sense was that they were the chosen people. They had found a text in the Bible which [said,] "But I am black though my brother is white". This convinced them that the peo-

ple of the old testament were negroes. The Israelites believed that modern Jews were imposters. Their wisdom was a deep ancestral knowledge of herbs and nature. They were always curing themselves with queer herbal remedies that they gathered from the fields. Once as we sat by the coke the most venerable and mild of the Israelites stretched out his hand. Below him lay the town of Danbury, which consisted of what might be called *filling-station architecture;* the country was the fine, small rolling land of Connecticut. One expected to see the flash of a deer's white scut as it jumped a boulder wall by a patch of unmelted snow. My friend stretched out his arm, and said, "Only man is miserable."[4]

Lowell commented that "this summed up my morals and aesthetics."

Jean Stafford was able to visit Danbury for an hour each Saturday. During the week she stayed in a small apartment in New York and spent much of her time warding off the recriminations that were now flowing freely down from Boston ("If we had only known how Bobby felt before he sent that declaration all this trouble could have been avoided").[5] Charlotte was convinced that Lowell had suffered another of his mental seizures and even talked of asking for him to be transferred to the psychopathic ward at Danbury. Jean, she felt, should have noticed the symptoms and alerted her earlier, but she reserved her bitterest ill-feeling for the Tates: she deplored their general influence on Lowell and blamed them for persuading him to give up his steady job at Sheed and Ward in order to encourage him "in the emotional excitement of poetry." Tate later commented: "I will never forget the phrase."[6]

Stafford was receiving $100 a month from Lowell's trust fund and was having a hard time surviving in New York. Her rent was $50, she sent $10 to Lowell and spent another $10 on her own medical expenses. This left $30 for "food, cigarettes, electricity, etc." In November she wrote to Mrs. Lowell about her difficulties and got an icily Bostonian reply:

I am glad to hear you say that you can, and are willing to support yourself while Bobby is in prison. I have just heard of a woman whose husband was recently sent to prison for 3 years, after first losing her entire fortune. Although this woman, having always had a great deal of money of her own, was completely untrained to work, she obtained a job in New York, suported [*sic*] herself, and her children, for 3 years, and when her husband was released from prison, she had managed to save quite a sum of money with which to help him to get started: Such conduct is certainly both admirable and heroic.

We think that Bobby has been extremely generous in wishing you to have all of the income from his trust fund while he is in prison. This is all the money that he has in the world, and he will be completely penniless when he is released from prison, if you care to impose upon his generosity.

I hope, Jean, for your own sake, as well as for Bobby's that you will see in the present situation an opportunity for courage, selfdevelopment, and integrity of purpose.[7]

Sharing a taxi to the prison with "two flashy looking articles . . . so opulent in their fur coats and highheeled shoes," Jean is perhaps to be forgiven for having felt "envious that their husbands had left them well provided for while they were off being castigated for their ideals."[8]

In addition to her money worries, Stafford was also running into trouble on the New York cocktail circuit. In one letter she describes a typical literary gathering at which Sidney Hook mockingly put it to her that Lowell could not—logically—be both a Catholic and a conscientious objector. Were not Catholics supposed to follow the Pope's lead? Taking up Hook's cue, "three quarters of the men there said that Cal was a fool or hysterical," and Stafford was soon reduced to tears. The next day she wrote to Peter Taylor:

I wish I could talk to you long and completely about literary people in New York. They are such cutthroats, such ambitious and bourgeois frights and yet I, in my stupid lack of integrity, continue to see them.[9]

With this same letter, she included quotations from the sermon she had just received from "Charlotte Hideous."

Although Stafford felt constrained to defend her "intrepid husband" against the skeptics in New York, she had her own doubts about the rationality of his position. At first, she had found his stand thrilling and admirable, but as the weeks passed she was getting more and more alarmed by his Catholic fanaticism; conversations with him, she said, had become so "insanely illogical" that they could be written into a case history of religious mania. She consulted a Jesuit priest in New York who had known and corresponded with Lowell and was relieved to have it officially confirmed that Lowell had indeed become "more Catholic than the church." But although this meant that *she* was not being a bad Catholic in her response to his religious fervor, it was of little help in reconciling her to what she saw as a drastic alteration in her husband's entire personality. The Lowell she visited at Danbury was, she says, "nothing like" the Lowell she had known at Kenyon. In February 1944 she writes a desperate letter to Peter Taylor:

> It is not right for me to burden you with this, just before you go overseas, but you are probably Cal's closest friend. I see I have given you no facts. Roughly this is it: after the war what Cal wants to do (he cries: "this is to be my life and I will not be hindered") is to be a sort of soapbox preacher with an organization called the Catholic Evidence Guilds which operate in city parks, etc, preach and answer the posers of hecklers. I cannot write this down without seeing you smile. . . . And when I inquire of him how we will live, he points to the Gospels and says that we must not worry about that, that God will take care of us, that one cannot be a wage slave but must have leisure in which to serve the Church. . . .
>
> I am frightened, feel that it will be three years before Cal has recovered from the pleasurable monasticism of the penitentiary. . . .[10]

In March 1944, Lowell emerged from the "closed order" of Danbury to face the more flexible requirements of parole. He was sent to Bridgeport, Connecticut, and given a job as a cleaner in the nurses' quarters of Bridgeport's St. Vincent's hospital. He was paid fifteen dollars a week and had to start work at 7 A.M. each day. Jean reported to Taylor that "he feels like Nancy Tate's valet [and] speaks distastefully of the 'pink things' hung out to dry in his work vicinity."[11] But the job was not entirely frivolous: as might be expected, Lowell managed to detect in it "a harsh somehow moral monotony."[12]

In Bridgeport, Lowell lived at first in a single room, sharing a bathroom with five others, and suffered the supervision of a fierce landlady who was convinced that he was a "draft-dodger." Jean had given up her apartment in New York, and while Lowell swabbed the nurses' floors she toured the Connecticut countryside in search of decent lodgings. Eventually she settled on Harbor View, Ocean

Avenue, Black Rock, Connecticut—an address that thoroughly delighted Lowell when he heard of it:

> We have a large room with a bay window and a fireplace, a smaller room and a bath. The harbor we view brings tears to Cal's eyes. He'd expected the ocean from the address and when he saw the pitiful little drop of water visible from our windows, he behaved as if he'd been deliberately cheated. We can however on a clear day see the Sound far far off and we have the illusion at least of being in the country.[13]

The house itself, which provides the location for two of Lowell's most celebrated poems ("Colloquy in Black Rock" and "Christmas in Black Rock"), is also brought to literary life in a story by Jean Stafford called "The Home Front." The doctor in the story is quite clearly Lowell:

> It was large, shapeless and built of yellow stone. It stood behind a high brick wall, its back windows overlooking an arm of the sea which, at low tide, was a black and stinking mud-flat. A dump had been made at the end of the water and here was heaped all the frightful refuse of the city, the high-heeled shoes and the rotten carrots and the abused insides of automobiles; when the wind blew, the odor from the dump was so putrid in so individual a way that it was quite impossible to describe. But on a clear day, the doctor could look the other way and see, far off, the live blue Sound and the silhouettes of white sailboats and gray battleships.[14]

Fortuitously, though, the house was owned by a Roman Catholic priest, and from the front steps it was possible to see the spires of both St. Stephen's and St. Peter's. Jean Stafford was also gratified to learn that the priest had bought it from a rum-runner who had used its location to good effect during Prohibition.

Although Lowell's release from his jail sentence was to become final in October 1944, there was still the possibility that he could again be inducted and, if he refused to serve, given a further spell in prison: quite likely, a far longer spell this time. In June, therefore, Lowell applied to join the army medical corps or some similar noncombatant branch of the forces: eventually he was classified 4F, "which means that save in the case of a great emergency, like the bombing of New York, he won't have to go into anything, neither prison nor the medical corps."[15]

During his term at Danbury, Lowell wrote no poems. He read Proust, and corrected the galleys of *Land of Unlikeness*. The book had been delayed several times, not least because of Lowell's inability (and this lasted all his life) to read a page of his own work without rewriting it. It had still not appeared by July, when Lowell, after almost a year's silence, began to write again; indeed, Jean Stafford writes to Peter Taylor on July 26 that "Cal . . . is working with the same intensity he did in that great period of fertility in Monteagle" and to Eleanor Taylor on the thirty-first: "Cal started writing poetry again and his intensity and industry make me feel completely worthless. I've done nothing at all this summer." By the time *Land of Unlikeness* appeared in the fall of 1944 Lowell had already completed seven poems in what he called "a new style, more lyrical and lucid" and rewritten several of the poems in his first volume.[16]

Land of Unlikeness was a considerable critical success. For a first volume put out as a limited edition by a small press, it had prominent reviews; and most of them could be taken as "encouraging." *Accent* placed it in a batch with Auden's *For the Time Being* and with books by William Carlos Williams and Marianne Moore; their reviewer, Arthur Mizener, was cagey about the book's sometimes "ludicrous" complexities and warned that "hysteria may be mistaken for directness, the accidental personal experience for the generally valid," but concluded that "When Mr. Lowell succeeds, what you hear is something like the voice of the prophetic poet, a voice which we have rarely heard since the seventeenth century; grand without grandiloquence and intimate without triviality or meanness."[17] In *Poetry*, John Frederick Nims coupled Lowell with Thomas Merton under the heading "Two Catholic Poets" and confessed that "After the glassy aureoles of Merton, it is good to discover the gnarled and oaken wainscot of Lowell's chapel." Nims goes on (a little unconvincingly) to praise the "brilliance" of Lowell's technique, claiming to have discerned in it "an intricate counterpoint of form and diction, form and matter, feeling and idea," and to express interest in "the strange marriage of Catholic belief and New England Puritanism." But his conclusion is lukewarm and almost daringly wide of the mark: "What Lowell lacks is sufficient emotional drive to make his disparate images organic."[18]

Luckily, no other reviewer contrived to reproach Lowell for his lack of powerful feeling, but there was an element of wariness in even the most glowing notices. Usually, there would be an assent to the book's power, its daunting physical attack, but a bewilderment about the poet's motives, the true sources of his intimidating anger. Even Randall Jarrell, in *Partisan Review*, seems mildly shell-shocked. His piece strains for superlatives:

> in a day when poets aspire to be irresistible forces, he is an immovable object.... Mr. Lowell is a serious, objective and extraordinarily accomplished poet.... some of the best poems of the next years ought to be written by him.[19]

But many of Jarrell's assertions seem to describe poems that he wishes Lowell to write rather than the ones that are actually before him: "his harshest propositions flower out of facts." This seems singularly wrong as a description of *Land of Unlikeness;* indeed, one might rephrase it: "*if only* his harshest propositions flowered out of facts."

Jarrell, though, is too good a critic not to see that Lowell's political satires have "a severe crudity," that his literary punning, his ubiquitous allusiveness, is often no more than "a senseless habit," that there is something "Bismarckian" in his surveillance of the moral world, and a tendency throughout to slip into an "Onward Christian Soldiers" style of battle rhetoric. Even so, such censure is well hidden, and Lowell had achieved what many would have thought impossible—he had disconcerted the notoriously definite Jarrell.

The other key review was by R. P. Blackmur and appeared in the *Kenyon Review* (Ransom later wrote to Lowell to apologize for Blackmur's "patronizing and superior remarks"[20]). Unlike any of the other reviewers, Blackmur meets the book's essential character head on, and his strictures may well have been the ones that Lowell brooded on most fruitfully:

> Lowell is distraught about religion; he does not seem to have decided whether his Roman Catholic belief is the form of a force or the sentiment of a form. The result appears to be that in dealing with men his faith compels him to be fractiously vindictive, and in dealing with faith his experience of men compels him to be nearly blasphemous. By contrast, Dante loved his living Florence and the Florence to come and loved

much that he was compelled to envisage in hell, and he wrote throughout in loving meters. In Lowell's *Land of Unlikeness* there is nothing
loved unless it be its repellence: and there is not a loving meter in the
book. What is thought of as Boston in him fights with what is thought
of as Catholic; and the fight produces not a tension but a gritting. It is
not the violence, the rage, the denial of this world that grits, but the
failure of these to find in *verse* a tension of necessity; necessity has, when
recognized, the quality of conflict accepted, not hated.[21]

Since leaving Kenyon, Lowell had written two substantial pieces
of literary criticism: on Hopkins and on Eliot's *Four Quartets.* [22]
They are both admiring, but where they do offer reservations it is
interesting that in each case those reservations could as easily be
turned against the poems Lowell himself was writing at the time.
Of Eliot he complains that "Occasionally the symbols are paradoxi-
cally too personal and too general to either exist in themselves or
carry sufficient symbolic meaning." As to Hopkins, his "rhythms
. . . have the effect of a hyperthyroid injection":

> As we know from the letters and personal anecdotes he lived in a state
> of exhilaration. But in some poems we feel that the intensity is man-
> nered, in others we could wish for more variety.

There is also in Hopkins, though infrequently, a tendency for lines
to "collapse in a style-less exuberance." Lowell quotes:

> This was that feel capsize
> As half she had righted and hoped to rise
> Death teeming in at her port-holes
> Raced down decks, round messes of mortals.

and comments: "*Messes of mortals!* This is a murderous example of
numb sprung rhythm and alliteration."

In November 1944 Lowell and Stafford moved to Westport, Connecticut. In a desultory manner, Lowell began to look for work that
would fit both his religion and his writing—at one point he speaks
of taking a job counseling juvenile delinquents, but this seems not
to have been followed through. His sense of Catholic mission was
sustained, he said, by a vision of a postwar world dominated by the
totalitarian threat: "there will be more wars, a universal materialistic

state [and] Christians will be driven underground." The time had come "to be very evident indeed about our Faith."[23]

Lowell's letters of this period are full of gloomy, grand-scale prognostications of this sort, but there is little real passion in them; in reality, he was enjoying a stretch of low-pressure domestic stability—working on new poems and feeling grateful that someone else was cleaning up the nurses' floors in Bridgeport. Jean's letters are jaunty and contented, studded with fond anecdotes of married life:

> We have two cats. Or rather, we had two cats, really just kittens. The little female, who was always unhealthily tiny, fell ill on Christmas Day and was dying until yesterday. I had wanted to take her to the vets to have her put away or to get the farmer near us to shoot her, but Cal couldn't bear it. He nursed her most tenderly, keeping her on a cushion in his study and tempting her with all sorts of things like liver broth.[24]

Lowell would often conclude his weighty sermons on the coming darkness with some modest and agreeable disclaimer:

> I am with you about the family being the primary social unit, but I don't think we will escape totalitarianism and another and worse war. However, all this will take time and might last forever. At worst, life is pretty wonderful; although anyone who has escaped this war has no right to talk. I don't care about anything except writing and trying to be a halfway decent Christian. Politics is a spider's web of unreality.[25]

And in another letter, perhaps most tellingly of all: "We who have accreted illusions all our lives, must read just to be able to see."

While they were living in Westport, Jean Stafford's novel *Boston Adventure* made its appearance and was an immediate success. Within a few months of publication 40,000 hardcovers were sold, and then a further 300,000 went via book clubs and overseas editions. Suddenly, Jean Stafford had some money; "We are neither respectable nor rich," Lowell wrote triumphantly to Allen Tate.[26] And Stafford took a special pleasure in reflecting that the source of her new wealth was a novel about Boston snobbery; shortly after the book appeared she made a point of visiting the Lowells:

> It was not a very good trip: we always expect things to be different and they never are. There are the same lectures and moral generalizations and refusals to countenance the way we live and the dredging up of all the mistakes of the past. I am more thoroughly, more icily, more deeply

disliked than ever on account of my book, even though it is generally
admitted that it's a damned good thing Bobby married someone who
makes money writing. This is the only way, you see, writing can be
justified. And my inimitable mother-in-law who, as always, would stop
a clock, said to Cal that his poetry was nice but valueless since "one must
please the many, not the few."[27]

With the proceeds of *Boston Adventure,* Jean planned to buy a
house in Maine where they would live for "all but the very coldest
months." In July 1945 their tenancy at Westport expired, and they
found a temporary base in a small furnished cottage at Boothbay
Harbor: "a sort of Maine Monteagle; the nights are cool, the scenery
is beautiful and the summer people, to the number of 15,000, are
atrocious. There are 27 gift and local color shops."[28] From there,
Jean began her hunt along the Maine coastline and, within a month,
discovered Damariscotta Mills, a village at the head of the Damariscotta estuary, seventeen miles from the sea. The house she bought
there was on a hillside and overlooked the remarkable Damariscotta
Lake, a lake "as long as the river, crowded with bass and salmon in
the summertime." For this alone, Lowell the fisherman would have
given quite a lot, but the house itself was "large and grandly Hel-
lenic" and to Jean "too wonderful to be believed in."

> It is about a hundred years old, has a barn attached to it which we are
> going to make into two vast studios, has fine old trees, a 12-mile lake in
> the back yard and within a stone's throw, the oldest R.C. church north
> of southern Maryland.[29]

They took possession in September 1945, too late to fortify the place
for winter living. It was decided to spend part of the winter in
Tennessee visiting Jarrell and Peter Taylor, who was now discharged from the army; after that they would base themselves at
Delmore Schwartz's house in Cambridge and make occasional trips
to Maine (or Jean would) to furnish and decorate the house in time
for spring.

8

When Randall Jarrell died in 1965, Lowell wrote of him: "Randall was the only man I have ever met who could make other writers feel that their work was more important to him than his own."[1] Twenty years earlier, in October 1945, Lowell sent Jarrell the manuscript of *Lord Weary's Castle;* it carried ten poems from *Land of Unlikeness,* each of these slightly revised, and thirty new poems.

Lowell could not have wished for a more rousing yet judicious mentor. Jarrell wrote back, declaring that *Lord Weary*

> will be the best first book of poems since Auden's *Poems.* . . . the best nine or ten of your new poems are better than any poem in *Land of Unlikeness;* not only that, I think they are some of the best poems anyone has written in our time and are sure to be read for hundreds of years. I am *sure* of this: I would bet hundreds of dollars on it. You know how little contemporary poetry I like—if I'm affected this way—unless I've gone crazy—it must be the real thing. I think you're potentially a better poet than anybody writing in English.[2]

And this, presumably, included Eliot, Auden, Frost—as well as the unselfish Jarrell. There were one or two qualifying footnotes: Lowell was perhaps too little interested in people and too often "harsh and severe," and Jarrell was glad to see that he had dropped his efforts at "contemporary satire"—"your weakest sort of poem . . . not really worth wasting your time on." Lowell's worst tendency, he thought, was "to do too mannered, mechanical, wonderfully-contrived exercise poems." All this said, though, Jarrell was finally persuaded by new poems like "The Quaker Graveyard in Nantucket," "The Exile's Return," the two Black Rock poems and

"Mr. Edwards and the Spider" to declare that "you write more in the great tradition, the grand style, the real middle of English poetry, than anybody since Yeats."

Breathtaking stuff, but the excessive strain in Jarrell's hymn of praise can be readily forgiven. If the two choices for a modern poet seemed to be, on the one hand, the learned, metrical, ironic line of Eliot and Auden and, on the other, the fiery, bardic line of Dylan Thomas (with the William Carlos Williams free-verse, "Americanist" model a kind of permanently "other" possibility), then Lowell's new poems undoubtedly would have seemed to be getting the best of every world. The Eliot line was sorely in need of some dramatic urgency; the Thomas line was self-evidently short on meter, scholarly allusion and, in the case of some of its wartime devotees, short too on elementary intelligence. In this context, Lowell's voice was arresting simply because it could not be shoved into any of these pigeonholes—it was fiery, yes, but it was also educated:

> The empty winds are creaking and the oak
> Splatters and splatters on the cenotaph,
> The boughs are trembling and a gaff
> Bobs on the untimely stroke
> Of the greased wash exploding on a shoal-bell
> In the old mouth of the Atlantic: It's well;
> Atlantic, you are fouled with the blue sailors,
> Sea-monsters, upward angel, downward fish:
> Unmarried and corroding, spare of flesh
> Mart once of supercilious, wing'd clippers,
> Atlantic, where your bell-trap guts its spoil
> You could cut the brackish winds with a knife
> Here in Nantucket, and cast up the time
> When the Lord God formed man from the sea's slime
> And breathed into his face the breath of life,
> And blue-lung'd combers lumbered to the kill.
> The Lord survives the rainbow of His will.[3]

Many a learned paper has been written on that final line of Lowell's "Quaker Graveyard in Nantucket," yet it is no "clearer," no less haunting than it ever was: it was lines like this (and there are perhaps thirty of them in *Lord Weary's Castle*) that reduced even a proudly analytical reviewer like Jarrell to using words like "magic."

Although Lowell had certainly become craftier and more resonant since writing *Land of Unlikeness,* in most of the new poems his posture—and, intermittently, his posturing—remained essentially the same: the hectic, crunchingly enjambed iambic line, the welter of grabbed myths and pseudosymbols, the impudent and hortatory prayers, the barely controlled retributive gusto and the linguistic flagellation—both of self (so that the poet's noble rage will not lazily abate) and of the fallen world (which, if it will not be redeemed, surely deserves further punishment). Like the earlier book, *Lord Weary's Castle* is marked throughout by what Gabriel Pearson called Lowell's "unacknowledged flight into the omnipotence of manic verbal control."[4]

Manic or not, though, the verbal control in *Lord Weary* is strikingly more at ease with its own mannerisms than in *Land of Unlikeness:* the thumping, unstoppable iambic line, the piled-up alliteration, the onomatopoeic consonants—Lowell uses these devices as if he now thinks of them as his, as if this is the way he happens to speak rather than a manufactured style. Also, in *Lord Weary,* the sillier puns are eliminated, the more hysterical "political" gesturing has given way to an elusive, almost taunting irony —and there is a new reliance on the restraining influence of a prose source. It is almost true to say that the most powerful pieces in the book—stretches of "The Quaker Graveyard," "Mr. Edwards and the Spider," "The Exile's Return" and "After the Surprising Conversions"—are so derived. And these pieces may in turn have led Lowell into the near-naturalistic monologues of the "Between the Porch and the Altar" sequence—a sequence that seems not to belong in the book, pointing forward as it does to Lowell's Browningesque next phase.

Perhaps more than any other twentieth-century poet, Lowell is now thought of as "autobiographical"; or, as Gabriel Pearson put it, "the materials of his own life are there to be made over to art." There is an interest, therefore, in reflecting how *little* of his life up to 1945 can be construed from the poems of *Lord Weary's Castle.* One can deduce something of his Boston background, his *Mayflower* ancestry—though nothing in the least precise. There are elegies in the book addressed to dead relatives, but these carry little direct feeling, nor do we get from them any clear sense of who these people were: would it be known, for instance, from "In Memory of Arthur Winslow" that Lowell had revered the old man in his youth, and spent the happiest of his boyhood holidays messing about at his grandfather's farm at Mattapoisett? Nostalgia could not, of course, sit easily with Lowell's vatic zeal.

Similarly, *Lord Weary's Castle* reveals little of the poet's adolescent storms; many of his Boston poems can, it's true, be seen as acts of vengeance, as suddenly unthwarted fits of youthful venom. Only in "Rebellion," though, do we get a glimpse of the circumstances:

> There was rebellion, father, when the mock
> French windows slammed and you hove backward, rammed
> Into your heirlooms, screens, a glass-cased clock,
> The highboy quaking to its toes. You damned
> My arm that cast your house upon your head
> And broke the chimney flintlock on your skull.
> Last night the moon was full:
> I dreamed the dead
> Caught at my knees and fell:
> And it was well
> With me, my father. Then
> Behemoth and Leviathan
> Devoured our mighty merchants. None could arm
> Or put to sea. O father, on my farm
> I added field to field
> And I have sealed
> An everlasting pact
> With Dives to contract
> The world that spreads in pain;
> But the world spread
> When the clubbed flintlock broke my father's brain.

The poem deteriorates into myth and melodrama, but in the first eleven lines there is enough clarity, respect for detail and variety of rhythm to suggest that, for Lowell, personal experience could have the same braking, liberating influence as the prose models of Thoreau or Edwards, which are heavily drawn on in "The Quaker Graveyard" and "Mr. Edwards and the Spider."[5] Again, though, it would have been impossible for the young Lowell to concede that the archangelic protagonist of these early poems could be trammeled by a mortal life, a single history. Thus, even the symbolically rich gesture of refusing the draft barely gets into a book written shortly after his release from prison. There is one poem, "In the Cage," which does seem to have been set in Danbury:

> The lifers file into the hall,
> According to their houses—twos
> Of laundered denim. On the wall
> A colored fairy tinkles blues
> And titters by the balustrade;
> Canaries beat their bars and scream.

And there is a similarly unusual mutedness and factuality in parts of "The Death of the Sheriff":

> We kiss. The State had reasons: on the whole,
> It acted out of kindness when it locked
> Its servant in this place and had him watched
> Until an ordered darkness left his soul
> A *tabula rasa;* . . .

But these are isolated clumps of clay in the elemental moonscape of *Lord Weary.*

Even at this early stage, though, it is probable that Lowell would have glimpsed where such low-keyed factuality might lead. And he would certainly have been struck by Ransom's choice of poems for the *Kenyon Review:* "Winter in Dunbarton" (with its middle section of fond, plainspoken elegy for a dead family cat), "Mr. Edwards and the Spider" (almost every line a direct quotation from Edwards's own writing) and "At a Bible House," a poem which, in spite of its intricate rhyme scheme, is almost Williams-like in its terse observation, its ungenerously short lines:

> At a Bible House
> Where smoking is forbidden
> By the Prophet's law,
> I saw you wiry, bed-ridden,
> Gone in the kidneys; raw
> Onions and a louse
> Twitched on the sheet before
> The palsy of your white
> Stubble . . .

Ransom wrote:

> I don't know who has grown up in verse more than you, these last
> few years; mostly, I think, by way of giving up the effort to com-
> municate more than was communicable, and by consulting the gen-
> tle reader's traditional range of intelligence rather than your own
> private article. These are nice.[6]

"Nice" is not a word even the gentle Ransom could have used about
"The Drunken Fisherman" or "Christmas in Black Rock"—or indeed about the majority of the poems in *Lord Weary's Castle*. But
he was right to sense that—for the purposes of poetry—Lowell's
saintly rage was almost spent.

In December 1945—at Jarrell's suggestion—Lowell mailed off the
manuscript of *Lord Weary's Castle* to Philip Rahv, co-editor of
Partisan Review: Partisan was negotiating a co-publishing contract with Dial Press and printed, or was about to print, a number of Lowell's new poems in the magazine; there seems to have
been some notion of *Partisan* and *Dial* jointly publishing these,
and others from *Land of Unlikeness*, as a book. On January 2,
1946, Rahv wrote back: "I have read your manuscript over the
weekend and think you did a wonderful job. I liked your inclusion of nine poems from your first book."[7] Rahv, though, went
on to say that the arrangement with Dial Press was far from settled, and that "there is a possibility of our going over to Henry
Holt—if that happens would you mind their publishing your
book?" Two weeks later, Rahv wrote again: "Since our negotiations with Dial tend to become rather protracted I've sent your
manuscript off to Lambert Davis."[8] Davis was an editor at Harcourt, Brace, but it was in fact Robert Giroux who read the
manuscript and urged its acceptance. Harcourt, Brace agreed to
bring the book out in the fall of 1946.

Meanwhile two midwinter weeks at Damariscotta Mills had persuaded Lowell that the new house, though splendid, was nowhere
near ready to be settled into. In January, Jean wrote exuberantly to
Allen Tate:

> We have had a taste of really rigorous country life: our pipes freeze and
> burst in the most heart-rending fashion and we were without water for

two weeks until an ingenious plumber came and moved every vital organ in the house. It has been 17 and 20 below several times. But I have never been in such top-notch shape in my life and do not even complain of the cold, a transformation in myself I do not altogether understand.[9]

Even so, in mid-January they decided to accept an invitation from the poet Delmore Schwartz to move in with him at his house on Cambridge's Ellery Street. Schwartz's marriage—to a *Partisan Review* book reviewer called Gertrude Buckman—had not long before come to an end, and he was eager to have others share his domestic chaos. The move meant, of course, a return to the Boston sphere of influence and, in particular, regular lunch visits to the Lowell home on Marlborough Street: a high price to pay, Jean Stafford thought, for the comforts of town living. She writes of one visit:

[it] left me in a state of traumatism from which I have not yet fully emerged. I have not been so persistently needled since before we were married: Your family is just a myth to me, Jean. In our little community here, we all marry our third cousins and know everyone; you are look- ing well, Jean, and putting on weight, but Bobby looks terribly thin and not at all well; is it that you don't like us that you didn't stay with us instead of with Mr. Schwartz? Three hours of it.[10]

At first, though, the arrangement with Schwartz worked out fairly well—a repeat version of Benfolly and Monteagle, with typewriters clattering in every room and arguments about the plumbing:

> We couldn't even keep the furnace lit!
> Even when we had disconnected it,
> the antiquated
> refrigerator gurgled mustard gas
> through your mustard-yellow house,
> and spoiled our long-maneuvered visit
> from T. S. Eliot's brother, Henry Ware . . .[11]

The visit Lowell writes of here had been maneuvered so that Henry Ware Eliot could arrange a Briggs-Copeland lectureship for him at Harvard, but the scheme eventually came to nothing. Schwartz was fond of inaugurating stratagems like this, and he enjoyed playing the senior literary figure to the youthful Lowells. But according to

Schwartz's biographer, James Atlas, the domestic balance soon became precarious:

> Delmore was envious of Lowell's Brahmin background, and his envy sharpened after Lowell took him to dinner at his parents' house on Marlborough Street. They weren't "that grand" Jean Stafford recalled [in an interview with Atlas in 1976] but Delmore was intimidated by the servants, heirlooms, and a certain reserve on the part of the Lowells. The elder Lowell's attitude towards Delmore can be guessed from his habit of telling his literary son that he "talked like a Jew." Delmore resented the way Robert Lowell kept bringing up a Jewish relative remote in time, Mordecai Myers, the grandfather of Lowell's grandmother. Lowell insisted that he himself was ⅛ Jewish, and made much of a portrait of Myers that hung in the drawing room on Marlborough Street.
>
> Things were never the same after that evening. Delmore baited Lowell mercilessly, made fun of his parents' home, and tried to destroy his marriage by circulating malicious rumors. Finally Lowell swung at Delmore, Jean Stafford had to separate them, and soon afterwards the Lowells left for Maine.[12]

In fact the visit lasted nearly three months, and as late as March 3 Stafford was writing to Peter Taylor: "We are having a splendid time with Delmore, but we must get back to Maine soon, because a house doesn't like to be left alone too long."[13] On March 24 she writes: "I am going home on Monday but Cal is going to the Trappists for eight days."[14]

These "Trappists" may have been the same Rhode Island monks who had entertained both Lowell and Stafford in June 1944: on that occasion they had had, according to Jean, "the most wonderful time imaginable . . . we went to all the services, to vespers, to Benediction and to Compline,"[15] but in 1946 Stafford's obsession was with homemaking at Damariscotta Mills, and it is hardly a surprise that her intensified activity on this score should have encouraged the contemplative in Lowell. During the next three months, however, he seems to have escaped from Maine as often as he could. In April "Cal went off to New York today, to be gone a week or more and I am again left here alone with the mice."[16] In May, Lowell writes to Peter Taylor: "I'll probably be passing through New York in a week or so and will see you."[17] And for those weeks when he did stay at Damariscotta he had devised an ingenious new means of stepping to one side of Jean's hectic refurbishing:

I go birding with field glasses every day and read a set of books called Birds of New England by a Mr. Forbrush who is the most eccentric writer of our times. His running attack on the "pernicious activities" of cats sets Jean's teeth on edge.[18]

But Lowell was not always in the mood to sidestep. Since Christmas, he and Stafford had been edgy and at odds. She, he would say, was drinking heavily, and so he attempted to ration her intake: this would produce the sort of quarrel Stafford later, and perhaps exaggeratingly, recalls in her short story:

> "What the bleeding hell?," I'd yell at him. "You drink as much as I do. You drink more!" and he'd reply, "A difference of upbringing, dear— no more than that. I learned to drink at home in the drawing room, so I know how. No fault of yours—just bad luck. You don't drink well, dear. Not well at all."[19]

This urbane, sneering Lowell figure doesn't quite fit with the accounts she was giving in letters at the time. In one of these she describes him returning from his April trip to New York: "When he came back and found the house fresh with all this wallpaper and this new paint, he exploded and said that it was cheap, that it was immoral, and that I had done the whole thing out of a sadistic desire to stifle him."[20] In "An Influx of Poets," she analyzes the incident more coolly:

> My nesting and my neatening were compulsions in me that Theron looked on as plebeian, anti-intellectual, lace-curtain Irish; he said I wanted to spend my life in a tub of warm water, forswearing adventure but, worse, forswearing commitment. My pride of house was the sin of pride. I took no stock in this, I knew it to be nonsense, but I did not know how to defend myself against his barbs, the cruellest of which was that I could not sin with style; as my dreams were wanting in vitality, so was my decoration of houses wanting in taste.

As the "Swiss-organdie glass curtains" were followed by "red velvet drapes" for the living room, and then the moss-green carpeting from Boston, the Theron-Lowell figure seethes with fury: "and all day and all night my God-fearing yokemate burned me at the stake in Salem." And it is overwritten lines like this that should encourage caution when it comes to construing real-life agonies from Stafford's fictional reconstructions.

Certainly, though, her nest-building obsessions[21] had come at almost precisely the wrong time for Lowell. His literary career was opening up at high speed, he was enjoying his trips to New York: Jarrell was there and so too—at this time—was Peter Taylor. Jean Stafford may have seen Damariscotta as a "temple" built in honor of her marriage; Lowell was beginning to see it as an overfurnished jail. And it should not be supposed that Stafford was silently long-suffering; in one of the very few moments in "An Influx of Poets" when she is moved to judge her own conduct, she confesses: "I make no plea for myself, for I had the tongue of an adder and my heart was black with rage and hate."

In spite of all this melodrama, Lowell seems to have kept busy through the spring of 1946, mostly writing book reviews for the quarterlies. The most noteworthy of these was a roundup of current poetry that eventually appeared in the Winter 1946 issue of the *Sewanee Review;*[22] it covered no fewer than nineteen newly published books of verse. Lowell is now thought of as having been shrewd and cautious in his public pronouncements on the work of his contemporaries—self-servingly so, it is implied, and certainly in his later years he became guardedly benevolent in his statements about other poets' work. It is therefore worth remarking that, at the age of twenty-nine, he was prepared to be almost Jarrell-like in his strictness. The first four books on his list are, he says, too awful even to be quoted from:

> I have nothing to say about the absurd phony-Lindsay clatter of Mr. Alan Baer Rothenberg, the ungrammatical pilfering of Mr. George J. Cox, the slick and sounding oratory of Mr. Carl Cramer or the harmless devotions of Mr. Lloyd Haberley. A few quotations would ruin these writers more effectively than any criticism, but I see no excuse for the exposure.

He then moves on to take fierce issue with C. Day Lewis ("verbal without craftsmanship; abstract without profundity"), Edmund Blunden (once a "small Hardy" but now "heavy, clumsy, careless, academic and sentimental") and Oscar Williams ("He never knows when to stop and can seldom write more than two or three lines that hang together").

Lowell spends rather more time on two dominating figures from his Harvard past: Robert Frost, who had once told him that he should "condense," is now scolded for having made *A Masque of Reason* "too long, random and willful"; and on his bygone mentor Richard Eberhart:

> Mr. Richard Eberhart writes a rough iambic line with subtle shifts in speed and tone. His best poems are entirely his own and masterful. Elsewhere his lines drag in a rhetorical doggerel, often relieved by strong lines and phrases. He has a paralyzing fascination for the mannerisms of Hopkins and likes to echo very famous lines from other poets. Sometimes his idealistic reflections on himself and the universe are remarkably foolish.

It should be said that Lowell does exempt "about five poems" from all this, including "The Fury of Aerial Bombardment"—still perhaps Eberhart's most memorable poem.

The meager rations of praise in Lowell's piece are reserved for Louis MacNeice ("perhaps the most observant eye in England") and Norman Nicholson ("readable and accomplished"). But throughout there is only one really charitable spasm. Lowell singles out Ralph Gustafson as "one of the best poets reviewed here," and it is easy to see why; there are clear hints of fellow feeling in his verdict that

> [Gustafson's] faults are never entirely overcome: they can be summed up by the word *jerky*. Monotonous alliteration, unidiomatic and ungrammatical sentences, jumps in subject-matter from one sentence to another, and monstrous mixed metaphors . . . but all his faults are present in all his poems and are inseparable from his virtues. No poem is a whole, but the most ambitious are the best. He has the ear and the power to become much better than he is.

Of Lowell's own poems in *Lord Weary's Castle*, two had appeared in magazines in 1945 (the first version of "The Quaker Graveyard" —lacking parts III and VII—in *Partisan Review* and "Colloquy in Black Rock" in the *Sewanee*). During the spring and summer of 1946 he was to have acceptances in all the leading magazines. In February a batch of three poems appeared in *The Nation* (where Jarrell was now the poetry editor) and Lowell made a further eight appearances in that magazine during the year—a total of twelve poems, including "The Exile's Return," "At the Indian Killer's Grave," "The Holy Innocents" and "Between the Porch and the Altar." Most of the other poems in the book appeared in *Partisan Review* (four poems, including "Christmas in Black Rock" and "After the Surprising Conversions") and *Kenyon Review* ("Mr. Edwards and the Spider," "At a Bible House" and "Mary Winslow"). He also made appearances in *Poetry* ("The Ghost"), *Commonwealth* ("The Dead in Europe") and in the first issue of a new periodical called *Foreground* ("In the Cage"). During 1946 it was barely possible to open a literary magazine without coming across Lowell's name; anticipation of the finished book was thus mounting for several months before it actually appeared.

The quarterlies, however, paid no more handsomely in the 1940s than they do today, and Lowell seems to have accepted that, along with Taylor, Jarrell and most of his other poet friends, he would sooner or later have to start looking out for teaching jobs. In May he was offered an instructorship at what he called "the Catholic University" in Boston ($2,500 a year for twelve hours' teaching per week), but negotiations foundered when Lowell requested shorter hours: he was interested, he said, in a job that left him free to write but not in "a lot of freshman composition courses."[23] In July, Jean Stafford wrote to Peter Taylor: "Our plans for the future remain vague. . . . We think now that we will stay on here as long as the weather allows and since that will be anyhow until November, we needn't worry for a bit yet."[24]

Towards the end of July the summer visitors began to arrive—the poet John Berryman and his wife, Philip and Natalie Rahv, and the critic R. P. Blackmur; the Parkers and the Clarks; also Robert Giroux, Lowell's editor at Harcourt, Brace, and a number of nonliterary friends—neighbors from Westport, the landlord from Boothbay Harbor, together with his wife and his wife's parents. As soon as one collection of guests moved on, another lot arrived. Jean had completed the shrine; now it was time to greet the worshipers. Needless to say, it didn't work that way:

> That awful summer! Every poet in America came to stay with us. It was the first summer after the war, when people once again had gasoline and

could go where they liked, and all those poets came to our house in Maine and stayed for weeks at a stretch, bringing wives or mistresses with whom they'd quarreled, and complaining so vividly about the wives and mistresses they'd left, or had been left by, that the discards were real presences, swelling the ranks, stretching the house, *my* house (my very own, my first and very own), to its seams. At night, after supper, they'd read from their own works until four o'clock in the morning. . . . They never listened to one another; they were preoccupied with waiting for their turn. And I'd have to stay up and clear out the living room after they went soddenly to bed—sodden but not too far gone to lose their conceit. And then all day I'd cook and wash the dishes and chop the ice and weed the garden and type my husband's poems and quarrel with him.[25]

It is not clear who issued the invitations that produced this summer "influx," but the upshot must surely have been easy to predict. Jean stepped up the drinking, and her quarrels with Lowell became more vicious and determined. Her fevers returned; she was also plagued with daily headaches—caused not just by large quantities of rum, nor, she says, by a diet of "too many iambs." As to Lowell, he very rarely unburdened himself in letters, and it is therefore hard to know how frenetic *he'd* become during these weeks. By August, though, he was sufficiently worn down to write to Peter Taylor:

I don't care for confessions, but I suppose I must tell you that everything is chaos between us. Jean is driving like a cyclone and we both have had about all we can stand and more. Right now I think I'll go to New York sometime in September and stay with the Jarrells and Lytle and then get a room and pick up some sort of temporary work. Jean has a lot of plans, none of them too good, including going to Hollywood. Anyway, we have got to *leave each other alone* and the future to time. Please just be an ear for this letter, and don't say anything to me or anyone else.[26]

The running conflict had taken a new and drastic turn. Shortly before Lowell wrote this letter, the "eighteenth guest since Memorial Day" had been flown into Damariscotta in a private plane that had been laid on by the last of her many summer hosts. Gertrude Buckman, the former Mrs. Delmore Schwartz, had come to stay. Jean was not on hand to welcome her; she had gone to see her doctor in Cambridge. In "An Influx of Poets," though, she makes it clear that many hours were later to be spent imagining this grand arrival:

> She came to us, quixotically and at the expense of her last host, in a Piper Cub, landing on an island in Hawthorne Lake, behind us, flown there by a Seabee so stricken with her that he loitered in the village several days afterward. If I had been there when she came, the outcome of my marriage would, I daresay, have been the same, but the end of it would probably not have come so soon. Certainly it would not have been so humiliating, so banal, so sandy to my teeth. But I was not there on that beautiful afternoon when her blithe plane banked and came bobbing to rest on Loon Islet and she came swimming to our landing.[27]

9

In "An Influx of Poets," Gertrude is portrayed as Minnie Zumwalt, raven-tressed and damask-skinned; having acquired a divorce from her murderously moody husband, the poet Jered Zumwalt, she is charming her way from house to house along the coast of Maine. She writes sharp little book reviews for *The Divergent*, but in life she is always ready to turn moon-eyed in the presence of a poet, and is therefore a hugely popular house guest. Poets' wives have no fear of her because Jered has unchivalrously—"in disgraceful and convincing detail"—told the world that she is frigid.

This may have been the rumor (and Delmore Schwartz's notebooks would seem to confirm it), but after Gertrude had been at Damariscotta for a few days, Jean Stafford began to have her doubts. She wrote to Peter Taylor:

> She lingered on and on. All day she read Cal's poetry and exclaimed over it or, when he mentioned something, she cried in her quite lovely voice: "read it aloud to me." And he would read to her from Boswell or Ben Jonson or Shakespeare (and you know how well he loved it! Ah, what a foolish woman I have been!) They would go to the lake early in the morning to swim and then in the afternoon, and then before dinner, and then late when the moon was full (one of Cal's chief and most bitter charges against me was that I did not know how to swim). They would walk to the village together, telling me that I was much too tired to go. They sat facing each other in the big chairs listening to records in the light of the fire. Gertrude told me things I had done wrong in my house, and Cal agreed with her, and she told me what I had done wrong in *The Mountain Lion* [Stafford's second novel] and Cal agreed with her. I was wormwood.[1]

And so it appears to have continued for the three weeks of Gertrude Buckman's stay. Later, Stafford was to accuse Buckman of deliberately "fouling my nest," of cold-bloodedly setting out to steal her husband: she "horribly flattered Cal, caused him to fall in love with her and caused herself to fall in love with him." She claimed that on returning to New York, Buckman wrote to Lowell and "all but said that she was in love." It was this letter, said Stafford, that encouraged Lowell to announce, in mid-September, that the marriage was over and that he wanted an immediate separation.

Buckman, on the other hand, recalls that throughout her visit to Damariscotta, Jean Stafford "was drinking herself into a stupor. . . . Most of the time she was just drinking—madly, madly, staying up all night and drinking," and that any closeness that developed between her and Lowell was more or less forced on them by Stafford's impossible behavior. She also claims that it was Lowell who made the first move to see her in New York: "He'd asked if he could come to see me. And I said, 'Certainly you can come and see me, with Jean, not by yourself.' And he said, 'But we're separating.' " Had Lowell then fallen for her at Damariscotta? "I don't know what his feelings were. How could I tell that? I suppose we were drawn to each other. He was so beautiful then. But I did think he was a very odd character, I must say. Unlike anyone else I've ever known."[2]

In September 1946 Lowell and Stafford traveled together to New York and said good-bye on the platform at Penn Station. Lowell rented a bug-infested room on Third Avenue and Jean Stafford stayed with friends. Over the next three weeks there were attempts at a reconciliation, but none of them lasted for more than twenty-four hours. Lowell had begun to see a lot of Buckman, using her apartment to work in during the day and moving in with her for a period when he caught influenza:

He would spend days in my flat working, and I would feed him. He was living in this ghastly rooming house on Third Avenue. I mean, he would get lice and crabs and everything, and he had no money. I really think he preferred that kind of thing. It was a haunt of pimps and prostitutes and God knows what.[3]

At times, Lowell was uncertain about what Buckman really meant to him, but any pressure from Stafford invariably drove him into a rage; he would tell her "over and over again in the indefatigable way only Cal can repeat, that I was possessive like his mother in not approving of so intimate a relationship with her."[4] In October, therefore, Jean changed her strategy and attempted to create a harmonious triangular arrangement. She agreed, for instance, that the three of them should make a Sunday trip to the Bronx Zoo—as doomed a project as could be imagined:

> I managed to get a hotel and that evening I telephoned G to say that I'd meet them the next morning to go to the zoo. The next morning Cal called me and blew up rhetorically and forbade me categorically to go (oh how can I shame myself further by telling you this juvenile tale. It is the want of dignity in the whole thing that most maddens me. The zoo, indeed). They came back and had dinner with me at my hotel and left very soon afterwards, very much like two married people obliged to dine with a boring relative. It was that evening that they began attacking people who were possessive and would not let other people alone.[5]

By this time, Stafford's control was visibly disintegrating, and the doctor she was seeing in New York arranged for her to go to a Catholic sanatorium in Detroit. She stayed there for eight hours ("I knew somehow that, if I let night fall I would be there for good") and then took a train to Chicago; from there she traveled on to Denver: "I was trying," she later wrote to Lowell, "to put as many miles between myself and you as I could do." She stayed with her sister in Denver for five days and swiftly "commenced to hate her because she judged me morally: 'Quit drinking for my sake.' " On her way back to New York she stopped over in Chicago:

> And then I did a pitiful thing. . . . I had not been able to read anything for weeks and so, in the station, when I still had some hours to wait, I bought a dollar edition of Boston Adventure and I tried to read it. I went into the women's room and tried to read it there and when I could not, the tears poured out and in a perfect rage I threw it in the trash container. It was, in its way, a little suicide.[6]

Soon after her return to New York, Jean Stafford was admitted to the Payne Whitney Clinic to undergo a "psycho-alcoholic cure";

she was to stay there for several months, and during that time she bombarded Lowell and Peter Taylor with a series of extraordinary letters. At first, she simply refused to accept that the marriage was over and confined herself to brilliant denunciations of the "stunted cowbird" Buckman. Lowell, she conceded, might have found the playmate he was always looking for (he had once told Stafford: "I don't want a wife. I want a playmate"), but she said:

> She is a child and if she wishes to eat the last piece of candy in the box, she will consult only her own desire. . . . [but] if you marry her, you will not be marrying a woman. Nor will you be any closer to the knowledge of what marriage is than you were with me. I knew more than you did, I think, and God knows I knew little enough.[7]

The trouble all along, she says, was that Lowell, with his "powerful alchemy," had turned her into a version of his mother and that subconsciously she had assented to this role "until [she] terrifyingly resembled her." And she, Stafford, had similarly confused Lowell with her dominating father. She wrote to Peter Taylor in November 1946:

> There was something wrong in me to marry him for he was so much like my father, whom first I worshipped and by whom I later felt betrayed. This is not psychiatric cant, even though the psychiatrists have told me that this is just what I did, married my father, just as the same perverseness made Cal marry his mother. But only in the past year did these people really emerge in us, and I suppose they emerged because we dug them out. We probably wanted it to be like this. I disobeyed him as I disobeyed my father. He was economically and domestically irresponsible as my father had always been. He read his poems aloud to me, as my father had read his stories for the pulp magazines. His manners were courtly or they were uncouth, and he was slovenly, as my father was. My father didn't have his wit, nor his brilliance. They were both violent men in every way.[8]

With this knowledge established, she would plead, surely she and Lowell could try again:

> I feel that somehow we will save one another and that our salvation will be unusual, for having suffered so much and having yet endured, we must have, both of us, extraordinary strength. I cannot help, with all this

lovely love of mine, wishing that we could live our lives together and feeling that we have a chance that no-one we have ever known has had.[9]

In the face of these pleas, Lowell remained stonily discouraging. He had shocked Jean by demanding a divorce and by announcing that he was no longer a Catholic; the Church, he said, had "served its purpose" (Jean commented on this that he probably meant that it had "served its *literary* purpose"). He would marry Gertrude Buckman, he told Peter Taylor, and when Taylor offered to act as an intermediary between him and Stafford, he refused. Taylor had suggested that they delay any final decisions for a year: "I feel like a parent whose two favorite children have had a bitter quarrel and are making a complete break and that's a pretty terrible feeling."[10] Lowell replied:

The time for considering and re-considering is long past. I'll only be counting the days.

Your letter was an honorable and warm-hearted one for you to have written. But what you imagine is not the same as my remembrance. You mustn't idealize what other people have to live. You mustn't.[11]

And, it must be said, Stafford's response to Taylor's plan does seem to bear out Lowell's view:

Peter, by this plan he will only be free to reject me in his brutal fashion over a longer period of time than he has done already. Mind you, I would take him back now, and I would forgive him, because I love him.[12]

Nearly all Stafford's letters waver agonizingly between savage recrimination on the one hand and pathetic pleading on the other. One day she will write in fury accusing Lowell of "Yankee trading" because he refuses to sign a quit claim on the house in Maine (Jean had put the house in their joint names and now wished to raise a mortgage on it to pay her medical expenses); on another, she will announce that she has stopped drinking, that her love has been purified of all selfish jealousies, and that she is now, at last, spiritually ready to make him a good wife: "Remember that I do love you and that I love you without reproach and that in wanting you, I realize that I am issuing a rather remarkable invitation, but one which will give me unmodified joy if it is accepted." They make harrowing reading, and although Jean persistently complains that Lowell, during these months, remained "so immovable, so utterly, so absolutely, utterly unaware of what I might be suffering," it is evident that with each letter she was—almost systematically—ruining her own cause. Lowell's plea throughout had been at least consistent: "Why can't we leave each other alone?" In her eyes, of course, this very consistency was nothing less than "calm, olympian brutality":

> It is Cal's doing, all of it. With serene greatness, he will be unsmirched. He will always be a Lowell. Forgive me for this deep bitterness. . . . If Cal had said, I am sorry, I could have borne it. If he had said, I am suffering too and the reason I am doing it this way is that I must end my suffering and yours. Perhaps he feels that, but he has never *said* it, he has never shown me anything in any of his letters but cold, self-justified hatred. He has even stooped to literal Yankee trading, and all I can feel now is, pray God that the day I can forget my Boston adventure will not be long in coming.[13]

Lord Weary's Castle had appeared in December 1946, but most of the reviews didn't start coming in until the following spring. With one or two fairly trifling exceptions, they added up to a chorus of acclaim. Randall Jarrell set the tone with a long piece in *The Nation:*

> When I reviewed Lowell's first book I finished by saying "Some of the best poems of the next years ought to be written by him." The appearance of *Lord Weary's Castle* makes me feel . . . like a rain-maker who predicts rain, and gets a flood which drowns everyone in the country. A few of these poems, I believe, will be read as long as men remember English.[14]

Selden Rodman in the *New York Times Book Review* attempted to go even further:

> One would have to go back as far as 1914, the year that saw the publication of Robert Frost's *North of Boston* or to T. S. Eliot's *The Love Song of J. Alfred Prufrock* to find a poet whose first public speech has had the invention and authority of Robert Lowell's. . . . The voice is vibrant enough to be heard, learned enough to speak with authority, and savage enough to wake the dead.[15]

And Anne Fremantle waxed mixed-metaphorical in *The Common-weal:*

> Robert Lowell . . . is a young, new poet of tremendous importance, who
> is both Catholic and classical. He writes in tight, tapestried meters,
> hierarchic in form and feeling. His verse, though full and rich, is trim
> as a yew quincunx, tailored as a box edging: he seems to have pared and
> whittled away every excrescence, every unessential, till the taut lines,
> clean as a whistle, dovetail effortlessly, polished like old, warm ivory.
> And always, at all levels, there is that continual awareness of his
> Maker. . . .[16]

The quarterlies were rather less ecstatic. Austin Warren in *Poetry*
was cautious and exegetical, but aware that here was something
new: "Lowell never sounds much like anyone else—and never like
Eliot or Auden." He suggests a comparison with Hopkins, Dylan
Thomas and John Wheelwright, but concludes: "Probably Lowell
can't imitate docilely even when he wishes."[17] Louise Bogan in *The
American Scholar* praised Lowell's "moral earnestness . . . it is extraordinary to find it at present in so pure a form,"[18] and Howard
Moss in the *Kenyon Review* greets him as "that surprising phenomenon, a religious poet who writes like a revolutionary," and confi-
dently ventures that "with this new book, Lowell can easily take his
place beside the few excellent contemporary poets America has
produced."[19]

The most eccentric review of the book was by Richard Eberhart
in the *Sewanee Review.*[20] Eberhart devoted the majority of his piece
to a rumination on the very earliest of Lowell's poems, those that
he had been privileged to view in manuscript twelve years before.
He even goes so far as to quote, approvingly, a particularly embarrassing lyric from those days: "A sight of something after death /
Bright angels dropping from the sky." Eberhart is at pains to point
out, not without a hint of mystery, that "experience" has darkened
the young poet's view since then: with *Land of Unlikeness*, "The
years had matured the wild early strains; much reading had been
assumed; much experience had taken its toll." The book had had
much "spiritual power," though, and also a "rugged, harsh New
England quality": "It was a manacle-forged mind I heard." He then
devotes a page and a half to itemizing the revisions Lowell has made
to the *Land of Unlikeness* poems that are reprinted in *Lord Weary's*

Castle. Eberhart does not approve of these: "in my opinion the cold-hearted tampering has in many cases dimmed the heat and originality of the prime utterance." There is an almost plaintive note in all this: as if Eberhart is letting Lowell know that he would have done far better to have consulted his old teacher. As to the new poems in *Lord Weary's Castle*—i.e., three-quarters of the book— Eberhart has a single paragraph on these. They are "passionate, forceful, sometimes choking and bursting from the rigorous moulds" and, on the whole, are "excellent."

April 1947 completed Lowell's extraordinary triumph. In that month he was awarded the Pulitzer Prize, a Guggenheim fellowship of $2,500, and an award of $1,000 from the American Academy of Arts and Letters. He was also sounded out for various teaching jobs —at Iowa and Chapel Hill, North Carolina—and was invited to spend two months at Yaddo, the writers' colony. To add a comic twist to all these solemn tributes, *Life* magazine produced a large photofeature on America's new great poet and this provoked an excited call from Hollywood. Robert Giroux, Lowell's editor at Harcourt, Brace, remembers:

> I got a call from a movie producer, who asked if Cal had ever been in the movies. I said, "What do you mean, writing scripts?" And he said, "No, has he ever acted?" "No, he certainly hasn't." "Well, we'd be interested in discussing this with him." Cal was very amused, very *pleased.* He was very handsome, in a masculine and classic very Roman way. Berryman called them "Cal's matinee-idol looks."[21]

During May, Lowell toyed with these various offers (although Hollywood seems never to have followed up its interest), and after a good deal of haggling over money he wrote off to Iowa on May 30 accepting $3,000 a year for "two or three hours classwork, just teaching writing." In June, though, he withdrew his acceptance, having been offered the prestigious post of Consultant in Poetry at the Library of Congress at a salary of $5,000 a year. This appointment would start in October 1947 and run for a year, and so Lowell decided to spend July and August at Yaddo before moving to Washington in September. In the space of a few months he had become unmarried, non-Catholic, the most promising young poet in America, and perhaps the first World War II CO to be offered a job in the government. Back in Boston, the *Sunday Globe* proclaimed him

MOST PROMISING POET IN 100 YEARS . . . MAY BE GREATER THAN JAMES AND AMY. And the paper carried a comment from "Robert Traill Spence Lowell, Annapolis graduate, retired navy officer and stockbroker"; "Poets," Lowell's father said, "seem to see more in his work than most other people."

During these months of triumph Lowell had been living mainly in New York. His only lengthy trip had been to Greensboro, North Carolina, where Peter Taylor had organized a Writers' Forum (really a kind of Kenyon reunion, with old classmates Robie Macauley and John Thompson there, as well as Taylor and Jarrell). Throughout this time, though, he had been getting weekly, sometimes twice-weekly, communications from Jean Stafford. Stafford stayed at Payne Whitney until summer 1947, and remained bitter and despairing: "I do not know what monstrous crime I did when I was a child to merit this punishment. These ghastly months in this ghastly asylum, this ghastly future which I face without *money.*"[22]

Money was very often the topic of her letters. One week, Jean would be renouncing all alimony claims; another, she would file some impossibly huge "minimum requirement." One week, she would be arranging to dismantle and sell the house in Maine; another, she would be determined to hang on to it. In March, Lowell wrote to Peter Taylor: "Things have been going very badly for Jean and I feel so depressed I almost dread seeing anyone."[23] At various times he did make financial offers—his first offer was $5,000 payable over ten years—but it was not always easy to talk business:

> If there were tears, really, when you read my letter, if you really re-read it, there would have been love, there would have been love and longing and the desire to return with gifts of understanding. Grief for me, unable to die although I live here in a tomb, would have never allowed your pencil to write down the word "alimony." You would have come to claim your presents that gather dust and you would have found them set with pearls of great price.[24]

And when Jean was prepared to talk, she would talk fairly tough:

> Your offer of $5,000 payable over a period of ten years shows remarkable business acumen but does not somehow really take me in. If this was

meant as a gesture of generosity, it falls rather short of the mark, I'm afraid. To be rather blunt about it, forty dollars a month, paid over a period of ten years, is not quite the same thing as what you got in six.[25]

After the announcement of Lowell's prizes and awards, it was perhaps to be expected that Jean would adopt an even harder line. Certainly as the year progressed, her demands did escalate. By September she was asking for $7,000 payable over five years, $800 for life and one-third of his trust fund, also for life. Lowell refused and was denounced as "Bostonian," "intransigent" and "shrewd."

The style of the negotiations, though, would always depend on Stafford's mood and on what she guessed to be the state of Lowell's relationship with Gertrude Buckman. Lowell was writing to friends throughout 1947 saying that his "remarriage" would be postponed until possibly a year after his divorce became final, and Gertrude Buckman would now say that marriage between them was never a serious possibility: "marriage with him would have been a crazy thing, really crazy. He wasn't husband material."[26] It is by no means certain that she thought this at the time; but it must be said that there was not much weight of feeling in a spoof verse review Buckman printed in *Partisan Review* in March 1947:

> So the symbolic wedding ring
> Often does not mean a thing
> And infidelity runs rife
> While everyday is simply strife
> And everyone loves another's mate
> And looks upon his own with hate.

It must have taken a certain impish bravery to publish this, under all the circumstances, and if Stafford saw it she could perhaps be forgiven for immediately adding a few hundred dollars to her alimony claim.

With matters still unsettled, Lowell left for Yaddo in June 1947 and hoped to "work like a steam engine" until Washington. He was translating *Phèdre* and planning a "symbolic monologue by an insane woman"; it would be a thousand lines long, he said, and made him feel like Homer or Robert Browning. Yaddo, he found, was "a marvellous place to work," but much of the fun was in observing his co-workers: mostly "goons," but "friendly and harmless." There was Theodore Roethke: "a ponderous, coarse, fattish, fortyish man —well read, likes the same things I do, and is quite a competent poet"; there was Mary McCarthy and her husband, Bowden Broadwater; and there was Marguerite Young—"really rather crucifyingly odd and garrulous."[27]

And Yaddo itself was a bizarre establishment, near Saratoga Springs. According to its brochure, it is built in "late Victorian eclectic style" and is modeled on an English country house—although it prides itself on touches of Gothic, Moorish and Italian Renaissance. Inside, the mansion is luxuriously furnished with "carpets, carved wood, ecclesiastical furniture from Europe, and period pieces"; its grounds are extensive and elaborately formal, and the Rose Garden is its special pride and joy. The original owner was a New York financier called Spencer Trask, and his wife, Katrina, had been particularly fond of roses: "Images of roses are evident throughout Yaddo in the stained glass windows, the furniture, paintings, woodwork, china and linen, for this flower was the motif of Katrina Trask."[28] It had been Katrina's idea that Yaddo should be turned into a "retreat" for artists, writers and composers; when Mr. Trask died before these plans were finalized, she married his close (and equally rich) friend George Foster Peabody; between them they opened the colony in 1926, with Elizabeth Ames as director—Mrs. Ames was an adopted relative of Mr. Peabody and, according to Lowell, you could "cut her liberalism with a knife."[29]

The faint absurdity of the place delighted Lowell, just as it had delighted Jean Stafford in 1943. She had written of it then:

> This place surpasses the Biltmore for luxury. The Mansion is full of three cornered Spanish chairs and tremendous gold plush sofas. The grounds are vast and perfectly beautiful. Full of innumerable lakes and pools and gardens and woodland walks. . . . The food is superb. The only trouble is the people.[30]

So, nothing much had changed. But Lowell liked the place well enough to ask for his stay to be extended and to write letters to his friends begging them to join him; and the "people" improved with the arrival of the short-story writer J. F. Powers, "a fine person" and admired by Jarrell. The wily, altogether worldly Catholic priests who populate his work would have had a timely appeal for Lowell;

certainly, Powers became one of his very few favorite American prose writers.

During July and August, Lowell continued to fiddle with his long poem—"but I must get down to things I'll really do"—and as early as July 3 he had completed three shorter pieces and "drafted a fourth." Just before leaving Yaddo, on September 2, he wrote to Gertrude Buckman: "I've finished another long poem of 127 lines and part of another of same length. This will make ½ of a book—not too bad for a summer."

> How is Truman? How is the French Ambassador, and Charles Luckman, and Senator Vandenberg? How is J. Edgar Hoover, and John L. Lewis? And Arthur Krock? Have you been asked to write a poem for Food Conservation? Have you learned the Dewey Decimal System?[31]

This, from John Thompson, was the typical response of Lowell's friends to his Washington appointment: delighted as they were, it was hard not to find something ribald in the idea of this notoriously ungainly and disheveled figure attempting to master an 8:30-to-5:00 office job.

The post of Poetry Consultant to the Library of Congress had been established in 1937, and the required duties were in fact attractively vague and flexible. The consultant was meant to keep an eye on the library's poetry shelves, to "survey" the existing collections and to recommend additions; he was also to solicit gifts of books and manuscripts from authors and collectors, answer "reference questions" that came in by mail and "confer with scholars and poets using the library's collections and facilities." By December, Lowell was writing to J. F. Powers:

> Paper and chaos pile up and I'm out of stamps and every day a retired major calls me and asks me to identify obscure quotations which may help him to win a radio contest, whose answer last week was Clara Bow. . . . Across the hall, a Senate Committee has been moved into the Division for the Adult Blind. No one sees the joke.[32]

Lowell's 1947 appointment happily coincided with the inauguration of a new scheme. The library wished to build up a collection of recordings of poets reading their own work, and it was to be the new consultant's responsibility to organize these recording sessions: to pick the poets, persuade them to take part and entertain them when they came to Washington. For Lowell, this was a thoroughly appealing chore: it would mean a steady stream of mostly congenial visitors, and also an opportunity to get to know poets he admired but hadn't met. He immediately sent off invitations to William Carlos Williams, Elizabeth Bishop—whose book *North and South* he had just admiringly reviewed, along with Williams's *Paterson* Book 1, in the *Sewanee Review* (Summer 1947)—and Randall Jarrell. He also invited Robert Frost, who wrote to him:

> Isn't it fine that the young promise I began to entertain hopes of when it visited me on Fayerweather Street Cambridge in 1936, should have come to so much and to so much more promise for the future.[33]

In Lowell's file at the Library of Congress there is a newspaper cutting—seemingly from the gossip column of a local paper. It praises his appearance—"Lowell looks the part of the poet. Dark-eyed, soulful-looking, esthetic and stuff"—but the writer is clearly piqued that he has refused to grant an interview. Hence some heavy innuendo about his marital status—although married, Lowell is living in Washington's men-only Cosmos Club—and a lightly ironical description of his World War II imprisonment: "he insisted that the danger to the U.S. was no longer imminent and that his services, perforce, were not necessary." Attached to the cutting is a memo dated October 27, 1947, from the Librarian to Personnel: "I'm concerned that normal personnel procedures didn't bring this out—this is the first time I've heard of this."

Nonetheless, Lowell was allowed to keep his job and he seems to have enjoyed it. Washington was full of distant and close Winslow relatives, and he wrote to his mother that, altogether,

> it's a nice combination of cousins and passing writers, and much as I hate to admit it, physically a pleasant city to live in. I've become very fond of Harriet and Mary and the Meades. Harriet's really a lot like you—tells the same kind of story. But I doubt if either of you would see the likeness.[34]

Harriet was the daughter of Arthur Winslow's brother Francis, and she was the Washington relative Lowell always felt closest to. "She was born to be a maiden lady and had certain classical aspects of the type," but she was also witty, generous, unshockable. She liked Lowell because he was so *interesting*—as she used to say, "there have been too many afternoon naps in the Winslow line."[35] In her "refined, not very ambitious way," Cousin Harriet was a figure in Washington society—"a true lady"[36]—but also roguish and worldly enough for Lowell to feel thoroughly at home with her.

Another Washington attraction was the presence in St. Elizabeth's Hospital of the imprisoned Ezra Pound. Lowell had long been fascinated by Pound: both by his poetry (although he thought the *Cantos* the "most self-indulgent long poem in English") and by his predicament. In their different ways they had both "betrayed" the American war effort; both had been arrested and locked up— and Pound's support of Mussolini's Italy might not have been so abhorrent to Lowell as it was to the *Partisan Review* crowd. He began regularly visiting Pound at St. Elizabeth's and as often as possible took visiting poets along with him. His letters of this time are full of Ezra Pound stories: Pound, he writes to Gertrude Buckman, is

> like his later prose and absolutely the most naive and simple man I ever
> met, sure that the world would be all right if people only read the right
> books. Pathetic and touching. He told about snatching up Confucius
> when the communists came for him with their tommy guns. This was
> all that saved him in the ensuing months.[37]

Pound was not the easiest person to visit, constantly inveighing against the "snakepit" of St. Elizabeth's and complaining that he was surrounded by "imbecilic mad niggers." Lowell's poet friends had varying reactions: Elizabeth Bishop said she was "really endlessly grateful for that experience";[38] Jarrell found him surprisingly mild-mannered but "obviously insane, and just childish about a lot of things,"[39] and John Berryman, who had "somehow expected him to be more normal," was disconcerted by Pound's aggressiveness. When Berryman—no doubt to keep the conversation going—said that "It would be interesting to know at what point piety becomes a vice," Pound had replied, "That sounds like a survival from the time when you believed in saying things that were clever."[40]

Most of these Pound anecdotes are in letters Lowell wrote to Gertrude Buckman. He also seems to have kept her informed on the divorce negotiations, and to have stressed the obstacles to their eventual marriage. In September, Buckman writes to him:

> I am baffled—I have never thought to come up against such determined wickedness, such abandon of scruples, such calculated and unabashed gold-digging; and cashing in on the Lowell name. Our persecutors, darling, are too strong for us. I don't know what to say to cheer you, except I don't think it's patience, as much as faith that will save us for a good and meaningful life together, which I want more than anything in the world.[41]

This is in response to Jean Stafford's demand for $7,000 plus extras; a demand described by Lowell as "the works."[42] But Buckman had also detected a cooling in Lowell's attitude since his arrival in Washington:

> My good dear, would you rather we didn't write? It does keep one keyed up too much, and perhaps we shouldn't. Why do you think we communicate badly by letter? Do you mean because I write emotional things that make you uneasy? I couldn't write you cold letters; that would be false. Tell my why. You didn't, you know. And I won't write if you don't enjoy getting letters from me—my vanity would be too hurt.[43]

Lowell spent Christmas, 1947, in Greensboro, North Carolina, with the Taylors and Jarrells, who were sharing a house there. In February he gave poetry readings at Harvard and Wellesley but seems to have paid only a brief visit to New York, and by the eighteenth of that month was back in Washington. It was around this time that he attended a dinner party given by Caresse Crosby (widow of the poet Harry Crosby) for the French poet St.-John Perse and was there introduced to a wealthy Georgetown neighbor, Mrs. Carley Dawson:

> I remember that later Robert said he'd noticed me because I'd had on dark stockings. This rather intrigued him. I don't remember what happened next—I may have invited him to dinner. And then we went to movies and so on and one thing led to another until we were engaged to be married.[44]

Carley Dawson's recollections of her six-month affair with Lowell are singularly joyless. "He was very handsome. I was very much in love with him," she says, but the relationship was for her a series of tests—most of which she failed:

> I met Jarrell at a luncheon with a lot of other people who I think were passing judgment on whether I was adequate for Robert. I'm sure I failed completely. I'd just been to the National Gallery and they kept asking me which pictures I liked. And I was quite nervous, because I knew why they were asking, that I was being needled. So I couldn't remember any of the things I really liked. I was absolutely terrified.[45]

The Washington Winslows cut her in public, she recalls, and when she visited the Lowells in Boston, Charlotte made a point of pouring her a large neat whisky; she couldn't finish it, she says, but she had the feeling that Mrs. Lowell thought she was acting a part: "Later Mrs. Lowell said that I was . . . something to the effect that I was a very *knowing* person, not a wise person but a knowing person. They thought I was acting."

Her most severe test, though, came with Lowell himself; she describes an evening when she and Lowell were sitting side by side on a sofa in her house. They were discussing" Shakespeare's plays:

> And I had argued something—just really for the sake of discussion, because I don't really know anything about Shakespeare's plays particularly. And all of a sudden Robert—who was sitting on my right—swung around and took my neck in his hands and swung me down onto the floor. And I looked at his face and it was completely white, completely blank. I can't describe it. The person inside was not there. And I have marvelous guardian angels. I think that if I had struggled at that time I wouldn't be here. But I said, "Robert, it's rather uncomfortable like this. Do you mind if I get back on the sofa?" And then he came back to himself, he was back in his body, and we sat down and continued our conversation. I didn't argue anymore.[46]

Although Carley Dawson knew from the start that there was "a Jewish girl in New York," it was not until May 1948 that Lowell wrote to Gertrude Buckman telling her that he had met someone else and, according to Buckman, "lashing himself for no reason at all." In April his divorce from Jean Stafford had come through, with Stafford finally settling for a single payment of $6,000. It was a Virgin Islands divorce and to get it Stafford had to fulfill a resident's requirement; she seems to have enjoyed the holiday:

My lawyer . . . says everything is going as smoothly as cream and if there are no mail delays and if you really do behave like the Top Flight Gentleman Bert you seem to be, I should be on my way home Saturday, 12th. This is my last week of residence and there are only four days left in it and not to put too fine a point on it, I will be happy as a clam when this whole thing is over.

I am sorry you are turning into a polar bert and think I should make a trip to Washington especially to show you how brown I am. I would be *so* proud to be browner than you.

A small, black, low-class Virgin Island bee stung me on the tip of my index finger and writing this letter hurts, but I wanted to tell you how nearly it's done and how I'll never stop thanking you if you do get your part of it done in record time. I am the only divorcee-to-be on the island who is married to a civilized man; or alas, perhaps I should state it another way and should say I am the only one whose husband wants to get rid of her as quickly as possible. But seeing them all, I cannot help feeling that in spite of all my hideous behavior in the first year of our separation, we have behaved better on the whole than most people know.

I want us both to marry again, don't you? We'll be so much wiser and so much calmer. It is my ambition to live the rest of my life at a low pitch.[47]

An ambition that was hardly likely to be fulfilled; but when she wrote this letter, Jean had already met Oliver Jensen, an editor at *Life* magazine, and had declared herself to be "in love." She married him shortly after the divorce. In June, back in New York, she met Lowell briefly, and told Peter Taylor:

At that moment I felt still married to him, but memory stayed my hand. He is an altogether magnificent creature and I am so glad that I never have to see him again that I could dance. He has got a new girl in Washington (very much older than he, natch).[48]

Carley Dawson had already had two troubled marriages. but she was finding it increasingly hard to fathom Robert Lowell. "It was amazing that a man of Robert's intellect should always be talking about bears . . . I think he really thought of himself as a bear." Her ten-year-old son used to watch Lowell doing his "Arms of the Law" act and one day proclaimed: "That man is mad, he's absolutely bonkers."[49]

In the summer of 1948, Lowell and Mrs. Dawson traveled to Maine to stay with the poet Elizabeth Bishop, who had borrowed Dawson's house at Stonington. And it was here that the end came:

> There was a question of going swimming, and we drove along the shore —but it was icy cold water, that Maine water. And I noticed that Robert was very different, he was different towards me, and I was extremely uneasy. He didn't seem to be himself at all. And that evening, or some evenings later, there was a question of him going to a group of poets somewhere, near Boston. And I was anticipating going with him, but he said no. And I remember that we talked all night long about this, and I realized something was very wrong with Robert. And so in the morning I went in as soon as I dared and woke up Elizabeth and told her that I thought Robert and I were finished. And she arranged to have a friend of hers drive me to the station, which was some way away from Stonington. And that was it. I never saw Robert again.

> *He didn't try to stop you going?*

> No, he was obviously determined that I would not go to this meeting. And the reason was that I wasn't intellectual enough, and also that he was going round the bend.[50]

Lowell has recorded his ungracious view of the matter in an unpublished poem called "The Two Weeks' Vacation." The poem is addressed to Elizabeth Bishop:

> "You and I, I and you,"
> The old stuck ballad record repeated—
> My Darling Elizabeth, we were alone
> And together—at last
> More or less hand in hand
> On the rocks at Stonington;
> For thirteen days we had been three . . .
> My old flame, Mrs. X—never left us,
> Each morning she met us with another
> Crashing ensemble,
> Her British voice, her Madame du Barry
> Black and gold eyebrows.
> She survived a whole day of handline
> Deep sea fishing for polock [*sic*], skate and skulpin [*sic*],
> Making me bait her hooks.
> And wearing a blue silk "ski-suit,"

Blouse, trousers, cape and even her gloves matched.
All this, for me! . . .

. . . on my next to last night, the thirteenth
I came down the corridor in pajamas,
No doubt arousing false hopes
And said . . . Well, who cares, my old flame left,
And I never heard from her ever after.[51]

Over the next few weeks, Lowell announced to several of his friends
that he was going to marry Elizabeth Bishop. A friend of both
Lowell and Bishop has recalled:

He never asked her. It did represent something he felt very strongly
about, but at a certain level he knew that it was not possible. He knew
perfectly well that she was homosexual. But that was a complicated issue
in Elizabeth's life. She did have affairs with men when she was younger
—she was about six years older than Cal. It was only when she moved
to Brazil in about 1950 that she lived with a woman permanently. Cal
and Elizabeth never made love—Elizabeth was very explicit about that.
She would joke and say that she never wanted to marry Cal but she
would have liked to have a child with him. And I think that was partly
a joke and partly serious.[52]

"The Two Weeks' Vacation," begun some ten years after the event,
seems to have been unfinished, but the second stanza reads (in part)
as follows:

So we sat, you talked of Marianne Moore
Taking her water cress sandwiches to
Tomfeed the Bronx Zoo "denizens."
How she stopped by a steel-point of Robert Burns
Saying, "But he couldn't have been *that* handsome!"
Dear Elizabeth,
Half New-Englander, half fugitive
Nova Scotian, wholly Atlantic sea-board—
Unable to settle anywhere, or live
Our usual roaring sublime. . . .[53]

Shortly after his Maine vacation—in August 1948—Lowell wrote
a strange letter to his mother, announcing that he had made a will
"which gives you everything I have during your lifetime and then

splits the trust between Randall Jarrell and Peter Taylor, the most needy of my friends."[54] Relations with his parents had been going through a placid phase since the success of *Lord Weary's Castle*, and Charlotte had been writing enthusiastically about his spreading fame: "wherever we go we are showered with congratulations on your achievements."[55] She had not taken to Carley Dawson and shortly after meeting her had told Lowell that she wished he could find a "nice" wife: "but until you do, remember that you have much more than most people to show for your 31 years even if it is not a wife and children."[56]

Lowell's drafting of a will may have been the result of anxiety about his father's health. Mr. Lowell had had a stroke earlier in the year and was no longer able to work. He had become "rather ashamed of himself, mastered by mother—and not knowing what to do with himself—and mother dreading the years of amusing him."[57] Around the time of Lowell's letter they were planning to move out of Boston for the sake of Mr. Lowell's health:

> Mother had bought the Beverly Farms house as a compensation for Father, whose ten years' dream of moving from Boston to Puget Sound had been destroyed by a second heart-attack. Fearfully, she had looked out of her windows at Beverly Farms, as though she were looking from the windows of a train that was drawing into the station; one station beyond her destination. From the beginning she . . . lived with one eye cocked toward Boston. She wanted to be in Boston, and she dreaded Boston's invasion and mockery of this new house, which was so transparently a sheepish toy-house for Father. Organizing and tidying with prodigal animosity, she kept her rooms alerted—not to be judged by visitors, but to judge them.[58]

Charlotte replied to Lowell's August letter by return of post:

> When I came to the part of your letter about leaving everything to me I almost cried. It reminded me of the time you gave us all of your allowance before starting to St. Mark's and we bought an electric toaster which we still use; it is sweet of you, Bobby, but I hope that you will inherit whatever I may leave, as I really would not care to live without you and Daddy.[59]

In September Lowell left Washington. His plans were to spend the winter at Yaddo, and he was scheduled to arrive there at the beginning of November. During October, though, his friends seem to have lost track of him, and on October 5 Allen Tate wrote a worried and unwittingly prophetic letter from New York to Peter Taylor:

> Cal seems to have catapulted himself from the L of C to the Adirondacks. No sight or word of him except by grapevine: he is forcing his poetry as he forced his religion. He should go back to his religion and force it again, if only to protect his poetry.[60]

10

Even after Lowell's arrival at Yaddo the grapevine continued to report that he was in a frighteningly "wound-up" state of mind. T. S. Eliot was said to be concerned that Lowell was drinking heavily and was on the verge of a crack-up. This story reached Jean Stafford and she wrote to Peter Taylor on December 22: "I can't believe it, and it makes me so sick at heart that I want reassurance."[1] Apparently, no reassurance came, and on January 1, 1949, she wrote to Lowell at Yaddo: "Is it true that you are drinking too much and going to pieces and that that ungainly bird Eliot is worried to death about you? So the story goes. . . ."[2]

The evidence of Lowell's own letters at this time suggests that his friends' fears were premature: the letters are relaxed and witty—he is enjoying Yaddo and is glad to be back at work after his bureaucratic spell in Washington. He was also no doubt relieved to have disentangled himself from Carley Dawson: Yaddo was, in so many ways, the perfect sanctuary. In December 1948 Lowell wrote to Caroline Tate (who would also seem to have been "worried to death" about him):

> I don't know how my soul is—pretty uncombed, I guess. But my spirits are fine. I have a small black room to sleep in (fine, but last night, the mattress suddenly dropped through the frame) and a largish light room to work in—five windows, four tables, three chairs, two lamps and one work-bed.
> I liked Washington, but what a delight to be done with it; and back to work. With what I've saved from the library and Yaddo and my Guggenheim, I can easily last two years before I have to think of teaching.[3]

And a letter to Robie Macauley suggests that Yaddo had lost none of its satiric appeal: apart from the young Southern novelist Flannery O'Connor and the critic Malcolm Cowley,

> . . . Yaddo is a little dim. O No, a man writing a history of Harvard, who almost swallows himself when he misses a ping-pong shot, who spent the first three dinners telling us long set-pieces on Harvard (leaving out crucial anecdotal facts, then recovering them). At the 4th dinner he said he wished he could afford to belong to the Harvard Club; at the 8th during a discussion on smoking "Have you ever tried Harvard Club tobacco?"; who has a six foot five son, and who finally, out of a blue sky, said: "Is there anything as perfect as an acorn?" (Holding one).[4]

Lowell was not required to spend Christmas in Boston with his parents; they had left for Florida for an extended holiday, which, it was hoped, would restore his father's health. His mother's letters were friendly and optimistic, and he had no new reason to be anxious on this score:

> How are you? And does the book progress satisfactorily: I think of you as walking in snow-filled woods or writing with such absorption that you cannot think of anyone or anything. Still you did remember us at Christmas! But do try to write to us occasionally. Your poems will live long after we are here no longer.[5]

In his first few days at Yaddo, Lowell had briefly encountered the novelist and book reviewer Elizabeth Hardwick—she had been at Yaddo during the summer and was about to leave as he arrived. Hardwick was a Southerner, from Kentucky, a friend of Allen Tate's. She had left the South in 1940 to do graduate work at Columbia University and had never properly returned. After two years at Columbia she had abandoned her Ph D and begun writing stories. In 1945 she published her first novel, *The Ghostly Lover,* and shortly afterwards started writing regularly for *Partisan Review.* By 1949 Hardwick had built up a reputation as one of that magazine's more fearsome critics. Peter Taylor, indeed, was one of her recent victims:

> How could any magazine print the tripe that Elizabeth Hardwick writes for criticism? I had never realized how truly dreadful she is till I saw her mind and her prose style at work on my own dear stories.[6]

And Elizabeth Bishop, on hearing that Hardwick was at Yaddo, wrote: "I forgot to comment on Elizabeth Hardwick's arrival—*take care.*"[7]

Lowell had met Hardwick before and had warmed to her—if only because she was a rich source of stories about Allen Tate (of these, Lowell could never tire since they usually involved some sexual folly). Taylor, for instance, had written to Lowell at Washington demanding ever more scandal about Tate: "I wish I knew what Madame Hardwick told you about Allen. After reading Sexual Behaviour in the Human Male I can believe anything about anybody."[8] Elizabeth Hardwick recalls their Yaddo meeting:

> I met him up at Yaddo. I'd been there in the summer—I was about to leave when he arrived—but we were both there for a couple of days and we talked quite a bit, and he said, "Why don't you come back?" We were all quite young then and living in furnished rooms and things like that. So I did go back after Christmas for a couple of months. And I suppose he had the beginning of his breakdown there. But I didn't know him well enough to know. It takes a lot of experience. And he was a very gripping sort of character. Anyway, I don't think I did know and everything got terribly wound up there.[9]

There is certainly a slight edge of hysteria in a letter Lowell wrote to T. S. Eliot in January 1949. He was corresponding with Eliot at Faber and Faber about a British edition of his poems—to be called *Poems 1938–49*. Lowell and Eliot had first met in 1946 (they were brought together by Eliot's American publisher, Robert Giroux), and it is unlikely that Eliot thought they were close enough for Lowell to address him as "Dear Uncle Tom":

> . . . After Washington, I had a tough two weeks of writing rubbish and knew it; then by rather sweating blood I got back. The poem is going to be long and long in doing. I have one book (?) between 600 and 800 lines coming into shape; I hope to have it all together in a couple of months. I'm not sure how long the whole will be; maybe some 3000 lines —I don't want to hurry—rather brood over it like a mother bear, till the form flashes (another fine mixed figure). . . .
>
> This is becoming chatter. . . . I guess everyone here feels like Timon's guests, and has to blow off steam, at times.
>
> I would like to get the judgment of Eliot the poet on my poems—off the record. Not so much judgment as the pointing out of things that are

good or on their way to being good, that I might usefully explore
further. The limiting negative kind of criticism I think I know something about (I always appreciate that too) but the other is limitless.

For "Eliot the editor" I've been trying to think of impossible typo-
graphical suggestions. But I don't give a damn really as long as you don't
split stanzas.

Ah, yes, Europe! I'd like to go. This is perfect, though barbarous and
isolated. If I could travel a little, then settle down and write day in and
day out, till my poem is over—with a little good company and joy.

FORGIVE ALL THIS CHATTER

This is sort of a monk's life, so you bend some one's ear off when you
have a chance.

Monk isn't right, of course. This letter is about as organized as one
of Merrill's; God help me. By the way, *I do not drink here the way I did
in Washington.* I begin to think Burgundy's about perfect for the long
run.

Wish Eliot the poet and Eliot the editor would take a look at Jarrell
and Bishop (Elizabeth).[10]

The "winding up" that Elizabeth Hardwick refers to seems to have
become intensified in February 1949 when a coincidence of circumstances offered a focus for Lowell's already disturbed sense of where
he stood. Tate was later to describe his situation at this point:

As I see Cal over the past twelve years, and no one I think knows him
better, three things held him together: the Church, his marriage and his
poetry. He gave up the Church; he gave up Jean; and some months ago
he virtually gave up poetry. He had been pushed forward too rapidly
as a poet and he had attempted a work beyond his present powers; he
couldn't finish it.[11]

It is likely that the work in question was Lowell's first attempt at
the long poem that became "The Mills of the Kavanaughs." During
1948 he had printed "Falling Asleep Over the Aeneid" and "Mother
Marie Therese," and it was to be over two years before he published
in magazines again.

Tate probably did know as much as anyone about Lowell's state
of mind during his first two months at Yaddo. In November he and
Lowell had gone on a fishing trip together and they had also been
in touch as members of the Library of Congress committee responsi-

ble for awarding the Bollingen Prize for Poetry (the committee members also included Conrad Aiken, Louise Bogan, W. H. Auden, T. S. Eliot, Robert Penn Warren and Karl Shapiro). It had been decided to award the prize to Ezra Pound for his *Pisan Cantos,* and nobody on the judging panel was in any doubt that this would provoke an outcry from the left and re-inflame (as it did) all the art-versus-politics disputes that had been raging on and off since the early 1930s. Indeed, an outcry was anticipated in the judges' citation:

> To permit other considerations than that of poetic achievement to sway the decision would destroy the significance of the award and would in principle deny the validity of that objective perception of value on which civilized society must rest.

The debate was to develop in the summer and autumn of 1949 (with Allen Tate as the most vigorous champion of Pound), but in February the essential argument was launched.

In April, William Barrett wrote an article in *Partisan Review* attacking the prize judges, and in the fall issue of *PR* there were replies from Auden, Shapiro and Tate—Shapiro had voted against Pound on the grounds that his anti-Semitism did indeed "vitiate" his art. Tate (almost) challenged Barrett to a duel. Later, two articles by Robert Hillyer in the *Saturday Review of Literature* kept things on the boil—in Tate's view, Hillyer exploited the Bollingen controversy in order to "sanction and guide" an attack on the whole of modern poetry, and in particular the New Criticism.[12] With John Berryman, Tate gathered seventy-three signatures for a letter in defense of the prize jury. The letter eventually appeared in the *Nation* on December 17, 1949. Radcliffe Squires, in a biography of Tate, writes:

> That pretty much ended the episode, for while an occasional article appeared in the next year or two, the excitement subsided. The triumph for Berryman and Tate, however, was that the Bollingen Foundation decided to continue the prize under the auspices of Yale University, with the same jury. The campaign had been trying.[13]

The Pound matter must certainly have been in Lowell's thoughts, and he would probably have held the view that those who most fiercely opposed the Bollingen Award were as pro-Communist as they were anti-Fascist. Although Lowell had printed more poems in *Partisan Review* than in any other quarterly, he had never been drawn into its political wrangling—indeed, by managing to be closely associated both with *Partisan* and with the Southern Agrarian reactionaries of the *Sewanee Review* circle, he had performed a small miracle of adroit noninvolvement. This was a period when every thinker had a label—Stalinist, anti-Stalinist, ex-Stalinist, ex-anti-Stalinist, Fascist, ex-Fascist, Catholic, ex-Catholic, and so on. In a year's time (February 1950) Senator Joe McCarthy was to make his first big speech alleging that the State Department had been infiltrated by Communists. In 1949 the climate for his witch-hunts was already building up.

Lowell, then, would have known as well as anyone who "the Stalinists" were, and according to Robert Fitzgerald, his general belief was that "since Marxism lost intellectual honor its adherents have been limited to those for whom such a loss has no particular meaning." If, in his already "wound-up" state, and with the Pound business in the air, Lowell needed an immediate target for his political hostilities, then Yaddo could hardly have been more obliging. Agnes Smedley, a writer on Far East politics, had lived at Yaddo until March of the previous year, had been there since 1943, and had enjoyed special privileges—a private telephone, for instance, and her own taxi instead of the one that regularly served the Yaddo guests. She was not known as a "creative writer," and her lengthy residence at Yaddo had long been thought odd by the "real artists," whose visits were limited to two or three months at a stretch; but it had been assumed that she had a close friendship with the director, Elizabeth Ames, and although Smedley was a known Marxist, this was simply thought to be a hangover from the days when Yaddo prided itself on its "anti-Fascist" hospitality.

On February 11, 1949, however, Agnes Smedley became front-page news. The *New York Times* announced:

TOKYO WAR SECRETS STOLEN BY SOVIET SPY RING IN 1941

The Army made public today a 32,000-word report on a Soviet spy ring in the Far East that was credited with a major development in diplomatic history and with having aided materially in the defeat by the Soviet Union of the Nazi armies invading Russian soil.

The report, put out under the name of General MacArthur, went on to identify Agnes Smedley as one of the spy ring's contacts; she had been, it said, "one of the most energetic workers for the Soviet cause in China for the past 20-odd years." Her writings on China had "hoaxed" a number of "high American officials," and the time had now come for her to be "exposed for what she is, a spy and agent of the Soviet Government." The *Times* then quoted a denial from Smedley: "I am not and never have been a Soviet spy or an agent for any country."

On February 12 the army issued a cautious statement pointing out that they didn't "necessarily agree with all of the MacArthur Report"; it had, after all, been written a year earlier. A week later, on February 19, they disowned it altogether: ARMY ADMITS SPY FAUX PAS; NO PROOF ON AGNES SMEDLEY. The report, the army now confirmed, "had not been edited properly, from the public relations point of view." On the twentieth, Agnes Smedley was reported to have thanked the army for "clearing her name"; in the same issue of the *Times* the Bollingen Award to Ezra Pound was officially announced under the headline: POUND, IN MENTAL CLINIC, WINS PRIZE FOR POETRY PENNED IN TREASON CELL.

During this week, or very shortly afterwards, two FBI investigators visited Yaddo. Four guests were by then in residence—Lowell, Flannery O'Connor, Elizabeth Hardwick and Edward Maisel—and of these the FBI men interviewed Hardwick and Maisel, who then reported back to Lowell and O'Connor. Yaddo, it transpired, had been under FBI surveillance for some time; the investigators had asked "highly circumstantial and specific questions" not only about Agnes Smedley, but about other Yaddo guests, and "seemed to have no confidence in either the words or the motives of the executive director of Yaddo, Mrs. Ames . . . but thought she had protected Mrs. Smedley to the point of misrepresentation."

According to the account prepared later by Robert Fitzgerald (and sent as an open letter to various literary figures in an attempt to explain Lowell's conduct during the weeks following the Smedley headlines), there was already at Yaddo a general feeling of unease; Lowell had early on felt "something unpleasant in the atmosphere of the place"—now he knew that this was "the result of long permeation by moods or influences that were politically or morally committed to communism. . . . The impression grew on Lowell that the outwardly benevolent institution had been given over to scandalous and sinister forces." As Fitzgerald concedes, "impressions of this kind come easily to the poetic imagination and are easily enforced by it," but in this case, he says, Lowell's suspicions were supported by "the fact that three other guests were likewise affected."[14]

Towards the end of February the four guests contacted the local directors of the Yaddo corporation and presented their misgivings. A meeting of the Yaddo board was convened, and Lowell was invited to present his case.

The transcript of the meeting makes fairly ugly reading.[15] Lowell's introductory statement demands that Mrs. Ames be "fired" and that this action be "absolute, final and prompt." The "exact" charges were that "It is our impression that Mrs. Ames is somehow deeply and mysteriously involved in Mrs. Smedley's political activities" and that Mrs. Ames's personality is such that "she is totally unfitted for the position of executive director." Lowell goes on from this to employ "a very relevant figure of speech." Yaddo, he says, is a "body" and Mrs. Ames "a diseased organ, chronically poisoning the whole system, sometimes more, sometimes less, sometimes almost imperceptibly, sometimes, as now, fatally":

> I want to say that we have not taken this matter up lightly, nor do we intend to drop it lightly. It is only fair to present to the attention of the Board that no matter what decision is taken by the board, the present guests intend to leave in a body on Tuesday, March first [Lowell's thirty-second birthday].
>
> If action is not taken by the Board that we consider adequate, I intend to confer with certain people in New York, among them Trilling, Rahv, Hook, and Haggin, and immediately to call a large meeting of the more important former Yaddo guests; at this meeting we will again press our case at great length.
>
> I think it only fair to tell the Board that I have myself influential friends in the world of culture, nine-tenths of whom in the course of my ordinary correspondence and conversation will be informed of this affair within three months. I want to give their names—I think it quite relevant: Santayana, Frost, Eliot, Williams, Ransom, Moore (in case you think I'm bluffing, I only know Miss Moore slightly but think she would agree), Bishop, Tate, Blackmur, Warren, Auden, Adams, Bogan, Empson. Of my own generation, Robert Fitzgerald, Jarrell, Bishop, Schwartz, Shapiro, Taylor, Powers, Stafford and Berryman. We shall also take steps to see that the important people in the world of music

and painting are fully informed. I should say, most of my friends are writers, but I have connections in Washington and I shall take steps to see that the matter is aired there, too.

Lowell then cross-examines the other guests, extracting from each of them a series of supposedly damaging "impressions." Hardwick, for example, testifies: "I personally feel that at times there is a discrepancy between Mrs. Ames's surface behavior and her true feelings, not towards me, but toward most matters. I only know the surface . . . I cannot read her heart." There is mention of other Communist writers who have been entertained at Yaddo, of a "proletarian novelist" called Leonard Ehrlich, who was a longtime friend of Mrs. Ames and a frequent visitor at Yaddo, of Agnes Smedley's proselytizing among the students at nearby Skidmore College, of mysterious Japanese and East German visitors, of suspicious jokes about "Molotov cocktail parties," of Mrs. Ames's unpatriotic caution in her dealings with the FBI, and so on. All in all, the "evidence" is a patchwork of devoured hearsay and rather desperate speculation: not one of the witnesses challenges Mrs. Ames's "surface" friendliness and efficiency. Lowell, however, seemingly content with the forcefulness of his presentation, goes on to harangue the board as follows:

> This may be impertinent but I think that the board cannot evade its moral responsibility because of any sentimental attachments or fear of any kind. I think of the Trasks [the founders of Yaddo] and I think it showed a touching innocent faith in the arts that they should have endowed Yaddo, and this faith has suffered hideous perversion, and I think the institution is faced with ruin.

The transcript continues for another thirty pages. There is lengthy testimony from Mrs. Ames's secretary, who admits to having been an FBI informer for the past five years—"I have, ever since I have been here, whenever I heard people talking very brilliantly red, I have written down their name and address and dropped it off at a certain place in Saratoga for forwarding to the FBI." And, after much haggling among the witnesses over small details of anti-Smedley gossip, there is a statement from Mrs. Ames herself: she explains that Agnes Smedley had been kind to her five years before when she (Ames) was nursing her dying sister, that she had "felt indebted to

[Smedley] after Marjorie died, as she had helped so much with the nursing and everything"; of Leonard Ehrlich she simply says: "He is a very good friend of mine and his brother and wife are. He was a very good friend of Russia and is still in the position so many of us are . . . of thinking we ought to try to reach some agreement." And she gives her version of the past few days' events:

> About immediate events: These are just factual statements. There were five (one man [the novelist James Ross] left yesterday, he did not want to be mixed up in this). Here have been these five people for several months, living in great apparent harmony and good will toward me. . . . when I have stayed away from dinner, asking why I did not come; every one of them asking for more time . . . some invited for the first time pressing for a chance to stay longer; Mr. Lowell asked to stay until August; Miss O'Connor wanting to stay until July, and come back next year. Mr. Lowell has written three or four of his friends whom he wishes to get here this summer, he started correspondence between me and them; he writes these letters telling about the ideal state of Yaddo; no reservations at all. They frequently came to my house for music or cocktails, a harmonious life, with now and then little affectionate notes. . . . then all of this changed with the morning of Tuesday, when they appeared at my door, looking extremely grave and upset, three of them. I asked them, and they stated that the FBI had questioned them the day before. I was very much upset and disturbed . . . it was quite a shock to me to hear that. When situations arise and people are disturbed I try to hold the line and seek for calm.

Mrs. Ames then describes her own interview with the FBI, which took place on the following Thursday; they questioned her about Agnes Smedley and about earlier visitors to Yaddo and she answered with "complete candor":

> They stayed with me for two and a half hours, and when they left, thanked me for my cooperation, shook hands with me, and said if anything else comes up, may we come back, and I said yes. That was on Thursday and to me it is a very unsettling thing to go through, anything like that.
> The next day, I did feel very tired out. As you know, I have not yet completely recovered from a serious operation ten months ago. On Friday, I came over for dinner, feeling very tired and very depressed and that night they say my attitude began to change. That is completely false.

What I want to stress is that they, after living here harmoniously, pressing for extensions of time, recommending their friends to come here . . . I can show letters they have written me . . . then like that, the whole thing changes. . . . I can attribute it to nothing but fear and hysteria. They are young people, in their 30's; I can understand it, faced with a world such as we have. Miss Hardwick had some experience with Communism in her early years; she is disillusioned and bitter. That is the story.

The directors agreed to discuss the matter again at their regular meeting in New York in three weeks' time. Lowell made one last appeal that Mrs. Ames be immediately suspended, but this was refused. Malcolm Cowley, a board member and a supporter of Mrs. Ames, wrote to a friend on March 8:

In the end nothing was done, nothing could be done, but everything was deferred to this new meeting in New York (in about two weeks or less) at which some sort of decision must be taken. The guests departed, vowing to blacken the name of Yaddo in all literary circles and call a mass meeting of protest. The directors departed. I stayed one day because I had to do a big review and would be too tired to finish it if I waited till I got back to Connecticut, but then I left too, feeling as if I had been at a meeting of the Russian Writers' Union during a big purge. Elizabeth went to a nursing home. Her secretary resigned. Yaddo was left like a stricken battlefield.[16]

Lowell felt thwarted and outraged by the board's indecisiveness; by now, according to Fitzgerald, the corruption of Yaddo had become symbolic of "the great evil of the world":

Moreover, as he confronted this evil, he found himself drawn at the same time by many tokens of a different kind of which normally he would not have been so hyperconscious, towards the church which opposes evil with holiness and communism with Christianity. The day after the abortive meeting he went with Miss O'Connor, who is a Catholic, to mass for the first time in over a year. The change taking place in him was like the process which sometimes occurs at a late stage in the formation of a work of art where everything begins to coalesce, to flow together into patterns that had not been foreseen: it is a stage of inspiration that is well beyond the deliberative.[17]

Charlotte Winslow, 1915.

Robert Traill Spence Lowell Sr. and Jr.,
about 1920.

Robert Lowell, about age five.

Robert Lowell, about age eighteen.

Frank Parker and Robert Lowell,
counselors at Brentwood Camp, 1934.

Robert Lowell, Jean Stafford and
Peter Taylor, in New Orleans, 1940.

Jean Stafford, in Boulder, 1936.

Frank Parker and his
cousin Ann Dick, in Boston, 1941.

Allen Tate, Marcella Comès,
Robert Lowell, in Monteagle,
Tenn., 1943.

Caroline Gordon Tate, Anne Goodwin Winslow, Andrew Lytle, Mrs. Andrew Lytle, Nancy Tate, Allen Tate, Robert Lowell, Jean Stafford, in Monteagle, Tenn., 1943.

Robert Lowell, Jean Stafford, Robert Giroux, in Damariscotta, Me., 1945.

Jean Stafford, 1947.

Robert Lowell,
in Greensboro,
N.C., 1946.

Randall Jarrell, Robert Lowell, Peter Taylor, in Greensboro, N.C., 1948.

Sara Layton, John Thompson, Jr., Helen Keeler Thompson, Jeanne Kelly, Robert Lowell, Garland Draper, George Rosen, in New York City, June 19, 1949.

On the following day, Lowell and O'Connor visited the Fitz-geralds, and Lowell announced that "he had returned to the Church that morning after receiving an incredible outpouring of grace." Sally Fitzgerald remembers that he was "shooting sparks in every direction,"[18] but at the time the Fitzgeralds were sympathetic, indeed gratified; and Robert wrote:

> During the rest of that week our friend labored under the strain and exaltation of religious experience: there were times when he was simply tired, interested and even amused, there were other times when every-thing he saw, everything that happened, seemed miraculous to him; when his steps were directed and his eyes were opened; when he felt that God spoke through him and that his impulses were inspired. . . . At the end of the week he visited a priest for absolution and then went off to make a week's retreat for absolution and counsel with the Trappists in Rhode Island.[19]

From Rhode Island, Lowell went back to New York, and at first seemed to have calmed down; friends like Fitzgerald, Tate and O'Connor were ready to view the whole incident as a symptom of his "reconversion"—although O'Connor had been worried by Lowell's insistence that she was a saint. On March 3, while Lowell was with the Trappists, Tate wrote to Elizabeth Hardwick: "Cal seems to have been reconverted to the church and I for one think it is a good thing." Tate, though, had not heard the full story of Yaddo, nor did he know the exact status of Lowell's relationship with Hardwick:

> Both Caroline and I thought at first that along with, or because of, or as a result of, his reconversion that he had fallen in love with you and was trying to marry you. Caroline said "Poor Miss Hardwick!" I knew Cal was in one of his manic phases but I could scarcely believe you had lost your reason.[20]

An entry in Fitzgerald's journal for March 4 records a telephone call from Lowell at six-thirty in the morning: "I want you to get a pencil and paper and take some things down." Lowell wanted to remind Fitzgerald that "Ash Wednesday was the day of the Word made Flesh," and that on that day Lowell had "received the shock

of the eternal word: tantum dic verbo et *sanabitur* anima mea."
Fitzgerald's notes continue:

> March 3 was the day of humors; I [i.e., Lowell] prayed to St. Anthony
> of Padua, who himself held the child (and prayed God to spare me His
> humor) and Elizabeth was miraculously purged of the pollution caused
> by her evasions. I prayed over her, and had to call on all the heavenly
> host, St. Michael and others, and prayed over her using the psalm (?)
> beginning "God said to the prophet, Even if the mother should forsake
> the child . . ." She was purged and became like that music of Haydn's.
>   Today is the day of Flannery O'Connor, whose patron saint is St.
> Therese of Lisieux.
>   Also: you are to take St. Luke the physician and historian as your
> patron saint.

> That morning, he said afterward, he filled his bathtub with cold water
> and went in first on his hands and knees, then arching on his back, and
> prayed thus to Therese of Lisieux in gasps. All his motions that morning
> were "lapidary," and he felt a steel coming into him that made him walk
> very erect. It came to him that he should fast all day and give up
> cigarettes. After mass and communion he walked, going in to a Protes-
> tant Church to observe and think about the emptiness and speculate as
> to how it could be filled—also the "nimbleness" there (for Protestants
> have some good things that Catholics don't) and then up to the Jesuit
> Church on 14th Street and then to the Church of St. Francis in the 30s
> feeling how in both love radiated from the altars. He went to the Guild
> bookshop to get Flannery a book on St. Therese of Lisieux but instead
> before he knew it bought a book on a Canadian girl who was many times
> stigmatized.
>   That night here he said to Elizabeth: It's no good telling you these
> things that have to be experienced; but Christ is present in the Eucharist
> and love is at the heart of the altar, and this is something perfectly real,
> just like getting your hand wet. That you must be told.[21]

On this same day, Fitzgerald wrote to Allen Tate and his wife,
Caroline Gordon (herself a devout Catholic):

> I think Cal's exaltation is natural, and that it does not exceed its cause,
> but I also think that there are other voices besides God's to be heard from
> him and that he must have guidance—just as Saint Teresa and others had
> to have it. This does not mean that I believe Cal to be any more a saint
> than I am. What I do believe is that God sometimes intervenes directly
> and unmistakably in our lives and that one effect of this, of the sense of

God's power and other perfections, is to unbalance the person acted upon. Why should it not? It is a power with which our own are incommensurable. All right: that is the essential thing that has happened in this case. Now for the disturbing thing: I'm quite prepared to believe that there are manic or paranoiac or schizophrenic tendencies in Cal (the terminology continues to be vague to me, I'm not a native of that territory; I mean he's liable to some sort of sickness) and that these tendencies have been awakened and are to be struggled against. We must merely distinguish between what has hit him and what it has induced in him. Now for the third thing: where there is convincing evidence of the intervention I spoke of, we may have a great deal of trust in the purposes that are being served and need not more than dutifully worry about the incidental difficulties. As a Catholic made alive by grace to some realities, I simply know that in these days we are called upon to bear witness perhaps more strenuously than may have been necessary in other days. Cal's intuitional powers have considerable range and value; what they bring up must stand criticism, but it must not be dismissed.[22]

In the three weeks leading up to the second directors' meeting, "Yaddo had become the favorite topic to discuss while holding a martini. New York was full of slanders, rumors, accusations and counter-accusations."[23] A second group of former Yaddo guests (Eleanor Clark, Kappo Phelan, John Cheever, Alfred Kazin and Harvey Breit) began circulating a statement supporting Mrs. Ames:

> . . . we reject as preposterous the political charge now being brought against Elizabeth Ames. We reject any insinuation that at any time she deliberately used the facilities of Yaddo for any other purpose than the furthering of the arts in America. Above all, it is a violation of elementary justice that such a charge and such insinuations should be deliberately confused with grievances of a purely personal nature, which cannot fairly be dealt with in an atmosphere of political tension.
>
> All of us have often gone on record as opposing the Communist Party. All of us have at one time or another, some of us for long periods, benefited from Elizabeth Ames's administration of Yaddo. We are anti-Stalinists. We feel that the charge currently being brought arises from a frame of mind that represents a grave danger both to civil liberties and to the freedom necessary for the arts. We feel this charge involves a cynical assault not only on Elizabeth Ames's personal integrity, but also on the whole future of Yaddo.

> We have lived at Yaddo; we have worked there; we want others to have the same opportunity. We are outraged, first, to see that opportunity jeopardized; and secondly, to see the human and political values we hold being debased through the use of a smear-technique that has so far not been honored in this country.[24]

Seventy-five copies of this document were sent out on March 21, and five days later fifty-one endorsements had been received by the organizers. "We also received several letters and telegrams from people acquainted with Yaddo but who had not been guests there." According to Fitzgerald, Lowell was "not only deeply wounded but incredulous at the kind of prose employed against him by people whom he had considered his friends" (among the pro-Ames signatories were Delmore Schwartz and Katherine Anne Porter):

> In the midst of what was becoming an ugly comedy, Lowell behaved gently but with increasing excitement. He had understandable difficulty in sleeping. He needed the reassurance of company. He and his friends made no attempt to counteract the circular letter with one of their own but they visited and remonstrated with one or two of those who had sent it.[25]

The petition served its purpose; when the Yaddo board re-met on March 26, they agreed that Lowell's charges be dismissed. Mrs. Ames's position as director was confirmed, though not without criticism of her too personal attitude towards inviting guests and extending the length of their visits. Later she would be deprived of those privileges, which were transferred to the Admissions Committee. Luckily, during the week before the meeting, Malcolm Cowley had been able to keep the story out of the newspapers: the *Herald Tribune* had intended to cover the controversy on Wednesday the twenty-third, but Cowley told them that if they held off until the actual meeting, he would see that they got an "exclusive"; as a result, a mild piece appeared in the paper's Sunday edition, and Cowley was able to write proudly to his friends that he had stumbled upon a first principle of Press Relations:

> Now I know how to have a story played down—give it to one morning newspaper as an exclusive to be published on Sunday; then the other papers won't bother with it on Monday, unless it is very big. If it had come out on a weekday, the World Telegram, Sun and Journal American would have had follow-ups.[26]

On the day of the Yaddo board meeting, Lowell put in an appearance at the Cultural and Scientific Conference for World Peace, which was being held at the Waldorf-Astoria Hotel in New York. The conference aimed to promote a conciliatory, if not craven, attitude to the Soviet Union; a number of Russian writers and artists were on the platform, for example, for the session on writing and publishing, and so too were a handful of American pro-Communists, including Agnes Smedley and three professors who had just been dismissed from the University of Washington for "alleged Communist Party membership." *Partisan Review* was well represented in the audience, and the Russians were thus given a fairly grueling time, with Dwight Macdonald and Mary McCarthy pressing them from the floor on matters of state censorship and the present whereabouts of writers like Pasternak and Babel. Lowell's contribution was rather more oblique. The *New York Times* reported it as follows:

"I am a poet and a Roman Catholic," Mr. Lowell declared. "I have two questions. The first is addressed to Mr. Pavlenko. What are the laws for conscientious objection in the Soviet Union? The second question is for Mr. Shostakovich. Will he tell us how the criticism of the Soviet Government can help an artist?"

Mr. Pavlenko replied that he didn't know what the Soviet laws on conscientious objection were. "I have had no personal acquaintance with them," he said. "When my country called, I fought. I hope to be able to fight when I am 100 years old."

Mr. Shostakovich, pale, determined-looking and a little nervous, replied to Mr. Lowell by affirming the criticism he had received for writing formalist music. "The criticism brings me much good," he said. "It helps me bring my music forward."[27]

Thirty years later, Shostakovich's memoirs appeared in the West; in them, he gave his account of the Waldorf affair:

I still recall with horror my first trip to the U.S.A. I wouldn't have gone at all if it hadn't been for intense pressure from administrative figures of all ranks and colors, from Stalin down. People sometimes say it must have been an interesting trip, look at the way I'm smiling in the photographs. That was the smile of a condemned man. I felt like a dead man. I answered all the idiotic questions in a daze, and thought, When I get back it's over for me.

Stalin liked leading Americans by the nose that way. He would show them a man—here he is, alive and well—and then kill him. Well, why say lead by the nose? That's too strongly put. He only fooled those who wanted to be fooled. The Americans don't give a damn about us, and in order to live and sleep soundly, they'll believe anything.[28]

Since leaving Yaddo, Lowell had been planning a missionary trip to Chicago and the Midwest—he would visit Tate at Chicago, Peter Taylor at Bloomington, Ransom at Kenyon. He would recruit allies for his contest against evil. Tate was alarmed at the prospect and much relieved each time Lowell postponed the actual date of his arrival: "We want Cal to come out but it would be better after he cools off a bit."[29]

Tate wrote this to Elizabeth Hardwick while Lowell was in retreat at Rhode Island, and he took the opportunity to insert some avuncular but firmly discouraging advice:

[Lowell] has got himself boxed into the corner that he has always wanted to be in; that is, the inescapably celibate corner. (1) he can't marry again, as a Catholic (2) as a strict Catholic, he can't commit adultery. He has been trying to get himself in this dilemma. I don't *predict* that he will become a monk but I do think it highly probable.[30]

Immediately after the Waldorf conference Lowell telegrammed Tate to expect him on March 29; the telegram was signed "Uncle Lig." The following day Tate wrote again to Hardwick:

Cal is here, and in 24 hours has flattened us out. I do not know what we can do. Fundamentally he makes a great deal of sense, but his mental condition is very nearly psychotic. We shall be able to get through the next ten days, till he goes to Kenyon: what worries me is his immediate future. What can he do? He says that God, or God through me, must tell him. I will not let him down, but the best help from others, if it is too much depended on, always lets us down. Perhaps a letter from you would help to calm him. He is pathetic. He constantly embraces us, and asks us to stand by him, since he is weak.[31]

A day later Tate had second thoughts: Lowell, he felt, was "better—distinctly so: he is quietening down hourly. . . . more than ever before he needs to be loved." Tate also adds that "His humor will save him in the long run."[32]

Two days after this, Tate was taking a less indulgent view of Lowell's sense of fun—possibly because one of Lowell's "jests" was to provide Caroline Tate with a list of Allen's lovers, and then to implore Tate to "repent." Also, there was much bear-foolery—the bear games that Lowell and Stafford had devised were not just verbal: on this occasion, according to Robie Macauley, Lowell did an "Arms of the Law" impersonation that ended with Tate being lifted into the air and then held at arm's length out of his second-floor apartment window; suspended thus, Tate was forced to listen to a bear's-voice recitation of his own most celebrated poem, "Ode to the Confederate Dead." ("Arms of the Law" was always Lowell's retributive joke-bear: "A Bostonian, an Irish policeman and a bear.")[33] Macauley's story is perhaps too good to be true, but certainly there was enough violence in those two days for Tate to lose patience and call the police:

> Saturday evening he made a scene in a restaurant, from which we extricated him with great difficulty. When we got him home, he raised the window and began to shout profanity and obscenity. This went on about 30 minutes. A crowd gathered and then five policemen appeared. It took four of them ten minutes to subdue and handcuff him. . . . I finally, with the help of Jim Cunningham, talked the police out of taking him to the station, and instead got them to take him to the University psychiatrist, who diagnosed his case as "Psychotic reaction, paranoid type." He thought Cal should be taken into custody, but I persuaded him and the police to turn him over to me for the night. We quieted him by three in the morning, and he slept a little. At breakfast, he was agitated, and announced that he had done something wonderful for us all. He then said he was going to Peter Taylor at Bloomington, Indiana. I saw no way to stop him short of calling the police and committing him. We put him on the train in great apprehension.[34]

While Lowell was on his way to Bloomington, Tate telephoned Peter Taylor "and explained what had happened"; he also suggested that Taylor meet Lowell's train with a police escort. Tate then fired off a thoroughly rattled letter to Elizabeth Hardwick in New York. He had heard that Lowell and Hardwick had begun an affair at Yaddo, and—as a former admirer of Hardwick's—he here takes a perhaps overprotective line:

Now my dear, *you must listen to what I say.* Cal is dangerous; there are definite homicidal implications in his world, particularly toward women and children. He has a purification mania, which frequently takes homicidal form. You must not let him in your apartment. . . .

It is not likely that he will get back to N.Y. At present he is quiet, feeling out, of course, the Taylors, but when they do not enter his world with full assent, he will become violent, as he did here. Overtly, we were all sympathy, but he began on Friday to suspect that we were the enemy.

While the police were subduing him, he shouted again and again: "Cut off my testicles."

You know what is wrong with him as well as I do.[35]

Tate then goes on to scold Hardwick, and to criticize Flannery O'Connor for having indulged Lowell in his campaign at Yaddo: "But you are a woman and Miss O'Connor is a woman, and neither of you had the experience or knowledge to evaluate the situation in public terms."

Lowell arrived in Bloomington on April 4 and Peter Taylor met him at the station. Taylor had already arranged to lodge Lowell at the University of Indiana Club—on Tate's advice; after all, the Taylors had recently had their first child, and from Tate's account of the upheavals in Chicago, it would be a risk having Lowell in their house. At first, Taylor had been reluctant to accept any such melodramatic diagnosis, but almost as soon as Lowell appeared it was evident that this was not just another of his famous "rages":

We were walking on the campus and talking about literary things, but I could see he was mad, the things he was saying, and I suddenly felt that all of our long conversations about literary things, about what we were going to do with our lives, at Kenyon, I felt they were all nonsense. And I felt that I was about to have a crack-up myself, I was so upset. . . . You see, I didn't know anything about psychiatry. I thought Cal was lost forever. He had "gone mad." I really thought that I had lost this friend forever.[36]

That same evening, Lowell separated himself from Taylor and set off to "explore" the town, and Taylor took this opportunity to telephone Merrill Moore in Boston and his old Kenyon friend John Thompson in New York; Moore agreed to tell Charlotte, and John

Thompson was ready to help in any way he could. Taylor then contacted the police.

Soon afterwards, there was a report that Lowell had stolen a roll of tickets from a theater box office and had come to blows with a policeman who tried to restrain him. A general alert was then put out to the effect that a disturbed poet called Robert Lowell was on the rampage in downtown Bloomington. As it turned out, the alert fitted neatly into Lowell's sense of his divine vocation. Robert Giroux recalls:

> Cal was walking the streets, and after a bit he went and rang a doorbell. And the door was opened by a policeman who was off-duty, in mufti, and he said to Cal, "You must be Robert Lowell." Cal nearly fainted; he thought this was divine intervention—this stranger knew his name.[37]

Among Lowell's drafts for *Life Studies* there is a fragment in which he tries to describe how it all seemed to him:

> Seven years ago I had an attack of pathological enthusiasm. The night before I was locked up I ran about the streets of Bloomington Indiana crying out against devils and homosexuals. I believed I could stop cars and paralyze their forces by merely standing in the middle of the highway with my arms outspread. Each car carried a long rod above its tail-light, and the rods were adorned with diabolic Indian or Voodoo signs. Bloomington stood for Joyce's hero and Christian regeneration. Indiana stood for the evil, unexorcised, aboriginal Indians. I suspected I was a reincarnation of the Holy Ghost, and had become homicidally hallucinated. To have known the glory, violence and banality of such an experience is corrupting. . . .[38]

When Peter Taylor next got word, Lowell was in a straitjacket at the Bloomington police station. "He'd had a terrible fight with a policeman," Merrill Moore later reported. "He had beaten up the policeman and the policeman had beaten him up, to the advantage of neither of them."[39] Taylor visited Lowell in his cell and was implored by him to kneel and pray; could Taylor not *smell* the sulfur and the brimstone? Lowell asked. Taylor prayed, and needless to say the prayers were of considerable length; meanwhile the duty officers at the station had been replaced by the night staff, who, when they checked the cells and saw Lowell and Taylor kneeling side by side, assumed that their daytime colleagues had bagged *two* religious maniacs. Taylor had difficulty persuading them to let him go.[40] He later wrote to Tate: "I suppose I was with him only a few hours, but they were the most truly dreadful hours of my life. It's still impossible for me to talk about it even to Eleanor."[41]

On April 6 Merrill Moore and Charlotte Lowell arrived, and Taylor helped them to get Lowell to the Chicago airport, where John Thompson was waiting to meet them. Lowell, says Thompson, was "foaming at the mouth," talking nonstop, and seemed likely at any moment to erupt into unmanageable violence:

> I remember we got to La Guardia and there wasn't a plane to Boston for hours. Merrill Moore went away to take a nap and write some sonnets. He didn't have as much as an aspirin on him. Cal was sitting on the floor at La Guardia. I had to carry him onto the plane to get him to Boston—to a place called Baldpate.[42]

At Baldpate, a small private hospital near Georgetown, Massachusetts, Lowell was put into a padded cell and, as Moore wrote to Taylor, "continued to be in a somewhat excited and confused state of mind." Moore's diagnosis was that Lowell was "having considerable conflict between religion and sexuality" and this had led to "a brainstorm which he will in time ride out."[43] Charlotte seems to have taken a similar approach. She wrote to Taylor thanking him for "Bobby's clothes, all so nicely washed," and for behaving "so wisely in a trying situation":

> You'll be glad to hear that all goes well with Bobby now. He seems to like the hospital and the doctors and he's eating and sleeping well. The doctors feel that this illness is largely hysterical due to overwork, over-stimulation, under-eating and sleeping, lack of exercise and physical care, combined with much mental strain and conflict. We expect him to be quite well again in a few months.[44]

Lowell was in fact refusing to allow either Merrill Moore or his mother to visit him at Baldpate, and Charlotte eventually had to ask Robert Giroux if he would act as an intermediary. Giroux recalls:

> The asylum was really like a prison. I drove out with Mrs. Lowell and Dr. Moore and they waited while I went in, having to pass through a series of locked doors—three or four—before I reached Cal's cell. The

attendant asked through an eye-level window if he wanted to see me, and Cal said "Yes." I was shocked to see that the room had no other windows, and the leather walls were indeed padded to prevent self-injury.

Cal was terribly pale and drawn, and looked anything but violent. He spoke piteously and very persuasively: "My mother wants to keep me here for the rest of my life. You've got to help me." I might have been convinced if, in an appeal to what he thought were my Catholic prejudices, he hadn't said: "She won't let me go to mass." I did not like Mrs. Lowell but I knew this was untrue and said, "Cal, your mother asked me to come to Boston because she's very upset at your refusal to see her." And he said, "No, no, I don't want to talk to her. I don't want to see her." Even people locked up in cells have rights, I thought, and went out and told them he was adamant.[45]

Meanwhile, in Chicago, Allen Tate had formed the same view of Charlotte's probable intentions and had written to T. S. Eliot "expressing anxiety lest Cal's mother should try to get him certified and locked up." Merrill Moore was enraged by this interference and immediately wrote to Tate that Lowell was, and would remain, a voluntary patient at Baldpate, and that Tate was quite wrong in his attitude to Mrs. Lowell: "she is a good mother, deeply interested in her son and fully aware of his talents and capabilities." Moore also felt that it was "not helpful to Cal's reputation here or in England to have rumors of this kind circulating about him."[46]

The rumors, though, had by this time already circulated, and invariably Tate was the source: he had told Jean Stafford, and she, he claimed, had spread the word around literary New York; he had also written to Malcolm Cowley, but this he said was because he wanted to protect Lowell against any possible libel suit from Mrs. Ames. Throughout, both Tate and his wife were nervously aware that they might be thought "heartless" in having foisted the sick Lowell on Peter Taylor, and they were anxious to head off any slanders of this sort. Tate's explanation was that he had not wanted to "engage with" Charlotte Lowell, that Charlotte had blamed him for too many things in the past—Lowell's marriage, his Catholicism, his conscientious objection, even his poetry—and he wanted no more of it:

. . . in the very nature of things, we cannot function as his parents.
Cal, in his emotional dependence, has caused us more anxiety in the

past twelve years than our own child has caused us in all her twenty-four. This has been particularly trying because he feels towards us something of the ambivalence of a child towards his real parents: love and hate, docility and disloyalty, etc. In view of this we had not sought his company since 1943; he had sought us.[47]

Charlotte, he said, "should be satisfied now"; and to establish this, Tate resurrected his earlier, pre-breakdown diagnosis of the "Lowell problem":

Cal gave up Jean, he has given up the Church (the recent reconversion was not real—he merely used the Church for a few weeks to establish his mania in religious terms), and he has given up poetry. I don't know whether he told you that he left the manuscript of his unfinished poem at Yaddo, in the hands of a virtual stranger. I am told that everything that paranoiacs do is symbolic action, and an objectivization of the delusion. In giving up these three things Cal has given up the three defenses against disintegration: but his mother will feel that he has given up all those wicked influences.[48]

At around the same time, Tate was also writing to Elizabeth Hardwick, urging her to acknowledge that Lowell "is homicidal, deeply and subtly. . . . You were in danger as long as you had him with you."[49] Even so, Hardwick was one of the first to visit Lowell at Baldpate and one of the very few visitors he welcomed.

During May, Lowell's letters were confused and ecstatic. He wrote to Tate that "I'm in wonderful shape in all ways but the days are long, long, long!!!";[50] to Jean Stafford, pleading that their Catholic marriage was still valid;[51] and to Randall Jarrell, instructing him to reread Paul and the Gospels: "you'll see that the truth is both with the Jews and the R.C. Church; or so God said." He also told Jarrell:

I've been thinking that you're perhaps the best poet in America (where are there better poets)—unless I am—I'm poor, helpless and conceited here—so bear (Arms) with me.

I've read Vanzetti's letter to Sacco's son for the first time. Their case is mine—I'm sure the pro-Russian traitors are secretely [sic] supported by *certain* rich men—those who have sold us (the poor—who's worse paid than the poet—even carpenters get more and work less) sold us for "a pair of shoes."

When I get out I'm going to do everything in my power to get the Sacco case re-opened, so that those responsible are imprisoned and *electrocuted.*

Mother of God, old Randible, there's no *man* I love more than you.[52]

Jarrell later described this letter as *"pathetic."*[53]

By the middle of June, Lowell had been given electric shock treatment and seemed well enough for Hardwick to spend two weeks near the hospital (at Frank Parker's house in Ipswich) and regularly visit him. When she returned to New York, she was wholly reassured and wrote to Lowell: "I feel so happy about you that I'm suspiciously dizzy and in fact it may be true, as the rumor goes much to my chagrin, that I've had a nervous breakdown."[54] He replied, "Gosh, your visit was wonderful and *SANING.* Hope you can stand me still,"[55] and then five days later wrote (on July 6):

How would you care to be engaged? Like a debutant. WILL YOU?
How happy we'll be together writing the world's masterpieces, swimming and washing dishes.
P.S. Reading *The Idiot* again.[56]

Hardwick agreed to "be engaged," and a few days later Lowell was discharged from Baldpate. The announcement of his engagement produced the by now almost ritual letter from his father:

I understand that you and Miss Hardwick plan to get married and live in Boston. . . . I think that it is much too soon to marry anybody—just after you have been discharged from a mental hospital, after shock treatment.

He had "nothing personal" to say against Elizabeth Hardwick, but:

I do feel that both you and she, should clearly understand, that if she does marry you, that *she* is responsible for you.
If, instead of marrying, you would like to come down here and convalesce here slowly, while working on your Guggenheim, we would, of course, be glad to have you.
At the present time, I do not feel that you are in any position to take care of yourself, let alone look out and provide for a wife, and we cannot approve.[57]

Mr. Lowell added that the fees at Baldpate had been deducted from money that Lowell had left with his parents for safekeeping, and that apart from the small income from his trust fund, he now had only $600 of his own. Elizabeth Hardwick had a one-room apartment in New York, but otherwise, as she recalls, "he literally had no place to go. He couldn't go home. And he'd never taught, he'd just written." Also, soon after leaving Baldpate, Lowell began to slide into a depression: "No one can care for me," he'd say to Hardwick. "I've ruined my life. I'll always be mad."

> So we got married, in his parents' house. He wanted to do it, and I wanted to do it. I don't think it was a very happy occasion for anybody else. He had just come out of an illness and here he was taking on something else. One doctor at the hospital said: "He certainly needs someone, but if I were you I wouldn't do it." Well, we did. . . .[58]

Frank Parker was Lowell's best man, and his wife, Lesley, a mildly appalled guest:

> Cal and Lizzie were staying with us in Ipswich, and also Mary McCarthy and Bowden Broadwater. Lizzie appeared in peacock-blue silk and a hat, and Mary McCarthy gave one look at her and said, "You cannot be married looking like that. No, you are going to wear my Balenciaga." So Lizzie went off in this very unaccustomed, perfectly beautiful black lace hat which belonged to Mary. Frank was best man, and he had, as I realized when we got there and all knelt down, two odd socks, one white and one black. The pastor's opening remarks were: "Dear friends, we are here for a wedding, not a funeral . . ."— looking around at everyone's glum faces.[59]

The honeymoon was at the critic F. W. Dupee's house in Red Hook, New York, and it could hardly be counted a success: Lowell's depression didn't lift; he remained "very self-critical, very tortured about himself, his future, almost on the point of tears."[60] Hardwick contacted John Thompson, and it was arranged for Lowell to see a doctor in New York. The diagnosis was "reactive depression," and it was agreed that Lowell should go into the Payne Whitney Clinic for treatment—at specially reduced rates. On his first night there he wrote to Hardwick: "Dearest, dearest, dearest Lizzie. I think of you all the time, and worry so about all

I have dumped on you. We are going to work it all out, dear, be as wonderful as you have been."[61] And shortly afterwards, on September 15, 1949: "This is a thorough and solid place—what I have long needed . . . in a week or so the craziness and insecurity will begin to go."[62]

At first, Lowell's admission to Payne Whitney was kept as quiet as possible. The fear was that rumors would spread that he had "cracked up" for a second time. In 1949 psychiatry was still fairly mysterious territory, even to most New York intellectuals, and Elizabeth Hardwick did not relish having to explain over and over again that Lowell's depression was the predictable down-curve of a manic-depressive cycle.

The doctors at Payne Whitney were cautious about making a diagnosis—for the first two weeks, Lowell was kept under observation, encouraged to mix with the other patients, play badminton and Russian Banker, do elementary carpentry, and so on. In the third week it was decided to label him "manic-depressive, which is not very serious, they say, since they seem certain it is psychogenic in origin." A course of mild psychotherapy was prescribed —Payne Whitney was not psychoanalytically inclined: Lowell would be encouraged to talk about himself, and be gently guided towards an understanding of his predicament, but he would not be urged to dig too deeply for its origins. The prognosis was highly optimistic. Elizabeth Hardwick wrote to Peter and Eleanor Taylor:

> I have spoken to the head doctor and to the doctor treating Cal and they both say there should not be an incapacitating attack either of elation or depression again. This isn't nonsense; on the contrary, these doctors can't resist taking a profound, mysterious and pessimistic line. They like to look at you, as if they were revealing a great discovery, and say, "you know there is a lot of anxiety beneath the calm surface."[1]

Lowell cooperated with the therapy as enthusiastically as he was able to, telling the doctors "all the sordid and awful things about myself I could think of."[2] As to the doctors, they felt that his willingness to reveal "all sorts of shameful and embarrassing things" was indeed a healthy sign, but they were worried that he was able to be so "impersonal and unemotional about these admissions."[3] To Peter Taylor, Lowell wrote:

> I am now in the Payne Whitney Clinic, where Jean was, and will probably be here two or three months for therapy. I seem to be in the other half, the down-half of what you saw in Bloomington—self-enclosed, unable to function, depressed.[4]

In fact, this letter was not sent, and it was late October before it became generally known that Lowell was at Payne Whitney. Hardwick had carried on living at Red Hook, commuting to make regular visits and staying over in hotels. During September, Lowell had had visits from both Tate and his wife. Allen urged him:

> Tell yourself every morning, five times, that you are one of the best poets and that your friends feel about you precisely as they always have; that is, devotedly. You should never think as well of yourself as other people do, but you ought to think better of yourself than you do now. And you will.[5]

Caroline, always more consistently sharp-tongued than her husband, found the whole visit "depressing," even irritating:

> He seems to be in much the same state he was in when he broke down in Chicago, only past the violent stage. I imagine that he summoned me partly for the same reason he came to see us in Chicago: to disclose his recently discovered secret of the universe. I guess it's no secret to you that it's Counter-Point! I choked back so many remarks in the hour and a half that I was there that I became almost apoplectic. I would go to see him again if I thought it would do any good but I can't see that it would.[6]

Caroline Tate goes on to recommend a Jungian approach to Lowell's illness; Jungians, after all, deal in the same materials as poets: "symbols, archetypes." And then, gratuitously: "It is pretty plain by this time that these attacks are cyclic, don't you think?"[7]

By the end of October, Lowell was well enough to be allowed out of the hospital on Wednesdays and on weekends, and he was able to spend these times with Hardwick in an apartment she had rented on Central Park West. He had been in Payne Whitney for nearly three months, but his parents had never been told. "It was my idea," Hardwick has recalled, "not telling them. Partly shame, partly not wanting to seem to be asking for help."[8] Eventually, they found out from Baldpate that Lowell was having "follow-up treatment" in New York, and Merrill Moore reassured them that a reactive depression was only to be expected. Moore had, in fact, written to Hardwick early in October that Mr. and Mrs. Lowell were so involved with their own problems and anxieties (Mr. Lowell had become "quite infantile and demanding and difficult") that it would be better for them to be kept at a distance:

> Actually from now on in they are not important and will not be any more. They are on their street car going to the end of the line where the car will stop and they will get off and walk the rest of the way.
>
> They can never do much for Cal (they never have) and if he tries or if you try to adjust to them at this stage it would waste priceless energy which they need for their life tasks and which you both need for yours.[9]

It was November 5 before Lowell communicated directly with his parents: he had been too "ashamed and puzzled," he said, to write to them before. He felt that he was "beginning to really learn something from the psycho-therapy" and added, in a postscript: "I've been trying to understand my first six or seven years and have many questions to ask you."[10] A week later his father wrote, praising Lowell for agreeing to take treatment—"I think it is such a very sensible and responsible thing to do"—and then drifting off into paternal emptiness:

> You had a wonderful career in college, and we certainly don't want your health to interfere with a brilliant career. So many literary people did not develop their bodies to keep pace with their brilliant minds.
>
> Psychiatry can do a lot for people but most people go, because someone else wants them to, and not because they really have any interest in it themselves, and it is not to be wondered at, that the results are not up to expectations.
>
> Saturday, we went to the Lunts in "I Know My Love"—a new

Theater Guild that started here. It is very well done, and I am sure you would enjoy it.[11]

By Christmas, 1949, Lowell was "functioning" again; his letters are brisk and busy, as if he was anxious to make it clear that he was finally back in the world of practicalities. To his mother he wrote:

> I have a world of things to do—preparing to leave hospital, my course at Kenyon, a lecture on Browning to be delivered at Kenyon, readings at St. Johns and here and the Commencement poem to be read at Harvard on the 19th of June—like James Russell Lowell, but I guess our poems will have little in common.[12]

The Kenyon course he mentions here was to take place in the summer at the newly instituted Kenyon School of Letters—an event organized by Ransom but not officially tied in with Kenyon College. Lowell's immediate hope was that Tate would be able to persuade Paul Engle, director of the writers' workshop, to offer him a job at Iowa similar to the one he had turned down in 1947. On January 1, 1950, he heard that Tate had been successful ("You are a wonderfully generous friend," Lowell wrote to him, "and I shall never forget"),[13] and that he was expected to arrive at Iowa by the end of the month. Lowell was discharged from Payne Whitney, having agreed to make contact with a psychiatrist in Iowa, and by January 25 he and Hardwick were installed in a one-and-a-half-room apartment in Iowa City: "a strange place . . . it's so flat and ugly and somehow has the air and look of a temporary town. Actually, any-thing over fifty years old is a landmark."[14]

Even so, within a week of their arrival, Lowell had got back to work; Elizabeth Hardwick wrote to Charlotte Lowell:

> Cal has started writing poetry again and has been steadily at it for the past week with his old inspiration and fantastic concentration. Even he must admit that what he has done is brilliant as ever and so he's fine and busy.[15]

And when classes started a week later, Lowell found them surpris-ingly agreeable. "There are no fireworks, nothing of the icy lucidity of the professional," but of the twenty-five poets in his class he thought that five or six were "really trying to do something" and that the atmosphere was "tame and friendly"—like almost everything else in Iowa City:

> Every afternoon a pack of very harmless and sorry-looking stray dogs settles on our pathway. This is one of the marks of Iowa City; the others are high-brow movies, the new criticism, and the Benalek murder trial, which Elizabeth is moving heaven and earth to enter as an accredited reporter.[16]

Lowell was making weekly visits to an Iowa psychiatrist, and in March he wrote to his mother: ". . . I am well out of my extreme troubles. There is a stiffness, many old scars, the toil of building up new habits. I definitely feel out of the old perverse dark maze."[17]

A new plan had been devised for 1950: after Iowa, there would be the visit to Kenyon, and after that "a frugal year abroad." With money saved from Iowa, the fee from Kenyon and the remainder of the 1947 Guggenheim, Lowell and Hardwick calculated that if they set off in September, they would be able to survive in Europe —"in Italy mostly"—until the following June. Lowell now felt that teaching would always be there to come back to; indeed, Iowa had assured him that there would be a position for him there on his return. And the European trip would, he thought, give him "the time, freedom and stimulation to finish his new book of poems."[18]

The Kenyon course was a success. Delmore Schwartz and Ransom were teaching there, and Lowell was able to show them the first draft of his long poem "The Mills of the Kavanaughs"; he gave lectures on Browning and on Frost and was applauded by Ransom for doing "a fine job for us here."[19]

After a short spell back in New York and a visit to Lowell's parents, Lowell and Hardwick were ready to leave. They had arranged to take a Norwegian freighter to Genoa—"it was all this youth stuff," Hardwick has recalled, although, in their early thirties, "we were not so young"—and in preparation they installed themselves and their luggage in a hotel. On August 26 Lowell's parents wrote to wish them "Bon voyage." Charlotte was anxious that they should always remember to contact the naval attaché at the appropriate American embassy, "and say that your father was a naval officer. That was helpful to us and gave us especial attention."[20] And, unusually, there was a note from Mr. Lowell;[21] he had enjoyed

their visit to Boston, he said, and would handle Lowell's mail while
he was away:

> We think it is nice to do well in your poems, but it is equally advisable
> to do well in a wife, and we think that you did.
> Hope you have a fine trip. Best love to you both.
> Affectionately,
> Your Dad

Four days later a telegram arrived: DADDY DIED VERY SUDDENLY AT
THE BEVERLY HOSPITAL.[22]

Lowell and Hardwick left their luggage at their New York hotel
and returned to Boston, where Lowell helped to organize his father's funeral. He later wrote:

> I was the only person Mother permitted to lift the lid of the casket.
> Father was there. He wore his best sport-coat—pink, at ease, obedient!
> Not a twist or a grimace recalled those unprecedented last words to
> Mother as he died, "I feel awful." And it was right that he should still
> have the slight over-ruddiness so characteristic of his last summer. He
> looked entirely alive, or as he used to say: *W & H:* Well and Happy.
> Impossible to believe that if I had pressed a hand to his brow to see if
> it were hectic, I would have touched the *cold thing!*[23]

And Elizabeth Hardwick has recalled:

> Cal was upset and there were some rather distressing things that had
> happened. He asked his mother, at Beverly Farms, about his father's
> will. His father didn't mention him in his will at all. And Cal said,
> "Didn't he even leave me his watch, or something?" And she said,
> "Oh, *Bobby.*" And he said he wanted to talk to his mother about how
> much money she had and what she was going to do with her life. She
> wouldn't discuss it. Instead she fell over and fainted, and crumpled
> down on the stairs. She would do rather dramatic things like that occa-
> sionally. But he was quite hurt that his father didn't mention him in
> his will.

But how could that have happened?

> What had happened was that Cal came into a small trust that went by
> will to him on his father's death. I mean, it was out of Mr. Lowell's
> jurisdiction, and so I suppose he thought that since Cal had that, there
> was no special reason to mention him in the will.[24]

Lowell and Hardwick stayed on at Beverly Farms for a month, and on September 29 they finally embarked for Europe. From the boat, Lowell wrote to his mother:

> Just a note to say goodbye and remind you must tell us anything that comes up and call on us for any help we can give. The last month has been a hard one and an instructive one—an education or its beginnings for us all. I'll miss you deeply.[25]

After a "rainless, sea-sickless"[26] voyage via Tangier, Lowell and Hardwick reached Genoa on October 10, 1950, and from there they made for Florence, intending to stay for a week before moving on to Rome. But Florence was not to be passed through so casually:

> We came here for a week, after we landed, and decided to stay permanently, goodness knows what influencing the decision besides the fact that Florence is interesting beyond limits—the churches, the galleries, etc. But I'm sure the suitcases made us decide upon it before even so much as visiting Rome. We rented the apartment the first week. . . .[27]

The five-room apartment they had found was "wonderfully furnished, beautiful dishes, sheets, silver, furniture and in a *chic* location," and $200 a month covered rent, food, heating and a maid. For Hardwick it was perfect: the maid meant that she could do her own work (she was writing a novel based on the Iowa City murder trial) and not be swamped by "the torture of the laundry, the cooking and the cleaning." As for Lowell, he had immediately launched himself into historic Florence, and was soon "in a daze about Italy."[28]

It became Lowell's habit over the next few months to search for an American parallel to each new European marvel; part of this was homesickness, but mainly it was an attempt to impose limits on his own excitement. Thus, Florence was Boston, Rome was New York, and Italy was "like America—a slightly older America, such as that of my childhood in the twenties."[29] Constantly, and not too convincingly, he would attempt to *place* each bewildering new place: "Even the greyest houses are attractive and you might think you were living in the glorious Victorian age in the poor Italian section of Boston, except for the posters and motor-bikes."[30]

The posters in Communist Florence mostly said things like

"Death to the criminal MacArthur," but that didn't worry Lowell. The Korean War had broken out in the summer of 1950, but in Florence "the people are divided every which way, and seem to be marking time—waiting for the giants, Russia and America, to act."[31] On the whole, he felt, the city was relaxed and slow, and in any case it was not modern political Florence he had come to see: "We'd get up at seven, and we'd walk all day and come back to wherever we were at 5—seeing everything."[32] And when Lowell was not looking, he was reading "grammars and art books" and Florentine histories. And his classical education gave him the pleasing illusion of being able to communicate with the natives:

> I have a theory that I can learn Italian simply by tossing about bizarre words and phrases—a new language is a joy as soon as you can be incomprehensible to your friends. Already, helped by Latin, I can say things to our maid that no one can understand; Elizabeth says things that I can't understand, and the maid says things that everyone in Italy can understand except us.[33]

During his first two months in Florence he was also "fussing with my Kavanaughs":[34] in other words, massively rewriting the whole book in galley proofs. Robert Giroux would write reminding him that printers charged real money for this kind of thing, and Lowell would take no notice. The book was now "much improved," he wrote to Peter Taylor.[35] It would be called *The Mills of the Kavanaughs* and would include the title poem along with the six other pieces he had completed since *Lord Weary's Castle*. It was scheduled to appear in the spring of 1951.

Lowell and Hardwick lingered in Florence from October 1950 until May 1951, with only intermittent excursions. There was a three-day trip to Monte Carlo—"no gambling, just sight-seeing"[36]—and further visits to Rome. For one luxurious ten-day spell they were entertained in the country villa of Princess Caetani, the publisher of an international literary magazine called *Botteghe Oscure*, and in Rome itself Lowell paid regular visits to George Santayana. A Boston Catholic, Santayana had been impressed by *Lord Weary's Castle* and had spoken of "the flames of piety that appear repeatedly, contrasting with the Bostonian and Cape Cod atmosphere of the background."[37]

Rome was the glittering metropolis—"much more lively socially and intellectually than Florence," Hardwick thought, but both she and Lowell were usually pleased to return to a city where "you can walk everywhere and learn your way about in a day."[38] In Florence they had met the poet Montale, "and had several sweaty, mute evenings of language difficulty and great displays of blundering affection. We walked up the Arno, I remember, and Montale, since we couldn't talk, sang into the night 'In Questa Tomba Oscura' and other songs."[39] In Florence, too, there was Bernard Berenson, the celebrated connoisseur of Italian painting and another self-exiled Bostonian. Berenson's villa was an "attraction" for visiting American intellectuals, and the old man himself was a dependable host figure, an "inn-keeper" almost: "He was too old," Hardwick wrote, "had been viewed and consulted far too much; you had the belated feeling you were seeing the matinee of a play that had been running for eight decades." In this same essay, Hardwick muses on the notion of expatriatism—and it seems that if she and Lowell ever thought of moving permanently to Europe, the example of Berenson was enough to give them pause:

> When we mailed a letter of introduction to him, he accepted it as a bizarre formality because, of course, he who saw everyone was willing and happy to see yet another. One was never tempted to think it was ennui or triviality that produced this state of addiction; the absorbing inclination seemed to be a simple fear of missing someone, almost as if these countless visitors and travelers had a secret the exile pitifully wished to discover.[40]

She felt the same about other, less renowned Americans who had tried to settle into the "dream-like timelessness of Italy":

> Everywhere in Italy, among the American colony, one's envy is cut short time and again by a sudden feeling of sadness in the air, as of something still alive with the joys of an Italian day and yet somehow faintly withered, languishing. Unhappiness, disappointment support the exile in his choice.[41]

For the mere traveler, though, there was still so much to see, and during the summer Lowell and Hardwick set off to "discover" Europe. They traveled in France with the Macauleys and to Greece and Turkey with the art critic Anthony Bower. Hardwick remembers it all as a period of

> gorgeous absorption and infinite passion for Italy and Europe, which both of us were taking in for the first time. We had the feeling that no life would be long enough. We shed tears when we opened the door of the Athens Museum and saw the Charioteer, standing serenely. Our plan was to take the boat from Bari to Piraeus, and then change to the boat for Turkey (we visited Greece on the way back). But while we were waiting for a change of boats, Cal got into a thrifty mood as a reaction to Tony's spendthrift nature and insisted on going to the Acropolis by subway. He managed to arrive there before we did and felt thereby very cunning and native.[42]

In October, Lowell wrote excitedly to Randall Jarrell:

> I feel and talk like a guide book—full of gaps, irrelevencies [sic] and amnesia. But it's overwhelmingly astonishing—so much that is harmonious, unbelievably wonderful, odd, unforeseen, varied—all one's European history to learn over, at least in sense that all one's facts and theories are hung onto new images.
>
> It's like going to school again—I fill up on everything indiscrimently [sic], and hope it will settle—a lot of French and Italian poetry, even some German and Latin, thousands of paintings, a lot of history, plays, opera, ballet—one feels so ignorant, so conscious that one won't have forever, that it's hard to stop.[43]

As it turned out, Lowell wasn't able to "stop" until late that autumn. The climax of his soaring and intense summer came in August with the arrival in Paris of the almost equally energetic Charlotte Lowell. Unfortunately, Charlotte's energies were not the kind that drove her into churches and art galleries; they were more to do with the shortcomings of bureaucrats and flunkies—wherever she went, Lowell wrote, she would leave "a wake of shattered chefs, ships-captains, hotel managers, Cook's agents etc. etc. . . . . truly, and I'm not exaggerating."[44] And for Hardwick,

> it was sheer torture. It was the routine: "You don't want another coffee, you don't want a cigarette, do you?" And I'd say, "Well, I think I do." It was like that. Little domestic things. I didn't find it pleasant. One thing I didn't like about Mrs. Lowell was that although she was very

protected and rather spoiled, she took a tough attitude towards other people's indulgences. That got rather tiresome.[45]

After a month of this, tension was running fairly high; as Mrs. Lowell later diagnosed: "It was a great adjustment for us all."[46] And it was in this atmosphere that Lowell suddenly announced his winter plans: he had decided they would go to Holland. Hardwick was appalled; she had expected that they would return to Italy as soon as Charlotte's visit had been coped with—after all, most of their luggage was still stored in Florence. Lowell would not be dissuaded; he wanted Hardwick to go ahead of him to Amsterdam to find somewhere to live; meanwhile he would escort Charlotte to the next bit of her holiday, at Pau. Hardwick, in the end, complied, but, she says:

> I was scared and miserable . . . I found it absolutely terrifying—I didn't know anyone there, I didn't know what to look for and so on. I was full of complaints—it all seemed so dour and hard to manage.[47]

Even though Lowell knew that Hardwick felt stranded and desperate in Amsterdam—she wrote to him of her "paralyzing anxiety"— he continued to argue that Amsterdam was where he needed to be:

> I am at the end of my road. I want to be located as soon as possible, and preferably in Holland. I have good reasons for this choice! The Anglo-Saxon's encounter with the Latin cultures has been worn to exaustion [*sic*]. Holland draws me because of the novelty, the freedom to pick and choose and the privacy which is so necessary for reactions that are at all personal or profound. . . . I *feel* I can make something out of Holland —one can never know, but the hunch seems crucially worth following.[48]

He wanted "sunlit rooms, a busy, perceptive, productive day and calm and joy between us."[49] He had been reading Motley's *Rise of the Dutch Republic* (which had given him "nightmares" when "still in short trousers";[50] he now describes it as a "magnificent, rather obtusely and fiercely Macaulayish anti-Catholic affair"[51]), and he had learned from it that "Catholic apologetics are more a splendid lawyer's harangue than the story of what happens."[52] He was anxious to see Dutch paintings; Rembrandt's *Syndics* in the Rijks-

museum had, he said, once been his "cause," and he badly wanted
to see it:

> Surreptitiously throughout my sixth form year at St. Mark's School, I
> had studied painting in Elie Faure's five volume *Histoire de l'Art,* cop-
> ied its photographs on tracing paper, penetrated the mysteries of "dy-
> namic symmetry" and finally spent twenty dollars, an entire term's
> allowance, on a copious, bake-finish Medici print of the Syndics which
> was hung in my alcove. This act, a very typical one, was unintelligible
> to my class mates. The *Syndics* had nothing manly or athletic about it;
> nor on the other hand was it at all arty, sophisticated, advanced. I was
> pitied by the class aesthetes, and nearly mobbed by its football play-
> ers.[53]

Chiefly, though, he wanted to rest for a time in a culture that was
in accord with "my own Protestant New England background."
    There was a note of desperation in all this, and Hardwick wrote
urging him:

> *take it easy, calm down* before things get any more absurd and destruc-
> tive. Living side by side as we do, without friends to advise and help,
> I get caught up in the whirl, utterly worn, bewildered and irritable and
> so I can't help you because my life becomes a nightmare, timeless, driven
> and irrational. You've been moving at a tremendous pace for half a year
> and it's time to stop physically and mentally.

Lowell continued to write almost every day from Pau; he didn't
want Hardwick to settle for Amsterdam unless she was genuinely
willing, but he also pleaded:

> I want to be a human and imaginative creature again—up till now
> I've been in a condition of blank drifting broken by manic enthu-
> siasms. . . .
>   Make up your mind on either Florence or Amsterdam in the next five
> days.

And in another letter:

> We must recover nervously and break this terrible wheeling of abuse
> and blind sudden fury. I now think getting *settled comfortably* and out
> of *the swim* comes before anything else.

On September 21 Hardwick wrote from Amsterdam that she had found a shabby but adequate two-room apartment. Lowell joined her there, having left Charlotte in Paris for the remaining three weeks of her vacation, and on October 6 he wrote to Randall Jarrell:

> So now we are stopped—after a trying and tumultuous visit from my mother. Amsterdam is outwardly a sort [of] eighteenth century Boston —all canals and lovely, small, baroquish brick houses, worldly, protestant, English speaking, the people sound and look German.[54]

And two weeks later he wrote to his mother just before she set off for home: "Amsterdam is on the whole a much handsomer (less beautiful) city than Florence—Life is more like it is in America and one feels more in control."[55]

During the first "rain-every-day months" in their tiny Amsterdam apartment, both Lowell and Hardwick felt claustrophobic and on edge; they both "suffered from the spleen and mastered . . . every wrinkle of domestic argument and sabotage."[56] Hardwick found Holland "not the land of tulips but the land of drudgery . . . it's a nightmare," but Lowell was gradually "calming down." He began work on a "poem about Florence after coming to the damp flats because it was *impossible* to write about Italy," and started reading "the complete records of the Nuremberg trials," which he borrowed, four volumes at a time, from the USIS library. At first Hardwick felt isolated and depressed, but things improved when they got to know a group of young Dutch intellectuals who had "read everything";[57] with one of these, Huyk van Leuwen, Lowell would "talk for hours about philosophy."

In February 1952 Lowell borrowed Van Leuwen's houseboat as a daytime workplace: "Poor dear, he's got it into his head that he's a strong, simple and capable man of the people, like a Dutchman." While Lowell was thus "at sea," Hardwick would sit at home "worried to death that he'll leave the gas on, trying to heat a can of soup, and I'm sure I'll have to trudge out tomorrow to see that he's all right."[58] From his houseboat, Lowell wrote to Jarrell:

> This has been a sedentary winter. . . . We read continuously, except when interrupted, then we sigh querulously, "But I never have any time to read." In this way I've gone twenty volumes of the Nuremberg trials,

a book by a psychiatrist on the prisoners, Hannah Arendt, Macaulay's History, Motley's Dutch Republic, a lot of Clarendon, a lot of North's Plutarch and a thousand other things . . . all of which you could no doubt have finished on a bus trip to North Carolina, and been at a loss for more before you were half there. . . .[59]

Holland had, after four months, almost served its purpose; it now seemed "a flat country with a flat grey climate that too often reminds one of Mount Vernon and Columbus." Dutch literature was "a sober review of other literatures": "Nowhere is the gay commercial bourgeois seventeenth century so present, nowhere do you meet so many people who put you at your ease. But this winter has been enough. . . ."[60]

From Amsterdam, they visited London and Belgium, and in both places Lowell made a characteristically wholehearted effort to educate himself in music: in Brussels he and Hardwick attended five Mozart operas in six nights, in London they saw *Der Rosenkavalier*, *Fidelio* and *Wozzeck*. Lowell declared himself "nuts about opera" and set about studying scores, quoting from Tovey's *Essays in Musical Analysis* and trying "to imagine, though tone deaf, modulating from the tonic to the dominant."[61] Hardwick's sardonic response to this new passion was to compare Lowell to "an advertisement I remember from America: 'Learn to play the piano in three weeks, no scales, no weary hours of practice and no talent required.' "[62]

In March, Lowell received an invitation to teach at the 1952 Salzburg Seminar, an annual American-organized event that ran through most of July and August; there was no salary involved, but there would be free passage, room and board, and it would be a way of seeing Austria. The invitation had come from the seminar's director, Shepherd Brooks, who had met Lowell at a cocktail party in Amsterdam and been beguiled by a brilliant account of his family's involvement in the slave trade:

To the best of my knowledge, the Lowells had no dealings whatever with slaves. Cal was making one of his extraordinary histories. But it struck me then that he would probably make a superb teacher so I invited him to teach at Salzburg.[63]

For Hardwick the prospect was exhilarating, not to say reviving: "I think only of leaving the Netherlands, my only thought, in fact, for the last seven months."[64] She busily arranged an itinerary that would take them through Germany to Vienna, after a short visit to Paris, where they "couldn't resist . . . at least a part of that fabulous 'Art of the 20th Century' conference." Tate would be in Paris for this event, along with Katherine Anne Porter, Auden, Spender and "even Faulkner."[65]

On May 4 Lowell and Hardwick set off for Brussels and were in Paris by May 16, when Hardwick wrote the Macauleys a more cheerful letter than she had been able to muster for some months:

> Allen Tate arrived [as a delegate to the Congress for Cultural Freedom] yesterday and I must say we were delighted to see him and had a marvellous time. . . . Cal still can't get used to this new pace, jumping into taxis every moment with Tate, meeting at Champs Elysées cafés, etc. Secretly, he's quite shocked that Tate won't retire to his hotel room in the afternoon, carefully study the text, and attend, in gallery seats, an evening performance at the Comédie. When Cal suggested this, Tate looked at him as if he had lost his mind. . . . As for me, I am most certainly enjoying the frivolity, except that by now Cal has me so well trained I sometimes feel as if I were failing all my school subjects.[66]

Lowell's comment on the Paris jaunt was: "We had a terrific time with Allen in Paris—religion seems to have freed him from all inhibitions."[67] Tate had become a Catholic in 1950.

It was almost a year now since *The Mills of the Kavanaughs* had appeared in the United States.[68] In fact, Lowell's "excitement" of the previous summer had coincided with his reading of the book's largely grudging and bemused reviews. Even Jarrell, though he extravagantly praised two of the book's six shorter poems, was in doubt about the 600-line dramatic monologue which gives the book its title. "Mother Marie Therese," he wrote, "is the best poem Mr. Lowell has ever written and 'Falling Asleep Over the Aeneid' is— is better." "The Mills of the Kavanaughs," however,

> does not seem to me successful as a unified work of art, a narrative poem that makes the same sort of sense a novel or a story makes. It is too much a succession of nightmares and daydreams that are half-nightmare; one counts with amusement and disbelief the number of times the poem becomes a nightmare-vision or its equivalent. And these are only too successfully nightmarish, so that there is a sort of monotonous violence

and extremity about the poem, as if it were a piece of music that consisted of nothing but climaxes. The people too often seem to be acting *in the manner of* Robert Lowell, rather than plausibly as real people act (or implausibly as real people act). I doubt that many readers will think them real; the husband of the heroine never seems so, and the heroine is first of all a sort of symbiotic state of the poet. (You feel, "Yes, Robert Lowell would act like this if he were a girl"; but whoever saw a girl like Robert Lowell?)[69]

Jarrell felt that the poem was "a sort of anthology of favorite Lowell effects," that Lowell "too often either is having a nightmare or else is wide awake gritting his teeth and working away at All The Things He Does Best." And there was an echo of Tate's view that Lowell had been "forcing" his talent in Jarrell's concluding quip: "As a poet Mr. Lowell sometimes doesn't have enough trust in God and tries to do everything himself: he proposes *and* disposes. . . ." Lowell replied to this in a letter to Jarrell in February 1952; he had, he said, been warned that Jarrell's review was hostile and had "worked up an imaginary rebuttal." Having now read Jarrell's piece, though, Lowell was pleasantly surprised: for all Jarrell's reservations, the title poem was still "a powerful and impressive poem, with a good many beautiful or touching passages and a great many overwhelming ones." Lowell wrote:

My defense was the same as your attack, i.e. that I had poured every variety of feeling and technique into it I knew of. The poem is meant to be grandiose, melodramatic, carried on by a mixture of drama and shifting tones, rather like Maud. I agree with most of what you say, except the heroine is very real to *me,* and that in a freakish way the poem has more in it than any of the others. Anyway I am delighted with your review and have read it many times out of vanity. Perhaps I agree with it all, but since I've finished nothing new I go on overrating the Kavanaughs.[70]

Another review that would have interested Lowell was by William Carlos Williams in the *New York Times Book Review.* Predictably, Williams rather skirts the question of what the title poem is about, and concentrates on "the formal fixation of the line" and on Lowell's use of rhyme, or "the rhyme-track," as Williams loftily describes it. Rhyme, he says, is clearly necessary to Lowell, if only so that he can appear to surmount it with his wrenched enjamb-

ments; you can judge the strength of the tide, he implies, by what
it does to the dams:

> In this title poem, a dramatic narrative played out in a Maine village, Mr.
> Lowell appears to be restrained by the lines; he appears to *want* to break
> them. And when the break comes, tentatively, it is toward some happy
> recollection, the tragedy intervening when this is snatched away and the
> lines close in once more. . . .[71]

A year earlier, Williams had called Lowell's rhyming "the finest I
know," though it reminded him of a "tiger behind bars." And
Lowell had praised the first two books of Williams's *Paterson* in
print—although more for their ability to "get everything in" than
for their prosody. Now Lowell had tried to get "everything" into
The Mills of the Kavanaughs but was being chastised for monotony.
Williams, he knew, would say that the source of this monotony, this
leveling, reducing factor, was an enslavement to traditional verse
forms. More and more, Lowell was inclined to learn from Williams.
Jarrell might laugh at Williams's "long dreary imaginary war in
which America and the Present are fighting against Europe and the
Past," but to Lowell—reading *Paterson* in Amsterdam—there was
a simple, subtle and perhaps alarming issue here that should be
pondered. In his letter to Jarrell, he is almost embarrassed to confess
his admiration for a writer he knew Jarrell regarded as naïve, as an
unthinking primitive who had somehow got it marvelously right
with *Paterson* Book 1 but had since got "rather steadily worse."
"Maybe," Lowell writes, "it's being away from home. . . . Well,
we'll wrangle it out when I see you."[72] To Williams he wrote,
almost wistfully, "I'd be as unhappy out of rime and meter as you
would in them," and from Amsterdam he had interestingly tried to
define the differences between them:

> I think I get what you mean about Eliot for the first time. You say, I
> think, that at the time the Waste Land appeared a whole flood of
> "American" poetry, that is poetry more in the present and more congen-
> ial to you was about to prevail. Then it was driven underground, into
> small privately printed editions, non-paying, ephemeral little magazines
> etc. There's a chance you are right, and of course you are right in a way.
> But it was fairly heroic of Eliot, whose personality and opinions are after
> all very special, not in tune with the times, not at all what anyone in

America or England really wanted—to have set out with all these disadvantages, and then by one's artistry and sincerety [sic] to dominate. . . . No, that's something! For the counts that you would think are against him, and they are against him are more amazing than what is superficially fashionable about his work. I think the field was open, and that the other poets had the more direct road. You shouldn't complain. Then for your method. I don't think it's good or bad. Your way of writing doesn't help without your eye, experience and sense of language. Your followers are mostly dull because none of them combine these qualities. Still I wish rather in vain that I could absorb something of your way of writing into mine.[73]

The other reviews of *The Mills of the Kavanaughs* had less to offer than those by Williams and Jarrell; in most of them respectfulness jostled with puzzlement, with mild "disappointment" the usual, cautious outcome. Indeed, such was the prevailing timidity that there is something refreshingly plainspoken about Rolfe Humphries's single-paragraph dismissal in the *Nation:*

> . . . I am sorry. I find him dull and I cannot make out what he is getting at; I am willing to take the blame for lacking whatever key is necessary to unlock the barriers in communication and understanding.[74]

Others had evidently run up against these same barriers but were not so ready to admit it. David Daiches in the *Yale Review* was fairly typical in speaking approvingly of Lowell's "poetic richness and dexterity" while wondering if, perhaps, there was not "an element of irresponsibility in the presentation."[75] And Richard Eberhart in the *Kenyon Review* wished he was able to devote his review to Lowell's revisions, but had had to content himself with not being able to understand "this ambitious poem of major complexity." The lines were "dense, close-packed, gnarled, intense and savage," and yet "the gold is embedded in schist," he said. But his review did have some interest in its attempt at a reply to the Williams type of stricture: "Lowell is a traditionalist. He is not going to throw over the iamb or anything of that sort," and also, on the question of the Williams requirement for a distinctively American poetic speech:

> there does not seem to be any poetic speech purely or exclusively American, certainly not in Lowell. . . . maybe the roughness, the turgidity, the boxer-like brilliance is the American thing.[76]

It is probable that most of the *Kenyon*'s younger readers would have been quite baffled by that "boxer-like" designation.

Jarrell was right to single out "Falling Asleep Over the Aeneid" as the most effective poem in *The Mills of the Kavanaughs;* certainly it is the one that most explicitly defines the difference in character between this book and *Lord Weary's Castle.* In it, an old man dreams over his Virgil and, when he wakes up, finds that he's too late for church—the Aeneid has served him as a Bible. And even in "Mother Marie Therese" it is the Mother Superior's delinquencies that are obliquely celebrated. Throughout the book, orthodox religious passion is viewed as either deranging ("Thanksgiving's Over") or debilitating (witness Father Turbot in "Mother Marie Therese"). The book is full of truants and delinquents, and there is no reduction in the level of self-loathing, but the Church no longer affords Lowell his symbolic armory; and without it he is—almost literally—unmanned. Whereas in *Lord Weary's Castle* autobiography made for clarity and exactness, in *The Mills of the Kavanaughs* it produces something close to chaos: the reason for this is that Lowell is attempting to adjust the instincts of the confessional to the decorum of an "objective" work of art, to speak of his most personal shames with supreme impersonality. Hence the cardboard characters, the dramatic monologues that all sound the same, the classical myths that don't quite fit, the narratives that weave in and out of dreamed and "real" experience, past and present actions, without ever yielding enough clues for us to sort out which is which.

Since the book is, in so many of its parts, impenetrable, the reader has to work in a piecemeal fashion, making the best sense of what *can* be made sense of. And much of this "making sense" can involve fitting the poem to what was happening, or had just happened, in Lowell's life when he wrote it. It is immediately noticeable, for example, that the book is a clamor of distraught, near-hysterical first-person speech, and that almost always the speaker is a woman. The men in the book are usually under attack. Thus, the rhetoric of "Thanksgiving's Over" and of large sections of the title poem can, not too fancifully, be heard as a fusing of two rhetorics—the enraged, erupting aggression of *Lord Weary* somehow loosened and given a new spitefulness by echoes of the letters Lowell had been getting—throughout 1947—from Jean Stafford, and echoes too (we might reasonably speculate) of the "adder-tongued" invective that she used to pour into their quarrels:

"If you're worth the burying
And burning, Michael, God will let you know
Your merits for the love I felt the want
Of, when your mercy shipped me to Vermont

To the asylum. Michael, was there warrant
For killing love? As if the birds that range
The bestiary-garden by my cell,
Like angels in the needle-point my Aunt
Bequeathed our altar guild, could want
To hurt a fly! . . . But Michael, I was well;
My mind was well;
I wanted to be loved—to thaw, to change,
To *April!* . . ."

And again:

"Husband, you used to call me Tomcat-kitten;
While we were playing Hamlet on our stage
With curtain rods for foils, my eyes were bleeding;
I was your valentine.
You are a bastard, Michael, aren't you! *Nein,*
Michael. It's no more valentines."

(If a hint of "You are a bastard, Michael, aren't you! *Nein*" found
its way into Sylvia Plath's "Daddy, daddy, you bastard, I'm
through," then Plath—it could be said—chose a thoroughly apt
poem to borrow from.) Lines like these could fit, without evident
strain, into almost any one of Stafford's pleading, vengeful letters:

What do I care if Randall likes my book? Or anyone? Why should it
console me to be praised as a good writer? These stripped bones are not
enough to feed a starving woman. I know this, Cal, and the knowledge
eats me like an inward animal; there is no thing worse for a woman than
to be deprived of her womanliness. For me, there is nothing worse than
the knowledge that life holds nothing for me but being a writer. But
being a writer and being a robbed woman whose robber will doubly
rejoice in her stolen goods.
     If you had loved me, you would love me now completely as I com-
pletely love you so that this is another dreadful truth that I must swallow: these bitternesses that I have tried to swallow still make me retch,
still after all these months and months of sickness and because I am as

sick now, I see no end and I wish, I wish, I wish, I wish to die. I do not see any other way except to live until I die: this is what it is now and what it is always to be.[77]

These are two paragraphs from a closely typed five-page letter; and throughout 1947 Lowell was for periods bombarded almost daily with similarly intense communications from his sick, abandoned wife. The voice is unmistakably the voice he borrows for Anne Kavanaugh. And the lines that Lowell's Anne puts in her husband's mouth seem meant to exemplify the "calm olympian brutality" which—according to Stafford's repeated accusation—was Lowell's actual posture at the time:

> . . . "Anne, my whole
> House is your serf. The squirrel in its hole
> Who hears your patter, Anne, and sinks its eye-
> Teeth, bigger than a human's, in its treasure
> Of rotten shells, is wiser far than I
> Who have forsaken all my learning's leisure
> To be your man and husband—God knows why!"

But Lowell was not just using poetry in order to recapture the flavor of marital quarrels. He seems genuinely to have been trying to fathom how *he* seemed to his women—to know this, and to judge it. And—being Lowell—to judge it without mercy. The paradox is that although he needed to do this in poetry, he could hardly bear to do it in public.

In her short story "A Country Love Story"[78] Jean Stafford has a narrator who is trapped in a sterile marriage to an ailing, intellectual husband; to sustain herself—and indeed the marriage—she invents an imaginary lover. Her husband doesn't guess this. In life, Lowell was susceptible to rumor about Jean's amorous fancies: there is evidence in letters that he was at various times led to believe she was interested in one or another of his friends, and that violent quarrels could result from these suspicions. With these two elements in mind—her restlessness, his jealousy—the central scene of "The Mills of the Kavanaughs" can easily be read as a parable of his marriage to Jean Stafford. In it, Anne Kavanaugh is in bed with her husband and dreams that she is being seduced by a young boy. Harry wakes and hears her speaking to her imaginary lover, attacks her in a jealous rage and then, in remorse, tries to destroy himself. The scene presents an extraordinary tangle of sexual angers and anxieties. It is worth quoting at some length (the "snowplow" mentioned in the first stanza here appears in Stafford's story and—years later—in "The Old Flame,"[79] where there is also reference to Stafford's "ghostly imaginary lover" whom "No one saw"):

> "You went to bed, Love, finished—through, through, through.
> Hoping to find you useless, dead asleep,
> I stole to bed beside you, after two
> As usual. Had you drugged yourself to keep
> Your peace? I think so. If our bodies met,
> You'd flinch, and flounder on your face. I heard
> The snowplow banging; its eye-headlights set
> On mine—a clowning dragon—so absurd,
> Its thirty gangling feet of angled lights
> Red, blue and orange. . . .
>
> . . . Then I slept. Your fingers held. . . .

> "You *held* me! 'Please, Love, let your elbows . . . quick,
> Quick it!' I shook you, 'can't you see how sick
> This playing . . . take me; Harry's driving back.
> Take me!' 'Who am I?' 'You are you; not black
> Like Harry; you're a boy. Look out, his car's
> White eyes are at the window. Boy, your chin
> Is bristling. You have gored me black and blue.
> I am all prickle-tickle like the stars;
> I am a sleepy-foot, a dogfish skin
> Rubbed backwards, wrongways; you have made my hide
> Split snakey, Bad one—*one!*' Then I was wide
> Awake, and turning over. 'Who, who, who?'
> You asked me, 'tell me who.' Then everything
> Was roaring, Harry. Harry, I could feel
> Nothing—it was so black—except your seal,
> The stump with green shoots on your signet ring."

Harry tries to strangle her; she threatens to "shout it from the housetops of the Mills" that her husband is mad, that he has tried to kill his wife "for dreaming." The next scene in Anne's reverie shows Harry:

"Looking in wonder at your bloody hand—
And like an angler wading out from land,
Who feels the bottom shelving, while he sees
His nibbled bobber twitch the dragonflies:
You watched your hand withdrawing by degrees—
Enthralled and fearful—till it stopped beneath
Your collar, and you felt your being drip
Blue-purple with a joy that made your teeth
Grin all to-whichways through your lower lip."

Harry doesn't recover his sanity; he lives on for a short time—"to baby-smile into the brutal gray / Daylight each morning" and to stare unknowingly at his "charts of . . . New England birds." What little we see of Harry's madness, in fact, has echoes of Lowell's later descriptions of his father's terminal days. And there are other strands in the poem that have as much to do with Boston as they do with events at Damariscotta Mills. Thus, at times, Anne is identifiably Stafford as Persephone—trapped in the underworld, half worshiping, half loathing her dead husband, but finally rejoicing in her freedom from his sexless tyranny. At other times the voice in which Anne despises Harry is more like the voice Lowell might have imagined his mother using to speak of *her* dead husband— although Lowell had begun writing the poem in 1948, it was completed after his father's death. Who else, one thinks, but Charlotte could he have had in mind when Anne declares:

"My husband was a fool
To run out from the Navy when disgrace
Still wanted zeal to look him in the face."

Harry's naval career in the poem might even be viewed as the kind of career Lowell would have had if he had been his father's son: it ended at Pearl Harbor.

Altogether, then, *The Mills of the Kavanaughs* is a confused, self-punishing, bleakly secular performance—and a crucial one in Lowell's development. But if one can catch his "own" voice—Lowell as Lowell—in the noise of those berating female voices he invents, then it is a voice that is perilously close to despair. If anything is yearned for in the book, it is silence, space, "sea-room"; in life, he seems to say, these must be stolen, but not so in death: "All's well

that ends: / Achilles dead is greater than the living." And it is surely
Lowell and not his Stafford derived heroine who speaks the anguished closing lines of "Her Dead Brother":

> O Brother, a New England town is death
> And incest—and I saw it whole. I said,
> Life is a thing I own. Brother, my heart
> Races for sea-room—we are out of breath.

After more Mozart and Strauss in Vienna ("the most dramatic show . . . in the world"[1]), Lowell and Hardwick arrived at Salzburg in July 1952. The Seminar in American Studies was held in an eighteenth-century rococo castle called Schloss Leopoldskron—it would have been hard to find a less mundane location for this multilingual gathering of some one hundred poets, artists and musicians from all over Europe. Lowell was entranced. After nearly two years in Europe he was no longer just a "literary man": his whole disposition now was to seek comparisons, connections, genealogies—painting, music, poetry held common ground, and that ground was international. And here was a castleful of European creativity. He had been assigned a group of about twenty poets, but his task was vague enough for him to be able to range as widely and excitedly as he pleased. In a matter of days, Shepherd Brooks, the seminar's director, has recalled, "he developed an extraordinary following. There was a series of very intense seminars. People were almost passionately involved with him—with his ideas."

Hardwick looked on apprehensively, and later wrote to Charlotte Lowell:

Cal was a huge success at the Seminar. I don't like to pay him empty compliments but as it worked out he was a gift from heaven for the whole session; he probably is, as much as anyone can be, a good representative of an intellectual American and he is also in love with Europe and has spent so much time on European literature and history in these last two years. It all paid off wonderfully. But the whole thing was exhausting simply because it was so stimulating, and he responded to nearly every one of the 100 students and worked much too hard, organizing poetry readings in nearly every known tongue, studying German poetry with a tutor on the side.[2]

By his own account, Lowell presented "all American poetry from Emerson to Jarrell." He organized readings in French, German and Italian—"which meant studying the stuff pretty intensely myself" —and gave seminars on Chaucer, Pope and Wordsworth:

My triumph and my most pretentious moment was a shot at Achilles' speech over one of Priam's sons, prefaced by "Greek quantities are anybody's guess": meaning, I think, verve must excuse sloppiness.[3]

He met a music student called Giovanna Madonia and, in Hardwick's phrase, "took up" with her. Salzburg was Mozart's birthplace, and Lowell now saw himself as a serious student of music. A real-life Italian with connections at La Scala was not to be viewed lightly. And, as with the Stafford/Buckman interlude, he expected his wife to sympathize with his intense new friendship.

It is probable that Lowell had been on the verge of a second breakdown in September 1951; then he had instinctively sought refuge and stability in Amsterdam. This time, though, he couldn't travel north, and in the souped-up atmosphere of Salzburg there was no possibility that he would simply "stop," "calm down" or "take it easy." For Lowell, the enticements of Art were supremely—some would say destructively—"not of this world." A few days before the end of the seminar—towards the end of August—he was missing for a day. He was eventually found wandering alone near the Austrian/German frontier and brought back to the Schloss. Shepherd Brooks describes what happened next:

Then the next night I came back to the castle about eleven and there were a number of police cars outside. My assistant told me that all the faculty were at one end of the castle and at the other Professor Lowell was on the top floor surrounded by police. . . . They were Austrian police. I met with John McCormick and Dr. Jerome Bruner and an Austrian psychiatrist who had come from the city hospital to discuss the situation. Cal was barricaded in his room and wouldn't come out.[4]

It was proposed that Lowell be taken to the city hospital, but Brooks and his staff opposed this; it would surely make things worse for

Lowell, "who lived so much in words," to be confined in a hospital where he couldn't understand the language. At this time Austria was still under occupation, and the American Army had its headquarters at Salzburg. Brooks contacted the military police, and, in a bizarre scene, the MP's came out to the castle and replaced the civil police who were standing guard outside Lord Weary's castle. Brooks recalls:

> A message then came through that Cal would not come out for anybody except me. So I went to his room—there was this surprisingly small military policeman standing just outside his door, rather frightened, a Southern boy. I went in, and there was Cal wearing just a pair of shorts, looking wild and terribly strong, and charged with adrenaline. I wasn't entirely sure what was going to happen next.[5]

Lowell agreed to go in the ambulance, but when he arrived at the Salzburg military hospital it was found that the six "violent rooms" were filled. After much argument, the army agreed to take Lowell in for one night, provided that someone stayed with him. Brooks's colleague Jerome Bruner volunteered. The army pedantically refused to take any further responsibility, and refused also to issue an order transferring Lowell to the nearest other military hospital —in Munich: it was somehow bureaucratically impossible for a Salzburg ambulance to cross the German frontier. The following day Brooks and a by now totally exhausted Bruner (Lowell had not slept all night) decided to smuggle their sick charge over the border in a private car. They set off with some nervousness:

> On the way Lowell kept talking about how terrible one lot of people were—the Austrians or Germans. I can't remember. He had categorized everybody in the one country as evil and everybody in the other as good. The good ones had good highways, cars that worked, trees that grew, happy ducks, and the peasants were attractive. The other had the opposite. Anyway, we had this little procession across the frontier—two cars, one with Cal and me and Jerry and the other with Elizabeth and my wife Esmé. And it was important to keep Esmé and Elizabeth's car out of sight—so Cal wouldn't notice. Jerry was in the front seat and Cal in the back of this tiny Hillman Minx car. Cal's shoulders were almost as wide as the seat. I could see his eyes in the rearview mirror—everything he said was exaggerated and he was having *fun*. He was creating his own reality and then responding to it, and everyone else had to go along with

it. It was extraordinary. So—it's almost 60 miles, the trip. It was pretty alarming. I felt at any moment he might put his arms around my throat, and that would have been the end of us.[6]

One particularly tricky moment came when Lowell suddenly remembered that the seminar still had three or four days to run and he hadn't written reports on any of his students. Brooks said, "Why don't you tell us now and I'll try to remember and then write it up when I get back to the Schloss." Lowell looked skeptical, but once he was launched, the day was saved: "He spent the rest of that trip describing the academic and artistic—as he saw them—qualifications of some fifteen or twenty poets and writers. And it was as if he had known each of them intimately."

When the car reached the hospital, Lowell developed a limp in his right leg; it was partially fractured, he said, and shorter than the other, and *this* was why he needed hospital attention, *this* was what the whole trip was about, *this* was why he had been held overnight at Salzburg, and so on. At first the Munich hospital's admissions sergeant said that he had no authority to accept a civilian, but Brooks and Bruner pleaded that Lowell was part of "America's national treasure," that he was ill and badly needed treatment: "So the sergeant bless him—in the great American tradition said, 'O.K., if he's that important, he's admitted. We'll sort out the details later.'"

So he was installed—in a locked ward full of disturbed military personnel. Hardwick took lodgings in a hotel in Munich's Schillerstrasse and visited the hospital each day. On her first visit she found Lowell rather pathetically trying to "get to know" his fellow patients:

He's just as preoccupied with the other patients as he was with the students. But this hospital is a terrible, terrible place for him. The other patients are of very low mentality; they don't like Cal at all and he's trying to talk to them, tell them what's what, etc. I'm afraid this terrible environment will cause an increase, if there are too many arguments, etc.[7]

Whether or not these arguments took place, Lowell's sojourn in the Munich jail did teach him something about earthy American vernacular—see "A Mad Negro Soldier Confined at Munich":

"We're all Americans, except the Doc,
a Kraut DP, who kneels and bathes my eye.
The boys who floored me, two black maniacs, try
to pat my hands. Rounds, rounds! Why punch the clock?

In Munich the zoo's rubble fumes with cats;
hoydens with air-guns prowl the Koenigsplatz,
and pink the pigeons on the mustard spire.
Who but my girl-friend set the town on fire?

Cat-houses talk cold turkey to my guards;
I found my *Fraulein* stitching outing shirts
in the black forest of the colored wards—
lieutenants squawked like chickens in her skirts.

Her German language made my arteries harden—
I've no annuity from the pay we blew.
I chartered an aluminium canoe,
I had her six times in the English Garden.

Oh mama, mama, like a trolley-pole
sparking at contact, her electric shock—
the power-house! . . . The doctor calls our roll—
no knives, no forks. We file before the clock,

and fancy minnows, slaves of habit, shoot
like starlight through their air-conditioned bowl.
It's time for feeding. Each subnormal boot-
black heart is pulsing to its ant-egg dole."[8]

If the character portrayed here was at all typical, it is clear that
Hardwick had good reason to be worried. Lowell's attitude to Hardwick remained unpredictable: he would try to goad her into argument or enrage her with insults ("Everybody has noticed that
you've been getting mighty dumb lately"[9]), but would become
anxious and suspicious if his vehemence failed to reduce her to tears:
"I can hardly bear it for more than five minutes. . . . These mixed
feelings terrify and oppress me, because I don't know how to respond for his own good."[10]

Inevitably, there were Lowellian moments of high comedy.
Hardwick recalls being summoned by the head of the hospital to

discuss the "case" and being asked for details of Lowell's army record:

> And I said: "Well, he didn't have an army record. He was a conscientious objector." And the lieutenant or whoever he was started screaming: "Get that son of a bitch out of here!" And I said: "But he's an American citizen. He's got no place to go."[11]

Of another visit, Hardwick wrote at the time to Robie and Anne Macauley:

> I can't resist one funny thing—there are many others, but I'm too gloomy today to remember them. Cal says Hiss is innocent and that his testimony was mostly a joke; full of a peculiar kind of wit like *mine!* At that point, I gave a strained, ha, ha.[12]

And the next day, when Hardwick called on Lowell's doctor for a report on her husband's progress, she was told: "He's fine. He's left the Church and wants to join the Army." Hardwick commented, "Dear old Cal, a born joiner"; and, at the end of the same letter, added, "I'm much more cheerful now and will keep an eye on Cal to be sure he doesn't recover and get shipped to the Korean front."[13]

Hardwick was able to write these letters to the Macauleys because they had been at Salzburg and witnessed Lowell's accelerating mania (indeed had been on the receiving end of some of his aggression), but she was anxious that this new episode be kept secret: "Given the tragedy of these attacks, the most important thing is to shield him when he's recovered." On August 25 she wrote again to the Macauleys:

> I want to impress on you the importance of not saying anything to *anyone* about this. If it "gets out" then you must minimize it, because he really is going to be well soon. I think I have managed the Seminar part as well as possible, and if there is not too much difficulty from American gossip filtering back from the school I'm sure I can pull Cal through the recovery period without too much pain.[14]

By October a rumor had reached Boston that Lowell had "suffered another severe mental breakdown," and Charlotte was writing angrily to Merrill Moore, blaming him—it would seem—for having mishandled the 1949 episode. By then, however, Hardwick had arranged for Lowell to be moved from the army hospital to a sanatorium at Kreuzlingen, in Switzerland:

> He still wasn't very well. But somebody had told us about this hospital in Switzerland. I can't describe to you the state we were in, with these old beaten-up suitcases—all this was travel by train, third class and so forth, no money, nothing, and Cal was in bad shape. He was so knocked out that he couldn't carry our three years' worth of suitcases —and I remember lugging them on to the train. But we got to this wonderful place—wonderful. Binswanger Sanatorium in Kreuzlingen.[15]

Lowell was *"utterly heartbroken,"* "shattered and ashamed,"[16] she said; he knew that he had behaved badly at Salzburg, but "since there are no great events to work through, he tries to recall feeling and tone, but he can't."[17] Once at Kreuzlingen, though, there was an immediate improvement; the place was spectacularly beautiful, set on a lake, and the amenities were luxurious:

> They clearly have the exquisite idea that the only thing wrong with mental patients is that they haven't enough comfort, service and good hotel management. In our case they were right, because we giggled all day long like a coal miner at the Ritz, in our connecting beautiful rooms, collapsed with sensuality in the deep baths and gasped at the four meals a day. All this for both of us at $15 a day. The horrid Munich cost that much for Cal alone.[18]

On September 15 Lowell wrote to the Macauleys:

> This is how the world looks when a man subsides—i.e. like home. We're even staying in a house that might have been designed by my grandfather. We're snugly resting together and doing Sunday crossword puzzles in preparation for Venice, to which we go in two days. Please forgive me for being such a vehement bore all summer. Teaching's strong medicine for the idle. . . .[19]

Later, Lowell was to describe the Salzburg episode to his mother: "Due to Elizabeth's alertness, the attack never went much beyond a state of nervous excitement," it was "a very mild repetition of the trouble that reached its climax before in Chicago and Bald Pate [*sic*]":

> in a period of twenty days I went through the three stages of exuberance, confusion and depression, and can now safely say it's all definitely over, without any likelihood of relapse or return. . . . I write all this to ease your mind, and perhaps a little out of pride so that you will appreciate my dear and intelligent Elizabeth. P.S. I'm not anxious to build up a reputation for poetic instability, so please reassure the Parkers.[20]

This was written on October 19; by then Lowell and Hardwick had moved on to Rome. After Kreuzlingen, they traveled with Allen Tate and Stephen Spender to Venice, where there was to be yet another "conference on the artist in the modern world" (this one organized by UNESCO). Lowell wisely kept to the sidelines of this portentous rally, but stayed on in Venice for three weeks—indeed, "did every stone of it"[21]—and then visited Padua, Verona and Torcello before settling into the "tremendous, quiet, slow tremendousness of Rome"[22] for the remainder of the winter; as Hardwick wrote:

> Now we are in Rome. Since I sent the postcard we have moved round the corner to the Pensione California. We have two rooms and plan to stay all winter, not looking for an apt. Actually, at least for this period of our lives, we have suddenly found by accident exactly what we want—two rooms in a pensione. It's just what we need, no household, no puttering about all day, and real privacy for working. Since we've been married Cal and I have spent 6 months of every year in a miserable furnished room together while travelling. The other six months were spent furnishing and managing a new apt. and then dismantling it. So far we are thrilled as babies with our new arrangements, and we are both working.[23]

Lowell was working on a poem for George Santayana, who had died earlier in the year, and in letters about his own work he continually talks of "going into new country," of not repeating his "old tricks."[24] In November he wrote to Allen Tate, "I'm full of stuff I had no notion of saying before,"[25] and a month later to Peter Taylor:

I haven't been writing at all until the last two months. . . . It's hell finding a new style or rather finding that your old style won't say any of the things that you want to, and that you can't write it if you try, and yet the petrified flotsam bits of it are always bobbing up where you don't want them.[26]

Lowell could now see Rome as a recuperative interlude; after two months there he began to compare its attractions with those of "the Maine countryside," a comparison farfetched enough to suggest that the city's fascination was very nearly spent. He began to talk more determinedly about getting back to work, of the need for "solitude and sweat."[27] Salzburg was now in the past, and—in any case—it had been only a mild attack. There was no longer any need to hide or to apologize; nor did he need to "take in" any more of Europe. The requirement now was to consolidate, to do something with whatever it was that he had learned from his two years of exile. By December his letters had become busier and wittier. He had been offered a job at Iowa as "resident lecturer in creative writing," and although the original intention had been to stay on in Rome until the summer, Lowell now felt:

We're getting much too poor to be proud, which is no fun and beyond the help of loans. It isn't just money, though, it's also a feeling of deracinated idleness, or rather a vision of such feelings increasing in the future—like lying in bed an extra two hours some half hungover morning, and delighting in the first hour and brooding greasily through the second and calling it pleasure or "life" as Cousin Ghormley would say.[28]

He accepted the Iowa job—which would be February through May —and also wrote to Ransom offering his services for the 1953 School of Letters (to be held that year at Bloomington):

I'd like to give a course called something like *Couplet, Blank Verse and Lyric*. It would be an unchronological survey of English poetry, in which I'd use the fixed metrical patterns as a jumping-off point for various comparisons of craft and content, and to show what tricks and limitations each poet has to work with.[29]

Lowell had completed versions of two poems while in Rome— "Epitaph of a Fallen Poet" (later to become "Words for Hart Crane")[30] and "Santayana's Farewell to His Nurses" (later "For

George Santayana, 1863–1952"),[31] and even in their earliest forms they showed that the "new country" Lowell was contemplating for his work was to involve some sort of quarrel with the regular iambic line. The School of Letters lectures would, he clearly thought, be part of this same exploration.

In fact, he completed one other work during this period, and this was in traditional meter. Lowell quotes it in a letter to Tate about Eisenhower's November 1952 election victory:[32]

Ike is a sort of symbol to me of America's unintelligent side—all fitness, muscles, smiles and banality. And Stevenson was so terribly better than one had a right to expect. We too feel too hurt to laugh. However, it's made me break into song. How's this to the tune of Yankee Doodle:

> Came to Boston, gave his speal [sic]
>   Smart as a buck pheasant:
> All those teeth inside his smile—
>   My god they're incandescent!
>
> His face is on your TV screen,
>   Got up with pancake powder,
> When he's scraped the barrel clean,
>   You'll see him swim in chowder.
>
> See me like an octopus,
>   A-hugging up Bill Jenner,
> I'd like to bust the bugger's puss
>   But Mamie loves a winner.
>
> My ghosts have told me something new
>   I'm marching to Korea;
> I cannot tell you what I'll do
>   Crusading's the idea
>   Yankee Doodle keep it up etc.

In January 1953 Lowell and Hardwick traveled back to the United States—in a ship carrying five hundred seasick immigrants to Canada—and on arrival in New York made straight for the Plaza bar: "we got a bill for $9 before we had barely eaten a potato chip and at that moment we knew we were at home."[33] From New York, they paid a short visit to Boston before journeying to Iowa. "I think

I really needed Europe to see how beautiful New England is," wrote Lowell;[34] and Hardwick was similarly re-beguiled. Boston was, she wrote, "enchanting, a really lovely city."

At any rate, it seemed so for three days, until they were reminded what living there would actually be like—until, that is, "the horrid reality of Mrs. L. battered and crushed us and we got on the train to Iowa in tears."[35] Lowell, Hardwick wrote, would gladly settle in Boston "for life"

> if it weren't for Mrs. Lowell. She is impossible, though; the detail of that judgement is infinite, but what it amounts to in the end is that in her presence all the joy goes out of existence. . . . there is not even a little corner left which you can fill up with affection or humor or respect or pleasure.[36]

At Iowa they moved into a comfortable three-room apartment and proceeded "frantically" to catch up on two years' worth of books and periodicals. Lowell's teaching duties were not strenuous —he had twenty-three poets in his charge and they would bring him their "life-works" two days a week, and he also undertook a course on French poetry: "a subject in which I have to acquire and give out knowledge almost simultaneously."[37] Visits from Tate and Peter Taylor enlivened the routine, but altogether, Lowell wrote in March, "life in Iowa is a pretty dormant, day to day thing."

He seems not to have been writing much. He was reworking the poems he had begun in Rome, and had completed "three or four highly-wrought short poems"—probably including "A Mad Negro Soldier" and "The Banker's Daughter" (he had, by February 1953, already published his first version of "Words for Hart Crane" and a poem for Ike's "Inauguration Day," and his Santayana poem came out in the Spring 1953 issue of *Perspectives USA*). In March 1953 he wrote to Peter Taylor:

> I'm at work on a long monologue. It's against my beliefs though. In this age of mounting populations in print nothing should go over 25 lines. What does War and Peace have that isn't more pregnantly said in a one-line Japanese—what shall I call it? "Westerly the blossoms of the apricot crumble against the shadow of the bamboo fishing pool." That's the way one of my poets writes.[38]

In April 1953 Lowell was offered the Chair of Poetry at the University of Cincinnati, an appointment that would run from January through June 1954. He was tempted but a trifle daunted; the job, he thought, would demand "written, publishable lectures, in fact a critical book. The prospect makes me feel squint-eyed, home-made and illiterate."[39] But the money was good, and since their brief visit to Boston in January Lowell and Hardwick had been spending a lot of time talking about money. In spite of Mrs. Lowell, they had decided that New England, if not Boston itself, was where they would eventually wish to settle. They had also decided that they were weary of apartment living. In April, Lowell was writing to his cousin Harriet in Washington that he and Hardwick hoped to buy a house "somewhere in New England."[40] The prospect of the Cincinnati job would make it possible for Lowell to borrow against his trust fund, and Iowa would always be prepared to have him for one term a year:

> I feel increasingly that Boston itself—the living twentieth century Boston at least as much as the old colonial Boston—is what I was born in and that only a sort of blind (O and I think necessary rebellion made me turn from it. That is I think I am now adult enough to be fairly conventional if not "proper" outwardly, and not shock (or be shocked by) people. One doesn't want to change too much though.[41]

Lowell accepted the Cincinnati job, spent the summer teaching at the School of Letters at Bloomington, and from there (feeling "seedy and subdued"[42]) he and Hardwick traveled to Gambier to spend August with the Taylors, Ransoms and Macauleys. Throughout, though, they had been searching and then negotiating for their New England home, and by September they had bought it: a house in Duxbury, Massachusetts, near Plymouth and an agreeable forty miles from Boston:

> It's a section heavy with Pilgrim history and monuments and immortalized by Longfellow; but charming, with a three mile beach. . . . the house was built in 1740 and has a 1950 oil furnace.[43]

It also had three acres of land, and Lowell looked forward to being "Mr. Lowell of Duxbury." Roof repairs were needed, though, and the house would not be ready for living in until the spring of 1954; but even Charlotte Lowell considered it had "possibilities" (although, according to Hardwick, "she seems in doubt that we, two middle-aged *infants*, will realize them"[44]).

Charlotte herself had spent a restless, irritable year in Boston, and had decided to go on a winter holiday in Europe. She had taken Italian lessons during the summer, and had rejected Merrill Moore's offer of a full-time job. Moore was concerned about her and, in July, had written an odd letter to Elizabeth Hardwick, suggesting that he and Charlotte might collaborate in writing "a book about Bobby, titled background of a poet, dealing with his early life up to the day he left Boston to go south and meet Ransom. This would cover the Boston period, St. Mark's and the fling at Harvard." Moore seemed to think that such a task would be good therapy for Charlotte, but when he proposed it to her he was given "a brush off":

> What worries me about Mrs. Lowell is that she is going off alone and really with no goal. She is studying Italian and is having a good time this summer, but I think it is tragic when women who are intelligent reach her age and are what I call disorganized. That is to say they slip; they spend a good deal of time in petty intrigue; they think mainly about themselves and on the whole, I can't think of it as a truly satisfactory life. . . .
> . . . I still wish she could be encouraged to collect or try to get together material for such a biographical sketch.
> Such a book was done was done [*sic*] about Rimbaud. I have a copy of it. Another was done about D. H. Lawrence recently. I think Bobby's life is as interesting (to me it is more so) as either of these men, so I wonder if you would explain it to Bobby and ask him what he thinks.[45]

Perhaps regrettably, nothing came of this enterprise, but Lowell did share Moore's unease about his mother's journey. In the month before she set off, he spent two weeks in Boston completing the purchase of the Duxbury house and was laid low with mysterious abdominal pains (eventually diagnosed as constipation). But it was the first time he had been alone with his mother for any length of time since 1951: "We were alone," he later said, "and talked over almost everything. That's how it was."[46] Also, perhaps prompted by these talks and by Moore's biographical suggestion, Lowell had been reading—rather, "gulping"—Freud: "I am a slavish convert," he wrote to Hardwick. "Every fault is a goldmine of discoveries. I am a walking goldmine. . . . It's all too much (especially while staying with mother). I long to be back."[47] Hardwick replied that she too had been doing some self-analysis ("mostly it's that baffling question of why one tortures the person he most loves and upon whom his happiness depends") and had just as instructively been studying a life of Browning:

> It seems that famous marriage was not at all propitious for writing in his case—he did most of his work before and after! And their relationship, intense as it was, was very peculiar; he kept saying "I put myself entirely in your hands." And she kept replying in horror, "Oh, no, you've got it all wrong. I want to put myself in yours." . . . But one should not draw private lessons from public history.[48]

Whatever small crisis was simmering here, it seems to have cooled down with Charlotte's departure for Europe on October 17. Charlotte telephoned Lowell in Iowa the night before she left, sounding terrified. "The poor old soul doesn't really want to go to Europe," Hardwick thought; it was even possible that the whole trip was a reproof to Boston, to those who she felt were neglecting her in her widowhood.[49]

For Lowell, there were almost too many coincidences in the air: Freud, his mother's trip, another house to be fixed up and settled into. And he was genuinely anxious about the Cincinnati lectures. Back at Iowa, he began teaching Homer in the original (with Hardwick as one of his students), supported the Iowa football team and joined a music club. The winter passed without incident, and by February 1954 he and Hardwick were safely installed in suburban Cincinnati. Some two weeks after their arrival, a cable reached them from Italy (four days late, having been sent to the wrong address in Boston): Charlotte had suffered a stroke and was in the hospital in Rapallo. Lowell took a plane from Cincinnati to Boston to New York to London to Paris. In Paris he contacted Blair Clark, who was working there as a CBS correspondent. Clark recalls:

> He stayed the night with me in Neuilly on his way to his mother. I had the feeling that he should immediately have gone to Rapallo if he wanted

to see his mother alive. But he didn't. He was in the early stages. I knew the symptoms by that time—he couldn't sleep, sat up all night talking and drinking and so on. Everything was racing. I would have gone down with him the next day but I just couldn't. I went down two days later—by this time his mother had died. She'd died that night—while he stayed with me.[50]

Lowell arrived at Rapallo (via Milan) at twelve-thirty on the night of Sunday, February 14. Charlotte had died an hour earlier, having had a second stroke. She had not known that her son was on his way, and in any case "she never really knew where she was." The doctors told Lowell that she had high blood pressure and arteriosclerosis and "couldn't have lasted long even if she had stayed at home."[51] To Hardwick he wrote: "Pretty rough. I spent the morning with her nurse who only speaks Italian, both of us weeping and weeping. I mean I spent it in the room with her body!"[52] Lowell describes this same morning in an unpublished prose piece he wrote some months after the event:

I arrived at Rapallo half an hour after Mother's death. On the next morning, the hospital where she died was a firm and tropical scene from Cezanne: sunlight rustled through watery, plucked pines, and streaked the verticals of a Riviera villa above the Mare Ligure. Mother lay looking through the blacks and greens and tans and flashings from her window. Her face was too formed and fresh to seem asleep. There was a bruise the size of an ear-lobe over her right eye. The nurse who had tended Mother during her ten days dying, stood at the bed's head. She was a great gray woman and wore glasses whose diaphanous blue frames were held together with a hair-pin. With a flourish, she had just pulled aside the sheet that covered Mother's face, and now, she looked daggers at the body, as if death were some sulky animal or child who only needed to be frightened. We stood with tears running down our faces, and the nurse talked to me for an hour and a half in a patois that even Italians would have had difficulty in understanding. She was telling me everything she could remember about Mother. For ten minutes she might just as well have been imitating water breaking on the beach, but Mother was alive in the Italian words. I heard how Mother thought she was still at her hotel, and wanted to go walking, and said she was only suffering from a little indigestion, and wanted to open both French windows and thoroughly air her bedroom each morning while the bed was still unmade and how she kept trying to heal the haemorrhage in her brain by calling for her little jars and bottles with pink plastic covers, and kept dabbing her temples with creams and washes and always, her quick cold bath in the morning and her hot aromatic bath before dinner. She kept asking about Bob and Bobby. "I have never been sick in my life." *Nulla malettia mai! Nulla malettia mai!* And the nurse went out. *Qua insieme per sempre.* She closed the door, and left me in the room.

That afternoon I sat drinking a cinzano with Mother's doctor. He showed me a copy of Ezra Pound's Jefferson and/or Mussolini, which the author had personally signed with an ideogram, and the quotations, "*Non . . . como bruti . . .*"[53]

On the Tuesday following his mother's death, Lowell went to Florence to pick up luggage she had left there, returning to Rapallo on the following day. He then helped to organize a small Episcopalian service in Rapallo's red-brick English chapel; for this he had purchased "a black and gold baroque casket that would have [been] suitable for burying her hero, Napoleon at Les Invalides":

And it wasn't disrespect or even impatience that allowed me to permit the undertakers to take advantage of my faulty knowledge of Italian and Italian values, and to overcharge me, and to make an ugly and tasteless error. They misspelled Mother's name on her coffin as *Lowel*. While alive Mother had made a point of spelling out her name letter by letter for identification. I could almost hear her voice correcting the workmen. "I am Mrs. Robert Lowell of One Seventy Marlborough St. Boston, L,O,W,E, *double* L."[54]

(In a letter to Blair Clark dated March 11, 1954, Lowell has the misspelling as "Charlotte Winslon," and in the poem "Sailing Home from Rapallo" as "Lovel.")

Arrangements had been made for Charlotte's body to be taken back to America by sea; the ship would leave from Genoa two days after the Rapallo service, and Lowell would accompany the coffin. Blair Clark traveled with him by train to Genoa and recalls:

on the way down Cal gave me an absolutely fascinating account of the Nuremberg trials. He'd spent a good deal of the winter of '51 reading it all up: the characters, Speer versus X and Y, the characters of the prosecutors, the witnesses. Spectacularly brilliant. I think it's accurate to say that an absolutely infallible indication of an impending manic episode was an interest in Hitler. Hitler was not a figure—but he was in the background of this two-hour monologue on the Nuremberg trials.[55]

Lowell has movingly described the ship journey to the States in "Sailing Home from Rapallo";[56] there is an almost equally powerful account of it in prose:

> On the Sunday morning when we sailed, the whole shoreline of the Golfo di Genova was breaking into fiery flower. A crazy Piedmontese Baron raced about us in a parti-colored sea-sled, whose outboard motor was, of course, unmuffled. Our little liner was already doing twenty knots an hour, but the sea-sled cut figure-eights across our bows. Mother, permanently sealed in her coffin, lay in the hold. She was solitary, just as formerly, when she took her long walks by the Atlantic at Mattapoisett in September, which she called "the best season of the year" after the summer people had gone. She shone in her bridal tinfoil, and hurried homeward with open arms to her husband lying under the White Mountains.[56]

Charlotte was buried in the family cemetery at Dunbarton, New Hampshire, and by March 11 Lowell and Hardwick were back in Cincinnati. During the Dunbarton funeral, Lowell had "in a funny way . . . felt close to Mother's friends. . . . I guess I am a black sheep forever, but it's calming not to be for a moment."[58]

I had a friend who had a formidable mother and he said he used sometimes to stop in the street and say "Is Mama *really* dead?" Not out of any sentimentality but from a genuine wonder that such a strange force could suddenly vanish. In my heart I do four times a day pay Mrs. Lowell the compliment of profound disbelief in this latest event. There is plenty of evidence to show that she seriously believed she'd outlive Cal and I thought so too and so did he! I am really sorry. She wouldn't have liked it at all! Think how furious this death would have made her and you can't help but feel it's a dirty trick.

I don't mean to be flippant about this. Mrs. Lowell's death is really a very interesting and amazing thing! I'm sure you know what I mean. And she had such a real death too! On far-away, sunny shores struck down at noon.[1]

This was Elizabeth Hardwick's candid response to news of Charlotte Lowell's death (she wrote this letter to Blair Clark while Lowell was still in Rapallo), and she was probably in part echoing what she imagined would be Lowell's own deepest reactions. For the moment, though, Lowell was not ready to engage in self-examination. His first response had been determinedly present tense: the drama of the death, the Napoleonic casket, the symbolic sea crossing, the ancestral burial at Dunbarton. The sheer metaphoric power of the whole episode was awesome. As to mourning, Lowell simply repeated that Charlotte's trip to Europe had been an appropriate "last fling," that staying in Boston would not have saved her life.

On his return to Cincinnati, though, a new voice is to be heard in Lowell's letters. There are, for instance, callously brisk accounts of his new financial gains: "Mother's death . . . has about doubled my income and given some fifty thousand dollars in cash. All very handy at this point."[2] He had become rich, he declared; he had been orphaned into a new and heady self-determination; he was starting a new life. Within ten days of returning to Ohio, he began issuing bulletins to friends:

> Dear Peter, This will come as a shock to you but I had better get it over with now. Elizabeth and I are separating. . . . I think that I will keep explanations to the minimum. We are perfectly friendly, oddly enough, still and both in very good spirits. There are no "sides." There is no great story to tell: we just exhausted each other, I more than Elizabeth, but we both did.[3]

This was written to Peter Taylor on March 19; two days later, in a letter to Blair Clark, Lowell was, if anything, more jaunty:

> I'd better start off with the *coup de foudre,* as Merrill Moore would say (You ought to have heard him struggling with various incorrect forms of this expression the last time I saw him, even spelling them out on an envelope, and so abashed and for once wordless about Mother's death!) Elizabeth and I are separating. You'll hear from her, and may have already; but my self-respect demands that I write too. But we don't have two camps and two versions. I'm not going to plumb the causes; briefly, we were worn thin by each other. We are on perfectly good terms and E is now in New York at the Algonquin looking for a comfortable apartment.[4]

Both letters, having disposed of tiresome private business, launch into speedy chat about his Cincinnati schedules, his views of Henry Adams's genius ("He's wonderful, by the way, on his and our manic-depressive New England character") and current politics: "Wasn't Nixon's speech the most servile mush you ever heard. I was amazed by Stevenson, the first long speech of his I've heard on the radio. You really learn from him."

The next round of letters, a week later, added a new piece of information; he had decided to remarry. During his week in Italy he had contacted Giovanna Madonia, the woman he had briefly, but intensely, focused on two years before in Salzburg. She had not, he'd found, "got over" him, although she had in the meantime married an Italian "man of letters" called Luciano Erba. Blair Clark recalls:

Somehow we met and had dinner with Giovanna and her husband, Luciano. It was very strange, all that. I didn't know how crazy Cal was at that point. I mean, I didn't think there was any great danger. Giovanna came to the opera and there was a lot of dodging around the pillars of La Scala to avoid the husband, and I saw some of it, like in an Orson Welles movie. I don't know quite what happened that night. Somehow the husband was spirited away—maybe I had something to do with it—and they had some time together, a couple of hours.[5]

For Madonia, Lowell's reappearance was miraculous, and on his return to the United States she wrote to him ecstatically: although, for those two years, she had "suffered, because of you, that which a normal woman suffers in two lives," she was now convinced that "you are giving life back to me: you must give me a happy life."[6] Her marriage to Erba was, she said, a torment:

Luciano lives through words, in this sense he is a real man of letters, and every day when I get home from work I am forced into conversations with him that last for hours and hours, conversations that leave me completely exhausted.[7]

With Lowell, she believed, it would be different. Lowell had told her that he had separated from Hardwick, and in response to this, Madonia (on March 21) pronounced herself

immensely happy . . . now that you are alone, only now, are you mine. I love you and you are mine and that is enough for me. That's all. Nothing other than you binds me to life. I want to live with you and for you. I want to have your child.[8]

Elizabeth Hardwick had indeed retreated to New York, but at first she was by no means sure that Lowell was entering another manic phase; he was puzzlingly "rational," she wrote to Blair Clark, even comically so:

Poor Cal! He's really a great comic character! "Uncle, honey, it's all over!" This was the way he announced the whole thing. And Blair, the way he has carried on over his mother's death is really extraordinary. I, of course, would never say this to anyone but you, but I think Cal is in an elation which is brought about by guilt feelings over his relief, quite unexpected, at his mother's death, guilt feelings complicated by his profiting from her death. Then Giovanna's telling him that she would never have married Erba except for him, that she was unhappy, etc.[9]

Lowell was producing some powerful rationalizations of their split: "Our marriage was really contra naturam for her as well as me. Marriage to me wronged her fundamental nature, her vocation—she was very gallant, but it gave her psycho-somatic jaundice."[10] And Hardwick was exhausted enough to see these—for a week or so, at any rate—as genuinely held beliefs:

> It is like coming out of a cave to be free of this. I don't know how I ever had the sense to pick up and go, but I suppose it was desperation. I feel fine, a bit bruised now and then. People have been awfully nice to me and I wish to forget the whole marriage and start all over. I want to marry a nice, sleepy old man who snoozes in front of the fire all day.[11]

Meanwhile, Lowell had announced to all his Cincinnati acquaintances that he was determined to remarry, and had persuaded them to stand with him on the side of passion. Some members of the faculty found him excitable and talkative during this period, but since the talk was always brilliant and very often flattering to them, they could see no reason to think of Lowell as "ill"; indeed, he was behaving just as some of them hoped a famous poet would behave. They undertook to protect this unique flame against any dampening intrusions from New York. Thus, when Hardwick became convinced that Lowell was indeed sick—over a period of two weeks his telephone calls to New York became more and more confused, lengthy and abusive—she ran up against a wall of kindly meant hostility from Lowell's campus allies. Her version of Lowell was not theirs, even when they were discussing the same symptoms; what to her was "mad" was to them another mark of Lowell's genius. She wrote to the chairman of the English Department pleading that he arrange for a doctor to see Lowell before the episode could gather full momentum, but was told that "Cal was fine, reading poetry, seeing friends, etc."[12] She persuaded Merrill Moore to write a letter and Moore was given the same style of rebuff. The view from Cincinnati was that the great poet was "better if anything" than he had been before; his tireless energy, his ranging eloquence were taken as signs of a newly liberated spirit and there was enchantment in the idea of his remote Italian lover—Hardwick was the ousted wife, to be handled sympathetically but firmly. As for Hardwick, her position had become, to say the least, exasperating. "I can't say: 'Cal wants to leave me, therefore he's crazy,' " but equally she didn't want Lowell "to come to with Giovanna at the docks, a not unlikely happening because if what he says is true she's moving fast."[13] And so she was. Encouraged by cables from Lowell, Giovanna was dismantling her marriage, arranging passport and visa, and—she vowed—would soon be on her way to Cincinnati.

But gradually, even some of the fond Cincinnatians began to have their doubts. One of them gave a party for Lowell, and he walked out after ten minutes, having insulted one of the other guests; he began making frequent visits to the Gaiety strip club—"every day, not just once but twice, and he didn't have enough money and one day, coming home, he jumped out of a moving taxi—to keep from paying."[14] George Ford, then of the Cincinnati English Department, remembers Lowell "talking like a machine gun with blazing eyes":

> My clearest memory of him was having him to our house for dinner, with only one other guest, Professor Carl Trehman, of the Department of Classics. Trehman asked a few questions about Virgil, Catullus, and other Roman poets, and Cal discoursed brilliantly about them, non-stop all through cocktails, dinner, and after dinner, as well. It was dazzling, but also alarming, and one felt that he might be on the edge of a breakdown. When the lectures resumed, the tensions increased. It was his habit sometimes to stop in the middle of a lecture, and stare at the audience, and give a little talk on American Republicanism. Sometimes he looked very belligerent indeed, and the Chairman of the Department, William S. Clark, became worried that some incident might happen in public. It seems weird to look back on it now, but we decided that some of the strongest and biggest members of the department should sit in the front row in case anything violent happened—being 6'2" and 200 lbs myself, I served in this capacity. But for some reason or another I was not present at the last of his appearances on the lecture platform.[15]

Lowell gave lectures on Ezra Pound and his madness, and on the darker aspects of Robert Frost's sensibility—on both occasions, Ford thought, he was "tense"; according to one member of the audience, Lowell's final lecture turned out to be on "Hitler, more or less extolling the superman ideology,"[16] and this seems to have been the one that persuaded the English Department that Lowell's "brilliance" needed to be curbed. By the time of this "Hitler lecture," though, Hardwick had decided to intervene. She traveled to Cincinnati with John Thompson and was eventually obliged to have Lowell detained under a court order. Thompson recalls:

> He had this circle of weak-minded Cincinnatians who were hiding him —from being arrested, from Lizzie. So I went out there with Lizzie— and I guess we finally called the cops on him and managed to get him committed. He would cave in at that point—once the cops came he would cave in. He'd say, "All right—I don't go willingly, but I'll go."[17]

A few Cincinnatians continued to "protect" Lowell; a lawyer called Gilbert Bettman was recruited, and it was some days before he could be persuaded that his efforts were misguided. Bettman and his wife, Elizabeth, had been on Lowell's "side" throughout, and had even written encouraging letters to Giovanna Madonia. As Mrs. Bettman now recalls: "We were not very 'up' on the course of mental illness in those days, and felt somewhat mousetrapped and awkward to be placed in a role which seemed contrary to Elizabeth's interests."[18]

Throughout these weeks of intensifying mania, Lowell had been writing frequently to Ezra Pound. On March 10 he told Pound of his mother's death:

> You didn't know my mother, so there is no point in going elaborately into our relationship. We were very much alike . . . only for most of her life she had no idea where or who she was. Most of our lives we weighed on each other like stones, but at the end (during the last ten months or so we were in a funny way speaking different languages, very close— the same metabolism, the same humor, the same boldness, and slowness.
>
> Well now to my reason for writing you—she died in the clinic of your friend Dr. Bacigaiupo—the young man, not his father. So for a week or so—I was also in Siena picking up Mother's belongings—I was very close to you. And I think I know better now my old friend, the man under the masks, under the "agenda" much better than I did—say when I was in Washington last November or December.[19]

On March 25 he announced his separation from Hardwick and his betrothal to Madonia:

> I am getting a divorce from my wife and can't afford to pay for anything I can get free. Don't you admire the casual way I introduced this

all-important item to me. I am going to marry an Italian girl—have been wasting half-dead, Ezra, now for two years.[20]

And on March 30, a week before his lecture, he writes Pound,[21] sending him a new poem, "An Englishman Abroad," which is an early draft of the poem later called "Words for Hart Crane":

Pardon this spate of letters, but for the moment you speak my language, and there's no telling how long that may continue. Yes, in spite of your Idaho humor, which is hardly the Tuscan of Ovid. Not reading Vergil is your furneral [sic], not his or mine. Imagine you thinking poor Mr. Dryden's translation had anything to *do* with the original! Sometimes I think you were born in Sioux City instead of Venezia.

Iambics—yes, you are partly right; but a man must sweat with his meters, if he is ever going to be a fabbro, and not just a prophet. Thirty-seven years has been too long for me. You've got a point, but I knew that in my cradle—you must have told me.

I can push my own Jambics [sic] where I want to—you can scratch your own back with your own. i.e. jambics.

Here's a new poem—no iambics—see what your cigar-store wooden Indian solid Kansas humor can do with it. Every syllable is meant to be there.

Con amore
Cal

Also, perhaps with this same letter, he enclosed "Adolf Hitler von Linz (Siegfried)"—it seems possible that *this* was the text of Lowell's so-called Hitler lecture. In fact, in the diary notes of Van Meter Ames, a philosopher at the university, there is complaining about the way Lowell had said of his "last poem" that "no one could follow [it] without coaching—lines from different parts of Juvenal, Dante, some of Hitler's German and some of Lowell's make-up German." The poem is a mischievous parody of Pound, and although too fidgety to make much continuous sense, it is quite clearly *not* a celebration of the Nazi "dumkopf." It reads as follows:

ADOLF HITLER VON LINZ
(SIEGFRIED)

Hitler Adolfus? Shall I weigh him?
Expende Hannibalem: quot libros in Duce summo

Invenies? Crepat ingens Sejanus.
The lungs of Luther burn. You might say
He laid his cards on the table face-up, and called the hands.
Short suits, short suits: a ten year Marathon talker
For ten years talking the State on his talking tongue
To plum-pudding. For what?
For six million Jews?
The salt of the earth has burned like flax
To dirt in the craw of the lime-pits of Auschwitz
Ach, das schreklichsten UnMench in diesem unmenchlicher Welt!
Vielleicht. Vielleicht? Das schrecklichsten!
He was. You were. *Du! Du!* Believing in Germany
Enough to break the Prussian spine.
Or the stiff neck of Europe?
Chiropractor, I went to jail
In my own country to save those German cities
You smashed like racks of clay pigeons,
Gyring through colored glass balls on Christmas trees
And Manchesters of Chicago Gothic—broken windows!
And my gorge stuck in my bowells [*sic*]
When they sent me down the Hudson, through neat Connecticut,
Through an alchemist's autumn, and hand-cuffed to two two-bit
Porto Ricans for Danbury, for my place of correction.
You nothing, whom we might have called Lucifer,
If only you'd lasted *un poco*—
una cosa picciola, animula blandula, believing in Italy,
Like no other German; no, not the Duce
Dragged for four hours by his bootstraps
Down the Uffizi *a Firenze*
By a thick Linz dumkopf cracked on the paint of Florence,
By a Barbarus Induperator, a German tourist,
Federigo Secondo, Manfredi, Winkelman,
By Freud!
Six million . . . Ma basta, un poco . . .
May the bastard rest in peace,
May the burn-out dust rest.[22]

On April 8, Lowell was committed to the Jewish Hospital in
Cincinnati on a 24-hour warrant, and Hardwick had to go through
the further ordeal of a court hearing before the committal was
confirmed. Giovanna was contacted by Blair Clark and persuaded
to await developments. Clark cabled Hardwick: GIOVANNA IN NICE

EXPECTING CAL HOTEL LUXEMBOURG STOP SHE KNOWS HE SICK FROM MAD CABLES AND RETURNS ITALY TOMORROW.[23]

The Jewish Hospital's first diagnosis was "hypomania," and it was explained to Hardwick that this latest episode was different in character from the "acute mania" of earlier attacks. In hypomania

> the patient has a lot of control, a lot of ability to function, while being at the same [time] extremely unwise, deranged. Dr. Piker says that he always tells his students that such a state is the most difficult one in psychiatry—usually even the family thinks the patient is all right and friends nearly always resent any restraint being put upon a man who has so much of his powers left.[24]

After a few days of sedative and warm-bath treatment, Lowell was put on a course of electric shock therapy, and for a month his condition fluctuated: frivolity alternating with reproach, and Giovanna still a constant (though increasingly more abstract) obsession. Hardwick wrote:

> You see he doesn't really know her—a curious state—and so he cannot know whether he prefers Giovanna to me! How disarming this wild situation is. Today, much better but still "gay" Cal said, "I'm just crazy about you, but I've got to get to Europe as soon as possible to see what Giovanna's really like. How can I say until I know!"[25]

Giovanna, it should be said, was in a somewhat similar position. As she wrote to Blair Clark:

> Cal's love for me is more phissical [sic] than anything else (actually we talked very little, also because it is very hard for me to understand his English . . .) so I know that he cannot change idea, at least untill [sic] this love will be less platonic.[26]

For Hardwick the Cincinnati breakdown was even more painful than the episodes that had centered on Chicago and then Salzburg. The Chicago breakdown had not involved hostility to her, and the Salzburg episode had been kept relatively quiet. This latest eruption was a grotesque public judgment of her marriage. At the beginning of April she had written a moving letter to Blair Clark:

I grow more doubtful every day. I am shocked and repelled by what Cal has done to me this time. It is true he doesn't seem to realize emotionally any of the real nature of his conduct; even, to mention the least, the unnecessary ungentlemanliness of it, the quite gratuitous bad manners. That is the superficial conduct, the rudeness, the meanness, the stinginess—and on a deeper level he has been of course indescribably cruel. I simply cannot face a life of this. I suppose I will sound self-righteous but no one has the slightest idea of what I've been through with Cal. In 4½ years, counting this present break-up, he has had four collapses! Three manic, and one depression. These things take time to come and long after he is out of the hospital there is a period which can only be called "nursing." The long, difficult pull back—which does not show always to others. I knew the possibility of this when I married him, and I have always felt that the joy of his "normal" periods, the lovely time we had, all I've learned from him, the immeasurable things I've derived from our marriage made up for the bad periods. I consider it all a gain of the most precious kind. But he has torn down this time everything we've built up—he has completely exposed to the world all of our sorrows which should be kept secret; how difficult these break-ups are for both of us. I've put on a show to some extent. But he has opened the curtain and let everyone look in. Now everyone knows that Cal goes off, says anything degrading he pleases about me, then comes to and I'm to nurse him back to some sort of sanity. There is nothing petty in my resentment of this—things like that cannot be pushed aside by a person of any pride.[27]

At the end of April 1954 Lowell's Cincinnati doctor—Philip Piker —wrote to Merrill Moore advising that Lowell seemed well enough to be moved to a hospital more suited to "convalescent purposes" (and also one that was rather less expensive).[28] Hardwick approached Payne Whitney, and although they were reluctant to treat patients who had not "kept up after their last treatment," they eventually took Lowell back for "extensive psychotherapy."[29] At the beginning of June—after a relatively calm and lucid interval— there was a new surge of "elation," of hostility to Hardwick, and a resurrection of the "Giovanna theme."[30] By mid-June there was a complete relapse:

Poor Cal—I feel nearly reduced to prayer at this point. Blair, isn't it terrible, this poor creature has acute mania again! I can hardly bear it for him. He's now cut off from all visitors, letters, calls—on the most

215

severly [*sic*] ill floor. I shudder to think how long it may be before he comes within reach again.[31]

When Hardwick wrote this letter to Blair Clark (on June 15), Lowell had been cut off from visitors for ten days; and the diagnosis was now leaning towards "acute schizophrenia": "This is not necessarily more serious . . . but it is very serious and while they expect Cal to pull out of this attack they don't expect the permanent relief that one gets in less serious cases."[32] In place of shock treatment, the Payne Whitney doctors were now trying "a new drug"—chlorpromazine, or (by its trade name) Thorazine.

As he relapsed, Lowell began writing again to Giovanna Madonia, who, according to Hardwick, now had for him the same function that the Catholic Church had served in earlier attacks. Lowell literally wanted to "join" Giovanna—and it was when he threatened to sign himself out of Payne Whitney in order to make tracks for Europe that the hospital had consigned him to one of their "acute" wards. As for Madonia, she knew by this time that Lowell was in a hospital, but she assumed that he had suffered a "nervous breakdown" in response to the stress of his separation from Hardwick. She too was under stress, she wrote, for similar reasons (her husband was refusing an annulment), she too was sick. As she saw it, both she and Lowell were struggling against a common foe; they had to make sure that they became "well and stable. . . . Before taking decisions we have all to be well—I am not dreaming. I want to spend my life with Cal, that's all."[33] On June 26 Madonia cabled Lowell: "I am serene and I am waiting," and on the same day wrote a letter saying that she would not travel to the United States until Lowell was completely "cured."

Lowell spent nearly three weeks in the locked ward at Payne Whitney. As with other hospitals he was admitted to, it has not been possible to consult his medical records. In this instance, though, Lowell set down his own—nonmedical—account of the "events" of June and July 1954. It is his most extensive and most richly detailed attempt to recapture the "tone and feel" of a psychotic episode:

When Mother died, I began to feel tireless, madly sanguine, menaced, and menacing. I entered the Payne-Whitney Clinic for "all those afflicted in mind." One night I sat in the mixed lounge, and enjoyed the new calm which I had been acquiring with much cunning during the few days since my entrance. I remember coining and pondering for several minutes such phrases as the Art of Detachment, Off-handed Involvement, and Urbanity: a Key to the Tactics of Self-control. But the old menacing hilarity was growing in me. I saw Anna and her nurse walk into our lounge. Anna, a patient from a floor for more extreme cases, was visiting our floor for the evening. I knew that the evening would soon be over, that the visitor would probably not return to us, and that I had but a short time to make my impression on her. Anna towered over the piano, and thundered snatches of Mozart sonatas, which she half-remembered and murdered. Her figure, a Russian ballerina's or Anna Karenina's, was emphasized, and *illuminated,* as it were, by an embroidered, middle-European blouse that fitted her with the creaseless, burnished, curved tightness of a medieval breast-plate. I throbbed to the music and the musician. I began to talk aimlessly and loudly to the room at large. I discussed the solution to a problem that had been bothering me about the unmanly smallness of the suits of armor that I had seen "tilting" at the Metropolitan Museum. "Don't you see?" I said, and pointed to Anna, "the armor was made for *Amazons!*" But no one took up my lead. I began to extol my tone-deafness; it was, I insisted, a providential flaw, an auditory fish-weir that screened out irrelevant sonority. I made defiant adulatory remarks on Anna's touch. Nobody paid any attention to me. Roger, an Oberlin undergraduate and fellow patient, sat beside Anna on the piano-bench. He was small. His dark hair matched his black flannel Brooks Brothers' suit; his blue-black eyes matched his blue-black necktie. He wore a light cashmere sweater that had been knitted for him by his mother, and his yellow woolen socks had been imported from the Shetlands. Roger talked to Anna with a persuasive shyness. Occasionally, he would stand up and play little beginners' pieces for her. He explained that these pieces were taken from an exercise book composed by Bela Bartok in protest against the usual, unintelligibly tasteless examples used by teachers. Anna giggled with incredulous admiration as Roger insisted that the clinic's music instructor could easily teach her to read more skilfully. Suddenly, I felt compelled to make a derisive joke, and I announced crypticly [*sic*] and untruely [*sic*] that Rubinstein had declared the eye was of course the source of all evil for a virtuoso. "If the eye offends thee, pluck it out." No one understood my humor. I grew red and confused. The air in the room began to tighten around me. I felt as if I were squatting on the bottom of a huge laboratory bottle and trying to push out the black rubber stopper before I stiffled [*sic*]. Suddenly, I knew [corrected in E.H.'s hand to "felt"] I could clear the air by taking hold of Roger's ankles and pulling him off his chair. By some criss-cross of logic, I reasoned that my cruel boorishness would be an act of self sacrifice. I would be bowing out of the picture, and throwing Roger into the arms of Anna. Without warning, but without lowering my eyes from Anna's splendid breast-plate-blouse, I seized Roger's yellow ankles. I pulled; Roger sat on the floor with tears in his eyes. A sigh of surprised repulsion went round the room. I assumed a hurt, fatherly expression, but all at once I felt eased and sympathetic with everyone.

When the head nurse came gliding into the lounge, I pretended that I was a white-gloved policeman who was directing traffic. I held up my open hands, and said, "No roughage, Madam; just innocent merriment!" Roger was getting to his feet; I made a stop-signal in his direction. In a purring, pompous James Michael Curley voice, I said, "Later, he will thank me." The head-nurse, looking bored and tolerant, led me away to watch the Liberace program in the men's television parlor. I was left unpunished. But next morning, while I was weighing-in and "purifying" myself in the cold shower, I sang

Rex tremendae majestatis
qui salvandos salvas gratis

at the top of my lungs and to a melody of my own devising. Like the cat-bird, who will sometimes "interrupt its sweetest song by a perfect imitation of some harsh cry such as that of the Great Crested Flycatcher, the squawl of a hen, the cry of a lost chicken, or the spitting of a cat" I blended the lonely tenor of some fourteenth century Flemish monk to bars of Yankee Doodle, and the *Mmm Mmm* of the padlocked Papagano [*sic*]. I was then transferred to a new floor where the patients were deprived of their belts, pajama-cords and shoe-strings. We were not allowed to carry matches, and had to request the attendants to light our cigarettes. For holding up my trowsers [*sic*] I invented an inefficient, stringless method which I considered picturesque and called *Malayan*. Each morning before breakfast, I lay naked to the waist in my knotted *Malayan* pajamas and received the first of my round-the-clock injections of Chloropromzene [*sic*]: left shoulder, right shoulder, right buttock, left buttock. My blood became like melted lead. I could hardly swallow my breakfast, because I so dread the weighted bending down that would be necessary for making my bed. And the rational exigencies of bed-making were more upsetting than the physical. I wallowed through badminton doubles, as though I were a diver in the full billowings of his equipment on the bottom of the sea. I sat gaping through *Scrabble* games unable to form the simplest word; I had to be prompted by a nurse, and even then couldn't make any sense of the words the nurse had formed for me. I watched the Giants play the Brooklyn Dodgers on television. . . . My head ached, and I couldn't keep count of the balls and strikes for longer than a single flash on the screen. I went back to my bedroom and wound the window open to its maximum six inches. Below me, patients circled in twos over the bright gray octagonal paving-stones of the courtyard. I let my glasses drop. How freely they glittered through the air for almost a minute! They shattered on the stones. Then every-one in the courtyard came crowding and thrusting their heads forward over my glasses, as though I had been scattering corn for pigeons. I felt my languor lift and then descend again. I already seemed to weigh a thousand pounds because of my drug, and now I blundered about nearly blind from myopia. But my nervous system vibrated joyfully, when I felt the cool air brushing directly on my eye-balls. And I was reborn each time I saw my blurred, now unspectacled, now unprofessorial face in the mirror.[34]

This account is taken from Lowell's original draft for the prose essay "91 Revere Street"; the tone in which Lowell remembers himself when "mad" is chillingly consistent with the tone he uses to recall childhood misdeeds. There is an amused, tolerant, near embarrass-ment as Lowell recalls the "mischief" he has done—in both school-room and asylum. The assault on Roger described here could almost have taken place at Rivers, and the expectation of punishment is casual but alert, just like a naughty boy's.

There is something similarly boyish in a letter Lowell wrote to Blair Clark on August 6:

I've been out of my *excitement* for over a month, I think, now, and am in good spirits, though I don't feel any rush of eloquence to talk about the past. It's like recovering from some physical injury, such as a broken leg or jaundice, yet there's no disclaiming these outbursts—they are part of my character—me at moments.

On the subject of Giovanna Madonia, Lowell said he had written to her that he "was staying married to Elizabeth":

However I wrapped my letters up in emotions (really felt at the time and made them as soft as I could). I haven't had an answer, and don't quite see what I can write her at this point. The whole business was sincere enough, but a stupid pathological mirage, a magical orange grove in a nightmare. I feel like a son of a bitch.

He wanted Clark to find out how she was: "I do know that I am responsible for whatever disturbances have happened in her life."[35]

In spite of its first side effects, Lowell had reacted swiftly to the Thorazine treatment, and Hardwick was mildly encouraged: "The most hopeful thing for the future is his extraordinary response to the new drug."[36] She was advised that Lowell's final diagnosis would, after all, be "manic-depressive" and not "schizophrenic"; the reassurance here being that schizophrenia was supposed to leave more "scarring" after an attack. By September 15 Lowell was ready to be discharged from Payne Whitney on condition that when he and Hardwick moved to Boston (where they intended to stay until the house at Duxbury was fixed), he maintain some kind of regular "psychotherapy." A fairly empty exhortation, it would seem, since —as Hardwick wrote to Clark:

> The doctors at Payne Whitney are not very hopeful about dramatic results from psycho-therapy for Cal. It isn't just putting in time with a doctor; you have to be the sort of person who can have detailed and changing insight into himself: you must do the work yourself. Of course Cal must take the psycho-therapy, but it will probably be most useful as a kind of support rather than a cure—or so they think now.[37]

At the end of September 1954 Lowell and Hardwick moved into a "half palazzo and half loft" apartment on Commonwealth Avenue. On October 24 Lowell wrote to Peter Taylor. "After months of walking in this maze, one is a little speechless and surprised to have eyes. We are both very well and send our love to you both. Cal."[38]

By February 1955 Elizabeth Hardwick was writing to friends that Lowell was "his old self again" and that he had begun work on a series of "remarkable" prose pieces: "They are reminiscences of childhood—that is the closest I can come—and I think of extraordinary beauty and interest." Lowell was at his desk each day for "sixteen hours or so and I've very nearly been feeding him through a tube."[1]

In the same month, Lowell wrote to Ransom seeking a reference for a teaching post at Boston University—he wanted a job, he said, "to keep my hand green and my mind mellow."[2] In the meantime, though, it did seem that his new prose project was discipline enough: his own retort, some would say, to the kindly promptings of the psychotherapists. An orphan and an heir, for the first time he could explore his Boston origins without any self-defensive rancor. His new therapist had encouraged him to adopt a strict daily regime—"get up at eight, shave, take walk etc"—and after their first three months in Boston Hardwick had reported: "Together we have managed so far to keep the depression from becoming incapacitating—it comes down upon us like a cloud but always lifts in a day or two."[3] The prose "reminiscences" were a way of cementing Lowell's new, timetabled calm—prose, Lowell found, need not thrive on bouts of high "enthusiasm."

Not that these pieces were mere therapeutic exercises; Lowell knew that during the later stages of this last episode his delusions had been neither Christ-like nor Napoleonic, and that more notably than in earlier episodes, there had been a regression to the infantile: the mother's boy no longer had a mother.

. . . after six or seven weeks at the Payne-Whitney Clinic, my bluster and manic antics died away. Images of my spoiled childhood ached inside me, and I would lean with my chin in my hand, and count the rustling poplars, so many leagues below me, which lined the hospital driveway and led out to the avenues of Manhattan, to life. I used to count the poplars, and gave them the names of old ladies. This one was my Great Aunt Sarah. That one was Cousin Susy Pickering. That was Cousin Belle Winslow. That was Mrs. Robbins. That was *Gaga* [the pet name of Lowell's maternal grandmother]. My grandfather Winslow had named his country house Chardesa for his children Charlotte, Devereux and Sarah.[4]

And on April 17, 1955, he wrote to Ezra Pound:

This has been a funny, eye-opening winter i.e. living in the Boston I left when I was seventeen, full of passion and without words. I suppose all young men get up the nerve to start moving by wrapping themselves like mummies from nose to toe in colored cloths, veils, dreams etc. After a while shedding one's costume, one's fancy dress, is like being flayed. I've just been doing a little piece of *Why I live in Boston*. I made it impersonal and said nothing about what I was looking for here—the pain and jolt of seeing things as they are.[5]

A further spur to autobiography came that same month, when Peter Taylor published his own autobiographical story, "1939." For Lowell, the coincidence was disturbing. What *was* this life that others found so fascinating, that Merrill Moore had wanted to "write up," that doctors were urging him to "probe," that his best friend had turned into fiction, and that had now—with his mother's death— been finally delivered into his own keeping? In response to "1939," he wrote to Taylor:

At first I was, how shall I put it, surprised and hurt—that's how the history of St. Mark's school speaks of my great-grandfather's novel, in which it was noted with surprise that Dr. Lowell's gentle humor had used members of the faculty as characters. If you'd used one of my poems instead of one of yours I think I would have sued. So I felt after reading; but since then I have [had] so many compliments—nothing I have ever written myself has ever gotten me such attention. . . . Well, I stand off, hat in hand, and thank you with grudging bewildered incomprehension. But were we really quite such monsters? Seriously, though the whole thing fascinates me—I have been trying to do the same sort of thing myself with scenes from my childhood with my grandfather, old Aunt Sarah, Cousin Belle etc. I want to invent and forget a lot but at the same time have the historian's wonderful advantage—the reader must always be forced to say "This is tops, but even if it weren't it's true." I think you've done the trick.[6]

Prose and psychotherapy aside, Lowell's first "grown-up" Boston spring was an "idle rather sociable" affair.[7] In April, Hardwick wrote to Cousin Harriet:

Everyone seems to come here, and so we feel rather more in the literary world than usual. We've had the Sitwells, Spender, John Crowe Ransom at Harvard last night, Lillian Hellman, and then magazine writers from Everywhere. T. S. Eliot is expected soon. Here in Boston we are somehow expected to do our part and so we are always giving luncheons and cocktails for the visitors and actually enjoying it all. It is alive here without being pulverizing like New York.[8]

As well as the cocktails and luncheons there were amateur theatricals and the occasional poetry reading or panel. Of these last, Lowell sardonically told Blair Clark:

poets are still a special species, like the two toed sloth, and a wonder for small audiences. Most of the poets who head discussions are formidably practical men, such as Eberhart and Macleish—they seem driven to insist that poetry is something sky-high, not only *on* the side of the angels, but *at* their elbow. My role on these occasions is to debunk. I begin to think that it is only at poetry conferences that I seem a practical man, with several strings to my fiddle.[9]

And in May he went so far as to attend the twentieth reunion of the St. Mark's Class of '35, and even persuaded Frank Parker to go along with him. But this visit could be explained away as "self-discovery":

I've been thinking back on my *break* with the boys, if I can call it that, for I was never at all close or firm with them. I think I gave myself a perhaps arbitrary dilemma, that of either sitting about inertly or of running blind. Nothing is more tantalizing than re-shaping one's silly former self; but the voice of middle-age says we are all warped old dogs set on lying in the sun and changing as little as rocks.[10]

(Lowell was thirty-eight when he wrote this letter; from now on, he would regularly affect a fatigued, world-weary tone of voice and, when "well," would usually seem older than his years. In depression, of course, he *was* fatigued, he *was* world-weary, and very often he was simply feeling the side effects of psychiatric medication; there is something touching, though, in the way he almost welcomed the label "middle-aged" as a means of explaining—to others, if not to himself—any prolonged stretches of enervation or low spirits.)

The summer of 1955 he and Hardwick spent partly in Duxbury and partly at the Castine summer residence of his cousin Harriet Winslow. Earlier in the year, Cousin Harriet had suffered a stroke and was now confined to her home in Washington. Since she herself could no longer make full use of Castine, she had offered it to Lowell as a summer retreat, an offer that would eventually make Duxbury superfluous. At Castine there was a house and a converted barn, which Lowell could use as a workplace. He later wrote of this to William Carlos Williams:

> I'm sitting in a little barn my Cousin Harriet made over and painted (against all town advice) with aluminum paint a sort of pewter color inside. It's right on the bay, which on one side looks like a print of Japan and on the other like a lake in Michigan as the rocky islands with pine trees ease off into birches and meadows.[11]

Lowell and Hardwick at once decided to buy a house in "proper" Boston. The pastoral life had never quite fulfilled its promise, and, in any case, part of the point of Duxbury had been its "safe" distance from Lowell's mother. They were now free to live anywhere they pleased.

The house they decided on was 239 Marlborough Street; "just exactly a block from the one I grew up in," Lowell wrote,[12] as if the choice had been weirdly fortuitous, and by the late fall of 1955 they had moved into a residence that was a fair copy of the one in which Lowell had spent much of his childhood. In November he wrote to Peter Taylor:

> We're having a good fall, and feel very lordly and pretentious in our new Boston house. . . . It's not really little and not at all unpretentious, and we despise everyone whose nerve for cities has failed, all country people,

all suburbanites, and all people who live in apartments, except for the Thompsons who are coming to visit this weekend. And are we priming ourselves to show off![13]

And to William Carlos Williams:

It's a unimpassioned, darkish, bricky, Londonlike street, still the mirror of propriety. . . . This is the first year since 1940 when I have spent two successive winters in the same city. We're fearfully relieved to be settled and doubt if we will ever move. We might even become Boston worthies, if it weren't for the worm of life in us.[14]

Lowell had, of course, come close to "settling down" before, and on at least two occasions the prospect had induced a lively panic; he had recoiled from Jean Stafford's nest-building efforts at Damariscotta Mills, and in the early stages of his Cincinnati illness had tried to sabotage the Duxbury move by sending abusive letters to the woman who was handling the interior decoration. But Marlborough Street, it seems, was utterly unthreatening; there is even a genuinely house-proud note in Lowell's first accounts of his new property:

The house has changed us in every way, but especially in my case: 1, I am about to explode any moment on a book-buying jag; 2, I have decided the only excuse for writing my autobiography is to make money. So I do a page a day, put in all the corn I can think of, then take my page down to Elizabeth and implore her to think of more. The book-buying is due to my not drinking, and to our for once having more unfilled shelves than can be counted.[15]

Lowell's "not drinking" had been decided on during a particularly "surly hangover mood" one Sunday in the spring and was yet another attempt to reduce the general level of "excitement." Also, in a course of drug treatment alcohol would have been "contraindicated." At first, he found that he was "twice as lazy as previously,"[16] but he had persisted throughout the summer—sustained by a bearlike pound of honey every day—and now could boast that he was at least a "harmless" driver. And in November 1955, as if to set a seal on his return to Boston, Lowell applied to rejoin the Episcopalian Church. The Reverend Whitney Hale, of the Church of the Advent on Mount Vernon Street, wrote to him as follows:

I am happy to report that Bishop Nash has formally restored you to communicant status and does not feel it is necessary for you to be "received back" by him with the usual ceremony used for Roman Catholics coming into our church inasmuch as you started out in the Episcopal church, but will do so if you desire it.

Also with your restoration I am now permitted to bless your marriage.[17]

Lowell's prose reminiscences had by now become a full-scale autobiography, and his letters throughout 1956 are full of weaving genealogies and dynastic coincidences. In February 1956 he wrote to Peter Taylor:

Just spent two days in delirious ancestor-worship, i.e. reading their writings. If my sudden line wasn't dwarfed by the Winslows, I'd say they were the most talented and charming people in the world. Have you run across any Devereuxs, Lanes, Pollocks, Mackies, Nelsons or Wilkinses?[18]

And in the same month to Harriet Winslow:

I had a little ancestor worshipping spree the other day and read up all we had in the house written by ancestors, and even worked out on four typewritten pages my family tree. How quickly it runs into the sands of the unknown. What sort of man was my grandfather Lowell, who died in his twenties, leaving only a Phi Beta Kappa key, a photograph, his name on a wall at St. Mark's school? He had only been married a few months, and Daddy, his first child was not yet born.[19]

When Ferris Greenslet was preparing *The Lowells and Their Seven Worlds* (1946), Lowell had refused to cooperate. His own copy of the book, though, is full of underlinings, and it is reasonable to assume that these were done in 1956. With Greenslet's help, he could track the fine detail of the "Traill-Spence" line and speculate about the Tyngs, the Duanes and the Myers. He could discover in himself a trace of Jewishness, of Scots; he could wistfully identify with the heroic Beau Sabreur (his great-grandfather's brother Charles, married to the sister of the celebrated Colonel Shaw and killed in the Civil War); he could conjecture about the mental illnesses that had afflicted both his great-grandfather's mother, Harriet, and her daughter Rebecca. And on the Winslow side there was equal scope for the kind of fanciful connections he delighted in; there were the Pilgrims, the frontiersmen, the Indian killers, the colonial governors, the Revolutionary War hero General Stark, and even a reputed witch—Elizabeth Hutchinson, who married Edward Winslow II (1634–82) was the granddaughter of Anne Hutchinson. And who *were* the Savages, the Davises, the Chiltons and the Ollyvers? Lowell wrote to his cousin Harriet in March 1956:

> A lot is lost and a lot was never seen and understood. We stand in our own characters, of course, and warp our own knowledge. Still, it's fascinating to see what one can fish up, clear up and write down. . . . it's like cleaning my study, like going perhaps to some chiropractor, who leaves me with all my original bones jumbled back in a new and sounder structure.[20]

The fragments of Lowell's autobiography which remain, and which are not early versions of "91 Revere Street," are mostly a series of false starts, the same page retyped, slightly revised and then seemingly abandoned. In one fragment, Lowell writes that he is working on his autobiography "literally to 'pass the time.' I almost doubt if the time would pass at all otherwise." The book, he said, would cover his early life up to 1934, the year of his first summer in Nantucket with Frank Parker. Lowell now viewed that summer as "a period of enthusiasm"; "enthusiasm" is a word he regularly uses to describe his manic episodes (the term probably derives from his reading in theology, where it would denote extreme religious zealotry, but by 1956 he would be more likely to accept the view of William Law, the eighteenth-century writer on Christian ethics and mysticism: "To appropriate Enthusiasm to Religion is the same ignorance of Nature as to appropriate Love to Religion: for Enthusiasm, a kindled inflamed spirit of Life is as common, as universal, as essential to human Nature, as Love is. . . .").[21]

Lowell felt that when his autobiography was completed, he would perhaps find that he had "*found* myself": "I also hope that the result will supply me with my swaddling clothes, with a sort of immense bandage for my hurt nerves."[22] In other words, this calm, industrious prose period of Lowell's life was a lot shakier than it seemed; every so often he would falter in his researches and stray off into agonized, present-tense unburdening:

For two years I have been cooling off from three months of pathological enthusiasm. I go to sleep now easily, but sometimes I wake up with a jar. In my dreams I am like one of Michael Angelo's rugged, ideal statues that can be tumbled down hill without injury. When I wake, it is as though I had been flayed, and had each nerve beaten with a rubber hose.[23]

And in another account, which in Lowell's manuscript runs on from his description of breaking his glasses at Payne Whitney:

Yet all this time [in context, the time-placing is a problem—"all this time" could mean the days immediately following the breaking of his glasses, or it could mean the two years' "cooling off" period, 1954–56, or, since Lowell is never reluctant to dovetail and amalgamate, it could mean both] I would catch myself asking whining questions. Why don't I die, die: I quizzed my face of suicide in the mirror; but the body's warm, unawed breath befogged the face with a dilatory inertia. I said, "My dreams at night are so intoxicating to me that I am willing to put on the nothingness of sleep. My dreams in the morning are so intoxicating to me that I am willing to go on living." Even now [i.e., in 1956] I can sometimes hear those two sentences repeating themselves over and over and over. I say them with a chant-like yawn, and feel vague, shining, girlish, like Perdita, or one of the many willowy allegoric voices in Blake's Prophetic Books. "For my dreams, I will endure the day, I will suffer the refreshment of sleep." In one's teens these words, perhaps, would have sealed a Faustian compact. Waking, I suspected that my whole soul and its thousands of spiritual fibres, immaterial ganglia, apprehensive antennae, psychic radar etc. had been bruised by a rubber hose. In the presence of persons, I was ajar. But in my dreams, I was like one of Michael Angelo's burly, ideal statues that can be rolled down hill without injury.[24]

The bulk of Lowell's manuscript "autobiography," however, is in the form of character sketches and anecdotes from childhood—his mother and grandfather are the characters most lovingly worried over, and there are some affectionately remembered minor figures. Lowell's father—the third principal—is usually made mock of, with his weakness a constant measure of the others' strength. Throughout there is a kind of double vision: the child's-eye view judged and interpreted by the ironical narrator, with a good deal of adult invention around the edges. It is a method that is particularly hard on Mr. Lowell. Lowell makes little effort to salvage any childish awe of

"Daddy" from his later hostility to the spinelessness of R.T.S. Among the "91 Revere Street" drafts, there is a touching paragraph in which Lowell explicitly confesses an injustice of this sort:

> As I try to write my own autobiography, other autobiographies naturally come to mind. The last autobiography I have looked into was a movie about a bull terrier from Brooklyn. The dog's name was, I think, *House on Fire*. The district he came from was so tough, that smoking had to be permitted in the last three pews at high mass. House on Fire's mother had been deserted by his father. House knows that his father is a great dog in the great world, either as a champion fighter or as a champion in exhibitions. House on Fire keeps saying with his Brooklyn accent, "I want to be a champ so that I can kill my father." In the end there is peace.
>
> My own father was a gentle, faithful and dim man. I don't know why I was so agin him. I hope there will be peace.[25]

Almost two-thirds of the material in Lowell's drafts is worked into "91 Revere Street," but in addition to the confessional material already quoted, there are two interesting anecdotal pieces that he also chose not to include, possibly because he found both tales so heavy with symbolism that they had become "significant to the point of being meaningless." In each case, Lowell was fascinated by the tangle of religiosexual suggestiveness, or "black magic," as he calls it. In the first story Lowell is aged three or four and the setting is Philadelphia, where, apparently, his parents got regular visits from a local Quaker lady, Martha Bent. Bent doted on the child Lowell and also developed coy and bantering relations with his father. Bob Lowell found Martha a "regular fella" because she listened to his naval yarns; Charlotte considered her "flaccid and flirtatious." As to the child Lowell: "I felt torn in two, and wanted to prove Martha both good and bad. She was an object to be wooed and despised." Martha wore around her neck "a plain black cord on which she had attached a cracked ivory elephant the color of jaundice and no bigger than a man's molar" and this modest ornament fascinated Lowell; it resembled rock candy and he wanted to possess it: "She must give me the ivory elephant. I wanted the elephant also because it was small, heavy, precious, useless, animal and the soul of Martha." Soon he does possess it; indeed, swallows it:

I was looking up and letting the ivory tap on my teeth as though it were a piece of rock candy. And then it went down. Doctors came. Mother kept saying with Gargantuan suavity, "Bobby has swallowed an elephant." Then it was unmentionably ascertained that the ivory elephant had come out in my chamber-pot. I was told that it was broken in three pieces so that I couldn't see it again. And even now I have no idea how Mother managed to mention the chamber-pot, my movement and the marvelous elephant all in one pure, smirking breath.[26]

The other story has similar ingredients: a surrogate maternal presence, a seductively (or so it seemed) sweet-tasting but forbidden token of the mother figure's "soul," a token that the child possesses, then destroys, and then a thrilling climax, an unmasking; in each story the child regains his real mother's attention by his theft of the adopted mother's "essence." The second incident in particular would have struck the adult Lowell as having been remarkably prophetic, and thus might be even more highly polished than the first. The setting is Brimmer Street in Boston, and Lowell is—he says—aged two:

When I was two years old I had a young nurse who was, herself, only eighteen or so years old and had come to Boston from Ireland. . . . Her name was Katherine. Katherine's rosary was a memorable work of religious mass-production. It was designed with a Celtic exaggeration and the beads were made of some material which had the appearance and texture of rock candy. These beads were so hard, cold and precious and of such fascination that immediately the fat, warm, wooden beads which decorated my crib lost all their appeal to me. But what I loved more than the beads of Katherine's rosary was the silver crucifix. It was heavy, intricate and important, as I could see from Katherine's awed and loving glance upon it. Katherine told me about Jesus and I regret to recall that my feelings were highly egocentric: I saw, with despair, that I was second fiddle even in my nurse's affections. And then suddenly the rosary disappeared and the house was disturbed by the mystery. I was questioned, but I merely gaped sweetly and presented myself as a figure of innocence, all sunlight and brown curls. I smiled and smiled and smiled, very much in the way my father smiled and smiled and smiled. A day or so later the rosary was found, hidden under the corner of the rug, where it had slipped by mistake according to the decision taken by the household. However, it was noticed that the Christus was missing and also, with embarrassment, that the chain of the rosary had been chewed. I returned to my denying smile, but later Mother saw me pushing a piece of paper down the register. "You will burn up the house" she said. But two days later she again saw me pushing a whole handful of paper strips down the register. "You are setting the furnace on fire," she said. I smiled and smiled, to her intense displeasure. "Yes, I know," I said. "That's where Jesus is."[27]

For nearly two years Lowell toiled on his prose reminiscences and continued tracking down remote ancestral possibilities. He would be delighted to get letters from eighth cousins in Springfield, Illinois, and to be told that the "maternal side of J. R. Lowell's ancestry has never been done justice. It was from them that he got his talent and his charm." He would compile lists of his literary antecedents and feel "mighty set up" when he managed to establish a (very) distant cousinship with Boswell.[28]

And the interest was not altogether antiquarian. On January 4, 1957, Elizabeth Hardwick gave birth to a daughter, Harriet; the Traill-Spence line of Lowells had actually been added to. In letters, Lowell seems both awed and captivated by this strange event. When, in May 1956, he had learned that he was to be a father, he wrote to J. F. Powers:

> We are in a state of tremendous excitement, we have just learned that like almost all other mortals we are to have a child . . . months ahead, but for certain unless there is some accident. It's terrible discovering that your one moral plank, i.e. an undiluted horror of babies, has crumbled! We're so excited we can hardly speak, and expect a prodigy whose first words will be Partisan Review.[29]

And again, after the birth:

> Yes, we do have a little girl, Harriet Winslow Lowell, born on the 4th of January. She is very various, yet sedate and makes her parents feel like infantile, stone-age cretins. She was born looking like the great—Ted Roethke, or times when her hair was in evidence—Churchill or Dylan Thomas. . . . Chaos grows like a snowball in our house; all values are standing on their ears.[30]

In two years Lowell had become a father, a university professor (he had taken up the Boston University job in 1956) and a house owner —all in all, a sober and industrious Bostonian. Throughout 1956 he and Hardwick had enjoyed showing off their grand new house and had won a small reputation for their stylish hospitality. When Marianne Moore visited them, she wrote to Elizabeth Bishop that she had had a "notable" tea with "R and E Lowell . . . I do like them —heartfelt, generous, genial, initiate and so prepossessing. . . ." and that she had greatly admired their "Boston-in-its-glory" residence on Marlborough Street.[31] In other words, Lowell was at last living the sort of life that Charlotte might have been impressed by. And—"tamed" and "tranquillized" by psychiatric drugs—he had avoided the "emotional excitement of poetry" for a full two years.

In March 1957 Lowell began his fortieth year with a reading tour of the West Coast; it was a strenuous trip, with readings "at least once a day and sometimes twice" for fourteen days, and he was later to describe it as an important influence on his quest for a "new style." The Beat poets had already trained Californian audiences to believe that poetry could be enjoyed by the untrained, and Lowell found himself willing to make some small compromises:

> At that time, poetry reading was sublimated by the practice of Allen Ginsberg. I was still reading my old New Criticism religious, symbolic poems, many published during the war. I found—it's no criticism—that audiences didn't understand, and I didn't always understand myself while reading.[32]

Lowell began simplifying poems as he read, adding syllables, translating Latin into English: "I'd make little changes just impromptu. . . . I began to have a certain disrespect for the tight forms. If you could make it easier by just changing syllables, then why not?"[33] In fact, Lowell's respect for tight forms had been crumbling since 1953; that is to say, he knew then (and probably earlier, with the reviews of *The Mills of the Kavanaughs*) that whatever he wrote next, it would not be in strict meter. Indeed, he had already written the odd piece that "broke meter": his poem on "Ford Madox Ford," for instance, was first published in the spring of 1954.[34]

Lowell's difficulty, however, was that rhyme and meter were for him very close to *being* the "natural speech" that William Carlos Williams and his followers were always calling for. The iambic pentameter was not an external, imposed literary method; after three books, it had become compulsive utterance. And it was probably harder for Lowell to discard rhymes than to invent them. Williams, he felt, was unique, but "dangerous and difficult to imitate." His disciples were spiritless and programmatic. Although Lowell was in regular, admiring contact with the older poet at this time and had been particularly dazzled by a reading Williams had given at Wellesley in 1956 ("somehow he delivered to us what was impossible, something that was both poetry and beyond poetry"[35]), he knew that the lessons he could learn from him would always be of the most general kind: loosen meter, abandon rhyme, use ordinary speech, introduce more characters, and so on. Even the very personal poems that Williams was writing in the mid-fifties were of a radiant simplicity that Lowell could marvel at but never think to copy: "Williams enters me, but I could never enter him."[36]

All the same, by 1957 Lowell had learned to mistrust both the means and the temper of his earlier work, the "used equipment," the "inertia of our old rhetoric and habits": for eighteen months the sober, therapeutic compromise had been to write in prose. And the compromise had been instructive. He had taken to studying prose texts in his poetry classes—"In prose you have to be interested in *what* is being said . . . it's very exciting for me, like going fishing."[37] He had discovered a (for him) new style of formal discourse— paradoxical, ironic, whimsically oblique but capable of elegiac weight. He had learned how to give voice to a wide range of what might be called the moderate emotions: affection, regret, nostalgia, embarrassment, and so on. He had become expert at contriving sentences that could be elevated and yet speakable, and had found a literary voice that could encompass something of his social self— that is to say, the teasing, mischievous, gently sardonic side of his own nature. The obvious next step for Lowell was to perceive that some, if not all, of these considerable gains could be carried over into poetry, that if elements of rhyme and meter could be injected into the sane and solid corpus of his prose reminiscences, he would in effect have found a new but "safe" function for many of the "old tricks" he had been ready to abandon. The "excitement" of poetry could vitalize and be restrained by the sturdy, detailed worldliness of prose:

> When I was working on Life Studies, I found I had no language or meter that would allow me to approximate what I saw or remembered. Yet in prose I had already found what I wanted, the conventional style

of autobiography and reminiscence. So I wrote my autobiographical poetry in a style I thought I had discovered in Flaubert, one that used images and ironic or amusing particulars. I did all kinds of tricks with meter or the avoidance of meter. When I didn't have to bang words into rhyme and count, I was more nakedly dependent on rhythm.[38]

And, of course, Lowell's prose "studies" not only suggested a new style; they also offered an almost limitless new subject. In 1976, looking back over his life's work, Lowell was to acknowledge that "the thread that strings it together is my autobiography, it is a small-scale *Prelude,* written in many different styles and with digressions, yet a continuing story. . . ."[39] In his first three books, autobiography had been oblique, almost clandestine; now he was free to be both distorting and direct. It seems never to have occurred to him that his personal history might not be of considerable public interest. And this, as Elizabeth Bishop pointed out to him, was his huge natural advantage:

And here I must confess (and I imagine most of your contemporaries would confess the same thing) that I am green with envy of your kind of assurance. I feel I could write in as much detail about my uncle Artie, say,—but what would be the significance? Nothing at all. He became a drunkard, fought with his wife, and spent most of his time fishing . . . and was ignorant as sin. It is sad; slightly more interesting than having an uncle practising law in Schenectady maybe, but that's about all. Whereas all you have to do is put down the names! And the fact that it seems significant, illustrative, American etc. gives you, I think, the confidence you display about tackling any idea or theme, *seriously,* in both writing and conversation. In some ways you are the luckiest poet I know![40]

From mid-August through October 1957 Lowell completed eleven poems in free verse—many of them turned into free verse from a first draft in couplets. He wrote to William Carlos Williams:

I've been writing poems like a house on fire, i.e. for me that means five in six weeks, fifty versions of each. I've been experimenting with mixing loose and free meters with strict in order to get one accuracy, naturelness [*sic*], and multiplicity of the prose, yet, I also want the state and surge of the old verse, the carpentry of definite meter that tells me when to stop rambling. There's no ideal form that does for any two of us, I think.

P.S. I see I forgot to say that I feel more and more technically indebted to you, growing young in my forties![41]

These poems included final versions of "Beyond the Alps," "Words for Hart Crane," "Inauguration Day: January 1953" and "To Delmore Schwartz" (this last a poem he'd begun in 1946). The new poems were "Skunk Hour," "Man and Wife" (though, interestingly, the superbly metrical first lines of this had been written three months earlier), "Memories of West Street and Lepke," "To Speak of the Woe That Is in Marriage" (originally part of "Man and Wife"), "My Last Afternoon with Uncle Devereux Winslow," "Commander Lowell" and "Terminal Days at Beverly Farms." In October he wrote—rather nervously—to Randall Jarrell:

> I've been writing poems lately again, my first in a good four years. And I want to try them out on you! Do you feel in the mood? I'll send one ["Skunk Hour"], and then if I get a peep out of you, will follow it with four or five more. I've been loosening up the meter, as you'll see and horsing out all the old theology and symbolism and *verbal* violence.[42]

Two weeks later he has heard that Jarrell does like "Skunk Hour," and he writes again:

> I've been working like a skunk, doggedly and happily since mid-August and have seven or eight poems finished (?) some quite long and all very direct and personal. They are mostly written in a sort of free verse that takes off from the irregularities of my Ford poem. I'll get them typed up for you next week and mail them off. I'll be very sad if you don't like them.[43]

In the first of these letters to Jarrell (October 11), Lowell remarks, "There's a new English poet called Larkin that I like better than anyone since Thomas. I've been reading him since the Spring and really like him better than Thomas." In his second letter (October 24) he recommends that Jarrell read the poems by W. D. Snodgrass which have appeared in an anthology called *The New Poets of England and America:* "I'm sure you remember him with his silly name and his Mahler songs. I had him off and on in classes at Iowa for years and thought that he had done one or two of the best poems that my students had written there."[44]

In the case of these two younger poets, Lowell's interest was not to do with matters of technique: Larkin used conventional forms, Snodgrass an intricate system of syllabics. It was more that, "unlike our smooth young poets," each of them "says something." Lowell spoke later, in an interview, of Snodgrass's "pathos and fragility . . . fragility along the edges and a main artery of power going through the center,"[45] and he admired the way in which Snodgrass's sequence "Heart's Needle" managed to treat with a kind of wry nobility a subject that in other hands might not have avoided sweetness and self-pity: the separation, by divorce, of the poet from his baby daughter. In Larkin he found irony, self-deprecation, a mockingly repressed unease, a willingness to speak directly out of intimate, if mediocre, states of feeling. With both poets the reader is more eavesdropper than audience; in both there is an anti-bardic element, an insistence on the poet as ordinary man, with ordinary life problems.

During 1957, Lowell had also been reading (and seeing) a lot of Elizabeth Bishop. He had often enough expressed his admiration of her "humorous commanding genius for picking up the unnoticed," and he had warmly reviewed her first book, *North and South*, in 1947; ten years later, poems like "Florida" and "At the Fishhouses" would have come back to him with an exemplary new vividness. In 1947 he had written indulgently of her "bare objective language" and merely noted that "Most of her meters are accentual-syllabic." In 1957, though, he saw her as "a sort of bridge between Tate's formalism and Williams's informal art." Again it was a combination of high, unfettered artfulness and "thinking-aloud" emotional directness that appealed to him. Bishop—with her intently charted shorelines, her humanly caught but still nonhuman creatures of the deep, her almost devout regard for humble details—offered a thoroughly "sound" model for a poet looking for ways into his own worldliness. And a poem like "Man-Moth" would have intensified his sense of fellow feeling; Bishop's fine poem showed that there were ways of writing about, as well as out of, desperation:

> Each night he must
> be carried through artificial tunnels and dream recurrent dreams.
> Just as the ties recur beneath his train, these underlie
> his rushing brain. He does not dare look out the window,
> for the third rail, the unbroken draught of poison,

runs there beside him. He regards it as a disease
he has inherited susceptibility to. He has to keep
his hands in his pockets, as others must wear mufflers.
         If you catch him,
hold up a flashlight to his eye. It's all dark pupil,
an entire night itself, whose haired horizon tightens
as he stares back, and closes up the eye. Then from the lids
one tear, his only possession, like the bee's sting, slips.
Slyly he palms it, and if you're not paying attention
he'll swallow it. However, if you watch, he'll hand it over,
cool as from underground springs and pure enough to drink.[46]

In the summer of 1957 Lowell spent hours in conversation with
Bishop. She had visited Boston from her home in Brazil; "Before she
had gone we had told each other almost everything that had ever
happened to us. She really has risen from the ocean's bottom."[47] Her
response to his new poems was all that Lowell could have wished:

> I find I have here surely a whole new book of poems, don't I? I think
> all the family group—some of them I hadn't seen in Boston—are really
> superb, Cal. I don't know what order they'll come in, but they make
> a wonderful and impressive drama, and I think in them you've found
> the new rhythm you wanted. Without hitches. Could they have some
> sort of general title. . . . "Commander Lowell," "Terminal Days at
> Beverly Farms," "My Last Afternoon with Uncle Devereux Wins-
> low" (the one I like best, I think. I think I'd like the title without the
> "my" maybe—to go with "Terminal Days" better?) "Sailing from
> Rapallo," which is almost too awful to read, but a fine poem. They all
> also have that sure feeling, as if you'd been in a stretch (I've felt that
> way for very short stretches once in a long while) when everything,
> and anything suddenly seemed material for poetry—or not material,
> seemed to *be* poetry, and all the past was illuminated in long shafts
> here and there, like a long-waited-for sunrise. If only one could see
> everything that way all the time! It seems to me it's the whole purpose
> of art, to the artist (not to the audience)—life *is* all right, for the time
> being. Anyway, when I read such an extended display of imagination
> as this, I feel it *for* you. . . .[48]

Bishop goes on to say that she still likes "the skunk one enormously"
("Skunk Hour" is dedicated to her), but she modestly supposes that
"it's exercises compared to the other ones."
    Lowell also sent his new poems to Allen Tate. Tate wrote back

to him on December 3. His letter confirmed the extent of Lowell's defection from the traditionalist camp, from the "rooftree" of Tate's influence. It was almost as if Tate had suffered a personal—or even filial—betrayal. The only poem Tate liked was "Skunk Hour" ("very fine"—perhaps because it is in neat sestets and has an almost regular rhyme scheme), and he grudgingly allowed that the rhymed and metrical "Inauguration Day: January 1953" could be published "without compromise." As to the rest:

> *all* the poems about your family, including the one about you and Elizabeth, are definitely *bad*. I do not think you ought to publish them. You didn't ask me whether they ought to be published, but I put the matter from this point of view in order to underline my anxiety about them. I do not mean to say that in some of these there are not sharp and even brilliant passages like the old Cal; it is simply that by and large, and in the total effect, the poems are composed of unassimilated details, terribly intimate, and coldly noted, which might well have been transferred from the notes from your autobiography without change.
>
> The free verse, arbitrary and without rhythm, reflects this lack of imaginative focus. Your fine poems in the past present a formal ordering of highly intractable materials: but there is an imaginative thrust towards a symbolic order which these new poems seem to lack. The new ones sound to me like messages to yourself, or perhaps they are an heroic effort of the will to come to terms with the harsh incongruities of your childhood and of your later struggles with your parents, and you are letting these scattered items of experience have their full impact upon your sensibility. Quite bluntly, these details, presented in *causerie* and at random, are of interest only to you. They are, of course, of great interest to me because I am one of your oldest friends. But they have no public or literary interest.[49]

To others, Tate was putting his objections even more forthrightly: these loose, self-centered poems made him wonder if Lowell wasn't on the brink of another manic episode. Elizabeth Hardwick was indignant when she heard that Tate was originating rumors of this sort. There had, she might have admitted, been a short spell during the summer when both she and Elizabeth Bishop had been worried that Lowell was getting dangerously "high," but by early December Bishop was able to congratulate her friend on somehow having averted a full-scale attack—"the whole phenomena [*sic*] of your quick recovery and simultaneous productivity seems to me in looking back to be the real marvel of my summer."[50] Later Bishop recalled that "one reason she left Castine—with her friend Lota—after a few days was that she felt Cal was getting sick and part of it was getting very amorous with her. There was this reawakened interest in her as someone he was in love with."[51] And it was almost at this point that Lowell wrote his poem "The Two Weeks' Vacation," which recalls his 1947 visit to Bishop and his rejection of Carley Dawson. The poem's final stanza reads, in part:

> And now ten years later, I see you to your plane in Bangor.
> You are thirty pounds lighter,
> Your uncertain fingers that float to your lips.
> And you kiss them to me, and our fellowship
> Resumes its old transcendence like a star.[52]

After Bishop's departure, Hardwick had reported to Cousin Harriet that "Bobby is fine. The happiest, healthiest couple are always writing the most brooding, neurasthenic works! This has indeed been one of our best times—this last year or so."[53] And as to the poems, Hardwick knew just how many hours of revision had gone into them (indeed she had herself helped with a good deal of the rewriting, and the manuscripts of Lowell's prose pieces bear extensive evidence of her editorial advice). She told Tate that the three and a half months in which Lowell had been working on *Life Studies* had in fact been "marvellously quiet ones with us": "he was not sick when he worked over and over those poems and I don't agree with you in the least about them."[54]

By the time Hardwick had got around to scolding Tate, however, his diagnosis, or prediction, had been "uncannily" proved right. In early December, after a reading trip to Washington and New York, Lowell was unignorably beginning to speed up. For Hardwick, it was the familiar dilemma: these excitements *could* burn themselves out, she would tell herself, they didn't *always* carry him "right off the track." For the moment, she would wait and see. Unhappily, she didn't have to wait for long. Dido Merwin, then married to the poet W. S. Merwin, recalls the day when Lowell decided to invite "le tout Boston" to an impromptu party—so impromptu that Hardwick learned about it only a few hours before the McGeorge Bundys actually arrived at her front door:

> And up the stairs they streamed. Ivor and Dorothea Richards, Frost, Edmund Wilson, Mrs. Edmund Wilson . . . I think Adrienne Rich was there. And Arthur Schlesinger—but everybody. Gertrude Buckman was in the kitchen crying. And Cal got Frost up into Harriet's night nursery. Edmund Wilson fell down, or someone knocked him down. There was a table covered in glasses and Cal came up to this corner where a number of us were circulating, including Lizzie, and he sat down in a chair and dashed the glasses off the table with his feet and sat there, with his feet on the drinks table, surrounded by broken glass, and shouted, "Lizzie, Bill [Merwin] says Hiss wasn't guilty." Dorothea and Ivor Richards were sitting on the sofa and Dorothea said to me, "What a lovely party. Everybody's having such fun!" There were punch-ups. There were insults. And Cal was just going round like the devil putting people against each other. It was the most extraordinary party—an absolute triumph for Cal. . . . The extraordinary thing was that nobody seemed to realize he was mad.[55]

In fact, probably everyone realized, but was too drunk to care. William Alfred, the Harvard medievalist who had recently become a close friend of the Lowells', remembers that his role at the party (agreed beforehand with Hardwick) was to see that all drinks were regularly stiffened: by this means, perhaps no one would *hear* when Lowell announced that celebrity X was indeed "the best second-rate poet in the city of Boston." The strategy proved an incomplete success.

Some seventy-two sleepless hours after the party, the police were called. Lowell's own psychiatrist had visited but had swiftly been sent packing. "It was terrible," Hardwick remembers. "Everybody was milling around and we couldn't do anything with him . . . he was just totally out of his mind."[56] In the end, Lowell was persuaded to accept treatment but insisted on being committed to one of the city's public hospitals; his preference was for the fearsomely named Boston Psychopathic. William Alfred describes what happened:

> Cal agreed to be admitted to the Boston Psychopathic, but only if he was accompanied by an old school friend of his, whom I would rather not identify. This friend was now an extremely elegant Boston swell

and when the circumstances were explained to him, he agreed to meet Cal at the police station. So the police arrived at Marlborough Street to take him away. Before he left, he wanted to sit for a few moments in Harriet's room and watch her sleep. He did this, with me telling the cops: "He won't be long." Then we left in the police wagon. And I remember the look on Cal's face—it was as if the real Cal, the Cal I knew, were looking out at me from within the mania. It was very moving. I'd never seen him crazy. Then when we got to the police station they treated him very roughly—they wouldn't even give him a glass of water. But his school friend arrived then, and he told the cop: "You will give Mr. Lowell a glass of water and you will keep a civil tongue in your head!" It was a bit better after that. Then we took him to the hospital. It was like taking a kid to a boarding school and then having to walk away, having to leave him there. They took his clothes away. When I left, he was standing there in his underclothes.[57]

During Lowell's brief stay at the Boston Psychopathic, he met a girl called Ann Adden, a "psychiatric fieldworker" from Bennington College, and almost immediately began to announce plans for a "new life." He was going to change his will and leave everything to his new love, he said; the source of his turmoil was his bad marriage, and so on. As for Ann Adden, she seems to have been thoroughly beguiled, and on more than one occasion helped Lowell play truant from the hospital; he would be found wandering on Boston Common or sitting in his lawyer's office hammering out the legal niceties of his rebirth.[58]

After a week or so the hospital discharged him; he had quieted down, the doctors said, and they thought that letting him out would be a "bold therapeutic measure."[59] It is hard not to suspect that they simply wanted to be rid of him. Certainly, he was far from well and for the next month seemed to be thoroughly adrift; he shuttled between Marlborough Street and a room on Harvard Square, some days protesting his love for Ann Adden and on others imploring Hardwick not to abandon the Marlborough Street house. A letter written on January 20, 1958, from Elizabeth Hardwick to Cousin Harriet, gives an idea of the almost tedious bewilderment that prevailed throughout these weeks:

Well, he's back, but even when I was talking to Bobby about the time you called I felt how unwise I was to have him here now. He is very, very far from well. On the telephone he sounds all right, calm and considerate, but in person the excitement, the unreal plans and demands, the unpredictability have hardly altered basically. There is a superficial alteration because of the drugs. But the deep underlying unreality is there, the fact that no one else's feelings really exist, wild projects, etc. I have not *taken him back*—awful phrase.[60]

But she would not refuse him refuge, and he could not bear to abandon his study, his books, his family furniture: "the most stabilizing factor has been the house! The last thing I would have thought for a person like Bobby." It was as if, at some level, Lowell knew very well that his adventure would not last; even as he grandly declared to Hardwick that "I promise nothing," he was ensuring that there would still be an old life to come back to. On the subject of Ann Adden, he seems to have been anxious to maintain at least a thin fog of uncertainty.

after completely dropping the poor girl I wrote you about, not even telephoning her when he got out of the hospital, not answering her calls —all of this seemed good when I heard it even though the girl, who had told everyone Bobby was in love with her and only needed to be rid of me to be well and happy, was described by a friend as in a "basket case condition" due to all the disappointment—now—hold your hats!—he had another girl! He said he spent the weekend with her, while he was away, and of course he is going to keep on. "This will make everything so much better with us. It's a wonderful thing for both of us," he said, us being myself and Bobby. By this time I felt so bored, so numb that I couldn't have cared less about the girl, but I did care about the deep derangement which such a conversation with me shows.[61]

It is probable that there was no other girl, that even the novelty of Ann Adden had had to be reinvented for the sake of a more stunning metaphor. As one friend of Lowell's has described it:

Cal had to be "in love." Poets were always in love. He adored the metaphor of these situations—him in hospital and some girl waiting for him in a ski-lodge in Vermont. But he'd quickly get bored—they wouldn't understand what he was talking about.[62]

For a few days at the end of January 1958 it seemed that this "boredom" had indeed begun to settle in. Lowell returned to Marlborough Street, and on January 24 Hardwick felt confident enough to announce that "Things are really much better!" He seemed "more himself," had begun teaching again and correcting student papers: "He seems to be settling down, quieting down gradually. I suppose underneath it had been harder for him to come back to the world than we know."[63] Lowell also began to focus once again on the new poems and, in particular, on Tate's scathing view of them. Also on the twenty-fourth he wrote to Tate:

> Let's not have a fight about my poems. I like them, and people as different as my Washington Winslow relation, Elizabeth Bishop, Philip Rahv and T.S. Eliot liked them and thought they topped my work. But you don't have to and I want us to stay as good friends as ever.
>
> You *were* uncannily right about my getting sick again. I had a bout of about a month in the Boston Psychopathic and am now back—in fact, I've been back teaching now for three weeks.[64]

On January 31 Tate replied, and his air of caution suggests that he still suspected Lowell to be worryingly high:

> I am a little baffled by your letter. I had no intention of having a "fight" with you or anybody else. I just don't feel angry. What I thought was quite simple, and it had nothing to do with thinking you had "betrayed the persona" I had of you. I simply thought that the poems contained intractable material, and that you were probably in a transition period from your early style to a new one. You have certainly reached the age when this is likely to happen. Nor did I think the poems *all* bad. It seemed to me that the personal poems were a little morbid, private and unorganized; and I was not put off because they were not *like* your old work; rather because they lacked the concentration and power, lacking as they seemed to lack, the highly formalistic organization of the old. Won't you just put down my dissenting opinion as the one negative vote, and let the opinions of others count? We can't expect *all* our friends to like what we do all the time.[65]

Tate also thanked Lowell for having praised *his* last group of poems, but pointed out, "There is a good deal of time between me and them, and they are beginning to look like old poems"; and, again, he tried to reassure his old friend that there *could* be criticism without quarrels. "Why should I 'cut' you in March? Come to, Cal. This is greatly beside the point."

But before Tate's letter arrived in Boston, Lowell had relapsed.

The brief lull seems merely to have recharged him, and before the end of January he was once again "active as electricity."[66] Hardwick arranged for him to be admitted to McLean Hospital outside Boston, and the doctors there pronounced him "truly under the complete domination of childhood fantasies."[67]

During his first week in a locked ward at McLean's, Lowell wrote a draft of the poem he later called "Waking in the Blue." The first draft is titled "To Ann Adden (Written during the first week of my voluntary stay at McLean's Mental Hospital)," and it reads as follows:

> Like the heart-toughening harpoon,
> or steel plates of a press
> needling, draining my heart—
> your absence . . . . .
> What use is my sense of humor,
> basking over "Jimmy", now sunk in his sixties,
> once a Harvard all-American (if such were possible from Harvard)
> still with the build of a boy in his twenties,
> as he lolls, ram-rod,
> with the luxuriance of a seal
> in his long tub,
> vaguely sulphurous from the Victorian plumbing.
> His bone brow is crowned with a red golf cap
> all day, all night,
> and he thinks only of his build,
> gobbling ice-cream and ginger ale—
> how to be more shut off from words than a seal.
>
> Thus day breaks in Bowditch Hall at McLean's;
> it ends with 'Hughey' 29,
> looking like Louis XVI
> released from his white whig [*sic*],
> reeking and rolly-polly as a sperm whale,

as he careens about naked,
horsing down chairs.
This fine figure of bravado ossified young.
In between the limits of day, here,
hours and hours go by under the crew haircuts,
and slightly too little non-sensical bachelor eyes
of the R.C. attendants
(there are no blue-blooded
old Boston screwballs in the Catholic Church)
Ann, what use is my ability
for shooting the bull,
far from your Valkyrie body,
your gold-brown hair,
your robust uprightness—you, brisk
yet discrete [*sic*] in your conversation!

II
(a week later)

The night-attendant, a B.U. student,
rouses his cobwebby eyes
propped on his Social Relations text-book,
prowls drowsily down our corridor. . . .
Soon, soon the solitude of Allah, azure day-break,
will make my agonized window bleaker.
What greater glory than recapturing the moment of glory
in *miseria?*

Snow's falling. Farther off in time,
a more illuminating snow:
on the slopes of the Mittelsell,
near Franconia, topped by Mount Washington,
you loom back to me, Ann,
tears in your eyes, icicles on your eyelashes,
bridal Norwegian fringe
on your coat, the wooly lining of a coat.

Your salmon lioness face is dawn.

The bracelet on your right wrist jingles with trophies:
The enamelled Harvard pennant,
the round medallion of St. Mark's School.
I could claim both,

for both were supplied by earlier,
now defunct claimants,
and my gold ring, almost half an inch wide,
now crowns your bracelet, cock of the walk there.

My Goddess. . . . But where in literature
has a goddess been able to stand up
to flesh and blood?
A lioness, then. With Descartes
I can almost lower animals to the realm of machines.
Ann, how can I charade you
In a lioness's wormy hide?—
massive, tawny, playful, lythe [*sic*]?

God be thanked, I now weigh 200 pounds,
have been a man for forty years;
You are 19,
see me still a St. Mark's sixth former,
my symbol the Evangelist's winged lion![1]

From these diffuse beginnings, the finished poem—worked on over a period of three months—was to become a supreme example of Lowell's new "informality," an informality seamed with high instinctive artifice (if such were possible!): small, almost whispered intrusions of alliteration and half-rhyme, a shrewd, suspenseful balancing of short and long lines, an almost ceremonial tightening here and there into strict meter or heroic couplet. In his first draft, Lowell really *is* informal, hasty, talkative; in the completed poem he makes every accent and line break earn its formal keep—he elevates exuberant chatter into haunting, measured eloquence:

WAKING IN THE BLUE

The night attendant, a B.U. sophomore,
rouses from the mare's-nest of his drowsy head
propped on *The Meaning of Meaning.*
He catwalks down our corridor.
Azure day
makes my agonized blue window bleaker.
Crows maunder on the petrified fairway.

Absence! My heart grows tense
as though a harpoon were sparring for the kill.
(This is the house for the "mentally ill.")

What use is my sense of humor?
I grin at Stanley, now sunk in his sixties,
once a Harvard all-American fullback,
(if such were possible!)
still hoarding the build of a boy in his twenties,
as he soaks, a ramrod
with the muscle of a seal
in his long tub,
vaguely urinous from the Victorian plumbing.
A kingly granite profile in a crimson golf-cap,
worn all day, all night,
he thinks only of his figure,
of slimming on sherbet and ginger ale—
more cut off from words than a seal.

This is the way day breaks in Bowditch Hall at McLean's;
the hooded night lights bring out "Bobbie,"
Porcellian '29
a replica of Louis XVI
without the wig—
redolent and roly-poly as a sperm whale,
as he swashbuckles about in his birthday suit
and horses at chairs.

These victorious figures of bravado ossified young.

In between the limits of day,
hours and hours go by under the crew haircuts
and slightly too little nonsensical bachelor twinkle
of the Roman Catholic attendants.
(There are no Mayflower
screwballs in the Catholic Church.)

After a hearty New England breakfast,
I weigh two hundred pounds
this morning. Cock of the walk,
I strut in my turtle-necked French sailor's jersey
before the metal shaving mirrors,
and see the shaky future grow familiar

in the pinched, indigenous faces
of these thoroughbred mental cases,
twice my age and half my weight.
We are all old-timers,
each of us holds a locked razor.[2]

The thread of marine images—seals, turtles, sperm whales—is in-sinuated with a casual air, but it serves to lend true elegiac weight to the near-cartoon images of Stanley and Bobbie: two highborn and historical New England "wrecks," each of them kingly, thorough-bred and ossified in the habits of their pampered childhoods, and each of them therefore a terrible mirror image for the strutting, grinning, cock-of-the-walk St. Mark's and Harvard poet: "We are all old-timers, / each of us holds a locked razor." (But could Stanley or Bobbie ever hope to pull off the rhyming triumph of those last five lines—"faces," "cases," and then the "a" sound of "age" and "weight" supplying the hoist forward to "locked razor": a final rhyme superbly softened, inexact and ominous?)

"Waking in the Blue" is twenty-five lines shorter than the origi-nal "To Ann Adden," and the missing lines are those that Lowell specifically addressed to his new love. It is not known whether or not Ann Adden saw "her" version of the poem; if she did, she probably didn't like it much. In spite of its air of high-spirited infatuation, its transmutations are surely too awesomely grand-scale: Ann Adden becomes lioness, Valkyrie, goddess—"massive, tawny, playful, lythe": a high price to pay for happening to be of Nordic origin. And there is a distinct note of menace in Lowell's reference to "earlier, now defunct, claimants" to the insignia she jingles on her wrist. She, too, the poem seems to say, will shortly be "defunct"—but only when Lowell has tired of his mischievous "charade," or has become bored with her both as metaphor and as reverential play-mate. William Alfred saw "the real Cal" looking out at him from within the mania; Ann Adden might well have felt the same when Lowell addressed her as

My Goddess. . . . But where in literature
has a goddess been able to stand up
to flesh and blood?
A lioness, then. With Descartes
I can almost lower animals to the realm of machines.

And sure enough, by the time Lowell was finished with his poem, he was also finished with Ann Adden: there is a near-chilling efficiency in his final excisions—"Waking in the Blue" reveals no trace of its first "inspiration." Ann Adden is both written out and written off. (Although later on, it should perhaps be said, there is further cause for uneasy admiration: in a poem called "1958," published in 1964,[3] and in "Mania" [1969],[4] Lowell resurrects half a dozen of the discarded "Ann Adden lines" and blithely recasts *them* into elegy.)

In January 1958, though, Ann Adden was still a lively presence. Although she was adopting a fairly guarded style—"This time you must get well and I must not interfere"—she was still a regular visitor to McLean's, and was assiduously following a reading program Lowell had devised for her; Hitler, she wrote to him, "has the greatest retrospective power," and she was also deep in Dante: "The X Canto is a beauty. Only sorry you're not present to read the Italian aloud." After Dante she would "delve into" Kant's *Critique of Pure Reason.* But what, she wondered, ought she to do about "the Picasso? . . . . If you want it sent to Marlborough Street, you better say something to Lizzie. I don't know where you ordered it or what you want me to do."[5]

For Hardwick, the girl's adoring presence was pure irritant, making it almost impossible for her, or any of Lowell's other "real-life" friends, to help him much: "These damned girls complicate everything; they keep me from acting in his best interests often because I don't want to seem pushing or jealous."[6] In early February, Hardwick retreated to New York and rested for a few days in the home of Blair and Holly Clark. "I needed it so much," she wrote to the Clarks on her return to "the inferno of suffering" in Boston:

> A thousand thanks for putting me up, putting up with me, feeding me, talking to me. . . . coming home, with such enormous responsibility. I spent all of Friday at the hospital and came home as if someone had been beating me all day.[7]

Lowell, she found, was calm, quiet, superficially "well," but insisting there was nothing wrong with him that could not be cured by a divorce:

> he says he must go to Reno immediately, marry someone or other, and *then* he will take treatment. He truly feels this is a life or death matter:

it is the only bearable plan for "curing himself" and he is clinging to it wildly. He becomes furious if you use the word "sick" and so on; he is profoundly aware that depressive symptoms—fear, remorse, uncertainty, anxiety, chaos—are always threatening him and he would truly rather wreck his whole life than have these symptoms for a moment. The doctors think he is scared to death and so do I—he is truly so desperate that he can't even allow himself to be helped. The whole thing is appalling—and it may go on and on. Control and a great deal of calm have returned, but he will not allow true realization that he has had another collapse to overcome him. Poor Cal! It is truly pathetic.[8]

The one "hopeful" aspect for Hardwick was that the doctors at McLean's agreed with her "on every point"; they were assuring her that Lowell indeed had a real commitment to her—"one of the few they can find in his life history." They encouraged her to try to "stand it," to stall about the divorce, which they believed "would be a disaster for him, etc."[9] On February 15 she wrote to Cousin Harriet describing the McLean's prognosis:

For the future, the unimaginable, frightening future which seems awful no matter what happens about the present: the doctors think Bobby can be cured, but that it would be hard, take years of serious working out with a doctor of his profound problems and fears. I spoke quite frankly to them, and said: "It is all very well to talk about cures, coping with problems, working it out, and so on. But do you really believe it? Do you really get these cures when someone is middle-aged, has had countless breakdowns, etc?" They assured me that they have begun in the last years to get permanent cures, that B. is not so seriously ill in terms of mental illness patterns, etc.[10]

On March 5 Blair Clark wrote a letter to Charles P. Curtis of the Boston law firm Choate, Hall and Stewart. Clark's letter has the value of being neutrally pitched and humbly factual, yet written from the very center of the "Lowell problem." It is quoted here in full:

Dear Mr. Curtis,
    This letter is to ask you for advice (or rather to ask if you would consider giving me some advice) on a very difficult matter concerning one of my oldest and closest friends. I refer to Robert Lowell who has been my friend since we were classmates at St. Mark's.

I would guess that you know that Lowell has had more than one severe mental breakdown during the last decade. Right now he is in McLean's sanitarium outside Boston, recovering from the violently irrational phase of his latest "episode." The indications are that he will stay there for at least another month, and perhaps more. Doctors have diagnosed Cal's illness as a recurring manic-depressive psychosis; I am using the terms inexpertly, but there have been four such seizures since the war serious enough to require hospitalization. In between, as you know, Cal functions brilliantly, and I mean this to apply not only to his writing but to his personal and family life.

The latest lull between the attacks was nearly four years long. During this period Cal's wife, Elizabeth, who is also an old and very dear friend of Holly's and mine, had a baby daughter, born when she was about forty. The child is Cal's only one (and Elizabeth's too, for that matter). When one of these attacks is coming on, and during the early stages of it, before he is made to go or voluntarily retreats to a hospital, his wife and child are by all accounts subjected to risks that so far, fortunately, have not gone beyond the threat of violence. I know, however, that Elizabeth has been badly frightened about the safety of the child and herself. I think that there is no one who has seen Cal in one of these crises who would not say that her apprehensions are thoroughly justified; she is not at all hysterically-inclined.

During this last period, it struck Elizabeth very forcibly that she was in a very difficult position with her husband as the one who was called upon to call the cops, so to speak—and, unfortunately, in fact, once or twice. And, from her accounts to me of what happened, the doctors involved took less responsibility for committing Cal, even for brief periods of observation, than one would have thought normal. So it was his wife, whom he naturally turned against in his irrational moments, who had to be the one who insisted that he should be taken off and treated as a sick person. She was his jailer.

I have now at last arrived at the point of my letter to you. It is to ask you whether you would think about, and advise me on, a device that would help to remove the entire burden of committal from Cal's wife's shoulders in any future episodes—(which all doctors who have seen Cal in the past say there will most likely be). Elizabeth knows, of course, that she cannot completely shuck her part in this; she has great common sense and no wish to duck all responsibility. But my question to you arises from talks I have had with her about the possibility of setting up something which would work at least in part automatically in the case of recurrence.

I am not thinking of anything as simple and crude as a signed-in-advance committal paper in a doctor's hands, although it might perhaps come to that. But it seems to me that the possibility should be explored of some legal method that would remove some of the burden of being her husband's keeper from Elizabeth without either taking needless risks with his liberties or leaving him with the constant apprehension that his freedom is subject to someone else's whim. As you can see, I have not been able to think this out to any sort of solution, and that is why I am consulting you. It seems to me that this is a matter of great delicacy, involving a whole range of human, medical and legal problems. I anticipate no easy or rapid solution, but I think that the possibility of easing the present situation should be examined, and I can think of no one who would be more apt to have valuable thoughts on it than yourself.[11]

Curtis wrote back with "advice as unhelpful as your problem is difficult":

I do not believe that any doctor will sign a committal paper in advance. I think that a new one will be required as and when an attack comes on. The fact is I don't know of any legal method that would remove the burden from Mrs. Lowell taking both the initiative and the responsibility of a committal to an institution.

He went on to speculate about the possibility of appointing a legal guardian of Lowell's person—a guardian other than his wife—or a conservator of his property, but he could not see the usefulness of taking either course: if such an appointment "is made when the individual is not well, and so he does not completely understand why he is assenting to the appointment, there is the risk that he will try to revoke it when he does become himself."[12]

An ironic footnote to this correspondence is provided by a letter Lowell wrote a few weeks earlier to Ezra Pound at St. Elizabeth's. Lowell too, it seems, was concerned about his future civic status: "Do you think a man who has been off his rocker as often as I have been could run for elective office and win? I have in mind the state senatorship from my district. . . ."[13]

During March, Lowell was allowed to spend weekends at home, and by March 15 he was well enough to begin the now familiar round of repairing and explaining. To Cousin Harriet he wrote apologizing for a "foolish, harsh letter" he had sent her from McLean's:

It's funny how the head fills with monstrous determination; all one's real loves and knowledges fly away; one stands reborn, scheming, lonely, silly. Please accept my brief and simple apology. I am deeply sorry the whole business happened and sorry that you had to hear about it.[14]

And on the same day, he wrote to Peter Taylor:

It's not much fun writing about these breakdowns after they themselves have broken and one stands stickily splattered with patches of the momentary bubble. Health; but not of kind which encourages the backward look.[15]

To both, Lowell was optimistic about his new course of "systematic therapy," but his assurances had an automatic ring. For the moment, his real need was to lie low, to "get to know" his old life once again:

Life is serene; we go to the movies, and concerts; Harriet takes us for long walks over the Public Gardens grass on Sundays; I've been translating some Italian and German poems and have a desk drawer full of fragmentary poems and autobiography. Elizabeth has been terrific, and we're awfully glad to be together.[16]

He felt that there were "good times ahead, and little Harriet will never see the shadow that has darkened us and gone. I don't think this is whistling in the dark."[17]

This tentative, "recuperating" mood, though, is most memorably caught in the poem Lowell began working on shortly after—or perhaps during his first weekend "release" from McLean's. It was the weekend of his forty-first birthday (March 1, 1958), and on March 2 Hardwick wrote:

I am feeling much better and so at last is Bobby. He was at home Friday afternoon—we went to the Symphony and then had dinner together; yesterday, Saturday, was his birthday and we went to the movies in the afternoon, bathed baby Harriet, had dinner here by the fire listening to Marriage of Figaro before B went back to the hospital. Next weekend he will be out to stay here, but will go back to the hospital on Sunday. He wants to come back to us. Gradually he has been getting better and then, what seems suddenly but really isn't, he is pretty much himself once more.[18]

Lowell's own account is called "Home After Three Months Away," and the second stanza describes baby Harriet's bath scene:

> Three months, three months!
> Is Richard now himself again?
> Dimpled with exaltation,
> my daughter holds her levee in the tub.
> Our noses rub,
> each of us pats a stringy lock of hair—
> they tell me nothing's gone.
> Though I am forty-one,
> not forty now, the time I put away
> was child's-play. After thirteen weeks
> my child still dabs her cheeks
> to start me shaving. When
> we dress her in her sky-blue corduroy
> she changes to a boy,
> and floats my shaving brush
> and washcloth in the flush. . . .
> Dearest, I cannot loiter here
> in lather like a polar bear.[19]

Sentimental? Well, almost—and that "almost" is of key importance in understanding what Lowell was now looking for in poetry. "Home After Three Months Away" probably owes something to the example of W. D. Snodgrass's "Heart's Needle," and it is worth remembering Lowell's response to an interviewer who suggested to him that Snodgrass's "best poems are all on the verge of being slight and even sentimental." Lowell said:

I think a lot of the best poetry is. Laforgue—it's hard to think of a more delightful poet, and his prose is wonderful too. Well, it's on the verge of being sentimental, and if he hadn't dared to be sentimental he wouldn't have been a poet. I mean, his inspiration was that. There's some way of distinguishing between false sentimentality, which is blowing up a subject and giving emotions that you don't feel, and using whimsical, minute, tender, small emotions which most people don't feel but which Laforgue and Snodgrass do. So that I'd say he had pathos and fragility—but then that's a large subject too.[20]

"Home After Three Months Away" is redeemed from sentimentality by its sheer technical control: in the lines above, see how the irregularly placed rhymes—"tub"/"rub," "put away"/"child's-play"—seem to be struggling towards the regularity, the calm of the ensuing couplets. In his new style, Lowell was becoming masterly in letting a poem's shape declare its mood. But there are other ways in which the poet here darkens a sweet domestic interlude—the poem is placed (in *Life Studies*) immediately after "Waking in the Blue" with its metal mirrors and its locked razors —simply to be able to shave freely has become a hard-won luxury for Lowell. And the line "Dearest, I cannot loiter here" is made doubly moving if we know that the poet is not really "home"—his weekend is over, he now has to leave his child and go back to the "house for the mentally ill." And, of course, it was Lowell's own "child's-play," his bearish foolery, that had required him to be "put away." The kingly references—"Is Richard now himself again," "my daughter holds her levee in the tub"—force us back to Stanley in his "long tub" and Bobbie, the "replica of Louis XVI," Lowell's McLean's playmates.

There are other, more secret ways in which "Home After Three Months Away" relates to Lowell's view of his own mania as "child's-play." The first stanza, for example, reads:

> Gone now the baby's nurse,
> a lioness who ruled the roost
> and made the Mother cry.
> She used to tie
> gobbets of porkrind in bowknots of gauze—
> three months they hung like soggy toast
> on our eight foot magnolia tree,
> and helped the English sparrows
> weather a Boston winter.

In life, the Lowells did have a "terrifying maid who hangs suet bones for the starlings on our poor little magnolia—this last is sober truth, but I don't ask belief."[21] Lowell had written this to Peter Taylor some two years before. And Hardwick has said:

> The fact is that we had a conventional Scotch nurse for a time and I did not like her at all, but was reluctant to let her go and finally got the

courage. The "suet" did not really happen to us. We saw it on a tree next door and thought it rather odd and sweet. (I was in a greatly distressed state about the nurse and I did "cry.")[22]

But hidden within the first three lines is something more than mere domestic data. For Lowell, Ann Adden had been the "lioness" to his "St. Mark's winged lion"; she had also been a "nurse" —literally so, when he first met her at the Boston Psychopathic. She too has now "gone," she will no longer make "the Mother cry." For a time, Lowell seems to be saying, he himself had been a "baby" and the nurse/lioness Ann Adden had displaced his real "mother," Elizabeth Hardwick. It was only in the very last versions of the poem that Lowell capitalized Harriet's "mother" into a "Mother" figure. It could hardly be a more subterranean apology; indeed, it is unlikely that anyone other than Lowell himself would have been able to make the "lioness" connection. Many readers, however, might have been puzzled by the rather too weighty inversion of the opening line, "Gone now the baby's nurse," and might therefore agree that the *gravitas* becomes more understandable if one accepts that Lowell here uses a real-life coincidence (the "terrifying maid" *had* left Marlborough Street by the time Lowell came out of McLean's) to smuggle in a very private renunciation of Ann Adden.

In one of his many drafts of "Home After Three Months Away" Lowell ended the poem as follows:

> For months
> My madness gathered strength
> to roll all sweetness to a ball
> in color, tropical . . .
> Now I am frizzled, stale and small.

The allusion is to Andrew Marvell's "To His Coy Mistress":

> Let us roll all our Strength and all
> Our Sweetness up into one Ball,
> And tear our Pleasures with rough strife
> Thorough the Iron gates of Life:
> Thus, though we cannot make our Sun
> Stand still, yet we will make him run.

A fine description, Lowell would have felt, of the manic resolve that he was now "cured" of; and also of the high energy and reckless idealism which, in theory and in others, he would always prize above timidity or common sense. The diagnosed "manic-depressive" will surely always have a buried yearning for the "tropical" terrain of his affliction; and the pursuit of "health" will in some measure always be more contractual than voluntary. The closing lines of "Home After Three Months Away" can be read as an expression of the cyclical, biochemical onset of "depression"; unscientifically, however, they are pure lament for the surrendered infancy of madness:

> Recuperating, I neither spin nor toil.
> Three stories down below,
> a choreman tends our coffin's length of soil,
> and seven horizontal tulips blow.
> Just twelve months ago,
> these flowers were pedigreed
> imported Dutchmen; now no one need
> distinguish them from weed.
> Bushed by the late spring snow,
> they cannot meet
> another year's snowballing enervation.
>
> I keep no rank nor station.
> Cured, I am frizzled, stale and small.

As always, Hardwick marveled at Lowell's "recuperative powers"; they were "almost as much of a jolt as his breakdowns; that is, knowing him in the chains of illness you could, for a time, not imagine him otherwise." And yet, she has said, he always managed to return to life "intact":

> . . . it seemed so miraculous that the old gifts of person and art were still there, as if they had been stored in some serene, safe box somewhere. Then it did not seem possible that the dread assault could return to hammer him into bits once more.
>
> He "came to" sad, worried, always ashamed and fearful; and yet there he was, this unique soul for whom one felt great pity. His fate was like

a strange, almost mythical two-engined machine, one running to doom and the other to salvation. Out of the hospital, he returned to his days, which were regular, getting up early in the morning, going to his room or separate place for work. All day long he lay on the bed, propped up on an elbow. And this was his life, reading, studying and writing. The papers piled up on the floor, the books on the bed, the bottles of milk on the window sill, and the ashtray filled.

He looked like one of the great photographs of Whitman, taken by Thomas Eakins—Whitman in carpet slippers, a shawl, surrounded by a surf of papers up to his lap. . . . Cal was not the sort of poet, if there are any, for whom beautiful things come drifting down in a snowfall of gift, the labor was merciless. The discipline, the dedication, the endless adding to his *store,* by reading and studying—all of this had, in my view, much that was heroic about it.[23]

Lowell spent the summer of 1958 completing the manuscript of *Life Studies* and in October was able to turn it in to Farrar, Straus and Cudahy. (Robert Giroux had moved there from Harcourt, Brace, and Lowell had followed him.) He attended weekly sessions with his new psychotherapist and during July and August shuttled between Boston and Castine—Hardwick had moved to Castine for the summer, but Lowell needed to be near his Boston doctor. So that he wouldn't be "sitting here idle," he had taken a summer teaching post at Harvard, and on October 31, 1958, he wrote to Peter Taylor: "I've got my book off at last. . . . I'm in the fine mood of an author with a new style and feel nothing else I've ever done counts." And in the same month Hardwick was able to report to Cousin Harriet that Lowell was "feeling in very good, but not *too* good spirits":

He has been hired again by Harvard for next summer, after first being told that he wouldn't be because certain people opposed it for reasons all too obvious. But then they changed their mind, which was gratifying. The summer teaching is a little bit of a bore, but this next will be the last I think. . . . financially he needs to do it; also he adores his teaching. It has never, strangely enough, been onerous to him as it is to so many others. He wants to work and this, outside his writing, is the only work he can do. We'll do the same, I expect, as last summer, which was a great success all round. I think this present doctor must be very good. Cal never talks about it—a good sign that something is going on, beyond useless pep talks. Anyway he's a delight, a wonderful pleasure to be with.[24]

A number of the *Life Studies* poems had appeared in *Partisan Review* earlier in the year ("Man and Wife," "Memories of West Street and Lepke" and "Skunk Hour" formed a powerful trio in *PR*'s issue for Winter 1958—i.e., January 1958), and a further batch was due to appear in January 1959. The finished manuscript offered twenty-four poems and was divided into four sections. Section One has four poems in Lowell's "old style," poems written before he had begun work on his prose autobiography. Of these four, "Beyond the Alps" is the only one that seems really to "belong" in the book. It serves to "clear the ground," not just stylistically but also autobiographically. If Lowell is about to abandon his old tricks, the poem suggests, it is because he no longer feels the fire and venom that sustained the hurtling iambic line; he has exhausted, and has become exhausted by, grand absolutes. In "Beyond the Alps" the old Lowellian ferocity, where it appears at all, is directed against what might be thought of as its source: the Catholic Church, which Lowell now berates for its temporal hypocrisies, its spiritual redundancy:

> When the Vatican made Mary's Assumption dogma,
> the crowds at San Pietro screamed *Papa*.
> The Holy Father dropped his shaving glass,
> and listened. His electric razor purred,
> his pet canary chirped on his left hand.
> The lights of science couldn't hold a candle
> to Mary risen—at one miraculous stroke,
> angel-wing'd, gorgeous as a jungle bird!
> But who believed this? Who could understand?
> Pilgrims still kissed Saint Peter's brazen sandal.
> The Duce's lynched, bare, booted skull still spoke.
> God herded his people to the *coup de grâce*—
> the costumed Switzers sloped their pikes to push,
> O Pius, through the monstrous human crush.

There is a flicker of yearning in that beautifully placed "O Pius," but it has little real-life consolatory usefulness.

The poem is about moving on, transition, the surrendering of large energies and aspirations—but a moving on to what? The poem's final image is one of Lowell's most perfect and impenetrable:

> Now Paris, our black classic, breaking up
> Like killer kings on an Etruscan cup.

It is entirely permissible to say of these extraordinary lines that

> The black of Paris is in contrast to the pure whiteness of the Alps; it appears pagan, sinister, mysterious. He has returned to the twentieth century, Etruscan in its remoteness—a buried world.[25]

This is as good an explication as any other, but the image continues to resist simple exegesis. And it can thus be taken as a kind of epigraph for a book which, in its bruised acknowledgment that poetry does indeed make "nothing happen," will seek to be refreshed by a direct, almost wide-eyed attentiveness to objects, places, personal experience. The only "task" of Lowell's new style will be to prove its own disconsolate and modest propositions; his one remaining faith, if one can call it that, is in the imaginable moral power of perfect speech. At worst, no one could say of *this* new book: "But who believed this? Who could understand?"

Part Two of *Life Studies* is the prose essay "91 Revere Street"—a highly polished slice of Lowell's autobiography. It centers on the poet's childhood from 1925 to 1928, and casts Mr. Lowell as the main character: his resignation from the navy, his business humiliations, his sad and amiable willingness to let himself be dominated not only by his wife, his friends, his employers, but also by his own low-level self-delusion. It is a merciless exercise; sorrowing, resentful, maliciously amused. The unforgiving child now armed, and armored, with grown-up literary poise.

Lowell liked to think of his presentation of his father as "tender," but only in the elegiac poems that appear in the fourth section of *Life Studies* does pathos outweigh ridicule. And even here the evidence of Lowell's drafts suggests that ridicule could as easily have been outweighed by something close to hatred:

> "Still doing things the hard way, Feller?"
> He'd tease me. Ten years later,
> When I came home from Kenyon
> College, an arm-chair *Agrarian*
> Quoting in Latin from the *Bucolics*
> And Pound's *ABC of Economics*
> He used to turn a puking green
> Reminding me how at fourteen
> He mailed a monthly check from Annapolis to his mother.[26]

This fourth section is arrived at by way of a group of chatty, affectionate pieces about literary figures: Ford Madox Ford, George Santayana, Delmore Schwartz and Hart Crane—a rather artificial yoking, this, of minor pieces with which Lowell had been tinkering for years. It is Part Four that actually bears the name "Life Studies"; and this is the section in which Lowell's "new style" is unequivocally on display. The studies open with family portraits and reminiscences—versifications, in the main, of the more powerful of his prose vignettes. There are times when the "poetry" adds nothing to the prose. For example:

> Almost immediately he bought a larger and more stylish house; he sold his ascetic stove-black Hudson and bought a plump brown Buick; later the Buick was exchanged for a high-toned, as-good-as-new Packard with a custom-designed royal blue and mahogany body. Without drama, his earnings more or less decreased from year to year.

This is from "91 Revere Street." Reset in free verse (in "Commander Lowell"), with some details added and some others dropped, it reads:

> whenever he left a job,
> he bought a smarter car.
> Father's last employer
> was Scudder, Stevens and Clark, Investment Advisors,
> himself his only client.
> While Mother dragged to bed alone,
> read Menninger,
> and grew more and more suspicious,
> he grew defiant.
> Night after night,
> *à la clarté déserte de sa lampe*,
> he slid his ivory Annapolis slide rule
> across a pad of graphs—
> piker speculations! In three years
> he squandered sixty thousand dollars.

The line breaks here seem random, and there is none of the rhythmic or imagistic subtlety that marks the later free-verse poems in the book. It is worth remembering that when Lowell first thought of "versifying" his prose autobiography, his instinct was to do it in metrical couplets. Here, for example, is a draft of a sonnet about the family graveyard at Dunbarton, in which Lowell's father is again to be found studying his graphs:

> Four years have left Dunbarton much the same,
> Mother, another stone, another name;
> And you, earth's orbit? You are things,
> No you, no person. Ah, the king of kings,
> Little Napoleon, whose bolting food
> So caught your fancy, caught your horror stood
> Blotting your minutes after Father died.
> No bustle, bustle, bustle. Groom and bride
> Lie cot by cot. Once more they feel the spark
> Dive through the unnerved marrow of their dark,
> A person breaking through his prison term,
> Where now as then, relapsing, Oh a germ,
> Studies his navel, graphs and charts and maps
> Gentle to all, and loving none perhaps.[27]

It is small wonder that when Lowell made the decision to shift from this kind of mechanical regularity to the spacious relaxation of free verse, he was somewhat dazzled by his own boldness; for a period, at any rate, he was content simply to "take liberties," to relish the sheer drasticness of what he'd done. The notion that free verse could be as intricate, dramatic and intense as anything he'd done before in meter seems not to have struck him until about halfway through the sequence of "family poems" in *Life Studies.* A letter to William Carlos Williams on February 19, 1958, is a bold and defensive statement to the archenemy of metrics that Lowell's "conversion" would, after all, be incomplete:

> In a month or so I'll mail you another little group of my own stuff, God willing. I now have four or five things you haven't seen. I wouldn't like ever to completely give up meter; it's wonderful opposition to wrench against and revise with. Yet now that I've joined you in unscanned verse, I am struck by how often the old classics get boxed up in their machinery, the sonority of the iambic pentameter line, the apparatus of logic and conceit and even set subjects. Still, the muscle is there in the classics, we re-read them with joy, and in a sense wherever a man has really worked his stuff outbraves time and novel methods. We would always rather read a good old sonneteer, such as Raleigh or Sidney than some

merely competent modern fellow who is on the right track. The excellent speak to the excellent.[28]

That "*we* would rather read . . ." observation is a kind of scolding bluff, since Lowell knew very well that Williams might *not* rather read a Raleigh sonnet than some new effort "in the American grain."

As it turns out, the inconsistency between the "early" and "late" poems of *Life Studies* does seem to have a point. The looser, more pedestrian "studies" are those in which the family is seen through the eyes of the child Lowell—"My Last Afternoon with Uncle Devereux Winslow," "Dunbarton," "Grandparents" and "Commander Lowell." These are elegant and witty pieces, and have some piercing moments—the ending of the Uncle Devereux poem for example—but the tone throughout is benign, detached and utterly unhurried. And one would be hard pressed to insist that they *need* to be set out as verse, not prose; indeed, their merits are prose merits.

The change comes when Lowell begins to draw on his adult experience of family life, and death; when the poet cannot avoid moving to the center of his own poems. It may be that by this stage Lowell was more sure—technically—of what he was about; or it may be that the subject was no longer half invented and remote. Certainly, with "Terminal Days at Beverly Farms" and the poems that follow it, there is a noticeable tightening: alliterations and assonances seem more deliberate, more shrewd and menacing; the dramatic shifts more calculated, brutal. Here is Mr. Lowell once again, thirty years older now but still clutching his ivory slide rule:

> Each morning at eight-thirty,
> inattentive and beaming,
> loaded with his "calc" and "trig" books,
> his clipper ship statistics,
> and his ivory slide rule,
> Father stole off with the *Chevie*
> to loaf in the Maritime Museum at Salem.
> He called the curator
> "the commander of the Swiss Navy."
>
> Father's death was abrupt and unprotesting.
> His vision was still twenty-twenty.
> After a morning of anxious, repetitive smiling,

his last words to Mother were:
"I feel awful."

There follow three more poems on Lowell's parents' deaths and
then a transitional piece—"During Fever"—in which the poet, a
father now himself, strains for a wise, forgiving view of his own
background. Then we are immediately thrust forward into the orphaned present tense, with "Waking in the Blue" and "Home After
Three Months Away." We have moved from "those settled years
of World War One" to the 1957 agonies of the family's afflicted heir,
from lazily chopped-up prose to a lyricism more delicately measured
than anything in Lowell's early meters. The matching of the poet's
maturity in free verse with the growing up of the child-hero of the
family poems may not have been planned out, but its dramatic
rightness does give credence to Lowell's contention that "I see the
'Life Studies' sequence as one poem, at least in the first section. It
really centers about my father and the parts are not meant to stand
by themselves."[29]
   Section II of the "Life Studies" sequence has four poems—each
of them bitingly personal but offering a broader view of Lowell's life
so far: in each he tries to face the crippling and destructive "side-
effects" of his recurrent mental breakdowns. One consequence is
that he no longer trusts his old intellectual vehemence and he knows
that others trust it even less: his verbal brilliance they now associate
with "the kingdom of the mad—its hackneyed speech, its homicidal
eye"; it frightens them. He knows too that when he was a "fire-
breathing Catholic C.O." and refused military service, he may well
have been in the grip of energies that must now, if he is to live any
sort of "normal life," be "tranquillized." It is no real comfort that
his own prescribed inertia is mirrored in the self-serving compla-
cency of Eisenhower's America, that

> even the man
> scavenging filth in the back alley trash cans
> has two children, a beach wagon, a helpmate,
> and is a "young Republican."

But then what are "ideals" worth if they can only be pursued in
mania? And what is a sane professor's life in Boston worth if "excite-

ment" or "enthusiasm" is always to be thought of as a symptom of destruction and collapse?

The first version of the poem "Man and Wife" was called "Holy Matrimony," and it included an early draft of what was later to become the separate "To Speak of Woe That Is in Marriage" (printed in *Life Studies* next to "Man and Wife"). Although uncompleted and unpolished, it provides a powerful insight into the "political" background of a poem in which references to "the Rahvs" (Philip Rahv was editor of *Partisan Review* during the most vehement period of *its* history) and "the traditional South" have seemed to some critics overintimate or incidental. "Holy Matrimony" also makes it clear that the "old-fashioned tirade" referred to in "Man and Wife" is in fact the substance of the next poem in the book—"To Speak of Woe That Is in Marriage"—although recast into the third person.

> At last the trees are green on Marlborough Street,
> Blossoms on our Saucer Magnolia ignite
> For their feverish five days white. . . .
> Last night I held your hands, *Petite*,
> Subtlest of all God's creatures, still pure nerve,
> Still purer nerve than I,
> Who, hand on glass
> And heart in mouth,
> Outdrank the Rahvs once in the heat
> Of Greenwich Village, and sat at your feet—
> Too boiled and shy
> And poker-faced to make a pass,
> While the shrill verve
> Of your invective scorched the solid South.
>
> On warm spring night [*sic*] though, we can hear the outcry,
> If our windows are open wide,
> I can hear the South End,
> The razor's edge
> Of Boston's negro culture. They as we
> Refine past culture's possibility,
> Fear homocide [*sic*],
> Grow horny with alcohol, take the pledge . . .
> At forty why pretend
> It's just the others, not ourselves, who die?

And now you turn your back,
Sleepless, you hold
Your pillow to your hollows like a child,
And once again,
The merciless Racinian *tirade*
Breaks like the Atlantic on my head:

"It's the injustice . . . you are so unjust.
There's nothing accommodating, nice or kind—
But *What can I do for you?* What can I do for you,
Shambling into our bed at two
With all the monotonous sourness of your lust,
A tusked heart, an alcoholic's mind,
And blind, blind, blind
Drunk! Have pity! My worst evil
Is living at your level.
My mind
Moves like a water-spider. . . .
The legs stick and break in your slough.
Why prolong our excruciation now?
What is your purpose? Each night now I tie
Ten dollar[30]

The draft version ends here, but the line finally (in "To Speak of Woe . . .") reads:

> Each night now I tie
> ten dollars and his car key to my thigh. . . .

The last poem in *Life Studies*—"Skunk Hour"—shows the poet free-lancing out on one of his nocturnal car rides. It is the most nakedly desperate piece in the book, and Lowell called it "the anchor poem of the sequence." "Skunk Hour" was the first of the *Life Studies* poems to be finished: after his tour of the West Coast in March 1957 Lowell "began writing lines in a new style," but

No poem . . . got finished and soon I left off and tried to forget the whole headache. Suddenly, in August, I was struck by the sadness of writing nothing, and having nothing to write, of having, at least, no language. When I began writing "Skunk Hour," I felt that most of what I knew about writing was a hindrance.[31]

He began the poem in mid-August 1957 and completed it in a month. It was modeled, he said, on Elizabeth Bishop's "The Armadillo." Both poems "use short line stanzas, start with drifting description and end with a single animal."[32]

The "drifting description" in the first four stanzas of "Skunk Hour" is of an ailing Maine sea town. The inhabitants are either anachronistic or nouveau-absurd: "our summer millionaire, / who seemed to leap from an L. L. Bean / catalogue"; "our fairy decorator." According to Hardwick, all these people "were living, more or less as he sees them, in Castine that summer. The details, not the feeling, were rather alarmingly precise, I thought. But fortunately it was not read in town for some time, and then only by 'people like us.' "[33] Perhaps because of the way the poem develops, explicators have been overeager to make these opening descriptive lines more weighty and sinister than they really are—in truth, they are meant as lightish social comedy: "I try to give a tone of tolerance, humor, and randomness to the sad prospect." As Lowell said, "all comes alive in Stanzas V and VI":

> One dark night,
> my Tudor Ford climbed the hill's skull;
> I watched for love-cars. Lights turned down,
> they lay together, hull to hull,
> where the graveyard shelves on the town. . . .
> My mind's not right.
>
> A car radio bleats,
> "Love, O careless Love. . . ." I hear
> my ill spirit sob in each blood cell,
> as if my hand were at its throat. . . .
> I myself am hell;
> nobody's here—

. . . This is the dark night. I hoped my readers would remember John of the Cross's poem. My night is not gracious, but secular, puritan and agnostical. An Existential night. Somewhere in my mind was a passage from Sartre or Camus about reaching some point of final darkness where the one free act is suicide.[34]

The closing image of the mother skunk risking all to feed her "column of kittens" is meant as ambiguous affirmation—the skunk family are to be seen as a "healthy, joyful apparition—despite their diet and smell, they are natural power."[35] The poet who feels lower than a skunk finds both comedy and renewal in the beasts' quixotically defiant march up Main Street. They are scavengers but could never be "Republicans." The skunks are both touching and funny, and, as much as anything else, it is Lowell's wit, his delight in the barbarous and the absurd, that rescues him from "final darkness." Read like this, the poem does indeed "anchor" a sequence that has asked, time and again, and in the worst of circumstances: "What use is my sense of humor?"

Apart from Allen Tate's "dissenting opinion," the response of Lowell's friends to the manuscript of *Life Studies* had been enthusiastic, and in November 1958 Lowell was particularly gratified to get a view of the finished book from William Carlos Williams, a view that (although rather confused in its expression—Williams was already a sick man) must have eased any lingering fears that the Williams influence was unassimilated:[36]

Dear Cal,
    Floss has just finished reading me your terrible wonderful poems. You have lost nothing of your art, in fact you have piled accomplishment upon accomplishment until there is nothing to be said to you in rebuttle [sic] of your devastating statements or the way you have uttered them. I'm trying to be not rhetorical but to approach the man you are with all defenses down.
    Either this has to be a long letter hinging [sic] growth in your sheer mastery of your skill in English composition or a heartbreaking statement of the human situation which has posessed [sic] you for the last ten years. To be a successful artist means a victory in the first place and then over the world you inhabit. Poverty as in the case of the painters Cezanne and Van Gogh—It was a mistake to bring that in here but I am merely stalling for words. You have nothing to do with that. Your problem was the English language. Your use of the words is aristocratic —sometimes you use rhyme—but thank goodness less and less frequently and that is an improvement, you speak more to us, more directly when you do not have to descend to it, your language gains in seriousness and ability in your choice of words when you abandon rhyme completely. I'm just fumbling around knowing I have much to say to you but without release.

The book must have caused you some difficulty to write. There is no lying permitted to a man who writes that way.

(Next day)

I couldn't go on. The book took too much out of me which I don't have any more to give. It's very impressive but I couldn't read it again. The one short lyric is really beautiful [probably "For Sale"], finished and beautiful.

Do you want me to return the manuscript, otherwise I'll keep it in my files—for some one of my literary executors to discover for himself and wonder at.

Keep well, Dear Cal

Bill

Oddly enough, *Life Studies,* the most "American" of Lowell's books, made its first appearance in Britain, in April 1959. Faber and Faber wanted to enter it for selection by the newly formed Poetry Book Society, and to qualify, the English edition had to be a "first edition." Charles Monteith of Faber recalls:

> we went ahead as fast as we could, which is why "91 Revere Street" isn't in it—we never even saw it until it appeared in the American edition —and I got page proofs ready in time and submitted them to the Poetry Book Society, and the upshot of all this was that it wasn't even recommended. The choice that time was *The Wreck of the Magyar,* by Patricia Beer.[37]

Apart from a review in the *Observer* by A. Alvarez which heralded "Something New in Verse,"[38] and more cautious tributes by G. S. Fraser in the *New Statesman* ("accomplished . . . interesting and touchingly 'human' ")[39] and Roy Fuller in the *London Magazine,*[40] the British reviews were fairly tepid. Frank Kermode's piece in the *Spectator* spoke of "a poet so sure of his powers that he does not recognise the danger of lapsing into superior doggerel when he too luxuriously controls it,"[41] and someone called Peter Dickinson in *Punch* announced that "few of the poems are in themselves memorable."[42] But perhaps the British review that would have mattered most to Lowell was by Philip Larkin in the *Manchester Guardian.* Larkin had already been in respectful correspondence with Lowell, and "respectful" is perhaps the best word to apply to his verdict on

Life Studies; the family poems he describes as "curious, hurried, off-hand vignettes, seeming too personal to be practised, yet none the less accurate and original," and of the whole book he writes:

> In spite of their tension, these poems have a lightness and almost flippant humour not common in Mr Lowell's previous work, matched with a quicker attention to feeling which personally I welcome. If these qualities are products of the stresses recorded in the final few poems of this book, Mr Lowell will not have endured in vain.[43]

The American reviews began to appear in May 1959. Richard Eberhart led the way in the *New York Times Book Review.* Uncertain about Lowell's new style, its "prosaic quality," Eberhart nonetheless elected to go overboard:

> Lowell's poems have a lasting tensile strength. They are made of finer blood, thrown together in a violence of imaginative reality controlled by sensitive knowledge of linguistics and cognitive nuances. . . . Savagery and sophistication meet in a style that is original, the Lowell idiom.[44]

But as usual, the important judgments came in the quarterlies. F. W. Dupee in *Partisan Review* rather regretted the abandonment of Lowell's old heroic stance: "He wrote as if poetry were still a major art and not merely a venerable pastime which ought to be perpetuated." On the other hand, though, these new works had none of the "contagion of violence, the excess of willful effort" that forced so many of the early poems to "run riot." Lowell was now seeking the "causes" of his "tragic imagination"; his "dark day in Boston" now produced "more humor and quizzical tenderness than fierce wit." There was, though, in *Life Studies* something "inconclusive":

> Where, Henry James would inquire, is your denouement? Still, the poems add up to something like the effectiveness of *Mauberley,* Pound's sequence of scenes and portraits from London life. They represent, perhaps, major poetry pulling in its horns and putting on big spectacles and studying how to survive. The once militantly tragic poet, who warred bitterly on himself, is pictured on the jacket of *Life Studies* wearing big spectacles.[45]

The *Kenyon* reviewer was John Thompson, the friend who on two occasions—in Chicago in 1949 and in Cincinnati in 1954—had faced the "kingdom of the mad" and helped to drag Lowell "home alive."

His review was by far the most intense and perceptive piece to be written on *Life Studies* and, indeed, still stands as one of the most intelligent and heartfelt estimates of Lowell's gifts. Thompson begins by announcing that these new poems are "a shock" and then takes on the not simple task of trying to define the difference between *their* shockingness and that of those "adventures in sensation" that can be found in "dozens of current novels and memoirs":

> in these poems there are depths of the self that in life are not ordinarily acknowledged and in literature are usually figured in disguise. Traditionally, between the persona of the creation and the person of the creator a certain distance exists, and this has been so even for lyric poets and their utterances, habitually inclined to the first person as they are. Devices of fiction or concealment large or small accomplish this estrangement. . . . Robert Lowell's new poems show that this distance between persona and poem is not, after all, important to art, but has been a reflection of the way our culture conceived character. This conception seems to be dwindling now to a mere propriety. And for these poems, the question of propriety no longer exists. They have made a conquest; what they have won is a major expansion of the territory of poetry.[46]

Thompson, an expert on traditional prosody, then describes the technical "shock" *Life Studies* also carries and is acute on how "The metrical form . . . works indirectly, even negatively" in these seemingly "free" poems; he draws on his long friendship with the poet to analyze the difference between a conventional "sense of history" (i.e., "glory of the past, misery of the present") and Lowell's unique way of living in the past: "the great past, Revolutionary America, the Renaissance, Rome, is all contemporary to him. He moves among its great figures at ease with his peers. For him the sense of declining glory is a permanent human feeling, not the special curse of our own time." And, in his conclusion, Thompson offers a verdict that, for all its generosity, amounts almost to a challenge; certainly, there is something daunting in its implied view of Lowell's possibilities—and duties?

> The voice of Robert Lowell's poetry has always had the authority of the extreme. No conflict is glossed over or rationalized by a system of ideas. His religion was always entirely eschatological; the world he describes, ancient or modern, is never influenced by religion but only threatened by it. It is as if he could bear to contemplate this world because he could momentarily expect its total destruction or total delivery.

Thus, the one thing this poet never worried about in his writing was how to go on living. This has given him great strength, which he still has. The new poems have abandoned the myths of eschatology and the masks of heroes, but the violence and guilt, the unalleviated seizure of experience, these remain. This is why, perhaps alone of living poets, he can bear for us the role of the great poet, the man who on a very large scale sees more, feels more, and speaks more bravely about it than we ourselves can do. He can speak now of the most desperate and sordid personal experience with full dignity. Nothing need be explained, accounted for, or moralized.[47]

Partisan and *Kenyon* published their reviews of *Life Studies* in their Summer 1959 issues. The *Hudson Review*'s contribution appeared three months later, even though the editor, Joseph Bennett, had picked himself as the reviewer of the book. Bennett's piece was brief and savage:

> This book does little to add to Lowell's standing as a poet. Lazy and anecdotal, it is more suited as an appendix to some snobbish society magazine, to *Town and Country* or *Harper's Bazaar*, rather than as purposeful work.[48]

Bennett goes on to sneer at the aristocratic Bostonians who in Lowell's book "romp through town mansions, country estates, seaside villas" and at the snobbishness that "we" find in Lowell's accounts of the McLean Hospital and West Street Jail: "we visit an insane asylum for Porcellian members; our jail in New York reminds us of the soccer court at St. Mark's School." There is no hint throughout the review that *Life Studies* might be anything other than "a collection of lazily recollected and somewhat snobbish memoirs, principally of the poet's own wealthy and aristocratic family."

In other reviews there were negative rumblings here and there; Thom Gunn in the *Yale Review* objected to "trivial autobiographical details, rambling and without unity" and to an overall "flatness" in the writing,[49] and M. L. Rosenthal in the *Nation* let it be known that his "first impression while reading *Life Studies* was that it is impure art, magnificently stated but unpleasantly egocentric— somehow resembling the triumph of the skunks over the garbage cans," but by the end of his review was sufficiently won over to proclaim that "*Life Studies* brings to culmination one line of development in our poetry of the utmost importance."[50] (Rosenthal was later to expand this review into an influential essay—called "The Poetry of Confession"—which claimed *Life Studies* to be "an outgrowth of the social criticism that has marked almost the whole sweep of poetry in this century. Thus, Lowell's poems carry the burden of the age within them.") Daniel Hoffman in the *Sewanee Review* believed the book to be "transitional. . . . The protagonist in Mr. Lowell's poems appears to be undergoing a regeneration, perhaps only just begun."[51]

Hoffman's review echoed a number of the other minor notices that greeted *Life Studies* on its appearance in May 1959. As Thom Gunn sardonically remarked: "The attitude of most critics I have seen is: this is not what we are used to from Lowell so let us play it safe by saying that it *may* lead to great poetry." It is not known how many of these notices Lowell saw at the time. On May 19, 1959, he was writing to Edmund Wilson from Bowditch Hall at McLean's: "I've been conditioning here for about a month, and feel swimming. . . ."[52] Lowell's second breakdown within a year had coincided with the publication of his revolutionary new book. The only review we know for certain that he saw was, ironically enough, in a letter from Allen Tate—written to McLean's on May 8: "you will be alright very soon. . . . your book is magnificent. All will be well."[53]

On his release from McLean's in June 1959 Lowell was once again pressed to engage in "uninterrupted psycho-therapy." As always, he agreed; but as Elizabeth Hardwick recalls, the agreement didn't mean that he expected it to do much good:

> Cal never cared anything about psychoanalysis—he went dutifully. It would be like going to mass because you're told to; told that you're going to be crazy all the time if you don't.[1]

Throughout the summer, Lowell obediently repeated the previous year's routine: commuting to Castine to be with his wife and daughter while keeping up his teaching and his therapy in Boston. He wrote one poem during 1959—"The Drinker," a rather meandering study in loneliness, or desertedness. It strives for a repellent accuracy on the rituals of the hangover (although truly hardened drinkers might find something quaint in the notion of "before-*breakfast*" —their italics!—"cigarettes"):

> Stubbed before-breakfast cigarettes
> burn bull's-eyes on the bedside table;
> a plastic tumbler of alka seltzer
> champagnes in the bathroom.

The drinker in the poem is a "beached whale" in whose warm-hearted blubber "barbed hooks fester":

> His despair has the galvanized color
> of the mop and water in the galvanized bucket.

Once she was close to him
as water to the dead metal.

He looks at her engagements inked on her calendar.
A list of indictments.
At the numbers in her thumbed black telephone book.
A quiver full of arrows.[2]

Hardwick had deliberately kept at a "certain distance" from Lowell during this latest illness. She had managed to patch together a
degree of optimism during the calm last months of 1958, and—on the
evidence of earlier attacks—had felt able to predict at least a two-
or even three-year respite. She had set up a European trip for May
and June of 1959: two weeks in London during May, then Amsterdam for a week, followed by a fortnight in Italy (Florence and
Venice, mainly) and a final ten days or so in Paris. The Tates (Allen
and his new wife, Isabella Gardner) and the Macauleys were in
Europe, and arrangements had been made for Harriet to be left
behind in Boston. On March 20, 1959, Hardwick had written the
Macauleys in Paris:

I'm very excited about the trip, but very reluctant, nearly ill really to
leave Harriet and very reluctant to be flying about everywhere, risking
her orphanage, if there is such a word. I at last feel she'll be all right here;
it is more myself, my own missing her, and wanting to get back safely
to her that bothers me.[3]

Lowell's collapse the following month seems therefore to have
come without much advance warning or buildup—and certainly,
this time, without a girl. He had, it is true, been "active" during
March, visiting Randall Jarrell in Greensboro, North Carolina, and
Peter Taylor in Columbus, Ohio, and on March 15 he had written
a slightly too breezy letter to John Berryman (who, he had heard,
was in the hospital, suffering from exhaustion):

I am just back from Greensboro, where Randall and [I] enjoyed (?)
ourselves lamenting the times. It seems there's been something curious
twisted and against the grain about the world poets of our generation
have had to live in. What troubles you and I, Ted Roethke, Elizabeth
Bishop, Delmore, Randall—even Karl Shapiro—have had. I hope your
exaustion [sic] is nothing very drastic; these knocks are almost a proof

of intelligence and valor in us. However, all in all, each year grows better and gayer and more serious.[4]

But for Hardwick, the suddenness of the attack, its closeness to the one before (it was just over a year since Lowell had been discharged from McLean's) raised new and wholly dreadful prospects. On June 1, she wrote, with some weariness, to Allen Tate:

> If only these things of Cal's were simply distressing; they cause me and other people real suffering. And for what? I do not know the answer to the moral problems posed by a deranged person, but the dreadful fact is that in purely personal terms this deranged person does a lot of harm. I don't know, Allen, what to do. This particular time I have kept at a certain distance from Cal, but he is terribly demanding and devouring. I feel a deep loyalty and commitment to him; and yet at the same time I don't know exactly what sort of bearable status quo I can establish with him. In any case I told him I envied you and Belle, and I do: that made him very angry.[5]

During Lowell's hospitalization at McLean's a year earlier, in the spring of 1958, he had tried his hand at translation—not for the first time, since there are versions of Rimbaud, Valéry and Rilke in *Lord Weary's Castle*. On April 1, 1958, he had written to Jarrell: "While I was in hospital and nothing original came I tried a few translations, mostly from an Italian poet of Eliot's generation, named Montale."[6] From Montale he had moved on to Ungaretti and to Rilke. Later in the year, having been "shatteringly impressed" by Pasternak (who had won the Nobel Prize in 1958), he had "changed one of [his] courses just to read Russian—it was meant to be something precise like the New Critics as prose writers."[7] And for the whole of 1959 he more or less gave up attempting to write anything "original." He felt "drained of new poems," and anything he did produce seemed "a dry repetitious version of something sufficiently and better said in Life Studies."[8] On January 3, 1960, he wrote again to Jarrell, who was in a similar predicament:

> How goes the Goethe? And what's happening to you? Flores German anthology just arrived in the mail, and I have read your bunch of translations with increased wonder.
> I'm deep in translations and have only finished one poem of my own since last winter. I have to bend and bend to enjoy new English and

Kenyon School of Letters: (*standing*) Philip Rice, Arthur Mizener, Robert Lowell, Kenneth Burke, Delmore Schwartz, Charles Coffin; (*sitting*) William Empson, John Crowe Ransom, L. C. Knights, 1950.

Lowell tips a foul ball, Kenyon College, 1950.

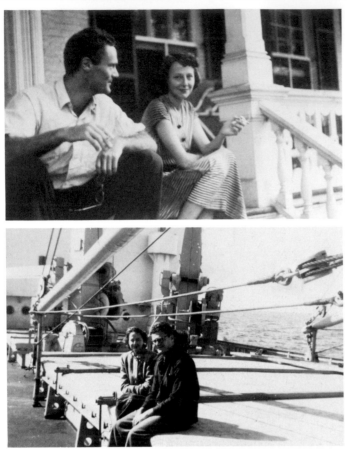

Robert Lowell and
Elizabeth Hardwick,
in Red Hook, N.Y., 1949.

Robert Lowell and
Elizabeth Hardwick
on the boat to Europe, 1950.

Left: Robert Lowell and Elizabeth Hardwick, in Florence, 1950. *Right:* Elizabeth
Hardwick, Florence, 1950.

© ROLLIE McKENNA

Robert Lowell, 1953.

Elizabeth Hardwick, 1955.

Right: Harriet Winslow's house in Castine, M

Right: Robert Lowell and daughter, Harriet, 19

Robert Lowell teaching in Boston, 1964.

OMB TESTS

Robert Lowell and Elizabeth Hardwick, in Castine, Me., 1960.

Robert Lowell with his daughter, Harriet, 1961.

American poems, but easily become pious and uncritical reading Pasternak and Montale. One wants a whole new deck of cards to play with, or at least new rules for the old ones. Maybe it's the times, or maybe it's being well in one's forties, or maybe it's all a private thing with me: but I feel wrung with altered views and standards—more than I can swallow. So many questions, one is almost speechless.[9]

The same note of "What next?" speechlessness is sounded in Lowell's address on receiving the National Book Award for *Life Studies*. [10] He talks in this of two "competing" types of poetry—"a cooked and a raw"—and clearly has in mind the challenge that Beat poets like Allen Ginsberg, Gregory Corso and Lawrence Ferlinghetti were then offering to the traditional or "academic" poets (of whom he, before *Life Studies*, would have been seen as a leading light). An anthology edited by Donald M. Allen called *The New American Poetry 1945–60* had, for example, presented a clamorous riposte to the authority of the *New Poets of England and America* collection put together two years earlier by Donald Hall, Robert Pack and Louis Simpson. By 1960 the battle lines were clearly drawn, and Lowell found himself in no-man's-land: "There is a poetry that can only be studied, and a poetry that can only be declaimed, a poetry of pedantry and a poetry of scandal." Lowell's "cooked" and "raw" definition became famous; this is how he elaborated it in a draft for his acceptance speech: "The cooked, marvellously expert and remote, seems constructed as a sort of mechanical or catnip mouse for graduate seminars; the raw, jerry-built and forensically deadly, seems often like an unscored libretto by some bearded but vegetarian Castro."[11] And as for his own poetry: "When I finished *Life Studies* I was left hanging on a question mark. I am still hanging there. I don't know whether it is a death-rope or a life-line."[12]

Ironically, this bleak curriculum is printed in the program for the Boston Arts Festival, which was held in June 1960, in Boston's Public Garden. Lowell had been asked to read a new poem at the festival, and since—as he said later—he could hardly have offered them "The Drinker" or even a version of Montale, he worked from January to June on a piece that is now thought of as a wholly triumphant answer to that "question mark." "For the Union Dead" can be both studied and declaimed; it is learned (and has provoked more reams of exegesis than perhaps any other poem by Lowell), but it also has vivid and personal ingredients—in the manner of *Life Studies*. And without doubt it provided a life-line, or at any rate a way forward to the next phase of Lowell's work.

The poem was the outcome of a cluster of coincidences: the coincidence of Lowell's sense of his own barrenness and the arrival of a "commission" from the Boston Festival. The subject of Colonel Shaw and his Negro regiment had long fascinated Lowell: Shaw was linked by marriage to Lowell's favorite ancestor, Beau Sabreur, and his suicidal mission had been celebrated in several poems, including one by James Russell Lowell. There was an additional prompting in the work Elizabeth Hardwick was doing at the time: she was preparing an edition of William James's letters, and it was James who had delivered the oration at the unveiling of Saint-Gaudens's memorial to Colonel Shaw:

> at the dedication,
> William James could almost hear the bronze Negroes breathe.
>
> Their monument sticks like a fishbone
> In the city's throat.[13]

Also, in October 1959 Lowell had become a member of the Tavern Club in Boston, and had dug out in the library there the text of Justice Oliver Wendell Holmes's "Harvard College in the War." Both James and Holmes spoke resoundingly of duty, self-sacrifice, heroic action: the formula for what John Thompson called a "glory of the past, misery of the present" study of the Boston spirit was readily to hand. Civil War heroism is set beside the threat of nuclear war; municipal barbarism (the ruining of Boston Common to build underground garages) is set against the natural barbarism of "the dark downward and vegetating kingdom / of the fish and reptile"; the Abolitionist struggle is mocked by television images of "the drained faces of Negro school-children." When he was a child, Lowell used to watch real fish in the Aquarium: but today

> The Aquarium is gone. Everywhere
> giant finned cars nose forward like fish;
> a savage servility
> slides by on grease.[14]

A melodramatic image, which recalls—in tone if not in meter—the poet-prophet of *Lord Weary's Castle,* the exalted punisher of Boston's ills. The difference is that Lowell now deals not in destruction but in decline, and he no longer pretends that God is on his side. "For the Union Dead" is an intricately organized poem, its chain of associated images seems fashioned with high cunning, and there is much subtlety in its manipulation of historical, personal and current political elements. If, in itself, it seems overdeliberate and without the energy and rhythmic grace of the best of the *Life Studies* poems (Lowell called it "the most composed poem I've ever written"),[15] it is nonetheless his first step towards extending the possibilities of his self-centeredness: towards treating his own torments as metaphors of public, even global, ills. It also marks a sorrowing and sour final truce with Boston.

For a year or more, Lowell had been writing in letters: "We are awfully sick of Boston. The only unconventional people here are charming screwballs, who never finish a picture or publish a line. Then there are Cousins and Harvard professors. All very pleasant, but . . ."[16] And Hardwick, in the December 1959 issue of *Harper's,* had published an article on "Boston: A Lost Ideal," which makes Lowell's scorn seem almost wistful and genteel. On "proper Bostonians" she writes that "the town has always attracted men of quiet and timid and tasteful opinion, men interested in old families and things, in the charms of times recently past":

> The importance of Boston was intellectual and as its intellectual donations to the country have diminished, so it has declined from its lofty symbolic meaning, to become a more lowly image, a sort of farce of conservative exclusiveness.

But in any case the Boston New Englander—i.e., the Anglo-Saxon —is now pure anomaly: the town is governed by Irish and Italians, and governed rather badly. Hardwick writes of Boston's "municipal civil backwardness," its "feckless, ugly, municipal neglect." The city has no night life—"In Boston the night comes down with an incredibly heavy, small-town finality"—no Bohemian or café life. It *does* have the "brilliantly exciting Boston Arts Festival held in the Public Garden for two weeks in June," it has Symphony Hall, lectures in nearby Cambridge, and so on; but the real action is "cozy,

Victorian and gossipy": "The "nice little dinner party"—for this the Bostonian would sell his soul":

> In Boston there is an utter absence of that wild electric beauty of New York, of the marvellous excited rush of people in taxicabs at twilight, of the great avenues and streets, the restaurants, theaters, bars, hotels, delicatessen shops.

By the time Lowell read his poem at the Boston Festival—to "an audience of thousands and encore after encore if that's what they're called when they're poems"[17]—he had already accepted a Ford Foundation grant to "study opera" in New York; the poet William Meredith had been given a similar grant, and he recalls:

> The Ford Foundation decided it would be interesting to take a group of established writers who had not written plays and attach them to repertory companies and see if they turn out to be good dramatists. More poets than fiction writers, I think. Anthony Hecht was attached to one of the repertory theaters in Manhattan, Richard Wilbur to the one in Houston. Lowell and I expressed an interest in opera and we were accredited to the New York City Opera Company and the Metropolitan for a season.[18]

The "study" would begin in September 1960, but as early as March, Lowell was writing to Meredith with the suggestion that they collaborate on a libretto based on Melville's story "Benito Cereno"; other possibles were Richard Hughes's *A High Wind in Jamaica* and Georg Büchner's *Danton's Death*—"the best modern political play I know of"[19]—but it was the Melville that excited Lowell, connecting as it did with his study of the Colonel Shaw exploit and with his own uneasy, ambiguous feelings about "the razor's edge of Boston's negro culture." As he paraphrased it for Cousin Harriet:

> Benito Cereno [is] the story of an honest but rather thick-skulled American sea-captain from Dunbury, Mass., who spends a day on board a Spanish slave ship in 1799, unaware that the slaves have seized the ship and killed most of the Spaniards. The hero is a sort of Henry Jamesian innocent abroad.[20]

"For the Union Dead" is, to be sure, an "abolitionist poem," and Lowell was later to say that in it "I lament the loss of the old Abolitionist spirit: the terrible injustice, in the past and in the present, of the American treatment of the Negro is of the greatest urgency to me as a man and as a writer."[21] But this correct thinking did not prevent him from responding to Melville's tale of a Jamesian innocent confronted with the realities of a successful black rebellion. On this subject, Lowell wrote to William Meredith:

> how can we handle the whole plot so as not to make it rather shockingly anti-negro: What I'd hope for would be something neutral, rather what's happening now, wrong blazing into a holocaust, no one innicent [sic]. But the action—in Melville the negroes with their bloodthirsty servility are symbolic drama—on the stage will be much more unbearable than read, or even worse, likely to seem a sadistic unfelt farce.[22]

(The phrase here, "bloodthirsty servility," forces one to look back to the final stanza of "For the Union Dead"—is the poem's vision of "savage servility" in truth Lowell's vision of wrong blazing into a black-against-white holocaust?)

Meredith was not enticed by the challenge of *Benito Cereno;* he thought it "full of problems. Quite possibly it is not the work we could best collaborate on."[23] His proposal was that they wait until September and then "hang around the City Center and the Met for the first four months" and try to "define our concept of the opera." Lowell, however, was not to be restrained, and during the summer of 1960, at Castine, he finished a draft of "the whole of Benito"—

> 47 pages, a sort of iambic free verse with a lot of show and charade and horror, more action than language. It went so quickly I am stunned and don't know whether it works or how it can work in with what you've done. I am eager to compare notes. My version is a play, not an opera, if it is anything.[24]

He also completed his heroic-couplet translation of Racine's *Phèdre* —prodded here by a commission for Eric Bentley's Classic Drama series—and started work on a group of Baudelaire "versions." Since the spring of 1959 he had published almost a dozen translations in magazines—his Montale and Rilke, as well as poems by Pasternak and Heine—and was beginning to think seriously of a collection. Although still "hanging on a question mark," Lowell was able to write to Meredith in August 1960:

> [I feel] wonderfully athletic, hackish and ready for opera, though I haven't done anything yet. I wonder if Phèdre or something like it could be given in a singing version, though I'm still keen on Benito.[25]

In September the Lowells moved from Boston to New York— the move was to be for the year of Lowell's Ford Foundation grant, and they had exchanged their Marlborough Street house for Eric Bentley's apartment at 194 Riverside Drive. Lowell and Meredith began to "hang around the Met," watching rehearsals and—Lowell boasted—attending "four Puccinis in a week."[26] In October, Lowell wrote to Peter Taylor, who was now in London working as a resident playwright at the Royal Court Theatre:

> We feel the same way as you about London about New York, very engagé and anonymous. There's a difference about my work, i.e. my total ignorance of music and opera. However, the rehearsals are great fun—full of things like Stokowski walking out and Christopher West walking out.[27]

Lowell's "theatrical" mood was sustained also by negotiations for a London and perhaps a Broadway production of his *Phaedra;* Lincoln Kirstein had shown Lowell's translation to the British producer George Devine, and the early signs seemed promising. "All very fantastic and unbelievable," Lowell wrote to Taylor, and was soon busy speculating about the members of his "ideal cast":

> Would Laurence Olivier really do for Theseus? etc . . . There's a terrific role for a young aging woman. The problem is whether any actor could deliver and any audience hear reams of heroic couplets of a rather pseudo 17th century grandiosity.[28]

Even the three-year-old Harriet, Lowell now spoke of as "very bossy and Broadwayish," and his letters to Taylor and Allen Tate in London were for a month or two full of rather boyish drama talk —the prospects for *Phaedra,* plans for future Brechtian spectaculars that would be "fierce and noble and indecent"[29] and jests about the

Met tenors who looked "like goons in the comic strip criminals."

Lowell and Meredith, it should be said, might be forgiven for not treating their visits to the Met too earnestly. Meredith gives an example of the way the Met viewed *them*:

> We sat in Rudolf Bing's office only once. When Bing found out that we were not members of the Ford Foundation staff but only grantees, he began to lose interest and be busy, and he suggested to Cal and me that as a beginning we might go up to Columbia University where there was an introductory course on the opera. I was about ready to bluster, but Cal said very sweetly, "You must understand, Mr. Bing, that Mr. Meredith and I are already professionals. We've come for some help in seeing how the opera company works." It was so much gentler than need be, the way he said it, but it was exactly the right thing to say. So we were allowed to go to live rehearsals and hang around backstage and were given house passes. By the end Bing was calling me Mr. Lowell.[30]

Lowell's excitement with the theater was really, Meredith believed, an aspect of his excitement with New York—he felt himself to be in the "capital of intellectual life," and of course "he could hold a larger court in New York" than he ever could in Boston. As early as October 1960 Lowell wrote to Peter Taylor:

> In a way we like New York better than Boston (though Boston has pleasant memories for me, is physically more human, is easier to get out of and other things) and we are thinking of moving permanently.[31]

By the end of the year the decision seems to have been made. In December, Lowell had written to Boston University that he wouldn't be able to teach either term next year: what he hadn't "yet written them" was that he intended living in New York. "Lizzie's even now roaming about town looking at houses."[32] In January 1961 an apartment on West 67th Street became available at a good price; both its location (no more than a hundred yards from Central Park) and its rather dramatically eccentric interior design seemed to Hardwick perfect, and on January 10 she wrote to Cousin Harriet:

> Our new apartment is absolutely definite now, more than that—irrevocable. I had some misgivings and clung a bit to Boston just because we were there. On the other hand, there was no profound reason why we shouldn't make the move. Bobby has wanted to even before this year and

we came here on the Ford grant to make certain and to look around. He never wavered and so there didn't seem to be any turning back. . . .

The apartment has "features" to say the least. It is a wonderful building, one of the few left here, built in the 1900's for artists. Many interesting people have lived here, and still do. It is very well-run, very cozy, very old-fashioned. We have had to have all sorts of meetings and inspections with the others of the 9 owners and Bobby said it was worse than the Tavern Club initiation. We have a two-floor in height, sky-lighted living room, dining room, kitchen and little room on the first— very large, strange and baronial. Then you go upstairs, to the balcony for the bedrooms.[33]

But the Marlborough Street house could not be sold until the summer, so Hardwick was in a sense still balanced between Boston and New York when, in February 1961, Lowell again began to show signs of speeding up. This time there was "a girl"—in the shape of a young New York poet called Sandra Hochman; and Lowell's protestations soon manifested what could now be thought of as "the usual pattern": the move to New York, he began saying, was a renunciation of Boston, and along with Boston, of Hardwick and the whole of his "old life." Hochman and New York offered him rebirth; it was all going to be wonderful. The difference this time, though, from Hardwick's point of view, was that the psychiatrist Lowell had been referred to in New York was adopting a quite different line from that of his doctors at McLean's: that is to say, she was not convinced that Lowell's "old life" was more "real" or more worthwhile than possible other lives that he might wish to change it for. Dr. Viola Bernard, whom Lowell had been seeing since his arrival in New York, was far more analytically inclined than any of his earlier "therapists" had been and more disposed therefore to seek existential "causes" for his sickness; she did not, in other words, assume him to be the victim merely of some metabolic imbalance that could be chemically set right. For Hardwick, understandably, this seemed like the last twist of the knife. In earlier episodes, when Lowell had turned on her, she had at least had the support of his physicians; now, it appeared, he had found a doctor who was prepared to encourage him in his delusions.

It was on March 3, 1961, that Lowell's new bout of "elation" reached its climax. Blair Clark recalls the circumstances:

It happened at my house. The middle of the night before he went in. I didn't know Sandra Hochman existed before then. Cal was in terrible physical shape, shaking, panicky, God knows what he was taking in the way of drugs. He was sweating, lighting cigarettes, talking nonstop. They both stayed overnight at my house. I locked my door and in the middle of the night she started beating on it; I think it was not so much that he was attacking her but that she was worried about him, because he was breathing badly, and drinking. So I spent the rest of the night trying to calm everything down, trying to get him to sleep. And I think the next day I took him to the hospital.[34]

On Viola Bernard's instructions, Lowell was taken to the Neurological Institute at the Columbia-Presbyterian Medical Center. Meredith recalls that he was in a locked ward on the twelfth floor; to visit him, "you had to be let through two sets of locked doors":

He wasn't dangerous to himself or others but he was so obstreperous. The thing that struck me about those visits was that he'd get through two pounds of chocolates and two packs of cigarettes. He was a factory of energy. I wasn't physically afraid of him. He was awfully gentle.[35]

On March 17 Meredith wrote to Adrienne Rich and Philip Booth, two poet friends of Lowell's who had sent letters to the hospital:

People who have seen these attacks at close hand before, as I have not, say that this is a mild one: there was no real violence, only a kind of modified social violence, at the outset, he went to the hospital of his own accord, etc. Elizabeth is very much shaken, although her friends here are taking care that she has company. No one predicts how long it will be before the drugs take hold & Cal begins to be himself again. Meanwhile he writes and revises translations furiously and with a kind [of] crooked brilliance, and talks about himself in connection with Achilles, Alexander, Hart Crane, Hitler and Christ, and breaks your heart.[36]

Lowell spent about six weeks in Presbyterian, but for a period after his discharge it was still, Hardwick says, "all Sandra":

It was all "I'm going to set up with her. You're wonderful, and Harriet's wonderful and everything's wonderful, but I'm going to live with Sandra." He was still in the hospital when he set up an apartment with her over on the East Side someplace. So at one time there was the Hochman apartment, the Riverside Drive apartment, the house in Boston and we had bought W. 67th Street. I was utterly petrified. I was terribly upset. This was one of the few times when I can say I was truly depressed, and crying, and just terrible. . . .[37]

Hardwick's instinct was to move back to Boston immediately. Lacking any support from Lowell's doctor, she could see no point in exposing herself to any further firsthand humiliations: "I wanted to take my little girl back up there, where we had someone to work for us, someone waiting for us to come home."[38] Dr. Bernard's view (gleaned from Lowell's friends: Bernard herself feels ethically bound not to discuss the matter) was that Lowell should break with his old habits—if he wanted to change his life, he should be allowed to do so. What if his manic breakouts were simply a measure of his essential discontent? Bernard was also reluctant to dampen Lowell's enthusiasm with any sustained drug therapy, although she seems to have assented to some drug intervention when the mania was at its height. It was not, according to Hardwick, that Bernard was especially pro-Hochman; she did believe, though, that Lowell should somehow "break the pattern" of earlier breakdowns.

It was Lowell himself who ensured that the pattern was restored. Not long after Hardwick had returned to Boston, Lowell walked out on Hochman: "He left her. He called up Dr. Bernard and said, 'I want to go home.' He came home very low and sad. Just shattered."[39]

On June 30 he wrote to T. S. Eliot:

We drive to Maine tomorrow. Our troubles are over and Lizzie and I are together again. The whole business has been very bruising, and it is fierce facing the pain I have caused, and humiliating [to] think that it has all happened before and that control and self-knowledge come so slowly, if at all. I have a very good doctor though and have unravelled many things. Life still has blood in it, and love has come back to our small family.[40]

In June 1961 Hardwick and Harriet had left Boston for Castine; Marlborough Street was sold, but the future still seemed shaky. On June 17 Hardwick had written to Lowell:

I am thinking about the winter and trying to see how I can learn to manage it—a very odd, ironical trick of fate that finds me worrying about New York. But I fear my own disintegration there, and I also fear the estrangement in our feelings—something the manifold necessities of life had not brought about until that terrible last winter. . . . At least I am determined to save myself, somehow, even if I don't know just how. And it means a lot to me to know that you'll be where you most want to be, leading the life and with the people you trust the most.[41]

When Marlborough Street was being sold, Lowell was at the Beverly Hills Hotel; he had gone to California to take part in a CBS film about Boris Pasternak, who had died the year before. He felt "dull and grieved," he wrote to Hardwick, that the Boston house had gone: "All that life! It haunted me during the long, whizzing, ten miles a minute jet flight. How I miss you, and how alone I feel here!"[42] From California he returned to New York and stayed there until the furniture arrived from Boston. An anxious letter from Hardwick suggests that for each of them the move still seemed provisional and hazardous:

I hope you won't become so vexed with the horrors of settling into our new life that you'll want to flee it. By the way, do you think you would be happy with a little apartment of your own? I don't see how we could ever afford it and yet several things you said on the way to the airplane haunt me. I really want to make the effort to give you—or allow you —the life that is most healthy for you and am going to make a really superhuman effort to improve as a wife so that your home and daily life won't make you sick again.[43]

As this letter hints, the intention was for Lowell to continue his sessions with Dr. Bernard, even though, his irony restored, Lowell was again treating these as necessary chores. Bernard, he wrote from California,

has decided my dreams are more rewarding than my actuality. This adds great plot, color and imagery to our sessions and seems to remove them to the for me safe and detached world of fiction—my disease in life is something like this.[44]

And, on the hotel stationery, he had even jotted down some of his Beverly Hills dreams; dreams almost too healthily Freudian to be believed:

1. Aunt Sarah's old maid complaining Cal has been rude to her and to Aunt S.
2. Surrounded by a wing or line of people, problem as in a game to meet or manipulate moves.
1. *Images*—a girl's legs said to have nothing on under her dress. But this merely meant no slip. Not particularly sexy image.
2. A girl in flamingo-red dress, beautiful. California tan and figure.
3. Small cannon, hand-sized, a toy but acquiring the strong hard materials and precise mechanism of a real cannon (modern).[45]

By July, Lowell was back with his family for the summer in Castine, calm and industrious again. In mid-August, Hardwick wrote that "this has been the best summer of all":

> Bobby goes to the barn [his regular workplace in Castine] at 9:30 with his lunch and writes . . . until 3:30. He comes back, we play tennis 4 to 6 and then have a bath, make a few dinner preparations, I have a drink; we dine at 7:30 or a quarter to eight. Play music or read and then in bed and asleep by ten. I don't think of this schedule as exciting reading and only put it in to show what a wonderful peaceful summer it has been.[46]

Between July and September, Lowell completed his play, *Benito Cereno*. It was, he said, "thunderously effective, though thin. . . . I feel like Randall, playwriting is so easy it's a crime."[47] As if to prove this, he had also done two other short plays—both based on short stories by Nathaniel Hawthorne. Lowell wrote to William Meredith on September 8:

> There are now three, Governor Endicott and the Puritans cutting down the May-pole at Merrymount, Hawthorn's [*sic*] My Kinsman Major Molineux and Benito. All told, they come to an evening and a hundred and ten or twenty pages. God knows if they are any good, but change is fascinating after short poems. One feels stuck with writing yet every so often, it becomes a wall, impossible to climb and unlikely to crumble. Plays seem an opening, if I can work them. I've always wondered why people like Eliot wrote them, but I see there's a sea of energy inside one that can't come out in poems and will come out this way.[48]

To this letter, Lowell added the postscript: "We've really had a wonderfully and much needed summer." He had been reading himself asleep over Dickens and had not had a drink since July: "I feel pretty used to not drinking now though a little grudging and unsociable around six o'clock as I swig my bottle of concentrated Walsh's [*sic*] grape juice. Our family is as calm as such nervous people can be."

By October 1961 the Lowells were settled at West 67th Street. Lowell spent October and November "in an aweful [*sic*] wrestle trying to get my play reworked so it will act,"[49] and also waiting for the reviews of his book *Imitations,* a collection of the sixty or so translations he had done since 1958. Lowell called the book a "small anthology of European poetry"; it ranged from Homer to Pasternak and "Lowellized" from originals in Greek, French, Italian, German and Russian. The verb "to Lowell" might usefully have been invented for this book; certainly, there was much hesitation about what exactly these "translations" should be called. For Lowell, they had simply been a way of moving "into a new air"; there had been nothing programmatic or even methodical about their making. At the outset, certainly, they had been speculative exercises: what would Rilke or Baudelaire be like if they "were writing their poems now and in America"?[50]

But by 1961 they had become a book, and they had to be presented with some measure of solemnity. At first, Lowell had thought of following Allen Tate's suggestion and calling the book *Versions.* T. S. Eliot, however, had written to Lowell in June, with his firm verdict on the title:

> I think that the right title for this is Imitations and I don't agree with Allen if he thinks that Versions would be better. I think also that a subtitle is a mistake: your translations are indeed imitations, and if you use the word translation in the subtitle it will attract all those meticulous little critics who delight in finding what seem to them mis-translations. You will remember all the fuss about Ezra Pound's *Propertius.* Keep the word translation out of it.[51]

Imitations was published in the United States in November 1961, and although it carried no subtitle, it did have a modest and challenging introduction by the author. In this, Lowell admits to recklessness with "literal meaning"—he had been more concerned, he said, to "get the tone" of the originals, to make "live English" out of them. Such a disclaimer might have mollified the "meticulous little critics" Eliot warned against, had Lowell shyly left it there. But, as Ben Bellitt later commented, there is a further paragraph in which "Mr. Lowell . . . delivers himself up to would-be assassins with the resolute fatalism of Caesar in the Roman Senate."[52] Lowell writes:

> Most poetic translations come to grief and are less enjoyable than modest photographic prose translations, such as George Kay has offered in his *Penguin Book of Italian Verse*. Strict metrical translators still exist. They seem to live in a pure world untouched by contemporary poetry. Their difficulties are bold and honest, but they are taxidermists, not poets, and their poems are likely to be stuffed birds. A better strategy would seem to be the now fashionable translations into free or irregular verse. Yet this method commonly turns out a sprawl of language, neither faithful nor distinguished, now on stilts, now low, as Dryden would say. It seems self-evident that no professor or amateur poet, or even good poet writing hastily, can by miracle transform himself into a fine metricist. I believe that poetic translation—I would call it an imitation—must be expert and inspired, and needs at least as much technique, luck and rightness of hand as an original poem.[53]

Having thus thoroughly failed to "keep the word translation out of it," Lowell goes on to list some of his many "licenses": Villon was "somewhat stripped," Victor Hugo "cut in half," Mallarmé "unclotted," and so on. In places, he said, he had even added verses of his own or shuffled stanzas from one poem to another: "And so forth! I have dropped lines, moved lines, moved stanzas and altered meter and intent."

The book version of Lowell's *Phaedra—A Verse Translation of Racine's Phèdre* was also published in 1961, and it was equipped with an introduction not dissimilar in tone to that of *Imitations:* "My version is free . . . I have translated as a poet." In many reviews it was coupled with *Imitations* as further evidence of Lowell's cultural imperialism. George Steiner's careful response in the *Kenyon Review* is perhaps the best summary of the prosecution case:

> I submit that *Phaedra* has an unsteady and capricious bearing on the matter of Racine. Far too often it strives against the grain of Racine's style and against the conventions of feeling on which the miraculous concision of that style depends. . . . what Lowell has produced is a

variation on the theme of Phaedra, in the manner of Seneca and the Elizabethan classicists. To link this version with Racine implies a certain abeyance of modesty. But modesty is the very essence of translation. The greater the poet, the more loyal should be his servitude to the original; Rilke is servant to Louis Labe, Roy Campbell to Baudelaire. Without modesty translation will traduce; where modesty is constant, it can transfigure.[54]

And modesty did turn out to be the theme of the several hostile notices that greeted *Imitations:* Lowell had presumptuously turned Rilke into Lowell, and the result was neither good Lowell nor recognizable Rilke. His howlers were itemized, his overburly modernizing was shown to be thuggish, disrespectful: respect for the original was spoken of as if it were something like respect for a parent, or grown-up. At least part of Lowell's crime was to have treated these great poets as his equals—as his playmates, almost. "I suppose," wrote Louis Simpson in the *Hudson Review,* "*Imitations* will interest some people as a mirror of Lowell's mind."[55] And Thom Gunn in the *Yale Review* complained that

> Hugo's suave gestures similarly become spasmodic jerks, Villon takes on the flat clinical sound of the "confessional" poems in *Life Studies,* and others I am not able to read in the original, Homer and Pasternak for example, all speak with the unmistakable voice of Robert Lowell. Preserving the tone of most of these poets is, in fact, the last thing he has done.[56]

Gunn also suggests that when Lowell doesn't make his originals sound like Lowell, as with Baudelaire, he turns them into Allen Ginsberg. A number of reviewers took the following comparison as a crushing indictment of the Lowell method:

BAUDELAIRE: Ainsi qu'un débauché pauvre qui baise et mange
    Le sein martyrisé d'une antique catin,
    Nous volons au passage un plaisir clandestin
    Que nous pressons bien fort comme une vielle orange.

LOWELL: Like the poor lush who cannot satisfy,
    we try to force our sex with counterfeits,
    die drooling on the deliquescent tits,
    mouthing the rotten orange we suck dry.[57]

In fact, the critics might more damagingly have quoted the limp translatorese that crops up throughout *Imitations:* the stale archaisms, the mechanical poeticizing—lines and stanzas, that is to say, that Lowell would never have wished to call his own:

> Lively boy,
> the only age you are alive
> is like this day of joy,
> a clear and breathless Saturday
> that heralds life's holiday.
> Rejoice, my child,
> this is the untroubled instant.
> Why should I undeceive you?
> Let it not grieve you,
> if the following day is slow to arrive.[58]

George Kay's prose translation of Leopardi reads as follows:

> Mischievous boy, this flowering age of yours is like a day full of joy, a clear cloudless day which precedes the holiday of your life. Have enjoyment of it, my son; a sweet state, a happy season, it is. I do not want to say anything more to you; but may your holiday which still hesitates to come, not be heavy.[59]

Lowell's version could not be accused of irreverent muscularity; its fault rather is to seem insipid and mechanical, the work of an amateur poet or an overworked professor.

In spite of spirited defenses by Edmund Wilson ("the only book of its kind in literature")[60] and A. Alvarez (a "magnificent collection of new poems by Robert Lowell, based on the work of 18 European poets"),[61] Lowell was taken aback by the vehemence of some of his assailants—although the review that seems to have most nettled him, by Dudley Fitts in the *New York Times Book Review*, was more condescending than fierce. It ended: "The book is fun; but schoolboys should read it in a salt mine."[62] In November, Lowell wrote to A. Alvarez, who was to print his superb Villon over a full page of the London *Observer:*

> Your remarks on my Villon are very opportune—Time Magazine in a longish panning review says half my poems bear the smudge of transla-

tion and the other half seem to have been written by some talented foreigner. Dudley Fitts in the New York Times says they should be read in a salt mine, with a grain of salt, and three hysterical Frenchmen writing to Encounter say my Rimbaud is an insane slaughter and hopeless trash. On the other hand, every decent judge from Edmund Wilson down like them or some of them. I feel misunderstood, not a bad feeling.[63]

And to Randall Jarrell:

I seem to be getting a rain of mangling reviews. Time magazine and now Dudley Fitts who says my poems should be read in a salt mine with grain of salt. I must know something about what I'm doing. I'm sure I do.[64]

To this, Jarrell fired back a bracing shaft of poet-to-poet lordliness:

I saw that stupid review in Time—Time's the cheapest magazine in the world and Dudley Fitts's the cheapest poetry reviewer; I can imagine what he was like when he had a chance to hurt a real poet in "*his* special field," translation—as if he had once in his life translated a line of poetry into a line of poetry.[65]

Jarrell could not have chosen a better moment to sound this note of solidarity. By November 1961 Lowell had at least two new poems of his own—an elegy for a St. Mark's schoolmate, "Alfred Corning Clark," and "Eye and Tooth," which Lowell described as "my farewell to contact lenses." By the end of the year he had five more —"Old Flame," "Water," "The Scream," "Middle Age" and "Fall 1961." These were his first poems in over eighteen months.

In his November 7 letter to Randall Jarrell bemoaning the reviews of *Imitations,* Lowell recalls the visit he made to Jarrell's home at Greensboro in the spring of 1959—just before the publication of *Life Studies:*

> I remember once, the last time at Greensboro, I think, when you came into my room and began talking out of a blue sky about the ills of our culture, and Mary [Jarrell] said that I worried about personal matters while you were upset about the world. The world is very much under my skin and really seems like a murderous nightmare when one looks outward. I am sick of nations armed to the teeth. It can't be true we must raise a finger or a whisper.[1]

The same apocalyptic note is sounded in other letters Lowell wrote during the fall of 1961. It was the period of the Berlin Wall crisis, and Lowell was not alone in feeling "the chafe and jar of nuclear war." In October, for example, he wrote to Cousin Harriet:

> The world's really strange isn't it? I mean the world of the news and the nations and the bomb testings. I feel it this fall and wonder, if it's just being forty three. Under a certain calm, there seems to be a question that must be answered. If one could think of the question.[2]

And, a few days earlier, to William Meredith:

> This is a weird year—less than last though. I haven't had a drink since July. The nuclear air gets on my nerves. It seems a hideous comedy that we should charge the globe with so much ruin. I guess I felt that way

about the bombing in the last war, but somehow it's now come to a head. I suppose I ought to join the unilateralist group, but I hate that arid, logic-chopping debater's world of the righteous cause.[3]

(Even so, Lowell did testify in a 1962 *Partisan Review* symposium on the "Cold War and the West": "No nation should possess, use or retaliate with its bombs. I believe we should rather die than drop our own bombs.")[4]

During these months of global tension, phrases from Lowell's letters keep spilling over into poems—as if, in the prevailing atmosphere of menace, there could be only a hairline separation between life and art. The poem "Fall 1961," Lowell's most direct response to the nuclear horror, can by itself be "over-heard" as an impassioned letter to a friend:

> All autumn, the chafe and jar
> of nuclear war;
> we have talked our extinction to death.
> I swim like a minnow
> behind my studio window.
>
> Our end drifts nearer,
> the moon lifts,
> radiant with terror.
> The state
> is a diver under a glass bell.
>
> A father's no shield
> for his child.
> We are like a lot of wild
> spiders crying together,
> but without tears.[5]

In fact, part of this poem is in Lowell's November letter to Jarrell:

Elizabeth Bishop has just blown in for a month. I find the talk and companionship here, particularly in little groups more up my alley than Boston. We are right off the Park, and I get a lot of nature taking Harriet to the amusements. The other day, Anton Webern's music was on the radio—she heard it and said, "It's like wild animals through the woods walking" and then "It's like a lot of spiders crying together but without tears."[6]

And writing on the same day to the British critic A. Alvarez, Lowell spoke of Alvarez's divorce and his separation from his young son: "It must be hell to be cut off from your child."[7]

In a similar way, the anguished last lines of "Eye and Tooth" (his "farewell to my contact lenses") echo a letter Lowell wrote to Isabella Gardner on October 10. The poem reads:

> Nothing! No oil
> for the eye, nothing to pour
> on those waters or flames.
> I am tired. Everyone's tired of my turmoil.[8]

And to Gardner Lowell writes: "Writing's hell, isn't it? I tire of my turmoil and feel everyone else has and long for a Horatian calm."[9]

The poems themselves are "small clear half-anguished things,"[10] obsessed with time, lost experience, blurred vision; they are nearly all poems written as if from the end of life, aching with nostalgia and remorse, and blankly futureless:

> At forty-five,
> what next, what next?
> At every corner,
> I meet my Father,
> my age, still alive.
>
> Father, forgive me
> my injuries,
> as I forgive
> those I
> have injured!
>
> You never climbed
> Mount Sion, yet left
> dinosaur
> death-steps on the crust,
> where I must walk.[11]

The short, five- or six-syllable, line is as bare as Lowell can make it; the point is *not* to seem craftsmanlike, melodic or composed. And in this sense the poems of fall 1961 and winter 1962 are far more "confessional" than the asylum or domestic poems of *Life Studies*. They follow on from the tormented soliloquy in "Skunk Hour" rather than from the pained tenderness of "Home After Three Months Away":

> Back and forth!
> Back and forth, back and forth—
> my one point of rest
> is the orange and black
> oriole's swinging nest![12]

There is a lot of counting in these poems—not syllables, but minutes. The poet mutters "one step, two steps, three steps": to steady himself but also to keep in rhythm with the global countdown.

> On the illuminated black dial,
> green ciphers of a new moon—
> *one, two, three, four, five, six!*[13]

> Back and forth, back and forth
> goes the tock, tock, tock
> of the orange, bland, ambassadorial
> face of the moon
> on the grandfather clock[14]

And when Lowell is not counting, he recounts: "Remember? We sat on a slab of rock." ("Water"); "My old flame, my wife! / Remember our lists of Birds! ("The Old Flame"); "Remember summer? Bubbles filled / the fountain, and we splashed." ("The Public Garden"). The impression is of a man writing what may be last letters to his friends; of memories which, in truth, might turn out to be memorials.

Lowell got through the winter of 1961–62 with nothing more serious than "tonsilitis, flu, bronchitis, one little fever giving ailment after another," and even did a small stretch of teaching at the New School for Social Research on West 12th Street. In the past four years, though, he had had three breakdowns at around this time (late winter, early spring), and a letter he wrote to John Berryman on March 18, 1962, suggests that the "cycle" had, but in a muffled way, completed its familiar process: an imagined death of the old self, a "rebirth" into the "new":

> All winter I've had an uncomfortable feeling of dying into rebirth. Not at all the sick, dizzy allegorized thing such words suggest and which I've felt going off my rocker. But the flat prose of coming to an end of one way of life, whittled down and whittled down and picking up nothing new though always about to. . . .
> What queer lives we've had even for poets! There seems something generic about it, and determined beyond anything we could do. You and I have had so many of the same tumbles and leaps. We must have a green old age. We both have drunk the downward drag as deeply as is perhaps bearable. I feel we have better work and better lives ahead.[15]

It seems possible that Lowell believed himself to have experienced the rhythms, as it were, of mania and yet not been thrust into a full-scale collapse. At the end of March he wrote to Edmund Wilson rather as he had written to Berryman two weeks earlier; Lowell had just returned from a short holiday in Puerto Rico and was "sunned and shaken"—

> shaken too by nights in a single bedroom, where I could wake up at all hours and read and smoke and speculate, and seem flooded by what is, without being able to define it, and somehow rejuvenated by it. Oh what could be less youthful than youth, mine anyhow, walking in its stiff necessary armor![16]

On May 11, 1962, Lowell attended a dinner at the White House in honor of André Malraux, the French Minister of Culture. It was to be a gracious Kennedy spectacular, and Lowell, it seems, was fairly high on the list of those "artists and intellectuals" whom the White House was anxious to flatter and parade. He had attended Kennedy's inauguration, and had sent the President an inscribed copy of *Life Studies;* and had responded to at least some of the "new dawn" glamour that surrounded the first months of the presidency —Kennedy was the same age as Lowell, had been at Harvard in 1936, was acquainted with Blair Clark. Of the inauguration, Lowell said: "When I was introduced to him he gave me the kind of compliment that indicated he'd really read the book, so I said to him 'You're the first President who's treated your peers as equals.' "[17] But the Bay of Pigs episode and the intensifying of the Cold War during 1961 had made the first year of Kennedy's government one of the most frightening since World War II. After the Malraux dinner, Lowell wrote to Edmund Wilson:

> I meant to write you a little fan note after Washington. Except for you, every one there seemed addled with adulation at having been invited. It was all good fun but next morning you read that the President has sent the 7th fleet to Laos, or he might have invaded Cuba again—not that he will. But I feel we intellectuals play a very pompous and frivolous role—we should be windows, not window-dressing. Then, now in our times, of all times, the sword hangs over us and our children, and not a voice is lifted. I thought of all the big names there, only you acted like yourself.[18]

And in an interview three years later, when asked if Kennedy had not introduced "some vague, fragile possibility of some kind of connection, even mutual interchange, between the representatives of the cultural life of the country and those of the world of power," Lowell enlarged on the view he had formed at the Malraux dinner:

> I was invited to the White House for Malraux's dinner there. Kennedy made a rather graceful joke that "the White House was becoming almost a café for intellectuals. . . ." Then we all drank a great deal at the White House, and had to sort of be told not to take our champagne into the concert, and to put our cigarettes out like children—though nicely, it wasn't peremptory. Then the next morning you read that the Seventh Fleet had been sent somewhere in Asia and you had a funny feeling of how unimportant the artist really was; that this was sort of window dressing and that the real government was somewhere else, and that something much closer to the Pentagon was really ruling the country.[19]

Before attending the White House dinner, Lowell accepted another small slice of government patronage when he agreed to visit South America under the auspices of the Congress for Cultural Freedom. He had several times half planned a trip to Brazil to visit Elizabeth Bishop; the offer of Congress funds simply jogged him into action. Bishop wrote asking, "Who pays for the Congress for Cultural Freedom, anyway?"[20] but the matter does not seem to have been pursued with any rigor.

Lowell flew to Brazil—with Hardwick and the five-year-old Harriet —during the first week of June 1962, and they were met in Pará by the Congress's representative, Keith Botsford. With Botsford, they journeyed down the coast of Brazil via Recife and Bahia to Rio, where the Lowells took up residence at the Copacabana Palace. Lowell's duties were fairly nebulous; he was expected to give interviews and press conferences and to attend dinners. As Botsford recalls:

> He was sort of vaguely there to be a famous literary man going through to pick up ideas. From the Congress's point of view he was an outstanding American to counteract, I suppose, Communist people like Neruda —our side's emissary.[21]

After Brazil, Lowell was meant to visit Paraguay and Argentina. Hardwick and Harriet were to return to the United States by ship on September 1, and a few days later Lowell would travel south with Botsford. Before leaving Rio, though, Lowell was beginning to seem "over-wrought," and he was drinking heavily. Elizabeth Bishop (to whom Lowell was once again declaring his true love) tried to persuade him to give up the remainder of his tour, but she "made no impression on him,"[22] and on September 4 he left for Buenos Aires. Botsford kept a journal of the Argentina visit, and the following account is based on his journal notes:

> When we got to Argentina, it was six double vodka martinis before lunch. And he made me drink with him. We went to lunch at the presidential palace, the Casa Rosada, and Cal promptly insulted the general, who was in fact about to be president of Argentina, and started one of the many diplomatic rumpuses he caused on that trip. There was the American cultural attaché, whose name I cannot remember, and Cal was sitting at this lunch in a very loud checked sports coat and open shirt, and all the generals were there, very uptight and distinguished. And there was this wonderful opening scene when Cal was introduced to the cultural attaché and talked to him for about three minutes. The guy was an absolute idiot and asked stupid questions and obviously

didn't know who Cal was. So Cal turned on him and said, "You're the cultural attaché?" "Yep, yep, sure am." And Cal said, "How can you be the cultural attaché? You're illiterate." That's how the lunch started, and it went on from there. After the lunch, Cal started his tour of the equestrian statues, undressing and climbing the statues. He insisted on being taken to every statue in B.A.—well, we didn't do every one, thank God. And he'd stop the car and start clambering up and sit next to the general on top of the statue.[23]

Keith Botsford says that he had no knowledge of Lowell's previous illnesses and, at first, simply thought that he had a very drunk and very sleepless poet on his hands. He took Lowell to meet the leading Argentine writers and set about trying to educate him in Latin American literature and history: "I considered it my task and my pleasure to inform him about a whole literature which I had discovered but which he knew nothing about." Needless to say, Lowell proved a tiring pupil:

One of the striking aspects was the tremendous expenditure of physical energy. I'd never realized how strong Cal was. He was a very powerful swimmer—very strongly developed shoulders and chest and great long arms. And indefatigable. He couldn't sleep. He couldn't do anything for himself. I had to do everything, pay for everything. He couldn't order breakfast. And it got very expensive. I kept having to cable for more money. Cal felt the Congress was paying his expenses and that meant he had carte blanche. He insisted on buying everyone expensive presents, leather jackets. I couldn't control any of it. And as he got higher and higher he began to treat me more and more as a flunky, a position which I resented. And all of a sudden for about a week he insisted I was homosexual. I think this was because he had a suitable component himself and was simply transferring it. But it was extremely burdensome to me and really rather painful. He kept on saying, "You're saying that because you're queer." His whole conversation became very fragmentary and disconnected. I used to think of it as a great knot which would twist and twist and twist and then a sentence would come out of it, pushed by a sort of strange breathy impulsion, and it was always in a totally unexpected direction. Eventually I was reduced to total flunkyism.[24]

One of Botsford's tasks was to send cables from Lowell to the Pope and to General Eisenhower: "America as the Roman Empire" was the theme. Just before he left New York, Lowell had read Edmund

Wilson's *Patriotic Gore* (indeed, he had written to Wilson saying, "I guess I pretty much agree. . . . The States have become a menace, sea-squids as you say, and I guess they never were too good"[25]), and Botsford remembers that he spoke of Wilson's book throughout the trip; although as he got higher he became more thrilled than repelled by the "menace" of American imperialism. He frequently pronounced himself "Caesar of Argentina" and told Botsford: "I want you to travel with me always. You are my lieutenant."

After five days, Botsford had had enough and returned alone to Rio, nursing a deep hangover. Elizabeth Bishop was furious when, two days later, she found out that Lowell had been left behind; she feared that he would get picked up by the police for drunkenness or, worse still, for his politics:

> When I finally got Keith I asked him what the HELL he thought he was doing; didn't he know Cal's history? (he did). WHY hadn't he called me before; what was he doing in Rio anyway, and WHY had he left Cal alone and sick in B.A.[26]

Under this pressure, Botsford agreed to return immediately to Buenos Aires. He contacted the American embassy there and got the name of a local doctor: Lowell had some days earlier thrown away all the pills he had with him. Botsford also contacted Blair Clark in New York and tried to cable Hardwick's ship.

The climax of Lowell's Argentine adventure came at a party given by the exiled Spanish poet Rafael Alberti. While Lowell and Alberti were locked in an arm-wrestling contest on the floor, Botsford went around trying to enlist help from the other guests: Lowell was sick, he explained, and should be persuaded to return to the United States for treatment. The reaction from Alberti's stoutly left-wing friends was that Lowell should at all costs be protected from this obvious CIA attempt to kidnap him.

When the party ended, Lowell returned to his hotel with an Argentine woman called Luisa: "She wanted none of him, but she was our only hope," says Botsford. While Luisa distracted Lowell's attention, an ambulance was called:

> And literally it took six very strong men to wrestle him into a straitjacket in the corridor of that hotel. I'd never realized the power of mania, physically. And it really was a close thing.[27]

Lowell was taken to the Clinica Bethlehem, and when Botsford visited him there next day,

> Cal was lying in the clinic bound with leather straps, arms and legs, and he was on, I think, 2,000 milligrams of Thorazine four times a day. And he was still violent underneath it. I was brought up as a composer, and all he wanted me to do was whistle. Sometimes it was "Yankee Doodle Dandy" or "The Battle Hymn of the Republic." Or it was Brandenberg concertos, Mozart piano concertos, anything. It was the one thing he craved, the one thing that would calm him. I'd be there two or three hours, just whistling until I was dry in the mouth. I'd whistle all the parts in the Ninth Symphony, or whatever, and he'd say, "Yeah, but do the tympani bit." He took great pleasure in this, and he was very tender and affectionate about it. I think there was in that strange manic state both love and hate.[28]

Shortly afterwards, Blair Clark arrived to take Lowell back to the United States. The clinic agreed to discharge him on condition that a doctor and a nurse accompany him to New York, and at huge cost (Clark recalls) this was arranged. There was one slight scare on the journey: by the time the plane reached its first stop—Asunción, Paraguay—Lowell had fallen in love with the stewardess. The stewardess left the plane at Asunción and Lowell demanded that he be allowed to go with her, get married, start a new life in South America. "But we got him back on the plane, and the next nervousness was Miami. He was talking all the way."[29]

Lowell's plane was met in New York by Hardwick and Dr. Bernard, and he was driven to the Institute for Living, a psychiatric hospital in Hartford, Connecticut. Although he was back at West 67th Street by November, it was not until January 1963 that he wrote to Cousin Harriet:

> For the last four months I have been writing almost every day. It seemed the best way to live through the slump that usually follows my attacks. Now at last, the last poem I've started is finished, and I feel free to look about me and take the air. Out of prison![30]

Before leaving for South America, Lowell had accepted a teaching job at Harvard University: "two classes, two days a week, from September thru December, $8,500 for two years. I'll commute from here [New York] and have the rest of the year to burn."[31] His illness had meant postponing his first classes, but by February 1963 he was writing quite jauntily about his "odd split week between Cambridge and New York."[32] Hardwick was now thoroughly settled in New York; indeed, she was beginning to think that the move from Boston had "saved my life, although I didn't know it at the time."[33] A turning point for her was the founding, in February 1963, of a new literary periodical, the *New York Review of Books.* In his January letter to Cousin Harriet, Lowell wrote:

> Lizzie is in a big undertaking and is on the masthead of a new book review for the moment being gotten together to fill in the gap left by the New York Times book section during the long newspaper strike. All the most distinguished and lively book reviewers and essayists in the country have been written or phoned for pieces. Now after two weeks they have almost all come through. The idea is to make the first number so dazzling that even after The New York Times returns, people will want to keep the new magazine floating.[34]

Lowell's own contribution to the magazine was fairly marginal, although he did guarantee a bank loan that helped to get it started; according to the editor Robert Silvers, he was "proud of the *Review* and would always talk about 'we.' But he didn't have a great deal to suggest about specific things."[35]

By the spring of 1963 Lowell had almost two-thirds of the poems that would go into his next book. To the fall 1961 group he had now added "Jonathan Edwards in Western Massachusetts," "Hawthorne," "Those Before Us," "The Lesson," "Caligula" and "Night Sweat." Apart from "Night Sweat," the group seems listless and academic—exercise poems. The Hawthorne and Jonathan Edwards pieces are ambling and agreeable; "Caligula" shows that Lowell can still turn a brutal couplet; "Those Before Us" and "The Lesson" are close to capturing the old immediacy but, in the end, seem casual and unfocused. "Night Sweat," however, is remarkable: not only does it resurrect something of the iambic early Lowell, the rhetorical surge, the heavy piled-up rhymes, the unabashed grandiloquence, but it does so without surrendering any of *Life Studies'* most important gains. The second stanza, certainly, proves that high rhetoric need not inflate or falsify:

Behind me! You! Again I feel the light
lighten my leaded eyelids, while the gray
skulled horses whinny for the soot of night.
I dabble in the dapple of the day,
a heap of wet clothes, seamy, shivering,
I see my flesh and bedding washed with light,
my child exploding into dynamite,
my wife . . . your lightness alters everything,
and tears the black web from the spider's sack,
as your heart hops and flutters like a hare.
Poor turtle, tortoise, if I cannot clear
the surface of these troubled waters here,
absolve me, help me, Dear Heart, as you bear
this world's dead weight and cycle on your back.[36]

In May 1963 Lowell was complaining to Randall Jarrell that "each new poem confronts me with the old familiar legions of my old tricks and accents";[37] it is not clear whether he means the old tricks of *Lord Weary's Castle* or the by now old tricks of his "new style." Either way, it seems a pity that he did not choose to build on the possibilities suggested by "Night Sweat."

In July, Lowell appeared at the Poetry International in London; he ate "Mongol food at the Empsons,"[38] had a Cambridge reunion with Frank Parker and William Alfred (both by chance in London at the time) and in two days "turned down about $1000 of drinks."[39] From London he went to Paris, where his "not drinking" hung "like a plague" over the city—but Mary McCarthy, he reported, was also "on the wagon," so with her he paid a sober visit to the Delacroix Exhibition at the Louvre before moving on to Nice, where he seems to have attended a literary festival. A postcard to Hardwick from Nice on July 24 reads: "In an hour I give first reading. I feel 'I should be dressed in shorts.' But I am not."[40]

Back in America, he resumed his shuttle between Harvard and New York. In New York he had talks with Jonathan Miller about the staging of his trio of plays, now titled *The Old Glory*. Miller remembers:

he asked me if I wanted to produce it, direct it. I read it and liked it, although I was slightly puzzled by some of it. Anyway, I was leaving for England in January 1964, and before I left I agreed to do it the following summer.[41]

There was a plan to hold preliminary readings of the plays before Miller left for London, but these had to be abandoned when, in December 1963, Lowell was once again committed to the Institute at Hartford. On December 7 Hardwick wrote to him there: "Don't worry about anything. Everything is fine at Harvard. Also talked to Jonathan yesterday. They are of course going ahead with the play as planned and will simply skip the readings." And a month later (January 9, 1964), with Lowell still in the hospital, she wrote to Allen Tate:

> Cal is fine, actually. I expect he'll be home in a few weeks. This thing just came on him and it is most discouraging because he tried awfully hard to push it away. He hasn't had a drink for a year; he goes to the doctor and does whatever is suggested. It doesn't seem to be under the control of the will at all, not even a little bit. This time the doctor sent him to Hartford, which was very sensible. He was noticeably better immediately because he wasn't surrounded by friends and the telephone. He's very *triste*, utterly bewildered. They tell him at the hospital that they think it is an organic affliction and it doesn't have to do except in the most indirect way, with what one does.[42]

Lowell had been committed to the hospital some two weeks after the assassination of President Kennedy. William Meredith remembers seeing him probably in late November 1963: "We were with some friends at the Opera Club and they all went into the box and we sat there talking and he said with a smile: 'Lyndon Johnson has asked me to be in the cabinet.'" It was evident that Lowell was manic, but even so, Meredith was puzzled by the smile:

> I saw him again when he came out of the hospital at Hartford, and I remember him saying to me, "This is always a very hard period for me because I have the embarrassment of remembering almost completely what I said and did." So I brought up the remark about Lyndon Johnson and I said, "What I want to know is why did you smile?" And he said, "I knew it was going to be hard for people to believe, and I thought if I told them these facts without confronting them I could tell them the truth and not be laughed at." So he hallucinated really successfully. He thought he was in the cabinet, but he didn't think I'd believe it and he

didn't want to be called a liar. That's pretty poignant, isn't it? A terrible insight into madness.[43]

By February 1964 Lowell was "himself again," and in March he wrote to T. S. Eliot as follows:

I want to apologize for plaguing you with so many telephone calls last November and December. When the "enthusiasm" is coming on me it is accompanied by a feverish reaching to my friends. After it's over I wince and wither. Fragments of the true man, such as he is, are in both phases. You are very dear to me always.[44]

For the next two or three months he was in a state of "dark, post-manic and pathological self-abasement." He was preparing his book *For the Union Dead* for publication and, on May 11, wrote to Randall Jarrell (who had evidently seen the manuscript):

It's awkward thanking you for liking my new book, but this came at a good time. One can judge so ill one's self, and sometimes I find a mean tameness and sour montony [*sic*] which I detest. *Life Studies* gave me an opening, and the problem for the last four or five years has been a hunt for the knack and power to fly.[45]

And during this same month, the letters he received tend to suggest that he had been writing to others in a similar, self-lashing way. Stephen Spender wrote to assure him:

You are in far too immediate contact with what makes you a poet, for your own happiness and comfort and of course this must worry those who are as grateful to you and as anxious to go on reading you—and that you should go on producing and teaching one so much—as I am.[46]

And, also in May 1964, there is a touching letter from Jean Stafford, written from New York Hospital:

There's no possible way of thanking you for your concern, for your lovely letters, for the books, the beautiful unpronounceable blue flowers. . . .
My dear, please never castigate yourself for what you call blindness —how blind we both were, how green we were, how countless were our individual torments we didn't know the names of. All we can do

is forgive ourselves and now be good friends—how I should cherish that.[47]

The final poems in the *Union Dead* collection had been written by the summer of 1963. They include the terza rima Tate pastiche "The Severed Head" and two stiff, well-meaning pieces about South America. "Buenos Aires" (published in the first issue of the *New York Review of Books* in February 1963) is a particularly sad example of Lowell hovering uncertainly between private agony and public obligation. There is also the charming "Soft Wood," a reflective, unrushed tour of Castine addressed to his cousin Harriet, who "was more to me than my mother":

> I think of you far off in Washington,
> breathing in the heat wave
> and air-conditioning, knowing
> each drug that numbs alerts another nerve to pain.[48]

In 1963 (two months before the Kennedy assassination) John Berryman had written to Lowell: "Hell of a year, isn't it? Mr. Frost, Ted [Roethke] and now Louis [MacNeice] whom I loved. Keep well, be good. The devil roams."[49] With Frost's death, there was a new pressure on Lowell to step up to the rank of "major poet." Even before the publication of *For the Union Dead* in the fall of 1964, Irvin Ehrenpreis had expressed what was a fairly widespread expectation: "From a glance at Lowell's most recent work, coming out in periodicals, one can prophesy that this next book will establish his name as that normally thought of for 'the' American poet."[50]

And most of the reviews did speak of Lowell in this way. Richard Poirier in the *Herald Tribune*'s *Bookweek* announced that "Robert Lowell is, by something like a critical consensus, the greatest American poet of the mid-century, probably the greatest poet writing in English."[51] And Stanley Kunitz, perhaps remembering that Eliot and Auden were still living, was only slightly less fullsome in the *New York Times;* for him, Lowell was "without doubt the most celebrated poet in English of his generation."[52] Praise of this sort issued from most sides, and Lowell was not disposed to challenge it: "My book is getting astonishing attention," he wrote to Allen Tate, "and I suppose I enjoy it all to the limit—a head of uncertainty curdled with vanity."[53] And when Kunitz asked him *why* he was so esteemed, his answer was: "It may be that some people have turned to my poems because of the very things that are wrong with me. I mean the difficulty I have with ordinary living, the impracticability, the myopia. Seeing less than others can be a great strain."

This note of faint unease, although it might sound like rehearsed modesty, was genuine. The deaths of near contemporaries like Roethke and MacNeice, and the suicide earlier in that same year of Lowell's former student Sylvia Plath, might well have made him feel that time shrank as the critics' expectations soared. Coronations were gratifying, but how do king-poets reign secure? And was there not a dreadful challenge in the conclusion of John Berryman's "obituary" letter: "But why publish verse anyway? It's all right for you to do, but why the rest of us?"[54]

Every evening at 8, at a drab brick building in Manhattan's Hell's Kitchen, the stage is set for the American Place Theatre production of Poet Robert Lowell's *The Old Glory*. Every Sunday at noon, with the addition of an altar, the same building is ready for the Holy Communion services of St. Clement's Episcopal Church, an off-Broadway mission parish serving the theatre community. Running both shows is the Rev. Sidney Lanier, 41, a lively, loquacious priest who as president of the theatre and vicar of St. Clement's is trying to bridge the gap between church and stage.

Thus, *Time* magazine on November 27, 1964. The American Place Theatre was founded in 1963 with the aim of persuading "writers of stature"—and, in particular, novelists and poets—to write plays. For its first year or so it had operated in semiprivate, offering its members readings and works in progress. With Lowell's *The Old Glory*, though, it was opening its doors; the 180-seat Church of St. Clement's would, it was proclaimed, become "a center of excitement, of talk, of argument, of ferment, of shared enthusiasm, of renewal of purpose."

This messianic function was not quite what Lowell had had in mind for his trio of short plays, but he doubtless savored the idea of having them performed in church. Of the plays themselves he had always spoken with some modesty. He had, he said, found playwriting "so easy—it's a crime," and it is a measure both of his standing as "*the* poet" of the day and also perhaps of the enfeebled state of the American theater in the early 1960s that *The Old Glory* should have been greeted as a major cultural event: a "cultural-poetic masterpiece," said Robert Brustein.[1] Comparing Lowell's texts with his prose originals—Melville's "Benito Cereno" and Hawthorne's "My Kinsman Major Molyneux"—it is hard to see now what the fuss was all about. Lowell's versions seem threadbare and—in an attempt for current political or social "relevance"—are often crudely underscored. And to call them "poetic" is charitable, since they are mostly written in an ambling prose; they don't elevate or intensify the words of the originals—they merely reorganize them. Thus, Melville writes:

> What, I, Amasa Delano—Jack of the Beach, as they called me when a lad—I, Amasa, the same that, duck-satchel in hand, used to paddle along the waterside to the schoolhouse made from the old hulk—I, little Jack of the Beach, that used to go berrying with cousin Nat and the rest—I to be murdered here at the ends of the earth on board a haunted pirate ship by a horrible Spaniard? Too nonsensical to think of. Who would murder Amasa Delano? His conscience is clean. There is someone above. Fie, fie, Jack of the Beach! you are a child indeed; a child of the second childhood, old boy; you are beginning to dote and drool, I'm afraid.

And Lowell "versifies":

DELANO   This ship is nothing, Perkins!
I dreamed someone was trying to kill me!
How could he? Jack-of-the-beach,
they used to call me on the Duxbury shore.
Carrying a duck-satchel in my hand, I used to paddle
along the waterfront from a hulk to school.
I didn't learn much there. I was always shooting duck
or gathering huckleberries along the marsh with Cousin Nat!
I like nothing better than breaking myself on the surf.
I used to track the seagulls down the five-mile stretch of beach
                                             for eggs.

How can I be killed now at the ends of the earth
by this insane Spaniard?
Who would want to murder Amasa Delano?
My conscience is clean. God is good.
What am I doing on board this nigger-pirate ship?

PERKINS   You're not talking like a skipper, sir.
Our boat's a larger spot now.

DELANO   I am childish.
          I am doddering and drooling into my second childhood.
          God help me, nothing's solid![2]

This is fairly typical of Lowell's "adaptation" of the Melville text; it is efficient, almost dutiful, but unadventurous. The creation of the character Perkins is forced on Lowell because most of Melville's "action" goes on inside Delano's mind. In the same way, Lowell supplies a brother for Robin to share his fears with in *My Kinsman Major Molyneux*. In both Melville and Hawthorne, of course, the central character is utterly alone—a Perkins or a young brother would have drastically reduced the eeriness.

Lowell's third play—*Endecott and the Red Cross*—was not included in the American Place Theatre's presentation of *The Old Glory* (it was later expanded and offered separately), and as Jonathan Miller admitted, this omission "seriously damaged the grand design."[3] Certainly, *Endecott* is the most subtle and revealing of the three plays; it too draws on prose sources (Hawthorne's stories "The Maypole at Merry Mount" and "Endecott and the Red Cross" and Thomas Morton's "New Canaan"), but at the heart of it is Lowell's own uneasy meditation on the exercise of power. Endecott the ruthless Puritan experiences a spasm of self-doubt; fleetingly, he is sickened by the emptiness of his own rhetoric, his "hollow, dishonest speech, half truth, half bombast":

> I now understand statecraft:
> a statesman can either work with merciless efficiency
> and leave a desert;
> or he can work in a hit-and-miss fashion,
> and leave a cesspool.[4]

In the character of Endecott, Lowell hints at his own indecision in these matters: his lifelong fascination with the "merciless efficiency" of historic generals and tyrants could not, he knew, fit with the correct liberalism required by his own epoch. As he tried to explain in an interview:

> One side of me . . . is a conventional liberal, concerned with causes, agitated about peace and justice and equality, as so many people are. My other side is deeply conservative, wanting to get at the roots of things, wanting to slow down the whole modern process of mechani-

zation and dehumanization, knowing that liberalism can be a form of death too.[5]

And these "two sides" of Lowell's political character are also in evidence in a letter he wrote to Blair Clark in August 1964 about the Republican party convention, at which Barry Goldwater was nominated as presidential candidate:

> We watched the convention of course and much roused by the night of turned down amendments. Goldwater's speech was ominously alive. I had a feeling that I was watching a dark little forlorn movement, the black splinter of an already shrunken party. But who knows? What you say about his possible election is true and dire. We would soon have a fascist state, for I think the Goldwater people would soon find themselves lurching into further extremes to keep going, and our country would be fearful to ourselves and the world. Sometimes now you get a little innocent gleam, innocent though dirtied with much brutality, jobbing and falseness, of someone genuinely wanting to move back to the old simpler times.[6]

Both "Benito Cereno" and "My Kinsman Major Molyneux" were attractive tales for Lowell because they evoke dilemmas of this kind. In each of them, an innocent representative of the "old order" strays into the aftermath of a successful uprising; neither at first knows or can bring himself to believe that the established rules no longer work. Each story, and each of Lowell's plays, is thus a process of unmasking: in "Benito Cereno," it is revealed that the blacks have taken over their own slave ship; in "My Kinsman Major Molyneux," it transpires that British rule has been usurped in Boston. In both plays the rebels are felt to be sinister, malign and even —in *Molyneux*—repellently disfigured; the ousted rulers, though, carry themselves with an exotic dignity even in ruin and humiliation —they are aristocrats, as if aristocracy were a species, not a rank. Lowell's versions are careful to expose the wrongs of the dislodged oppressor (indeed, adding to Melville, Lowell makes Delano shoot down the leader of the blacks and say, "This is your future"), but they are in no sense dramas of indignation or of revolutionary zeal.

Jonathan Miller began preparing his production of *The Old Glory* in the early fall of 1964. He stayed in a small studio upstairs from the Lowells' apartment at West 67th Street and was able to have regular, not always fruitful consultations with his author:

> I don't think Lowell had a really intrinsic sense of the theater. I don't think he had a good visual sense either, of how things might look. He was tremendously open to suggestion, totally humble about that. If you said, "I don't think these pages work," he'd say, "I guess not. We can print them later in the book." And he was always amused and entertained by bits of business. He'd laugh a lot and be very amused by seeing how things were staged. It was Elizabeth who would say, "That young man is so vulgar. Cal, you must tell him." And Cal would then say, "I guess he is. I guess . . . could you get him to wear his hat a little bit less cockily." She was more interested in the theater anyway, and she also had what I think a lot of New York intellectuals have, which is a very sharp, *Variety*-reading, Broadway sense of what's going to work and how you're going to make a fool of yourselves in front of the critics. He was not so socially fastidious about how something would look on the stage.[7]

As the date for the production neared, Miller found that Lowell was beginning to wind up: "It was all very subliminal. You only very gradually noticed." He was becoming "tenacious of schemes and ideas"; he would want Miller to sit up "a little bit later at night, and then later and later" and would become "hectic and slightly impatient" if he was refused.

> He talked a lot about literature and about poetry and about art, and invented a lot of games and would arrange hypothetical weekends and say, "How would it be if you had a weekend with Joinville and Lionel Trilling? Who'd be the best chess player?" All history became a simultaneous event where it was possible for everyone to meet everyone. Famous, important, great people would encounter one another. I think that in his full-blown lunacy all the distinctions of time vanished altogether, and the world was populated by a series of tyrants and geniuses all jostling with one another, competing with one another in knowledge or in sexual skill.[8]

Lowell began writing new acts for his plays, insisting on one memorable occasion that, at the end of *Endecott,* Sir Walter Raleigh's wife should come onto the stage carrying her husband's severed head. "Blood streams from the severed neck," he said. "I guess that could be done with ribbons." But when Miller persuaded him that such lurid treats might not fit too easily with this drama of Puritan self-scrutiny, Lowell would quite happily submit: "He'd just say, 'I guess not.' And abandon it. 'We might do it on opening night as a special.' "[9]

The Old Glory opened on November 1, and in spite of some grumbles from the *New York Times* critic (he found *Major Molyneux* "a pretentious arty trifle" and *Benito Cereno* "labored"), the production was a great success, winning five Obie awards for the 1964–65 season, including the award for Best Play. W. D. Snodgrass declared that he had "never been in a more excited and hopeful audience. We may yet have a theater of our own,"[10] and Randall Jarrell wrote a letter to the *Times:*

> I have never seen a better American play than "Benito Cereno," the major play in Robert Lowell's "The Old Glory." The humor and terror of the writing are no greater than those of the acting and directing; the play is a masterpiece of imaginative knowledge.[11]

In January 1965 *Benito Cereno* was transferred to the Theatre de Lys in Greenwich Village for a regular off-Broadway run, and by this time Lowell had, in Miller's words, "gone over":

> He tended to go into these things when there was something in the offing, where fame, a great deal of attention, or notoriety was probable. I used to see on his bookshelf what seemed a rather fat copy of *Les Fleurs du Mal.* I never took it off the shelf, but it seemed much larger than it ought to be, and I wondered if it was an annotated edition or something. And then I suddenly noticed one day in the same place on the bookshelf a book of identical size without a dust jacket and it was *Mein Kampf.* And I remember him meeting me at the airport and I could see him on the mezzanine, sort of sweating, and his spectacles seemed steamed over, and he came down to greet me and he was wearing an open-necked shirt and there was a huge medallion of Alexander bouncing on his chest. And as he greeted me there were three or four Hasidic rabbis coming off the plane and a sort of mischievous look came into his eyes, and he said, "Oh, Jonathan, the Germans were not responsible for World War Two."[12]

Even after *The Old Glory* had completed its run at St. Clement's church, Lowell continued to attend services there—and on one occasion was allowed to preach a sermon. It was at St. Clement's that he met the Latvian dancer Vija Vetra. Her program of Indian sacred dances was to be featured in one of Sidney Lanier's church services; Lanier wished to "bring dance for the first time into his church." Vetra describes her first meeting with the famous poet:

> I arrived early to get everything ready. And Robert also came early. I had never heard of Robert Lowell. I had never even heard of the Lowell family. So I was absolutely ignorant, which was delicious. And he sees me in my Indian costume—very unusual to see something like that in his church, of course. So he comes straight along, stretches out his hand and introduces himself: "I am Robert Lowell." Thinking I would crumble with being so impressed, or squeak with delight. I think he expected that, you know—at least make big eyes. So we talked a bit, but the others wanted to get on with the preparations and they pushed him away. But he came always back and wanted to talk more and more. Then he found out I am born in Latvia and he started putting questions about the Russians and Communism. He was very political also.[13]

Lowell invited Vija Vetra to the off-Broadway opening of his play; indeed, invited her to pretheater drinks at West 67th Street:

> And I knew I couldn't disappoint him. So he picked me up and he said, "We're having a gathering first at my home of some friends and all of us together will go to the theater." So fine. I had no bad conscience towards his wife because nothing had yet happened that I should be afraid of her spurn. So we went there, and he introduced me to his friends and to his wife, of course, and she greeted me coldly as ice. And I thought, Oh, I should not have come. What he had told her, in his naïveté, I don't know. . . .[14]

After the performance, Lowell took Vetra backstage to meet the actors, and Hardwick went home. Lowell decided he was going to stay the night with his new friend:

> So he took me home, and he said, "I am going to stay here. I'm not going to go home." And I said, "No, Robert, please don't complicate things further. Don't do that to me—and to her." So he blackmailed me then. "All right, then, would you like me to run under a bus? I have all this sedation. Anything can happen." He could always take a taxi, of course. But he used it more or less as an excuse. And luckily I did have two couches, in a sort of triangle, so I made a bed for him. And I thought,

if he uses that kind of blackmail, all right, I'll give in, but next day he'll go. He stayed there for a week or two. That was Robert.[15]

During that "week or two," Lowell began introducing Vetra as his future wife; he leased an apartment at 16 West 16th Street in their joint names (they signed "Robert and Vija—Mrs. Robert—Lowell") and began buying furniture. Vetra could see that he was "a bit overexcited . . . But I have dealt with artists all my life and I didn't think it was anything special." And in any case: "He was excited like anybody normally would be in having a prospect, a new beginning." As for Vetra, she too had become "enthusiastic":

> Of course I got more and more close to him, more and more enmeshed with him, and I can really say that I began to fall in love with him. And I got caught up in his enthusiasm to go further, to solidify it. I felt that having come here, to America, it would be wonderful to have a new life with someone I could really love and cherish. I felt very lonely at that time too.[16]

Before Lowell and Vetra could move into their home, Blair Clark intervened. He arranged for Vetra to meet Dr. Bernard:

> Bernard told me, surely, don't I see that he's in this condition—as if saying that someone could love me only if he's crazy, or in a depressed mood. Saying wouldn't it be better if for a while he was separated from me and put into a rest home. But he didn't want to go.[17]

Lowell's new scheme was that he and Vetra should "go and live in Maine, because he absolutely adored Maine, and Lizzie can stay where she is, and that station car we will take and the other car she can have." But Clark and Dr. Bernard continued to put pressure on Vetra—in her words, "to do their damnedest to get rid of me." And in the end,

> they rather convinced me that it might after all be best for him, and if it is so, then I thought I'll give it a try, knowing that I'm risking losing him altogether. I knew that, but I thought maybe by some chance it will work well. So I thought if I could help, maybe I should do it. Because I was the only one whose word he would follow. I knew that and he knew it and everybody else knew it. So I told him what they had told me and we talked it over. And he said, "I really don't want to go, but

if you think . . . And of course as soon as I come out we will marry
then."[18]

On January 25 Blair Clark accompanied Lowell and Vetra to the
Institute for Living in Hartford; he had hired a limousine, and the
three of them sat in the back seat: "Blair on one side, Robert in the
middle, me on the other, holding hands all the way. Poor thing. He
just felt he was sent to the slaughtering house, you know, like a
lamb."

Vetra returned to New York and moved into the West 16th Street
apartment, and for two weeks heard nothing: "I thought I would
take my life, that's how down I was." Lowell was not allowed to
make telephone calls, nor—at first—to receive visitors. He wrote
daily letters to Vetra, but these were sent to West 67th Street: "They
were sending the whole bunch to his wife."

> then one day he rang me: "Now I am allowed to make one call to you.
> Why don't you send me letters? Why don't you answer?" So then we
> found out that they had all been sent to Lizzie. He was furious and rang
> her, or wrote to her, and demanded that my letters be sent to me. So
> one day they arrived, the whole stack at once.[19]

For the first ten days of his hospitalization, Lowell continued to be
adamant about his new life with Vija Vetra. His letters to her are,
in the main, desperate entreaties:

> Please don't change your mind, mine only grows more set in determina-
> tion to marry you.
> Dearest Love, Love, Love you wanted letters, but I only want to return
> to you as soon as possible.[20]

But by February 5 he is beginning to have doubts; indeed, some kind
of climax seems to have been reached with his anger over the side-
tracking of his Vetra letters. He writes to Hardwick:

> Thanks for the wire. I was really very upset about the letters business.
> If I am irrational, then I'm full of irrational turbulence. So, that's over.
> How do I feel? Really, it's complicated, and there'll be a melancholy to
> any possible decision. Surely, there's some terrible flaw in my life that
> blows a bubble into my head every year or so. It mustn't continue,

though I suppose that's only partly up to me and partly of [*sic*] to fate, nature, God and whatever.[21]

By February 9 he had made up his mind. He had been reading Elizabeth Hardwick's edition of *Persuasion*:

And now I feel like Sir Walter Elliot, as a [*sic*] read your many notes, and try to feel important and dignified to hide what a mess I've made of my human ties. If you and Harriet want me, I am yours. Vija is coming up here tomorrow, and I ought, I suppose, make no decision till after then. Still I know now for certain that I can't avoid returning to my two girls, if they'll have me. I am sorry from my heart for having put us all through the hoops.[22]

The following day, Vetra traveled up to Hartford, her first visit there since Lowell had been admitted two weeks earlier:

So I saw him, and he felt as if he had been walked on, so unsure of himself. "Well, I guess it will be best if I went back home." Like a vegetable. I don't know what they did. More drugs, of course, maybe even shock treatment, I don't know. He felt so guilty he had to tell me this, but it had been decided that it would be best to call it off for a while and go back home and see what happens. He was so happy to see me and we had a talk, and before I left, he was wearing this striped shirt, and I said, "Give me a souvenir. Give me the shirt that you are wearing." And he said, "But I have a new one." "I don't want that. I want the one you wore." So he took it off and gave it to me. I still have it.[23]

A fortnight later, Vija Vetra received another souvenir in the shape of a letter from Lowell's attorneys, Migdal Low and Tenny:

In order to terminate any responsibility Mr. Lowell may have with respect to the apartment at 16 W. 16th St, without undue hardship to you or additional expense to him, it is advisable that we meet as soon as possible.[24]

At this meeting, Vetra was given two days to vacate the apartment: "Heartless, absolutely heartless. That's the American way. Very ugly." She retaliated, Hardwick recalls, by sending Lowell "a lot of bills with demanding notes. He dropped them on the floor and I picked them up and paid them."[25]

Shortly after his discharge from the hospital, Lowell and Hardwick left for a two-week visit to Egypt, at the invitation of the American University of Cairo. He gave two lectures in Cairo and then they took a short tourist's trip to Upper Egypt. By the time he returned to New York, Blair Clark had "tidied up . . . the Vija Vetra problem."[26]

"When your private experience converges on the nation's experience you feel you have to do something."[27] Lowell had already "done something," in response to the nuclear threat, in a handful of poems in *For the Union Dead*, but it was not until 1965 that he began to present himself as an authoritative public figure, someone whose prose voice would carry weight in matters of political debate. As Blair Clark remembers it, Lowell's concern about American activity in Vietnam began to show itself in the spring of 1965:

> The first time I realized that there was going to be a big revulsion against Vietnam was '65, when I had an argument with Cal. Spring of 1965, when we were already slightly involved. I say "slightly"—we had about 75,000 to 100,000 troops there. But Cal was already outraged by it, and I—a much more "political" person than Cal—I pooh-poohed it, and said to Cal I didn't think Johnson would get caught in that trap. Of course, he was right.[28]

American bombing raids on Communist targets in Vietnam had begun in February 1965, and during March Johnson stepped up the dispatch of combat troops. In April and May the first antiwar demonstrations were held, both in Washington and in colleges across the country. In April, also, Johnson had sent over twenty thousand marines into the Dominican Republic "to protect the lives and property of United States citizens."

It was in this atmosphere that the President gave his blessing to a White House Festival of the Arts, to be held on June 14. The organizer, Eric F. Goldman (a "special consultant" to the President), concedes that the festival was in some measure "a tool to quiet opposition to the war," but doubts that Johnson took the event very seriously: "Overall, LBJ appeared to think of it as a pleasant day, the sort of thing a President ought to do in view of all the interest in art around the country, one that would particularly please the ladies, and that was that."[29] Goldman drew up an invitation list, which included figures from the worlds of "painting, sculpture, literature, music (serious and jazz), the cinema, and photography." For "literature" he chose Mark Van Doren, Saul Bellow, John Hersey, Edmund Wilson and Robert Lowell. Wilson immediately refused "with a brusqueness that I have never experienced before or after in the case of an invitation in the name of the President and First Lady."[30] Lowell, telephoned by the White House at the end of May, agreed to attend and give a poetry reading.

But a few days later Lowell changed his mind. The circumstances are not entirely clear, but Robert Silvers, editor of the *New York Review,* remembers the weekend in question:

> It's very hard to remember exactly, but I remember it was a Saturday morning and I was down in the Village and Philip Roth was living there and I happened to meet him in the street. And he said, "It would be very sad if Cal turned up at that," and I agreed, and he said, "Well, I hope you'll talk to him about it." I tried to ring Cal but he wasn't there, so I wrote him a note about it and dropped it off at the house.[31]

When Silvers called round later that day, Lowell had already written a letter to Johnson and planned to release it to the *New York Times.*[32] The letter read:

DEAR PRESIDENT JOHNSON

When I was telephoned last week and asked to read at the White House Festival of the Arts on June fourteenth, I am afraid I accepted somewhat rapidly and greedily. I thought of such an occasion as a purely artistic flourish, even though every serious artist knows that he cannot enjoy public celebration without making subtle public commitments. After a week's wondering, I have decided that I am conscience-bound to refuse your courteous invitation. I do so now in a public letter because my acceptance has been announced in the newspapers and because of the strangeness of the Administration's recent actions.

Although I am very enthusiastic about most of your domestic legislation and intentions, I nevertheless can only follow our present foreign policy with the greatest dismay and distrust. What we will do and what we ought to do as a sovereign nation facing other sovereign nations seem now to hang in the balance between the better and the worse possibilities. We are in danger of imperceptibly becoming an explosive and suddenly chauvinistic nation, and may even be drifting on our way to the last nuclear ruin. I know it is hard for the responsible man to act; it is also painful for the private and irresolute man to dare criticism. At this anguished, delicate and perhaps determining moment, I feel I am serving you and our country best by not taking part in the White House Festival of the Arts.

> Respectfully yours,
> Robert Lowell

As Goldman records, his first reaction to this letter was "fury. This, I told myself, was arrant troublemaking and publicity-seeking." On reflection, though, he decided that Lowell was a "sincere and troubled man" and therefore might be persuaded to change his mind about publishing his letter in the *Times;* he telephoned Lowell and argued that since his acceptance of the invitation had not been widely publicized, it would surely be proper for him to withdraw now "for personal reasons":

No, Lowell replied, he wanted to go ahead.

> Throughout the conversation, the poet was gracious, free of self-righteousness about the position he was taking, and thoroughly understanding of the complications he was causing. I hung up the telephone with the impression of a fine human being. I also hung up with the feeling that all hell was about to break loose.[33]

Goldman drafted a reply to Lowell and sent it to Johnson for his signature; it spoke of Johnson's full and deep respect for Lowell's disagreement with "certain phases of the Administration's foreign policy."[34]

> The roar in the Oval Office could be heard all the way into the East Wing. The instruction came back. Answer the letter under my own name and make it "just an acknowledgement." I decided that "just an acknowledgment" could include this much:

> Dear Mr. Lowell,
>   As you requested, I have sent your letter on to President Johnson.
>   Needless to say, I regret very much that the White House Festival of the Arts will be deprived of your distinction and talents.
> > Sincerely yours,
> > Eric F. Goldman

The next morning the *New York Times* carried the story on its front page, and swiftly followed it with another report under the headline: "Twenty Writers and Artists Endorse Poet's Rebuff of President."[35] Robert Silvers and the poet Stanley Kunitz had organized a telegram to Johnson expressing support for Lowell and "dismay at recent American foreign policy decisions." The signatories were: Hannah Arendt, John Berryman, Alan Dugan, Jules Feiffer, Philip Guston, Lillian Hellman, Alfred Kazin, Stanley Kunitz, Dwight Macdonald, Bernard Malamud, Mary McCarthy, Larry Rivers, Philip Roth, Mark Rothko, Louis Simpson, W. D. Snodgrass, William Styron, Peter Taylor, Edgar Varese and Robert Penn Warren. "An impressive array of talent," even Goldman had to admit, but for Johnson the telegram was more infuriating than the letter; it smacked of organization, of a conspiracy between "these people" to insult him and his office, and "to hurt their country at a time of crisis":

> They were not only "sonsofbitches" but they were "fools" and they were close to traitors. A minor event, a mere ceremonial festival of the arts, was blowing up into a situation which could have anything but minor significance.[36]

Silvers and Kunitz had arranged the telegram "so that Cal wouldn't be alone in what he did but would have the support of a group of people who felt concerned about the war and the bombing. There was the Dominican intervention too, which was highly controversial. But that the American B-52s were bombing was a source of consternation."[37] Certainly, for Lowell the "bombing" was the issue. As Blair Clark has commented: "Boy, Cal's politics—they're a study. He was so anti-Communist in one way, and yet he had this moral thing about the bombing."[38]

Clark also perceived that Lowell had a "shrewdness" in handling his public persona, and that the "LBJ letter" was an example of his "brilliant timing":

> You have to say that that was a very successful operation of high-level cultural publicism. Cal the public figure—he knew what he was doing. I'm sure there were people who were terribly envious of his ability to manipulate himself as a public figure. He did it without any pomposity —but he definitely believed that he *was* a public figure.[39]

It is true enough that the reverberations of Lowell's grand gesture were felt for some weeks afterwards—at any rate, in the columns of the *New York Times*. Arthur Schlesinger, speaking to the American Booksellers Association, was reported to have "gently ridiculed" the Lowell stand. To this, Philip Roth protested, "to me it does not seem nearly so ironic for a poet of stature to protest American foreign policy as for an Administration so insensitive to human values in its dealings with other nations to sponsor 'a festival of the arts.' But then each man to his own sense of the ridiculous."[40] Schlesinger replied that he had not ridiculed Lowell—whom he "cherished" as a friend and "admired" as a poet—but had merely said that he preferred the methods of Dr. Linus Pauling, who, when invited to dinner by President Kennedy, had picketed the White House for a day and then gone in to eat his food.[41]

This hint was perhaps on Dwight Macdonald's mind when, after having signed the telegram supporting Lowell, he received *his* invitation to the festival: it had been held up in the mail. Macdonald promptly accepted, but arrived at the White House bearing a petition that read: "We should like to make it clear that in accepting the President's kind invitation to attend the White House Arts Festival, we do not mean either to repudiate the courageous position taken by Robert Lowell, or to endorse the Administration's foreign policy." By the end of the evening he had collected nine signatures, and had almost come to blows with Charlton Heston, who felt Macdonald to be short of "elementary manners": "Are you really accustomed to signing petitions against your host in his home?" Macdonald later wrote an amusing account of his escapade for the *New York Review of Books.*[42]

President Johnson put in a brief and extremely reluctant appearance at the festival, but he left it to Lady Bird to attend the actual readings. Each of these, Goldman writes, was a possible source of embarrassment. Mark Van Doren, for instance, had been invited to introduce the writers' section of the festival, and the speech he had prepared was almost exclusively in praise of Lowell; in its first version it "included no word of appreciation for the sponsorship [of the Festival] by the President and the First Lady." Goldman pleaded with him to rewrite the speech, and eventually Van Doren agreed to do so; in his revised version he merely noted Lowell's absence "with regret":

He may or may not have been correct . . . nor do I commit any of the writers present here to agreement or disagreement. . . . I have been troubled as to whether I should speak of it at all; I do so now, after several previous attempts merely as honoring the scruple of a fine poet who, in his own terms, was "conscience-bound" to stay away.[43]

and then went on to thank his hosts for "their magnificent and gracious hospitality" and to pronounce that "we are all proud and happy to participate."

Goldman's other worry concerned John Hersey, who, on the day of Lowell's letter to the *Times,* had said that he would make *his* protest by reading to the President some extracts from his book on Hiroshima. Hearing this, Johnson once again saw red: he and his wife did not want "this man to read these passages in the White House." Goldman retorted that it "would be White House censorship" if they tried to prevent Hersey from reading his own work, and Johnson eventually compromised by ordering a "black-out" of all press and television coverage of the festival; a one-hour television special was canceled and photographers were banned. He also ordered an FBI check on all the invitees. Hersey, meanwhile, had decided that he wished to read a preface to his extracts from *Hiroshima;* this preface would point out, he said, that "The step from one degree of violence to the next is imperceptibly taken and cannot easily be taken back. . . . Wars have a way of getting out of hand." With some nervousness, Goldman concurred, and on the night of the festival, Hersey not only read his admonitory preface but also made a point of "occasionally lifting his eyes to look straight at Mrs. Johnson, who sat in the front row. When he finished, there were a few seconds of silence, then vigorous applause. The First Lady, who clapped for all other readings, sat motionless."[44]

The harassed Goldman was relieved that his remaining poet guest was the light versifier Phyllis McGinley. But even she was determined to contribute to The Lowell Problem. She added a new verse to her poem "In Praise of Diversity":

> And while the pot of culture's
>   bubblesome,
> Praise poets even when
>   they're troublesome.

As Goldman describes it, the Lowell letter hung challengingly over the entire event. Even those writers, such as Saul Bellow, who believed that Lowell's gesture had been inappropriate, became "decidedly unsettled"—he was, he said, "under pressure from the New York crowd" to withdraw or to make some form of protest; he had been accused of "turncoating for publicity and preferment." There were similar complaints from Ralph Ellison. Almost everyone who turned up, it seemed, felt the need to explain what he was doing there; and so far as Johnson was concerned, the White House had been taken over for the night by a gang of conspirators and traitors. All in all—and largely thanks to Lowell—the event was "an unmitigated disaster":

> Almost everything that happened after Lowell's letter and President Johnson's reaction to it had added bricks to a wall between the President and these groups. Mercifully, much of the story was unknown. But enough had become public to make the wall seem as impassable as the barbed concrete between East and West Berlin.[45]

Six weeks after the festival, President Johnson increased still further the U.S. "presence" in Vietnam, and asked Congress for a further billion dollars so that "all that we have built" would not be "swept away on the flood of conquest." And on August 4 he added his own comic postscript to the Lowell letter. Addressing thousands of students on the lawn of the White House, he told them that he was as "restless" as they were, and as young in spirit. He went on:

> Robert Lowell, the poet, doesn't like everything around here. But I like one of his lines where he wrote: "For the world which seems to lie out before us like a land of dreams." Well, in this great age—and it is a great age—the world does seem to lie before us like a land of dreams.[46]

The line he quotes is, of course, from Matthew Arnold's "Dover Beach." Lowell, however, had used it as an epigraph for his book *The Mills of the Kavanaughs,* and clearly Johnson's speech writer, in a hurry to supply an upbeat Lowell quote, had not adventured past the title page. LBJ was once again a laughingstock in the smart intellectual circles which his festival had at first been meant to woo.

Lowell's own comment on Johnson's speech was appropriately laconic; he told the *New York Times:* "I think I like things as much as the President."[47]

Lowell emerged from his skirmish with the President feeling both "miscast" and yet "burdened to write on the great theme, private, and almost 'global.' "[48] His difficulty was that his image of America was not too sharply different from his image of himself. America he thought of in terms of *Moby Dick:* "the fanatical idealist who brings the world down in ruins through some sort of simplicity of mind." Such a tendency, he said, was "in our character and in my own personal character."[49] In other words, Lowell knew that in his own life an excess of idealism had often issued in destruction. From what seat of virtue, therefore, could he now chastise the President? He felt there to be a hollowness, a fraudulence in the wise-prophet stance he was now being tempted to adopt. And yet he was tempted.

In Castine during the summer of 1965 Lowell worked on a group of poems in a meter borrowed from Andrew Marvell's equivocal "Ode upon Cromwell's Return from Ireland." In their final versions, at least two of these poems seem more "public," more addressed to an audience, than anything that Lowell had done before. Indeed, "Waking Early Sunday Morning" is now thought of as a key "political poem" of the 1960s:

> O to break loose. All life's grandeur
> is something with a girl in summer . . .
> elated as the President
> girdled by his establishment
> this Sunday morning, free to chaff
> his own thoughts with his bear-cuffed staff,
> swimming nude, unbuttoned, sick
> of his ghost-written rhetoric!
>
> No weekends for the gods now. Wars
> flicker, earth licks its open sores,
> fresh breakage, fresh promotions, chance
> assassinations, no advance.
> Only man thinning out his kind
> sounds through the Sabbath noon, the blind

> swipe of the pruner and his knife
> busy about the tree of life . . .
>
> Pity the planet, all joy gone
> from this sweet volcanic cone;
> peace to our children when they fall
> in small war on the heels of small
> war—until the end of time
> to police the earth, a ghost
> orbiting forever lost
> in our monotonous sublime.[50]

The first three lines here do, almost explicitly, equate the poet's manic elation—his "something with a girl in summer"—with the excited self-belief of the military establishment, but the shift into "global" elegy in the last stanza is also a shift away from any risk that the poem might be read as holier-than-thou polemic.

"Waking Early Sunday Morning" went through several versions before its publication, and—as Alan Williamson has valuably pointed out[51]—there is much to be learned from the stanzas Lowell eventually left out. Many of them express a distaste for the type of "ambition" that Lowell's admirers were now expecting from him; the wish to "break loose" into the "criminal leisure of a boy" is far purer and more powerful than the impulse to pretend that poetry can save the world:

> Time to dig up and junk the year's
> dotage and output of tame verse:
> cast-iron whimsy, limp indignation,
> liftings, listless self-imitation,
> whole days when I could hardly speak,
> came barging home unshaven, weak
> and willing to show anyone
> things done before and better done
>
> . . . .
> For days now, or is it a week,
> I run away from busywork
> to lie in my far barn apart,
> and when I look into my heart,
> I discover none of the great

> subjects, death, friendship, love or fate,
> I look for doorknobs, marbles, sad,
> slight, useless things that calm the mad.
>
> Now on the radio the wars
> blare on, earth licks its open sores,
> fresh breakage, fresh promotions, chance
> assassinations, no advance!
> Only man thinning out his kind
> sounds through the Sunday noon, the blind
> swipe of the pruner and his knife
> busy to strip the tree of life.
>
> I cannot take it. One grows sick
> of stretching for this rhetoric,
> this hammering allegoric splendor,
> top-heavy Goliath in full armor
> toddling between two hosts, all brass,
> except its breast-plate, lump and mass,
> propped on its Brobdignagian staff
> bull-throated bombast stuffed with chaff.[52]

In an even earlier version, Lowell portrays himself as "running from crisis into crisis—/Prufrock in love with Dionysus." As he rewrote the poem, though, he depersonalized it; the directly self-lacerating elements are pruned away and President Johnson becomes the empty rhetorician. Similarly, the wars that are here "on the radio" get moved to the very center of the poem. In the end, it could be said that Lowell aims for just that tone of millennial *gravitas* which in these early drafts he is "sick of stretching for." But is this any different from saying that because of his distrust of easy rhetoric he finally—indeed triumphantly—achieves a rhetoric that we can trust; a rhetoric of painful and profound "unease"?

> Pity the planet, all joy gone
> from this sweet volcanic cone;
> peace to our children when they fall
> in small war on the heels of small
> war—[53]

The other poems that Lowell wrote during the summer of 1965 are less "burdened" with political "unrest." None of them, however, moves with great assurance, or even clarity, and the Marvellian couplet often encourages a tripping, near-doggerel effect:

> Behind a dripping rock, I found
> a one-day kitten on the ground—
> deprived, weak, ignorant and blind,
> squeaking, tubular, left behind—
> dying with its deserter's rich
> Welfare lying out of reach:
> milk cartons, kidney heaped to spoil,
> two plates sheathed with silver foil.[54]

This is from a poem called "Central Park," in which Lowell tries to manifest compassion for those trapped in "fear and poverty"; all that comes over is a generalized revulsion, and the poem's last lines —sometimes cited as a memorable evocation of urban violence—are almost offensively facile and complacent:

> We beg delinquents for our life.
> Behind each bush, perhaps a knife;
> each landscaped crag, each flowering shrub,
> hides a policeman with a club.[55]

"Fourth of July in Maine" is a chatty, reverent verse letter to Cousin Harriet; it is light, sentimental and well-mannered, and has some nice Lowellian guinea pigs, but it barely gets beyond the family circle. "Near the Ocean" is a nightmarish, obscure reverie on marriage, both vengeful and apologetic: it seems to review earlier points of crisis in Lowell's relationship with Hardwick, and to offer, in the end, a scarred, exhausted truce:

> Sleep, sleep. The ocean, grinding stones,
> can only speak the present tense;
> nothing will age, nothing will last,
> or take corruption from the past.
> A hand, your hand then! I'm afraid
> to touch the crisp hair·on your head—
> Monster loved for what you are,
> till time, that buries us, lay bare.[56]

Both poems in their very different ways speak of marital conflict, of "energies that never tire / of piling fuel on the fire," of "wild spirits and old sores in league / with inexhaustible fatigue," and the conclusion of "Fourth of July in Maine"—although its yearning for lost "gentleness" is rather pat—again suggests a gutted, stoic compromise:

Far off that time of gentleness,
when man, still licensed to increase,
unfallen and unmated, heard
only the uncreated Word—
when God the Logos still had wit
to hide his bloody hands, and sit
in silence, while his peace was sung.
Then the universe was young.

We watch the logs fall. Fire once gone,
we're done for: we escape the sun,
rising and setting, a red coal,
until it cinders like the soul.
Great ash and sun of freedom, give
us this day the warmth to live,
and face the household fire. We turn
our backs, and feel the whiskey burn.[57]

The episode with Vija Vetra had been galling for Hardwick, not because she considered Vetra a formidable rival (she says now that this was "the only affair I know Cal to have been truly, honestly ashamed of; there was regret sometimes, but not shame of choice"). Her real fury was with the "enlightened" line that had been taken by Lowell's doctor. As with Sandra Hochman, Hardwick had received little backing from Dr. Bernard; "the great thing in this 'event' was my fury with Dr. Bernard, my feeling of helplessness with regard to her; her idea of living out these 'test cases' as if tying yourself up for life, or years, was a little workout in the gym to get yourself in shape."[58] Shortly before Lowell was hospitalized, Hardwick wrote as follows to Blair Clark:

I have been thinking it all over. If Cal seems all right except for V.V. and if he doesn't want to go to the hospital, I begin to feel that I at least ought not to insist. It is only his own welfare that matters. If it is all right for him to set up a new life, I don't think my feelings against it are very much to the point. I begin to think perhaps Cal should make one last effort to cure himself or at least to be happier, if only temporarily, than he is with me. And maybe that will ultimately cure him. For myself I do not want him to be violently treated with drugs and then sent back home in a depression—back to a home he probably doesn't want to come to. I feel that isn't good for either of us. If he is not doing harm to himself; if perhaps gradually with a smaller dose of the drugs he can get back to some routine and work in his new situation, then he must do that.

You can send this letter to Dr. Bernard. I am all right. And I begin to think Harriet is now old enough to be able to make the break from Cal if she has to. I know it would be hard for her, but I might gradually put her in a slightly happier situation than apartment life here. I won't stay absolutely the same forever and neither will she.

I say all this to you, darling friend, in good faith. I do not want to force Cal back. I don't feel any longer that he loves me. And I always felt before that he did, or I would not have fought so hard. You and Dr. Bernard do what you think is best.[59]

Both Clark and Bernard thought it "best" for Lowell to be treated in the hospital, and for the Vija Vetra involvement (which even Bernard seems to have thought somewhat outlandish) to be distanced until Lowell was able to make a sane judgment of its possibilities. But what is a "sane judgment"; how much of the penitential depression that followed each of Lowell's manic "seizures" was caused by the lowering effect of his drug therapy? Lowell's renunciation of Vetra, his genuinely remorseful (and in this case, it seems, embarrassed) feelings about the havoc he had caused: were these more "true" than his exhausted, sheepish pleas to Hardwick—for forgiveness, for another chance? And how could Hardwick simply pretend that she had not been abused and humiliated; how could she take him back without some lingering rancor, and without wondering what horrors his next "test case" would bring? When, from Hartford, in February 1965, he told her that he had given Vetra up and wanted to come home again, Hardwick wrote back to him:

Dear one: I got your Friday note today. Cal my heart bleeds for you, but remember what greatness you have made of your life, what joy you have given to all of us. My purpose, beloved, is to try to see *what can be done to help us all.* I hate for you to get sick. I would kill myself, if it would cure you. There must be something more we can lean on—medical, psychiatric, personal, the dearest love goes out to you from your apartment here on 67th St.

I long to talk to you again.[60]

In the hospital at Hartford in February 1965 Lowell learned of the death of the critic R. P. Blackmur. Lowell had not been an intimate of Blackmur's, although they had over the years visited each other's country homes in Maine, and Lowell had always been grateful for the acute review Blackmur had written of *Land of Unlikeness*. He was, in Lowell's view, "an awesome critic"[1] and also "a good poet, weird, tortured, derivative, original—and more a poet in his criticism."[2] The news of his death, though, was for Lowell not just a personal blow; it was yet another sign of the unsteadiness of his whole world of literary friends and mentors. Blackmur had died at sixty-one, but Lowell said, "he always seemed to me like a young man, just a little my senior."[3]

A month earlier T. S. Eliot had died; two years earlier it had been Robert Frost and Theodore Roethke. Roethke, again, had not been a close friend. Lowell had first met him at Yaddo in 1947; he had liked him as a drinking and croquet companion, but had not greatly admired his work: "My final judgment on his poetry," he wrote to J. F. Powers, "is pretty complicated—a fairly small thing done, at its best, with remarkable clarity and freshness." And he had from the start been both repelled and fascinated by Roethke's blatant careerism: "if somehow he could forget about renown and arriving and all that . . . but it's easy to say this about someone else—hard to practice."[4]

Lowell knew that he was every bit as ambitious as Roethke; he too, in 1947, wanted to arrive, to be "major," to be "*the* poet," and he was always to keep a shrewd eye on the fluctuations of rank in the poetry world. But his own professional persona could hardly have been more unlike Roethke's. Lowell affected (and often genuinely felt) humility and tentativeness, and would manifest a shy, disclaiming pleasure in whatever praise might swim his way. Roethke, however, was openly hungry for acclaim, and insatiable: he would quote over and over again from his favorable reviews, and smart terribly if the critics fell even slightly short of downright eulogy. Quite simply, Roethke wanted to be Champ.

This being so, he was forever watchful of contenders, and from the beginning he had Lowell marked out as a threat. "The best of his stuff has a rough power," he conceded in 1947, but "it's not all that R. Jarrell says it is."[5] He would be scathing about "the patty cake Lowell and Jarrell play in print,"[6] and would say of some new poem of his own that it was the "answer" to Lowell's latest effort. Towards the end of his life, Roethke wrote of the poems that were to be collected in his posthumous book *The Far Field:* "I've got old Cal beat, but really."[7]

As to Lowell, he was never wholly converted to Roethke's work, although he would politely name him in any list of his favorite contemporaries. And—in championship terms—he seems never to have felt uneasy about Roethke's claims. In letters to Roethke there is often a faintly avuncular note; and often he would merely be responding to Roethke's constant need for reassurance: "There's nothing wrong with your brain . . . you are one of the most intelligent men in America."[8] But his praise for Roethke's actual poems never quite rings true. Often it would be offered in the form of a hurried P.S.: "Yes, I do think you are tops as a poet in your new book,"[9] or, "One of the things I marvel at in your poems is the impression they give of having been worked on an extra half day."[10] On one occasion, in 1961, Lowell confesses to having "mislaid" a batch of poems that Roethke had sent him: "—before I had read them! Well, I've recently read some strong poems of yours in I think The Observer and another in the New Yorker. No diminishment!" Noticeably, Lowell doesn't ask Roethke to send copies.[11]

There were other ways, though, in which Lowell felt a real bond with the older poet (Roethke was born in 1908). There was the coincidence of Roethke's notion of himself as a sort of dancing bear. He was a big—some might say gross—man and yet at poetry readings he would literally dance to his own rhythms:

> And I have made a promise to my ears
> I'll sing and whistle dancing with the bears.[12]

When he first met Roethke, Lowell was full of his own bear jokes and thought it delightful that there should be a bear-poet more shaggy and ungainly than himself. For a period he addressed Roethke in letters as "Dear Bear."

A further coincidence was that Roethke, since 1935, had suffered recurrent manic-depressive illnesses. Over the years, Lowell wrote him moving letters about this:

> I feel great kinship with you. We are at times almost one another's shadows passing through the same jungle. Things have lately risen for me considerably. Getting out of the flats after a manic leap is like our old crew races at school. When the course if [*sic*] half-finished, you know and so does everybody else on the boat, that not another stroke can be taken. Yet everyone goes on, and the observer on the wharf notices nothing.[13]

> Our troubles are a bond. I, too, am just getting over a manic attack. Everything seemed to be going swimmingly, then suddenly I was in the hospital—thorozine [*sic*], windy utterances, domestic chaos . . . the old story. Now it's passed; I'm back in my study; my feet are on the floor. When you come we can spill out to each other.[14]

Elizabeth Hardwick comments on this "kinship": "I think Cal admired Roethke's work, but no room could contain the two of them at the same time. They were competitors in symptoms. I remember that Cal told me that he and Roethke were someplace around Boston, traveling in and out of the city on the train. And Cal said, 'Would you believe it, he expected *me* to get the tickets, *me* to make all the arrangements.' "[15]

On July 10, 1963—less than a month before Roethke died of a heart attack—Lowell wrote him a letter that was strikingly more candid and searching than any of his earlier communications: closer, at any rate, to what seems to have been the truth of their relationship:

> I remember Edwin Muir arguing with me that there is no rivalry in poetry. Well, there is. No matter what one has done or hasn't done (this sounds like a prayer) one feels each blow, each turning of the wind, each up and down grading of the critics. We've both written enough and lived long enough perhaps to find this inescapable. Each week brings some pat on the back or some brisk, righteous slur, till one rather longs for the old oblivion. Well, it would be terrible if there weren't many

frogs in the pond, and even many toads. It does make me happier that
you exist, and can do so many big things that I have no gift for. We
couldn't be more different, and yet how weirdly our lives have often
gone the same way. Let's say we are brothers, have gone the same
journey and know far more about each other than we have ever said or
will say. There's a strange fact about the poets of roughly our age, and
one that doesn't exactly seem to have always been true. It's this, that to
write we seem to have to go at it with such single-minded intensity that
we are always on the point of drowning. I've seen this so many times,
and year after year with students, that I feel it's something almost
unavoidable, some flaw in the motor. There must be a kind of glory to
it all that people coming later will wonder at. I can see us all being
written up in some huge book of the age. But under what title? Anyway,
Ted, I do love and honor you.[16]

Roethke was fifty-five when he collapsed on a tennis court on Bain-
bridge Island, Washington, on August 1, 1963.

On February 5, 1965, Lowell wrote to Elizabeth Hardwick from
the hospital at Hartford:

Mournful thoughts on death: it's [*sic*] seems so irrational for Frost, Eliot,
Blackmur and Roethke all to have died in about the same twelve months,
all different in age and the consummation of their careers. No, everything that is isn't right![17]

Of Eliot's death he wrote to Robert Giroux:

I have reached an age when all my elders are disappearing, and can't
reconcile myself to the fact. I must say there was no one who spoke with
such authority, and so little played the role of the great man. He was
a good and patient friend to both of us.[18]

And to Eliot's widow, Valerie:

Too long a time has passed since Tom's death. I wept when I heard
about it, and for weeks caught myself rather inanely saying, "This is
sheer loss, without recompense." Sheer loss for us. I have reached an age
when all my elders are disappearing, and can't reconcile myself to the
fact. Their wit and guidance are irreplaceable and each year one seems
to withdraw further from the friendly shade and walk in the noonday
glare.

I don't want to go into a critical tribute now, but I must say that there was no one else who could both write and tell us how to write, no one who spoke with such authority and so little played his roll [*sic*] of the great man. There was no doubt of the greatness. Even in the modest silences and the patient courtesy with the boring and humdrum, and least of all in the loud laughter and little phases and whole narrations of wild irony.

He was a good and patient friend. I think we laughed at the same things and hated the same things, and no older man so touched something personal in my depths.[19]

To Charles Monteith, at Faber and Faber, he summarized: "So many friends of mine have died this year and yet his though long on the verge seems the most impossible and intolerable of all."[20]

The year 1965 was to bring another death, a death even more "impossible and intolerable." In April, Lowell heard that Randall Jarrell had suffered a bad mental breakdown; Lowell was shocked —for all the passion and nervous edginess of Jarrell's intellectual style, Lowell had always thought of him as invulnerably rational, somehow protected by his cleverness from any serious psychic upheavals. It is significant that Lowell rarely wrote to Jarrell on personal matters, and through the course of their friendship Jarrell had always managed to avoid direct involvement in the dramas that attended Lowell's breakdowns. Their mutual friend John Thompson believed that Jarrell's sense of his own precariousness was what made him keep Lowell's madness at arm's length;[21] but it is probably also true that for Lowell, Jarrell's real usefulness was as critic, as poetic conscience almost—and this function would certainly have been imperiled by excessive intimacy:

> I have never known anyone who so connected what his friends wrote with their lives, or their lives with what they wrote. This could be trying: whenever we turned out something Randall felt was unworthy or a falling off, there was a coolness in all one's relations with him. You felt that even your choice in neckties wounded him.[22]

And when Lowell came to summarize their friendship, it was as if he were excusing Jarrell for what others might have judged to be lack of human warmth:

> Randall had an uncanny clairvoyance for helping friends in subtle precarious moments—almost always as only he could help, with something

written: critical sentences in a letter, or an unanticipated published book review. Twice or thrice, I think, he must have thrown me a life-line.[23]

It was with some tentativeness, then, that Lowell wrote to the suffering Jarrell on April 29, 1965: in a sense, he didn't know whom he was writing to.

Dear Randall,

I have thought twice about intruding on you, but I must say that I am heart-broken to hear that you have been sick. Your courage, brilliance and generosity should have saved you from this, but of course all good qualities are unavailing. I have been through this sort of thing so often myself that I suppose there's little in your experience that I haven't had over and over. What's worst, I think, is the grovelling, low as dirt purgatorial feelings with which one emerges. If you have such feelings, let me promise you that they are temporary, what looks as though it were simply you, and therefore would never pass does turn out to be not you and will pass.

Please let me tell you how much I admire you and your work and thank you for the many times when you have given me the strength to continue. Let me know if there's anything I can do. And *courage*, old friend![24]

Six months later, in October 1965, Lowell heard of Jarrell's death. The newspaper reports said that he had been "struck by an automobile as he walked along the heavily traveled Chapel Hill by-pass"; a witness reported that he had "lunged into the side of the car that hit him";[25] it could have been an accident, but few of Jarrell's friends believed it was. Lowell for years afterwards was deeply reluctant to admit that this "noble, difficult, and beautiful soul"[26] had died by suicide.

Within weeks of Jarrell's death, Lowell collapsed again—his ninth episode since 1949. But this time there was a wildly novel twist. A year earlier Lowell had formed a slight friendship with Jacqueline Kennedy. He had sent her copies of his books and she had "read them many times." In January 1965 she had written to thank him for his poems—not that she had much "enjoyed" them.[27] They saddened her, she said, because they made her think of her dead husband. If Kennedy were still alive, it would now be his inauguration, and Lowell would surely be an honored guest.

During 1965, of course, Lowell became something of a public figure himself: his refusal to attend the White House Arts Festival disrupted an event that had—in part—been meant to demonstrate that the Johnsons were no less cultivated than the Kennedys, that Lady Bird could compete with Jackie in matters of graciousness and taste. Also during 1965 Jacqueline Kennedy was from time to time "escorted" by Blair Clark, who had been a classmate of John Kennedy's at Harvard. According to Clark, Lowell began to feel a certain schoolboy rivalry, and "there was much jostling about who was going to be closer to Jackie." As to her feelings about Lowell, Clark surmises:

> She was interested. She was a collector—not of *personages* exactly, but personalities. She was genuinely interested in him as a personality. I don't think there was any more than that. She was interested in the sense that he was unique, interesting as a character.[28]

In November—on the anniversary of her husband's assassination—Lowell presented Jackie Kennedy with a signed copy of *The Old Glory* and was delighted by her fairly warm response—although she addressed him formally as "Dear Robert Lowell."[29] She was grateful, she said, for the play, as she had been for the books he had given her the year before. She would have been glad, though, if Lowell had announced himself—why didn't he tell her in advance when he was planning one of his Santa Claus appearances? Did he just leave his presents and run off? Or did he have to haggle absurdly with her Secret Service bodyguards? Anyway, she was genuinely touched—this was the worst bit of the year for her, and it was somehow strengthening to have this "Friend Across Central Park," as Lowell later described himself in a poem:

> I, in my Dickensian muffler, snow-sugared, unraveling—
> so you phantasized—in the waste thaw of loss:
> winter and then a winter; unseared, your true voice seared,
> still yearningly young; and I, though never young
> in all our years, and younger when we meet.

A week later, on December 1, 1965, Lowell's interest in Jackie Kennedy had become a gossip item: he was pictured with her on the front page of *Woman's Wear Daily*—they were attending the first night of *Hogan's Goat*, a play by Lowell's Cambridge friend William Alfred. A week after that, Lowell was telephoning his friends to tell them of his fierce new admiration.

He also reported that he had acquired a marvelous new art *objet* —a bust of the Indian chief Tecumseh. It had cost him $3,500, and he had put it on his dining table at West 67th Street, replacing a bust of Napoleon. His new prize had been made in Rome in 1854. Taylor wrote to Allen Tate:

> One has to laugh at his antics, but it is heartbreaking. I wonder if there is nothing more that can be done for him than is being done. And I wonder how long his health and his luck can hold out. Some sort of violent end seems inevitable.[30]

The climax of this episode came with an evening at the opera, an evening that Robert Giroux—who was Lowell's host that night— described later as "a combination of Walpurgis night and the Marx Bros."[31] Giroux tells how the evening began:

> I'd asked him and Lizzie and the Fred Dupees. and it was a black tie night. We were going to have dinner at the opera—a rather festive occasion. But during the day Lizzie called me and said "Cal's in terrible shape. I'm sorry we can't come." Anyway, we'd just sat down for drinks in the Met Club room when the door opened and in walked Cal in the most exalted state I've ever known him to be. He was brilliant—but superhuman, so to speak. His first remark was "I'm so sorry, Lizzie can't come, she's not feeling well." And then he went into this nonstop talk —he was in a fugal state of some kind, but very articulate, talking about "brilliant women"—Lizzie, Mary McCarthy, Jacqueline Kennedy. He just talked a blue streak about them. You couldn't get a word in; we all sat there absolutely bedazzled by this performance. Well, we went in for the first act, but he'd no sooner sat down than his head fell forward and he began to snore.[32]

But not for long. In one account of Lowell's night at the opera, he is said to have risen to his feet and, from the front of Robert Giroux's private box, begun conducting the orchestra. In another, he is seen backstage congratulating one of the performers. Sidney Nolan gives the following account:

I do remember that night at the opera in New York, with Bob Giroux. There was a dinner with a course between each act. And Cal was pretty high and he kind of did in the dinner. The opera was *Don Carlos.* And as we were having the first course Cal started quoting remarks that some dead friend had made about the various people present. Things like "Oh, Bill always said you were a nice girl but you had legs like a table." That was the name of the game—you know, dead friends can't be contradicted. And he kept it up all night. It was quite awkward. And there's a scene in *Don Carlos* where a chap is shot in the dungeons. So there's this shot and dead silence, and Cal said in a loud clear voice, "Oswald!" And we went around afterwards to see the chap, an Italian tenor—we finally got to see him and Cal said to him, "You were a king tonight." And he said, "No, no, I sang well, but no king, not a king, just a tenor." And Cal said, "You are a real king, do you understand?" And then turned to his wife, who was there, and said, "Your man is a king, a king amongst men." And I thought, Oh God. Then Cal said, "Since you are a king, I've brought the Duke of Wellington to meet you." And the man's face fell—and I had to disentangle and get out.[33]

In Robert Giroux's account, the opera was Tchaikovsky's *The Queen of Spades* (or *Pique Dame*), and after the first act he spotted Nolan in the audience:

The hero of the evening was gentle Sidney Nolan. I saw him in the box (he was probably William Meredith's guest), and told him how sick Cal was, and wondered how we could persuade Cal to leave. He said, "I don't think Cal likes opera that much. I'll suggest that the three of us go back and discuss my illustrations for his book." I was amazed that it really worked; Cal seemed happy to go. We sat him between us in the taxi, and when we reached his apartment on West 67th Street there, standing in the doorway, with her arms folded, was his doctor. When he wouldn't get out of the taxi, she actually said to him, "Cal, how can you do this *to me*?" She got in the front seat. Again Nolan was the hero, and suggested we drive around Central Park. The driver, a typical New York taxi man, said, "What's this all about?" I told him to keep the meter running and drive around the park. The second time around, Nolan quietly directed the driver to Cal's hospital. He was much calmer now, and when we got there, Nolan said, "Cal, why don't you and I go in the hospital. You know you want to get this settled." He quietly got out with Nolan, and the doctor joined them. I drove back to *The Queen of Spades,* and called Elizabeth before I went in for the last act, in which mad Hermann keeps muttering, "Three cards! Three cards!" before he's done in by the *Pique Dame*.[34]

These were clearly two different nights at the opera and two quite separate escapades—there is an understandable tendency for Lowell's friends to muddle the events of one illness with those of another, and during this period Lowell was a frequent opera-goer. What seems certain, though, is that after a day in a hospital in New York, Lowell was driven up to Boston with Nolan and admitted to McLean's on December 7, 1965. The following day, Dr. Bernard wrote to Blair Clark: "Mr. L. reached McLean yesterday by car, accompanied by Mr. Nolan—left with good feeling toward wife and myself and pleased to be going to McLean's." On December 30 Lowell had a letter from Jackie Kennedy.[35] She thanked him for a book he had sent her for Christmas—a book on Alexander the Great —and assured him that she had been assiduous in her reading of Joinville and Cato: two earlier Lowell recommendations, it would seem. About Alexander, she was puzzled about Lowell's reasons for introducing her to the less than lovable world conqueror. It is a touching, slightly bewildered note—she rather envies Lowell, she says, for being "in retreat" over the Christmas season. If she were he, she would stay in McLean's forever; but Lowell, she believed, had more courage than she did, and would no doubt soon be back in town.

Just as there is a tendency for the details of Lowell's episodes to get blurred in his friends' memories, so there was almost a probability that his antics would get distorted or embellished as reports of them went into general circulation. There were now "Cal stories" that could be swapped at dinner tables and chuckled over at literary gatherings. The Jackie Kennedy story, the Tecumseh story, the Latvian dancer story, and so on: the more celebrated Lowell became as a poet and as a public figure, the more avid the requirement for fresh pranks. And, more troublingly for those who cared for him, his enemies could all too easily construct from accounts of his delusions a portrait of Lowell as a sort of near fascist—How was it, they could disingenuously wonder, that this renowned spokesman for correct liberal causes persistently "revealed," in mania, a fascination with tyrants and monsters of the right? Lowell was by now a much envied "star" of literature, and with each new breakdown, each new

round of malign gossip, he seemed—almost willfully—to be mocking the supposed invulnerability of his position and prestige.

As for Lowell's closest friends, they knew that in his illnesses
there was always an element of simple mischief, of sly, childishly
perverse outrageousness—"I am going to appall you by doing, or
being, the worst thing you can imagine," and so on. But by now
they had seen it all so many times, the shock tactics no longer had
much sting. In letters these friends would now make only passing
reference to Lowell's latest "crack-up." It was not that "everyone's
tired of my turmoil"—although many were; it was more that everyone was now used to it, and knew that it was almost certainly
incurable. A letter from Allen Tate to Peter Taylor, written a week
after Lowell had been admitted to McLean's, provides some indication of the tone that was now being taken by his friends—still deeply
sympathetic, but resigned and (as Taylor himself said) "one has to
laugh":

> I was in N.Y. last week and heard a play-by-play account by Stanley
> Kunitz of the purchase of Tecumseh. The statue, it appears, is now back
> with the dealer, who will not refund the $1,000 deposit; it remains with
> him as a credit towards the purchase later of another "work of art." I
> have not heard about Cal's debut as an opera conductor. All this is very
> sad. Stanley fears that the gap is closing, that the seizures are becoming
> more frequent. Elizabeth assured me on the telephone that the present
> upset is milder than the others; at least there was no Lady Poetess, or
> dancer, this time. I feel that the crush on Madame Jacqueline is an
> improvement in the direction of sublimation. Perhaps we should en-
> courage it, even going so far as to implore Madame's assistance as a sort
> of therapy-at-a-distance. Wystan Auden told me that Cal had told him
> that I had written last summer 800 lines because I was away from "that
> stupid girl from Boston." I wrote 200. To exaggerate only fourfold
> indicates real restraint in Cal.[36]

A week before Lowell was admitted to McLean's he had agreed that
his name be put forward as a candidate for one of England's more
eccentric academic posts: the Professorship of Poetry at Oxford.
Even if Lowell had not been in an elated mood, he would have
relished the sheer quaintness of the job, and the small, donnish
dramas that surrounded it. The Poetry Professorship was not a
conventional university appointment; indeed, it was famous for

offering "no power, little work, and less money." For three lectures a year the Professor would receive a token £300 (then $840); and he would be expected to serve a five-year term. The drama of the thing, though, derived not from the job itself but from the time-honored method of deciding who should get it. The Poetry Professorship was the one Oxford chair that was decided by election. Every five years the university's thirty thousand or so Masters of Arts were entitled to vote for one or another of the nominated candidates— but they had to vote in person, and they had to wear the regulation cap and gown. It was all faintly absurd, but Oxford loved it; during the buildup to an election, high tables would be abuzz with barter and intrigue, and the weightier national newspapers would follow the campaigns with full front-page solemnity.

It is not clear how much Lowell knew about the job when Charles Monteith, of his London publisher Faber and Faber, proposed his nomination; it may well have been enough for him that the post had in the past been held by some illustrious figures—Matthew Arnold, W. H. Auden, Robert Graves—and that, were he to be elected, he would be Oxford's first non-British Poetry Professor. On November 27 he cabled to Monteith: "Propose my name if you have the courage to do so."

With Lowell's agreement secured, Monteith began recruiting sponsors for his candidacy, and within days had enlisted the support of substantial Oxford figures, such as Sir Maurice Bowra (the Warden of Wadham College), Isaiah Berlin, Professor Nevill Coghill (Merton Professor of English Literature) and Mr. Alan Bullock (Master of St. Catherine's). He also persuaded W. H. Auden and Cecil Day Lewis (another previous Professor) to sponsor Lowell's candidature. Auden's agreement was offered, though, with a cautionary postscript:

> I am entirely in agreement. . . . I think, however, that his supporters should be aware, if they aren't already, that Cal has times when he has to go into the bin. The warning signals are three a) He announces that he is the *only* living poet b) a romantic and usually platonic attraction to a young girl and c) he gives a huge party.[37]

By the time Auden's reply arrived, Lowell was of course already in "the bin." News had reached Monteith of his performance at the opera, and there was an uneasy period when it seemed likely that

Lowell might make an appearance in London (he had agreed to do a BBC interview with Malcolm Muggeridge). But the visit was canceled; Monteith wrote back in reassuring terms to Auden, and the campaign continued to build strong support.

The Lowell lobby in Oxford, however, had already made a vital tactical mistake. They had neglected to solicit the support of Enid Starkie, the reader in French literature at Somerville College. Miss Starkie had organized the campaigns of Day Lewis in 1951 and Auden in 1956, and was indeed celebrated for her labors in this field (as well as for wearing red underwear and a French sailor's hat, though not, so far as anybody knew, "a turtle-necked French sailor's jersey"). Starkie was piqued by the oversight, and set about organizing a campaign of her own; her candidate was the very English, indeed very Oxford, poet Edmund Blunden (well known for his writings on the First World War, but associated also with the premodernist Georgian poets: a critic in the thirties had nicknamed him "the Merton fieldmouse," and Lowell in 1946 had called him "heavy, clumsy, careless, academic and sentimental"). It was, Monteith concedes, "an inspired choice":

> I think the truth is that Enid was extremely miffed that she hadn't been approached first. I think if only we'd had the nous to approach her straight away, we'd have wrapped it up. And she picked Blunden, which was of course an inspired choice on her part. It untapped a great deal of crypto-xenophobia, I think. Blunden had of course been a fellow of Merton, and he was liked very much. There were lots of people around who remembered Blunden very well and liked him—and he was a very nice man. And a large number of people came floating in like backwoods peers to vote for the British poet, the war hero, all that kind of thing. When it came to the actual voting, I remember myself running into people like Roger Fulford brought down from the wilds of north Lancashire simply to vote proudly for Blunden—it was like voting for England. It was a brilliant choice.[38]

A week before the election (to be held on February 5, 1966) Starkie had collected over three hundred signatures to support Blunden's candidacy, and although Lowell was evidently backed by the students and by the London literary magazines, his nomination was endorsed by a mere forty names. Lowell's men would contend that theirs were "quality names," and that only a handful of Starkie's three hundred were in the same league. Starkie, even so, toiled on right up to polling day, and Lowell's chief Oxford backer, Maurice Bowra, was soon reduced to blustering protests about her vulgar methods:

> When I knew she was going to fight me, we both agreed we wouldn't go round collecting names. It degraded the whole thing. This was a serious academic affair until Dr. Starkie turned it into something like the Oxford and Cambridge boat race. We'll be standing on Magdalen Bridge selling rosettes next.[39]

On February 6 the *New York Times* announced:

LOWELL DEFEATED FOR OXFORD CHAIR:

> Oxford has repelled the American poetical invasion. . . . The new professor of poetry at the university will be Edmund Blunden of Britain. The voting was 477 to 241. . . . Mr. Lowell said here yesterday of Mr. Blunden's victory, "I think it's a swell choice. I have read his poetry and admired it for years."

The report in the *New Statesman* was headed "Someone Has Blundened," and Stephen Spender wrote a letter to the London *Times* suggesting that, next time round, the undergraduates should be allowed to vote. Lowell himself may well have been more irked by the result than he pretended. It was a month after the event that he wrote to Charles Monteith:

> I hope you haven't [*sic*] I have retired into a morose silence after Oxford. I very much enjoyed your cable and letter and the stream of clippings —a marvellous comic novel, every word, not American, but English. Then I'm glad Blunden got it in the end; he is a good poet and I was encroaching on his yard.[40]

Throughout the summer of 1966, Lowell worked on an adaptation of Aeschylus' *Prometheus Bound*—this in response to a commission from Peter Brook of London's Royal Shakespeare Company—and prepared his volume *Near the Ocean* for the press. The book was to be illustrated with drawings by Sidney Nolan, and would include his "Near the Ocean" sequence, two other short poems (an elegy for Roethke and the poem "1958," much of which he had salvaged from the first draft of "Waking in the Blue"). He also included a number of imitations—of Dante, Juvenal and Horace, as well as the two seventeenth-century Spanish poets Góngora and Quevedo. These had been written during the summer of 1962 and could therefore have been included in *For the Union Dead;* it is probable, though, that Lowell had not then thought them worthy of book publication. The Dante and the Juvenal are painstakingly closer to their originals than anything in *Imitations*—"Maybe I felt ragged by people telling me I wasn't close enough"[41]—and these take up eighteen of the book's forty or so pages. Lowell's prefatory note to *Near the Ocean* has a rather strained and hopeful ring: "The theme that connects my translations is Rome, the greatness and horror of her Empire. . . . How one jumps from Rome to the America of my own poems is something of a mystery to me."

Lowell seems to have written no poems of his own throughout 1966; indeed, not since the summer of 1965. His decision to put together a new volume at this stage suggests either that he felt himself to be at something of a dead end, or that the public or occasional aspect of poems like "Waking Early Sunday Morning" made him see the book as his timely contribution to the intensifying antiwar campaign. But there was no suggestion of haste in the book's actual production. When it appeared in the spring of 1967, its lavish appearance was derided by most of the reviewers:

> It is a pretentious volume; printed on expensive paper, bound in heavy cloth and stamped in three colors, decorated with twenty-one drawings by Sidney Nolan, designed lavishly and wastefully in an outsized format, jacketed in varnished sixty pound stock—in short, a very self-conscious looking collector's item.[42]

Or, as David Kalstone put it, more equably, in *Partisan Review:* "the slick coffee-table design of the volume entirely misrepresents the poems, which, at their best, challenge things that are shiny and bright."[43] Perhaps, sensing a strain of vulgarity in his wish to get a book out quickly, Lowell had been anxious that its physical appearance should seem leisured and aloof. According to Hayden Carruth in the *Hudson Review,* the book's publication "had been postponed several times, and . . . the price had been announced progressively at $4.95, $5.50 and $6.00. Why?"

There were moments during the summer at Castine when Lowell would confess that his retreat into the "prosing" of Aeschylus might simply be a way of "escaping my destiny." He could, he said, "bury" himself in *Prometheus:* "Often three or four hours would go by before I looked up, and saw low tide changed to high." But on the other hand, "Oh destiny, where is it?"[44] He wrote this on July 16, 1966, two days after learning of yet another death. On July 11 Delmore Schwartz's body had been found in a corridor of the Columbia Hotel in New York; he had suffered a heart attack. Lowell had not been close to Schwartz since those months in 1946 when he had shared a house with him in Cambridge; they had quarreled then over Schwartz's supposed flirtation with Jean Stafford, and a year later Schwartz had been none too pleased to hear of Lowell's association with his ex-wife, Gertrude Buckman. In 1959, though, Schwartz had responded warmly to the poem Lowell addressed to him in *Life Studies* and had lavishly praised the "new style" poems in that book: "an intensity so moving it is heartbreaking." In the same letter, he also thanked Lowell "for the money and for the very nice things you say about my own work."[45]

Lowell, in fact, had for some time been nervous of the *idea* of Delmore Schwartz, of his decline from early promise, of the ways in which he had wasted his real talent, and towards the end he had avoided Schwartz because of "his suspiciousness, his paranoia, his setting of people against each other."[46] In 1966, though, Lowell remembered the Schwartz of "humorous early days—all good sense and promess [*sic*]!" Some of this, he felt, had lasted, but "in flashes, and mostly with young acquaintances in bars."[47] On hearing of his death, Lowell wrote to William Meredith:

Oh destiny, where is it? I have been thinking of Delmore. You probably heard of his death, a heart-attack, alone, outside a cheap hotel room in New York. I felt frightened to be with him for years—needlessly, in a way, but I was sure it would lead to confusion and pain. Then I think back on his low voice, so intuitive, reasonable, a great jag of my education, from weak hands into weak hands perhaps, more than I could use, but much of it has stayed. Two things had hold of him, when I knew him best, the first dark rays of his paranoia, often lighting up things, but unbearable to friends, and his long effort to write in quiet, underwritten style—maybe a crippling venture, maybe not. I think the later poems have more flow and joy than suited his genius. His destiny seemed the most hopeful of any young poet in 1940, then the downward road, some germ in the mind, the most dismal story of our generation perhaps, and maybe a lot more to the writing than one knew.[48]

The notion of there being a sort of generic curse on the poets of his generation was recurring time and again in Lowell's letters of this time, and it was encouraged on all sides by critical articles that proposed Lowell and John Berryman as victim heroes of the age— "each of them salvaging his work from the edge of some kind of personal abyss" (A. Alvarez). Lowell's own identification with Berryman as a co-explorer of risky psychological terrain was certainly becoming more and more heartfelt as, one by one, the others of his generation were cut down by early deaths. In 1966 the news of Berryman was persistently of his bad health, his drinking and his breakdowns, and Lowell seems to have followed the reports with a resigned dread. In recent years his regard for Berryman's poems had deepened. In 1959 he had been undecided about Berryman's idiosyncratic "new language" as it appeared in *Homage to Mistress Bradstreet* and the very first of the "Dream Songs." He had written to him then:

> I wonder if you need so much twisting, obscurity, archaisms, strange word orders, & signs for *and* etc? I guess you do. Surely, here as in the Bradstreet, you have your voice. It vibrates and makes the heart ache.[49]

By 1964 he had been won over to the style and he wrote a guardedly favorable review of 77 *Dream Songs* for the *New York Review of Books,* but he still had the deepest sort of reservations. After writing his review, he wrote to William Meredith:

> My Berryman piece is perhaps of some value as a record of a man's struggle with the text, a climbing of the barriers. In this book, he really is a new poet, one whose humor and wildness make other new poets seem tame. I read him with uncertainty and distress and quite likely envy, which is a kind of tribute. I think it's only here and there that I read him with the all-out enjoying amazement that I feel for Bishop, Plath, Larkin and much of Roethke. A handful of the songs now seem part of what we are proudest of.[50]

With the death of Randall Jarrell, though, it was to be expected that Lowell would look towards Berryman as the only truly formidable talent of around his own age—Berryman was three years older than Lowell, as Jarrell had been. Also, Berryman had been an admirer of Jarrell's. Berryman could never have Jarrell's "senior" role in Lowell's life, but it *was* possible for him to be thought of as an endangered, brilliant equal. In March of 1966 Lowell wrote to him:

> This is really just to say that I love you, and wonder at you, and want you to take care . . .
>
> Let me beg you to take care of yourself. You must be physically fragile. If anything happened to you, I'd feel the heart of the scene had gone.[51]

In October 1966 Lowell got a group of new Berryman dream songs, to which he responded more warmly than he had to anything that Berryman had done before. They were called "Opus Posthumous" and were really, Lowell thought, "his own elegy and written from the dirt of the grave."[52] He cabled Berryman in Dublin: YOUR POSTHUMOUS POEMS ARE A TREMENDOUS AND LIVING TRIUMPH LOVE CAL, and in reply got "a sad letter"; he wrote to Philip Booth that Berryman "was very very sick, spiritually and physically, I guess":

> there is personal anguish everywhere. We can't dodge it, and shouldn't worry that we are uniquely marked and fretted and must somehow keep even-tempered, amused, and in control. John B. in his mad way keeps talking about something evil stalking us poets. That's a bad way to talk, but there's truth in it.[53]

Berryman's "Opus Posthumous" poems are indeed "amused and in control," but in truth they are suicide notes, and none more explicitly than his elegy for Randall Jarrell. This, certainly, Lowell would have wondered at and envied, and—on behalf of his "marked" generation—been most proud of:

> Let Randall rest, whom your self-torturing
> cannot restore one instant's good to, rest:
> he's left us now.
> The panic died, and in the panic's dying
> so did my old friend. I am headed west
> also, also, somehow.

> In the chambers of the end we'll meet again
> I will say Randall, he'll say Pussycat
> and all will be as before
> whenas we sought, among the beloved faces,
> eminence and were dissatisfied with that
> and needed more.[54]

From the accounts we have of Lowell's teaching methods, it seems likely that he would have found Oxford's insistence on formal lectures something of a burden. There have been a number of essays on "Lowell in the Classroom," both at Boston University during the 1950s and from 1963 at Harvard. They speak of his mild, myopic manner, his chain-smoking and his Southern accent (acquired from Tate and Ransom, it is usually supposed, although Blair Clark remembers that "he spoke that way when he was at St. Mark's").[55] Richard Tillinghast has written:

> I picture him at Harvard slouched in a leather chair, a penny loafer dangling from one foot, shoulders scrunched up toward his massive head, his hands framing a point in the air, held up before his face as though to protect it from attack, now and then righting the black-rimmed glasses that kept sliding down the bridge of his thick nose.[56]

About his actual teaching, it has been said that he taught "almost by indirection," "he turned every poet into a version of himself," "he told stories [about poets' lives] as if they were the latest news." The various accounts seem best summarized by Helen Vendler:

> Lowell began his classes on each successive poet with an apparently indolent, speculative, and altogether selective set of remarks on the poet's life and writing; the poet appeared as a man with a temperament, a set of difficulties, a way of responding, vocation, prejudices. The remarks were indistinguishable from those Lowell might have made about a friend or an acquaintance; the poets *were* friends or acquaintances; he knew them from their writing better than most of us know others from life. This, in the end, seems to me the best thing Lowell did for his students; he gave them the sense, so absent from textbook headnotes, of a life, a spirit, a mind, and a set of occasions from which writing issues—a real life, a real mind, fixed in historical circumstance and quotidian abrasions.[57]

On student poems, Lowell was less attentive to the poet's quotidian abrasions; he could be "arbitrary, petty and cruel," said Judith Baumel, one of his Harvard students, "and had very little help to offer in the form of direct, constructive criticism of line, structure, intent, execution of student drafts. He would say, rarely, 'This line is quite nice' or 'I like it, this is my favorite part.' "[58] And the poet Anne Sexton, who attended Lowell's classes at Boston University, wrote in 1961: "He works with a cold chisel with no more mercy than a dentist. He gets out the decay. But if he is never kind to the poem, he is kind to the poet."[59]

In 1966 one of the poets he was "kind to" was Grey Gowrie, an Irish earl who had arrived at Harvard a year earlier and had attended his classes in creative writing. Gowrie was given a job as Lowell's assistant, and with his wife, Xandra, he seems to have provided Lowell with a kind of "alternative" Cambridge life, or at any rate a social circle younger and merrier than he had in New York. Lowell spent two or three days a week in Cambridge and had a pair of grimly functional rooms in Quincy House; in the evenings he would tend to welcome company. Some of his contemporaries in Cambridge disapproved of his association with the Gowrie "fast set" —they believed Lowell to have been beguiled by the whiff of British aristocracy, and by what they saw as the "decadence" of the Gowrie ménage. Said one: "He would go around with this rather wild young set; they flattered him and over-excited him—sometimes he would turn up with them all and it would be like Comus and his crew." Gowrie recalls:

When I first got to know him, he was absolutely in peak form. He was less bardic than he was later. He was very, very good-looking, and very quiet, rather modest and well dressed, a very elegant figure, rather New England and elegant, with sort of Englishy clothes. And apart from liking and admiring his work, I actually got on with him because he was very funny and ironic and English in his humor, and if you were a young married couple in America, there was a slight shortage of that. He made very much the same sort of jokes as my mates at Oxford or Eton.[60]

One of Gowrie's more eccentric aspects, for Lowell, was his admiration for the poet Charles Olson. Olson was the revered master of Black Mountain poetry, or Objectivism; the theory of Objectivism derived from the Americanist beliefs of William Carlos Williams, but in its more extreme manifestations it was far more liberated from traditional European influences than Williams could ever bring himself to be—it built poems out of what the eye could see, and the only formal rules it would yield to were those dictated by the breathing and the pulse rate of the individual poet. Polemically, it set itself against the so-called academic poetry, of which Lowell was now monarch—and during the mid-sixties the separation between the two camps was almost total. With the death of Williams, Olson became "the" poet of the Americanist avant-garde, and it amused and puzzled Lowell that this British earl should have sympathy for a figure who was notoriously hostile to any Eng. Lit. presence in America. Gowrie's account of this small corner of his relationship with Lowell has interest both as biography and as a reminder that there *were* other poetic kingdoms besides Lowell's:

> He thought of me as someone who liked Black Mountain very much, which I didn't, but I was a great friend of Charles Olson; he had lived with me when his wife died, and I felt great loyalty to him. There was a lot of rivalry on Olson's side, because Olson always thought that Cal had sort of popularized and chiced and smarmed up the matter of New England, which was enormously his field of interest and endeavor. It wasn't as bitchy as English literary backbiting. It was more as if you were a very passionate socialist and someone you admired very much insisted on being a member of the Tory party. It was that kind of feeling, that immense gifts were being used on the wrong approach. I was very fond of Charles, and Cal was a great tease about this. He erected a sort of Olson/Gowrie world and it was very light and funny.[61]

Around November 1966, though, Gowrie began to notice that the teasing about Olson was becoming obsessive, "very possessive and detailed . . . and it reached a stage when the world he had invented had become quite real to him":

> It was very odd for me because he started to look rather like Charles Olson, who was absolutely enormous and chain-smoking and heavy-breathing, and nuts, but dotty old sea-captain sort of nuts. Whereas Cal was just very funny and quick and not like somebody who's nuts at all. But then, he would become this huge person drinking vodka and milk and breathing like a bull.[62]

As the Olson obsession built up, it would lead into other obsessions: with politics and power. Harvard in the mid-sixties had what Gowrie calls "this intense Washington nexus. . . . People didn't think they were making it as professors unless they were constantly on the plane down to advise committees." Gowrie's wife, Xandra, worked for the Kennedy Center and was a friend of the then not famous but "altogether astonishing" Henry Kissinger. Lowell would make jokes about Kissinger, and again by November these jokes were becoming darker, more insistent and more tiresome. Jokes about the Harvard Law School and School of Government and their bustling Washington connections gradually turned into not so funny soliloquies on "issues of power . . . or about his own war experience as a conscientious objector, and about the Lepke poem." When not manic, Lowell had seemed to Gowrie fairly shrewd and sensible about politics; "that is, he would say, roughly, that democracy is a terrible system until you think of the alternatives, and he had the proper liberal horror of the alternatives. Nothing unusual, the perfectly ordinary civilized person's approach, with an impatience with the pseud and the over-Americanly intense or ambitious." But as he began to speed up,

> it would always go very much towards the right, but always on personalities, not policy, never "What this country needs is a strong man" or "Put down the Negroes." It was about the misunderstanding of the nature of personality. It wasn't what they did, it was the issue of the will and the personality.[63]

Xandra Gowrie was also seeing a lot of Lowell at this time; for her, the worst feature of his mania was when, in the early stages, he would say "awful things about people he was really very fond of. And when Cal said awful things they were always spot-on, so people quailed and got very angry. He'd say it absolutely directly to them. You know, you're so stupid you never should have taken up writing, or, the pity about you is that your husband never sleeps with you." The tyrant delusions she found easier to stomach:

> It seemed to me that if you were manically mad, as he was, so that you were on the edge of physical violence all the time, there was a sort of refuge in images of historical tyrants and violent characters which I suppose you could say was in itself a sort of safety valve. It was better

to be raving on about Hitler than to be actually murdering people or breaking up the furniture. . . . the logistics of it were that he woke earlier and earlier, and felt worse and worse about the cruelty he had handed out the night before, and drank earlier and earlier in the day to forget it, so that in the end he was drinking vodka and milk at half past ten in the morning. And then he'd be high again, so that the remorse would turn to a high again, with the next day's vitriol. And then he couldn't sleep at all. So it turned into a 24-hour binge. And then it was the historical obsession—Hitler or Napoleon or James IV. And into all this came the Kennedys—you know, where's Jackie's telephone number, or where's Bobby's, and if only Bobby had been something to do with James IV.[64]

On Christmas Eve, 1966, the police were called to Frank Parker's house in Cambridge. Xandra Gowrie recalls that

there were eight policemen. God knows why, but there they were, with guns and everything, and Cal sort of leaning back against the sink and looking round. And you knew that the whole history of his violence and vitriol had to be part of this final scene, and he looked around and there was a milk bottle—Cal was terribly strong, he was an embryo footballer, so you knew he could be, and sometimes was during that time, very frightening and violent—but that was just an agonizingly sad gesture, a token of symbolic violence, and that milk bottle was thrown at the policeman, who just moved aside and then walked up to him and took him away. It was just incredibly sad. We were just exhausted by him, like everybody was, and no one else at Harvard at that point would take him on, because they'd all seen it and been through it and they were only too glad that some new acolyte would do it.[65]

Lowell was again admitted to McLean's, although he was still in contact with Dr. Bernard in New York. Elizabeth Hardwick had been ready to let the Gowries handle this latest collapse; indeed, on one occasion Grey Gowrie had flown with Lowell to New York, and Hardwick had made it clear that, in her view, Gowrie should take him back to Cambridge and arrange for treatment there. Gowrie has described the trip:

It became clear that he should go back to go inside. Lizzie and I had no disagreement personally about it. Lizzie said, "He's listening to Grey at the moment. Grey's the person who's got to get him inside." I took him in a Fleetwood Cadillac, I remember—an enormous thing, something hired for corporation presidents. I got him to the airport, and on the way I thought he'd died. He went completely out and I really thought he was dying. When I got to the airport, I went looking for a stretcher or an ambulance. And then to my amazement, I saw that he'd got out of the car and was at the news stall buying *Playboy*. [66]

Lowell's medical treatment up to 1967 seems always to have combined "drugs" (one or another of the phenothiazines) and "therapy"; that is to say, supportive talk sessions with psychiatrists.
Although he had had brushes with analysts, he had never "gone into
analysis." The probability is that even had he wished to be analyzed,
it would have been hard to find someone willing to accept a patient
with his history of psychotic illness. In 1954 it had been thought that
Thorazine (chlorpromazine) was the "wonder drug" that would
stabilize him, but thirteen years later it was evident that Thorazine
had no preventive function.

In 1967 a new wonder drug made its appearance: lithium car-
bonate. First tested in Denmark, it had shown remarkable results
with manic-depressive patients: its effect was to balance the suff-
erer between the two poles, as it were, of his affliction—between
the extremes of elation and depression. And it seemed to have
none of the physical side effects of Thorazine: lithium users did
not become sluggish, dazed, somnambulistic. Rather, they might
appear suspended, uninvolved, disinclined to "follow through"
their feelings: above the battle, they might sometimes seem to be
striving for the old intensities, but it would be as if they were
always being tugged back to "safety," to the middle ground; such
"side effects," however, would probably be apparent only to the
patient's closest friends.

The drug itself is a salt formed by reacting the metal lithium with
carbonic acid. The theory is that manic-depressives are deficient in
this salt; regular blood tests will establish the extent of the deficiency
and the appropriate lithium dosage will correct it. The prognosis is
that properly monitored lithium treatment can keep a patient stabi-

lized for life. Lowell was at first cautious and whimsical about his new treatment, which seems to have begun shortly after his discharge from McLean's in the spring of 1967. Perhaps he had been told that the metal lithium was sometimes used in cooling systems for nuclear reactors (though not often, because of its corrosive tendencies) or that, rather poetically, "it burns in air with a brilliant white flame." But he was ready to give almost anything a try. In June 1967 he wrote to Peter Taylor:

> Oh, dear, I now have 3 glasses: far, reading and my old good for nothing which I prefer. Pills for blood pressure, no more tennis singles. But really it's nothing. I'm in terrific shape! I even have pills that are supposed to prevent manic attacks, something (probably a sugar pill unnoticed when taken or after but which supplies some salt lack in some obscure part of the brain and now for the rest of my life, I can drink and be a valetudinarian and pontificate non-sense.[1]

Since March, he told Taylor, he had been "on the run"—a performance of his *Phaedra* in Philadelphia and a visit to London for the opening of *Benito Cereno*—"the reviews were lousy," he said. "There were a lot of complaints about it being too short." Perhaps in order to enliven his brief visit, he announced to the British press that he might now write plays about either Trotsky or the recently killed Malcolm X: "I could probably get him talking. But all the Negroes around him,—I don't know how they'd talk."[2] His worries on this score were respectfully reported in the quality London papers.

Jonathan Miller had again directed *Benito Cereno,* and during Lowell's visit the two of them discussed their next joint project: a Yale Drama School production of Lowell's adaptation of *Prometheus Bound.* The National Endowment for the Arts had provided Yale with a $25,000 grant; $10,000 of this would go to Lowell, so that he could attend rehearsals and also hold occasional classes with the Drama School's "student playwrights." Lowell wanted Miller to direct, and Robert Brustein, the school's recently appointed dean, was thoroughly in favor; after all, as drama critic of the *New Republic,* Brustein had been the most fervent champion of Lowell's "prose style" in *Benito Cereno. Prometheus* did not pretend to be in verse. Brustein has written of the Lowell/Miller partnership:

The two men complemented each other strangely, Lowell taciturn and soft-spoken, mournful and reserved; Miller dynamic, convivial, hyper-active, marvelously funny, a cascade of anecdotes and insights always pouring from his lips.[3]

(Lowell's mental state in April 1967 can be judged by Brustein's distribution of adjectives—a few months earlier his description of Miller might happily have fitted Lowell.)

According to Brustein, the production of *Prometheus* at Yale almost faltered at the outset:

> Later I learned that the grant had almost been canceled. President Johnson, enraged to discover that a government agency had awarded money to someone he believed had insulted him, demanded that the award be withdrawn. To the credit of the endowment—then under the chairmanship of Roger Stevens—Johnson's efforts were resisted. But this represented the first attempt by government to politicize the decisions of the agency.[4]

President Johnson, though, could hardly have seen the text of Lowell's *Prometheus,* since it was not finished until the last moment; nor is it likely that he had heard rumors that Lowell's Zeus, in his more dangerously potent moments, might easily be seen as a cartoon of LBJ.

Opening night was on May 9, 1967, and according to the New Haven newspapers, it was "a major social and literary event." The contingent of notables from New York included "David Merrick, Robert Motherwell, Stephen Spender, Philip Roth, George Plimpton and Susan Sontag." Opinions afterwards were mixed: there was some complaint about Miller's decision to set the play in what seemed to be a ruined seventeenth-century castle, and also some uneasiness about Lowell's "manhandling" of the original. He had, it was complained, turned Io into a dominating mother figure and Prometheus into a mumbling victim of "radical intellectual anxiety." This last phrase came from R. W. B. Lewis, Yale's professor of English and American Studies, who also thought that Lowell's Zeus was "at once vaguer and more frightful than President Johnson"; it was more plausible, he thought, to see the dreadful god as "the true and demonic begetter of the fiercely muddled emotions that Johnson more or less accidentally arouses in us. . . . the result is a heroic demonstration of the near-impossibility of composing drama under the contemporary circumstances."[5]

"It is impossible," says Lowell's Prometheus, "to think too much about power," and Lowell's own nonmanic reflections on this topic had been aired in an interview with the *Observer* during his March visit to London:

> Once you get that enormous Government machine connected with power and world ambition it's terrifying. And there are a lot of other machines in the world besides America's: Russia's is another. I'm haunted by the First World War, when these huge countries, despite inertia—or through inertia—went to war. Nobody could stop it; not even the people running the Governments. We've seen this twice in one century, and it's impossible to see that very much has been done to prevent a third.
>
> I think the best thing—it's a little chilly to me—would be a sort of pax Americo-Russiana: just coming to terms by trying to keep the lid on the world: and Europe might be in this. I think that's a strong possibility. It will be very much 'Two Cheers for Democracy'; *faute de mieux* kind of thing: an attempt at peace and just-under-peace. . . .[6]

Optimistic musings of this sort occasioned Lowell's next appearance in the headlines of the *New York Times*. On May 17, 1967, he introduced a poetry reading by the Russian poet Andrei Voznesensky, and announced that "both our countries, I think, have really terrible governments. But we do the best we can with them and they'd better do the best they can with each other or the world will cease to be here." The *Times* reported an "audible sharp intake of breath" from the audience; Lowell, they said, had not been available for further comment and "Mr. Voznesensky, who has avoided mentioning the Soviet and United States governments during his tour, turned away when asked to comment on the American poet's remarks." Lowell, however, had gathered that "Russian writers loathe Mao and couldn't care less about Ho and what we are doing in Vietnam" and had genially added to his platform speech: "One wishes that in another year there would be a third poet here—a Chinese and a good poet, and one more detached than Chairman Mao."[7] But no one seems to have been much amused.

In June 1967 Lowell was in the newspapers again. He had declined to sign a public appeal to President Johnson to support Israel
in its war with the Arab nations. The organizer of the appeal,
Charles E. Silberman, explained that "Mr. Lowell's reason was opposition to all war," but Lowell swiftly corrected him: "I thought
we should have guaranteed the boundaries of Israel and, if necessary, helped to defend them. I did not think the United States should
have forcibly opened the Gulf of Aqaba." He went on to praise
Johnson's neutral stance as "correct and humane" but added, "This
war should never have happened; for this Russia and America, the
suppliers of weapons, are to blame."[8] But privately he wrote to Peter
Taylor: "I am pretending my great-grandmother Deborah Mor-
decai was a Syrian belly dancer."[9]

The real issue for Lowell, though, in 1967 was Vietnam, and
throughout the year he was in demand as a speaker and petition
signer. He was vehemently opposed to the war, but equivocal about
being identified too closely with the "peace movement": there were
many views he did not share with the more fiery of the "peaceniks"
and it was not in his nature to join movements that he had no wish
to lead. His friend Esther Brooks recalls an occasion in Cambridge
that seems aptly to dramatize his general stance:

> he found himself committed to read at Harvard for a group which, as
> it turned out, was one of the many disruptive organizations abounding
> on the campus at that time. The major part of its members weren't
> students of the university at all but were outsiders, there for the purpose
> of stirring up violence. When my husband and the poet William Alfred
> and I arrived at the theater and took this fact in, we tried to warn Cal,
> but he was late getting in from New York and suddenly he was there
> before us on the reader's platform—tall, awkward, disheveled, somewhat
> diffident, and gazing around him in what appeared to be a rather vague
> and absent way. Then he sat down. Someone wearing a red arm band
> came from the back of the hall to introduce him as "the great poet of
> the Revolution," and a voice somewhere in back of me yelled, "Let's
> have the poem 'Che Guevara.' " Then another voice—"Yay, man, Che
> Guevara, *viva la Revolución!*" Cal stood up, muttered something about
> being a poet, not a revolutionary, and began to read a poem he had
> written to his daughter Harriet. And so for forty minutes or more he
> read some of his early poems and some more recent ones, while from
> time to time a voice from somewhere in the audience would call out for
> "Che Guevara, man, let's have the Che Guevara!" But Cal kept on: a

new poem for Allen Tate, an older one for George Santayana, something from *Life Studies,* but no poem for Che Guevara, no Caracas, no March 1 or 2, not a single political poem. However vague or diffident or vulnerable he had seemed at the beginning, he had grasped the situation almost instantaneously and he had set out to defuse its potential explosiveness. He had turned a radical protest meeting into a poetry reading. He had fulfilled his commitment to read but he had not been used.[10]

In September 1967 Lowell was one of three hundred and twenty signatories to a statement pledging "to raise funds to aid youths who resist the draft and the Vietnam war." The statement, published as an advertisement in the *New York Times* and *New Republic,* called on "all men of good will to join us in this confrontation with immoral authority." And on September 21 it was announced that "a sizable number" of the signers of the statement would take part in "an act of civil disobedience at the Department of Justice on October 20." Lowell was one of this number, and his participation has been memorably described by one of his co-protesters, Norman Mailer, in *The Armies of the Night.*[11] Mailer doesn't just report the event: he also has some shrewd insights into Lowell's personality—shrewd enough for Lowell later to describe the book as "one of the best things ever written about me." At first, Mailer presents Lowell as a superior, strangely wounded spirit, a man of high, aristocratic guilts and cosmic sorrows, disdainful of the swirl of opportunism and radical overeagerness in which his ideals have, for the moment, trapped him—but determined, nonetheless, to see the whole thing through.

On the night before the draft-card demonstration there is a public meeting in Washington at which Mailer, Lowell, Dwight Macdonald and Paul Goodman are scheduled to appear. Mailer gets very drunk beforehand, and insists on appointing himself master of ceremonies; he then harangues the audience with obscure jokes and vivid obscenities. Lowell sits on the platform and on his face there is "the expression . . . of a dues payer who is just about keeping up with the interest on some enormous debt. . . . I am here, but I do not have to pretend to like what I see."

As Mailer vigorously rambles on, Lowell continues to sit "in a mournful hunch on the floor, his eyes peering over his glasses to scrutinize the metaphysical substance of his boot, now hide? now machine? now, where the joining and to what? foot to foot, boot to earth—cease all speculation as to what was in Lowell's head." But there is little need for speculation:

> Lowell looked most unhappy. Mailer, minor poet, had often observed that Lowell had the most disconcerting mixture of strength and weakness in his presence, a blending so dramatic in its visible sign of conflict that one had to assume he would be sensationally attractive to women. He had something untouchable, all insane in its force: one felt immediately that there were any number of causes for which the man would be ready to die, and for some he would fight, with an axe in his hand and a Cromwellian light in his eye. It was even possible that physically he was very strong—one couldn't tell at all—he might be fragile, he might have the sort of farm mechanic's strength which could manhandle the rear axle and differential off a car and into the back of a pickup. But physical strength or no, his nerves were all too apparently delicate. Obviously spoiled by everyone for years, he seemed nonetheless to need the spoiling. These nerves—the nerves of a consummate poet—were not tuned to any battering.

Mailer then turns on Lowell with some imagined invective: What right have "you, Lowell, beloved poet of so many" to condemn me, Mailer, the ruffian whose element is "dirt and the dark deliveries of the necessary"; "How dare you scorn the explosive I employ." This was Lowell's reward for having, at one moment, looked up from his shoe and given Mailer a "withering glance, saying much, saying 'Every single bad thing I have ever heard about you is not exaggerated.' " And now, with the meeting reduced to near disarray by Mailer's boorish clowning:

> Lowell with a look of the greatest sorrow as if all this *mess* were finally too shapeless for the hard Protestant smith of his own brain . . . fell backward, his head striking the floor with no last instant hesitation to cushion the blow, but like a baby, downright sudden, savagely to himself, as if from the height of a foot he had taken a pumpkin and dropped it splat on the floor. "There, much-regarded, much-protected brain, you have finally taken a blow" Lowell might have said to himself for he proceeded to lie there, resting quietly. . . .

Earlier on the same evening Mailer had had an exchange with Lowell at a cocktail party; they had sought each other's company as the only fit company available and Lowell had praised Mailer: "You know, Norman . . . Elizabeth and I really think you're the finest journalist in America." Mailer knew that Lowell thought this, because the poet had written him a postcard once using almost the same words: but Mailer distrusted Lowell's praise—he remembered that Lowell had told him privately how much he admired his, Mailer's, first and only book of poems, but had never voiced the opinion in public when the book received a mauling from the critics. He had also noted that Lowell's postcard calling him America's best journalist had been timed to coincide with a review by Elizabeth Hardwick of *An American Dream*—a review, Mailer remembered, that had "done its best to disembowel the novel":

> Lowell's card might have arrived with the best of motives, but its timing suggested to Mailer an exercise in neutralsmanship—neutralize the maximum of possible future risks. Mailer was not critically equipped for the task but there was always the distant danger that some bright and not unauthoritative voice, irked at Lowell's enduring hegemony, might come along with a long lance and presume to tell America that posterity would judge Allen Ginsberg the greater poet.

Back at the meeting, though, Mailer found himself stirred into true admiration by Lowell's reading of "Waking Early Sunday Morning" and also by his stylish handling of the audience: "We can't hear you," they shouted, "speak louder," to which Lowell replied, "I'll bellow, but it won't do any good."

> He was not a splendid reader, merely decent to his own lines, and he read from that slouch, that personification of ivy climbing a column, he was even diffident, he looked a trifle helpless under the lights. Still, he made no effort to win the audience, seduce them, dominate them, bully them, amuse them, no, they were there for him, to please *him*, a sounding board for the plucked string of his poetic line, and so he endeared himself to them. They adored him—for his talent, his modesty, his superiority, his petulance, his weakness, his painful, almost stammering shyness, his noble strength—*there* was the string behind other strings. . . . Mailer discovered he was jealous. Not of the talent. Lowell's talent was very large, but then Mailer was a bulldog about the value of his own talent. No, Mailer was jealous because he had worked for this audience, and Lowell without effort seemed to have stolen them.

On the day after the reading, Mailer and Lowell, together with other notables like Dr. Spock and Noam Chomsky, led a march of about five hundred draft-resisters, sympathizers and media men to the steps of the Department of Justice. The idea had originally been for each of the notables to accompany a resister up the steps and stand beside him as he deposited his draft card in a bag. Lowell in particular had been repelled by this suggestion and had said to Mailer, "It seems . . . that they want us to be *big buddy.*" In the end it was decided that each of the notables would make a short speech in support of the demonstration. And here again Mailer was captivated by Lowell's diffident, dignified performance:

> In the middle of these speakers, Robert Lowell was called up. He had been leaning against a wall in his habitual slumped-over position, deep in revery at the side of the steps—and of course had been photographed as a figure of dejection—the call for him to say a few words caught him partly by surprise. He now held the portable hand microphone with a delicate lack of intimacy as if it were some valuable, huge, and rare tropical spider which he was obliged to examine but did not have to enjoy. "I was asked earlier today" he began in his fine stammering voice which gave the impression that life rushed at him like a series of hurdles and some he succeeded in jumping and some he did not, "I was asked earlier this afternoon by a reporter why I was not turning in my draft card," Lowell said with the beginnings of a pilgrim's passion, "and I did not tell him it was a stupid question, although I was tempted to. I thought he should have known that I am now too old to have a draft card, but that it makes no difference. When some of us pledge to counsel and aid and abet any young men who wish to turn in their cards, why then you may be certain we are aware of the possible consequences and do not try to hide behind the technicality of whether we literally have a draft card or not. So I'm now saying to the gentlemen of the press that unlike the authorities who are running this country, we are not searching for tricks, we try to think of ourselves as serious men, if the press, that is, can comprehend such an effort, and we will protest this war by every means available to our conscience and therefore not try to avoid whatever may arise in the way of retribution."
> It was said softly, on a current of intense indignation and Lowell had never looked more dignified nor more admirable. Each word seemed to come on a separate journey from the poet's mind to his voice, along a winding route or through an exorbitant gate. Each word cost him much —Lowell's fine grace was in the value words had for him, he seemed to

emit a horror at the possibility of squandering them or leaving them abused, and political speeches had never seemed more difficult for him, and on the consequence, more necessary for statement.

So Mailer applauded when Lowell was done. And suddenly liked him enormously for his speech, and decided he liked him truly. Beneath all snobbery, affectations of weariness, literary logrollermanship, neutralsmanship, and whatever other fatal snob-infested baggage of the literary world was by now willy-nilly in the poet's system, worked down intimately close to all his best and most careful traditions and standards, all flaws considered, Lowell was still a fine, good and admirable man, and Norman Mailer was happy to be linked in a cause with him.

Shortly after Lowell's speech, Mailer was arrested for trying to cross the police line. Lowell and Macdonald allowed themselves to be turned back by the MP's and later joined in a sit-down demonstration outside the West Wall of the Pentagon. There, Chomsky was seized by the police, but Lowell and Macdonald were ignored. "They left, unhurt," writes Mailer, "and eventually went home, Lowell to begin a long poem a few days later (when next Mailer saw him a month later, 800 lines had already been written!)." When Lowell first read Mailer's account of him, he was visiting his aunt Sarah in Manchester, Massachusetts. Hardwick remembers: "There we were, in the scenery, very proper Bostonian and so on, and Cal said to me, 'You know, in Boston they think I'm Norman Mailer, and in New York they think I'm Robert Lowell.' "[12]

> Where two or three were heaped together, or fifty,
> mostly white-haired, or bald, or women . . . sadly
> unfit to follow their dream, I sat in the sunset
> shade of their Bastille, the Pentagon,
> nursing leg- and arch-cramps, my cowardly
> foolhardy heart; and heard, alas, more speeches,
> though the words took heart now to show how weak
> we were, and right. An MP sergeant kept
> repeating, 'March slowly through them. Don't even brush
> anyone sitting down.' They tiptoed through us
> in single file, and then their second wave
> trampled us flat and back. Health to those who held,
> health to the green steel head . . . to the kind hands
> that helped me stagger to my feet, and flee.[13]

The "800 lines" that Mailer refers to were not, as he seems to have supposed, lines inspired by events outside the Pentagon. The mild, debunking piece above is one of two poems on the subject; in the other, Lowell also presents himself as rather comically inept and timid: "lovely to lock arms, to march absurdly locked / (unlocking to keep my wet glasses from slipping)." But it is certainly true that Lowell *was* producing lines at an extraordinary rate, and had been doing so since June of 1967. And they were all, like this one on the Pentagon sit-in, slack fourteen-liners—unrhymed, unmetrical, uneven. By Christmas, 1967, he had written over seventy such pieces and, during the following year, was composing at the average rate of four "sonnets" every week. After nearly two years of silence (if one leaves aside translations) he had become as profligate as Merrill Moore. Suddenly, *everything* could be "got into" poetry: headlines, domestic trivia, chance conversations, private anecdotes, as well as his continuing autobiographical obsessions. By the end of 1968 Lowell had written nearly four thousand publishable lines.

It is hard not to speculate about the "sources" of this new abundance. One influence, which Lowell has himself acknowledged, was John Berryman's *Dream Songs:* seventy-seven of these had been published in 1964, and since then they had been appearing by the dozen—each song comprising eighteen (or sometimes nineteen) lines divided into three stanzas. Lowell found most of the songs sloppy, "not quite intelligible," relentlessly indulgent—but he could also see that their cumulative power, their congested, worldly vigor, could only have been captured at the expense of that shaping carefulness over individual lines, individual stanza breaks, which, throughout his own career, Lowell had assumed to be art's first, most nobly difficult requirement. Lowell had poured his whole self into lyrics that could be offered to the world as "finished"; he had made his personal predicaments stand as fit metaphors for the terrors of the globe. But, with Berryman's example in mind, he could now see how much of random circumstance, how much of life's haphazard, interesting flow, was by rule excluded from poems that held their own intensity and artifice in awe. This is how, in 1964, he had described *Dream Songs:*

> The scene is contemporary and crowded with references to news items, world politics, travel, low-life, and Negro music. . . . The poem is written in sections of three six-line stanzas. There is little sequence, and

sometimes a single section will explode into three or four separate parts. At first the brain aches and freezes at so much darkness, disorder and oddness. After a while, the repeated situations and their racy jabber become more and more enjoyable, although even now I wouldn't trust myself to paraphrase accurately at least half the sections.

. . . Several of the best poems in this sequence are elegies to other writers. His elegies are eulogies. By their impertinent piety, by jumping from thought to thought, mood to mood, and by saying anything that comes into the author's head, they are touching and nervously alive. . . .

. . . All is risk and variety here. This great Pierrot's universe is more tearful and funny than we can easily bear.[14]

Two other sprawling, catch-all epics had haunted Lowell for years: Williams's *Paterson* and Ezra Pound's *Cantos*. But he had never trusted himself to veer that far away from the formalist stringency he had learned from Tate and Ransom. *Life Studies* had marked the limits of his disobedience—thereafter he had gravitated back to rhyme and meter. What appealed, though, in the Berryman model was the illusion of structure: the predetermined sectioning. There was in Berryman a beguiling sense of being on parole: the freedom to break lines at will, to be prosy, talkative, discursive, jokey, and yet still have the constraint of being "boxed up" by the "machinery" of a repeated line count.

Other influencing factors can be thought of. The death of Randall Jarrell had removed the one critical voice that Lowell was in fear of—What will Randall think of *this?* had always been one of his first worries. It is possible that Jarrell might have found most of these new fourteen-liners slack, near-journalistic, or too much like casual diary jottings; they might have seemed to him too mumblingly unrhetorical, too self-indulgent. This is guessing; but there *is* a sense in which Lowell's new surge of eloquence is also a surge of truancy from the idea of some absolute critical authority, a "breaking loose" from the requirement *never* to write badly.

Another element—but to be thought of with the utmost caution —was the effect of the drug lithium, which Lowell had begun taking in the spring of 1967. There is evidence that Lowell believed he had finally been "cured" by lithium. Certainly, by Christmas, 1967, he knew that he had escaped his annual breakdown and was writing to friends praising his new medication. Allen Tate wrote to him in

February 1968: "The best news in your letter is the new pill you are taking. It's not at all *so late!* You have twenty years ahead, if not more. That you missed this last December is a wonderful thing."[15] And the novelist Richard Stern has a journal entry dated December 27, 1968, in which he describes a visit to Lowell in Chicago:

> He is sitting in bed in socks, a blue pocket-buttoned shirt, loose tie. Poems, the new "fourteen-liners" are spread and piled on the red quilt. Cal reads ten or twelve of them aloud. The last is about an odd Christmas tree of artificial roses which his daughter was "too unconventional to buy." There were many "annotations"; Harriet calls these "footmarks." He'd written the Christmas tree poem the night before. Since June, he's written seventy-four of them. It was after he'd started the lithium treatments. He went in to shave and came out every now and then, face half-mooned with cream. He showed me the bottle of lithium capsules. Another medical gift from Copenhagen. Had I heard what his trouble was? "Salt deficiency." This had been the first year in eighteen he hadn't had an attack. There'd been fourteen or fifteen of them over the past eighteen years. Frightful humiliation and waste. He'd been all set to taxi up to Riverdale five times a week at $50 a session, plus (of course) taxi fare. Now it was a capsule a day and once-a-week therapy. His face seemed smoother, the weight of distress-attacks and anticipation both gone.[16]

Certainly, there is a low-keyed agreeableness in most of the new sonnets: a passivity, or receptivity. There is also a slackening of grandeur and ferocity in the way he views his own obsessions, a new willingness to accord near-equal status to whatever happens to have happened. Many of the sonnets are recognizably by Robert Lowell; they employ his verbal tricks—his triple adjectives, his gnomic oxymorons—and they are frequently dense with obscure details from his autobiography. And yet there is something glazed and foreign in their manner of address, as if they sense an audience too far-off, too blurred to be worth striving for. Or is this fanciful? It would be safer, maybe, to conjecture that the important "side effect" of Lowell's lithium treatment was in how it seemed to him: in that sense of "it is all so *late*" which Tate replies to in his letter. Lowell's fourteen-liners are, without doubt, hungry for content, as if they had been starved for years. As Lowell later said, "Accident threw up subjects, and the plot swallowed them—famished for human chances."

In December 1967 Lowell and Hardwick visited Caracas, Venezuela, to attend a Congress for Cultural Freedom conference along with Jason Epstein, Jules Feiffer and Lillian Hellman, and in January 1968 Lowell visited the Jesuit priest Ivan Illich's Center for Intercultural Documentation in Cuernavaca, Mexico. It was around this time that Illich was lecturing America on the dire consequences of her "innate . . . compulsion to do good." "I was speaking mainly," he said, "to resisters engaged in organizing the March on the Pentagon. I wanted to share with them a profound fear: the fear that the end of the war in Vietnam would permit hawks and doves to unite in a destructive war on poverty in the Third World."[17] As Robert Silvers recalls, Lowell had been much impressed by Illich, whose essays had been appearing regularly in the *New York Review*:

> Cal seemed fascinated by his vision of a society that would be stripped of the unnecessary, where a lot of the professional institutions that dominate life—in education, in medicine—would be demystified and their functions taken over by austere communities in which people would cooperate in devising more rational arrangements. At Cuernavaca Illich had a language school, where people were said to learn Spanish quickly by using tapes, and a "center for documentation." He described training local people who would collect information on a host of subjects such as development, technology and medicine and publish it in booklets sold to libraries all over the world. He was a tall, thin, cosmopolitan Yugoslav with an intense energy and charm—practically cinematic; a priest who would say he was theologically conservative but set against the false priesthood of modern secular professionalism in the advanced countries, whether communist or capitalist. Cal seemed delighted, in his skeptical way, by the man's unexpected ideas and qualities.[18]

Lowell's sequence of sonnets "Mexico"[19] suggests that he found others in Cuernavaca rather less impressive; one sonnet describes a visit to "the monastery of Emmaus" at Cuernavaca, where the monks seem to have gone "into" psychoanalysis:

> A Papal Commission camped on them two years,
> ruling analysis cannot be compulsory,
> their cool Belgian prior was heretical, a fairy. . . .
> We couldn't find the corpse removed by helicopter;
> the cells were empty, but the art still sold;

> lay-neurotics peeped out at you like deer,
> barbwired in spotless whitewashed cabins, named
> *Sigmund* and *Karl*. . . . They live the life of monks,
> one revelation healing the ravage of the other.

Most of the "Mexico" sonnets, however, are love poems—and these
have a candor and clear-sightedness which Lowell has never before
allowed himself when writing of his "affairs"; for the first time, the
"girl" has a real dramatic presence:

> The difficulties, the impossibilities,
> stand out: I, fifty, humbled with the years' gold garbage,
> dead laurel grizzling my back like spines of hay;
> you, some sweet, uncertain age, say twenty-seven,
> unballasted by honor or deception. . . .

The insisted-on "impossibility" of the relationship provides the
theme; he, middle-aged, the famous poet, the husband and father
with a complicated life back home; she the innocent, the creature of
nature, the near-child: "—how can I love you more, / short of turning into a criminal?"

> Sounds of a popping bonfire; no, a colleague's
> early typing; or is he needing paregoric?
> Poor Child, you were kissed so much you thought you were
>   walked on;
> yet you wait in my doorway with bluebells in your hair.

and there is one fine, summarizing poem—certainly one of the most
sharp-edged, most tenderly "composed" pieces in the "notebook"
which Lowell was busily adding to each day:

> No artist perhaps, you go beyond their phrases,
> a girl too simple for this measured cunning. . . .
> Take that day of baking on the marble veranda,
> the roasting brown rock, the roasting brown grass, the breath
> of the world risen like the ripe smoke of chestnuts,
> a cleavage dropping miles to the valley's body:
> and the following sick and thoughtful day
> of the red flower, the hills, the valley, the Volcano—
> this not the greatest thing, though great; the hours
> of shivering, ache and burning, when we'd charged

so far beyond our courage—altitudes,
then the falling . . . falling back on honest speech:
infirmity, a food the flesh must swallow,
feeding our minds . . . the mind which is also flesh.

The girl was called Mary, was probably Irish—one poem speaks of the two lovers as "Potato-famine Irish-Puritan, and Puritan"—and she seems to have been working at Cuernavaca as one of Illich's assistants. Lowell left Cuernavaca on January 9, and the following day Mary wrote to him:

> yesterday I waited till after your plan [*sic*] lifted . . . did you fly safely? I hope you slept, you seemed tired. but also a little happy, and so I was happy.
> I wanted to run over and give you the blue flower I was wearing. But then I thought how it would begin to die and wither on the way home, and I didn't want you to have anything but a sense of life, not withering. . . .[20]

It was, of course, the "time of the year" for Lowell to have "something with a girl," but in January 1968 he appears to have been able to judge the liaison's real-life possibilities, to have restrained himself from any wild commitment, from fantasies of rejuvenation and rebirth. To have been able to do so makes him all the more fretfully "feel his age"—and throughout the "notebook" poems (they were to be published under the name *Notebook*) there is every so often a flicker of nostalgia for the majestic lunacies of his pre-lithium winters. And there is much caricaturing of himself as weary, middle-aged voyeur—"O my repose, the goat's diminishing day," "I stand between tides":

> The cattle get through living, but to *live:*
> Kokoshka at eighty, saying, 'If you last,
> you'll see your reputation die three times,
> and even three cultures; young girls are always here.'
> They *were* there . . . two fray-winged dragonflies,
> clinging to a thistle, too clean to mate.[21]

In Lowell's world at Harvard there were also girls, and during 1967 there had been a "serious" involvement with a young Cambridge poet; she asks not to be named, but agrees that her presence can be felt in *Notebook*. She, like Mary, was a non-manic attachment; she was not led to suppose that Lowell wished to abandon his marriage; she was aware that he looked to her for "renewal" and companionship. And another Cambridge girlfriend from around this time has said of him:

> I never got the overpowering tyrannical side of him. Exactly the opposite. If he'd wanted to be tyrannical and overpowering I would have been the perfect subject. One of the things I really miss in Cal—you know, it's incredibly seldom you ever know anyone who has that extremely strong instinct for focusing on you and what you're about and what you're trying to do. He did that more than anyone I've ever known. He may have been more like that with girls, I don't know. I think he found a tremendous solace in women. I think he had what I think of as a rather corny simplistic and too easily categorized view of women as being less contrived and closer to the truth of behavior. He talked an awful lot about Ophelia as someone who had failed his idea of women. She'd copped out, yes, but he thought she knew what she was getting into with Hamlet and that she was quite a smart little come-on girl. He was very cozily physical. He liked to hold your hand, or if he walked with you, he liked your arm linked in his. The times I slept with Cal he wasn't crazily sort of sexy at all. He was very huggy. He'd hug you all night, and the minute he woke up he'd hug you. But I think he was quite panicked by thoughts of impotence.[22]

During 1968 Lowell's public persona achieved its remarkable apotheosis. He was already as well known to nonliterary Americans as a poet could reasonably hope to be: he had refused Johnson's White House invitation, he had marched on the Pentagon, he had —in February 1968—called for "a national day of mourning" . . . "for our own soldiers, for the pro-American Vietnamese, and for the anti-American Vietnamese," for all those people "we have sent out of life."[23] These were acts of witness and verbal protest, and they issued from the sidelines: Lowell was cast as spokesman for the angry and impotent intellectual community, and was addressing himself to a President notoriously indifferent to the responses of his "sort of people." In the fall of 1967, though, an odd accident propelled him to the center, or to very near the center, of "real politics."

Eugene McCarthy, the senator from Minnesota and a friend both of Allen Tate and of Lowell's novelist friend J. F. Powers, announced that he intended to challenge Johnson in some of the forthcoming primary elections for the Democratic party's presidential nomination: McCarthy's simple platform was opposition to the Vietnam war. Not only did McCarthy know Tate and Powers, he was also an admirer of Lowell's poems; indeed, in his spare time, he was himself a poet.

In the early days of McCarthy's campaign, Lowell agreed to speak for the senator at New York fund-raisers. The two became friends, each flattered by the attention of the other: Lowell was astonished that this real if idealistic politician should also be stylish and ironic ("it's hard to imagine anyone less like a great statesman . . . and more like a good writer"),[24] and McCarthy enjoyed both the weight of Lowell's prestige and the light relief of his company. They formed an odd, teasing partnership: righteous yet disdainful of self-righteousness, heroically altruistic and yet sardonic about the mechanics of power-seeking. Jeremy Larner, one of McCarthy's speech writers, has captured rather well—though sneeringly—the spirit of the "campaign" in its early stages:

I got my first glimpse of McCarthy fifteen days before New Hampshire, when some wealthy backers arranged a cocktail party at a posh town house in Manhattan. There were carefully collected show-business people, arts and writing people, rich people: come with curiosity and a bit of trepidation. . . .

McCarthy looked grave and weary. Eventually, he made a little talk with allusions to poets, expressing his sense of the country's divisions. The President could not travel openly, he commented. But one's mind wandered. . . .

Before that, Robert Lowell had supplied a rambling introduction. "You're supposed to be artists," he said to the beautiful people, "I don't see any artists here." But his audience knew better—they had signed the artists and writers petition against the war. Finally, Lowell turned to the candidate, who sat beside him, in an antique chair. "You haven't got a chance, you know that, don't you?"

McCarthy sat motionless, his face set, his eyes to Lowell with no expression, no acknowledgment. The room was silent. No one spoke, not even the official backers. Lowell resumed his introduction with grim satisfaction. What on earth were we doing there?[25]

In spite of this elegant inertia at the top, McCarthy attracted huge support among the young; indeed, he was the sole "legitimate" rallying point for the diverse groups and factions that opposed the Vietnam war. Pundits wrote condescendingly about the "McCarthy kids," "the Children's Crusade," and it was casually prophesied that in McCarthy's first real test—the New Hampshire primary on March 12, 1968—he would be lucky to get 10 percent of the vote, even though Johnson had done no campaigning in the state. Of McCarthy himself, one commentator wrote: "His obvious dislike of campaigning, his low-key style, his virtual political obscurity at a national level—all this put him, if not beyond the pale, at least crawling on the fringes."[26] On March 12, though, came what this same writer called "the most sensational political upheaval in recent American history." McCarthy captured a stunning 42 percent of the vote to Johnson's 49 percent. The Children's Crusade had turned out to be a grown-up electoral reality. Four days after New Hampshire, Lowell wrote to Peter Taylor:

> I've been all over the place and followed McCarthy three days in New Hampshire going through two sweater factories, one shoe factory and one wood factory, one Lions and Kiwanis club, and two ladies clubs. My line was that if I spoke he'd lose the few votes he had. It's a miracle how such a quiet and in many ways soporific campaign worked.[27]

(McCarthy himself recalls that Lowell almost *did* lose him votes by telling the owners of the sweater factories that the workers in the shoe factory seemed so much happier than their own employees: "But we've got very good industrial relations!" "Yeah, but they just seemed happier somehow, maybe it's something to do with the shape of the shoes, or the leather. . . .")[28]

Within days of McCarthy's triumph in New Hampshire, Robert Kennedy announced that he would enter the presidential race. Up to this point, he had been careful neither to back McCarthy nor to deplore him. For Lowell, Kennedy's intervention presented a small challenge to his loyalty. Since 1965 he had been playfully intrigued by Bobby—or, at any rate, by the idea of him as a driven, fated prince. He would ask people which character in Shakespeare Bobby could most aptly be compared with. Also, according to Blair Clark, Jackie Kennedy "was busy educating Bobby. Cal was one of the educators—upgrading the savage Bobby into the cultural hero that he became."[29] Lowell had, for instance, given Jackie Kennedy a marked copy of Plutarch's *Lives* and was much excited when he later learned that Bobby had borrowed it and read it: "Bobby was very conscious of the nobility and danger of pride and fate."[30] After Plutarch, Kennedy and Lowell met a few times and exchanged letters. On February 18, 1966, Kennedy wrote to Lowell:

> You have probably read it as I understand you have read everything but when I found the following in Edmund Wilson's book "The Bit Between My Teeth" I thought of you.
> "That hour is blessed when we meet a poet. The poet is brother to the dervish. He has no country nor is he blessed with the things of this world; and while we poor creatures that we are, are worrying about fame, about power, about riches, he stands on a basis of equality with the powerful of the earth and the people bow down before him."
>   Pushkin
> When are they going to write those kind of things about those of us in politics.
> See if you can start a trend in that direction.[31]

And Lowell, not long out of McLean's and in a "down" period, answered on February 25:

> I have always been fascinated by poets like Wyatt and Ralegh, who were also statesmen and showed a double inspiration . . . the biggest of these must be Dante, who ruled Florence for a moment, and would never have written about Farinata and Manfred, without this experience. Large parts of the Commedia are almost a Ghibelline epic. Then there are those wonderful statesmen, like Lincoln and Edmund Burke, who were also great writers.
> Well, I do think you are putting into practice that kind of courage and ability that your brother so subtly praised in his *Profiles*, and know how to be brave without becoming simple-minded. What more could one ask for in my slothful, wondering profession?[32]

Kennedy, however, was no docile student, and he could easily become impatient with Lowell's grand historical perspectives. Grey Gowrie, who sometimes dined with Lowell and the Kennedys (Jackie and Bobby), believed that "Bobby was rather funny about Cal. He sort of admired him but at the same time he thought his politics were absolutely bananas. But that was in late '66 and Cal was reasonably bananas at that time."[33] He also thought that Lowell was slightly envious of Bobby's effortless charisma. And an anecdote related by William Vanden Heuvel, a Kennedy campaign aide in 1968, does rather comically ring true:

> [Bobby] and Lowell discussed *The Education of Henry Adams*. Bobby said he found it a boring book and pulled it off a bookshelf. Robert Lowell took it and proceeded to read the part of it that describes the funeral of John Quincy Adams—which is a very moving and eloquent chapter of the book. Bobby suddenly got up and excused himself. Lowell followed him right to the door of the bathroom, still reading. Bobby shut the door and said "If you don't mind." Lowell said: "If you were Louis XIV you wouldn't mind."[34]

It was perhaps because of such lapses of *grandeur* that Lowell decided to stick with McCarthy even after Kennedy had made his declaration. He wrote to Peter Taylor:

> My heart, such as it is, will have to be with McCarthy to the end, personally and because he is much the better candidate as far as I can judge and then (this almost means most) because he hoped and dared when no other politician in the whole country hoped or dared, when there was no hope.[35]

And two months later, speaking for McCarthy in Oregon, Lowell —after first admitting that he personally liked and admired Kennedy—was uncharacteristically bitter about Kennedy's "shy, calculating delay in declaring himself" and "the shaggy rudeness of his final entrance":

> And who can look forward to the return of the old new frontiersmen? They don't look as good as they once did, after eight years. These men, tarnished with power and thirsting to return to that power. We cannot forgive Senator Kennedy for trying to bury us under a pile of gold.[36]

The next primary after New Hampshire was Wisconsin, and on March 22 Lowell set off for Milwaukee "with somehow a heavy heart . . . the odds seem set against our getting any but the two worst candidates. What a nightmare to be in all this."[37] It is not surprising that the *New York Times* detected a certain failure of enthusiasm in both Lowell and his candidate:

Senator McCarthy, a reader of poetry and a secret poet himself, not only feeds somewhat bemused audiences of Rotarians and dairy farmers quotations ranging from Walt Whitman to an ancient Irish bard named Caduc the Wise, but also has traveling with him an authentic poet, the distinguished Robert Lowell of Harvard.

When candidates speed from town to town, they usually spend their time in close conversation with aides about the peculiar characteristics and problems of the next stop, rehearsing the names and sensitivities of the important local politicians.

But not Gene McCarthy. He rides with Robert Lowell, whose knowledge of politics extends no further than the Guelphs and Ghibellines in 14th-century Florence and whose total interest in the campaign is embraced by his statement: "I am for peace."

Arcadians both, Mr. McCarthy and Mr. Lowell discuss poetry and divert themselves with a kind of "in" conversation, of which the following is a sample:

LOWELL: Can they draft monks?

McCARTHY: No.

LOWELL: Well, that's a loophole.

McCARTHY: Do you suppose we could get some bishop to give all our student supporters minor orders?[38]

This kind of levity was, of course, thoroughly disquieting to McCarthy's fervent aides: "We tried to keep Lowell from McCarthy at very crucial times because we always thought he took the edge off. Every time Lowell and McCarthy would get together, Lowell, or so we thought, would convince McCarthy that really he was above all this." At times, they would book McCarthy into hotels under a false name, "to hide him, not from the press but from people . . . like Robert Lowell." But Lowell "had a very good nose" and would invariably track him down.[39] McCarthy himself still chucklingly recalls the day he kept James Reston waiting for an interview: he was deep in literature and jokes with Lowell "and could not be disturbed";[40] for the aides, he remembers, this was almost the unforgivable last straw. Lowell might later have been blamed for distracting McCarthy from his duties, but it is evident that the senator was a more than willing collaborator in these truancies. Several accounts picture the two of them as chortling naughty boys, and Lowell's most convinced tribute to McCarthy later on was to the "brilliance" of his jokes. As for McCarthy, his fondest memory is of Lowell inventing the slogan "Porky Pig is for Lyndon"; "and everywhere we went he kept pointing out these empty lots and saying: 'That would be a great place for one of my Porky Pig billboards.' "[41]

On March 31, 1968, Lyndon Johnson threw the whole contest into magnificent confusion by announcing that he would not be seeking reelection. It was now McCarthy versus Kennedy—and the winner would almost certainly face Hubert Humphrey in August. McCarthy had a walkover in Wisconsin, and defeated Kennedy in Oregon, but the key confrontation, it was generally believed, would come in California in June. Lowell joined the McCarthy entourage at the Fairmont Hotel in San Francisco, having already—it seems —formed the view that if McCarthy lost in California, "his people should support Kennedy and vice versa." Without consulting McCarthy, Lowell arranged a meeting with Kennedy, who was staying in the same hotel. Arthur Schlesinger, in his biography of Kennedy, records:

> They had a fairly unsatisfactory talk. Kennedy, in Lowell's view, was making debater's points. Lowell said: "You mustn't talk to me this way." Kennedy said mildly that he guessed there was not much more to say. Lowell said: "I wish I could think up some joke that would cheer you up, but it won't do any good." Afterward, he told McCarthy: "I felt like Rudolf Hess parachuting into Scotland."[42]

McCarthy and Kennedy were about to face each other in a televised debate; the McCarthy camp believed this to be the crucial test and were anxious that their candidate should at least *seem* to take it seriously. Again, though, the memoirists recall that Lowell's presence was disruptive:

> Finney [Thomas Finney, McCarthy's chief adviser in California] was trying to brief him à la Kennedy, with little cards that let him know things that were important and would come up, and how he felt McCarthy should respond. And McCarthy was very, very good. He was going through all this and taking pieces of paper from Finney, looking at them and dropping those on the floor that he'd studied carefully. You're never sure about McCarthy. It *looked* like he was attentive and interested. But then, of course, Lowell got to him fifteen minutes beforehand, and they started to drink, the two of them, and went downstairs. . . .
> McCarthy and Lowell got into the same limousine. On the way to the

studio, McCarthy wanted to see Alcatraz. And so they took a detour, and McCarthy looked at the prison. He and Lowell composed, I think, a twentieth-century version of "Ode to St. Cecilia's Day" in the backseat. So, by the time he got to the studio, yes, he was then like Henry V at Agincourt.[43]

McCarthy himself is dismissive of the theory that Lowell was responsible for his poor showing in the TV debate: "There was no point in preparing for that debate because you couldn't anticipate what lies Kennedy would come up with."[44] And Blair Clark, who by a strange chance ("Cal had nothing to do with it") had become McCarthy's campaign manager, would also absolve Lowell from the blame:

A lot of people say that McCarthy lost the debate with Bobby Kennedy in San Francisco in May 1968 because he spent the morning joking with Cal, Mary McGrory and me in the hotel room instead of boning up on Kennedy's record on housing. But that's not why he lost the debate. He lost the debate out of not wanting to win it, and out of some contorted resentment of the Kennedys. That's why he lost the debate. And it cost him California.[45]

Lowell had left California by June 5, the day of Robert Kennedy's assassination, and although he continued to speak for McCarthy right through to the Democratic Convention in Chicago at the end of August, his heart does not seem to have been in it. In July, he wrote, in a speech called "For McCarthy":

One longs for our old opponent, Senator Kennedy; Robert Kennedy had his scrappy, abrasive qualities but it was hard not to honor him, and even feel something close to ardor: he had feelings of his own, fire, the spirit of vertigo. Little of this remains in many of Kennedy's chief lieutenants; solemnly, woodenly, they troop to Humphrey. Mr. Humphrey rubs no one the wrong way, at least personally: he goes down easily, as if he himself were one of the products of the druggist he once aspired to become.[46]

Four days before the Democratic Convention the Russians occupied Czechoslovakia, and McCarthy's faint hopes were thus effectively killed off. At the convention itself, the bloody showdown between

demonstrators and police was for Lowell the final, numbing irony
—the "five nights of Chicago: police and mob" left him feeling
"tired and had":

> The police weren't baby-sitting at 5 a.m.:
> in our staff headquarters, three heads smashed, one club;
> Five days the Hilton was liberated with troops and cars—
> a fallen government. The youth for McCarthy
> knew and blew too much: their children's crusade![47]

And in September, with Humphrey now lined up against Nixon,
and with George Wallace rather sinisterly in the wings, Lowell
wrote to his Castine friend, the poet Philip Booth:

> New York is insufferable, the election, the talk about the election, the
> depression, the frustration, the moisture,—and there's noise twenty
> hours a day. Such the insight of my jaundiced eye, my jaundiced ear.
> Strange moods of testiness; very productive, but not sociable. . . .
> . . . Yet quite likely the future will be desultory, depressed and moist,
> and maybe peaceful. Luckily our only completely dangerous "leader"
> is Wallace, a man of perhaps too little articulation to win power.[48]

Lowell continued to speak against the war when asked, and in
November 1968 was stung to engage in an acrimonious dispute with
Diana Trilling in the pages of *Commentary:* she believed him to be
"soft" on student violence (she was writing on the Columbia riots
of April 1968), and he believed her to be evasive on the Vietnam war.
To the "soft on students" charge, Lowell made the following reply:

> I answer that I might wish to be a hundred percent pro-student, but the
> other morning, or some morning, I saw a newspaper photograph of
> students marching through Rome with banners showing a young Clark-
> Gable-style Stalin and a very fat old Mao—that was a salute to the
> glacier. No cause is pure enough to support these faces. We are fond of
> saying that our students have more generosity, idealism and freshness
> than any other group. Even granting this, still they are only us younger,
> and the violence that has betrayed our desires will also betray theirs if
> they trust to it.
> I would like to tell Mrs. Trilling one thing very clearly. I had nothing
> to do with the student strike at Columbia. I was at Columbia just once
> two or three weeks before the troubles. I spoke for four or five minutes

against President Johnson's Vietnam War. I received tame applause. Also, I want to explain to her, finally I hope, that I have never been new left, old left or liberal. I wish to turn the clock back with every breath I draw, but I hope I have the courage to occasionally cry out against those who wrongly rule us, and wrongly lecture us.[49]

And the end of Lowell's political adventure is tersely marked by the sonnet he calls "November 6th": on the previous day Richard Nixon had narrowly defeated Humphrey at the polls:

> Election Night, the last Election Night,
> without drink, television or a friend—
> wearing my dark blue knitted tie to classes . . .
> No one had recognized that blue meant black.
> My daughter telephones me from New York,
> she talks *New Statesman*, 'Then we're cop-outs! Isn't
> not voting Humphrey a vote for Nixon and Wallace?'
> And I, 'Not voting Nixon is my vote for Humphrey.'
> It's funny-awkward; I don't come off too well;
> 'You mustn't tease me, we were clubbed in Chicago.'
> *We must rouse our broken forces and save the country:*
> we often said this, now the fallen angels
> open old wounds and hunger for the blood-feud
> hidden like contraband and loved like whiskey.[50]

For almost a year Lowell had been writing his fourteen-line poems at the rate of three or even four a week. By July 1968 he was talking of the "long poem" he had almost finished—"I want this book to hit with a single impact: the parts are not meant to stand by themselves"[1]—but it was in October 1968 that he decided that the movement of his *Notebook*'s plot should be from summer 1967 through the fall of 1968:

> It is not a chronicle or almanac: many events turn up, many others of equal or greater reality do not. This is not my diary, my confession, not a puritan's too literal pornographic honesty, glad to share private embarrassment, or triumph.[2]

Although *Notebook* makes much of its framework of public events —Lowell lists the year's principal upheavals in a note at the end of the published text—and although Lowell's own year had been hectically political, there are few poems that are explicitly "about" the headline sensations of 1967–68. Indeed, anyone reading the book now, without aid from any of the histories, would find it hard to recall even the main outlines of what happened. As Lowell notes, in explanation of his list of dates: "Dates fade faster than we do. Many in the last two years are already gone; in a year or two, most of the rest will slip."[3]

The book's real scope, of course, is the scope of Lowell's consciousness: and here he does not provide us with a list of dates, nor does he offer many footnotes. The assumption throughout is that we will somehow know as much about his life as he does: a necessary assumption, he implies, for the purposes both of reticence and of tone. In poem after poem, there is an unbending intimacy between the poet and his addressee; Lowell uses snatches of conversation, secret jokes, idly resurrected incidents from youth and childhood, quotations from books, private letters, gossip, and "much more that I idly spoke to myself." Having chosen his structure, Lowell gives it freedom to ingest at random. His themes—Power, Middle Age, and Art—are huge enough to seem consistently pursued; his plot— the passage of the year fitted to the chronology of his own life—is loose enough to be lost track of and picked up again at will.

It would take a whole book to annotate *Notebook,* and the labor would not always be worthwhile. Now and again, though, there are poems that gain hugely from some knowledge of their "background." Here, for instance, is a sonnet called "The Next Dream":

> 'After my marriage, I found myself in constant
> companionship with this almost stranger I found
> neither agreeable, interesting, nor admirable,
> though he was always kind and irresponsible.
> The first years after our first child was born,
> the daddy was out at sea; that helped, I could bask
> in the rest and stimulation of my dreams,
> but the courtship was too swift, the disembarkment
> dangerously abrupt. I was animal,
> healthy, easily tired: I adored luxury,
> and should have been an extrovert: I usually
> managed to make myself pretty comfortable. . . .
> Well,' she laughed, 'we both were glad to dazzle.
> A genius temperament should be handled with care.'[4]

And here, from a draft of Lowell's autobiography, is its remarkable prose source:

A few months after Mother's death in 1954, I went through her papers and discovered a note-book written in 1937, when she had just begun to have interviews with a psychiatrist. The spelling is a miracle of inaccuracy due to ignorance, but also due to impatience. The notes soon became mere quotations from psychiatry books that Mother was reading. However, the first five or six pages are personal: they are an autobiographical sketch disguised as a third person description of Miss B.

Mother's account shows courage and self-knowledge, and refuses to evade. Here are excerpts exactly as she wrote:

"Miss B's father was a conscientious disciplinarian, so busy in uprooting what was bad that he destroyed and damaged much that was good. Her mother was suppressed and unhappy, rather superficial, but was completely dominated by her husband, who insisted on running everything, with constant criticism and direction." As a child Miss B was "self-conscious, introverted, aggressive and rather deceitful." Her Father's discipline was "erratic but severe." "Being a rather lonely and maladjusted child, retreated into a world of dreams and unreality, and spent an increasing amount of time in this way (Began at about 10 years, encreased [*sic*] till about 26, and lasted until over 40)." She was "absolutely powerful and perfect in this and resisted exeration [*sic*] of any kind."

Miss B married, because she thought it was time to. She was not at all in love with the man, nor did she really admire him. But he seemed the best that was offered. She rather enjoyed his admiration, and thought she might improve him, and would be free herself, and away from the constant family frictions and quarrels, which she thought degrading.

But she also thought she was doing a very wrong thing in marrying this man whom she did not love, and often felt that she would be punished for it, as she was always punished for doing what was wrong.

After this marriage . . . having to live in constant companionship with this comparative stranger, whom she found neither agreeable, interesting, nor admirable, was a terrible nervous strain. She became increasingly critical and unappreciative. She wished to do nothing and see no one. She was utterly hysterical, and would have liked to die, but the idea of (Playing the game) kept her from doing it. So to the world, her family, and her friends she appeared happy and serine [*sic*]. She was determined not to whine and be a Coward; but what a lot of care she made for herself.

Her husband "could not understand at all, was always kind, though irresponsible; and thought her half crazy.[5]

For Lowell, few documents could have held more fascination; in the poem, he turns Miss B back into the first person and adds to his mother's self-description quotations from his own memories of childhood. (For example, again in his draft autobiography, he tells that "When visitors praised Mother's house, she would smile and answer in a cosy, humorous removed voice: 'I usually manage to make myself pretty comfortable.' ")[6] Readers without access to Lowell's papers could hardly fathom the full weight or even rightly gauge the direction of this poem: who, or what, they might wonder, is the poet quoting from, and to what purpose? Although much of *Notebook* thrives on the neglect of such considerations, there are large stretches of it that can be altered into a new forcefulness by "biographical" support.

And there are other stretches that cannot. For example, a poem like "The Misanthrope and the Painter"—one of many that recount gnomic dialogues between we-know-not-whom—will tend to leave most readers wondering, So what? It goes like this:

> 'The misanthrope: a woman who hates men.
> Women are stronger, but man is smarter.' 'Mostly
> woman hates his drinking and his women,
> hates this in all men; she will not permit
> Cassio to escape tragedy.'
> 'Hear the artist on her fellow artist,
> woman on woman?' 'The only way she can
> repaint this one is for her to lie under a truck.'
> 'I pick up lines from nothing.' 'I'm not nothing, Baby.
> When I am in a room, Wyeth is invisible.'
> 'When Rembrandt had painted the last spot of red
> on his clown's nose, he disappeared in paint.
> I pick lines from trash.' 'I'm not garbage, Baby.
> You may have joie de vivre, but you're not twenty.'[7]

There is, admittedly, a comic near motto for *Notebook* in the exchange: " 'I pick lines from trash.' 'I'm not garbage, Baby.' "; but all in all what can be made of this? Who are these two people; where are they; is one of them meant to be Lowell? And so on. The "key" is provided by Sidney Nolan:

I was with Cal and this girlfriend of his in Boston, and at one point she said, "When I'm in the room, the Rothko disappears." That's what *she* said. So I said, "That isn't fair to Rothko." So we changed it to that realist, the famous chap who did *Saturday Evening Post* covers—not Rockwell. It then says, "You may have joie de vivre, but you're not twenty-one." That was her talking to *me*. The point is, she wanted me to get out of the way.[8]

Nolan had gone to Milwaukee with Lowell in 1968, and had also seen him regularly in Boston and New York. There are at least a dozen poems in *Notebook* that he can similarly "explain" but not illuminate: he will recognize snatches of his own conversation, or lines from books that he knew Lowell was reading at the time, and he can also identify characters and situations. But, as with "The Misanthrope and the Painter," the poem in question very often stays elusive—or if not that, then trifling or self-indulgent.

Other friends can provide a service of this sort with other poems; there are letters in libraries which will reveal that "Friend Across Central Park" (p. 66) is addressed to Jackie Kennedy, or that Irving Howe is the "New York Intellectual" (p. 112), or that Allen Tate couldn't remember telling Lowell's daughter, Harriet: "I love you now, but I'll love you / more probably when you are older" (p. 73); and the score or so amusing literary anecdotes—about Eliot, Ford, Jarrell, Pound—can be verified or contradicted. Such knowledge does not always generate forgiveness, and often Lowell's opacity seems merely mischievous or vain. In the end, though, nothing much can be got from *Notebook* without giving some measure of assent to the hit-or-miss manner of its composition: for Lowell himself, it remained a text that he could tamper with, add to, and finally break into separate parts. It is a weird, unshapely monument to his belief that his experience had somehow not been served respectfully if it had not been transmuted into literature: the near literature of *Notebook* made it possible for him to "meathook" the mundane.

Published in June 1969, *Notebook 1967–68* was received in most quarters with awkward respectfulness—"complex and imperfect . . . a propitiatory act to the modern god of chaos," said William Meredith in the *New York Times Book Review*. The book's sheer size was felt to compensate for its obscurity, its line-by-line unevenness, and the historic sketches—a gallery, this, of Lowell's favorite "despotic gangsters": Attila, Caligula, Napoleon and Hitler —caused several reviewers to marvel at his understanding of "the violence of our history and the moral stench of power." A year later, Lowell was to publish a revised version, which he called simply *Notebook*—"about a hundred of the old poems have been changed, some noticeably. More than ninety new poems have been added"—and there was by then rather more resistance to his new fecundity: Donald Hall, for instance, spoke of "the seedy grandiloquence" of *Notebook* and dismissed the whole thing as "self-serving journalism."[9] In 1969, though, the feeling was that this almost official "major U.S. poet" had estimably tried to land The Big One.

Lowell had completed his final revision of *Notebook 1967–68* in February 1969. In January he visited Canada and Newfoundland— "the setting of my grandfather's longest and best-loved novel the New Priest of Conception Bay (really, you can look on a large Northern map)"[10]—and at the end of February he set off for a two-week tour of Israel. The plan then was for Lowell to go to Italy for a performance in Turin of *The Old Glory* and then to meet up in Spain with Hardwick and the Nolans (Sidney and his wife, Cynthia). Relations with Hardwick, though, seem to have been tense during the winter of 1968–69. Lowell again got through these months without a breakdown, but a letter he wrote Hardwick on January 9, 1969, suggests that the two years since his last illness had not been free of turbulence: there were his Cambridge infidelities (which he seems to have made little effort to hide) and also, it seems, a new attachment to the stimulus of alcohol:

> I have been hard going the last couple of years, tho when haven't I been? I am going to do everything to cut down on the drinking, even stop if I must. . . . Also, even harder, a pledge to try to do my duties and answer things. Can I become the pillar never absent from the family hearth? I love: your varied interests, your refreshing teaching, your neat clothes, your capacity for keen conversation and argument and most for our lovely child. You know it's hard, I seemed to connect almost unstopping composition with drinking. Nothing was written drunk, at least nothing was perfected and finished, but I have looked forward to whatever one gets from drinking, a stirring and a blurring? I'll really try as a child might say, but even the Trinity can't make the crooked stick straight—or young again.[11]

Lowell arrived in Tel Aviv on March 6, 1969. His itinerary would take him to Nazareth, the Golan Heights, Jerusalem and Jericho: he was expected to give readings, to visit libraries, and to do the rounds of local literary figures, although—as he later reported—"At the University of Texas I met far fewer Americans than here." On March 6 he wrote to Hardwick:

But I have the shakes. When I lift the coffee cup to my lips at breakfast table, I don't know whether I can get it there. God, have mercy on me —may I not die far from you! Love (This is lovely if I woke a 100 years younger. Love again I miss you so.

And, in the same envelope:

My dearest, adored Lizzie
    My hand almost shakes too much to write. I'll see a doctor in a few minutes. I only pray to God that I see you and Harriet again, dearest!

Not surprisingly, when this letter reached Hardwick three days later, it "hit [her] like a bomb":

After a few attempts to get Dr. Platman, unavailing, a few wondering fears of how I could get to you, I just collapsed in tears and called Barbara [Epstein], and put to good experience her executive years on the phone at the NYR by getting my loved one on the phone. I'm utterly relieved that you were there, thankful. And of course ecstatic to find you better. . . . Darling, I won't let you go so far away ever again.[12]

By the time Hardwick wrote this letter Lowell had recovered sufficiently to move on to the King David Hotel in Jerusalem. From there he wrote to her on the tenth:

Dear Heart: I guess this has time to arrive before you depart. So loved to hear your voice—4 days ago I went thru a trauma and daze of thinking it couldn't be possible I'd never meet you again. Not so much trouble, just high blood pressure, trembling of foot and hand—remedy don't climb high places, overdrink, stay up too late (all the old things), and take pressure pills.

Lowell's attack was never satisfactorily explained, although Hardwick thinks it was caused by thyroid medication prescribed by Lowell's doctors to combat a possible side effect of lithium. Later on, Lowell wrote about his "trauma" to John Berryman:

I thought I'd had a stroke, but it turned out to be largely a wrong prescription. These wretched little black splinters mortality hits us with. Well, we both know it. I'd like to scorn it, not quite a Yeats. It seems silly to triumph that much. He too knew he couldn't.[13]

Lowell spent the summer of 1969 in Castine with Hardwick and Harriet—"very cozy times here with hot weather and cold"—and in September resumed his split life, shuttling between Harvard and New York. His view of New York was as "jaundiced" as it had been a year earlier: "I've come back to New York for some reason with feet of stone . . . this place hammered together with stone, dirt and bad sounds! Anyway I feel autumnal, my feet drag."[14] And Cambridge offered only "riches of solitary speculation":

> Most of my close friends are gone from Harvard. . . . Is there anything more last man alive than a dinner with one's self: One resolves to stop doing what one doesn't enjoy. But of course it's not that easy. It's not that easy to say one now knows better what one wants than in earlier days. Still, it's all pretty good, if we could only slow and hurry time at will.[15]

The Gowries had by this time left Harvard, and Lowell's two closest Cambridge friends were William Alfred and the poet Frank Bidart. Bidart had joined Lowell's writing class in 1966:

> I was auditing it as a graduate student, and I was showing him poems of mine in his office hours. I've never known anyone else who did anything like this. He had what amounted to an open workshop once a week for two, two and a half hours, from, say, eight-thirty or nine in the morning to about eleven or twelve. He had this instead of having individual conferences with his students. People would bring their poems and sit around a desk and pass them around and everybody would talk about them. You didn't have to be connected to Harvard at all. He welcomed anybody. That was what was so extraordinary. Obviously, if your poems were liked you were a little more encouraged to come back, but a lot of people came again and again who had nothing to do with Harvard.[16]

Towards the end of the fall semester, 1966, Lowell had begun to speed up: "It was so painful in class," Bidart recalls, "because this very brilliant person would start reading a student poem aloud and he couldn't get through a line. He would read half of one line and his eye would skip down to the next line" Bidart visited Lowell at McLean's in January 1967 and their friendship had developed from this point; but it was not until the fall term of 1969 that they formed what Bidart calls their "working relationship":

When Grey Gowrie left for England and Richard Tillinghast left for Berkeley, Cal was a lot lonelier and I got to know him much better partly because he didn't have his closest friends anymore—his closest friends among the students, I mean, because he would of course see Bill Alfred a lot. He had a real sense of loss that the people he felt most comfortable with were gone. Cal was always eager to hear criticism. He wanted you to like his poems, obviously, but he didn't want you just to be a yes man. He once said the best reader of your work was someone who was crazy about your work but didn't like all of it—and that's certainly the way I felt. I can remember one afternoon in his rooms at Quincy House—I said I didn't think this line was quite right, or something, and he changed it right in front of me, and it was unnerving, it was scary. It was a little like going into a museum and you say, "I'm not crazy about that arm," and the statue moves. It was really unnerving. In a way, one didn't want to have that much effect.[17]

By fall, 1969, Lowell was already at work on revisions to *Notebook 1967–68*, and he enlisted Bidart as a kind of chief adviser or assistant:

He started making lists of revisions, and we started going through these revisions and really talking about them. And that was really the beginning of our working relationship. I liked the poems very much, but I thought they were often too hard, too obscure. He often did not know when something was unclear. It's not that he was trying to write something that opaque. So at that point I started seeing everything, I think, and particularly these two- and three-line revisions that he was making lists of.[18]

In December 1969 Lowell was back in New York, and he asked Bidart to join him there to continue the *Notebook* revisions. Bidart stayed in the studio at West 67th Street for a week in January 1970 and "we worked all day for about a week":

These pages of revisions were very complicated and Farrar Straus wanted cleaner copy, so he asked me to help him put it together. That was the first time I ever stayed with him. He was making more revisions, but we were also typing these one- and two-line revisions into copies of the poems so the printer would be able to decipher all this. He was typing in one room and I was typing in the other. He just never stopped. He couldn't type a poem without making a change.[19]

During the same fall semester that Lowell began working with Bidart, he formed another friendship with one of his students. Martha Ritter, at twenty-one, had joined Lowell's class that fall and was writing a thesis on *Notebook:*

> He said I could come and sit in on sessions he had with Frank Bidart. Every week the poems he had written that week were gone over by Frank and Cal. He told me, in that funny way he had of being sardonic and friendly at the same: "If you keep quiet in the corner, you can listen and take notes."[20]

Ritter would occasionally be allowed to contribute one or two revisions of her own: "And I'd feel terrific, as if I'd become one of the guys."

> It was quite soon that I started seeing him alone—probably about October. He had a lot of invitations—to publishing parties, all kinds of readings, that kind of stuff. But he did feel quite alone. I would go to his rooms at Quincy House and spend quite a lot of time with him. Yes, I fell in love with him: gradually, during that fall. We developed these very secret kind of domestic interstices. I would go and cook things and type up poems and make typographical errors and invent new words.[21]

Lowell made it clear to Ritter that he "was very proud of the fact that he was one of the very few people he knew who'd had such a long marriage." Unless he got sick, he said, he would never think of leaving Hardwick:

> I think one of the attractions was that I was quite untouched; I was a virgin, and this fascinated him. He told me he had never slept with a woman who was a virgin. I think for him women were somehow distant, mythological, as if they were to be studied—as if he was watching them, like a child. Yes, he was conscious he was treading on dangerous ground. He would talk about it and was upset about it—almost ashamed. But we couldn't keep away from each other. He said something to me, acknowledging that my love was greater than his. He said that most people can say that they love, but very few people can say they have been loved. And the fact that I loved him so deeply was an incredible thing to him.[22]

Towards the end of the fall semester, Lowell accepted a visiting professorship at All Souls, Oxford, for the spring of 1970. Ritter suggested that she abandon her thesis and join him in Oxford; Lowell persuaded her that she should complete her academic work: "Even though the effort was to keep his marriage together, this didn't rule out the far future." Ritter determined that she would graduate and *then* follow Lowell to All Souls; or, indeed, to wherever he might be.[23]

Lowell's All Souls appointment would begin in April 1970, and he planned first to holiday in Italy with Hardwick. Between January and March he saw Ritter a few times in New York; looking back, Ritter now thinks that by this time he was "trying to distance, to change things." But there had been no explicit break before he left for Europe, and he was aware that Ritter's intention was to follow him.

Lowell's own intention was to have his wife and daughter join him for a year in England. Arrangements had been made for Harriet to take time off from her New York school and for West 67th Street to be let to the novelist Carlos Fuentes. Hardwick also gave up her teaching job at Barnard College for one year. After Italy, Lowell would travel on to Oxford and shortly afterwards Hardwick would return to New York to settle the last details of their move.

22

Before his arrival at All Souls, Lowell received another English offer: a teaching appointment at the University of Essex, to begin in October 1970. The two jobs could hardly have been less alike. All Souls was unique among Oxford colleges: it had no students, either graduate or undergraduate, and a number of its fellows had no academic function. They might be politicians, clergymen, bankers; selected in the first place for their intellectual distinction, they might use the college as a retreat from their momentous lives in London. From time to time, it is contended, Britain's political destiny has been decided over claret at All Souls—in the late 1930s Lord Halifax discussed Hitler's "limited intentions" with the editor of *The Times,* and as one disaffected Fellow wrote in 1966:

> in the common room beneath the high towers some of the most cata-
> strophic decisions of the age were contested in vain—the refusal to bring
> down Mussolini, the refusal to help Republican Spain, the refusal to
> collaborate with Russia, the refusal to defend Czechoslovakia.[1]

By the time Lowell got there, All Souls' reputation for "truly epoch-making political blunders" had largely been forgotten, but—in a period of "student power" and rattled academic self-questioning—the college was now being jeered at as a magnificent anomaly: one of Oxford's oldest, richest and most beautiful but, to the "radical" observer, provocatively pointless.

Essex, on the other hand, was purposeful, ill-favored and post-war. Built in parkland outside Colchester, this "new university" (as the new universities were called) had been the scene of some of the most fiery student riots of the 1960s. The poet Donald Davie had recently resigned his professorship of literature on the grounds that Essex was overrun by Trotskyists and sociologists, and had indeed decided to abandon not just Essex but the whole of Britain in favor of what he called the "luxury of expatriatism." Professor Philip Edwards, in his letter offering the job to Lowell, said that after Davie left, "the morale of the department went right down, and tempers were very short. Our well-publicized student riots of May, 1968 made things worse, since Davie found himself on one side of the fence and most of his colleagues on the other."[2] And Davie, when he heard that Lowell was thinking of accepting the Essex post, wrote from Stanford, California, in commiserating terms: "I have despaired of my country, as perhaps you have despaired of yours."[3] Lowell wrote to tell Hardwick of the Essex offer, suggesting that when she came over to England they could inspect the place before finally deciding.

Lowell arrived at All Souls on April 24, and wrote to Hardwick: "Here I am . . . a half lost soul in All Souls." He had "eaten in gown . . . and handled a 14th century psalm book."[4] A few days later he was no less bemused: "The second sex doesn't exist at All Souls. I feel fourteen again. Vacationing at St. Mark's. . . . But there's so much I like here; it's an education. for what?"[5] And later still: "All Souls is elderly and stiff, yet a pleasant seat on the sidelines to watch the storm."[6]

On April 30 there was to be a party at Faber and Faber in Lowell's honor, and he had been asked to prepare a guest list of his English friends: "Jonathan Miller, the Gowries, the Alvarezes, the Isaiah Berlins, the William Empsons, the Stephen Spenders"—he suggested twenty or so names. And a few days before the party, Lowell invited another London acquaintance—Lady Caroline Blackwood, a close friend for some years of the *New York Review*'s Robert Silvers, and a friend also of the Gowries: she too was of Irish aristocratic background,[7] a member of the wealthy Guinness clan (although, as Lowell later wrote, she "loathes the stout which was fed her as nourishment as a child").[8]

Blackwood was thirty-eight, had been married to the painter Lucien Freud, and her second husband, with whom she had three daughters, was the musician Israel Citkovitz. Her own gifts, though, were literary. She had contributed articles and stories to *Encounter* and the *London Magazine,* and Lowell may well have come across her work; for example, in the 1959 issue of *Encounter,* which published C. P. Snow's "The Two Cultures," Philip Larkin's "The Whitsun Weddings" and Auden on Hannah Arendt, there had been a witty piece by Caroline Freud about "the Beatnik":

> Supposedly revolutionary, the 'Beatnik Movement' is unique in that it enjoys the recognition, support and succour of the very society whose dictates it pretends to flout. It has all the trappings of the subversive, the meeting in the darkened cellar, the conspiratorial whisper behind the candle in the chianti bottle, the nihilistic mutter, without the mildest element of subversion. No one in the future, when filling in an official form, will ever be made to swear that they have never been a Beatnik.[9]

She ends with an acid portrayal of Lawrence Lipton, the Beat "Grand Lama," at his pad in Venice West, Los Angeles: Lipton philosophizes, and Lady Caroline transcribes, and every so often, "we had a long silence" . . . "Once again we had a silence," and

> As I was leaving, 'The Lama' stood in the doorway of his shack. 'We have many Artists down here in Venice West', he said, 'all of them living in dedicated poverty. Some of them are among the most creative talents in America. I should very much like you to have a look at them. I will telephone you as soon as I have arranged to have you shown round their pads'. Suddenly I became cool, visionary. I saw that 'The Lama' had already, mystically, ruthlessly, appointed my future Duties. He had ordained how my life from then on was to be spent. Like a Florence Nightingale. Or a conscientious inspector of an Insane Asylum. Making daily rounds of condemned Artists in padded cells.[10]

In October 1959, not long after Lady Caroline completed her appraisal of Beat poetry readings in L.A., Lowell had been awarded an odd prize in London: a prize awarded annually by the brewing family's own poet, Bryan Guinness, otherwise Lord Moyne, and a cousin of the Blackwoods. Lowell's response to the Guinness Poetry Prize was almost as sardonic as Lady Caroline's view of the U.S. avant-garde: "I much admire the Guinness people's belief in the occasion; they seemed quite surprised that I wouldn't be there— jetted in perhaps. I feel in touch with some old tradition, such as Ben Jonson's bottle."[11]

Some seven years later Lowell and Blackwood met for the first time in New York. As with the "Grand Lama," Blackwood remembers the event chiefly for its "silences":

when I was with Bob [Silvers], he used to take me to dinner at West 67th Street. And I couldn't speak. I'd been told—which was nonsense—that Cal couldn't speak about anything except poetry. That was the legend about him: everything else bored him. If you know that about anyone, it's terrifying. So there were these ghastly silences. I thought it was better, if he only wanted to talk about poetry, not to talk at all—better than to say, "Do you like Housman?" or that kind of thing. So I just used to sit absolutely silent. I was always put next to him. And it used to be my dread. To break the silence once, I said I admired the soup. And he said, "I think it's perfectly disgusting." And then we had a silence.[12]

The dinners were during one of Lowell's manic periods, and Blackwood remembers that "a day or two after one of these dinners, I nearly ran him over":

I was in a taxi in New York, and suddenly there was a frightful swerve and I looked round and there was Cal. He'd stepped right in front of my taxi. He was just weaving through the traffic, looking neither to the right nor the left—cars screaming and screeching. And I felt very concerned for him—it was *so* dangerous. I remember thinking, He's not going to last very long, and feeling awfully sad.[13]

It was therefore with less than total enthusiasm that she accepted Lowell's invitation to the Faber party; she went, though, and that night Lowell stayed at her apartment:

After the Faber party, he moved into Redcliffe Square—I mean instantly, that night. He had this fantasy that Bob Silvers had given him my telephone number because he wanted Cal and me to get married. Of course, that was the last thing Bob wanted. But Cal persisted with that fantasy always—that this was fate, organized by Bob.[14]

For much of the next month, Lowell and Lady Caroline conducted their romance in semi-secret. She recalls clandestine visits to All Souls—"this place that was secret to men"—and trips to Ireland and the Lake District. Hardwick meanwhile was waiting in New York for news of the London accommodation that Lowell was meant by now to have arranged. On May 17, he wrote to Blair Clark, from All Souls:

Time whizzes by here as everyone told me it must—with scarcely time
to write letters of refusal to the things I can't do. We've decided to move
here for a year or two. I'll teach at Essex and live in London, Harriet
and Lizzie will live in London and I'll commute. Almost the same salary,
subjects, time etc. as Harvard. . . . Lizzie will come over about the tenth
or twelfth to strengthen my dawdling house-hunting.

Things seem rasped and low in America, and here I sigh gladly
into the somewhat different air. I'm thankful to get away for a
stretch.[15]

On May 26, though, he was writing defensively to Hardwick:

What's up? Such boiling messages, all as public as possible on cables and
unenclosed postcards. It's chafing to have the wicked, doddering, genial
All Souls porter take down your stinging cable. It matters not: everything must be pressing you this moment in New York.[16]

It was the end of June before Hardwick—in Robert Giroux's
words—"learned the worst." He wrote to Charles Monteith:

It was the uncertainty and the worry about Harriet that was hardest for
her to take. The next day she learned (from friends of theirs in London)
the name of the person with whom he is staying. "I had to burst out
laughing," she said. She thinks from this and other evidence that Cal is
probably ill, and she is consulting his doctor. She called him [Lowell]
next day and described his telephone manner as low-keyed, "not vindictive and even solicitous."[17]

For a week or so, however, she sent further "boiling messages." Did
he *realize*, she wanted to know, the damage he had done: Harriet,
for example, had no school to go to—the "safe" New York City
schools were full; and as for her own work:

I want to add my absolute horror that you two people have taken away
something I loved and needed. My job at Barnard, which I tried to get
back, but it is filled for this year and the budget is filled.
 . . . My utter contempt for both of you for the misery you have
brought to two people who had never hurt you knows no bounds.[18]

By the first week in July it was evident to Blackwood that Lowell was indeed "ill." At All Souls during May and June there had

been scenes that are still vividly recalled by certain Fellows—he made not altogether unrequited overtures to one of the dons' wives, and his high-table conversation was rarely as poised or even coherent as it might have been—but it was still possible then to think of him as simply drunk or rather boorishly "poetic." To Blackwood, he had seemed "very elated, but I wouldn't then have known for certain." The climax for her came in the first week of July:

> He locked me in the flat upstairs [Blackwood's house in Redcliffe Square is divided into three separate apartments], and he wouldn't let me telephone—and I had the children downstairs. But I didn't dare go down to see them, because I knew that he'd come too. And I simply didn't want him in the same flat as the children in the state that he was in. Neither did I want to be locked in with him. It was the longest three days of my life.[19]

On July 9 Lowell was admitted to Greenways Nursing Home in London's St. John's Wood. Hardwick was telephoned by Mary McCarthy (from Paris; McCarthy had heard the news from Sonia Orwell). On July 17 Sonia Orwell telephoned Blair Clark: "Dr. says if Caroline will take resp. he can leave nursing home. Caroline in Ireland—confidentially, Caroline is through."[20]

Shortly after Lowell was admitted to Greenways, Blackwood sent a note to the hospital. Lowell later quoted from it in his poem "Marriage?": "I think of you every minute of the day;/I love you every minute of the day."[21] But she added that it would be better if she did not see Lowell or talk to him again until he had recovered. To this, Lowell replied:

> I love you with my heart and mind, what can I do, if you give me nothing to go on? I can't crowd in on you. Let's for God's sake try again, cool and try. So much love should go on to something.
>   P.S. If I were with you I'd do all within my defects. Can you pretend to be the same? O try![22]

Blackwood was horrified by the suggestion that Lowell might be discharged into her care; horrified for her children as well as for herself. She decided that she would simply "disappear." She wrote to him that she might herself become ill if they remained in contact, and made it clear that before the relationship could move forward, Lowell must get well again. She loved him, certainly, but the future was a blank.

Over the next week Lowell wrote to Blackwood once, sometimes twice a day; she arranged for him to be told that she too had had a breakdown, and this news seems to have greatly excited him: they were suffering "simultaneous sickness," they really were meant for each other—"If we can both be well, I'll walk the ocean. But we will be well," and "(Sonia says) I must get well completely before you could. I take this." On one occasion he left Greenways and went to her house in Redcliffe Square: and "so terrified the cleaning lady that she ran off and was never seen again. And that's what his *appearance* did!" Throughout this week Blair Clark was recording almost daily phone calls:

> *R. Silvers phone conv. with B.C.* 21/7/70
> —worrisome situation: Cal was at Caroline's in London, got cleaning woman to let him in—he was drunk—Car. can't stand it yet doctors say he can't be told. They won't answer for consequences.
> *E. Hardwick conv. with B.C.* 21/7/70
> —"I talked to Cal about 2:30 and he said she'd had a nervous breakdown just like me and will be in hosp. for 2 weeks."
> *B. Silvers conv. with B.C.* 22/7/70
> —Caroline is closing house in London—vanishing concerned that he not track her down
> —Car. quotes "I can't take responsibility" but "hasn't thought through what ought to happen ultimately"
> *Jonathan Miller—phone conv. with B.C.* 23/7/70
> Cal in limbo—no social or therap. nexus—Drs. don't know history— Car. not going to stay with him—she's swept along in the energy of his dissolution, not understanding that she's part of the illness
> —he's in "mood of curious, penitential, false meekness."
> *E.H. phone conv. with B.C.* 26/7/70
> —(Cal) said as if saying he had a cold—"Trouble is that Caroline had had a nervous breakdown too"[23]

On July 29 Hardwick decided she would go to London: there were reports that Lowell was able to wander out of the hospital at will, that he was drinking in the local pubs, that the doctors were incompetent, and so on. She telephoned Blair Clark:

—made up my mind—Bill Alfred going with him [*sic*]—I won't have him killed—destroyed
—allowed to go out—in pyjamas—out to pubs—steals from hand-bags—(she weeps)—they don't understand—he drinks—I'll talk to doctors—brilliant, proud, dignified man, not an ape—
—Car. thing is secondary: he can marry her if he wants
—He might keel over dead, with drugs and beer
—Bill will go to pub, cut his hair, buy him shoes—until they can control him—sit there with him. Cal is really a marvelous person, not this detached idiot—not in emotional contact with his real personality[24]

Hardwick was reassured by her visit. She found Lowell heavily drugged, "hardly able to get across the street," but she felt he was in good hands: the hospital *was* a real hospital, even though it had the appearance of a rather shabby-genteel private residence. She had lunch with him downtown and took him to the film *Patton*, which he liked a lot: he was not "saying outrageous things," but on the other hand, there was "no rapport." She decided to return to New York and left him a note saying: "If you need me, I'll always be there, if you don't, I'll not be there."[25] And the next day Lowell wrote to her:

> You[r] last not[e] and much else that you said and have said through the yeras [*sic*] go through my heart. You couldn't have been more loyal and witty. I can't give you anything of equal value. Still much happened that we both loved in the long marriage. I feel we had much joy and many other things we had to learn. There is nothing that wasn't a joy and told us something. Great Joy. Love. Cal.[26]

Blackwood returned to London in August. Lowell was calm, she found, but "he wasn't normal," and she refused to allow him back to Redcliffe Square. He wrote to her:

> I assume *ceteris paribus* that when I am in a certain state you are too. I could come out in a week or two, if I could have a place to stay. Do come and see me, it's the best slow step we could make. Then I'd like to have the bottom rooms. We could be together without meeting till evening.[27]

But the risks still seemed too high:

I told him he must get a flat of his own. Which he minded terribly—
he was very wounded. But it was like it always was—he *wasn't* all right:
he was terrified of being alone. I think that was because he was terrified
of being mad alone. He really couldn't bear a night alone. But Israel
[Blackwood's estranged husband, Israel Citkovitz, who lived in one of
the three Redcliffe Square apartments] said rightly, was saying, "I really
don't want a madman with the children." I had to tell Cal that. Because
Israel could have taken the children away from me.[28]

Lowell rented an apartment at 33 Pont Street (about five minutes'
taxi ride from Redcliffe Square); his landlord was "a man named the
Knight of Glyn, the only title of its kind in England. His mail comes
addressed that way and his towels are marked K of G,"[29] and on
September 11 he wrote to Blair Clark:

I am settled fairly near Caroline and we do things together, most things.
I am well and not depressed. College begins early next month, and I'll
have to rub my eyes to know I'm not leading the old life. Yet I am not
at all and it gives food for thought. A new alliance or marriage and a
new country.[30]

A month later Lowell writes again to Clark; he is planning a Christmas visit to New York but "there's a problem whether to come with
Caroline":

it seems callous humanly for me to *arrive* in New York, in Lizzie's home
city, with Caroline. Or am I being meaninglessly scrupulous? Until the
divorce is made, and it looks as though it will, and that I will marry
Caroline—it still remains uncertain in my mind. When friends of mine
have been in this dilemma, I've always thought they should stop tortur-
ing themselves and everyone else, and make a quick clean severance. But
it's not easy, unless one becomes some sort of doll only capable of fast
straightforward action.[31]

To Hardwick, he had been evasive, writing fond and chatty letters,
but no more. On October 15 William Alfred wrote urging him to
tell her "something clearcut about what you mean to do. Your
letters, written in kindness though they are, only serve to deepen
her conviction that you are of two minds about the years ahead.
That makes her miss you more."[32] Three days later, Lowell wrote
as follows:

Dearest Lizzie,

I don't know whether I've said or written I feel like a man walking on two ever more widely splitting roads at once, as if I were pulled apart and thinning into mist, or rather being torn apart and still preferring that state to making a decision. Is there any decision still for me to make? After all I have done, can I go back to you and Harriet? Too many cuts.

Time has changed things somewhat since we met at Greenways. I am soberer, cooler. More displeasing to myself in many little ways, but mostly about you. A copy of my new book came the other day, and I read through all the new and more heavily revised poems. A sense of the meaning of the whole came to me, and it seemed to be about us and our family, its endurance being the spine which despite many bendings and blows finally held. Just held. Many reviewers saw this, though it was something I thought pretentious and offensive to push in my preface, I saw it too. I have felt as if a governing part of my organism were gone, and as if the familiar grass and air were gone.

I don't think I can go back to you. Thought does no good. I cannot weigh the dear, troubled past, so many illnesses, which weren't due to you, in which you saved everything, our wondering, changing, growing years with Harriet, so many places, such rivers, of talk and staring—I can't compare this memory with the future, unseen and beyond recollection with Caroline. I love her very much, but I can't see that. I am sure many people have looked back on a less marvelous marriage than ours on the point of breaking, and felt this pain and indecision—at first insoluable [*sic*], then when the decision had been made, incurable.

I don't think I can come back to you, but allow me this short space before I arrive in New York to wobble in my mind. I will be turning from the longest realest and most loved fragment of my life.[33]

And again, on October 22, he writes that he is going through "the usual, once annual depression" and that "whatever choice I might make, I am walking off the third story of an unfinished building to the ground":

I don't offer this as a good description, it's too vague and grand, but to show you why my useless, depressed will does nothing well. Just the usual somberness after mania, jaundice of the spirit, and yet it has so many absolutely actual objects to pick up—a marriage that was both rib and spine for us these many years.

Caroline isn't (if you really want me to be free to talk about her) one of my many manic crushes, rather this and everything more, just as you were at Yaddo and after. She is airy and very steady and sturdy in an

Robert Lowell and Elizabeth Bishop, in Rio de Janeiro, 1962.

PHIL. MacMULLAN/NEWSWEEK

Robert Lowell, 1964.

Roscoe Lee Brown and
Robert Lowell during
a rehearsal of *The Old Glory.*

Left: Robert Lowell and Jackie Kennedy at Sidney Lanier's theater party at The American Place for *Hogan's Goat*, November 30, 1965. *Right:* Robert Lowell at Paris Review party at the Village Gate, May 15, 1967.

Robert Lowell on the March on the Pentagon, October 21, 1967.

John Crowe Ransom's eightieth birthday. (*Clockwise from top*): Robert Lowell, Susan Thompson, John Crowe Ransom, Eleanor Ross Taylor, Robie Macauley, Elizabeth Hardwick, Jack Thompson, Peter Taylor, David McDowell, G. Lanning, in Gambier, Ohio, 1968.

Elizabeth Hardwick,
Castine, Me., 1969.

Robert Lowell,
Harriet Lowell,
Elizabeth Hardwick, 1969.

Robert Lowell, in Venice, 1970.

Robert Lowell and
Nicholas Nabokov,
in Venice, 1970.

Robert Lowell and
Harriet Lowell,
in Venice, 1970.

Robert Lowell and
Elizabeth Hardwick leaving
Venice, saying good-bye to
Esther Brooks, 1970.

Caroline Blackwood,
Peter Taylor,
Robert Lowell, 1971.

Caroline Blackwood.

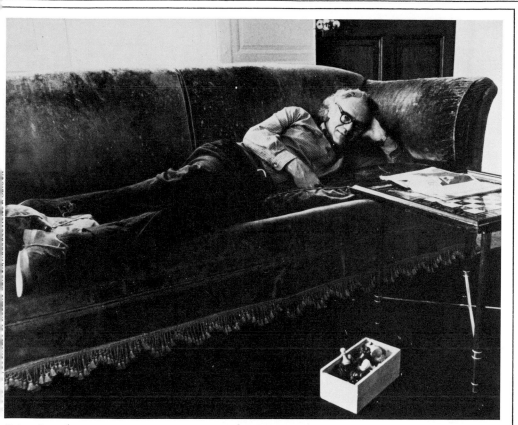

Robert Lowell at Milgate, 1973.

Robert Lowell at Milgate, 1973.

Robert Lowell at the grave of his cousin Harriet Winslow, in Washington, D.C., 1974.

Robert Lowell, 1977.

Elizabeth Hardwick,
Robert Lowell,
Dr. Carl Cori,
in Castine, Me., August 1977.

Robert Lowell,
Castine, Me.,
August 25, 1977.

odd way. She has been very kind to me. I think we can make out. I love her, we have been together rather a long time—often and intensely. I have doubts that I by myself, or anyway, can make out, that dear you and Harriet can make out. I think somehow that Christmas will help us all. Great troubles but no longer everyone unreal to everyone, and Christmas is the season to lighten the heart.[34]

Three weeks later, on November 7, he seems to have made up his mind; he asks Hardwick, "I wonder if we couldn't make it up? . . . Maybe you could take me back, though I have done great harm." Of course, she may not want him back; she may feel "happily rid of [her] weary burden." A week later he is still pressing: "I will do all I can to make things work: I think we can—we have after all for more years than I have the wits to count, tho all remains remembered." And to friends, throughout November, he writes, though warily, of a reconciliation. To Peter Taylor, he summarizes the year's events as follows:

I fell in love, part manic, was sick in hospital a good part of the summer, got well, stayed in love. There was great joy in it all, great harm to everyone. I have been vacillating. I think Lizzie and I will come back together, if that can be done. Anyway, I'll be home in New York during Christmas.[35]

And to Blair Clark: "I think now, but it is hard to be very confident, that Lizzie and I will come together again. . . . When we are depressed, our only support seems to be old habits—mine for a quarter of a century.[36]

Lowell speaks in this same letter of his "baffling vacillation," the "jerky graph of the heart," but he does not seem seriously to have entertained the thought that Hardwick might finally have had enough, that it wasn't merely a question of *his* vacillation. On October 23 Hardwick wrote to Blair Clark about Lowell's proposed visit to New York:

For my business with Cal a visit is not necessary. I do not expect that any of us, even Harriet, will get anything out of it really and I will be glad when it's over. . . . Caroline would never come. That is his fantasy and his need to keep a sense of our competing over him going. She has never competed for anyone in her life and I do not want Cal back under any circumstances. But I don't see him coming here, supposing Caroline would, and having a honeymoon visit when the whole purpose of the trip was to spend a bit of the Christmas with Harriet, to make arrangements for the future. This is the last time he will see me—something I don't think he realizes, since he is reluctant just to face the lack of drama that the end of this would mean. Also I have the idea that he is afraid to budge one inch from Caroline—she might not be there when he got back. I don't think he is really well, and he is kept going on this false sense of people competing for him.

I could not put Harriet and me through the giddy unreality I know Cal would be sunk in if he came over with Caroline. I feel it would be the end of Caroline's feeling for him too, because she would see how he has to exploit or boast or else things aren't real. In a way I doubt *he* will come. In all the months he has been gone I've heard from him a lot and he has never answered one question that I have put to him, or discussed really anything, me or Harriet or practical things or Caroline—except himself.[37]

By the end of November, Lowell seems to have grasped that his "choices" might indeed be illusory: on the one hand, "it comes to me that I can't pull this new marriage off," that Blackwood might not wish to marry him; and on the other, that Hardwick's response to his latest escapade was puzzlingly volatile.[38] On November 21 he wrote to Clark:

It must be like migraine getting stuck with all my affairs, from all sides. . . . Here's what's going on in me. I am haunted by my family, and the letters I get. There seems to be such a delicate misery. Lizzie's letters veer from frantic affection to frantic abuse. Then somehow she and Harriet are fused as one in her mind. It's not possible, but I get the impression they really are in Lizzie's mind. It's crazy, but I can't from a distance do anything about it, perhaps less on the spot.

The thing is I am perfectly happy with Caroline. At first I was afraid of not being married—old feelings of being outlawed. But I see it doesn't matter much. We can go on permanently as we are. We are permanent no matter what our status. Caroline has always been afraid of legal marriage. Not being married, somehow loosens the bond, man and woman's mutual, self-killing desire to master the other. Then we might get married anyway when we knew we didn't have to. I don't know yet what will happen, but I increasingly fear for the blood I'll have to pay for what I have done, for being me. Anyway, I'll be coming to you around the 14th alone.[39]

Lowell carried on living in Pont Street until his departure for New York; since October he had been teaching two days a week at Essex and finding his poetry classes there "rather retarded after Harvard. The college looks like Brandeis, if Brandeis had been built on a fiftieth the money, and with no Jews."[40] Otherwise, he had been leading "a mole's life," with occasional readings—in Bristol and Cambridge and in London at the Mermaid Theatre and the Institute for Contemporary Arts—and a weekly lunch with Sidney Nolan. At his readings he would be told by the organizers that he had attracted "a record small audience," and all in all he was enjoying England's "famous more mumbled and muffled pace."[41] As to America, he wrote to Hardwick that he dreaded "the *Review* circuit and the buzz of American politics." One of the nice things about England was that "an American isn't expected to follow issues."[42] But in mid-December he set off "home"—with nothing re-solved, and no clear idea of what would happen next. After he left, Caroline Blackwood wrote him a letter, which, again, he was later to put into a poem ("With Caroline at the Air Terminal"): "If I have had hysterical drunken seizures,/it's from loving you too much. . . ." This is, almost word for word, the opening of Black-wood's letter. She went on to say that she was uncertain whether they would ever meet again; unsure, even, that they should. What-ever happened, though, she wanted Lowell to know that the happi-ness he had given her was unique, that if there was misery ahead, she would never regret having known him, and so on. Lowell responded to all this with a terse cable from New York: I AM NOT A CRIPPLE LOVE CAL.

23

"If I have had hysterical drunken seizures,
it's from loving you too much. It makes me wild,
I fear . . . We've made the dining room his bedroom—
I feel unsafe, uncertain you'll get back.
I know I am happier with you than before.
Safer. . . ." The go-sign blazes and my plane's
great white umbilical ingress bangs in place.
The flight is certain . . . Surely it's a strange joy
blaming ourselves and willing what we will.
Everything is real until it's published.[1]

Since July in Greenways, Lowell had again been "turning out poems at a great rate,"[2] and like this one, they were transcriptions of the day-to-day shifts and swells of his dilemma. When he wrote to Blair Clark that he had been "through baffling vacillation, and letters would have been like a jerky graph of the heart," he might easily have said the same of this new spate of fourteen-liners, or "belles lettres," as—with some irony—he called them. In September he had "thirty or so new poems in the old meter";[3] by the end of November he had ninety: "Poems at a great rate, even scribbling lines down during a dinner. I suppose I may have a book, a little notebook, ready by next fall. Then a new tune, a new meter, a new me. The last never I suppose."[4] Throughout October and November, he said, he had done "nothing but bury my indecisions in many many poems."[5]

Before flying to New York, he had asked Frank Bidart to meet him there: he wanted Bidart to help him sort out the "tall house of draft and discard" which, along with the ninety or so "finished" poems, he had accumulated since July.

In mid-December I got a letter or telegram asking if I could meet him in New York. He was going to be in New York for Christmas. That's the Christmas that's in *The Dolphin* [the book title Lowell was to give to these 1970 sonnets]. It's certainly the case that before he came, there was a sense that the thing with Caroline might be over. But Lizzie, when she met him at the airport, was terribly upset because she knew right away—I think he announced immediately that he was going back. So the whole trip, which he had been very much looking forward to, was right away poisoned for her. He was staying at Blair Clark's apartment, not with her.[6]

Lowell's New York visit, in Bidart's view, was not just "to see Harriet" or to sort out his affairs: "I think he wanted to see what it felt like, and to talk to old friends—just to touch base. . . . I don't think he really knew exactly what was going to happen":

I think I went to see him around December 28—though it may have been before Christmas. I flew to New York, and it seems to me it was early in the day. . . . Maybe I stayed over at Blair Clark's that night, I'm not sure. Anyway, we talked a little bit about his personal situation, but he had the beginning of *The Dolphin*. At that time there was no image of the dolphin in it, so the whole controlling symbolic scheme was not there. It was more nakedly a ninety-odd-sonnet narrative, but very much without an ending. He'd already begun writing the Christmas stuff—he was absolutely writing it as he was living through it. I was there long enough to read some ninety odd sonnets. Then I went back to Cambridge and after a few days he went back to England. I didn't hear from him for a long time and didn't know what was happening.[7]

Lowell returned to London in January with matters still unsettled. He was committed, he felt, to at least one more term at Essex and he had rented the Pont Street apartment until spring: these, he pleaded, were two concrete reasons for not lingering in New York. Shortly after his return, though, he was still vacillating. He wrote to Hardwick (in a letter from Pont Street dated simply 1971):

What shall I say? That I miss your old guiding and even chiding hand. Not having you is like learning to walk. I suppose though one thing is worse than stumbling and vacillating, is to depend on someone who does these things. I do think achingly about you and Harriet.

In February 1971 Caroline Blackwood learned that she was pregnant. As Frank Bidart recalls:

> He told me later that it was when he got back that Caroline said she was pregnant. I guess the point of this is that at this time [December 1970] he was intending to stay with Caroline regardless of the pregnancy. It wasn't the pregnancy that precipitated that. It may have sealed it, that spring, I don't know, but it certainly wasn't any simple cause and effect. He said to me, later, that he would not have been upset if girlfriends he had had earlier had got pregnant, but there was no sense he would have left Lizzie for them.[8]

Certainly, Lowell welcomed the pregnancy; from March 1971 his "vacillating" stops. On March 14 he wrote to Harriet telling her that he and Caroline were going to have a child:

> There can't ever be a second you in my heart, not even a second little girl, to say nothing of a boy.
>
>   You are always with me, you and your mother. I want you to visit us whenever you wish and can. We're not ogres and bears. I think you may find that you will love Caroline. She has never been harsh to her own girls.

Hardwick's first response to the news was angry and self-protective, or rather protective of her own and Harriet's future, although Lowell had offered her the whole of his "unearned income." Blair Clark, who saw Lowell in London in March 1971, wrote to him on returning to New York:

> your relations with Harriet depend almost entirely on what *you* do about them. You absolutely cannot count on any help from Eliz. That well is poisoned, whatever the formal position of Eliz. is. As we agreed, no campaign for Harriet can now be undertaken, but I think you must gently keep in touch with her, not expecting much response. . . . you can count on no good will from Eliz. in any of this. I would say that any chance of that disappeared when you got off the plane in Dec. wearing that ring, and now, with the child in prospect, it has receded into unimaginable distance. I think she is and will remain extremely bitter, Cal, and I repeat that the most foolish thing I ever heard said was Lady Jean Mailer's "I always love everyone I've ever loved." In any case, Eliz. not being an upper-class swinger, such friendliness is inconceiva-

ble. So, in my strong view, you're on your own in an uphill battle for the affections of Harriet.[9]

Lowell wrote back to Clark that he thought Hardwick "a little puts on her demonic . . . mask with you," that he had just had "the most friendly [letter] I've ever gotten from Lizzie speaking of my lovely letter to H." and that "I'm very hopeful, with forebodings of course."[10] Indeed, hopefulness surges through every letter Lowell writes throughout this spring and summer. In March, to Bill Alfred, he announces:

Caroline and I are having a child. It will be born early in October, and most people we've met know by now. Many problems, but somehow a calm has come for the last month and a half that is quite surprising. Like walking through some gauze screen that allowed one to see real things without touching them, but what we see is different. Anyway, for me and Caroline a peace we haven't known, perhaps ever. Ah well who knows . . . what's around the corner? It's easier to face.[11]

And in May he writes to Peter Taylor:

Caroline's almost five months pregnant and looks nine. Fearful dread of twins and indeed Allen [Tate] who behaved very badly about us to Lizzie, has already offered himself as a godfather. Even so, if there is only one child we might call him, until after the divorce, Lowell Guinness. It's a great comfort, soothes us, and somehow takes away from the wilfulness of my action. I feel that I have more than half lost Harriet, not through anyone's fault but through distance. It's more than I can bear sometimes, but this will make up. We have three other children, lovely little girls, so "Lowell" will have a nest waiting. One child is already knitting him mittens. Everything in our house is a girl except me—two rabbits, two kittens, a small guineapig named Gertrude Buckman etc.

Do you think you might ever come over here? We could give you a wonderful brick ruin and a stocked troutstream about the width of a typewriter ribbon. England has everything you love, safe schools, no negroes, quaint old people, absolutely nutty ones our age, whiskey without ice. You could renew your old academic and ecclesiastical connections. . . . I miss America, and thought of coming over this spring, but it seemed too complex and jolting. It would be better probably after the baby is born. I've just finished another book of poems, after working frantically, sometimes six days a week. . . .

> Caroline and I haven't quarrelled for four months, an absolute record for me with anyone. We are both slovenly, but essentially sane.[12]

The spring visit to America that Lowell planned for May was abandoned, he told Blair Clark: "I sensed the time wasn't very lucky for visiting Lizzie and Harriet, with my mind over my shoulder back in England. I miss Harriet constantly, and Lizzie too. Perhaps almost stronger than the missing is the feeling of not seeing something through. This isn't the kind of thing I usually bedevil myself with, but twenty years is like a full life time, one never to be filled."[13] To both Taylor and Clark he speaks of being "reborn" at fifty-four and to Clark that he feels "stunned by my good luck":

> Caroline is in blooming health, sheer woman humanity. She looks as if we were going to have twins, but I think its just her usual swollen pregnancy. . . . Forgive this spring fever letter. I detect a smugness peeping through its nostalgia.[14]

During the spring of 1971 Lowell had formed a friendship with the young British writer Jonathan Raban. Raban had done a glowing radio review of *Notebook,* and Lowell had invited him to lunch:

> Lunch was extraordinary. We started off talking about literature and going through the inevitable roster. Then I started talking about fishing, about which Cal got instantly enthusiastic. We started arranging imaginary fishing trips all over England. And then I had to come back to Redcliffe Square to read the draft of *The Dolphin*—I took it off with me to read in a spare room. Cal expected me to read the entire book and make suggestions in the course of an hour while he sat nervously in the next room opening the door every so often and asking me which poem I'd got to.[15]

It was not until two weeks later, Raban says, that he realized Lowell "was on the edge of a manic high." At first he had thought "he was behaving just as Robert Lowell might be expected to behave— massively enthusiastic, schoolboyish, frantically playful." They had gone together to the London Dolphinarium on Oxford Street, and Lowell had been thrilled. On May 4 he wrote to Harriet:

I've been to see two performing dolphins, Baby and Brandy, in a tank on Oxford St. They can jump twenty feet, bat a ball back to their trainer, pretend to cry for fish . . . bigger brained than man and much more peaceful and humorous.

After this, Raban recalls, "he took to going down the Kings Road and buying incredibly expensive stone dolphins from places like the Antique Hypermarket, where he discovered these things were going for hundreds of pounds." And at Blackwood's country house, Milgate (near Bearsted in Kent), he arranged for dolphins to be placed "at either side of the front door, dolphins in the garden, dolphins as hatstands":

Dolphins were his high obsession at that time. What was interesting about it was that it was a manic attack which this time he fought off. This was early in his relationship with Caroline; she was two or three months pregnant, I think. Cal was able to hold off the mania by some kind of effort of will—hitting the brink of it and being able to voluntarily draw back, in a way he wasn't able to later. They were both treating each other with a sense of each other's fragility. I mean, Cal holding himself back because he saw the panic in Caroline, and Caroline in a way holding herself back from her thing, from her fear of Cal. They treated each other with an almost drunken delicacy, and you could feel a massive amount of self-restraint on both sides, and terror —terror that if one of them flipped, the whole thing would crash. It was a rather remarkable time, because I think it was almost the first manic attack Cal had which he actually fought off—sort of saw through to the end without actually going over the top. So the obsession was with dolphins—it never got into great men. Which was a triumph.[16]

In July 1971 Raban accompanied Lowell on a trip to the Orkneys. Blackwood's cousin, Gareth Browne, owned a recording company that specialized in poets reading their own work, and had arranged a recording session with Orkney poet George Mackay Brown. Lowell and Raban were invited to join Browne's "entourage"; for Lowell it was an opportunity for a genealogical adventure —he would track down the source of the "Spence negligence," make contact with a line in his ancestry that had always intrigued and amused him. As soon as he arrived he became "enormously excited":

We got a car to take us to Stromness, which is about twenty miles from the airport, and on the way Cal leant over the seat and said to the driver: "I'm Robert Traill Spence Lowell." The driver just grunted. And Cal said, "Do you know the Traills or the Spences?" And the driver said, "Yes." Absolutely tightlipped. Cal was terrifically excited: you know, *Where are the Spences, where are the Traills?* And the driver—he could obviously see a rich American and didn't want to lose his custom, but, at the same time, clearly, the Spences and the Traills had utterly disgraced themselves, they were the most terrible people to be associated with.[17]

When they reached Stromness, Lowell continued his researches; he went into shops and post offices and asked, "Do you know any people around here called Spence or Traill?" The response was always monosyllabic and suspicious:

I think they'd been rack-rent landlords and had fled the country with money that had properly belonged to Orkney—or something like that. Anyway, it was absolutely clear that the Spences and the Traills had disgraced themselves in Orkney. It was total shame.[18]

Lowell might have failed to dig out his own niche in British history, but in July—on his return from the Orkneys—he was rather pleased to find himself equipped with at least the trappings of a social "rank": he had been promoted to the role of country squire. Blackwood had decided to move from London to her country house, and on July 25 Lowell wrote contentedly to Clark:

In the last weeks we've been moving *permanently* to the country. We'll keep part of Redcliffe Square to visit, but all will be here: the younger children's school (the oldest is off to boarding school) my commuting to Essex. Already one feels reborn. Our child too will be born here. No more weekly full family stampedes from London to Kent, and now it will be possible to put this house in reasonable shape. And so on. Up till now we were really sort of half-camping in two houses. Also it attenuates our uneasy closeness with poor Israel [Citkovitz, still legally married to Blackwood and, of course, the father of the three young girls]. The pregnancy and birth and first months will be worlds easier for Caroline. We are already interviewing couples.[19]

Milgate was, he said, fifty miles or so from London, "an hour by train from London and about two hours door to door from Essex"; for Lowell it was a British Castine, with some eccentric old-world extras. He described the surrounding terrain as "a mixture of Connecticut semi-suburban and Pennsylvania professional farming" and the house itself as "early eighteenth-century Palladian and very old-South messy"; the gently crumbling interior and the blithely overgrown fields and gardens in which the house was set presented a comic and endearing challenge to his "New England creed that morality is tidiness." In August he wrote to Philip Booth, who was still summering in Castine:

After the first grindings, I think we are all much calmer, much happier than two years ago. But Peter Taylor wrote me (humorously) count no man happy till he's in his coffin. I think of Lizzie and Harriet hourly, yet the strain of the motor was shaking us all screwloose. Climate here is much like Castine, clouds by day and fires by night; I can see drifting sheep and cattle from my desk; this morning, two grouse on the walk—some of the same visitors, Blair, McCarthy, Bob Silvers —still, no ocean, no many summers-tried neighbours.[20]

All in all, though, Lowell enjoyed playing squire at Milgate: "He loved the idea," says Raban, "of being a gentleman with his own estates who lived in a house that had once belonged to the original Rosicrucian [Robert Fludd, 1574–1637], with all this eighteenth-century furniture and a desk looking out over a kind of Kent that Robert Lowell, squire and poet, might well have actually owned, as far as the eye could see. There was a terrific glamour in that for him."[21]

The squire, however, still had to earn his living, and Lowell was beginning to find his weekly trips to Essex University a slightly tiresome chore. In relation to Milgate, geographically, Colchester was nothing like as well placed as he describes it in his letters, although he did have a jokily simplified notion of the map of England:

He thought of England as totally circular. All places were simply beyond the other place. The starting point was London and then England was a direct straight line and all places were simply spread out on that line. Milgate was 40 miles away from London and Colchester was 60 miles from London—so Colchester must be 20 miles beyond Milgate.[22]

In fact, to get to Colchester from Kent by rail meant an hour's train ride to London, a change of stations, and then another hour's ride out of London. The trip from door to door could easily take more than four hours, and even by chauffeur-driven car (a method sometimes resorted to by Lowell!), it was an irksome journey. His real grumble, though, with the University of Essex was the low caliber of the students; he found most of them "inaudible and polite and sluggish":

> when I ask an Essex student if he doesn't think that Act Two Scene Four in Lear has most of the play's struggles, the students start mutely mumbling their text. How do you teach, if the students don't do your work? So, in life, in all things.[23]

Professor Edwards confesses that "academically, I don't know that you could call the arrangement a great success. I was very conscious that Essex wasn't Harvard and embarrassed that half our students hadn't even heard of him."[24] And Dudley Young, a colleague with whom Lowell often lodged on his one or two nights at Essex, says:

> The students were brash, unbuttoned and street-wise; and though suspicious of anyone as old or as famous as Lowell, they enjoyed telling him [Bob] Dylan's stuff was more important (an argument he would engage with some ferocity).[25]

According to Young, Lowell's "radical credentials, which would have appeared impeccable in 1967, were by then looking dubious to many"; also, several of Lowell's admirers on the faculty were uneasy about the *Notebook* poems. Edwards agrees: "I didn't much like the poetry he was writing at the time; it wasn't to my mind anything like as good as the poetry that made us invite him." Dudley Young, in his own words "a stripling of 30 and unquestionably hippoid," recalls nightly "blow-outs":

> Evening festivities in the first year were variously attended, by staff and students, and were not unlike those conducted by Delmore Schwartz, as transcribed by Bellow's *Humboldt*. At sub-manic velocity the man

was truly amazing, the range dazzling, the anecdotes endless and funny and fine. To bring us back from high talk, or just to silence some bore, he would ask Deg, my sagacious labrador, lying by the fire, what *he* thought; and there would follow a doggy discourse, regal and hilarious, usually along the line of "What fools these mortals be." Cal loved the dog, and these bouts of ventriloquism were altogether magical. But often, as the evening progressed the speed increased; and the mono-mania would sound, the language come unstuck, and we'd all go to pieces. With any luck it would then be bedtime.

Beneath the fun, never far away, was the seriousness; for they were seriously crazy times. Gradually, a resistance to milord's monomania developed amongst us, particularly in me, his manservant, more exposed to it than anyone else.[26]

There are others at Essex who recall Lowell's oppressive mono-logues, his rudeness and egotism; and even those who liked and valued him would not pretend that he had "fitted in." Gabriel Pearson, one of Lowell's best critics and a member of the Essex faculty, describes him as "seeming always submarine, as if he was looking out at the world through the windows of a fishtank,"[27] and Philip Edwards's most vivid recollection is of a myopic, displaced figure:

I can picture him now getting to the top of a flight of stairs in the university, gazing suspiciously to right and left, failing to recognize any landmarks and inevitably taking the wrong direction. We took him down to the saltings on the Colne estuary and he looked about him and said it reminded him of the coast of Maine.[28]

In his first term at Essex, in the late fall of 1970, Lowell found he had an extra student in one of his classes: Martha Ritter had indeed followed him to England. "He didn't know I was coming. I ap-peared in his class. It was very dramatic. He was wearing a tie I'd given him, but he had a ring on his left finger. It was very impulsive of me, but I'd been given every reason to feel that this was going to be picking up where we left off." Ritter too remembers Lowell as "out of place" at Essex:

he said that he had met a woman, and he couldn't decide whether or not to leave Lizzie. I had become a confidante, a person who he knew loved him deeply and would do anything for him. And I had lunch with him every day and we talked about which woman he should choose. It was a bit masochistic perhaps, but he was in really bad shape. So we would talk and talk and walk about the grounds of this place where nobody gave a damn about his existence, and asked him to analyze Beatle songs. It was horrible. He was aware of the pain that was being caused by this situation in me, and he was in pain himself, but I felt almost that he was dependent on me. I tried to be strong and kind, but I couldn't handle it and finally left.[29]

Sheridan Lowell was born on September 28, 1971. The last few days of Blackwood's pregnancy were tense; in fact, she was moved by "midnight ambulance" from the local hospital in Maidstone to University College Hospital in London because of possible complications. Throughout all this drama, Lowell had "continual nosebleeds for eight days" and in the end was himself sent to the hospital for tests: "It's my old wavery blood pressure . . . the blood goes high then drops—not with inner anguish but mysteriously. I guess it's not too serious. Like me."

During the week of Sheridan's birth, Lowell had a letter from Hardwick, which suggested that she had by now heard rumors about a "new book of poems" that made use of her letters, cables, and so on: during the summer, Lowell had shown the manuscript of *Dolphin* to several of his American summer visitors, and had asked advice about the rights and wrongs of publishing such intimate material. On September 29 he wrote back to Hardwick:

> I only partly understand your second paragraph about "recent shocks." One of course is my book, but it doesn't have a publication date, need not come out ever. It's not defamatory, it's like your *Notebook*, probably less astringent. My story is both a composition and alas, a rather grinding autobiography, what I lived, though of course one neither does or should tell the literal or ultimate truth. Poetry lies. I'll send it to you if you wish (when it's in neater shape), you won't feel betrayed or exploited but I can't imagine you'll want to scrape through the sadness and breakage now.[30]

He wrote again, on the same matter, two days later:

Whatever you do, don't burn *your* Notebook![31] I hope to live in it long after I'm dirt. What you showed me was some of your tenderest, and easiest writing. I wrote you that mine need not be published ever. It won't be published, but kept. I won't burn all but a few blue parts, so you mustn't. Maybe in calmer times we can publish the two books in one volume. I think in years to come, if we are still here, my poems will seem less disturbing to you. It's my best (last) work maybe—isn't an author always his own best critic? Particularly of a lately finished book.[32]

During the next week Lowell added more poems to *The Dolphin*, and was more and more tempted to at least toy with the possibility of publication. In December he wrote to Frank Bidart:

Could you come here after Christmas or early January: Here's the agenda, as Pound would say. My new book, the Dolphin about eighty poems, shorter than when you saw it, but with many new poems (it now ends in a long pregnancy and birth (one poem) sequence) everything endlessly rewritten, and about 40 poems about England statuary, demos, etc. taken out, not because they are bad but because they clog the romance 2. To find something to do with the rejected poems; they can't be a narrative, but could have a mounting drive of similarity. 3. Here's where I need you most; I've tried to reduce *Notebook* to personal narrative. Mostly the Historic, the metaphysical and the political go, though it keeps bits of each, then go the personal poems that fit well enough but are inflated, uninspired or redundant. I've done a sort of jerrybuilt first draft, and am not sure whether it works (half my new revision will go? etc) You can see how your advice and care would be unique and invaluable. This all began by trying to get round the mounting pressure on me not to publish The Dolphin (for moral reasons) And indeed, it must wait.[33]

Bidart arrived at the beginning of January and "ended up staying, I think, six weeks." By 1972 Lowell literally had more poems than he knew what to do with, and had also massively revised the whole of *Notebook;* for two years, he had been carrying around his copy of the English edition of *Notebook* and "he had been writing, in pencil, corrections and revisions and possible changes all over these poems, on every single page." He had become dissatisfied, according to Bidart, with the "aesthetic" of the book, its "whole desire for immediacy":

The aesthetic of *Notebook* had been very much connected to the whole desire for immediacy. It's not that [in 1967–68] he was interested in disposable poetry—but there had been that feeling that art can be much more connected to fleeting feelings, insights, perceptions, marginal half-thoughts and how all these bear down on one's life. . . . But I think that he was not at all happy with that aesthetic. And also he was simply not happy with the writing.[34]

Even so, Lowell felt that he could not now publish a *third Notebook* and, by the time Bidart arrived in England, had already begun to break the book up into at least two possible "new" volumes. He had culled fifty or so "historical" subjects from the book, revised them heavily, and put them into chronological order: this, he thought, might make a book called *Heroes*:

He had these separately typed, as I remember, and as we started going through them he started putting more *Notebook* poems into it and as it grew the title "Heroes" just seemed too narrow, and that became *History*. Essentially, almost everything that was not family poems from *Notebook* could go into *History*, and also the poems that didn't fit very well in *Dolphin*.[35]

The "family poems" would themselves make a book, and this Lowell decided to call *For Lizzie and Harriet*, even though it was to include, for example, the "Mexico" poems and other nonhistorical items which Lizzie and Harriet might reasonably feel were not addressed to their best interests. For example, Martha Ritter is the "dolphin" in the poem "Morning" (called "Dawn" in *Notebook*):

> In this ever more enlightened bedroom,
> I wake under the early rising sun,
> sex indelible flowers on the air—
> shouldn't I ask to hold to you forever,
> body of a dolphin, breast of cloud?
> You rival the renewal of the day,
> clearing the puddles with your green sack of books.[36]

Really, these are poems that "cover" the period of Lowell's personal life in which, whatever his vagaries, he continued to feel unshakably committed to his wife and daughter; in narrative terms, they prepare the ground for the anguished indecisions of the *Dolphin* tale. For most of the six weeks that Bidart stayed at Milgate the chief task was to turn *Notebook* into two polished, separate books. For the moment, the matter of the new *Dolphin* poems was postponed:

> The working pattern we developed was that I would cut sonnets out of a copy of *Notebook*—he would tell me which ones he wanted, in which order—and paper-clip them on to big legal-size sheets. . . . He would lie on his work-bed with his marked copy of *Notebook* and dictate across the room revisions which I would write in in the margin across from where the poem cut out from *Notebook* was paper-clipped. Usually he would dictate about four, one sheet, and then I would read them and we'd talk about them and argue about them. And sometimes he would change the order, or he would make more revisions, or sometimes he would go back to what he had before. There were some that we continued to argue about and that I never liked but most of them I liked a lot. I was always able to say just what I thought. I would be no use to him if I weren't. By this time he knew I adored his work, and I loved him, and he was just never insulted by that sort of thing. And Caroline would wander in and read something and she was always full of criticisms and suggestions. She never had the slightest hesitation in saying she didn't like something.[37]

When Bidart left, in February, "there was the text of *History* and *For Lizzie and Harriet* and *The Dolphin*. *The Dolphin* ended with the birth of Sheridan and essentially followed the real chronology of what happened—but I had much less to do with that than with the others." Bidart and Lowell did, however, discuss the problem of how, if ever, *The Dolphin* might be published: "it had to give Lizzie pain, he was very aware of that," to have these intensely private torments paraded in a poem, to see herself portrayed as the ousted, vengeful wife, to have snatches of her letters, telegrams, phone conversations used as the all too raw material for Lowell's lightly fictionalized drama of *his* indecision. And yet, as Bidart saw it, these were poems: "the only thing posterity will not forgive you for is a bad book." The idea was floated of a very limited edition—perhaps as few as one hundred copies—and some moves had indeed been made in this direction. Olwyn Hughes, sister of the poet Ted Hughes, had proposed publishing such an edition, and Lowell was for a time convinced that this was the best compromise.

During the spring of 1972 Lowell continued to fret about *The Dolphin*, but the worry was no longer about *if* the book should be published: what he was looking for was the least painful (for Hardwick) way to get the poems out. Letters from friends in America who had seen the version of *Dolphin* which Bidart had taken home with him were almost unanimously shocked that he should even think of releasing such material. In April, Stanley Kunitz wrote to him:

> As for *Dolphin*. I should be less than honest if I didn't tell you it both fascinates and repels me. There are details which seem to me monstrously heartless. I will grant that parts of it are marvelous—wild, erotic, shattering. (Who else had the nerve for such a document of enchantment and folly?) But some passages I can scarcely bear to read: they are too ugly, for being too cruel, too intimately cruel. You must know that after its hour has passed, even tenderness can cut the heart. What else need I say to you, dear Cal, not as your judge—God Save me! —but as your friend. In any event, these are matters that I have not discussed with another soul.[38]

(Lowell responded to these strictures with what Norman Mailer would certainly have seen as an example of "neutralsmanship"—he offered to dedicate the book *History* to Kunitz, who was moved to reply: "What could I cherish more. . . . if you were here, I would embrace you."[39] The dedication in the end was to both Kunitz and Bidart, in spite of a plea from Elizabeth Bishop that Lowell dedicate it solely "to Frank . . . he has worked so damn hard. When he came back here last winter I don't think he thought of anything else for months—he used to call me up and recite sonnets and sonnets from memory, re-arranging lines and commas and so on—it's fantastic.")[40]

Bishop herself had strong views on *The Dolphin*, in its first version, and on March 21, 1972, wrote:

> Dearest Cal:
>   I've been trying to write you this letter for weeks now, ever since Frank & I spent an evening when he first got back, reading and discussing THE DOLPHIN. I've read it many times since then & we've discussed it some more. Please believe I think it is wonderful poetry. It seems to me far and away better than the NOTEBOOKS; every 14 lines have some marvels of image and expression, and also they are all much *clearer*. They affect me immediately and profoundly, and I'm pretty sure I understand them all perfectly. . . . It's hell to write this, so please first

do believe I think DOLPHIN is magnificent poetry. It is also honest poetry —almost. You probably know already what my reactions are. I have one tremendous and awful BUT.

If you were any other poet I can think of I certainly wouldn't attempt to say anything at all; I wouldn't think it was worth it. But because it is you, and a great poem (I've never used the word "great" before, that I remember), and I love you a lot—I feel I must tell you what I really think. There are several reasons for this—some are worldly ones, and therefore secondary (& strange to say, they seem to be the ones Bill [Alfred] is most concerned about—we discussed it last night) but the primary reason is because I love you so much I can't bear to have you publish something that I regret and that you might live to regret, too. The worldly part of it is that it—the poem—parts of it—may well be taken up and used against you by all the wrong people—who are just waiting in the wings to attack you.—One shouldn't consider them, perhaps. But it seems wrong to play right into their hands, too.

(Don't be alarmed. I'm not talking about the whole poem—just one aspect of it.)

Here is a quotation from dear little Hardy that I copied out years ago —long before DOLPHIN, or even the *Notebooks,* were thought of. It's from a letter written in 1911, referring to "an abuse which was said to have occurred—that of publishing details of a lately deceased man's life under the guise of a novel, with assurances of truth scattered in the newspapers." (Not exactly the same situation as DOLPHIN, but fairly close.)

"What should certainly be protested against, in cases where there is no authorization, is the mixing of fact and fiction in unknown proportions. Infinite mischief would lie in that. If any statements in the dress of fiction are covertly hinted to be fact, all must be fact, and nothing else but fact, for obvious reasons. The power of getting lies believed about people through that channel after they are dead, by stirring in a few truths, is a horror to contemplate."

I'm sure my point is only too plain . . . Lizzie is not dead, etc.—but there is a "mixture of fact & fiction," and you have *changed* her letters. That is "infinite mischief," I think. The first one, page 10, is so shocking —well, I don't know what to say. And page 47 . . . and a few after that. One can use one's life a [*sic*] material—one does, anyway—but these letters—aren't you violating a trust? IF you were given permission—IF you hadn't changed them . . . etc. *But art just isn't worth that much.* I keep remembering Hopkins' marvellous letter to Bridges about the idea of a "gentleman" being the highest thing ever conceived—higher than a "Christian" even, certainly than a poet. It is not being "gentle" to use personal, tragic, anguished letters that way—it's cruel.[41]

In England, Lowell was also soliciting advice: he wanted to see how the poems appeared to people for whom Hardwick's feelings would not be of personal concern. In March he wrote to Christopher Ricks, the British critic and scholar; Lowell and Ricks had become friends since their first meeting in May 1970:

> My book problems are complicated and I would like to ask your advice. My new book is a small one, some eighty poems in the meter of Notebook—the story of changing marriages, not a malice or sensation, far from it, but necessarily, according to my peculiar talent, very personal. Lizzie is naturally very much against it. I am considering publication in about a year; it needn't be published, but I feel clogged by the possibility of not. This awkward exposition shows my painful embarrassment.[42]

In April, Lowell invited the British poet Alan Brownjohn to Milgate for a weekend; Brownjohn had written admiringly of *Notebook* in the *New Statesman*. At this first—and, for Brownjohn, uneasy—weekend ("It was like being invited down to visit Milton or Chaucer or someone") the *Dolphin* issue wasn't raised, but in May Lowell wrote to him that "My ms. problem is this: a book of a little over 60 poems about the last two years, the end of my old marriage and then the beginning. I suppose what you are so expert on (truth of tone) is all-important."[43] Brownjohn then called at Redcliffe Square:

> After I'd been I had the impression that he was enormously determined to get a number of views on the decorum of publishing some of these personal poems about Elizabeth. I gather he'd taken that dilemma around to several people. When I got to Redcliffe Square on that particular day [June 6, 1972] I realized it wasn't just a question of making a few comments on the new poems he'd been writing. There was the question of the propriety of publishing these kinds of transcribed telephone conversations or letters. He asked that question fairly outright and said, "These are poems written straight out of verbatim letters, and I've talked to one or two people and some people say they shouldn't be published in that form. What do you think?" And I think in sheer nerves, reading the photocopied drafts as he set them in front of me, I said, "I think it's all right." I suppose if pressed I would have defended this by saying there is a kind of entitlement of poets to transmute, to use any kind of material that life, personal and public, offers them. And if Lowell isn't entitled to do this, who is? . . . It seemed to me he clearly wanted to do

it and one didn't feel like saying no on behalf of someone one had never met.[44]

Jonathan Raban was another "detached" English figure whose advice Lowell solicited. Raban remembers "egging him on to do it. . . . I was really out of what the effect in New York would be": he suggested to Lowell that perhaps he could "test" the American reaction by letting Faber put the book out first in England:

> I was very much on the side of publishing, because it seemed to me that *Dolphin* wouldn't really be a book at all if it didn't have that suggestion of documentary, and fragments of other people's conversations and letters. I thought they were some of the best poems in the book. So, for literature's sake, the book ought to be published in exactly the way he'd written it and not edited out of fear of what Lizzie was going to say.[45]

Raban, like Brownjohn, felt that Lowell had made up his mind; "he loved the feeling of being vulnerable to everybody else's advice and criticism." As early as April 1972 he had begun revising and rearranging the *Dolphin* poems with a view to publication. He had been stung by Elizabeth Bishop's letter, and also by Bill Alfred's view that certain of the poems "will tear Elizabeth [Hardwick] apart, important though I agree they are to the wholeness of the book. I have to say that." Alfred also reported in this letter (March 12, 1972) that he had just met W. H. Auden for the first time: "He spoke of not speaking to you because of the book. When I said he sounded like God the Father, he gave me a tight smile. I write to warn you."[46] Lowell was indignant about this—"How could he stop speaking to me about a book he hadn't seen"—and cabled Auden: DEAR WYSTAN ASTOUNDED BY YOUR INSULT TO ME WITH WILLIAM ALFRED.[47]

On April 10 Lowell wrote to Frank Bidart that he intended to modify *Dolphin;* principally, he had decided to move Sheridan's birth forward in the narrative, so that it would appear that the new child was a factor in his Christmas, 1970, dilemma. He had also made other, softening alterations:

> I've read and long thought on Elizabeth's [Bishop's] letter. It's a kind of masterpiece of criticism, though her extreme paranoia (for God's sake don't repeat this) about revelations gives it a wildness. Most people will

feel something of her doubts. The terrible thing isn't the mixing of fact and fiction, but the wife pleading with her husband to return—this backed by 'documents'. So far I've done this much: 1) most important —shift *Burden* before *Leaving America* and *Flight to New York.* This strangely makes Lizzie more restful and gracious about the "departure." I haven't changed a word to this effect, but one assumes she knows about the baby's birth. *Burden* now begins with *Sickday* and I think gains much by the baby's birth not being the climax. 2) Several of the early letters, From my Wife, are now cut up into Voices (often using such title) (changing mostly pronouns) as if I were speaking and paraphrasing or repeating Lizzie. Most of the later letters I haven't been able to change much or at all. 3) Changes for my style, not to do with this business.

Now the book must still be painful to Lizzie, and won't satisfy Elizabeth. As Caroline says, it can't be otherwise with the book's donnee. However, even fairly small changes make Lizzie less a documented presence. A distinct, even idiosyncratic voice isn't the same as someone, almost fixed as non-fictional evidence, that you could call on the phone. She dims slightly and Caroline and I somewhat lengthen. I know this doesn't make much sense, but that's the impression I get reading through the whole. Then Sheridan is somewhat a less forced and climactic triumph; as E's problem of the getting back to England and into pregnancy is gone, and the very end of *Flight,* with the shark is less Websterian and Poeish.[48]

Bidart was against the proposed change of structure, feeling that "it blurred the dramatic movement of the poem. You know, the Christmas thing does feel different if you imagine him coming back to America having already had a child with Caroline. There was much more sense in the original that it was a real crisis, a real question of whether he might stay."[49] Lowell, though, was firm on this point: "The thing is," he wrote on May 15, "I *must* shift the structure and somehow blunt and angle the letters."[50] He had promised Faber, he said, that he would have the manuscripts of all three books *(History, For Lizzie and Harriet* and *Dolphin)* by August, and he again asked Bidart to help with the final revisions.

when I got to England in June, he still wanted to make this structural change but also, he had done an enormous amount of rewriting. And I felt that the structural change, when I read it with all these revisions, was possible. It did change the book, but it didn't wreck it. And in the earlier version, which ended with the birth of Sheridan, it had come out a little bit like a happy ending, and that was somewhat of a problem. On the other hand, it did make the book less a drama. The emotional movement is somewhat murky.[51]

In September, Lowell wrote to William Alfred that baby Sheridan had learned to walk and was destructive, "even to books, and even after Milton appeared to him in a vision saying: 'If you kill a man you only kill a body, but if you destroy a book you destroy an immortal soul.' " *The Dolphin,* muted and "written much better—both for art and kindness," was scheduled for publication in summer, 1973.[52]

24

The winter of 1971–72 was later remembered by Lowell as one of his most momentous and chaotic. There had, of course, been Sheridan's birth and the problems (both textual and moral) of *The Dolphin*. In addition, there were two worrying domestic dramas. In October 1971 a general handyman at Milgate suddenly became "violent, almost insane, with many unpleasant side-effects. We were left with two little girls, a boy still at the breast, and a large, somewhat remote country house—all rather spooky for a week or so, but now over, I think."[1] And in January 1972 Lowell's stepdaughter Ivana (now aged six) overturned a kettle of boiling water and was badly burned; she spent three months in the hospital, where Lowell visited her several times and marveled at her courage. Children had always rather bored him; now, after two years of being surrounded by small girls, he found himself willing to concede that they could have an unreal kind of attractiveness—as curiosities, however, rather than as bona fide humans:

> Small-soul-pleasing, loved with condescension,
> even through the cro-magnon tirades of six,
> the last madness of child-gaiety
> before the trouble of the world shall hit.
> Being chased upstairs is still instant-heaven,
> . . . .
> Though burned, you are hopeful, experience cannot tell you
> experience is what you do not want to experience.[2]

Throughout this same winter, Lowell had been making the first moves towards a divorce settlement with Elizabeth Hardwick.

In October, just three days after Sheridan was born, he wrote to her:

> On the will—I mean the settlement—can't your friendly lawyer draw up what seems right, and then I without a lawyer will object to what I wish to. I'd like to avoid lawyer costs. Though I pay less than my share, my expenses for the baby are heavy, will be. Also my royalties for this half [?] were only a little over $4000—with $7000 last spring. This give [*sic*] me only 11 or 12 thousand. A drop? Or is there some catch? On the other hand I'll have 140 thousand in trust from Harvard. Oh I'm well enough off.[3]

The Harvard money Lowell speaks of here would come as a result of the sale of his papers to the Houghton Library—all his manuscript material and letters up to 1968. Lowell's American royalties during the period 1965–70 had risen from $6,500 to over $15,000 (*Life Studies* and *For the Union Dead* were his best-selling volumes): the "11 or 12 thousand" he mentions in this letter was therefore a slight falling off. Also, his income from poetry readings had necessarily declined: in Britain the fees for such appearances were tiny, and some of the grander colleges expected their poets to perform for nothing. With teaching, Lowell could probably depend on a minimum earned income of $20,000. He was "well enough off," but he would have to work.

Formal divorce proceedings began in September 1972, shortly after Lowell delivered to his publishers the manuscripts of his three books. Dealings with Hardwick through the year had been "cordial," and of Harriet's visit at Milgate for eight days in the summer Lowell wrote: "We had the loveliest time, as though she were the same and a grown-up, very young and humorous and kind to her father. We exaggerate the forks made by our choices, or do we?"[4]

In October, Lowell and Blackwood flew to New York. A financial agreement had been drawn up (with Blair Clark's help): essentially, it gave Hardwick and Harriet most of the income from Lowell's trust fund—some $20,000 a year. Hardwick would also get the New York apartment together with "all tangible personal property—furnishings, works of art, household goods." As soon as the papers were signed, Lowell and Blackwood flew on to Santo Domingo for a package divorce/marriage. Lady Caroline explains:

We got married there for technical reasons. It can be done very quickly. You get divorced the same day and then they hurry you to the wedding, which is in a sort of shed. Talk about lack of solemnity. It doesn't make you feel panic, because it doesn't feel at all like a marriage. Blair Clark arranged the whole thing—it's terribly expensive. You go on this honeymoon flight, people who don't want to get divorced, people who aren't going to get married to someone else. So it's a very sinister flight, in a sense. We stayed in Santo Domingo for a couple of days. It was lovely there. It's a place with grotesque hotels and wonderful rum punches, and the most frightening-looking men you've ever seen—international crooks. Cal loved it, because it was so mad. It's so laid-on, like a package tour—a limousine meets the plane, takes you straight to the place where you get divorced—it was a double divorce, of course, because I was divorcing Israel. The limousine waits and then on to the marriage, which was just a shed with a lot of people typing. They typed all through our marriage. There was no pretense. The typing didn't stop at all, deafening typing. And the ceremony is in Spanish, of course.[5]

The newlyweds arrived back in England in November (they were to be known as "Robert and Lady Caroline Lowell," he announced), and Sonia Orwell gave them a wedding party in London. Lowell commented on this: "I feel we should appear in black mourning the disgrace of lost alimony, like soldiers who lose a redout [*sic*]. But we've gained more than I can say by the divorce —more than I can say because so much of it is undefinable comfort of mind."[6] Even so, he said he felt

taken by the divorce settlement, though there was nothing I could do about it. And perhaps anyway after the divorce I am drained of anything to say. I must keep up with her [Hardwick] to keep up with Harriet— and a thousand good memories. All cancelled? No, probably just my mood today.[7]

In May 1973 Lowell was still nursing this mild sense of grievance over what he called "a barracuda settlement," and he was resentful also that Hardwick was planning to sell the Castine house—on this, he hesitated for a time over signing a necessary deed:

I don't intend to hold up the deed, much, but it's naturally sad for me to have the house sold. What are you getting? Should I let it go without worries and suggestions, as if it had only been air to me?

Also I must have things, personal things, like the eagle, country clothes etc. Not worth much but dear, if I were to see them I would recognize them. I have no legal right to ask this.[8]

And again, five days later:

it's a desolate thought that all I have from the past is grandpa's gold watch and some fifteen books. . . . I am not trying to hold you up more than I have written (except why should I sign away my claim to all my Castine property? The barn isn't being sold.) I am rather irritated about this being sprung on me suddenly.[9]

Perhaps it comforted Lowell that he might have a legitimate grievance against Hardwick; he knew that in July *The Dolphin* would be published, and that there would surely be a scandal. He hoped that for those with no personal involvement his three books (*The Dolphin* was published simultaneously with *History* and *For Lizzie and Harriet*) would be read simply as books, and that praise of the poetry might outweigh the human blame. In fact, the books mostly *were* reviewed as books, but not with quite the warmth that Lowell seems to have expected. There was much agreement that his revisions were improvements, although Calvin Bedient in the *New York Times Book Review* was alert to "repeated reversals of meaning [which] create the sinking impression that all is arbitrary. 'Often the player's outdistanced by the game' runs a line in *Notebook*; 'often the player outdistances the game' runs the revision."[10] As Jonathan Raban has observed, Lowell's revisions were usually

a kind of gaming with words, treating them like billiard balls. For almost every sentence that Cal ever wrote if he thought it made a better line he'd have put in a "never" or a "not" at the essential point. His favorite method of revision was simply to introduce a negative into a line, which absolutely reversed its meaning but very often would improve it. So that his poem on Flaubert ended with Flaubert dying, and in the first draft it went "Till the mania for phrases dried his heart"—a quotation from Flaubert's mother. Then Cal saw another possibility and it came out: "Till the mania for phrases enlarged his heart." It made perfectly good sense either way round, but the one did happen to mean the opposite of the other.[11]

Few reviewers seemed to mind about this kind of thing; the general line was "if the poems taken from *Notebook* are improved, they are at least more perfectly imperfect." On *The Dolphin*, however, the "disinterested" critics were less charitable: there was widespread impatience with the book's "half fiction" indecisiveness. In *Poetry* Stephen Yenser wrote:

> "Half fiction": the phrase, whether intended to exculpate others or not, betrays a concern, felt throughout, that might be thought irrelevant. It makes little difference to the principals whether it happened, one would think, but only whether it were true. Just as no amount of fictionalizing could diminish the actual anguish, so no amount of such anguish can create the necessary fiction. My own doubt has nothing in common with the silly complaint lodged anonymously (in a "scouring voice of 1930 Oxford") against Yeats and Proust in one of these poems, that some things are too "personal" to be published, but arises from the feeling that *The Dolphin* is more gossip (fact, data, raw material) than gospel (parable, pattern, truth). Lowell's sequence is so relentlessly documented (even if the documents are doctored, as the familiar style of the quotations from letters and conversations itself suggests) that the pattern of experience cannot emerge.[12]

The *Sewanee Review* was even more dismissive, caricaturing Lowell's stance as "Here are the facts, dreams, events, whatever; I present them; they are unimportant, incomprehensible and boring," and deciding that, yes, "poetically, they are"—Lowell's "famous talent is everywhere manifested: the poems are not given a chance."[13] And even a sympathetic reviewer like William Pritchard in the *Hudson Review* felt obliged to concede that "one should feel uneasy about this, should say at some point, yes Lowell has finally gone too far; you can't turn life into literature twenty minutes or a year later; many of these sonnets are almost inaudible, don't rise above a private mumble, resist being dragged into the social relationship of poet and reader."[14]

The field was thus wide open for the "personal" reviews, and in this category the most savage onslaught came from Adrienne Rich, at one time a close friend of Lowell's but they had been out of touch for years. In June 1971 Rich had written to Lowell reproaching him for his treatment of Hardwick; at that time, she probably had no knowledge of the poems he was writing, and certainly did not know of any plans to publish them:

I feel we are losing touch with each other, which I don't want. . . .

I feel a kind of romanticism in your recent decisions, a kind of sexual romanticism with which it is very hard for me to feel sympathy . . . my affection and admiration for Elizabeth make it difficult to be debonair about something which—however good for her it may ultimately be—has made her suffer.[15]

In the September–October 1973 issue of the *American Poetry Review* Rich wrote as follows:

There's a kind of aggrandized and merciless masculinity at work in these books. . . .

Finally, what does one say about a poet who, having left his wife and daughter for another marriage, then titles a book with their names, and goes on to appropriate his ex-wife's letters written under the stress and pain of desertion, into a book of poems nominally addressed to the new wife? If this kind of question has nothing to do with art, we have come far from the best of the tradition Lowell would like to vindicate—or perhaps it cannot be vindicated. At the end of *The Dolphin* Lowell writes:

> I have sat and listened to too many
> words of the collaborating muse,
> and plotted perhaps too freely with my life,
> not avoiding injury to others,
> not avoiding injury to myself—
> to ask compassion . . . this book, half fiction,
> an eelnet made by man for the eel fighting—
>
> my eyes have seen what my hand did.

I have to say that I think this is bullshit eloquence, a poor excuse for a cruel and shallow book, that it is presumptuous to balance injury done to others with injury done to myself—and that the question remains, after all—to what purpose? The inclusion of the letter poems stands as one of the most vindictive and mean-spirited acts in the history of poetry, one for which I can think of no precedent: and the same unproportioned ego that was capable of this act is damagingly at work in all three of Lowell's books.[16]

Adrienne Rich's review was the most vehement statement of the prosecution case, and Lowell was able to rationalize its intense tone as a symptom of Rich's dogmatic feminism: in conversation, though, he would refer to it time and again—it always unnerved him to make enemies of friends. For Hardwick, of course, these weeks of publication were acutely painful; her conduct, and her suffering, had been set up for idle public comment—the humblest of hack book reviewers was entitled to muse on the half-fiction characters of "Harriet" and "Lizzie" and to ask which bits of letters were "real" bits, which burst of scolding dialogue was "fact," and so on. One review, by Marjorie Perloff in the *New Republic*, even went so far as to venture half-judgments on the half-real personalities presented in the poem:

> Poor Harriet emerges from these passages as one of the most unpleasant child figures in history . . . her cloying moral virtue. It is therefore difficult to participate in the poet's vacillation, for Lizzie and Harriet seem to get no more than they deserve. And since these are, after all, real people, recently having lived through the crisis described, one begins to question Lowell's tone.[17]

This piece infuriated Hardwick: now, it seemed, the sixteen-year-old Harriet was to be morally examined in the intellectual weeklies. "I never want to hear from you again," she told Lowell,[18] and she wrote letters to his English and American publishers denouncing them as "contemptible." Robert Giroux recalls: "She said I should have checked out permissions. I hadn't, for the simple reason I had no idea they were her letters. It seemed to me a strictly personal matter between him and her. I hadn't known until after *Life Studies* was published that "To Speak of Woe That Is in Marriage" made use of private letters or conversation, and no one objected."[19] Lowell wrote her calming, hopeful letters: "Most of the hurting reviews . . . will look very dim by September. . . . I'm sorry I brought this on you, the ghastly transient voices, the lights";[20] "I can't defend myself too much, or anyway shouldn't at this moment if I could. Nothing in the books was dishonestly intended. . . . I think I am living through many of your feelings. I suffer."[21] Sensibly, Hardwick decided to take a vacation at Lake Como. As for Harriet, she had been at Milgate while the worst of the American reviews were coming out, and by the end of July had set off with a friend to bicycle around in Ireland; according to Lowell, she thought "the trouble was over an imaginary real estate dispute—long since settled in Lizzie's favor."[22]

In Britain, Lowell claimed, *The Dolphin* was "just another book of poems," and to Blair Clark he wrote in injured tones:

> I have hardly had one real, uninsulting review in America, but many of the English are all that I could ask—comparisons with Yeats' last poems. Well, that's secondary—I feel rather like one of the black scorched grasshoppers in Hemingway's fishing story—burned by notoriety.[23]

In the same letter, he discusses his plans for returning to Harvard in September; he had rented a house in Brookline and would resume his old teaching pattern (Elizabeth Bishop had been filling in for him since 1970). On August 31 he wrote to William Alfred:

> It does seem strange returning. The summer tho quiet has been worrying. I am afraid relations with Lizzie are broken off; at least I haven't heard from her for about two months. The reviews fanned the fire, but I now think the exposure of publication was bound to do it. . . . I do think the business is blowing away. Was it Calvin or Harry Levin that said acting is a choice of evils. It so often is in little things (that makes them so irritating) then every so often something big is. I must have been right to publish. How could I know?[24]

Even so, there was a certain exhilaration in the idea of reappearing at the scene of his most recent crime; he was looking forward to "students who talk," he said, to his "long religious and gossipy talks" with Alfred, and to the loyal companionship of Frank Bidart. On September 7 he and his English family would arrive in Boston: "weary, plane-squashed, all ages, hardly able to speak our language."[25]

In Lowell's August 31 letter to William Alfred there is a note of both exhaustion and relief, as if a reckless and turbulent chapter of his life had been heroically survived. He had left his country, he had signed away his wealth, he had risked the condemnation of his dearest friends: the worst, he now might think, was over—and literally "the worst." Even Lowell could not imagine misdemeanors grander or more comprehensive than those already lived through, or inflicted. Now he could count the profit and the loss in the "familiar air" of Harvard:

> The summer's end and the month's end, and now the English heat wave has so far retired that my hands are still and cold as I write. In a week we will be in Brookline. Harvard seems a recovered universe; if I looked in the mirror, I imagine I would have the white beard of father time.
>
> I don't know why I am writing you this way. From not having written verse perhaps.[26]

For nearly seven years Lowell had written only "sonnets"; between September and December 1973 he wrote nine poems in a relaxed, almost meandering free verse:[27] "single poems in short free verse lines about being 56–57."[28] They were also about returning from exile (indeed, one of them was a rewriting of a poem from *Lord Weary's Castle* called "Exile's Return"); the poet sees himself as Ulysses "circling" the geography of the life he left behind:

> He circles as a shark circles
> visibly in the window—
> flesh-vain, sore-eyed, scar-vain,
> a vocational killer
> foretasting the apogee of mayhem,
> breaking water to strike his wake.

The colors in these new poems are autumnal: "firm brown and yellow, / the all-weather color for death"; "I cannot read everything I've written, / it's a greenless brown"; "things wrong / clothe summer / in gold leaf." And in all of them there is an elegiac, penitential note:

> Past fifty, we learn
> with surprise and a sense
> of suicidal absolution
> that what we intended and failed
> could never have happened—
> and must be done better.

He writes to his parents, as if for one last time attempting to resolve their ancient quarrels. In "To Mother" he writes:

> I've come home a third time to your Boston,
> I almost lifted the phone to dial you
> forgetting you have no dial. . . .

> Your exaggerating humor,
> the opposite of deadpan
> and so unfunny to a son, is mine now . . .
>
> It has taken the years since you died to discover
> you are as human as I am. . . .

And there are two linked poems: "What We Were" (a monologue spoken by his father) and "Before We Are," his own middle-aged address to Sheridan—"Three ages are a moment, / the same child in the same picture, / he, I, you, / chockablock, one stamp. . . ." To his old friend Peter Taylor he addresses "The Afterlife," which, in a letter to Blair Clark, he rightly calls "about the grandest" of the group. In this poem the drastically shortened lines seem, and are probably meant to seem, a symptom of the poet's shortened breath, his diminished aspirations:

> Southcall—
> a rival couple
> two Tennessee cardinals
> in green December outside my window
> dart and tag and mate—
> young as they want to be.
> I'm not;
> my second fatherhood
> and four years in England
> have made my friends and connections
> twenty years older.
> We are dangerously happy,
> our book-fed faces
> streak like the red birds,
> dart unstably
> ears cocked to catch
> the first shy whisper of deafness.
> This one year killed
> Pound, Wilson, Marianne Moore and Auden;
> the daughters and nieces lose their bloom,
> the inheritors grow
> large and red on middle-age,
> like red roses
> nodding, nodding, nodding.
> Peter, in our boyish years,
> 30 to 45,

when Cupid was still the Christ of love's religion,
time stood on its hands.

Sleight-of-hand.

Of the deaths that Lowell lists here, the one that mattered most
to him was Pound's, and in January 1973 he had spoken at a Pound
memorial gathering in New York:

> It's not my duty as fellow poet, critic and his friend to defend or clear
> Pound's record. I can't see him as a bad man, except in the ways we all
> are. I do see him as a generous man to other artists, and this in a way
> none of us will touch. The Broadcast smears seem, if not acts of madness,
> at least acts of dementia and obsession. . . .[29]

In the same speech he recalled his last meeting with Pound in
Rapallo, in March 1965 (when he himself had been fleeing to Egypt
in the wake of the Vija Vetra upheaval). Pound was "emaciated, neat
in blacks and whites, silver beard, he looked like the covers of one
of his own books, or like an El Greco, some old mural, aristocratic
and flaking."

> He held up his blotched, thinned away hands, and said, as if he were
> joking at them, "The worms are getting to me." Later, I must have said
> something about Hamilton or Pennsylvania College, where he had stud-
> ied. He said "Yes, I started with a swelled head and end with swelled
> feet." He was thinking of Oedipus. I said, "You are one of the few living
> men, who has walked through Purgatory." Watching me like a cat, and
> catching my affectation and affection, he answered, "Didn't Frost say
> you'd say anything once—for the hell of it?"[30]

Pound was almost the last of Lowell's revered "elders." A year
before, there had been the suicide of John Berryman, certainly the
last of Lowell's "generically" doomed generation. Berryman had
jumped to his death (aged fifty-seven) from a bridge over the Missis-
sippi near the University of Minnesota. The papers said: "Mr. Berryman apparently left no note, and the only identification on his
body was his name on a pair of glasses and a blank check." A
malicious joke (said by many to have originated with Auden) was
that Berryman *did* leave a note. It read simply: "Your move, Cal."

If Lowell never heard the joke, he did respond to the spirit of it, and in his elegy for Berryman he wrote:

> I used to want to live
> to avoid your elegy.
> Yet really we had the same life,
> the generic one
> our generation offered. . . .
>
> We asked to be obsessed with writing,
> and we were. . . .
>
> You got there first.
> Just the other day,
> I discovered how we differ—humor . . .
> even in this last *Dream Song,*
> to mock your catlike flight
> from home to classes—
> to leap from the bridge.[31]

In an obituary article in the *New York Review* Lowell says of Berryman that in recent years "as he became more inspired and famous and drunk, more and more John Berryman, he became less good company and more a happening," and he describes their last meeting in New York:

I met John last a year or so ago at Christmas in New York. He had been phoning poems and invitations to people at three in the morning, and I felt a weariness about seeing him. Since he had let me sleep uncalled, I guess he felt numbness to me. We met one noon during the taxi strike at the Chelsea Hotel, dusty with donated, avant-garde constructs, and dismal with personal recollections, Bohemia, and the death of Thomas. There was no cheerful restaurant within walking distance, and the seven best bad ones were closed. We settled for the huge, varnished unwelcome of an empty cafeteria-bar. John addressed me with an awareness of his dignity, as if he were Ezra Pound at St. Elizabeth's, emphatic without pertinence, then brownly inaudible.

His remarks seemed guarded, then softened into sounds that only he could understand or hear. At first John was ascetically hung over, at the end we were high without assurance, and speechless. I said, "When will I see you again?" meaning, in the next few days before I flew to England.

John said, "Cal, I was thinking through lunch that I'll never see you again." I wondered how in the murk of our conversation I had hurt him, but he explained that his doctor had told him one more drunken binge would kill him. Choice? It is blighting to know that this fear was the beginning of eleven months of abstinence . . . half a year of prolific rebirth, then suicide.[32]

For four years Lowell had felt himself to be reborn, but by 1974 the persistent obsession is with death. The comparison of *The Dolphin* with the last poems of Yeats had been both heartening and chilling. Lowell had grown his white hair long, and friends were disturbed by his willingness to *seem* old: his white mane unkempt, his movements effortful, his clothes those of a man who has stopped caring how he looks. In spite of all this, though, Lowell monitored his own health and the health of his friends with a kind of fatalistic dread: "As we get older," he wrote to Frank Bidart, "we are incurables." Peter Taylor had had a heart attack, and in the first months of 1974 there was "a deluge of strokes, Hannah Arendt in Scotland, Lillian Hellman in Paris, Frank [Parker] in Cambridge. I'm afraid the strain of giving up cigarettes is suicidal."

In January 1974 Lowell and his family returned to England, and Lowell revised his new poems for magazine publication in the spring. In April he visited America again, for a reading tour of Southern colleges—"Vanderbilt, Charlottesville, South Carolina, Washington, almost all the south"—and when he returned to London, there was yet another death, this time unsettlingly close to home: "When we got back we discovered that Israel [Citkovitz] did not answer his telephone. The fire brigade broke into his flat because the police refused and he was found dead in his bed."[33] Citkovitz had had a stroke earlier in the year and had been partly paralyzed and in the hospital for weeks; Lowell had seen him there and had found him "Ten years older in an hour." A fond, low-key elegy called "In the Ward" has an almost conspiratorial ring:

> You are very frightened by the ward,
> your companions are chosen for age;
> you are the youngest
> and sham-flirt with your nurse—

> your chief thought is scheming
> the elaborate surprise of your escape.
>
> Being old in good times is worse
> than being young in the worst.[34]

To William Alfred, Lowell wrote: "I don't think you ever met Israel Citkovitz, Caroline's former husband. He died of a stroke about two weeks ago, not unexpected—maddening, grotesque, rather lovely man. We have lived in the world of his death."[35] And then, as if in some rehearsed drama, July brought the death of Lowell's Kenyon mentor, John Crowe Ransom. Ransom had been ill for some time, so his death also was "not unexpected." Its timing, though, helped to plunge Lowell even more deeply into a "grey blank." He wrote to Peter Taylor:

> John's death. It does seem right, right that his death should show an untroubling anyone courtesy [Ransom died in his sleep, aged 86]. . . . He was my teacher and kept me from breaking myself. I'm struggling to write on him.[36]

Taylor was also low and fearful after his heart attack, and Lowell writes to him as a companion in "death's shadow":

> In depression and even more in travelling, I too go over my life trying to understand it—I think in a way, I never understood it, that it is addition not to be understood just completed. . . . Yet I can't live that way, must live with a point to be reached—even a reward card to be won.[37]

In October 1974 Lowell was at a party given by the London publisher George Weidenfeld. He was not drinking; indeed, to aid in this latest of several efforts to renounce alcohol, he was taking the drug Antabuse. On October 9 he writes again to Taylor:

> The other night at a large party I suddenly felt an acute nausea as if I had been drinking heavily, then a rather comforting feeling of changing inside to ice, then I was being rolled about by six merry people on a low table, like a gentle practical joke. I had fainted. It may have been from accidentally drinking something like vodka and orange juice, or it may

not. The doctors can't tell. Anyway it's not serious but it made me feel
close to you. I've written you a second poem about this and about the
years that brought us to now. . . .[38]

The poem read, in part, as follows—Lowell revised it for book
publication:

> My thinking is talking to you—
> last night I fainted at dinner
> and came nearer to your sickness,
> nearer the angels in nausea.
> The room turned upside-down;
> I was my interrupted sentence,
> an accident tumbled alive
> on a low, cooling black table.
> . . . .
> 1974,
> the Common Market,
> the dwarf-Norman fruit-tree
> espaliered to the wall—
> the old boys drop like wasps
> from windowsill and pane.
> This year for the first time,
> even cows seem transitory.
> The Psalmist's glass-mosaic Shepherd
> and bright green pastures
> seem *art nouveau* for our funeral.[39]

And around the same time, Lowell wrote a similar reminiscing,
near-elegiac poem to Frank Parker; it recalls their early friendship
at St. Mark's, the high ambitions they evolved during their 1935
summer at Nantucket: "I want to write," "I want to paint":

> We once claimed alliance with the Redskin. . . .
> What is won by losing,
> if two glasses of red wine are poison?[40]

After his fainting attack, Lowell was examined by a London heart
specialist and "was cleared of any heart trouble, as earlier of lung
trouble,"[41] but for weeks afterwards he brooded on the incident. In

December he responded reassuringly to concerned letters from Elizabeth Hardwick—"my heart and lungs are completely cleared by science. Nothing is durable or easy-moving at our age"[42]—but to Taylor he continued to dwell on symptoms of decline:

> For several years I haven't felt my "true self." Most embarrassing, when I get out of one of the large taxis, the driver sometimes asks if I need help; I take stairs too with a considered seriousness, I forget names and faces as always only more; if I give someone a comic name . . . I am liable to think it is his name. I forget things, have no memory of where I put my cigarette lighter after a few minutes, no recollection even after I find it irrationally lying on a distant bureau. I act, as all flesh must, my age.[43]

In October, Lowell was also writing of "troubled times with the stock market and with Caroline. She is having what we call an acute nervous depression." He would go to Harvard in the spring without her—"I don't think we are up to the great expense and weight of moving our whole family to Cambridge"—but he was also now pondering the possibility of a permanent move back to the United States: "There's the now insoluble question of whether we should live in England or come to America where I can earn and make connections. Well, this will solve itself?" In December it was decided that Blackwood and the children would, after all, join him for the Harvard spring semester, and she flew over to Boston for a week to look at houses. On December 14 Lowell wrote to Frank Bidart:

> I am unable to thank you sufficiently for Caroline's week, it's [sic] pleasure and success. I did not want to force her hand about coming to Boston, or even try to make a delightful prospect, until she had seen and judged for herself, both the kind of house and the whole atmosphere. . . . I see now, as I saw when Caroline determined to fly, that everyone coming with me meant more to me than I know how to say, running through all my nerves . . . like our San Domingo marriage. . . .[44]

It was unlikely that Lady Caroline would have agreed to any permanent resettling in America, whatever the financial advantages. She believed that Lowell became dangerously excited whenever Harvard was in prospect:

> In a new place he wasn't as threatened by his inner things as he was in the place of his birth. At Harvard it was always touch and go. He was

so edgy at Harvard and he was so on the brink all the time—encouraged by all those hangers-on who tried to make him sit up all night drinking.[45]

Although lithium had for over four years prevented a full-blown manic attack, there were certainly periods when Lowell's friends had thought that he might be "on the brink." During Lowell's "exile's return" in the winter of 1973, Jonathan Raban had been teaching in Boston, and he remembers that he and Blackwood had devised a code: if Lowell began to show symptoms of mania, she would telephone Raban and say something to him about "laundry" —Raban should then call for help. The code was never used, but its very devising suggests something of Blackwood's continuing anxiety. The memory of her 1970 "lock-up" was keen enough for her to be watchful of any "highs"; she was convinced that there were grave risks involved whenever Lowell set foot on his home ground. And there is no reason to suppose that her anxiety did not communicate itself to Lowell.

Before setting off for Harvard in February 1975, Lowell visited Dr. Paul Brass and demanded a medical report for his Boston doctor, Curtis Prout. He refused to give Brass Prout's address. In the end Brass handed over a sealed envelope. Lowell opened this on the flight over and was shaken.

> This delightful man has been a patient of mine since his arrival in England. The two problems he has had over here are at present under treatment. He suffers from chronic manic depression controlled with large doses of lithium, and he also has had a raised blood pressure over the last four years. The blood pressure is controlled at about 150/100 on three tablets of methyl dopa 250 mgm per day. His pulse remains constantly at 100 per minute and I must say he never really looks particularly well.
>
>   You probably know that he had a tendency in the past to drink excessive amounts of alcohol and to smoke too much. Of his own accord he has been taking Abstem tablets one daily and has more or less been on the wagon for the last four months. He has even cut down on his cigarette smoking to about 20 a day.[46]

The report goes on to describe Lowell's fainting fit at the Weidenfeld party—he "might inadvertently have taken some alcohol"—and to pass on the results of his October examination by "an eminent cardiologist." It was this specialist's opinion that shook Lowell:

Chest X-ray showed a slightly odd-shaped heart, but I think it was within ordinary limits. All his ECG's show left axis deviation compatible with left anterior block. There is some delay in right ventricular conduction, but this does not amount to bundle branch block. PR Interval is normal.[47]

No new treatment was suggested, but the family doctor proposed that if dizziness recurred "we should consider a pacemaker. . . . I have not discussed this with him, particularly I have not mentioned a pacemaker. He is extremely apprehensive and this would certainly make him very worried about his future health." There is also mention in the report of "severe chest pains . . . starting in his back and radiating round to the right side. X-rays show quite considerable osteo-arthritis in his dorsal spine."

For Lowell, this talk of pacemakers and "bundle branch block" was deeply alarming; and in spite of reassurances from his Boston doctor—who wrote to Blackwood that Lowell looked "twenty years younger since I last saw him because he's been off alcohol"— he continued to see himself as a victim of heart illness. In the spring of 1975 he collapsed again, in New York; the circumstances are not entirely clear, but it would seem that, in fear of a manic attack, he overdosed on lithium. Robert Giroux recalls:

We had lunch on that day in Greenwich Village, at an Armenian restaurant, the Dardanelles, that he liked. After we ordered our food (he did not ask for a drink), to my horror his head fell forward and he slumped down in his seat. I said, "Cal, you're not well. Let me get a taxi," but he said, "No, I really want some food. I'll be all right, I'm just tired." To my surprise, after he began to eat, he visibly improved and began to seem his old self. When we finished, I suggested we ride uptown together (my office is downtown), but he insisted he was all right. Late that afternoon he collapsed again, and the doctors at Mount Sinai diagnosed his condition as toxic. Food apparently was an antidote. Lithium requires strict monitoring, which Cal was incapable of. The doctors did not seem to understand that asking *him* to "have the levels checked" was absurd; he could not take care of himself in this way.[48]

Lowell was kept in Mount Sinai for a few days' observation, and Robert Silvers visited him there:

I saw him the night before he went in. We'd all been to the opera, and at the restaurant afterwards Cal seemed in terrible shape—exhausted, excited, incoherent. He slumped at the table drinking glass after glass of orange juice. The next day at Mount Sinai he talked in a wandering way about Alexander the Great—how Philip of Macedon had been a canny politician but Alexander had been able to cut through Asia.[49]

In May 1975 Lowell was back in Boston, and Dr. Prout writes to him at 34 Cypress Street, Brookline:

A week ago, you called me because you were feeling lethargic and sleepy. You had felt unwell and thought perhaps you needed to take more lithium to prevent a manic attack, and you had gone, from your usual five, up to as many as eight tablets a day. Your blood level, at that time, was 1.5, and we consider the desirable range to be something in the order of 0.5 to 1.0. As you know, I saw you at home several times. Your heart and blood pressure continue to be good, but you didn't feel right in the head. There was also some apprehension about the possibility of a stroke, which I helped to allay.

Perhaps, because I was overly concerned with the overdose, I over-estimated the length of time it would take to reduce the lithium in your blood, because the sample taken on May 12 was 0.2, which is too low. I therefore asked you to go back to, and stay on, your five tablets, regularly, a day. I don't think you ought to go above it or below it and I do think you might have this level checked in England in about four weeks.[50]

In July, Lowell was writing from Milgate that apart from "coughs, pinkeye and palpitations" there was "nothing wrong,"[51] and, three weeks later, that "I don't have sleepy sickness if I don't mix heart slowers with lithium—not a 100 per cent answer."[52] And in August he felt strong enough to attend a fairly drunken and contentious poetry festival in Ireland: " 'too much drinking and too many poets read,' as someone said to me, but glorious. Three or four gates to climb from where we were staying to a salmon river—the heat had driven them into the wilds."[53] In September 1975 he reported to Blair Clark that he had had "a quiet, hard working and at times American hot summer. . . . We go to London almost weekly, but when we see strange and numerous people are so unpractised we can hardly speak, tho I think Caroline can sometimes." He would resume his Harvard teaching in February 1976; this time, however, he and Blackwood would live in New York and he would "commute to Harvard as once before."[54] As he explained also to Frank Parker: "It's really almost easier for me to fly to classes from New York than to drive in from Brookline. I hope to have rooms in one of the houses and stay two nights a week. I count on seeing you a lot."[55]

During the summer and early fall of 1975 Lowell had prepared a *Selected Poems* for the press; and he also had a book of his prose essays which he hoped to publish under the title *A Moment in American Poetry*. Over thirty new poems had been finished and he was thinking that this would be "about enough" for a new book; "I'll keep writing till November, and come out in the Spring."[56]

It was agonizing to watch. That was the saddest. It would start with a feeling in his spine. And he'd suddenly say, "Honey, Christ, I'm going to have an attack." It's as if you said to me in the middle of a conversation that you were going to have an attack. But he would say: "I can feel it. In the spine. It's a funny, creepy feeling. It's coming up the spine from the lower back, up." Once at Milgate he said he was going to have an attack. And we had one hope: that if he had a massive Valium injection, it might stop—you know, that thing where they do it right in the vein. So I said: "Let's get right on the train and go to Dr. Brass" [their London doctor]. When we set off he was talking a lot, but he was making sense. By the time we reached Victoria, he wasn't. He'd gone, flipped. I got him to Redcliffe Square and Dr. Brass came round and gave him the massive Valium. He was there all night giving him more Valium—he said that people have their nose off and their leg amputated under the doses he'd given Cal. But Cal was still walking around talking and waving his arms. And Dr. Brass said, "That man is like a bull." He'd never seen anything like it. But in an hour he'd gone—between Milgate and Victoria station.[1]

In November 1975 Lowell was admitted to a private hospital called the Priory in Roehampton, a south London suburb; for many of Lowell's London friends, this was the first time that they had experienced one of his attacks; indeed, for several of them, it was as if literature was eerily transmuting itself back into life. The tyrant delusions, in particular, were disconcerting; after all, there was nothing much in the "mad" poems to prepare the unversed visitor for the daunting impact of the poet's actual madness.

I went to visit Cal one afternoon and met one of those gangly mental patients hanging around in the corridors. I asked him where Mr. Lowell was, and he said, "Oh, you mean the Professor. He's going around with his piece of steel. He's got this very important piece of steel." Anyway, I found Cal wandering out on the lawn, carrying what looked like a piece of motor car engine, or part of a central heating system, and Cal was standing there holding it up and saying, "The Chief Engineer gave me this. This is a present from the Chief Engineer." I said, "Oh yes." And he said, "You know what this is? This is the Totentanz. This is what Hitler used to eliminate the Jews." I said, "Cal, it's not. It's a piece of steel. It's nothing to do with the Jews." And then this awful sad, glazed look in his eyes, and he said something like "It's just my way. It's only a joke."[2]

But it was not so easy to laugh off the tyrannical elements in Lowell's own behavior: "I think it was only when he was in hospital that he ever stood up to his full height. He sort of grew. And there was also a sort of ferocity. If one disagreed with him, he would begin to blaze. He could be very frightening."[3] Certainly, Caroline Blackwood found him so, and over the next three months she came close to despair. After Lowell had spent two wild, oppressive weeks in the Priory, he discharged himself. Blackwood was taking a course of acupuncture for a back complaint that had troubled her for many years, and Lowell decided that his problem could be similarly treated. Blackwood's doctor reluctantly agreed to have a try, and after a single session Lowell pronounced himself entirely cured.

Indeed, for a time, it did seem that the needles had worked miracles. Lowell spent December at Milgate, seemingly much calmed. Before the end of the year, though, he was admitted once again to Greenways, the hospital that had treated him in July 1970. And on January 4 he discharged himself from Greenways. At this point, with the acupuncture "miracle" in mind, Blackwood decided that she had had enough of orthodox medicine, and for the next three weeks Lowell was treated at Redcliffe Square by a strange combination of homeopathy and acupuncture; nurses were engaged and Blackwood retired to Milgate with the children—she would commute from there to London.

I was so desperate at that point I would have gone to a miracle worker. But my heart sank when the doctor came round with these ridiculous little pills. Here was Cal, this enormous man with these enormous problems. You've seen homeopathic pills—they're absolutely minute. You just couldn't believe they could work on such a huge physique.[4]

A few entries from the logbook kept by Lowell's nurses during these three weeks provide a chastening view of "the Professor" as mere patient. In the functional jottings of his professional custodians, he becomes a humbled, pitiable figure—a huge child to be watched over night and day. The notebook is titled "Mr Robert Howell," and the General Instructions read as follows:

> Professor Lowell discharged himself from Greenways. His Dr. is Dr. Lederman who is very helpful. The professor must not be left alone at any time. The day nurse must go out with him and the night nurse must sit in his room. He must not be allowed to touch alcohol in any form.
>
> Don't leave him alone to go shopping. He is very untidy and one has to clear up all the time. He likes orange juice and drinks gallons of milk but is a little sketchy about other things. He does like soup and toasted crumpets. He is always mislaying his cigarette holder and lighter. Smokes incessantly—
>
> Small hints on professor's behaviour. Has claimed to have swallowed Dettol. Has put hair lacquer in pubic area producing rash. Has put olive oil in orange juice.
>
> Don't leave anything at all doubtful lying about.[5]

Most of the day-to-day entries are to do with diet, homeopathic pills and mixtures, visits from the acupuncturist. During the nights Lowell is regularly reported as "Restless and did not sleep for long intervals." Now and then a note of mild alarm is sounded: "Visited Westminster Abbey briefly and returned home 3.30 p.m. No apparently harmful effect." (As a result of this visit, Lowell decided he wanted to change his nationality so that he could be in Poets' Corner.) "Had lunch with literary agent and three others at l'Escargot in Greek Street. Was told not to drink anything but had some white wine." (At l'Escargot, Lowell tried to enlist help from the waiters and from strangers lunching at adjoining tables— help in compiling an "anthology of world poetry." He told them that he was king of Scotland but that the anthology's selection process would be wholly democratic.) "Left flat *unaccompanied* in taxi for Portobello Rd. without waiting for Miss Conway. Dr. Lederman informed. (7.30 a.m.); Professor Lowell *returned* from

Portobello Road at 10.20 a.m. Very flushed and seemed *over* delighted with his purchases of books, etc." (Among his purchases that day was a large knife, soon itself to feature in a Report by Lowell's night nurse: "He pointed a knife at me—joking he said— a funny joke.")

And so it went on for fifteen days. On January 21, though, he was readmitted to Greenways. Caroline Blackwood remembers his final forty-eight hours at home as involving "every sort of horror," and it is easy to see why. The nurses, however, icily recorded the events as follows:

9 a.m. Rather tired and drowsy during morning. Had small amount of breakfast. Dr Lederman phoned.

10 a.m. Asked for pt. to have 2) Orphenidrine.

12 a.m. To Harley Str. Very drowsy in taxi—for acupuncture.

1.30 p.m. When leaving taxi (I had to pay taxi-driver as Prof. Lowell had forgotten his wallet) he slipped away.

3.35 p.m. Returned in company of a friend (later Prof Lowell said he was a director of plays). He said he had found the professor in a pub and he had had an amount to drink. Patient did not appear in any distress, and not noticeably drunk. (Had had lunch in Hamburger Heaven).

4.30 p.m. Friend left after reading poems to professor and conversing.

4.45 p.m. Lady Caroline came to see her husband.

5 p.m. Dr Lederman informed of Professor's drinking and said not to give him any further sedation.

8 p.m. Dr Lederman gave acupuncture.

8.30 Had a bath

9.30 p.m. Quite normal. Walking around the flat. Smoking a lot.

10.00 p.m. Dr Lederman phoned (prescribes medication)

11.00 p.m. Gone off to sleep.

1.00 a.m. Awake and walking around. Drinking lots of juice and coffee (medication given)

5.00 a.m. Awake and restless. (more medication given) Slept until 7.30 a.m. Got dressed by himself and went out with me to buy the papers.

8.30 a.m. Professor got undressed and went back to bed.

9 a.m. Dr Lederman rang (prescribes different medication) and asked for Lady Caroline to encourage as many visitors as possible to visit the Professor. Said Prof not to go to acupuncture.

12 Noon. But pt. wanted to go to Harley St. with Lady Caroline. Not so restless during morning. Returned from acupuncture.

1 p.m.–2 p.m. Slept.

2 p.m. Had consomme and toast and orange juice and coffee. Up to lounge. Continues to be extremely untidy in appearance and dirty in habits. Smoking incessantly, but appears calmer and not so agitated.

3 p.m. Took the bread knife and started taking strips off the walls. Lady Caroline informed Dr Lederman. G.P. will be coming. Not violent or difficult to manage but insisting on taking bread knife.

3.30 p.m. Dr Brass came and gave valium injection.

3.30 p.m.–5 p.m. Pt. slept.

5 p.m. Prof rang psychiatrist (a different one from the one who was attending him before). Dr Brass will probably bring psychiatrist to see Professor. To be put into Greenways.

5.30 p.m. Had a bath. Spray prescribed by Dr Brass applied to areas where he had shampooed himself with hair lacquer.

5.30–7 p.m. Resting quietly. Had a bottle of milk.

7 p.m. Dr Benaim (psychiatrist) rang and will get in touch with Dr Brass.

6.30–8 Slept.

7 p.m. Had plate of lentil soup and toast

8 p.m. Appears cheerful

That night Lowell slept longer than on almost any previous night recorded in the nurses' logbook. At 7 A.M. on the following day he "got dressed and went out to buy newspapers. Behaviour quite normal." This is the final entry in the logbook. Later on that same day Lowell returned to Greenways. Again, though, Blackwood was haunted by the fear that he would be "let out too soon." It was all too easy for him to "escape" from Greenways, and after one or two alarms, Blackwood decided that she would have to have him legally "committed"—and committed, moreover, to a hospital far enough from London for her to feel safe from the threat of a surprise appearance. The hospital was St. Andrews in Northampton, some sixty-odd miles from London, and Lowell was taken there by ambulance towards the end of January 1976. In the poem "Home," Lowell writes poignantly about one of Blackwood's visits: there will always be some sense of desertion when a loved one disappears "round the bend," some sense of *"You chose to go / where you knew I could not follow:*

> at visiting hours, you could experience
> my sickness only as desertion . . .

Dr. Berners compliments you again,
"A model guest . . . we would welcome
Robert back to Northampton any time,
the place suits him . . . he is so strong."
When you shuttle back chilled to London,
I am on the wrong end of a dividing train—
it is my failure with our fragility.

If he has gone mad with her,
the poor man can't have been very happy,
seeing too much and feeling it
with one skin-layer missing.[6]

Lowell spent only two weeks in St. Andrews. In mid-February, he wrote to Frank Bidart:

So good to hear your voice. I had just been talking to Lizzie, and felt a rush of health. My recovery has been easy in most ways, but I am weighed down by the new frequency of attacks. How can one function, if one is regularly sick. Shades of the future prison. But all's well for the present. The doctors differ somewhat but are optimistic. So am I. We sit by the fire paying bills. Caroline has written three chapters of a novel. I've written a short heart-felt poem.[7]

On March 4 Lowell wrote a rather shamefaced and gloomy letter to Peter Taylor, who had visited Britain during the later days of Lowell's attack: "I got well shortly after your visit and wish to god it had been sooner so that you would have been spared my antics. However now I am the most halting and tedious person on earth."[8] To Blair Clark, on the same day, he writes:

I finally deciphered the crucial word "tricky" in your lithium warning. I think you mean the blood has to be taken every month or so to check the amount of lithium in the system. I've been doing that, though hating the blood needle. However, the air is full of rumours against lithium, hard to check on because it is almost a universal faith with English doctors. It's the preventative effectiveness that shakes me, I can't really function against two manic attacks in one year.

This one was drawn out, but not too bad. I've been home a month now, rather downlooking at first, then thawing, all the while writing with furious persistence.

Outside the sun is shining. Harriet is arriving tonight. A coal and wood fire warms the large bright-window room, and we swim along happily writing and rewriting.[9]

And, in a P.S. to this, he writes: "Tell me if you come across anything more detailed on lithium. I am trying to find a substitute."

Two poems—"The Downlook" and "Thanks-Offering for Recovery"—suggest that Lowell knew what had been lost, perhaps irretrievably, by his drawn-out winter antics. He was to place the poems, unchronologically, at the very end of his book *Day by Day*, as if to locate the precise point of damage in his relationship with Blackwood:

> Last summer nothing dared impede
> the flow of the body's thousand rivulets of welcome,
> winding effortlessly, yet with ambiguous invention—
> safety in nearness.
>
> Now the downlook, the downlook—
> . . . .
>
> How often have my antics
> and insupportable, trespassing tongue
> gone astray and led me to prison . . .
> to lying . . . kneeling . . . standing.[10]

And, from "Thanks-Offering for Recovery": "This winter, I thought / I was created to be given away."

In April, Lowell and Lady Caroline flew to New York for a performance of *The Old Glory* at the American Place Theatre (it was put on as part of the American bicentennial celebrations). "The production," Lowell thought, "didn't come up to Jonathan's of course and was often like the original coin restamped in plaster." He wrote this to Elizabeth Hardwick, whom he had visited on the day before he left, and added: "I miss having you to talk to. I feel deeply all you had to put up with me for so many years."[11] And in the poem "Off Central Park" there is clear nostalgia for "our light intimacy of reference," for the solid detail of shared history. There are the "old movables . . . / . . . I can give the dates when they entered our lives," the bureau where he could always find "fresh shirts," and

> In the bookcase, my Catholic theology,
> still too high for temptation—
> the same radical reviews
> where we first broke into print
> are still new to us.

The reestablished old familiarity is such that Lowell feels able to hazard a direct quote from Hardwick without fear of *Dolphin*-style recriminations:

> "After so much suffering," you said,
> "I realize we couldn't have lasted
> more than another year or two anyway."[12]

Before leaving England, Lowell had written to Clark resurrecting the idea of a permanent move back to America, but this brief April visit had made New York, at any rate, seem "too fast and fallen for us."[13] He still felt the tug, though, and was evidently much relieved that he was once again on "talking" terms with Hardwick. Indeed, in July he wrote to her again, as if seeking a final peace on the matter of *The Dolphin:*

> I regret the Letters in Dolphin. The only way to make a narrative was to leave a few. I hesitated to send you a copy of the Selected Poems, but Giroux acted on his own; which was right because the bulk of them were written under your eyes.
>
> Autobiography predominates, almost forty years of it. And now more journey of the soul in my new book. I feel I, or someone, wrote everything beforehand. If I had read it at twenty would I have been surprised, would I have dared to go on?[14]

A month later Hardwick visited London for a PEN conference, and shortly after this Lowell wrote: "I can't find the words or maybe the style to say how comforting and enjoyable your visit was. It was so strange seeing you and Caroline easily together, that I almost feel I shouldn't refer to it."[15]

The "haunting transatlantic problem" continued to haunt Lowell throughout the summer. In America, "both Caroline and I would be decisively better off, yet the move would be a shattering one for us as a family, getting the children resettled etc. or paying them flying visits, the groaning effort of abandoning houses, finding something new."[16] In Britain, he was beginning to feel "an expensive, parasitical burden," and this uneasiness was sharpened when, in September, Blackwood decided to sell Milgate, which "just got too expensive to run, £900 a quarter for electricity, etc." They would look for a smaller place, perhaps near Oxford, "costing as much, but cheaper to run."[17] There was no need for an immediate decision, he believed. A house had been rented in Cambridge, Massachusetts, for the fall semester (September through January), and he expected that Milgate would still be intact on his return. In September he wrote to Frank Bidart that "we arrive Flight BA 561 2.05 p.m. on Wednesday the 15th. . . . I'm surprised how glad I am to be getting back to Harvard this fall, and to you the center of it." And in a P.S. he tells Bidart that Milgate is "on the market. It won't go soon, I suppose. The unfixed future is bewildering."[18]

As it turned out, Lowell did not travel on Flight BA 561; shortly before the fifteenth he was again in Greenways. And this time Blackwood could not take it: "I'm no use to him in these attacks. They destroy me. I'm really better if I'm away if he has one"; "It's like someone becoming an animal, or someone possessed by the devil. And that's what tears you apart. You think, I love this person, but I hate him. So where are you?"[19] This time, however, in mid-October, she flew to America with Sheridan and Ivana, and from the rented house in Cambridge she telephoned Blair Clark, who made notes of their conversation:

> She said she'd come with Sheridan for a few weeks because Cal was threatening to leave the hospital—a doctor had done a phoney "miracle" and said he was all right and was ready to release him. The only way to handle that was to come here. She said then "nobody could take *it* on." She said she'd talked to Cal this morning on the phone, and he had said he was better and might come "out" (i.e. to the U.S.) in 2 weeks. She said this was a straight crackup on the eve of his coming to Harvard, —no drug problem.[20]

On October 30 Lowell wrote to William Alfred that he was "three days out of hospital, but ninety percent certified healthy." His worry was that "Caroline is very sick with habitual overdrinking" —but she, like him, "makes miraculous turnabouts."[21] And in the poem "Runaway" he wrote: "At the sick times, our slashing,/ drastic decisions made us runaways."[22]

In Cambridge the confusion was exacerbated: Blackwood was convinced that Lowell was still sick, and he was convinced that she needed help far more than he did. On November 25 Lowell called Blair Clark, as Clark records:

> Cal Lowell called, I having called him. He was at Frank Bidart's in Cambridge. He said, in effect, that he'd left the house and Caroline for a while to get some peace. He said Caroline was in real trouble, that the late night "tirades" after drinking were bad. There was a suicide attempt (I gathered this was not recent). He had a doctor at McLean's who said he might be able to help her. And this doctor would tell Harvard he was OK and could bring him out of a manic breakdown "in a week" if that happened. I got impression Caroline would go back to England in a couple of weeks, with Sheridan but that Cal might not go. He said it was bad for her to have to go because of taxes (he mentioned 80%). He said he was "crazy about" her and there was no one else for him, but it was hard now. We agreed we'd talk this week and he might stay with me when he was down for "Y" reading Dec. 8th.[23]

Lowell stayed at Bidart's apartment for ten days ("he was just unbelievably grateful and relieved to be in an atmosphere that was not this terrific turmoil, anger, drama, tension"[24]). Five days before Lowell's reading at the YMHA in New York (a reading at which he read "two very negative poems about Caroline"[25]), Blackwood returned to England. With some hesitation, Lowell followed her in mid-December. They spent Christmas in Scotland, and then— much against her wishes—Lowell returned to Cambridge in January 1977. Frank Bidart recalls:

> I went to pick him up at the airport, let's say, Thursday or Friday night. The school term (he had not taught at all in the fall, and Harvard had agreed to let him teach the spring semester instead) was to start, say, the following Tuesday or Wednesday, and it was arranged he was to stay in Dunster House, but he'd stay with me first for like a week or so. It was terrifically cold, and the second night about two in the morning— we'd both been asleep—he knocked on my door and said that he couldn't breathe and he felt he had to go to the infirmary. So we got dressed and went downstairs and got into my car. My car was quite old and it was terribly cold and my car wouldn't start. And he was just incredibly gracious about it. I mean, he was having trouble breathing and you might have expected that he would be somewhat angry with

me for having this car that was so unreliable, but there was a kind of resigned patience to the way the world works—a sense that, well, this is the way it is, we have to go back inside now and call a cab. I don't think he climbed back up again, but anyway, I got a cab and we went to the infirmary.[26]

A doctor examined Lowell but could find nothing, and it was arranged that he should have tests at McLean's on the following Monday. Lowell gives his account of Monday's events in a letter to Caroline Blackwood:

I should tell you about the hospital, though it is a tame story—that's its point. After my cardiograph came out irregular, I waited a long moment, then was practically handcuffed in a sort of sitting up stretcher, bounced down a stairless gangway (all this was in McLean's) then banged in an ambulance to Mass. General. More waits, while I absorbed the imaginable seriousness of my condition. Death? Ivan Illich: But there was no pain at all, and it seemed to me that death would be nothing. What gentler thing could one ask for, except, though painless, it had absolutely no meaning, no long private message. Of course, I was soon reassured, when new tests I had already been given at McLean's removed the drama.[27]

The diagnosis was congestive heart failure; in Lowell's definition: "the lungs filled with water because the heart can't squeeze enough." He stayed for about ten days in Phillips House at Massachusetts General—much intrigued by the memory that his grandfather had died in "almost" the same hospital room—and Hardwick came up from New York to visit him. During the week he contacted his Aunt Sarah (Cotting), the oldest surviving member of his family; Aunt Sarah had refused to speak to him since his marriage to Lady Caroline, but he now "asked her to come in to see him, to bury the hatchet, and she came. He was afraid he would die with the sun going down on his wrath with Aunt Sarah."[28] In spite of such fears, Lowell "was in no sense a good patient." Helen Vendler, who had been asked to take over Lowell's first Harvard class if he was still in the hospital when term began, remembers that "he didn't particularly obey the instructions given to him by the hospital. He did take the diuretics that he was supposed to take, but he did not stop drinking. . . . And he was supposed to stop smoking of course. And he didn't."[29]

On his release from Mass. General, Lowell took up residence in Dunster House ("very small, two rooms, fireplace, view of the Charles, two desks, bookcases. third floor, meals if I want them"), and felt himself to be "an old student among students." On his first day there he wrote to Blackwood: "I don't think I've ever been so on my own, so firmly pinned down to emptiness. . . . The mind goes numb reading through about thirty student poems. The body goes numb in its little room, too enervated to read through Anna Karenina as one resolved."[30]

On February 23, however, there was light relief when Lowell gave a reading in New York with Allen Ginsberg. He read "Phillips House Revisited," a new poem about his stay in Massachusetts General (and confided to the audience that he was now suffering from "water in the lungs"), "Man and Wife," "To Speak of Woe That Is in Marriage," and—by popular request—"Waking Early Sunday Morning" and "For the Union Dead." Towards the end of the evening (possibly because the reading took place in St. Mark's-in-the-Bowery, where he had been married to Jean Stafford) he read "To Delmore Schwartz," and when he finished and was about to begin "Ulysses and Circe," a "genial if sloshed young man, who was sitting with his wife and baby near the front, suddenly shouted: 'Robert, you left out that great line about paranoid' " ("the paranoid inert gaze of Coleridge"). Edgar Stillman reported the ensuing banter for the *Soho Weekly News:*

> "Point taken," Lowell answered. He continued talking about "Ulysses and Circe": "It's wonderful to write about a myth especially if what you write isn't wholly about yourself."
> "You're treating us like a classroom," the young man now called.
> "That's nice," said Lowell, "because I am a teacher." He continued reading, but not for long.
> "Please don't talk to me while I'm trying to read," Lowell begged, peering over his glasses at the young man.
> "Near the end of 'Ulysses and Circe' I believe when the old hero and Penelope were sitting down naked at table . . ." "I'll applaud that," the young hero shouted, shuttling his baby to his wife.
> Several called shut up.
> "Don't tell me to shut up," the young man said.
> "Lord, this is not good," Lowell muttered, and the mike caught mild consternation in his voice.
> Looking like an extremely good-natured if brown-bearded Santa

Claus, Allen Ginsberg said, "Perhaps we should all tell him to shut up."
    The crowd yelled: "Shut up."
    The baby cried.
    "It was quiet," the father said. "It *woke* the baby."
    Lowell said, "We're having a happening."
    The baby cried, but not very hard.
    "My son is happy, my son is laughing," the father said. Someone persuaded the little family to leave. First Dad held his boots up to an amused and friendly crowd. He needed time to put them back on.
    When Lowell finished "Ulysses and Circe" he was given a long standing ovation. Afterwards scores of young people crowded round him and Allen Ginsberg holding up their books, letters, fragments of paper for their autographs. Lowell, sweating, his eyes tired and even wild, enclosed by a mob of eager faces and hands, protested.
    "I'm afraid this will have to be the last. My fingers are giving out."[31]

The "young man" who heckled Lowell was in fact Gregory Corso, the renowned Beat poet, who in the early 1960s was often mentioned as an "alternative" to Lowell. All in all, the evening sealed an amiable truce between the Palefaces and the Redskins, the cooked and the raw. Before returning to Cambridge, Lowell had a premature birthday party with Hardwick and Harriet at West 67th Street. They gave him a laurel wreath. On March 1 he would be sixty.

Lowell's sixtieth birthday coincided with news from Blackwood that Milgate had been sold, and that she had taken an apartment in a huge Georgian stately home at Castletown, near Dublin. The house was the headquarters of the Irish Georgian Society, and most parts of it were open to the public. Desmond Guinness, Lady Caroline's cousin and the Society's president, had suggested that she rent one of the house's small private apartments; for tax purposes, it was sensible for her (and perhaps for Lowell also) to establish residence in Ireland—and for Blackwood, certainly Castletown offered a convenient interim arrangement. According to friends, Lowell complained that the sale of Milgate had gone through without any consultation: "After all, it had been their home together. But she just sold it, and said she was moving to Castletown for reasons of taxes and all that." To Blackwood, though, he wrote:

What strikes me in this order is the teenager flat, the likeness to the Louvre (a vague feeling that we will live there as old royal Louvre pensioners, and the nearness of the Liffey). . . .

But it has taken away a huge, undefined vagueness, my only way since I left of imagining our future—an infinite stairway of Dunster House cafeteria dining halls.[32]

He agreed to join Blackwood and the children at Castletown for Easter (March 31 to April 10), and on March 18 he wrote to her again:

I love you so much and I wish I could do everything for you. What did you mean on the phone that I had nearly lost you? I am excited about the house. But do you really want me back? Sometimes, you sound indifferent. I'm not, though my voice may sound low and subdued coming from so far.[33]

But the Easter visit was not a success, and on his return to Cambridge, Lowell told friends that he had decided that the marriage should be ended. Castletown he had found isolated and overpowering; too large-scale for any sort of convincing domesticity (although the apartment itself was, in relation to the whole, distinctly poky) and too far from Dublin to promise even a rudimentary social life: "It meant making sort of state arrangements to, say, meet the Heaneys for lunch. It wasn't a viable life at all, he didn't feel." And of his marriage, he believed now that it couldn't work. Helen Vendler saw Lowell often after his return from Ireland and she says:

he was in great distress about it, in that he represented himself as being still in love with her—a state he certainly gave a very good imitation of. He had a picture of her in his room, the one in a gondola, and would stop very often, looking at it and saying, "Isn't she beautiful? Have you ever seen anyone more beautiful? Doesn't she have a wonderful face?" But he simply said that life with her was impossible, because of what they were like together. He didn't blame her. There wasn't any recrimination or ill-speaking of her. He almost spoke of her as though she were a child, haplessly gone wrong, almost, and that there was no way he could live in the turbulence of their mutual life. But he had obviously never fallen out of love with her. Lizzie was talking to him every day. She called up when I was there one day, and he said, "Helen Vendler's here, I'm showing her my new poem," and talked to her in the most affectionate and old-shoe sort of terms. He was extremely grateful to her for being willing to take him back. He said that.[34]

Lowell's poem "Last Walk?"—with its "Liffey, torrential, wild, accelerated to murder," its "Explosion is growing common here"— tells something of Lowell's Easter dramas. A more direct and powerful statement, though, is made in "Seesaw":

> The night dark before its hour—
> heavily, steadily,
> the rain lashes and sprinkles
> to complete its task—
> as if assisting
> the encroachments of our bodies
> we occupy but cannot cure.
>
> Sufferer, how can you help me,
> if I use your sickness
> to increase my own?
>
> Will we always be
> one up, the other down,
> one hitting bottom, the other
> flying through the trees—
> seesaw inseparables?[35]

Certainly this is close in tone and substance to the letters Lowell wrote to Blackwood after his return from Ireland:

I don't know what to say, our problems have become so many-headed and insuperable. Nothing like the sunshine of the years we had together—when it shone, as so often—so blindingly.

(April 14)

Us? Aren't we too heady and dangerous for each other? I love you, am more dazzled by you, than anyone I've known, but can't I be a constant visitor? Then there will be no wrinkles to steam-iron out. Ireland seems so far from home and help . . . who and what I know, though a kind of paradise to come to with you and Sheridan and all the girls there, and the big winey dinner in big rotting house.

(April 19)

And us? I really feel too weak and battered by it all. I fear I do you more harm than good. I think your blackness would pass if you didn't live in fear of manic attacks. And they don't seem curable—almost thirty years. How's that for persistence? I miss you sorely.

(April 22)

[In Ireland] . . . in a way you are nearer to your neighbours and a part of your past. But how lonely and dark it might become. But of course I know nothing about what is going on in your heart.
(April 30)

Shortly after writing this last letter, Lowell spoke on the telephone with Blackwood, and she suggested joining him in Cambridge. On May 3 he wrote:

Dearest—

I'm writing about three or four hours after your call—in great confusion, not knowing how or what to say. I am afraid of your visit, because I am afraid nothing will be done except causing pain. How many lovely moments, weeks, months, we had. Sunday I sat by the Charles River watching the strollers, the joggers, the sunners—and the river. And I seemed to follow it back through our seven years, the great multitude of restaurants, the moment when everyone was in the bathroom when I bathed, the long summer of your swelling pregnancy, the rush to London, the little red man's appearance—or earlier trapped in All Souls, and a thousand things more. But the last two years have been terrifying for us both—and neither of us have made it any better for the other. It hasn't been a quarrel, but two eruptions, two earthquakes crashing.

Well, we should talk . . . always. I really can't do anything till June in New York or the end of May here, or I could visit Ireland mid- or later summer. I feel you ended things during my Irish visit, ended them wisely and we can't go back. I have had so much dread—the worst in my life—that I would do something, by my mere presence I would do something to hurt you, to drive you to despair. Who knows cause. . . .

Five days later, Blair Clark set down some "notes for a never-to-be-written 'memoir' ":

About three weeks ago I had lunch with Cal at the Italian Pavilion. He was back a couple of weeks from an Easter-break visit to Ireland and was down from Harvard for a day or two. He soon said that he guessed his marriage was over. He had gone to the two apartments in a castly place that Caroline had moved to, apparently (according to Eliz.) without asking him, after the Bearstone [*sic*] place was sold. They seem still to have a kind of access to the London flat though there are complications about the occupancy; there is nothing as straight as a lease, as usual for tax reasons. Cal's description of the Irish place was that it was near lots of Guinness relatives and that there was much visiting back and forth and parties for the children, and thus pleasant for them though not his kind of life.

About Caroline he said that she could not take his manic periods, that they frightened and exhausted her. I had the impression that she was at least as much for the end of the marriage as he was. He rather quickly said that he was sort of moving back with Lizzie, and could he have the apartment on the third floor back, the one I've been renting since last Sept. from Eliz. I said of course he could and when did he want it. Soon, he said, and he was going to Maine this summer with Lizzie and Harriet.

We talked about children and he said that now Harriet was someone he could talk with, that he never had been much interested in children when they were young. I tried my notions of why even small children are fascinating, as I have before, but he doesn't see it that way. It isn't rejection, he just finds them boring, totally incomprehensible beings.

In all this Cal's tone was quite flat, as if he were talking of someone else's life. Something he said gave the impression that he still had romantic-erotic feelings about Caroline. About Eliz. he talked of what they had in common, mainly literature but also Harriet. He did not talk as if he were formally "going back to her"; it was some other kind of arrangement, looser, vaguer.[36]

Since his April lunch with Lowell, Clark had talked with him again about Blackwood's suggested visit; he "had done everything to discourage her from coming, telling her on the phone that the marriage couldn't be 'mended.' "

In May, Lowell was to receive a $10,000 award from the American Academy of Arts and Letters, and Lady Caroline told him that she wanted to attend the ceremony with him. Lowell was reluctant, but according to a friend,

Caroline insisted on coming over for that. She spent about a week in New York and insisted he stay with her in a hotel. It was absolute hell on earth, because she was doing everything to get him back and he was not saying yes. He was really quite afraid that she would kill herself. But she didn't and she went back to England.

By this time, it seems, the "impossibility" was clear to both of them. Blackwood's fear of Lowell's mania was such that she could barely distinguish "health" from "sickness"; any sign of excitement, high-spiritedness, was now a possible symptom. For example, in several letters to Blackwood, Lowell referred to an incident in which Sheridan had corked a moustache onto his upper lip in imitation of a Hitler he had seen on television. Jestingly—in cheery one-line throwaways—Lowell would say, "I am trying to find a genuine Mein Kampf with a young photograph of Hitler to checkmate Sheridan," or—with reference to a postcard he had sent his son— "Hitler cards are unattainable." For Blackwood, the mere mention of Hitler was a danger sign; thus, an otherwise quite sensible letter would take on a threatening glow. The constraint that this imposed on Lowell was intolerable; on the other hand, Blackwood could not simply unlearn the traumas of the last two years. Lowell wrote to her in July 1977:

> a voice inside me says all might be well if I could be with you. And another voice says all would be ruin, and that I would be drowned in the confusion I made worse. If I were to get sick in Ireland? But here it can all be handled. But it's the effect my troubles have on you. It's like a nightmare we all have in which each motion of foot or hand troubles the turmoil it tries to calm.[37]

Lowell wrote this letter after returning from a ten-day visit to Russia as a member of an American delegation to the Union of Soviet Writers in Moscow; Elizabeth Hardwick was also in the delegation, along with Edward Albee, William Styron, Norman Cousins (editor of the *Saturday Review*), Vera Dunham, a professor of Slavic languages, and Leo Gruliow, editor of *Current Digest of the Soviet Press*. A bizarre way for Lowell and Hardwick to be reunited, remembering the circumstances at Yaddo in 1948, but neither of them took seriously the proposal that they were now furthering Soviet-American relations; the discussions mainly would be about copyright laws, Lowell thought, and therefore of not much interest to a poet. William Styron recalls:

Cal (and, I think, Lizzie) seemed as skeptical as I about the fruitfulness of the trip but it could be regarded as a nice all-expenses-paid-for junket to a new and fascinating country, so we set off in fairly good spirits. Before we got to Moscow I enjoyed seeing two examples of Cal's disregard for convention—a nonconformity which I had seen him display before and which I really admired. Cal chain-smoked . . . and on the Boeing 747 we were seated in a nonsmoking section. Cal smoked anyway, much to the annoyance and finally the fury of a nonsmoker whose protests to the stewardesses were of no avail. Cal referred to this man contemptuously as an "environmentalist," and kept smoking the entire way to Frankfurt, despite all efforts on the part of the staff to make him stop. I was rather tickled by his obstinacy; after all, it was Pan American which had made the mistake in seating, and he was standing by his rights.[38]

Lowell's other small rebellion was against a "rather fussy bureaucrat" from the Kettering Foundation (which was paying for the trip); the bureaucrat had told the writers that the hotel they were staying at in Frankfurt was very expensive and that they "should display caution and discretion in ordering, especially meals":

no one was more insulted by the edict than Cal. To my great delight, Cal led a revolt in the restaurant and, in clear sight of the man in question, ordered four of the most sumptuous and expensive bottles of white German wine that any of us had ever tasted. It was a clear victory of individual choice over bureaucracy.[39]

In Moscow, however, Styron remembers Lowell as "tired and melancholy"; and to another delegate—Nathan Scott, a professor of religious studies at the University of Virginia—he seemed "utterly spent and exhausted." At the discussion sessions he said little; according to Scott, Lowell made one short speech in which "having been more than a little tried by some harangue that we'd been listening to, he reminded our Russian hosts of Auden's word about poetry not making anything happen."[40] For Styron, Lowell did not need to say anything:

I'll never forget how touched I was at the boring writers' sessions when I would glance over and let my eyes rest on the brooding, sorrowing Beethovenesque head. I don't know why that head and face so often touched me through sheer presence—so much suffering contained there, I suppose.[41]

From Moscow, Lowell and Hardwick made their way back to Castine, with some days in New York and Cambridge, where Lowell had further heart tests at McLean's. Frank Bidart remembers:

The doctor told him that his heart was in very good shape and that he was in very good shape and that he was much better. He was going to spend the rest of the summer working on a prose essay on New England writers.[42]

From Castine, Lowell wrote to Caroline Blackwood: "I talked to Bingo [Gowrie] who said you were fine; but Natalia [Blackwood's eldest daughter] didn't say you were fine but were on the verge of tears all day, and needed a rest. You are always with me—deep and in rapid images."[43] He would visit her in Ireland in September, he said.

Lowell stayed at Castine with Hardwick throughout the summer, and in the last week of August Frank Bidart visited him there.

I was there for, I believe, two nights. Lizzie had sold the house they had lived in together, that she had inherited from Cousin Harriet, and had redone the barn into a house. They were quite nice to each other—extremely warm and comfortable—but at the same time he seemed, emotionally, in a kind of suspended animation. I had never seen him like this. He was working in a little sort of boathouse he had rented, and he was carrying Caroline's letters around with him in an envelope. He showed me some of them, and they were not full of vituperation and anger. They were very sort of ironic and full of jokes, and she was very much wanting him to come back. The plan was that he was going to spend a week in Ireland seeing Sheridan and Caroline, but there was absolutely no explicit purpose of going back to Caroline. He took great pleasure in the view of the harbor from the boathouse. He was, as always, working hard.[44]

Before leaving Castine, Lowell wrote to Blackwood: "I haven't quite lost my muse." He tells her that he has been working on "an old piece of prose . . . a series of vignettes":

Cotton Mather, Ben Franklin, Emerson, Hawthorne, Thoreau, Lincoln, Wallace Stevens, Santayana—almost all New England, and worthies. I've got 19 pages and at worst as many again to write. Because I'm working on it, I think it my best critical prose.[45]

Of these essays, Hardwick says: "The work he was writing stunned me by its brilliance, the memory—for he wrote these American portraits almost without any books to go on—was a phenomenon, I thought. But then, I should not have been surprised because the saturation in the texts had been his life and the originality of his thoughts about American literature—well, that was just his beautiful, free independent intelligence still hourly, daily, there for him to call upon."[46] He had also written two poems, and he showed these to Bidart in Boston on the night before he left for Ireland. They had dinner with Helen Vendler in Lowell's favorite Athens Olympia Greek restaurant, on the edge of Boston's "combat zone" (or red-light district). Both Bidart and Vendler thought that Lowell was "dreading" his visit to Ireland because "he knew Caroline would be wanting him to come back. He wanted to see her and he wanted to see Sheridan, but he was very scared." Vendler recalls seeing him off at the airport:

> Frank and I put him on the plane that night. We took him to Logan Airport, and the last I saw of him he was going down the entry way to the plane clutching a big ship model. And that night, before we went out to dinner, Frank and I started talking about Dunbarton, and Cal said, "It's in Dunbarton, but you know it's not the same place I talk about in the poem. The cemetery has been moved because they put a dam in and the Army Corps of Engineers had to come in and move the whole private graveyard to a place that wasn't going to be flooded" . . . And Frank said to me, "Let's go up there sometime in the fall," and Lowell said, "That's where I'm going to be buried." So I said, "You mean you've arranged it already?" And he said, "Yes, I've arranged everything, it's in my will. I'll be buried with a solemn high mass at the Church of the Advent." I was really shocked that he would do that, and he was immensely amused at my anticlericalism, so to speak, and he said: "That's how we're buried." Meaning the family.[47]

The two poems Lowell showed Bidart were called "Loneliness" and "Summer Tides." Bidart typed fair copies of each of them; "and Cal gave me things to keep for him, because he was coming back

in a week. So I had that packet of Caroline's letters, for example."
"Summer Tides" mixes in Lowell's Castine harbor view with his
favorite photograph of Blackwood in a gondola; and the poem's final
image Bidart could identify from "the week before when I saw him
in Castine":

That line about "trembles on a loosened rail"—literally, the front part
of the lawn gave onto a precipice and there was a railing there and this
was being eaten away and the whole thing was about to fall down. So
this was a real thing—there was a lot of talk of it costing $10,000 to
rebuild. To make that into a metaphor of something happening in his
life was amazing.[48]

SUMMER TIDES

Tonight
I watch the incoming moon swim
under three agate veins of cloud,
casting crisps of false silver-plate
to the thirsty granite fringe of the shore.
Yesterday, the sun's gregarious sparklings;
tonight, the moon has no satellite.
All this spendthrift, in-the-house summer,
our yacht-jammed harbor
lay unattempted—
pictorial to me like your portrait.
I wonder who posed you so artfully
for it in the prow of his Italian skiff,
like a maiden figurehead without legs to fly.
Time lent its wings. Last year
our drunken quarrels had no explanation,
except everything, except everything.
Did the oak provoke the lightning,
when we heard its boughs and foliage fall? . . .
My wooden beach-ladder swings by one bolt,
and repeats its single creaking rhythm—
I cannot go down to the sea.
After so much logical interrogation,
I can do nothing that matters.
The east wind carries disturbance for leagues—
I think of my son and daughter,
and three stepdaughters

on far-out ledges
washed by the dreaded clock-clock of the waves . . .
gradually rotting the bulwark where I stand.
Their father's unmotherly touch
trembles on a loosened rail.[49]

Before he left, Lowell's new book, *Day by Day*, was published in America, and Helen Vendler reviewed it in the *New York Times Book Review* for August 14 under the heading "The Poetry of Autobiography"; "this new collection," she said, recounted the "attrition" of his marriage:

> There is no use denying that these poems . . . need footnoting. One has to know (from previous work) his reading, his past and his present and one has to re-construct the scenario behind this book—Lowell's life in Kent, his hospitalization in England, his wife's sickness, their temporary stay in Boston, their separation, a reconciliation, a further rupture, a parting in Ireland, Lowell's return to America.[50]

Day by Day not only chronicles Lowell's most recent dramas. It also seems intent on some final settlement with the obsessions of a lifetime. Key chapters of the "Lowell life" are resurrected: his parents, the schoolmates at St. Mark's who mocked him for his Caliban-like savagery (they would say "my face / was pearl-gray like toe-jam—/ that I was foul / as the gymsocks I wore a week? / A boy next to me breathed my shoes, / and lay choking on the bench"); his early treatment at the hands of Merrill Moore: Lowell remembers Moore telling him when he was in college that "You know, you were an unwanted child," and wonders still, "Did he become mother's lover?" Moore is mocked for the "million / sonnets he rhymed into his dictaphone," but his "Tennessee rattling saved my life." In other poems there are the years at Kenyon with Peter Taylor, at Baton Rouge with Robert Penn Warren; a "Letter" to Jean Stafford with talk of her "novels more salable than my poems" and "Our days of the great books, scraping and Roman mass"; and fond addresses to Cousin Harriet, William Meredith ("Morning After Dining with a Friend"), Frank Parker. It is almost as if Lowell was anxious not to leave anybody out.

Many of these poems are loose, chatty, confidentially *verbatim*, and there are moments throughout the book when Lowell calls into question his whole "way of writing"; he envies the imaginers, the mythmakers, the fabulists, or even those "like Mallarmé who had the good fortune / to find a style that made writing impossible." "Alas, I can only tell my own story," he writes in "Unwanted," and the suggestion throughout *Day by Day* is that perhaps the last chapter of the story has been told. The "Day by Day" sequence in the book ends with a poem called "Epilogue":

> Those blessèd structures, plot and rhyme—
> why are they no help to me now
> I want to make
> something imagined, not recalled?
> I hear the noise of my own voice:
> *The painter's vision is not a lens,*
> *it trembles to caress the light.*
> But sometimes everything I write
> with the threadbare art of my eye
> seems a snapshot,
> lurid, rapid, garish, grouped,
> heightened from life,
> yet paralyzed by fact.
> All's misalliance.
> Yet why not say what happened?
> Pray for the grace of accuracy
> Vermeer gave to the sun's illumination
> stealing like the tide across a map
> to his girl solid with yearning.
> We are poor passing facts,
> warned by that to give
> each figure in the photograph
> his living name.[51]

And among the drafts for Lowell's Castine essays on New England writers, there is a moving local footnote to the poem. Lowell is writing about George Santayana:

He had spent a lifetime trying to drive back the New England he had been born to, its fashions, its morals, its reigning minds. They were too hateful, and in a way too cherished, for him to quite deny their existence. He said "I have enjoyed writing about my life more than living it."[52]

Lowell arrived at Castletown on September 2, and stayed there for ten days. Blackwood recalls that "He was fine at the beginning when he came. He was just totally happy to be home. Like a little boy. And then there was this thing that he'd committed himself to going back to Harvard. And then it started." Lowell became increasingly agitated, she says, "he never stopped moving from room to room. He couldn't make up his mind—he was changing his mind every five minutes." She believed that this restlessness signified impending mania.

> He said, "Will you come with me?" And I said, "But I don't have a house. I can't come with Sheridan and be in a motel." And as he was getting madder, I wasn't sure if I wanted to. I thought, perhaps if he can make the crossing, I'll make up my mind then. . . . But I also thought —he'll have to have an attack because he'd made such a fool of himself. He'd gone back to Lizzie, publicly. He'd made a mess. Would there be more letters, another *Dolphin?* It was too awful. And he knew that.[53]

After ten days of turbulence, Lowell telephoned Elizabeth Hardwick in New York. He was coming home early, he said, because things had become "sheer torture" at Castletown. Lady Caroline, he said, had left for London, and he would get a flight to New York on the following day—Monday, September 12. (His original intention had been to fly to Boston on the fifteenth.) On the Sunday night, Lowell was alone in Castletown, and as he wrote to Blackwood, he freakishly became "immured" in the vast mansion: first the telephone failed, then the electricity.[54] He tried to leave the house to make calls from the nearby village of Celbridge but, in the dark, was unable to locate a latch on the one door (a side door in the basement) that could be opened from inside without a key. It could not have been easy even to find his way back to his top-floor apartment; when the cleaning woman "released" him in the morning, he complained that Castletown "was a very bad place; it needs an elevator"; then, she says:

> he went down with one lot of suitcases and then he came back up again and gave me three dollars and shook hands and said he'd see me again.

He was a bit fussed about being locked in and that but otherwise he
seemed in very good form. He left a letter for Lady Caroline in there
under the lamp and asked me would I see that she got it. . . .[55]

Lowell arrived in New York on the afternoon of September 12, and
took a taxi from Kennedy Airport. When the driver reached West
67th Street, he saw that Lowell had slumped over in his seat; he was
holding a large brown-paper parcel and he seemed to be asleep.
Elizabeth Hardwick was called from the house and rode in the taxi
to Roosevelt Hospital: "But I knew that he was dead."[56] Hours
afterwards Hardwick opened the parcel Lowell had been carrying
—it was a portrait of Lady Caroline. He had brought it over to be
"valued" in New York.[57]

Lowell's death was described in the newspapers the next day as
the result of a heart attack, and the obituaries unanimously mourned
him as "perhaps the best English language poet of his generation."
At his funeral on Beacon Hill there were six hundred mourners; the
pallbearers included friends from five chapters of his life: Blair
Clark, Frank Parker, John Thompson, Peter Taylor, Robert Fitzgerald, Grey Gowrie, Robert Giroux and Frank Bidart. After the
requiem mass there was a private burial at Dunbarton, and ten days
later a memorial tribute in the American Place Theatre in New
York.

"He was resigned to dying. He knew he was going to die," says
Lowell's Cambridge friend Bill Alfred, and there are other friends
who would agree. Lowell had often said that he did not expect to
live beyond sixty; both his parents had died at sixty, he would point
out (although they didn't), "and it was as if he felt that he should
too." Caroline Blackwood calls his death a "suicide of wish": there
were "various things he said" at Castletown during his last week
which made her think that he did not expect to live. And in Frank
Bidart's view: "There was an intense sense that spring and summer
that things were building up to some crunch, that something had
to give. I didn't think it was going to be Cal that gave, but it was."
Peter Taylor simply felt "angry with Cal," as if Lowell had voluntarily elected to walk out on his old friend.[58]

Certainly, in many of the formal tributes that appeared just after
Robert Lowell's death, there was just this sense of both grief and
grievance: a feeling that the world had been robbed of a phenomenon. But there was also an acknowledgment that Lowell had per-

haps properly completed both his life and his life's work. Bidart, in a *Harvard Advocate* issue in honor of Lowell, wrote that "Valéry's words about Mallarmé come irresistibly to mind: 'Near him while he was still alive, I thought of his destiny as already realized.' "[59] And Christopher Ricks quotes words that I myself was privileged to read out at Lowell's memorial evening in New York on September 25, 1977. On Lowell's death, Ricks says, "there came to me the words of Empson on King Lear":

The scapegoat who has collected all this wisdom for us is viewed at the end with a sort of hushed envy, not I think really because he has become wise but because the general human desire for experience has been so glutted in him; he has been through everything.

We that are young
Shall never see so much, nor live so long.

NOTES

The libraries referred to are the following:

Beinecke Library, Yale University, New Haven, Conn.
Berg Collection, New York Public Library, New York City
Chalmers Memorial Library, Kenyon College, Gambier, Ohio
Columbia University Library, New York City
Dartmouth College Library, Hanover, N.H.
Firestone Library, Princeton University, Princeton, N.J.
Houghton Library, Harvard University, Cambridge, Mass.
Library of Congress, Manuscripts Division, Washington, D.C.
Newberry Library, Chicago, Ill.
University of Minnesota Libraries, Manuscripts Division, Minneapolis, Minn.
University of Washington Libraries, Manuscripts Collection, Seattle, Wash.

Chapter One

1. This and—except where indicated—all other quotations in this chapter are from Lowell's draft ms for an autobiography (Houghton Library) written in 1955–57. Some of Lowell's "memories" should be treated with caution; it is likely that he added colorful details here and there, polished up or elaborated some of his quotations, and from time to time simply invented episodes from childhood.

2. "91 Revere Street," *Life Studies* (New York: Farrar, Straus and Cudahy, 1959), pp. 23–24.

3. Ibid., p. 24.

Chapter Two

1. See Chapter One, note 1.

2. Edward Tuck Hall, *St. Mark's School: A Centennial History* (Stinehour Press,

1967), p. 82. Tuck Hall quotes from St. Mark's 1926 Report as published in St. Mark's *Bulletin,* December 1926.

3. John P. Marquand, letter to I.H., June 10, 1981.

4. Frank Parker, interview for BBC TV (1978).

5. Blair Clark, interview with I.H. (1979).

6. Ibid.

7. Ibid.

8. R.L., "Moulding the Golden Spoon." Orations in the state contest of the Ohio Inter-Collegiate Oratory Association, February 16, 1940.

9. Blair Clark, interview with I.H. (1979).

10. *Vindex* 59 (1935), pp. 156–58.

11. Frank Parker, interview with I.H. (1980).

12. Blair Clark, interview with I.H. (1979).

13. R.L. to Richard Eberhart, July 10, 1935 (Dartmouth College Library).

14. Ibid., August 1935 (Dartmouth College Library).

15. *Vindex* 59 (1935), p. 215.

Chapter Three

1. Revised and printed as *The Mad Musician,* in *Collected Verse Plays of Richard Eberhart* (Chapel Hill: University of North Carolina Press, 1962), pp. 131–66. Eberhart, in a letter to I.H., November 26, 1981, writes: "What you ought to do is reprint my entire play about him . . . wherein I try to tell the truth way back then."

2. Blair Clark, interview with I.H. (1979).

3. R.L. to Arthur Winslow, May 18, 1935 (Houghton Library).

4. Frank Parker, interview with I.H. (1980).

5. This and subsequent quotations from Anne Dick are from an interview with I.H. (1979).

6. Charlotte Lowell to R.L., August 1936 (Houghton Library).

7. Anne Dick to Charlotte Lowell, July 1936 (Houghton Library).

8. R.L. to Frank Parker, n.d.

9. R.L. to Richard Eberhart, August 23, 1936 (Dartmouth College Library).

10. R.L., "Visiting the Tates," *Sewanee Review* 67 (1959), pp. 557–58.

11. Ms in Richard Eberhart collection (Dartmouth College Library).

12. Robert Lowell Papers (Houghton Library).

13. Anne Dick, interview with I.H.

14. R.L. to Richard Eberhart, n.d. (Dartmouth College Library).

15. Charlotte Lowell to Anne Dick, 1936 (Houghton Library).

16. R. T. S. Lowell to Mrs. Evans Dick, December 22, 1936 (Houghton Library).

17. R. T. S. Lowell to Evans Dick, December 23, 1936 (Houghton Library).

18. Evans Dick to R. T. S. Lowell, December 23, 1936 (Houghton Library).

19. Robert Lowell, *Notebook 1967–68* (New York: Farrar, Straus & Giroux, 1969), p. 37.

20. R.L. ms, c. 1956 (Houghton Library).

21. Frank Parker, interview for BBC TV (1978).
22. Frank Parker, interview with I.H. (1980).
23. R.L. to Sarah Cotting, March 24, 1937 (Houghton Library).
24. R.L. to Mrs. Arthur Winslow, March 24, 1937 (Houghton Library).
25. R.L., BBC radio portrait of Ford Madox Ford, c. 1960.
26. R.L. to Anne Dick, n.d. (Houghton Library).

Chapter Four

1. R.L., "Visiting the Tates," *Sewanee Review* 67 (1959), p. 557.
2. R.L. to Richard Eberhart, n.d. (Dartmouth College Library).
3. R.L., "Visiting the Tates."
4. Ibid.
5. Ibid.
6. Allen Tate, "An Open Letter," May 24, 1937, in John T. Fain and Thomas D. Young, eds., *Literary Correspondence of Donald Davidson and Allen Tate* (Athens: University of Georgia Press, 1974), Appendix C.
7. R.L. to Charlotte Lowell, May 24, 1937 (Houghton Library).
8. Ibid.
9. Ibid.
10. R.L., draft autobiography, 1955–57 (Houghton Library).
11. R.L. to Charlotte Lowell, May 24, 1937 (Houghton Library).
12. R.L., "Visiting the Tates."
13. R.L. to Richard Eberhart, n.d. (Dartmouth College Library)
14. Ibid.
15. Arthur Mizener, *The Saddest Story* (London: The Bodley Head, 1971), p. 439. Janice Biala to George Davis, June 21, 1937.
16. R.L. to Richard Eberhart, n.d. (Dartmouth College Library).
17. R.L. to Charlotte Lowell, July 5, 1937 (Houghton Library).
18. Blair Clark, interview with I.H. (1980).
19. Anne Dick, interview with I.H. (1979).
20. Ford Madox Ford to Dale Warren, June 11, 1937 (Mizener, p. 441).
21. R.L. to Richard Eberhart, n.d. (Dartmouth College Library).
22. Peter Taylor, interview with I.H. (1980).
23. R.L. to Charlotte Lowell, July 31, 1937 (Houghton Library).
24. Robie Macauley, quoted in Mizener, p. 443.
25. R.L., "Ford Madox Ford," *New York Review of Books*, May 12, 1966.
26. Mizener, p. 442.
27. Jean Stafford, Author's Note, *The Collected Stories of Jean Stafford* (New York: Farrar, Straus and Giroux, 1969).
28. R.L. to Charlotte Lowell, August 24, 1937 (Houghton Library).
29. Mizener, p. 598.
30. R.L. to Charlotte Lowell, August 24, 1937 (Houghton Library).
31. Ibid.
32. R.T.S. Lowell to R.L., n.d. (Houghton Library).

Chapter Five

1. John Crowe Ransom to Allen Tate, October 10, 1937. Thomas Daniel Young, *Gentleman in a Dustcoat: A Biography of John Crowe Ransom* (Baton Rouge: Louisiana State University Press, 1976), p. 292.

2. R.L., "Tribute to John Crowe Ransom," *New Review* 1, no. 5 (August 1974), pp. 3–5.

3. John Thompson, *New York Review of Books* 24, no. 17 (October 17, 1977).

4. Peter Taylor, interview with I.H. (1980).

5. Ibid.

6. Ibid.

7. Ibid.

8. Ibid.

9. Ibid.

10. John Thompson, interview with I.H. (1980).

11. Peter Taylor, interview with I.H. (1980).

12. Ibid. Later Lowell was to wonder "who can doubt that bears are the wisest, most amiable, most benevolent, most virtuous and shaggiest of creatures?"—R.L. to Gertrude Buckman, March 1948.

13. Peter Taylor, "1939," *The Collected Stories of Peter Taylor* (Farrar, Straus & Giroux, 1969), p. 335.

14. Ibid., pp. 336, 337.

15. R.L., "Tribute to John Crowe Ransom."

16. R.L. to John Crowe Ransom, December 8, 1961 (Chalmers Memorial Library, Kenyon College).

17. *Kenyon Collegian*, December 15, 1974.

18. Peter Taylor, interview with I.H. (1980).

19. Ibid.

20. R.L. to Richard Eberhart, November 12, 1937 (Dartmouth College Library).

21. Richard Eberhart to R.L., 1937 (Dartmouth College Library).

22. R.L. to Richard Eberhart, November 27, 1937 (Dartmouth College Library).

23. Richard Eberhart to R.L., February 7, 1938 (Dartmouth College Library).

24. R.L., review of *The World's Body*, in *Hika*, October 1938.

25. Ms (Dartmouth College Library).

26. R.L. to Richard Eberhart, November 27, 1937 (Dartmouth College Library).

27. John Thompson, interview with I.H. (1979).

28. R.L. to Frank Parker, n.d.

29. Peter Taylor, "1939," p. 338.

30. Ibid., pp. 343, 347, 348.

31. *The Collected Stories of Jean Stafford* (Farrar, Straus & Giroux, 1969), pp. 179–93.

32. Blair Clark, interview with I.H. (1980).

33. Seattle *Times*, December 29, 1938.

34. Charlotte Lowell to Merrill Moore, May 27, 1939 (Library of Congress).

35. *Day by Day* (New York: Farrar, Straus & Giroux, 1977), p. 122.

36. R.L., "Tribute to John Crowe Ransom."

37. Blair Clark, interview with I.H. (1980).

38. Ibid.

39. Merrill Moore to R. T. S. Lowell, June 27, 1939 (Houghton Library).

40. Merrill Moore to R.L., July 11, 1939 (Houghton Library).

41. R.L. to Merrill Moore, n.d. (Houghton Library).

42. Merrill Moore to R.L., July 11, 1939 (Houghton Library).

43. Merrill Moore to Charlotte Lowell, July 26, 1939 (Library of Congress).

44. Ibid.

45. Charlotte Lowell to Merrill Moore, November 12, 1939 (Library of Congress).

46. Merrill Moore to Charlotte Lowell, March 24, 1941 (Library of Congress).

47. Ibid.

48. Merrill Moore to Charlotte Lowell, May 4, 1951. Moore notes that this was "a little game Mrs. Lowell and I are playing with each other. She said that I reminded her of the King in 'The King and I' and she identified herself when she saw it with Anna, the governess, who was always in conflict with the King. It is a little game we keep going just for fun" (Merrill Moore Papers, Library of Congress).

49. Peter Taylor, interview with I.H. (1980).

50. Orations in the state contest of the Ohio Inter-Collegiate Oratory Association, 1940.

51. R.L. to Charlotte Lowell, n.d. (Houghton Library).

52. Ibid.

53. R.L. to A. Lawrence Lowell (typed copy in Houghton Library dated "Wednesday").

54. A. Lawrence Lowell to R.L., February 21, 1940 (Houghton Library).

55. Merrill Moore to R.L., February 28, 1940 (Blair Clark papers).

56. R. T. S. Lowell to R.L. (Houghton Library).

57. R. T. S. Lowell to Richard Eberhart, December 20, 1938 (Dartmouth College Library).

58. R.L. to Charlotte Lowell, July 9, 1939 (Houghton Library).

59. Ibid., April 22, 1940 (Houghton Library).

60. Peter Taylor, interview with I.H. (1980).

61. R.L. to Charlotte Lowell, n.d. (Houghton Library).

Chapter Six

1. Peter Taylor, interview with I.H. (1980).

2. Ibid.

3. R.L. to Robie Macauley, 1940.

4. R.L. to Charlotte Lowell, April 22, 1940 (Houghton Library).

5. R.L. to Mrs. Arthur Winslow, n.d. (Houghton Library).

6. R.L. to Robie Macauley, 1940.

7. Typescript, n.d. (Houghton Library). Parts of this poem are incorporated in

"Park Street Cemetery" (*Land of Unlikeness*) and "At the Indian Killer's Grave" (*Lord Weary's Castle*).

8. R.L. to Robie Macauley, n.d.

9. Peter Taylor, interview with I.H. (1980).

10. Jean Stafford, "An Influx of Poets," *New Yorker*, November 6, 1978, p. 49.

11. Jean Stafford to Robie Macauley, n.d.

12. Jean Stafford, "An Influx of Poets," p. 49.

13. Ibid.

14. Patrick Quinn, interview with I.H. (1981).

15. Peter Taylor, interview with I.H. (1980).

16. Jean Stafford to Peter Taylor, November 1942.

17. Robert Giroux, interview with I.H. (1980).

18. Frank Parker, interview with I.H. (1980).

19. Jean Stafford, unpublished interview with Joan (Cuyler) Stillman, Westport, Conn., October 16–17, 1952.

20. Jean Stafford, "An Influx of Poets," p. 49.

21. R.L. to Robie Macauley, 1943.

22. Jean Stafford to Peter Taylor, October 1941.

23. R.L. diary (1974).

24. R.L. to Charlotte Lowell, August 1943 (Houghton Library).

25. R.L., "Sublime Feriam Sidera Vertice," *Hika*, February 1940, p. 17.

26. "On the Eve of the Feast of the Immaculate Conception 1942," *Land of Unlikeness* (Cummington, Mass.: Cummington Press, 1943), p. 12.

27. Transcript of talk, undated but c. 1960 (Houghton Library).

28. Jean Stafford to Peter Taylor, August 1943.

29. Ibid., November 1942.

30. Ibid., March 30, 1943.

31. R.L. to Charlotte Lowell, August 1943 (Houghton Library).

32. Ibid.

33. Jean Stafford to Peter Taylor, July 20, 1943.

34. Ibid., August 3, 1943.

35. R.L. to Charlotte Lowell, August 1943 (Houghton Library).

36. Typescript in Houghton Library.

37. R.L. to Charlotte Lowell, September 7, 1943 (Houghton Library).

38. R.L. to Mrs. Arthur Winslow, n.d. (Houghton Library).

39. Ms in Houghton Library.

40. R.L. to Mrs. Arthur Winslow, October 12, 1943 (Houghton Library).

41. R.L. to Peter Taylor, October 13, 1943.

42. Jim Peck, interview with I.H. (1980).

Chapter Seven

1. Ms in Houghton Library.

2. Jim Peck, interview with I.H. (1980).

3. Ibid.

4. R.L., draft autobiography, 1955–57 (Houghton Library).

5. Charlotte Lowell to Jean Stafford, October 31, 1943.

6. Allen Tate to Peter Taylor, April 10, 1949.

7. Charlotte Lowell to Jean Stafford, November 10, 1943.

8. Jean Stafford to Peter Taylor, December 22, 1943.

9. Ibid., n.d.

10. Ibid., February 11, 1944.

11. Ibid., n.d. Nancy Tate is the daughter of Allen and Caroline Tate.

12. R.L. to John Crowe Ransom, July 13, 1944 (Chalmers Memorial Library).

13. Jean Stafford to Peter Taylor, n.d.

14. Jean Stafford, "The Home Front," *Children Are Bored on Sunday* (New York: Harcourt, Brace, 1945), pp. 104–42. In 1946 Robert Lowell wrote to Richard Chase: "Jean's story 'The Home Front' is about where we lived in Black Rock—next to a huge dump and a horrible inlet of mud and refuse" (Columbia University Library).

15. Jean Stafford to Eleanor Taylor, November 16, 1944.

16. R.L. to Allen Tate, July 31, 1944 (Firestone Library).

17. Arthur Mizener, "Recent Poetry," *Accent* 5 (1944–45), 114–20.

18. John Frederick Nims, "Two Catholic Poets," *Poetry* 65 (1944–45), 264–68.

19. Randall Jarrell, "Poetry in War and Peace," *Partisan Review* 12 (1945), 120–26.

20. John Crowe Ransom to R.L., December 12, 1945 (Houghton Library).

21. R. P. Blackmur, "Notes on Eleven Poets," *Kenyon Review* 7 (1945), 339–52.

22. R.L., review of T. S. Eliot, "Four Quartets," *Sewanee Review* 51 (Summer 1943), 432–35; "A Note/on Gerard Manley Hopkins/," *Kenyon Review* 6 (Autumn 1944), 583–86.

23. R.L. to Peter Taylor, January 12, 1945

24. Jean Stafford to Peter Taylor, December 29, 1944.

25. R.L. to Peter Taylor, July 18, 1943.

26. R.L. to Allen Tate, n.d. (Firestone Library).

27. Jean Stafford to Cecile Starr, May 5, 1945.

28. R.L. to Allen Tate, July 7, 1945 (Firestone Library).

29. Jean Stafford to Cecile Starr, n.d.

Chapter Eight

1. Robert Lowell, "Randall Jarrell, 1914–1965," in *The Lost World* (New York: Collier, 1965). Reprinted in *Randall Jarrell, 1914–1965*, ed. Robert Lowell, Peter Taylor and Robert Penn Warren (Farrar, Straus & Giroux, 1967), pp. 101–12.

2. Randall Jarrell to R.L., October 1945 (?) (Houghton Library).

3. "The Quaker Graveyard in Nantucket," *Lord Weary's Castle* (Harcourt, Brace & Company, 1946).

4. Gabriel Pearson, "Robert Lowell," *Review*, no. 20 (March 1969), 3–36.

5. See Hugh B. Staples, *Robert Lowell: The First Twenty Years* (London: Faber & Faber, 1962) for a study of Lowell's use of his prose sources.

6. John Crowe Ransom to R.L., October 5, 1945 (Houghton Library).

7. Philip Rahv to R.L., January 2, 1946 (Houghton Library).

8. Ibid., January 16, 1946 (Houghton Library).

9. Jean Stafford to Allen Tate, January 4, 1946 (Firestone Library).

10. Jean Stafford to Cecile Starr, February 1946.

11. Robert Lowell, "To Delmore Schwartz," *Life Studies* (Farrar, Straus & Giroux, 1959), pp. 53–54.

12. James Atlas, *Delmore Schwartz* (New York: Farrar, Straus & Giroux, 1977), Also, Eileen Simpson in *Poets in Their Youth* (New York: Random House, 1982), pp. 123–24, writes: "Delmore, the intriguer, had hinted . . . that [Jean] was interested in another man (himself perhaps?). He had even insinuated this to Cal, whereupon Cal had socked him. The fistfight that ensued brought the Ellery Street winter to a dramatic close."

13. Jean Stafford to Peter Taylor, n.d.

14. Ibid., March 24, 1946.

15. Ibid., June 29, 1944.

16. Ibid., April 15, 1946.

17. R.L. to Peter and Eleanor Taylor, May 23, 1946.

18. Ibid.

19. Jean Stafford, "An Influx of Poets," *New Yorker,* November 6, 1978, pp. 46, 51, 52, 55.

20. Jean Stafford to Peter Taylor, December 19, 1946.

21. Cecile Starr, in a letter to I.H. (September 30, 1981), writes: "I think her love of household was at the center of her marriage to Cal."

22. R.L., "Current Poetry," *Sewanee Review* 54 (Winter 1946), 340–41.

23. R.L. to Peter Taylor, August 19, 1946.

24. Jean Stafford to Peter Taylor, July 15, 1946.

25. Jean Stafford, "An Influx of Poets," p. 43.

26. R.L. to Peter Taylor, August 13, 1946.

27. Jean Stafford, "An Influx of Poets," p. 43.

Chapter Nine

1. Jean Stafford to Peter Taylor, December 19, 1946. Eileen Simpson writes, in *Poets in Their Youth:* "Aquaphobia, which [Jean Stafford had] suffered from since childhood, kept her from swimming or boating. She confessed that as a child taking a bath had made her so anxious she had been able to manage only by organizing an elaborate ritual around it (like Molly in *The Mountain Lion*)" (New York: Random House, 1982), p. 134.

2. Gertrude Buckman, interview with I.H. (1980).

3. Ibid.

4. Jean Stafford to Eleanor and Peter Taylor, December 13, 1946.

5. Jean Stafford to Peter Taylor, December 19, 1946.

6. Jean Stafford to R.L., n.d. (Houghton Library).

7. Ibid., n.d. (Houghton Library).

8. Jean Stafford to Peter Taylor, November 26, 1946.

9. Jean Stafford to R.L., n.d. (Houghton Library).

10. Peter Taylor to R.L., November 19, 1946.

11. R.L. to Peter Taylor, December 27, 1946.

12. Jean Stafford to Peter Taylor, December 31, 1946.

13. Ibid., n.d.

14. Randall Jarrell, "From the Kingdom of Necessity," *Nation* 164 (1947), 74–77.

15. Selden Rodman, "Boston Jeremiads," *New York Times Book Review*, November 3, 1946, pp. 7 ff.

16. Anne Fremantle, review of *Lord Weary's Castle*, *Commonweal* 45 (1946–47), 283–84.

17. Austin Warren, "A Double Discipline," *Poetry* 70 (1947), 262–65.

18. Louise Bogan, "Experiment and Post-Experiment," *American Scholar* 16 (1947), 237–52.

19. Howard Moss, "Ten Poets," *Kenyon Review* 9 (1947), 290–98.

20. Richard Eberhart, "Four Poets," *Sewanee Review* 55 (1947), 324–36.

21. Robert Giroux, interview with I.H. (1980).

22. Jean Stafford to R.L., n.d. (Houghton Library).

23. R.L. to Peter Taylor, March 10, 1947.

24. Jean Stafford to R.L., n.d. (Houghton Library).

25. Ibid.

26. Gertrude Buckman, interview with I.H. (1980).

27. Descriptions from a letter by R.L. to Gertrude Buckman (July 8, 1947); quoted to I.H. in interview (1980).

28. Yaddo brochure.

29. R.L. to Gertrude Buckman, July 8, 1947; quoted to I.H. (1980).

30. Jean Stafford to Peter Taylor, July 10, 1943.

31. John Thompson to R.L., October 13, 1947 (Houghton Library).

32. R.L. to J. F. Powers, December 1, 1947.

33. Robert Frost to R.L., July 17, 1947 (Houghton Library).

34. R.L. to Charlotte Lowell, February 18, 1948 (Houghton Library).

35. Elizabeth Hardwick, interview with I.H. (1982).

36. Marcella Winslow, letter to I.H., February 19, 1982.

37. R.L. to Gertrude Buckman, October 1, 1947.

38. Elizabeth Bishop to R.L., May 1948 (Houghton Library).

39. Gertrude Buckman to R.L., April 13, 1948 (Houghton Library).

40. R.L. to Peter Taylor, February 18, 1948.

41. Gertrude Buckman to R.L., September 22, 1947 (Houghton Library).

42. R.L. to Allen Tate, September 24, 1947 (Firestone Library).

43. Gertrude Buckman to R.L., September 22, 1947 (Houghton Library).

44. Carley Dawson, interview with I.H. (1980).

45. Ibid.

46. Ibid.

47. Jean Stafford to R.L., n.d. (Houghton Library).

48. Jean Stafford to Peter Taylor, June 26, 1948.

49. Carley Dawson, interview with I.H. (1980).

50. Ibid.

51. "The Two Weeks' Vacation," unpublished ms, c. 1957 (Houghton Library).

52. Interview with a friend of R.L. and Elizabeth Bishop (1982). The friend wishes to remain anonymous but says, "I know I mustn't be the source of this, but I'm sure Elizabeth Bishop told me these things because she wanted them to be on the record to some extent."

53. "The Two Weeks' Vacation," unpublished ms, c. 1957 (Houghton Library).

54. R.L. to Charlotte Lowell, August 24, 1948 (Houghton Library).

55. Charlotte Lowell to R.L., June 22, 1947 (Houghton Library).

56. Ibid., August 1948 (Houghton Library).

57. R.L. to Peter Taylor, May 12, 1948.

58. R.L., draft autobiography 1955–57 (Houghton Library).

59. Charlotte Lowell to R.L., August 26, 1948 (Houghton Library).

60. Allen Tate to Peter Taylor, October 5, 1948.

Chapter Ten

1. Jean Stafford to Peter Taylor, December 22, 1948.

2. Jean Stafford to R.L., January 1, 1949 (Houghton Library).

3. R.L. to Caroline (Gordon) Tate, December 1948 (Firestone Library).

4. R.L. to Robie Macauley, n.d.

5. Charlotte Lowell to R.L., December 25, 1948 (Houghton Library).

6. Peter Taylor to R.L., June 28, 1948 (Houghton Library).

7. Elizabeth Bishop to R.L., December 31, 1948 (Houghton Library).

8. Peter Taylor to R.L., October 11, 1948 (Houghton Library).

9. Elizabeth Hardwick, interview with I.H. (1979).

10. R.L. to T. S. Eliot, January 18, 1948.

11. Allen Tate to Marcella Winslow, April 20, 1949.

12. Robert Hillyer, Saturday Review of Literature: "Treason's Strange Fruit" (June 11, 1949) and "Poetry's New Priesthood" (June 18, 1949).

13. Radcliffe Squires, Allen Tate (New York: Pegasus, 1971), p. 188.

14. Robert Fitzgerald, Open Letter to T. S. Eliot, Allen Tate, John Crowe Ransom, Robert Penn Warren, William Carlos Williams, J. F. Powers, Randall Jarrell, Peter Taylor, Katherine Anne Porter, Louise Bogan, Leonie Adams, Elizabeth Bishop, Marianne Moore, John Berryman, R. P. Blackmur, George Santayana, May 26, 1949.

15. Transcript of a Yaddo directors' meeting, February 26, 1949 (Malcolm Cowley Papers, Newberry Library).

16. Malcolm Cowley to Louis Kronenberger, March 8, 1949 (Newberry Library).

17. Robert Fitzgerald, Open Letter.

18. Sally Fitzgerald, interview with I.H. (1980).

19. Robert Fitzgerald, Open Letter.

20. Allen Tate to Elizabeth Hardwick, March 3, 1949 (Houghton Library).

21. Robert Fitzgerald Journal, March 4, 1949.

22. Robert Fitzgerald to Allen Tate, March 4, 1949.

23. Malcolm Cowley to Allen Tate, March 27, 1949 (Newberry Library).

24. Petition in support of Elizabeth Ames, March 21, 1949 (Newberry Library).

25. Robert Fitzgerald, Open Letter.
26. Malcolm Cowley to Granville Hicks, April 5, 1949 (Newberry Library).
27. *New York Times*, March 27, 1949.
28. *Testimony: The Memoirs of Dmitri Shostakovich*, as told to and edited by Solomon Volkov (Harper & Row, 1979), p. 198.
29. Allen Tate to Elizabeth Hardwick, March 8, 1949 (Houghton Library).
30. Ibid.
31. Ibid., March 30, 1949 (Houghton Library).
32. Ibid., March 31, 1949 (Houghton Library).
33. Robie Macauley, interview with I.H. (1980).
34. Allen Tate to Malcolm Cowley, April 4, 1949 (Newberry Library).
35. Allen Tate to Elizabeth Hardwick, April 4, 1949 (Houghton Library).
36. Peter Taylor, interview with I.H. (1979).
37. Robert Giroux, interview with I.H. (1979).
38. Ms (Houghton Library).
39. Merrill Moore to Allen Tate, April 12, 1949 (Firestone Library).
40. Peter Taylor, interview with I.H. (1979).
41. Peter Taylor to Allen Tate, April 21, 1949 (Firestone Library).
42. John Thompson, interview with I.H. (1979).
43. Merrill Moore to Peter Taylor, May 24, 1949.
44. Charlotte Lowell to Peter Taylor, April 16, 1949.
45. Robert Giroux, interview with I.H. (1979).
46. Merrill Moore to Allen Tate, May 10, 1949 (Firestone Library).
47. Allen Tate to Merrill Moore, n.d. (Library of Congress).
48. Allen Tate to Peter Taylor, April 10, 1949.
49. Allen Tate to Elizabeth Hardwick, April 18, 1949 (Houghton Library).
50. R.L. to Allen Tate, May 5, 1949 (Firestone Library).
51. Jean Stafford to Peter Taylor, May 9, 1949.
52. R.L. to Randall Jarrell, May 21, 1949 (Berg Collection).
53. Randall Jarrell to Peter Taylor, n.d.
54. Elizabeth Hardwick to R.L., June 24, 1949 (Houghton Library).
55. R.L. to Elizabeth Hardwick, July 1, 1949.
56. Ibid., July 6, 1949 (Houghton Library).
57. R. T. S. Lowell to R.L., July 13, 1949 (Houghton Library).
58. Elizabeth Hardwick, interview with I.H. (1979).
59. Lesley Parker, interview with I.H. (1981).
60. Elizabeth Hardwick, interview with I.H. (1979).
61. R.L. to Elizabeth Hardwick, dated "First Night" from the Payne Whitney Clinic.
62. Ibid., September 15, 1949.

Chapter Eleven

1. Elizabeth Hardwick to Peter and Eleanor Taylor, October 20, 1949.
2. Ibid., September 20, 1949.
3. Elizabeth Hardwick to Peter and Eleanor Taylor, October 20, 1949.

4. R.L. to Peter Taylor, n.d. (Houghton Library).
5. Allen Tate to R.L., October 11, 1949 (Houghton Library).
6. Caroline (Gordon) Tate to Elizabeth Hardwick, n.d. (Houghton Library).
7. Ibid.
8. Elizabeth Hardwick, interview with I.H. (1982).
9. Merrill Moore to Elizabeth Hardwick, October 5, 1949 (Houghton Library).
10. R.L. to Charlotte Lowell, December 26, 1949 (Houghton Library).
11. R. T. S. Lowell to R.L., November 11, 1949 (Houghton Library).
12. R.L. to Charlotte Lowell, November 5, 1949 (Houghton Library).
13. R.L. to Allen Tate, December 29, 1949 (Firestone Library).
14. Elizabeth Hardwick to Charlotte Lowell, February 5, 1949 (Houghton Library).
15. Ibid.
16. R.L. to Allen Tate, March 15, 1950 (?)(Firestone Library).
17. R.L. to Charlotte Lowell, March 10, 1950 (Houghton Library).
18. Elizabeth Hardwick to Charlotte Lowell, May 13, 1950 (Houghton Library).
19. John Crowe Ransom to R.L., September 7, 1950 (Houghton Library).
20. Charlotte Lowell to R.L., August 26, 1950 (Houghton Library).
21. R. T. S. Lowell to R.L., August 26, 1950 (Houghton Library).
22. Cable to R.L. and Elizabeth Hardwick at the Little Hotel, 33 West St., N.Y.C. (Houghton Library).
23. Autobiography, draft ms, 1955–57 (Houghton Library).
24. Elizabeth Hardwick, interview with I.H. (1979).
25. R.L. to Charlotte Lowell, October 10, 1950 (Houghton Library).
26. Postcard from R.L. to Charlotte Lowell, October 10, 1950 (Houghton Library).
27. Elizabeth Hardwick to Robie and Anne Macauley, November 12, 1950.
28. Ibid.
29. R.L. to Charlotte Lowell, December 26, 1950 (Houghton Library).
30. R.L. to Peter Taylor, January 15, 1951.
31. R.L. to Charlotte Lowell, December 26, 1950 (Houghton Library).
32. Elizabeth Hardwick, interview with I.H. (1979).
33. R.L. to Peter Taylor, January 15, 1951.
34. Ibid.
35. Ibid.
36. R.L. to Charlotte Lowell, December 26, 1950 (Houghton Library).
37. George Santayana to R.L., July 25, 1947 (Houghton Library).
38. Elizabeth Hardwick to Robie and Anne Macauley, November 12, 1950.
39. Elizabeth Hardwick, interview with I.H. (1982).
40. Elizabeth Hardwick, "Living in Italy: Reflections on Bernard Berenson," in *A View of My Own* (New York: Farrar, Straus & Giroux, 1962), pp. 203–14.
41. Ibid.
42. Elizabeth Hardwick, interview with I.H. (1982).
43. R.L. to Randall Jarrell, October 6, 1951 (Berg Collection).
44. R.L. to Harriet Winslow, n.d. (Houghton Library).
45. Elizabeth Hardwick, interview with I.H. (1979).
46. Charlotte Lowell to R.L., October 18, 1951 (Houghton Library).

47. Elizabeth Hardwick, interview with I.H. (1979).

48. R.L. to Elizabeth Hardwick, from Hotel Bristol, in Pau, France, n.d.

49. Ibid., September 17, 1951.

50. R.L., draft autobiography, 1955–57 (Houghton Library).

51. R.L. to Randall Jarrell, October 6, 1951 (Berg Collection).

52. Ibid.

53. R.L., draft autobiography.

54. R.L. to Randall Jarrell, October 6, 1951 (Berg Collection).

55. R.L. to Charlotte Lowell, n.d. (Houghton Library).

56. R.L. to Peter Taylor, April 30, 1952.

57. Elizabeth Hardwick to Robie and Anne Macauley, November 29, 1952.

58. Ibid., February 22, 1952.

59. R.L. to Randall Jarrell, February 24, 1952 (Berg Collection).

60. Ibid.

61. R.L. to Peter Taylor, April 24, 1952.

62. Elizabeth Hardwick to Robie Macauley, April 15, 1952.

63. Shepherd Brooks, interview with I.H. (1980).

64. Elizabeth Hardwick to Robie Macauley, May 7, 1952.

65. Ibid.

66. Elizabeth Hardwick to Robie Macauley, May 16, 1952.

67. R.L. to Peter Taylor, July (?) 1952.

68. *The Mills of the Kavanaughs* (New York: Harcourt, Brace & Company, 1951).

69. Randall Jarrell, "A View of Three Poets," *Partisan Review* 17 (1951), 691–700. Reprinted in *Poetry and the Age* (London: Faber & Faber, 1965).

70. R.L. to Randall Jarrell, February 24, 1952 (Berg Collection).

71. William Carlos Williams, "In a Mood of Tragedy," *New York Times Book Review,* April 22, 1951, p. 6. Reprinted in *Selected Essays* (New York: Random House, 1954).

72. R.L. to Randall Jarrell, February 24, 1952 (Berg Collection).

73. R.L. to William Carlos Williams, from Amsterdam, n.d. (Beinecke Library).

74. Rolfe Humphries, "Verse Chronicle," *Nation,* 173 (1951), 76–77.

75. David Daiches, "Some Recent Poetry," *Yale Review* 41 (1951), 153–57.

76. Richard Eberhart, "Five Poets," *Kenyon Review* 14 (1952), 168–76.

77. Jean Stafford to R.L., 1947 (Houghton Library).

78. Jean Stafford, "A Country Love Story," *The Collected Stories of Jean Stafford* (New York: Farrar, Straus & Giroux, 1969), pp. 133–45.

79. *For the Union Dead* (New York: Farrar, Straus & Giroux, 1964), p. 6.

Chapter Twelve

1. R.L. to Peter Taylor, n.d.

2. Elizabeth Hardwick to Charlotte Lowell, August 26, 1952 (Houghton Library).

3. R.L. to Blair Clark, September 15, 1952.

4. Shepherd Brooks, interview with I.H. (1980).

5. Ibid.

6. Ibid.

7. Elizabeth Hardwick to Robie and Anne Macauley, August 24, 1952.

8. "A Mad Negro Soldier Confined at Munich," *Life Studies* (New York: Farrar, Straus & Giroux, 1964), p. 8.

9. Elizabeth Hardwick to Robie and Anne Macauley, August 25, 1952.

10. Ibid., August 24, 1952.

11. Elizabeth Hardwick, interview with I.H. (1979).

12. Elizabeth Hardwick to Robie and Anne Macauley, August 24, 1952.

13. Ibid., August 25, 1952.

14. Ibid.

15. Elizabeth Hardwick, interview with I.H. (1979).

16. Elizabeth Hardwick to Robie and Anne Macauley, September 2, 1952.

17. Ibid., September 5, 1952.

18. Ibid., October 19, 1952.

19. R.L. to Robie and Anne Macauley, September 15, 1952.

20. R.L. to Charlotte Lowell, October 19, 1952 (Houghton Library).

21. Elizabeth Hardwick to Robie and Anne Macauley, October 19, 1952.

22. R.L. to Blair Clark, September 15, 1952.

23. Elizabeth Hardwick to Robie and Anne Macauley, October 19, 1952.

24. R.L. to Allen Tate, November 5, 1952 (Firestone Library).

25. Ibid.

26. R.L. to Peter Taylor, December 7, 1952.

27. Ibid.

28. R.L. to Blair Clark, December 3, 1952.

29. R.L. to John Crowe Ransom, November 24, 1952 (Chalmers Memorial Library).

30. *Life Studies* (New York: Farrar, Straus & Giroux, 1964), p. 55.

31. Ibid., pp. 51–52.

32. R.L. to Allen Tate, November 5, 1952 (Firestone Library).

33. Elizabeth Hardwick to Blair and Holly Clark, February 3, 1953.

34. R.L. to Harriet Winslow, September 26, 1953 (Houghton Library).

35. Elizabeth Hardwick to Blair and Holly Clark, February 3, 1953.

36. Elizabeth Hardwick to Robie and Anne Macauley, n.d.

37. R.L. to Charlotte Lowell, March 3, 1953.

38. R.L. to Peter Taylor, March 25, 1953.

39. Ibid., April 29, 1953.

40. R.L. to Harriet Winslow, April 29, 1953 (Houghton Library).

41. Ibid., September 26, 1953 (Houghton Library).

42. R.L. to Peter Taylor, October 11, 1953.

43. R.L. to Allen Tate, December 2, 1953 (Firestone Library).

44. Elizabeth Hardwick to Blair Clark, October 16, 1953.

45. Merrill Moore to Elizabeth Hardwick, July 22, 1953 (Houghton Library).

46. R.L. to Peter Taylor, March 11, 1954.

47. R.L. to Elizabeth Hardwick, September 10, 1953.

48. Elizabeth Hardwick to R.L., September 12, 1953 (Houghton Library).

49. Elizabeth Hardwick to Blair Clark, October 16, 1953.

50. Blair Clark, interview with I.H. (1980).

51. R.L. to Blair and Holly Clark, n.d.

52. R.L. to Elizabeth Hardwick, n.d.

53. R.L., draft autobiography, 1955–57 (Houghton Library).

54. Ibid.

55. Blair Clark, interview with I.H. (1980).

56. *Life Studies*, pp. 77–78. In an early draft of the poem "Sailing from Rapallo," Lowell writes:

> The young, very au courant hospital doctor
> Owned a presentation copy
> Of Ezra Pound's *Cantos*.
> Worried by my hypo-mania
> He gave me a bottle of chlorpromazene [*sic*].

56. Autobiography, draft ms, 1955–57 (Houghton Library).

57. R.L. to Blair Clark, March 11, 1954.

Chapter Thirteen

1. Elizabeth Hardwick to Blair and Holly Clark, February 20, 1954.

2. R.L. to Blair Clark, March 21, 1954.

3. R.L. to Peter Taylor, March 19, 1954.

4. R.L. to Blair Clark, March 21, 1954.

5. Blair Clark, interview with I.H. (1981).

6. Giovanna Madonia to R.L., March 21, 1954; translated from the Italian by Holly Eley (Houghton Library).

7. Ibid.

8. Ibid.

9. Elizabeth Hardwick to Blair Clark, March 27, 1954.

10. R.L. to Blair Clark, March 30, 1954.

11. Elizabeth Hardwick to Blair Clark, March 27, 1954.

12. Ibid, April 1, 1954.

13. Ibid, n.d.

14. Diary of Van Meter Ames, read to I.H. by Elizabeth Bettman (1981).

15. George Ford, letter to I.H. (1981).

16. Elizabeth Bettman, interview with I.H. (1981).

17. John Thompson, interview with I.H. (1979).

18. Elizabeth Bettman, interview with I.H. (1981).

19. R.L. to Ezra Pound, March 10, 1954 (Beinecke Library).

20. Ibid., March 25, 1954 (Beinecke Library).

21. Ibid., March 30, 1954 (Beinecke Library).

22. Ms poem (Beinecke Library).

23. Cable from Blair Clark to Elizabeth Hardwick, April 12, 1954 (Houghton Library).

24. Elizabeth Hardwick to Blair Clark, April 10, 1954.

25. Elizabeth Hardwick to Blair and Holly Clark, May 4, 1954.
26. Giovanna Madonia to Blair Clark, March 19, 1954.
27. Elizabeth Hardwick to Blair Clark, April 4, 1954.
28. Philip Piker to Merrill Moore, April 26, 1954 (Houghton Library).
29. Elizabeth Hardwick to Blair Clark, May 15, 1954.
30. Ibid., June 9, 1954.
31. Ibid., June 15, 1954.
32. Ibid., June 22, 1954.
33. Giovanna Madonia to Blair Clark, May 23, 1954.
34. R.L., draft autobiography, 1955–57 (Houghton Library).
35. R.L. to Blair Clark, August 6, 1954.
36. Elizabeth Hardwick to Blair Clark, August 31, 1954.
37. Ibid.
38. R.L. to Peter Taylor, October 24, 1954.

Chapter Fourteen

1. Elizabeth Hardwick to Peter Taylor, February 10, 1955.
2. R.L. to John Crowe Ransom, February 24, 1955 (Chalmers Memorial Library).
3. Elizabeth Hardwick to Blair and Holly Clark, November 29, 1954.
4. R.L., draft autobiography, 1955–57 (Houghton Library).
5. R.L. to Ezra Pound, April 17, 1955 (Beinecke Library).
6. R.L. to Peter Taylor, April 11, 1955.
7. R.L. to Blair Clark, May 7, 1955.
8. Elizabeth Hardwick to Harriet Winslow, April 22, 1955 (Houghton Library).
9. R.L. to Blair Clark, May 7, 1955.
10. Ibid.
11. R.L. to William Carlos Williams, June 24, 1957 (Beinecke Library).
12. R.L. to Peter Taylor, November 6, 1955.
13. Ibid.
14. R.L. to William Carlos Williams, December 2, 1955 (Beinecke Library).
15. R.L. to Peter Taylor, November 6, 1955.
16. R.L. to Blair Clark, May 7, 1955.
17. Rev. Whitney Hale to R.L., November 12, 1955 (Houghton Library).
18. R.L. to Peter Taylor, February 12, 1956.
19. R.L. to Harriet Winslow, February 13, 1956 (Houghton Library).
20. Ibid., March 8, 1956 (Houghton Library).
21. Quoted in Christopher Dawson, "Religious Enthusiasm," *The Month* (1951).
22. R.L., draft autobiography.
23. Ibid.
24. Ibid.
25. Ibid.
26. Ibid.
27. Ibid.
28. R.L. to Harriet Winslow, April 10, 1957 (Houghton Library).

29. R.L. to J. F. Powers, May 16, 1956.

30. Ibid., February 6, 1957.

31. Elizabeth Bishop to R.L., September 4, 1956 (Houghton Library).

32. Robert Lowell, Interview, *Review*, no. 26 (Summer 1971).

33. Robert Lowell, interview with Frederick Seidel, *Paris Review* 25 (Winter–Spring 1961), 56–95.

34. In *Encounter* 11 (April 1954), 32.

35. Robert Lowell, "William Carlos Williams," *Hudson Review* 14 (1961–62).

36. Ibid.

37. R.L. to Randall Jarrell, October 24, 1957 (Berg Collection).

38. R.L., "After Enjoying Six or Seven Essays on Me," *Salmagundi*, no. 37 (Spring 1977), 112–15.

39. Ibid.

40. Elizabeth Bishop to R.L., December 14, 1957 (Houghton Library).

41. R.L. to William Carlos Williams, September 30, 1957 (Beinecke Library).

42. R.L. to Randall Jarrell, October 11, 1957 (Berg Collection).

43. Ibid., October 24, 1957.

44. Ibid. In 1951, Jarrell had written to Lowell from Princeton: "I had a boy at Colorado last summer who was good (an excellent Rilke translation) and most of his poems were excellent though unconscious imitations of you. You'd had him in a class. De Witt Snodgrass, poor ill-named one! When you influence people, when your poems influence theirs, that is—you really mow them down. . . ." (Houghton Library).

45. Seidel, *Paris Review* interview.

46. Elizabeth Bishop, "The Man-Moth," *The Complete Poems* (New York: Farrar, Straus & Giroux, 1969), p. 15.

47. R.L. to Randall Jarrell, October 24, 1957.

48. Elizabeth Bishop to R.L., December 14, 1957 (Houghton Library).

49. Allen Tate to R.L., December 3, 1957 (Houghton Library).

50. Elizabeth Bishop to R.L., December 11, 1957 (Houghton Library).

51. Friend of R.L. and Bishop to I.H. (1982).

52. Ms (Houghton Library).

53. Elizabeth Hardwick to Harriet Winslow, November 22, 1957 (Houghton Library).

54. Elizabeth Hardwick to Allen Tate, December 16, 1957 (Firestone Library).

55. Dido Merwin, interview with I.H. (1980).

56. Elizabeth Hardwick, interview with I.H. (1981).

57. William Alfred, interview with I.H. (1981).

58. Christina Lowell Brazelton, interview with I.H. (1980).

59. Elizabeth Hardwick to Harriet Winslow, December 15, 1957 (Houghton Library).

60. Ibid., January 20, 1958 (Houghton Library).

61. Ibid.

62. Esther Brooks, interview with I.H. (1981).

63. Elizabeth Hardwick to Harriet Winslow, January 24, 1958 (Houghton Library).

64. R.L. to Allen Tate, January 24, 1958 (Firestone Library).

65. Allen Tate to R.L., January 31, 1958 (Houghton Library).

66. Elizabeth Hardwick to Harriet Winslow, February 2, 1958 (Houghton Library).

67. Elizabeth Hardwick to Blair Clark, February 16, 1958.

Chapter Fifteen

1. Ms (Houghton Library).

2. *Life Studies* (New York: Farrar, Straus & Giroux, 1964), pp. 81–82.

3. *Near the Ocean* (New York: Farrar, Straus & Giroux, 1967), p. 41.

4. *Notebook 1967–68* (New York: Farrar, Straus & Giroux, 1969), p. 89.

5. Ann Adden to R.L., n.d. (Houghton Library).

6. Elizabeth Hardwick to Harriet Winslow, January 2, 1958 (Houghton Library).

7. Elizabeth Hardwick to Blair and Holly Clark, February 16, 1958.

8. Ibid.

9. Ibid.

10. Elizabeth Hardwick to Harriet Winslow, February 15, 1958 (Houghton Library).

11. Blair Clark to Charles P. Curtis, March 5, 1958.

12. Charles P. Curtis to Blair Clark, March 13, 1958.

13. R.L. to Ezra Pound, January 29, 1958 (Beinecke Library).

14. R.L. to Harriet Winslow, March 15, 1958 (Houghton Library).

15. R.L. to Peter Taylor, March 15, 1958.

16. Ibid.

17. R.L. to Harriet Winslow, March 15, 1958 (Houghton Library).

18. Elizabeth Hardwick to Harriet Winslow, March 2, 1958 (Houghton Library).

19. "Home After Three Months Away," *Life Studies,* p. 83.

20. Seidel, *Paris Review* interview.

21. R.L. to Peter Taylor, February 12, 1956.

22. Elizabeth Hardwick, interview with I.H. (1982).

23. Ibid.

24. Elizabeth Hardwick to Harriet Winslow, October 20, 1958 (Houghton Library).

25. Hugh B. Staples, *Robert Lowell: The First Twenty Years* (Faber & Faber, 1962), pp. 71–72.

26. *Life Studies* ms (Houghton Library).

27. Ibid.

28. R.L. to William Carlos Williams, February 19, 1958 (Beinecke Library).

29. R.L. to Hugh B. Staples, December 24, 1958.

30. *Life Studies* ms (Houghton Library).

31. R.L. on "Skunk Hour," in *The Contemporary Poet as Artist and Critic,* ed. Anthony Ostroff (Boston: Little, Brown, 1964), pp. 71–110.

32. Ibid.

33. Elizabeth Hardwick, interview with I.H. (1982).

34. R.L. on "Skunk Hour," in Ostroff (ed.), *The Contemporary Poet* . . .

35. R.L. to Hugh B. Staples, December 24, 1958.

36. William Carlos Williams to R.L., November 24, 1958 (Houghton Library).

37. Charles Monteith, interview with I.H. (1980).

38. A. Alvarez, "Something New in Verse," *Observer*, April 12, 1959, p. 22. Reprinted in *Beyond All This Fiddle* (London: Allen Lane, 1968).

39. G. S. Fraser, "I, They, We," *New Statesman* 57 (1959), 614–15.

40. Roy Fuller in *London Magazine*, no. 6 (August 1959), 68–73.

41. Frank Kermode, "Talent and More," *Spectator* 300 (1959), 628.

42. Peter Dickinson, "More and More Poems," *Punch* 246 (1959), 659.

43. Philip Larkin, "Collected Poems," *Manchester Guardian Weekly*, May 21, 1959, p. 10.

44. Richard Eberhart, "A Poet's People," *New York Times Book Review*, May 3, 1959, pp. 4 ff.

45. F. W. Dupee, "The Battle of Robert Lowell," *Partisan Review* 26 (1959), 473–75. Reprinted in F. W. Dupee, *The King of the Cats and Other Remarks on Writers and Writing* (New York: Farrar, Straus & Giroux, 1965).

46. John Thompson, "Two Poets," *Kenyon Review* 21 (1959), 482–90.

47. Ibid.

48. Joseph Bennett, "Two Americans, a Brahmin and the Bourgeoisie," *Hudson Review* 12 (1959), 431–39.

49. Thom Gunn, "Excellence and Variety," *Yale Review*, 49 (1960), 295–395.

50. M. L. Rosenthal, "Poetry as Confession," *Nation* 190 (1959), 154–55.

51. Daniel G. Hoffman, "Arrivals and Rebirths," *Sewanee Review* 68 (1960), 118–37.

52. R.L. to Edmund Wilson, May 19, 1959 (Beinecke Library).

53. Allen Tate to R.L., May 8, 1959 (Houghton Library).

Chapter Sixteen

1. Elizabeth Hardwick, interview with I.H. (1981).

2. *For the Union Dead* (New York: Farrar, Straus & Giroux, 1964), pp. 36, 37.

3. Elizabeth Hardwick to Robie and Anne Macauley, March 20, 1959.

4. R.L. to John Berryman, March 15, 1959 (University of Minnesota Libraries).

5. Elizabeth Hardwick to Allen Tate, June 1, 1959 (Firestone Library).

6. R.L. to Randall Jarrell, April 1, 1958 (Berg Collection).

7. R.L. to Peter Taylor, October 31, 1958.

8. R.L. to Harriet Winslow, August 9, 1959 (Houghton Library).

9. R.L. to Randall Jarrell, January 3, 1960 (Berg Collection).

10. Address of Robert Lowell, National Book Awards, March 23, 1960.

11. Ms (Houghton Library).

12. Program, Boston Arts Festival, June 1960.

13. Title poem of *For the Union Dead*, p. 71.

14. Ibid., p. 72.

15. R.L. to Allen Tate, November 18, 1960 (Firestone Library).

16. R.L. to Randall Jarrell, February 15, 1960 (Berg Collection).

17. Elizabeth Bishop to R.L., June 29, 1960 (Houghton Library).

18. William Meredith, interview with I.H. (1981).

19. R.L. to William Meredith, March 3, 1960.

20. R.L. to Harriet Winslow, July 31, 1961 (Houghton Library).

21. R.L., letter to the *Village Voice,* November 19, 1964, p. 4.

22. R.L. to William Meredith, March 3, 1960.

23. William Meredith to R.L., March 28, 1960.

24. R.L. to William Meredith (summer 1960), n.d.

25. Ibid., August 25, 1960.

26. Washington *Star,* November 1, 1960.

27. R.L. to Peter Taylor, October 12, 1960.

28. Ibid.

29. Ibid., December 17, 1960.

30. William Meredith, interview with I.H. (1981).

31. R.L. to Peter Taylor, October 12, 1960.

32. R.L. to Edmund Wilson, December 16, 1960 (Beinecke Library).

33. Elizabeth Hardwick to Harriet Winslow, January 10, 1961 (Houghton Library).

34. Blair Clark, interview with I.H. (1981).

35. William Meredith, interview with I.H. (1981).

36. William Meredith to Adrienne Rich and Philip Booth, March 17, 1961.

37. Elizabeth Hardwick, interview with I.H. (1981).

38. Ibid.

39. Ibid.

40. R.L. to T. S. Eliot, June 30, 1961.

41. Elizabeth Hardwick to R.L., June 17, 1961 (Houghton Library).

42. R.L. to Elizabeth Hardwick, June 16, 1961.

43. Elizabeth Hardwick to R.L., June 17, 1961 (Houghton Library).

44. R.L. to Elizabeth Hardwick, June 18, 1961.

45. Ms (Elizabeth Hardwick).

46. Elizabeth Hardwick to Marcella Winslow, August 19, 1961 (Houghton Library).

47. R.L. to Peter Taylor, August 7, 1961.

48. R.L. to William Meredith, September 8, 1961.

49. R.L. to Randall Jarrell, November 7, 1961 (Berg Collection).

50. *Imitations* (New York: Farrar, Straus & Giroux, 1961), pp. xi–xiii (Introduction by R.L.).

51. T. S. Eliot to R.L., June 1, 1961 (Houghton Library).

52. Ben Bellitt, "*Imitations:* Translation as Personal Mode," *Salmagundi* 1, no. 4 (Winter 1966–67), 44–56.

53. R.L., Introduction to *Imitations,* pp. xi–xii.

54. George Steiner, "Two Translations," *Kenyon Review* 23 (1961), 714–21.

55. Louis Simpson, "Matters of Tact," *Hudson Review* 14 (1961–62), 614–17.

56. Thom Gunn, "Imitations and Originals," *Yale Review* 51 (1962), 480–89.

57. "To the Reader," *Imitations,* p. 46.

58. "Saturday Night in the Village," *Imitations*, p. 28.

59. George Kay (ed.), *Penguin Book of Italian Verse* (London, 1958), p. 287.

60. Edmund Wilson, *New Yorker*, June 2, 1962, p. 126.

61. A. Alvarez, *Observer*, May 26, 1962.

62. Dudley Fitts, "It's Fidelity to the Spirit That Counts," *New York Times Book Review*, November 12, 1961, pp. 5 ff.

63. R.L. to A. Alvarez, November 7, 1961.

64. R.L. to Randall Jarrell, November 7, 1961 (Berg Collection).

65. Randall Jarrell to R.L., n.d. (Houghton Library).

Chapter 17

1. R.L. to Randall Jarrell, November 7, 1961 (Berg Collection).

2. R.L. to Harriet Winslow, October 25, 1961 (Houghton Library).

3. R.L. to William Meredith, October 20, 1961.

4. "The Cold War and the West," *Partisan Review* 29 (Winter 1962), p. 47.

5. *For the Union Dead* (New York: Farrar, Straus & Giroux, 1964), p. 11.

6. R.L. to Randall Jarrell, November 7, 1961 (Berg Collection).

7. R.L. to A. Alvarez, November 7, 1961.

8. "Eye and Tooth," *For the Union Dead*, p. 11.

9. R.L. to Isabella Gardner, October 10, 1961; quoted in Steven Gould Axelrod, *Robert Lowell: Life and Art* (Princeton, N.J.: Princeton University Press, 1978).

10. R.L. to John Berryman, March 18, 1962 (University of Minnesota Libraries).

11. "Middle Age," *For the Union Dead* p. 7

12. "Fall 1961," *For the Union Dead*, p. 12.

13. "Myopia: a Night," *For the Union Dead*, p. 33.

14. "Fall 1961," *For the Union Dead*, p. 11.

15. R.L. to John Berryman, March 18, 1962.

16. R.L. to Edmund Wilson, March 31, 1962 (Beinecke Library).

17. R.L., interview with Richard Gilman, *New York Times*, May 5, 1968, pp. D1 ff.

18. R.L. to Edmund Wilson, May 31, 1962 (Beinecke Library).

19. R.L., interview with A. Alvarez, in *Under Pressure* (London: Penguin, 1965).

20. Elizabeth Bishop to R.L., April 4, 1962 (Houghton Library).

21. Keith Botsford, interview with I.H. (1981).

22. Elizabeth Bishop to Elizabeth Hardwick, September 13, 1962 (Houghton Library).

23. Keith Botsford, interview with I.H. (1981).

24. Ibid.

25. R.L. to Edmund Wilson, March 31, 1962 (Beinecke Library).

26. Elizabeth Bishop to Elizabeth Hardwick, September 13, 1962 (Houghton Library).

27. Keith Botsford, interview with I.H. (1981).

28. Ibid.

29. Blair Clark, interview with I.H. (1979).

30. R.L. to Harriet Winslow, January 23, 1963 (Houghton Library).

31. R.L. to Philip Booth, January 15, 1962.

32. R.L. to Allen Tate, February 15, 1963 (Houghton Library).

33. Elizabeth Hardwick, interview with I.H. (1981).

34. R.L. to Harriet Winslow, January 23, 1963 (Houghton Library).

35. Robert Silvers, interview with I.H. (1981).

36. "Night Sweat," *For the Union Dead,* p. 69.

37. R.L. to Randall Jarrell, May 7, 1963 (Berg Collection).

38. R.L. to Elizabeth Hardwick, July 24, 1963.

39. Ibid., n.d.

40. Ibid., July 24, 1963.

41. Jonathan Miller, interview with I.H. (1980).

42. Elizabeth Hardwick to Allen Tate, January 9, 1964 (Firestone Library).

43. William Meredith, interview with I.H. (1981).

44. R.L. to T. S. Eliot, March 4, 1964.

45. R.L. to Randall Jarrell, May 11, 1964 (Berg Collection).

46. Stephen Spender to R.L., May 1964 (Houghton Library).

47. Jean Stafford to R.L., May 8, 1964 (Houghton Library).

48. "Soft Wood," *For the Union Dead,* p. 64.

49. John Berryman to R.L., September 13, 1963 (Houghton Library).

50. Irvin Ehrenpreis, "The Age of Lowell," *Stratford upon Avon Studies* 7, ed. John Russell Brown and Bernard Harris (London: Edward Arnold, 1965).

51. Richard Poirier, "Our Truest Historian," *New York Herald Tribune Weekly Book Review,* October 11, 1964, p. 1.

52. Stanley Kunitz, "Talk with Robert Lowell," *New York Times Book Review,* October 4, 1964, pp. 34–39.

53. R.L. to Allen Tate, October 9, 1964 (Firestone Library).

54. John Berryman to R.L., September 13, 1963 (Houghton Library).

Chapter Eighteen

1. R.L., *The Old Glory,* rev. ed. (New York: Farrar, Straus & Giroux, 1968), p. 217 (Introduction by Robert Brustein).

2. "Benito Cereno," *The Old Glory,* pp. 180–81.

3. Jonathan Miller, "Director's Note," *The Old Glory,* p. 221.

4. "Endecott and the Red Cross," *The Old Glory,* p. 48.

5. R.L. interview with Stanley Kunitz, *New York Times Book Review,* October 4, 1964.

6. R.L. to Blair Clark, August 1, 1964.

7. Jonathan Miller, interview with I.H. (1980).

8. Ibid.

9. Ibid.

10. W. D. Snodgrass, "In Praise of Robert Lowell," *New York Review of Books* 3 (December 3, 1964).

11. Randall Jarrell, "A Masterpiece," *New York Times,* November 29, 1964, II, p. 3.

12. Jonathan Miller, interview with I.H. (1980).

13. Vija Vetra, interview with I.H. (1981).

14. Ibid.

15. Ibid.

16. Ibid.

17. Ibid.

18. Ibid.

19. Ibid.

20. R.L. to Vija Vetra, January 30, 1965.

21. R.L. to Elizabeth Hardwick, February 5, 1965.

22. Ibid., February 9, 1965.

23. Vija Vetra, interview with I.H. (1981).

24. Migdal, Low and Tenny to Vija Vetra, February 24, 1965.

25. Elizabeth Hardwick, interview with I.H. (1982).

26. Blair Clark, interview with I.H. (1979).

27. R.L., interview with Richard Gilman, *New York Times,* May 5, 1968.

28. Blair Clark, interview with I.H. (1979).

29. Eric F. Goldman, *The Tragedy of Lyndon Johnson* (New York: Knopf, 1969), p. 421.

30. Ibid.

31. Robert Silvers, interview with I.H. (1981).

32. *New York Times,* June 3, 1965, p. 1.

33. Goldman, *Lyndon Johnson,* p. 429.

34. Ibid.

35. *New York Times,* June 4, 1965, p. 2.

36. Goldman, *Lyndon Johnson,* p. 447.

37. Robert Silvers, interview with I.H. (1981).

38. Blair Clark, interview with I.H. (1979).

39. Ibid.

40. Philip Roth, "Festival of the Arts Now?" *New York Times,* June 15, 1965, p. 40.

41. Arthur Schlesinger, "What Schlesinger Said," *New York Times,* June 21, 1965, p. 28.

42. Dwight Macdonald, "A Day at the White House," *New York Review of Books* 5 (July 15, 1965), pp. 10–15.

43. Mark Van Doren, quoted in Goldman, *Lyndon Johnson.*

44. Goldman, *Lyndon Johnson.*

45. Ibid.

46. *New York Times,* August 5, 1965.

47. Ibid.

48. R.L. interview, *Review,* no. 26 (Summer 1971).

49. R.L., interview with A. Alvarez, *Observer* (London), July 21, 1963.

50. *Near the Ocean* (New York: Farrar, Straus & Giroux, 1971), pp. 19–20.

51. Alan Williamson, Lowell Special Number, *Agenda,* 18, no. 3 (1980).

52. Ms (Houghton Library).
53. "Waking Early Sunday Morning," *Near the Ocean,* p. 20.
54. "Central Park," *Near the Ocean,* p. 33.
55. Ibid., p. 34.
56. Title poem of *Near the Ocean,* p. 38.
57. "Fourth of July in Maine," *Near the Ocean,* pp. 28–29.
58. Elizabeth Hardwick, interview with I.H. (1982).
59. Elizabeth Hardwick to Blair Clark, n.d.
60. Elizabeth Hardwick to R.L., n.d.

Chapter Nineteen

1. R.L. to Elizabeth Hardwick, February 5, 1965.
2. R.L., interview, *Review,* no. 26 (Summer 1971).
3. R.L. to Elizabeth Hardwick, February 5, 1965.
4. R.L. to J. F. Powers, February 5, 1948.
5. Theodore Roethke to Kenneth Burke, September 18, 1947, in *Selected Letters of Theodore Roethke,* ed. Ralph J. Mills, Jr. (Faber & Faber, 1970), p. 134.
6. Theodore Roethke to Dylan Thomas, December 1, 1952, in *Selected Letters,* p. 182.
7. Theodore Roethke to Isabella Gardner, February 17, 1963, in *Selected Letters,* p. 258.
8. R.L. to Theodore Roethke, December 18, 1961 (University of Washington Libraries).
9. Ibid., April 10, 1957.
10. Ibid., July 10, 1963.
11. Ibid., October 10, 1961.
12. Theodore Roethke, "Four for Sir John Davies," *The Waking* (New York: Doubleday, 1953).
13. R.L. to Theodore Roethke, June 6, 1958 (University of Washington Libraries).
14. Ibid., March 1958.
15. Elizabeth Hardwick, interview with I.H. (1982).
16. R.L. to Theodore Roethke, July 10, 1963 (University of Washington Libraries).
17. R.L. to Elizabeth Hardwick, February 5, 1965 (Houghton Library).
18. R.L. to Robert Giroux, April 8, 1965.
19. R.L. to Valerie Eliot, April 12, 1965.
20. R.L. to Charles Monteith, February 26, 1965.
21. John Thompson, interview with I.H. (1979).
22. R.L., Peter Taylor and Robert Penn Warren (eds.), *Randall Jarrell, 1914–1965* (New York: Farrar, Straus and Giroux, 1967), pp. 101–12.
23. Ibid.
24. R.L. to Randall Jarrell, April 29, 1965 (Berg Collection).
25. *New York Times,* October 15, 1965.

26. R.L. et al. (eds.), *Randall Jarrell, 1914–1965,* p. 112.

27. Jacqueline Kennedy to R.L., January 5, 1965 (Houghton Library).

28. Blair Clark, interview with I.H. (1979).

29. Jacqueline Kennedy to R.L., November 24, 1965 (Houghton Library).

30. Peter Taylor to Allen Tate, December 7, 1965 (Firestone Library).

31. Robert Giroux to Charles Monteith, January 31, 1965.

32. Robert Giroux, interview with I.H. (1979).

33. Sidney Nolan, interview with I.H. (1980).

34. Robert Giroux, interview with I.H. (1979).

35. Jacqueline Kennedy to R.L., December 30, 1965 (Houghton Library).

36. Allen Tate to Peter Taylor, December 14, 1965.

37. W. H. Auden to Charles Monteith, December 20, 1965.

38. Charles Monteith, interview with I.H. (1980).

39. *New York Times,* February 1, 1966.

40. R.L. to Charles Monteith, March 8, 1966.

41. R.L., interview with D. S. Carne-Ross, *Délos* 1 (1968).

42. Hayden Carruth, "A Meaning of Robert Lowell," *Hudson Review* 20, no. 3 (Autumn 1967).

43. David Kalstone, "Two Poets," *Partisan Review,* 34 (1967), 619–25.

44. R.L. to William Meredith, July 16, 1966.

45. Delmore Schwartz to R.L., April 12, 1959 (Houghton Library).

46. Frank Bidart, interview with I.H. (1982). Bidart is here quoting R.L. on Schwartz.

47. R.L. to James Laughlin, August 31, 1966.

48. R.L. to William Meredith, July 16, 1966.

49. R.L. to John Berryman, March 15, 1959 (University of Minnesota Libraries).

50. R.L. to William Meredith, October 3, 1964.

51. R.L. to John Berryman, March 10, 1966 (University of Minnesota Libraries).

52. R.L. to Philip Booth, October 10, 1966.

53. Ibid.

54. John Berryman, "Op. post. no. 13," *His Toy, His Dream, His Rest* (Faber & Faber, 1969), p. 15.

55. Blair Clark, interview with I.H. (1981).

56. Richard Tillinghast, "Robert Lowell in the Sixties," *Harvard Advocate,* November 1979, 14–16.

57. Helen Vendler, "Lowell in the Classroom," *Harvard Advocate,* November 1979, 25–29.

58. Judith Baumel, "Robert Lowell: the Teacher," *Harvard Advocate,* November 1979, 32–33.

59. Anne Sexton, "Classroom at Boston University," *Harvard Advocate,* November 1961.

60. Grey Gowrie, interview with I.H. (1980).

61. Ibid.

62. Ibid.

63. Ibid.

64. Xandra Gowrie, interview with I.H. (1980).

65. Ibid.

66. Grey Gowrie, interview with I.H. (1980).

Chapter Twenty

1. R.L. to Peter Taylor, June 4, 1967.

2. R.L., interview with John Gale, *Observer,* March 12, 1967.

3. Robert Brustein, *Making Scenes* (New York: Random House, 1981), pp. 31–32.

4. Ibid. p. 31.

5. R. W. B. Lewis, *Yale Daily News,* May 24, 1967.

6. R.L., interview with John Gale, *Observer,* March 12, 1970.

7. *New York Times,* May 18, 1967.

8. Ibid., June 14, 1967.

9. R.L. to Peter Taylor, June 4, 1967.

10. Esther Brooks, "Remembering Cal," in *Robert Lowell: A Tribute,* ed. Rolando Anzilotti (Pisa: Nistri-Lischi Editori, 1979), pp. 37–44.

11. Norman Mailer, *The Armies of the Night* (New York: New American Library, 1968). All quoted matter concerning the event is from Mailer's book.

12. Elizabeth Hardwick, interview with I.H. (1982).

13. *Notebook 1967–68* (New York: Farrar, Straus & Giroux, 1969), p. 27.

14. R.L., "The Poetry of John Berryman," *New York Review of Books,* May 28, 1964.

15. Allen Tate to R.L., February 7, 1968 (Houghton Library).

16. Richard Stern, *Tri-Quarterly* 5 (Winter 1981), 270–71.

17. Ivan Illich, *Celebration of Awareness* (London: Penguin, 1976), p. 21.

18. Robert Silvers, interview with I.H. (1981).

19. *Notebook 1967–68,* "Mexico" sequence, pp. 58–63.

20. Mary to R.L., January 9, 1968 (Houghton Library).

21. *Notebook 1967–68,* p. 8.

22. Anonymous, interview with I.H. (1980).

23. R.L., "Day of Mourning," *New York Review of Books,* February 29, 1968.

24. R.L. to Peter Taylor, March 16, 1968.

25. Jeremy Larner, *Nobody Knows* (New York: Macmillan, 1969), p. 187.

26. Max Hastings, *America 1968, The Fire This Time* (London: Gollancz, 1969).

27. R.L. to Peter Taylor, March 16, 1968.

28. Eugene McCarthy, interview with I.H. (1980).

29. Blair Clark, interview with I.H. (1979).

30. Arthur M. Schlesinger, Jr., *Robert Kennedy and His Times* (New York: Houghton Mifflin, 1978). R.L. quoted.

31. Robert Kennedy to R.L., February 18, 1966 (Houghton Library).

32. R.L. to Robert Kennedy, February 25, 1966. R.F.K. papers, in Schlesinger, *Robert Kennedy and His Times.*

33. Grey Gowrie, interview with I.H. (1980).

34. Jean Stein and George Plimpton (eds.), *American Journey: The Times of Robert F. Kennedy* (New York: Harcourt Brace Jovanovich, 1970), p. 193.

35. R.L. to Peter Taylor, March 16, 1968.
36. Stein and Plimpton (eds.), *American Journey*.
37. R.L. to Elizabeth Hardwick, March 22, 1968.
38. E. W. Kenworthy, "Poet and Politician Orchestrate McCarthy Overtures to Voters," *New York Times*, March 29, 1968.
39. Andreas Teuber, special assistant, McCarthy campaign, quoted in Stein and Plimpton (eds.), *American Journey*, pp. 311–12.
40. Eugene McCarthy, interview with I.H. (1980).
41. Ibid.
42. Schlesinger, *Robert Kennedy and His Times*, pp. 910–11.
43. Andreas Teuber, quoted in Stein and Plimpton (eds.), *American Journey*, pp. 311–12.
44. Eugene McCarthy, interview with I.H. (1980).
45. Blair Clark, interview with I.H. (1979).
46. Ms (Houghton Library).
47. *Notebook 1967–68*, p. 138.
48. R.L. to Philip Booth, September 30, 1968.
49. R.L., *Commentary*, April 1969, p. 19.
50. *Notebook 1967–68*, p. 140.

Chapter Twenty-one

1. R.L. to A. Alvarez, July 30, 1968.
2. *Notebook 1967–68* (New York: Farrar, Straus & Giroux, 1969), p. 159.
3. Ibid.
4. *Notebook 1967–68*, p. 17.
5. R.L., draft autobiography, 1955–57 (Houghton Library).
6. Ibid.
7. *Notebook 1967–68*, p. 92.
8. Sidney Nolan, interview with I.H. (1980).
9. Donald Hall, *Review*, 29–30 (Spring–Summer 1972). See also review by I.H. in *Times Literary Supplement*, December 25, 1970, reprinted in *A Poetry Chronicle* (London: Faber & Faber, 1973).
10. R.L. to Peter Taylor, February 6, 1969.
11. R.L. to Elizabeth Hardwick, January 9, 1969.
12. Elizabeth Hardwick to R.L., March 9, 1969 (Houghton Library).
13. R.L. to John Berryman, September 9, 1969 (University of Minnesota Libraries).
14. Ibid.
15. Ibid., September 25, 1969 (University of Minnesota Libraries).
16. Frank Bidart, interview with I.H. (1981).
17. Ibid.
18. Ibid.
19. Ibid.
20. Martha Ritter, interview with I.H. (1981).

21. Ibid.
22. Ibid.
23. Ibid.

Chapter Twenty-two

1. David Caute, "Crisis in All Souls," *Encounter* 26, 3 (March 1966).
2. Philip Edwards to R.L., April 2, 1970 (Houghton Library).
3. Donald Davie to R.L., April 4, 1970 (Houghton Library).
4. R.L. to Elizabeth Hardwick, April 25, 1970.
5. Ibid., April 27, 1970.
6. Ibid., June 1, 1970.
7. The eldest child of Maureen Guinness, marchioness of Dufferin and Ava; her father, whose full name was Basil Sheridan Hamilton-Temple-Blackwood, fourth marquess of Dufferin and Ava, had been killed in Burma in 1945.
8. R.L. to J. F. Powers, February 18, 1973.
9. Caroline Freud, "The Beatnik," *Encounter* 12, no. 6 (June 1959).
10. Ibid.
11. R.L. to Charles Monteith, October 1, 1959.
12. Caroline Blackwood, interview with I.H. (1979).
13. Ibid.
14. Ibid.
15. R.L. to Blair Clark, May 17, 1970.
16. R.L. to Elizabeth Hardwick, May 26, 1970.
17. Robert Giroux to Charles Monteith, June 29, 1970.
18. Elizabeth Hardwick to R.L., June 26, 1970.
19. Caroline Blackwood, interview with I.H. (1979).
20. Blair Clark's notes, July 17, 1970.
21. "Marriage?" *The Dolphin* (London: Faber & Faber, 1973), p. 26.
22. R.L. to Caroline Blackwood, n.d.
23. Blair Clark's notes, July 21–26, 1970.
24. Ibid., July 29, 1970.
25. Ibid., August 9, 1970.
26. R.L. to Elizabeth Hardwick, August 6, 1970.
27. R.L. to Caroline Blackwood, n.d.
28. Caroline Blackwood, interview with I.H. (1979).
29. R.L. to Peter Taylor, November 1, 1970.
30. R.L. to Blair Clark, September 11, 1970.
31. Ibid., October 9, 1970.
32. William Alfred to R.L., October 15, 1970 (Houghton Library).
33. R.L. to Elizabeth Hardwick, October 18, 1970.
34. Ibid., October 22, 1970.
35. R.L. to Peter Taylor, November 1, 1970.
36. R.L. to Blair Clark, November 7, 1970.
37. Elizabeth Hardwick to Blair Clark, October 23, 1970.

38. R.L. to Blair Clark, November 7, 1970.

39. Ibid., November 21, 1970.

40. R.L. to Elizabeth Hardwick, November 16, 1970.

41. Ibid., November 28, 1970.

42. Ibid., November 30, 1970.

Chapter Twenty-three

1. R.L., *The Dolphin* (New York: Farrar, Straus & Giroux, 1973), p. 72.

2. R.L. to Elizabeth Hardwick, November 28, 1970.

3. R.L. to Frank Bidart, September 11, 1970 (Houghton Library).

4. R.L. to Elizabeth Hardwick, November 28, 1970.

5. Ibid., November 30, 1970.

6. Frank Bidart, interview with I.H. (1981).

7. Ibid.

8. Ibid.

9. Blair Clark to R.L., March 17, 1971.

10. R.L. to Blair Clark, April 1, 1971.

11. R.L. to William Alfred, March 20, 1971.

12. R.L. to Peter Taylor, May 13, 1971.

13. R.L. to Blair Clark, May 15, 1971.

14. Ibid.

15. Jonathan Raban, interview with I.H. (1979).

16. Ibid.

17. Ibid.

18. Ibid.

19. R.L. to Blair Clark, July 25, 1971.

20. R.L. to Philip Booth, August 19, 1971.

21. Jonathan Raban, interview with I.H. (1979).

22. Ibid.

23. R.L. to Elizabeth Hardwick, March 9, 1972.

24. Philip Edwards, letter to I.H., January 28, 1982.

25. Dudley Young, letter to I.H., January 27, 1982.

26. Ibid.

27. Gabriel Pearson, interview with I.H. (1980).

28. Philip Edwards, letter to I.H., January 28, 1982.

29. Martha Ritter, interview with I.H. (1981).

30. R.L. to Elizabeth Hardwick, September 29, 1971.

31. Elizabeth Hardwick in interview with I.H. (1982): "Re. my 'Notebook,' I told Cal I was writing a sort of memoir, putting it in a handsome leather book with fine paper which had been given to me as a present by John Thompson. Cal had certain grandiose ideas about this 'Notebook,' also known as, my title, a joking one, 'Smiling Through.' I did very little of it, came upon it later and threw it away. Cal, I think, hoped it would be deliciously acerb and 'interesting.' Instead the little I wrote was sentimental and I tore it up like many another false start."

32. R.L. to Elizabeth Hardwick, October 1, 1971.

33. R.L. to Frank Bidart, n.d. (Houghton Library).

34. Frank Bidart, interview with I.H. (1981).

35. Ibid.

36. R.L., *For Lizzie and Harriet* (New York: Farrar, Straus & Giroux, 1973), p. 21.

37. Frank Bidart, interview with I.H. (1981).

38. Stanley Kunitz to R.L., April 19, 1972 (Houghton Library).

39. Ibid., August 16, 1972 (Houghton Library).

40. Elizabeth Bishop to R.L., October 26, 1972 (Houghton Library).

41. Ibid., March 21, 1972 (Houghton Library).

42. R.L. to Christopher Ricks, March 21, 1972.

43. R.L. to Alan Brownjohn, May 16, 1972.

44. Alan Brownjohn, interview with I.H. (1980).

45. Jonathan Raban, interview with I.H. (1980).

46. William Alfred to R.L., March 12, 1972 (Houghton Library).

47. R.L. to William Alfred, n.d.

48. R.L. to Frank Bidart, April 10, 1972 (Houghton Library). In the original ms of *The Dolphin*, the section called "Burden" comprised eleven poems. In the published book, ten of these (heavily revised) are placed in the section called "Marriage." They are "Knowing," Question," "Overhanging Cloud," "Gold Lull," "Green Sore," "Letter," "Late Summer at Milgate," "Ninth Month," "Morning Away from You" and "Robert Sheridan Lowell." A comparison of the ms Dolphin with the published text suggests that Lowell's efforts to "depersonalize" were minor and halfhearted. Certainly nothing very "outrageous" was suppressed; and fairly often his revisions have slightly muddied the meaning of the original.

49. Frank Bidart, interview with I.H. (1981).

50. R.L. to Frank Bidart, May 15, 1972 (Houghton Library).

51. Frank Bidart, interview with I.H. (1981).

52. R.L. to William Alfred, n.d.

Chapter Twenty-four

1. R.L. to Frank Bidart, n.d. (Houghton Library).

2. *The Dolphin* (New York: Farrar, Straus & Giroux, 1973), p. 64.

3. R.L. to Elizabeth Hardwick, October 1, 1971.

4. R.L. to Philip Booth, 1972.

5. Caroline Blackwood, interview with I.H. (1979).

6. R.L. to Blair Clark, n.d.

7. Ibid.

8. R.L. to Elizabeth Hardwick, May 21, 1973. On the Maine property, Hardwick explains (in an interview with I.H. in 1982): "The property was left in its entirety to me by Miss Winslow. Cal had no claims at all on it, but I always felt it was left to me for reasons of practicality and was not meant as a rebuke to Cal. When we

were together, he and I decided that I would sell part of it in order to improve the barn on the water where he worked. That was done. When we were divorced, I wanted to live in the barn as more suitable for me and Harriet. I had to sell the house on the Commons in order to make a house of the barn. Under Maine law, Cal, as my former husband, was required to sign. Only his signature was required, but he refused for a good while, seeming to think the signature indicated that indeed the property had been left to both of us. I explained, the Maine lawyer explained, but he would not for a long time accommodate and I almost lost the sale of the other house. Behind this was, in my view, his sadness, not his greed, that Cousin Harriet, much loved by both of us, had done what she did."

9. R.L. to Elizabeth Hardwick, May 26, 1973.

10. Calvin Bedient, "Visions and Revisions—Three New Volumes by America's First Poet," *New York Times Book Review*, July 29, 1973, pp. 15 ff.

11. Jonathan Raban, interview with I.H. (1979).

12. Stephen Yenser, "Half Legible Bronze," *Poetry* 123 (February 1974), pp. 304–9.

13. Paul Ramsey, "American Poetry in 1973," *Sewanee Review* 82 (Spring 1974), pp. 393–405.

14. William Pritchard, "Poetry Matters," *Hudson Review* 26 (Autumn 1973), pp. 579–97.

15. Adrienne Rich to R.L., June 19, 1971 (Houghton Library).

16. Adrienne Rich, *American Poetry Review*, September–October 1973.

17. Marjorie Perloff, "The Blank Now," *New Republic*, July 7 and 14, 1973, p. 24.

18. R.L. to Blair Clark, July 31, 1973.

19. Robert Giroux, interview with I.H. (1979).

20. R.L. to Elizabeth Hardwick, July 12, 1973.

21. Ibid., July 16, 1973.

22. R.L. to William Alfred, August 31, 1973.

23. R.L. to Blair Clark, July 31, 1973.

24. R.L. to William Alfred, August 31, 1973.

25. Ibid.

26. Ibid.

27. The texts of poems quoted on pp. 436–38 are as they first appeared in *New Review* 1, no. 1 (April 1974). They were revised for book publication in *Day by Day* (New York: Farrar, Straus & Giroux, 1977).

28. R.L. to Blair Clark, February 22, 1974.

29. Ms (Houghton Library).

30. Ibid.

31. *Day by Day* (New York: Farrar, Straus & Giroux, 1977), p. 27.

32. R.L., "The Poetry of John Berryman," *New York Review of Books* May 28, 1964.

33. R.L. to Peter Taylor, May 13, 1974.

34. *Day by Day*, p. 38.

35. R.L. to William Alfred, May 20, 1974.

36. R.L. to Peter Taylor, July 13, 1974.

37. Ibid.

38. Ibid., October 9, 1974.

39. *New Review* 2, no. 20 (November 1975). Revised for publication in *Day by Day* (1977).

40. Ibid.

41. R.L. to Elizabeth Hardwick, October 13, 1974.

42. Ibid., December 13, 1974.

43. R.L. to Peter Taylor, n.d.

44. R.L. to Frank Bidart, December 14, 1974.

45. Caroline Blackwood, interview with I.H. (1979).

46. P. R. Brass to Curtis Prout, February 5, 1975 (Houghton Library).

47. Ibid.

48. Robert Giroux, interview with I.H. (1982).

49. Robert Silvers, interview with I.H. (1981).

50. Curtis Prout to R.L., May 1975 (Houghton Library).

51. R.L. to Peter Taylor, July 1, 1975.

52. Ibid., July 21, 1975.

53. R.L. to Frank Parker, September 11, 1975.

54. R.L. to Blair Clark, September 11, 1975.

55. R.L. to Frank Parker, September 11, 1975.

56. R.L. to Frank Bidart, August 7, 1975.

Chapter Twenty-five

1. Caroline Blackwood, interview with I.H. (1979).

2. Jonathan Raban, interview with I.H. (1979).

3. Ibid.

4. Caroline Blackwood, interview with I.H. (1979).

5. This and the ensuing quotations are from the nurse's day book, January 1976.

6. *Day by Day* (New York: Farrar, Straus & Giroux, 1977), p. 114.

7. R.L. to Frank Bidart, February 15, 1976 (Houghton Library).

8. R.L. to Peter Taylor, March 4, 1976.

9. R.L. to Blair Clark, March 4, 1976.

10. "The Downlook," *Day by Day,* p. 125.

11. R.L. to Elizabeth Hardwick, April 29, 1976.

12. *Day by Day,* pp. 44–45.

13. R.L. to Frank Bidart, April 15, 1975 (Houghton Library).

14. R.L. to Elizabeth Hardwick, July 2, 1976.

15. Ibid., September 4, 1976.

16. R.L. to Blair Clark, March 4, 1976.

17. R.L. to Peter Taylor, September 4, 1976.

18. R.L. to Frank Bidart, September 4, 1976 (Houghton Library).

19. Caroline Blackwood, interview with I.H. (1979).

20. Blair Clark's notes, October 21, 1976.

21. R.L. to William Alfred, October 30, 1976.

22. *Day by Day,* p. 103.

23. Blair Clark's notes, November 25, 1976.

24. Frank Bidart, interview with I.H. (1981).

25. Ibid.

26. Ibid.

27. R.L. to Caroline Blackwood, February 28, 1977.

28. Frank Bidart, interview with I.H. (1981).

29. Helen Vendler, interview with I.H. (1981).

30. R.L. to Caroline Blackwood, January 31, 1977.

31. Edgar Stillman, "Robert Lowell Revisiting," *Soho Weekly News*, March 3, 1977, p. 53.

32. R.L. to Caroline Blackwood, March 2, 1977.

33. Ibid., March 18, 1977.

34. Helen Vendler, interview with I.H. (1981).

35. *Day by Day*, p. 107.

36. Blair Clark, "The Lowells . . . notes for a never-to-be-written 'memoir,' " May 8, 1977.

37. R.L. to Caroline Blackwood, July 17, 1977.

38. William Styron, letter to I.H., July 1, 1981.

39. Ibid.

40. Nathan Scott, letter to I.H., March 27, 1981.

41. William Styron, letter to I.H., July 1, 1981.

42. Frank Bidart, interview with I.H. (1981).

43. R.L. to Caroline Blackwood, n.d.

44. Frank Bidart, interview with I.H. (1981).

45. R.L. to Caroline Blackwood, n.d.

46. Elizabeth Hardwick, interview with I.H. (1982).

47. Helen Vendler, interview with I.H. (1981).

48. Frank Bidart, interview with I.H. (1981).

49. Uncollected. *New Review* 4, no. 43 (October 1977).

50. Helen Vendler, "The Poetry of Autobiography," *New York Times Book Review*, August 14, 1977.

51. *Day by Day*, p. 127.

52. Ms (Houghton Library).

53. Caroline Blackwood, interview with I.H. (1979).

54. R.L. to Caroline Blackwood, n.d.

55. Mrs. Dignam, interview with I.H. (1979).

56. Elizabeth Hardwick, interview with I.H. (1979).

57. The painting of Caroline Blackwood is by her first husband, Lucien Freud.

58. Quotations in foregoing paragraphs from interviews with I.H. (1979–81).

59. *Harvard Advocate*, November 1979, p. 18.

INDEX

About the Author

IAN HAMILTON was born in 1938 and educated at the Darlington Grammar School and Keble College, Oxford. He is the author of two books of poetry, *The Visit* and *Returning,* and two books of criticism, *The Little Magazines* and *A Poetry Chronicle.* He has also edited two collections of poetry, *The Poetry of War 1939–45* and *The Modern Poet,* and has been the editor of the *Review* (1962–72) and the *New Review* (1974–79).